Learn OpenShift

Second Edition

Master container orchestration with OpenShift 4 – architecture, deployment, and operations

Aleksey Usov

Aleksandr Varlamov

Denis Zuev

<packt>

Learn OpenShift

Second Edition

Portfolio Director: Kartikey Pandey
Relationship Lead: Deepak Kumar
Project Manager: Sonam Pandey
Content Engineer: Sayali Pingale
Technical Editor: Simran Ali
Copy Editor: Safis Editing
Indexer: Rekha Nair
Production Designer: Vijay Kamble
Growth Lead: Shreyans Singh

First published: July 2018
Second edition: January 2026

Production reference: 1230126

Published by Packt Publishing Ltd.
Grosvenor House
11 St Paul's Square
Birmingham
B3 1RB, UK.

ISBN 978-1-83588-240-5
www.packtpub.com

Contributors

About the authors

Aleksey Usov is a principal architect at Li9 Technology Solutions. He is primarily focused on containerization, virtualization, DevOps, CI/CD, IaC, and automation. As part of his job, he works with Linux, OpenShift, Ansible, Terraform, GitLab, and many other technologies on a daily basis. As an architect, Aleksey is deeply involved in all aspects of working with his customers, gathering requirements, designing a solution, doing hands-on work, and presenting it to the customer. Some of his largest customers include Wells Fargo, Credit Suisse, Sutter Health, and Shambaugh & Son. He is also a proponent of constant education, which earned him the status of Red Hat Certified Architect Level XXV (world record) in 2023 and Kubestronaut in 2025.

Aleksandr Varlamov is an architect and hands-on SRE focused on building secure, scalable cloud-native platforms. His work spans Linux, containers, Kubernetes, OpenShift, GitOps, DevSecOps, automation, and cloud-native security. He holds a master's degree and multiple industry certifications, including Red Hat OpenShift and Kubernetes credentials. He has led enterprise platform and architecture initiatives for large organizations, including governance and compliance automation across financial services, healthcare, insurance, technology, automotive, and media streaming.

Denis Zuev is widely known in the IT industry for his ability to design systems of any complexity from scratch, as well as his extensive mentoring background. Having started his career as a network engineer, working with Cisco and Juniper products and performing consulting services for prominent businesses such as CenturyLink (now part of Lumen Technologies), UPS, AT&T, and Bell Integrator, Denis now works as a solutions architect for Broadcom, delivering high-quality services to his customers. He is also a passionate self-learner who has earned perhaps the highest number of certifications in the industry. Among his credentials are CCIE, JNCIE, CCDE, and HCIE. Currently, Denis lives in Littleton, CO, with his wife and two boys.

About the reviewers

Iuliia Kozlova is a lead QA expert at Simbirsoft, Russia. As an expert on software testing and Kubernetes, she has provided her expertise to a number of businesses of national significance, automating the QA process and helping build business-focused teams. Having passed all Kubernetes-related certifications from the Linux Foundation, she also possesses the title of Kubestronaut, the first in her country. Iuliia has also made numerous other contributions to the industry in the form of book reviews and scientific articles. In her work, she uses Kubernetes to build isolated and disposable test environments as part of software integration and delivery pipelines and has developed an interest in OpenShift as one of the leading Kubernetes distributions.

Sergei Dudnik is an experienced IT professional and certified infrastructure architect. He is a **Red Hat Certified Architect** (**RHCA XX**) and a **Red Hat Certified OpenShift Architect** (**RHCOA III**), as well as a **Certified Kubernetes Administrator** (**CKA**) and an IBM Certified Advanced Technical Expert. Sergei specializes in enterprise Linux platforms, OpenShift and Kubernetes-based infrastructures, and the design of scalable, highly available, and secure production systems.

Table of Contents

Chapter 2: Kubernetes and OpenShift 27

Part 2: Post-Installation, Configuration, and Application Deployment 109

Chapter 4: Post-Install Configuration 111

Chapter 6: Exploring Scalability with OpenShift 169

Chapter 7: Application Security and Isolation 191

Chapter 8: Working with Persistent Storage 247

Chapter 9: Developing for OpenShift 287

Chapter 10: Deployment to OpenShift 329

Chapter 11: Deploying Applications with Helm and Kustomize 369

Part 3: Logging, Monitoring, Observability, and Advanced OpenShift Services 411

Chapter 12: Logging in OpenShift 413

Chapter 13: Monitoring in OpenShift 433

Chapter 14: Understanding Service Mesh and Distributed Tracing 469

Part 4: Extending, Maintaining, and Upgrading OpenShift 565

Chapter 16: Understanding Operators and the Operator Framework 567

Chapter 17: Upgrading OpenShift 605

Preface

When we started our paths in IT, the cloud-native ecosystem looked different. Containers were still in their early days, orchestration was immature, and there was no widely accepted platform standard. The problems were familiar – consistency across environments, repeatable deployments, security boundaries, compliance controls, and operability at scale – but the tooling and patterns were fragmented.

Then Docker arrived, followed by Kubernetes, and the direction became clear. Kubernetes became the standard foundation for modern platforms, and Red Hat OpenShift emerged as a practical enterprise implementation, bringing opinionated operations, integrated security capabilities, and a path for organizations that need more than "just a cluster."

Cloud computing is a model for delivering computing resources on demand – typically through self-service portals and APIs – without requiring customers to purchase and operate the underlying hardware. In practice, cloud offerings are often described through service models that reflect how much control the customer has.

- **Infrastructure as a Service** (**IaaS**) provides building blocks such as networks, storage, and virtual machines. Customers manage the operating system and runtime stack, while the provider manages the hardware. Examples include Amazon EC2 and OpenStack.
- **Platform as a Service (PaaS)** provides a managed runtime and deployment experience. Customers focus on application delivery, while the provider (or platform team) manages the operating system and much of the runtime. Examples include AWS Elastic Beanstalk, Heroku, and Red Hat OpenShift.
- **Software as a Service (SaaS)** provides complete applications delivered as a service, where customers primarily configure and use the software. Examples include Salesforce and Microsoft 365.

In this book, we focus on Red Hat OpenShift, an enterprise Kubernetes platform often used as a foundation for enterprise-grade PaaS platforms. OpenShift has evolved significantly over time, with the most notable shift being the move to Kubernetes at its core in OpenShift 3. Today, OpenShift builds on Kubernetes and adds opinionated operations, integrated security capabilities, and a broad ecosystem of extensions.

One lesson we learned repeatedly is that OpenShift is never only OpenShift. Real adoption is shaped by everything around it: identity and access management, governance, compliance automation, software supply chain practices, observability, and the operational processes that keep a platform reliable under pressure. That is the lens we use throughout this book.

The first edition of this book used OpenShift 3.9 and focused on installation and core operations. For this second edition, we wanted to go further – covering the capabilities and practices that make OpenShift genuinely useful in real organizations, not only as a lab environment. We chose **OpenShift 4.16** as the baseline for this edition because it is an **Extended Update Support** (EUS) minor release and fits perfectly for teams that prefer a longer-lived upgrade cadence.

While we were writing, OpenShift continued to move forward – as it always does. Newer releases (including 4.20) introduce additional features and refinements, but the foundational ideas and operational patterns remain stable, and that is precisely what this book emphasizes.

You will start with a grounding in containers and Kubernetes, then build an OpenShift cluster on VMware vSphere and complete key day-2 tasks to make it operable. From there, we move into scalability, authentication and authorization, security, and application delivery. We include templates for context, but focus on Helm and Kustomize as the more common approaches in modern Kubernetes environments. The second half of the book covers observability and additional services often deployed alongside OpenShift, and we close with operators, upgrades, troubleshooting, and maintenance.

Our goal is simple: help you adopt OpenShift with less friction, fewer surprises, and a clearer model of how the platform fits into real organizations. We don't give you a single "right" solution, but we aim to provide direction – and the patterns to make good decisions under real constraints.

And because this space keeps moving, we don't see this as the final word. As OpenShift and the surrounding ecosystem evolve, you'll want to stay current and build on the foundations in this book.

Who this book is for

This book is for architects, DevOps engineers, SREs, platform engineers, and anyone who wants to understand OpenShift 4 – both the platform's capabilities and the business value it enables. To get the most from the material, you should be comfortable with Linux basics, the command line (Bash), and core networking concepts.

What this book covers

Chapter 1, Understanding Containers, introduces the concept of containers, explains how they are different from virtualization, the technologies behind Linux containers, and why they have become so popular.

Chapter 2, Kubernetes and OpenShift, starts with the history of Kubernetes, establishes the definition of a Kubernetes distribution, discusses the architecture of Kubernetes, and then moves on to compare vanilla Kubernetes and OpenShift, highlighting the features that OpenShift brings to the table. In this chapter, you are also introduced to OpenShift Local for non-resource-intensive exercises.

Chapter 3, Getting Started with OpenShift, discusses OpenShift installation methods, establishes prerequisites for installing OpenShift on VMware vSphere using the UPI approach, and then walks you through the installation process step by step. Here, you also get an opportunity to refresh your knowledge of Kubernetes core APIs and learn about the OpenShift API deprecation policy.

Chapter 4, Post-Install Configuration, demonstrates how to complete some of the most common day-2 configuration items, such as setting up and using infrastructure nodes, encrypting etcd, and replacing default ingress and public API certificates.

Chapter 5, Navigating Authentication and Authorization, explores the concepts of authentication and authorization and how they are interrelated, various identity providers (with an emphasis on HTPasswd and LDAP), and role-based access control, and wraps up with how service accounts can be used to grant access to the OpenShift API to external systems.

Chapter 6, Exploring Scalability with OpenShift, explains how horizontal scaling is different from vertical scaling and what makes it the preferred way of adding capacity to your cluster. We will also glance over how to remove nodes manually, should manual intervention be required. Lastly, we will explore how autoscaling works in OpenShift, specifically the MachineAutoscaler and ClusterAutoscaler APIs.

Chapter 7, Application Security and Isolation, starts with a discussion about projects and how they are different from Kubernetes namespaces. This sets the scene for project guardrails, namely ResourceQuotas, LimitRanges, and NetworkPolicies. In this chapter, we also talk about the security context of your workload and how SecurityContextConstraints are used to limit what it can do. We wrap up this long chapter with what Pod Security Policies are and how to use them.

Chapter 8, Working with Persistent Storage, explains the need for persistent storage by highlighting the differences between stateful and stateless applications, and teaches you about OpenShift APIs involved in the lifecycle of storage volumes, such as PersistentVolume, PersistentVolumeClaim, and StorageClass, and types of volumes. In this chapter, we also expose you to the **Container Storage Interface** (**CSI**), the architecture of **OpenShift Data Foundation** (**ODF**), and walk you through the process of installing ODF on your cluster.

Chapter 9, Developing for OpenShift, begins with an overview of features that OpenShift provides to developers and then moves on to set up OpenShift Local on your laptop. As a next step, we guide you through using odo to deploy and introduce changes to a sample Go-based application, while observing the results of those changes in real time. The second part of this chapter is dedicated to the discussion of images, the Cluster Samples Operator, the integrated image registry, and ImageStreams. Finally, we talk about using **Source-to-Image** (**S2I**) and how to use it to build a sample application, as well as using ConfigMaps and Secrets to supply your applications with configuration, including best practices around them.

Chapter 10, Deployment to OpenShift, explains how templates can be useful for deploying complex multi-tier applications, what options you have for building images directly in OpenShift, the basics of Tekton Pipelines, as well as the differences between Kubernetes-native Deployments and OpenShift-specific DeploymentConfigs. Next, we will proceed to talk about deployment strategies, their use cases and limitations, an overview of architectural differences between Kubernetes and OpenShift, and microservices. We will close this chapter with a discussion about scaling, node selectors, and placement rules.

Chapter 11, Deploying Applications with Helm and Kustomize, opens with an introduction to Helm and how it acts as a package manager of Kubernetes, simplifying the management of applications' lifecycle. As an exercise, we will guide you through writing a simple Helm chart of your own and installing it on your cluster. In the second part of the chapter, we show you how to use Kustomize to manage configuration differences of your application across different sites and environments. On the final note, you get to see how Kustomize can be integrated into a Git-based workflow, facilitating collaboration and auditing.

Chapter 12, Logging in OpenShift, begins the discussion of observability by introducing the concept of logging and why it matters (especially in distributed systems), and details the steps needed to configure log collection on OpenShift 4. As part of that process, the chapter also explains each step and how to install and configure each component of the logging stack.

Chapter 13, Monitoring in OpenShift, continues the topic of observability with the exploration of the monitoring stack, its architecture, a brief history of Prometheus, and different types of metrics. In this chapter, you will also learn how to configure the cluster monitoring stack for persistence and how to enable monitoring for user-defined projects. As a wrap-up, we walk you through installing Grafana and configuring it to display metrics from a sample application.

Chapter 14, Understanding Service Mesh and Distributed Tracing, exposes you to the concept of Service Mesh and how it can help enforce policies for distributed microservices and secure communication between them, and guides you through the installation of Service Mesh 2. In this chapter, you also learn how distributed tracing can help identify issues with microservices, isolate problematic applications, and even inject faults deliberately.

Chapter 15, Exploring Additional Services in OpenShift, discusses how OpenShift's capabilities can be extended with extra services, usually provided in the form of operators or Helm charts. As examples of such services often used by large businesses, we will examine Serverless, Windows containers, and GitOps.

Chapter 16, Understanding Operators and the Operator Framework, introduces you to the concepts of operators, operator patterns, and the Operator Framework. In this chapter, you will learn what operators are, how they are built and distributed, how they marked the transition from OpenShift 3 to 4, their capability levels, and finally, get to build a simple operator of your own.

Chapter 17, Upgrading OpenShift, sheds light on what happens under the hood when you initiate a cluster upgrade, as well as limitations and OpenShift components involved in this process. In this chapter, you will also learn about different upgrade channels, when one might be preferable over another, and the release cadence of OpenShift.

Chapter 18, Troubleshooting and Maintenance, the final chapter of this book, exposes you to general troubleshooting techniques and maintenance procedures, including some of the tools that you may find useful.

To get the most out of this book

- You should be comfortable working with command-line interpreters on Linux and macOS X, such as sh, bash, zsh, and others. Experience with Windows PowerShell is not required, but basic familiarity will be useful in *Chapter 15, Exploring Additional Services in OpenShift*.
- This book uses `vi` as the default text editor; however, you are free to use others, such as `nano`. Keep in mind that `vi` is used by default when editing OpenShift objects live with `oc edit`, so if you prefer a different editor, set the `EDITOR` environment variable in your shell accordingly – for example, `export EDITOR=nano` for all subsequent commands or `EDITOR=nano oc edit ...` for a one-time override.
- This book does not assume any prior knowledge of OpenShift or Kubernetes; however, having such experience will make it easier to understand the differences between the two and why OpenShift is considered an enterprise-grade PaaS solution.

Download the example code files

The code bundle for the book is hosted on GitHub at `https://github.com/PacktPublishing/Learn-OpenShift-Second-Edition`. We also have other code bundles from our rich catalog of books and videos available at `https://github.com/PacktPublishing`. Check them out!

Download the color images

We also provide a PDF file that has color images of the screenshots/diagrams used in this book. You can download it here: `https://packt.link/gbp/9781835882405`.

Conventions used

There are a number of text conventions used throughout this book.

`CodeInText`: Indicates code words in text, database table names, folder names, filenames, file extensions, pathnames, dummy URLs, user input, and Twitter handles. For example: "Before we start, run the following command to export the `kubeconfig` file for your cluster into your shell."

A block of code is set as follows:

```
apiVersion: config.openshift.io/v1
kind: OperatorHub
metadata:
  name: cluster
spec:
  sources:
  - name: community-operators
    disabled: true
```

Any command-line input or output is written as follows:

```
$ oc get -o yaml clusterversion/version
```

Bold: Indicates a new term, an important word, or words that you see on the screen. For instance, words in menus or dialog boxes appear in the text like this. For example: "Now, refresh the web console in your browser, then click **Add access** and then on the **Role** drop-down list. You should see only the **view** role."

Warnings or important notes appear like this.

Tips and tricks appear like this.

Get in touch

Feedback from our readers is always welcome.

General feedback: If you have questions about any aspect of this book or have any general feedback, please email us at `customercare@packt.com` and mention the book's title in the subject of your message.

Errata: Although we have taken every care to ensure the accuracy of our content, mistakes do happen. If you have found a mistake in this book, we would be grateful if you reported this to us. Please visit `http://www.packt.com/submit-errata`, click **Submit Errata**, and fill in the form.

Piracy: If you come across any illegal copies of our works in any form on the internet, we would be grateful if you would provide us with the location address or website name. Please contact us at `copyright@packt.com` with a link to the material.

If you are interested in becoming an author: If there is a topic that you have expertise in and you are interested in either writing or contributing to a book, please visit `http://authors.packt.com/`.

Free benefits with your book

This book comes with free benefits to support your learning. Activate them now for instant access (see the "*How to Unlock*" section for instructions).

Here's a quick overview of what you can instantly unlock with your purchase:

EPUB PDF

DRM-Free PDF Version

Download DRM-free PDF and ePub copies of this book.

7-Day Packt Library Access

Get 7-day unlimited access to 8,000+ books and videos. No credit card required.

Available for first-time Packt+ trial users only.

Next-Gen Reader Access

Read this book on Packt Reader with progress sync, dark mode and note-taking.

How to Unlock

Scan the QR code (or go to `packtpub.com/unlock`). Search for this book by name, confirm the edition, and then follow the steps on the page.

UNLOCK NOW

Note: Keep your invoice handy. Purchases made directly from Packt don't require one

Stay Sharp in Cloud and DevOps – Join 44,000+ Subscribers of CloudPro

CloudPro is a weekly newsletter for cloud professionals who want to stay current on the fast-evolving world of cloud computing, DevOps, and infrastructure engineering.

Every issue delivers focused, high-signal content on topics like:

- AWS, GCP & multi-cloud architecture
- Containers, Kubernetes & orchestration
- Infrastructure as Code (IaC) with Terraform, Pulumi, etc.
- Platform engineering & automation workflows
- Observability, performance tuning, and reliability best practices

Whether you're a cloud engineer, SRE, DevOps practitioner, or platform lead, CloudPro helps you stay on top of what matters, without the noise.

Scan the QR code to join for free and get weekly insights straight to your inbox:

`https://packt.link/cloudpro`

Share your thoughts

Once you've read *Learn OpenShift, Second Edition,* we'd love to hear your thoughts! Scan the QR code below to go straight to the Amazon review page for this book and share your feedback.

`https://packt.link/r/1835882412`

Your review is important to us and the tech community and will help us make sure we're delivering excellent quality content.

Part 1

The Basics and Installation

This part is intended to expose you to theoretical knowledge about OpenShift, its features, and architecture. Upon completion, you will have a working OpenShift cluster ready for hosting applications.

This part of the book includes the following chapters:

- *Chapter 1, Understanding Containers*
- *Chapter 2, Kubernetes and OpenShift*
- *Chapter 3, Getting Started with OpenShift*

1

Understanding Containers

Containers and virtualization have changed the way we think about running applications. They've made things faster, more efficient, and much easier to manage – especially as environments grow more complex. In this chapter, we'll take a closer look at what containerization is, how it compares to virtualization, and why it's become such a big deal in the world of modern infrastructure.

Containerization is a lightweight way to package and run software consistently across environments – from a laptop to production. Unlike **virtual machines** (**VMs**), which each run a full operating system, containers share the host's kernel, making them faster and more efficient.

While both containers and VMs allow multiple apps on one machine, they use different approaches. That distinction affects performance, resource use, and deployment speed – topics we'll break down with clear examples. It's also worth noting that containerization doesn't replace virtualization; it builds on it. In fact, the two can work well together. This chapter will take you through a hands-on example where you'll create a VM using VMware Workstation or Fusion. That VM will be your safe space to experiment with Podman, a container engine that's like Docker but offers some key advantages, especially in rootless environments.

By the end of this chapter, you'll understand how containers fit into the bigger picture of application delivery, and you'll have some hands-on experience to go with it. That way, when we dive into more advanced topics later, you'll already have the groundwork in place.

We will cover the following main topics in this chapter:

- Benefits of containerization
- Containerization versus virtualization
- Containers and microservices
- Setting up the lab environment
- Podman overview
- Podman versus Docker

Let's get started!

Free Benefits with Your Book

Your purchase includes a free PDF copy of this book along with other exclusive benefits. Check the *Free Benefits with Your Book* section in the Preface to unlock them instantly and maximize your learning experience.

Technical requirements

In this chapter, you will need the following:

- Internet access
- Shell terminal and SSH client
- CentOS 9:
  - Based on a Type 2 hypervisor: VMware Fusion or VirtualBox
  - Based in the private or public cloud
- Firefox or another modern web browser

You can access this book's GitHub repository at `https://github.com/PacktPublishing/Learn-OpenShift-Second-Edition`.

Benefits of containerization

Containerization has reshaped the way we build, run, and manage applications. With tools such as Docker, it's now easy to package an app – along with everything it needs – into a compact, portable container that runs anywhere.

In the sections that follow, we'll look at the key benefits that have made containers such a vital part of modern software development, such as the following:

- **Consistency and portability:** Inconsistencies between development, testing, and production are common and often cause problems. Containers solve this by packaging everything the app needs, so it runs the same everywhere – on your laptop, on-premises, or in the cloud. With Docker images, you build it once and run it anywhere with confidence.
- **Agility and speed:** Containers start fast and use less space because they share the host's operating system, unlike VMs that run a full OS. This makes development quicker, deployments faster, and updates easier.
- **Resource efficiency and density:** Because containers are lightweight, you can run more of them on the same server. This means better use of hardware and lower costs. Docker also lets you control how much CPU and memory each container uses.

- **Scalability:** Scaling apps up or down to match demand is key. Containers make this easy – Docker can start or stop them in seconds. With tools such as Kubernetes (used in OpenShift 4), this scaling can happen automatically to keep things running smoothly.
- **Simplified deployment:** Docker makes deployments more consistent and less error-prone by packaging everything your app needs. With tools such as OpenShift 4, handling updates and rollbacks becomes much easier.
- **Enhanced security and isolation:** Containers improve security by keeping apps isolated from each other. This helps prevent one app from affecting another. Docker uses built-in Linux features such as namespaces and **control groups (cgroups)** to add extra layers of protection.
- **Improved collaboration and microservices:** Containers are a great fit for microservices, where big apps are broken into smaller parts. Docker makes it easy to package and manage each piece, so teams can work faster and more independently.

Here is a diagram of the main architectural differences between applications running on top of an OS on physical or virtualized hardware and applications running in containers:

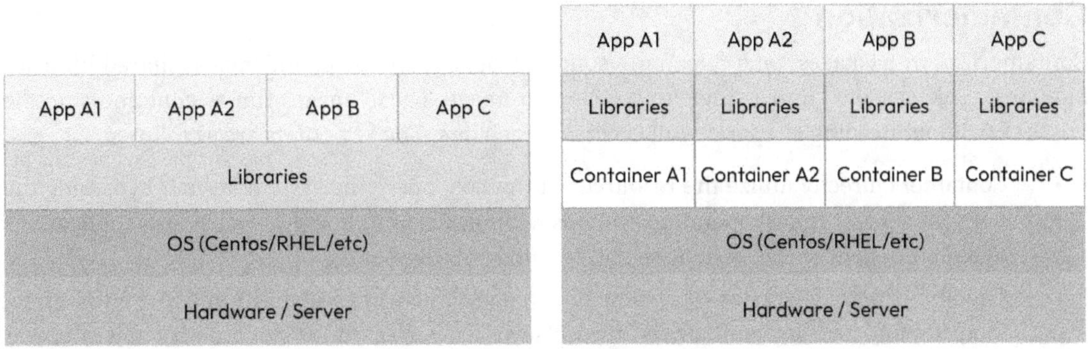

Figure 1.1: Bare metal and VM versus containerization

While both bare-metal apps and containerized apps run on the same operating system, containers add a lightweight layer that separates each app from the OS. This lets every container run with its own libraries and dependencies, keeping apps isolated and avoiding conflicts.

Understanding how containers and Docker work is essential in the OpenShift 4 world. In the coming chapters, we'll dive deeper into how OpenShift uses these foundations to manage complex, container-based applications.

Containerization versus virtualization

While both containerization and virtualization aim to optimize resource utilization and easy application development and deployment, they operate at fundamentally different levels and have distinct use cases. Let's clarify the differences.

Virtualization

Virtualization uses software to let one physical machine run multiple VMs. Each VM has its own operating system and simulates full hardware such as CPU, memory, and network. The key points are as follows:

- Virtualization involves creating VMs on top of a physical server using a hypervisor. Each VM simulates complete hardware (CPU, memory, disk, and network interfaces) and runs its own isolated operating system and applications. All that hardware, albeit virtual, needs time to initialize. It is not uncommon to disable unnecessary devices, such as USB ports and a wireless card, on a VM to speed up startup time. However, this approach has limits.
- VMs offer robust isolation and compatibility with diverse operating systems, and are well suited for migrating legacy applications.
- The inclusion of a full operating system per VM introduces overhead, resulting in slower launch times, larger image sizes, and somewhat reduced density compared to containers.

Containerization

Containerization packages an application's source code and all its dependencies (shared libraries, modules, packages, etc.) into a single unit called an image. These images run as containers on the host's OS without needing a separate full OS inside each one. The key points are as follows:

- Containers directly utilize the resources of the host operating system kernel, bypassing the need for separate guest operating systems within each unit. Instead, they house applications and their dependencies in lightweight, isolated environments.
- Containers provide greater efficiency, agility, portability, and scalability due to their minimal footprint and near-instant launch times. They are a perfect fit for cloud-native and microservices-based architectures.
- Containers running on a host must share the same OS kernel, making them less suitable for hosting applications with vastly different operating system requirements.

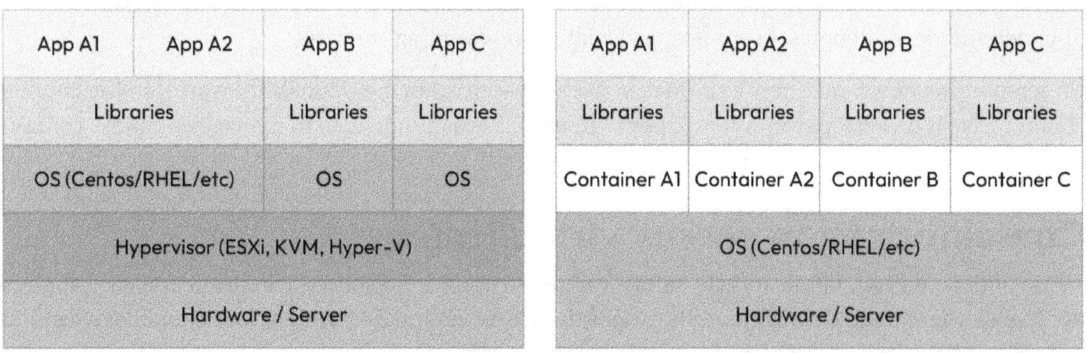

Figure 1.2: Virtualization versus containerization

Choosing between containers and VMs depends on your needs. As innovative as containerization turned out to be, it isn't an answer to all problems. In some scenarios, VMs may be preferable over containers, as in these examples:

- If you're running older, monolithic apps or need to support different operating systems.
- When running a resource-intensive application that requires dedicated resources or a special hardware configuration.
- When an application requires special kernel modules or settings. Containers cannot make these changes unless they're running in privileged mode, which negatively impacts security posture.
- When stronger security and isolation are required, for example, because of untrusted applications or compliance requirements.

On the other hand, if you're building with microservices, need to scale fast, or want lightweight, portable apps, containers (such as Docker) are usually the way to go.

OpenShift and hybrid approaches

Modern platforms such as OpenShift 4 support both containers and VMs, giving you flexibility in how you run your applications. It's common to see containers running inside orchestrated VMs – this setup combines the speed and portability of containers with the strong isolation that some legacy apps still need.

The following table summarizes the differences between virtualization and containerization:

Feature	Virtualization	Containerization
Approach	Emulates complete physical hardware (hypervisor)	Shares the host OS kernel
Unit of isolation	VM	Container
Operating system	Each VM runs a full guest operating system	Containers use the host operating system kernel
Resource overhead	Higher (each VM has its own OS)	Lower (shared OS kernel)
Startup speed	Slower (full OS boot required)	Significantly faster
Image size	Larger (includes full OS)	Smaller (application + dependencies)
Application portability	Good, VM runs independently	Excellent for similar OS environments
Ideal use cases	Legacy apps, OS diversity, and strong isolation	Cloud-native, microservices, high density, and agility

Table 1.1: Virtualization versus containerization summary

Now let's talk about how containerization helps in implementing a popular architectural pattern: microservices.

Containers and microservices

Containerization took off alongside the move to microservices. Instead of building one big, all-in-one app, microservices break things down into smaller units that can be built, deployed, and updated on their own. Containers make this much easier; they're a great way to package and run each service separately. This setup comes with several advantages, such as the following:

- **Granular isolation and deployment:** Each microservice, with its specific dependencies, can reside within a dedicated container. This promotes isolated environments, preventing conflicts and allowing independent updates without impacting other components of an application.
- **Scalability by design:** Microservices work best when you need to scale specific functions of an application under load. Containers facilitate rapid scaling by quickly replicating instances of the microservice in question. Orchestration platforms such as Kubernetes (on which OpenShift 4 is built) excel at managing these containerized microservices at scale. In the case of a monolith, you must scale an entire application, which is much slower and leads to inefficient use of computing resources.
- **Enhanced agility and resilience:** Smaller, focused microservice code bases promote faster development cycles and iterative updates. Microservices within containers can be modified and redeployed without disrupting the entire application system. This isolation provides better fault tolerance, as issues in one microservice are less likely to have a cascading effect and take down the whole application. Other microservices can often gracefully handle such failures, improving overall application uptime. One way to accomplish that is to connect all microservices together via a service mesh, which provides failover capabilities and circuit breaking to prevent propagation of failures, among other features. We will discuss this approach in more detail in *Chapter 14, Understanding Service Mesh and Distributed Tracing*.
- **Diverse development and technology flexibility:** Microservices allow you to choose appropriate technologies for different components of your application. Containers readily support this heterogeneous environment, as each microservice can have its own tailored tech stack within the container's boundaries. Each microservice can use the most suitable stack (databases, programming languages, etc.), independent of other services. This avoids being locked into a single technological stack.
- **Agility and development speed:** Smaller, focused services within a microservice architecture lead to faster development and release cycles. Teams can work independently on specific services, update them frequently, and deploy changes without major disruptions to the whole system.
- **Maintainability:** Small, well-defined microservices are inherently easier to understand, modify, and test compared to large, complex monolithic applications.

> Despite being an attractive design pattern, microservice architecture is not a silver bullet. There are cases when monoliths are preferable to microservices, for example, legacy applications, small teams without DevOps experience, rapid prototyping, learning, POCs, or a lack of supporting infrastructure, such as a service mesh.

OpenShift 4 builds upon this containerization foundation for its orchestration capabilities. It supports seamless deployment, scaling, networking, and management of containerized microservices. As you progress through this book, you'll understand how its tooling leverages containers to power highly dynamic microservice environments.

Now, let's talk about the technical foundation of containers.

How containers work

A container engine creates a union filesystem by merging container image layers. Because container image layers are immutable, a container engine adds a writable layer for runtime file modifications. Containers are designed to be ephemeral, which means that the container engine removes the writable layer when you remove the container. There are ways to preserve a container's state using Docker and Podman – with (see `docker/podman commit` and `docker/podman save`) or without metadata and history (see `docker/podman export`); however, it is considered an anti-pattern, and the recommended way to persist a container's data involves volumes. We will examine how they're implemented in Kubernetes and OpenShift in *Chapter 8*, *Working with Persistent Storage*.

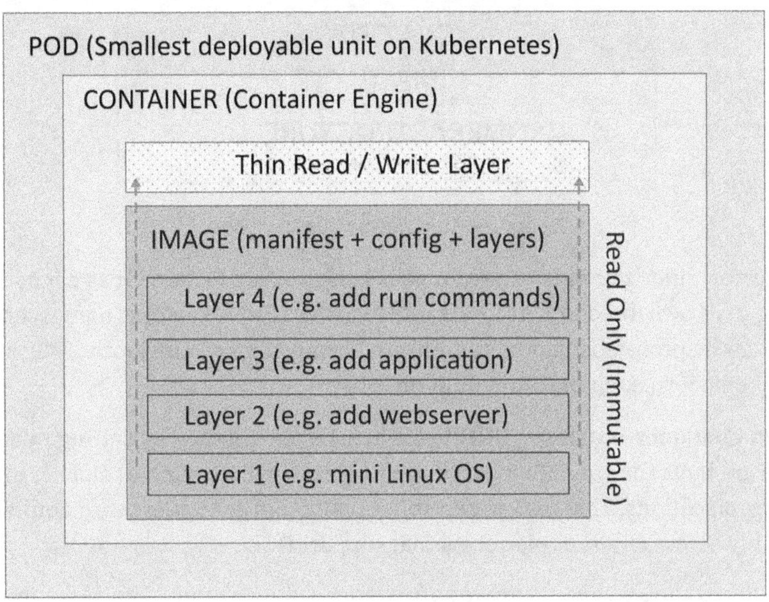

Figure 1.3: Container images

Containers rely on Linux kernel features, such as namespaces and cgroups. Cgroups are used for resource management, such as CPU time allocation and system memory. Namespaces, specifically `network`, `UID` (**user ID**), `IPC` (**inter-process communication**), `UTS` (**Unix Timesharing System**, isolates hostname and NIS domain), `PID` (**process ID**), and `mount`, provide the functionality to isolate processes within containers from each other and from the host system.

> When we're talking about namespaces in the context of containerization, we're referring to Linux kernel namespaces as process attributes, **not** Kubernetes namespaces (these are a completely different concept and will be discussed in detail in *Chapter 7, Application Security and Isolation*). This is to clarify the difference for those of you who may already be familiar with some Kubernetes entities.

If you run your Linux-based containers on Windows or macOS with solutions such as Podman Desktop or Docker Desktop, they will run containers in an isolated virtualized environment, in other words, in a VM with a Linux-based OS.

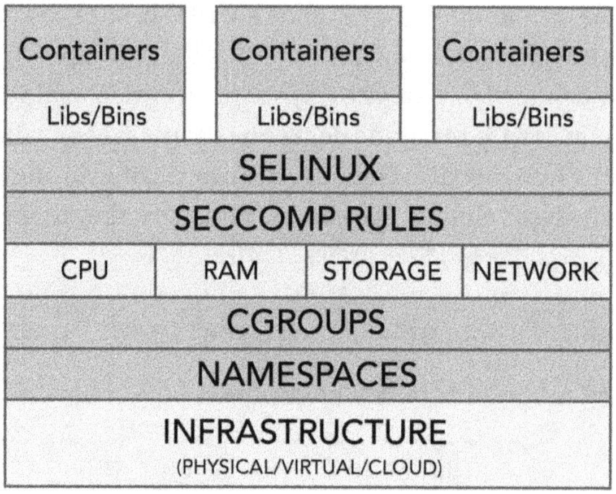

Figure 1.4: Containers under the hood

The idea behind containerization isn't new; it goes back to Unix tools such as `chroot`, which let you isolate a process in its own directory. As Linux evolved, new features such as namespaces and cgroups were added to handle process isolation and resource control more efficiently. These built-in kernel features are what modern containers are built on today.

Today, the **Open Container Initiative** (OCI) helps ensure consistency by setting open standards for how containers are built and run. Most popular container engines, such as Docker and Podman, follow these OCI specifications. That means developers can build containers with confidence, knowing they'll run reliably across different platforms that support OCI.

Setting up the lab environment

There's a saying, "*One good test is worth a thousand expert opinions.*" We follow the same principle in this book, and whatever we talk about, we try to verify in the lab, and urge you to follow the same advice. Trust but verify.

In *Chapters 1* and *2*, we mainly use a single instance of CentOS 9. In later chapters, we are going to utilize a mix of **OpenShift Local** and **OpenShift 4 UPI** (which stands for **User Provisioned Infrastructure**) multinode clusters built in a VMware vSphere environment. You don't need a dedicated server with a lot of resources to follow the labs in this book. You can complete most of the tasks on your laptop, provided that it has enough CPU and RAM, but we encourage you to have your own dedicated servers to be able to run a full OpenShift 4 installation.

Lab deployment options

There are multiple ways of creating the same virtual environment we have in this book. If you are proficient with cloud or virtualized environments such as VMware, Hyper-V, or KVM, feel free to use those.

We cannot cover all lab installation options in this book, as it's not our main focus, but we want to emphasize that it can be deployed on most of the systems, platforms, and cloud environments.

RHEL-based OS

For Podman and for testing overall, it is a good idea to have a production-like OS. Despite the significant amount of Linux flavors available, enterprises usually focus on the Red Hat products, and **Red Hat Enterprise Linux** (RHEL) could be called a de facto standard. Other popular enterprise Linux distributions are **SUSE Linux Enterprise Server** (SLES), Ubuntu LTS, and Oracle Linux, so containerization is not limited to only RHEL derivatives.

If you prefer to use something open source in your lab, you can always go with **Community Enterprise Operating System** (CentOS), which is an open source Linux distribution that will work well for your lab and is well suited for Docker and Podman testing and running, or just as a developer's workstation. Another good choice is Rocky Linux, a CentOS successor that is binary compatible with RHEL and provides Podman through its package manager.

Public cloud providers

You can use any cloud provider, such as **Amazon Web Services** (AWS), Microsoft Azure, Google Cloud, or others, to deploy both CentOS 9 and OpenShift 4 while you are going through this book. There might be minor differences in installation and deployment, but overall, they are very similar. If you are using one of these public cloud providers, make sure that you have enough CPU, RAM, and storage.

> When running on AWS, we do not recommend using Amazon Linux 2023. It may seem like a natural choice on Amazon; however, it has compatibility issues with CentOS and Fedora, and it doesn't support installing Podman via the package manager.

Private cloud providers

There are many private cloud providers that also would work perfectly and can be used for the purpose of this book. Please feel free to use any if you have access to those, such as VMware and KVM-based solutions, and, of course, Microsoft Hyper-V. In this book, we will pay special attention to VMware, since it is the most common private cloud solution we usually see in large enterprises, so we believe it may be helpful to you in your journey.

VMware ESXi and vSphere

VMware ESXi and vCenter are both components of the VMware vSphere virtualization platform. ESXi is a hypervisor that creates and manages VMs on a single physical server. vCenter Server is the centralized platform for managing vSphere environments.

We use VMware ESXi and vSphere to deploy a full OpenShift by leveraging the UPI installation method. You are not required to have the same setup to complete all the tasks, but it will make your experience better if you have a similar setup as we have in this book.

Refer to the official installation documentation to install VMware ESXi on your server from [1].

VMware was acquired by Broadcom at the end of 2023 and is going through a lot of transition in its documentation. If the preceding direct link stops working, refer to the Broadcom documentation at [2].

QEMU and KVM

The KVM acronym is self-descriptive: it stands for **kernel-based virtual machine.** Essentially, it is a kernel module that turns your Linux into a hypervisor. KVM is very often used together with **QEMU**, which stands for **Quick EMUlator**. QEMU is an open source machine emulator, which allows you to emulate (or virtualize) a complete system, including CPU, memory, disks, and so on. When QEMU works with KVM, it relies on KVM's ability to virtualize "hardware" at near-native speed. Both QEMU and KVM are available for the majority of OSs, and can be easily installed and controlled over CLI (`virsh`) and GUI (`virt-manager`).

Please refer to the documentation at [3] to read more about how to enable and use it in RHEL.

Microsoft Hyper-V

Microsoft Hyper-V is a hardware virtualization from Microsoft that lets users create and run VMs on the Windows OS. The free, standalone version of Hyper-V has been discontinued as of Windows Server 2025 (Standard and Datacenter editions). It is now available as a Windows role whose activation is free; however, Windows itself, as well as running VMs, must be properly licensed. Read more at [4].

You can enable it either on Windows 10/11 (only Pro and Education editions) or Windows Server if you have a dedicated server. We won't be covering this deployment option in this book, but you can refer to the Microsoft documentation on enabling the Hyper-V role and use the same installation methods from this book to deploy OpenShift 4.

Consult with the official installation documentation at [5] to install Hyper-V on your system.

VirtualBox

Oracle VM VirtualBox is a free, open source virtualization software that allows users to create and run VMs on their laptops. It's a cross-platform tool that can virtualize x86 and AMD64/Intel64 computing architectures.

Refer to the official installation documentation at [6] to install VirtualBox on your server.

VMware Fusion and VMware Workstation

VMware Fusion and VMware Workstation are both VM tools that allow users to run multiple operating systems from a single Mac or PC. The main difference between the two is that they run on different platforms:

- **VMware Fusion**: A Mac-specific version of VMware Workstation. Supports both x64 and ARM-based processors.
- **VMware Workstation**: Allows Intel-based desktops to run different operating systems inside a VM on a Windows-based host OS.
- **VMware Workstation Player**: A free desktop application that lets users run a single VM on a Windows or Linux PC. It can also create its own VMs and run existing ones.

Both VMware Fusion and VMware Workstation are commercial products, but as of the time of writing, both VMware Fusion and desktop versions were recently made free for personal use. VMware was acquired by Broadcom in late 2023, and in early 2024, it made VMware Fusion/Workstation available for personal use.

Installing CentOS 9

For the next sections, you need to deploy a VM with CentOS 9. Depending on your preferences, please select a platform: either a public or private cloud, a virtualization platform such as VMware vCenter, or just use your laptop to install VirtualBox or VMware Fusion.

Please ensure you can reach the VM over SSH and you have a “root” privilege to execute the package manager commands that we provide in the next section of this chapter.

You can download CentOS for your platform from the official repository at [7].

Podman overview

Containers are transforming software development. They package applications and their dependencies into portable units, ensuring that they run the same way on any compatible system, be it your laptop or a massive cloud-based cluster. This streamlines deployment, promotes consistency, and empowers microservice architectures. Podman offers a unique way to harness the power of containers.

What is Podman?

Podman is a command-line tool designed for managing containers and related components: images, volumes, and even groups of containers known as **pods**. Here’s how it differs from Docker:

- **Daemonless architecture**: Unlike traditional container runtimes, Podman doesn’t rely on a central, long-running background process (daemon). This translates into security advantages and sometimes better integration with system administration tools.
- **Kubernetes compatibility**: Podman closely aligns with Kubernetes concepts and can manipulate pods directly. This is key for developers aiming to mirror their development experience closely to a Kubernetes-based production environment.

- **OCI compliance**: Podman plays a nice role in the broader container ecosystem as it works with images compliant with the OCI standards. This ensures that the images you build will work across other container tooling.

Why choose Podman?

If containers are so revolutionary, why not just use a tool such as Docker? Here's where Podman shines:

- **Security-conscious design**: Its daemonless approach reduces the attack surface and minimizes the privileges that the tool requires.
- **Rootless containers**: Podman enables running containers without administrative (root) privileges. This promotes secure practices, as even a breached container has far less ability to inflict damage.
- **Developer-friendly focus**: Podman's compatibility with Kubernetes vocabulary and concepts creates a smoother transition from local development to large-scale deployment scenarios.
- **Part of a rich ecosystem**: Projects such as Buildah (focused on image creation) and Skopeo (image repository inspection) complement Podman, creating a toolkit that aligns with open source standards.

Let's look at the rootless aspect of Podman in more detail.

Benefits of rootless containers

While Docker is built on a client-server model, with the Docker daemon running as root and handling requests from the Docker client (usually, the Docker binary), Podman has a fundamentally different architecture: it can run containerized processes as a regular user. This approach has several benefits:

- **Reduced risk of privilege escalation**: Even if a container is exploited, it won't be able to obtain privileges beyond those of a user that the container runs as, limiting the blast radius.
- **Reduced attack surface**: Without a daemon running with root privileges, there is less to exploit and less opportunity to damage the host system.
- **No need for elevated privileges**: Unprivileged users can run their own instances of Podman without having to obtain root access on the host machine, leading to better isolation, security, and less headache for system administrators.

Getting started with Podman

To start running containers with Podman, we are going to use CentOS 9, as we previously discussed. Go ahead and log in using your credentials. In our case, the user's name is `redhat`:

```
$ ssh redhat@192.168.164.134
Warning: Permanently added '192.168.164.134' (ED25519) to the list of known
hosts.
redhat@192.168.164.134's password:
[redhat@localhost ~]$
```

You can also set up SSH key-based authentication using the following command:

```
$ ssh-copy-id redhat@192.168.164.134
```

Here, `192.168.164.134` is the IP address of your CentOS 9 VM.

The IP address of the VM that you have might be different, and you can get it by using the `ip address` command in your terminal.

We also assume that you are familiar with the Linux CLI basics, but to clarify, $ will follow the command executed by an unprivileged user (`redhat`, in our case), and # will follow the command executed by the root user.

You might need to follow the Podman documentation for the installation procedure if Podman is not installed by default. You can find it at [8].

Depending on how you deploy a VM to run exercises in this chapter, there are many ways to obtain the VM's IP address. Use platform-specific means of doing so. For example, Vagrant can create KVM-based VMs, and after a VM is up and running, you just need to run `vagrant ssh` to connect to it. Learn more about Vagrant and how it manages the VM lifecycle at [9].

Run the following command to install Podman on your VM. You'll need to provide the root password from the initial setup:

```
$ sudo dnf -y install podman
We trust you have received the usual lecture from the local System
Administrator. It usually boils down to these three things:
    #1) Respect the privacy of others.
    #2) Think before you type.
    #3) With great power comes great responsibility.
[sudo] password for redhat: Redhat1!
...
<output omitted>
...
Complete!
```

Now, we can pull a simple HTTP server using the `nginx` image from the public repository:

```
$ podman pull nginx
✓ docker.io/library/nginx:latest
...
<output omitted>
...
760b7cbba31e196288effd2af6924c42637ac5e0d67db4de6309f24518844676
```

You can check the status of the downloaded image, as follows:

```
$ podman images
REPOSITORY      TAG          IMAGE ID      CREATED     SIZE
docker.io/library/nginx latest  ..cbba31e 8 days ago 196 MB
```

Nice, there's the container image we have just downloaded. Let's run it:

```
$ podman run -d -p 8080:80 docker.io/library/nginx
```

In case you haven't used Docker or Podman before, here's what the flags from the preceding command mean:

- `-d`: Run a container as a daemon, so that it disconnects from the terminal and keeps running in the background
- `-p`: Forward connections from `localhost:8080` to port `80` inside the container, so that we can reach the application by sending a request to `localhost:8080` instead of having to obtain the container's IP address

You can verify that the container is running by running the following command:

```
$ podman ps
```

Run the `curl` command to verify that the web server is available:

```
$ curl localhost:8080
<!DOCTYPE html>
...
<output omitted>
...
</html>
```

It works! We can safely stop and remove this running container using its ID or using the following command:

```
$ podman rm -f $(podman ps -qa)
d4b1ce044bfa
```

This quick demo showed you how easy it is to bring the `nginx` web server up and down using Podman.

Core concepts: images, containers, and pods

These are the main concepts of running containers:

- **Images:** An image is a binary artifact that packages an application, its dependencies, and metadata in a special format that is understood by compliant container engines. On a lower level, they are implemented as filesystem snapshots containing differences and layered on top of each other. They contain all the files and instructions needed to create a self-contained, executable environment. You typically fetch prebuilt images from registries such as Docker Hub.

- **Containers:** Containers are running instances of your images. You can have multiple containers derived from the same image, each potentially configured slightly differently. They are generally ephemeral, designed to be replaced as you update your software.
- **Pods:** A pod in Podman is a group of related containers. They share resources such as network namespaces and storage, mirroring many pod scenarios on full-blown Kubernetes clusters. Strictly speaking, any pod in Podman and Kubernetes/OpenShift includes at least two containers: an `app` container and a so-called `pause` container that is responsible for creating a network namespace, acquiring an IP address, and keeping that namespace alive so that if the app container crashes, it can rejoin the namespace without losing its address and having to obtain a new one. Learn more about `pause` containers at [10].

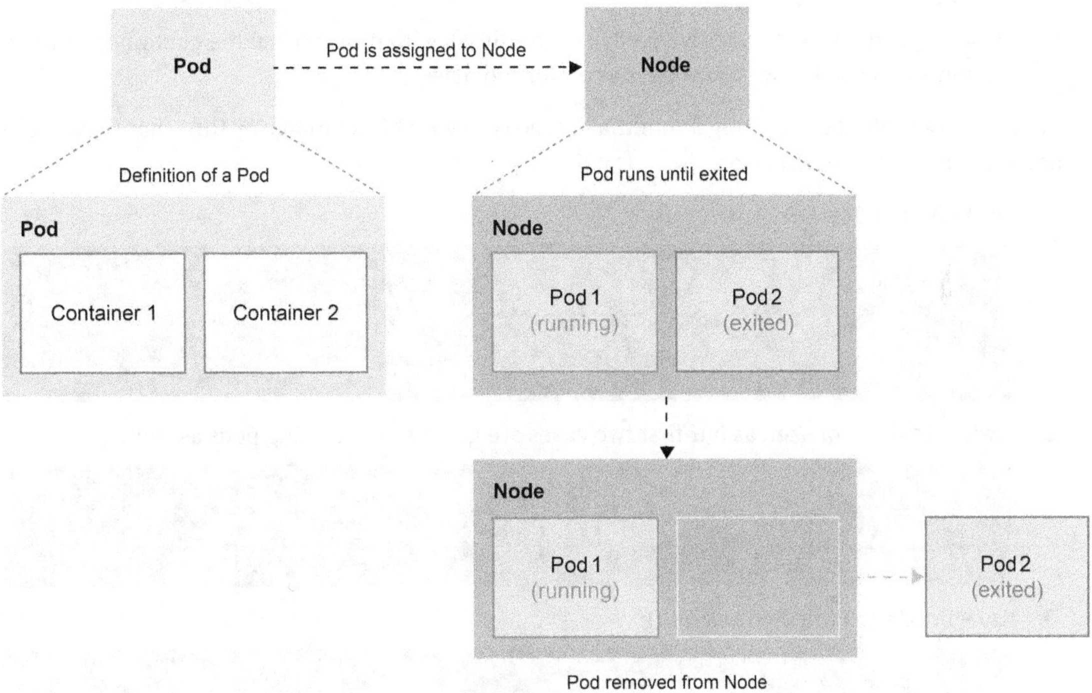

Figure 1.5: Pod overview

Managing everyday tasks

Podman offers intuitive commands such as the following:

- **List images:** `podman images`
- **List running containers:** `podman ps` (add `-a` at the end of the command to see stopped containers, too)
- **See inside a container:** `podman exec -it <container_name or ID> sh` (this launches an interactive shell inside the container)
- **Tailing logs:** `podman logs -f <container_name or ID>` for monitoring output live

These basic commands will enable you to experiment with various containerized software readily. Try them on your own and see how they work.

Root versus rootless

We have already discussed some of the benefits of rootless containers in this chapter, and now it's time to see it in action. We are going to look at four main use cases running containers with Podman:

- Running Podman as root, with processes in the container running as root
- Running Podman as root, with processes in the container running as non-root
- Running Podman as an unprivileged user (rootless), with processes in the container running as root
- Running Podman as an unprivileged user (rootless), with processes in the container running as non-root (also known as rootless as a non-root user)

Let's prepare our lab VM by pulling a minimal image (**Universal Base Image** or **UBI**) that we will use to demonstrate all those scenarios:

1. SSH into our CentOS 9 VM:

```
$ ssh redhat@192.168.164.134
Warning: Permanently added '192.168.164.134' (ED25519) to the list of
known hosts.
[redhat@localhost ~]$
```

2. Switch to the root user, as our first two cases are going to be running pods as root:

```
[redhat@localhost ~]$ sudo -i
[sudo] password for redhat:
[root@localhost ~]#
```

3. Download `ubi9` (the Red Hat UBI):

```
# podman pull ubi9
Resolved "ubi9" as an alias (/etc/containers/registries.conf.d/001-rhel-
shortnames.conf)
...
<output omitted>
...
Storing signatures
b5b4e09c00c5d19e1506d6439f94a583443ac7871b27d498d98f67a1a2a79450
```

Now, let's get to the scenarios themselves, starting with running everything as root.

Running Podman as root, with processes in the container running as root

Run the container as the root user:

```
# podman run -it ubi9 id
uid=0(root) gid=0(root) groups=0(root)
```

Here, we are running a container as the root user with a UID of `0` inside the container, and `0` from the host OS perspective.

Running Podman as root, with processes in the container running as non-root

Run the container as a non-root user:

```
# podman run -it -u sync ubi9 id
uid=5(sync) gid=0(root) groups=0(root)
```

Here, we are running a container as a `sync` user with a UID of `5` inside the container, and `5` from the host OS perspective.

Running Podman as an unprivileged user (rootless), with processes in the container running as root

Exit from the root user back to the `redhat` user and run the following command:

```
# exit
$ id
uid=1000(redhat) gid=1000(redhat) groups=1000(redhat)
$ podman run -it ubi9 id
uid=0(root) gid=0(root) groups=0(root)
```

Here, we are running a container as the root user with an UID of `0` inside the container, and a `redhat` UID of `1000` from the host OS perspective.

> We use an account called `redhat` here just as an example. Depending on how you provisioned your VM and created a non-root user, it may have a different UID or name. If your user is different, but you want to mirror examples in this chapter more closely, you can create it with the following command: `useradd -u 1000 redhat`.

Running Podman as an unprivileged user (rootless), with processes in the container running as non-root (also known as rootless as a non-root user)

Run the following command:

```
$ id
uid=1000(redhat) gid=1000(redhat) groups=1000(redhat)
$ podman run -it -u sync ubi9 id
uid=5(sync) gid=0(root) groups=0(root)
```

Here, we are running a container as a sync user with a UID of 5 inside the container, and a different UID from the host OS perspective.

Here is a summary of these four options from the security point of view:

Scenario	Can create new processes inside the container	Can kill processes inside the container	Can kill processes outside the container	Security considerations
Podman as root, container as root	Yes	Yes	Yes, the root has full power on the host system	Least secure option; exploit gives total control
Podman as root, container as non-root	Yes	Yes, root-equivalent within the container	No (unless severe misconfiguration)	Mitigates damage, but Podman itself is still vulnerable
Podman as non-root, container as root	Yes, but confined by user namespace restrictions	Yes, within the container	Very limited: only if host resources are improperly exposed	Significantly more secure with careful setup
Podman as non-root, container as non-root	Yes, with similar restrictions as outside the container	Yes, within the container	Practically impossible (except extreme misconfiguration)	Most secure; limits potential damage drastically

Table 1.2: Root versus rootless comparison

Now that we've explored various combinations of host and container UIDs, let's take a look at how Podman differs from Docker, an older engine that pioneered containerization as it is known today, back in March 2013.

Podman versus Docker

The world of containerization often centers around Docker, the tool that brought containers into the mainstream. Podman, however, provides a good alternative that meets the demands of developers and administrators. Let's look at their core differences and advantages, and when to choose one over the other:

- **Docker's daemon:** In contrast to Podman, Docker relies on a central, long-running daemon process (`dockerd`). This daemon handles image management, launching containers, networking, and most interactions with the Docker command-line tool (`docker`).
- **Podman's liberation:** Podman eschews the daemon. Instead, it uses the `fork/exec` model: it spawns child processes when necessary for running containers and managing images.

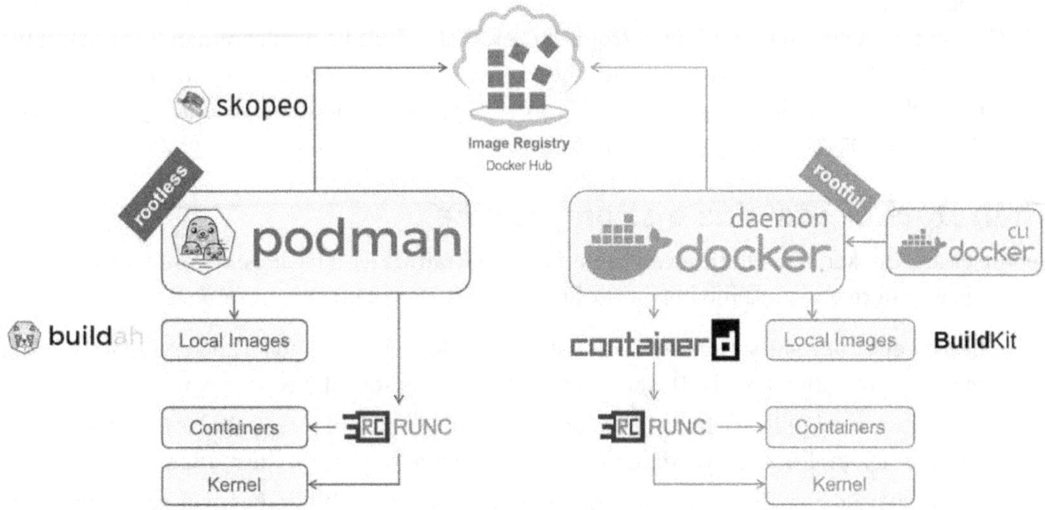

Figure 1.6: Podman versus Docker

Security plays a huge role in the world of containers, and while Docker came first, it couldn't address all the issues and demands of real-world needs as it evolved; this is where Podman comes into the picture.

Security implications

The daemon approach introduces potential concerns with elevated privileges and expanded attack surface:

- **Elevated privileges:** The Docker daemon often runs as root, giving it vast control over the host system. A vulnerability in the daemon has far-reaching implications.
- **Expanded attack surface:** A running daemon is another process that attackers can target, increasing the area where risks reside.

These issues are perfectly handled by Podman's architecture, as follows:

- **Rootless by design:** Podman encourages (and in many cases, enforces) running containers without root privileges, limiting the damage a compromised container could inflict.
- **Smaller footprint:** Without a long-running daemon, there's less background activity for an attacker to potentially exploit.

Developer friendliness and Kubernetes

Though Podman is a dedicated project and initiative, it is backward compatible with Docker and further extends its capabilities:

- **Command parity:** Podman was designed to be familiar to Docker users. Many commands (`build`, `run`, `ps`, and `images`) translate directly, easing the learning curve.

- **Pod emphasis:** Pods, groups of tightly coupled containers, are first-class citizens in Podman, so on top of commands adopted from Docker, it also adds its own commands for manipulating pods. Developers targeting Kubernetes find that this mirrors production environments more closely, providing a *practice field* of sorts. One useful command, `podman generate kube <POD_NAME_OR_ID>`, can generate a pod's YAML for Kubernetes, easing migration.

When Docker remains a strong choice

In some cases, Docker can still be a valid solution, especially if it's a legacy environment with small local projects where users are relying on Docker Desktop. Here are some examples:

- **Legacy environments:** Organizations with heavy Docker investments and established tooling may find transitions costly. Docker's maturity remains advantageous in some contexts.
- **Docker Swarm:** Docker's built-in orchestration solution, while less popular than Kubernetes, provides a simplified onboarding experience for smaller-scale orchestration needs.
- **GUI focus:** Docker Desktop provides a graphical interface. While Podman has its own functionally similar GUI project [11], backed by **Cloud Native Computing Foundation** (CNCF, part of the Linux Foundation), Docker Desktop has had more time to mature and may appeal to a more conservative audience.

Additional considerations

You also need to consider the following criteria in order to make the right choice. It's not always obvious how to do it, but this is where the companies that provide professional services shine:

- **Ecosystem growth:** Podman is part of the Red Hat ecosystem, driving adoption. Its community and related tooling continue to expand rapidly.
- **Specific features:** Some edge cases exist where niche capabilities reside only in one tool or the other. Deep investigation of these becomes necessary for specialized use cases.
- **Vendor support:** If using commercially supported enterprise Linux, consider that Podman may be the officially supported container runtime, influencing your decision.

When to pick Podman

Security and containerization-focused development are key points in the Kubernetes world. That is why a lot of attention is going toward the following:

- **Security:** Podman's design inherently promotes better security practices. Choose it for environments handling sensitive data.
- **Development:** Working on projects intended for Kubernetes? Podman provides a more seamless mirroring of the production environment.
- **Rootless Containers:** For situations where containers must not gain excessive privileges, Podman is often the better fit.

> Docker Swarm is not supported by Podman. As of the time of writing this book, there is no planned feature similar to it in Podman, the main reason being that Kubernetes is now the recommended container orchestration engine. Read more at [12].

When Docker still makes sense

But there are still cases where Docker works better than Podman:

- **Docker-centric workflows:** Migrating existing Docker-based setups takes time and effort. If a compelling reason is absent, staying with Docker might be the most efficient path in the short term.
- **Ease of use (GUI):** For those who strongly prefer graphical interfaces, Docker Desktop provides a more streamlined experience than the current Podman GUI tools.
- **Small-scale, well-understood workloads:** Docker's daemon model, when security is well managed, might be perfectly acceptable for contained, less security-sensitive deployments.

As container technology continues to grow, both Docker and Podman offer solid solutions, each with its own strengths.

Docker helped kick off the container movement by making things easier to use and more accessible to developers. It runs on a background service (called a daemon), which handles container operations behind the scenes. Docker Desktop is the most common developer-friendly solution, which allows developers to work locally, control deployments, images, and volumes, and even allows them to run a local version of Kubernetes, all with enterprise-grade support.

Podman, as the CLI tool, dramatically differs from Docker, providing a security-focused and lightweight alternative. Podman is a daemonless solution, available across Red Hat-based operating systems (RHEL, Fedora, and CentOS), and allows rootless container support, which provides better security.

Podman mimics Docker's CLI, and the transition from Docker to Podman and vice versa is usually very simple. Podman Desktop doesn't have an enterprise version or some of the nice features that Docker Desktop has. However, for those who are planning to use OpenShift, it may be preferred, since it not only has a local version of Kubernetes but also allows you to simply run a development OpenShift cluster.

Understanding the strengths of both will help you choose the right tool – whether you're supporting today's workflows or planning for a more scalable, secure future.

Summary

In this chapter, we briefly covered what containerization is, how it benefits the modern world by itself, and how it lives together with and differs from virtualization.

Most importantly, we discussed how containers work in OpenShift 4, as this is the main product we will use in this book. This book is full of practical exercises, so we need to build multiple lab environments; one of the simplest and most accessible ones is running on the local laptop as a VM. We brought up a Linux VM and completed several practical tasks with Podman basics. We went over essential concepts such as images, containers, and pods, and how they work together. From there, we compared root versus rootless containers and their different implementation scenarios and outcomes.

Finally, we did a comprehensive comparison of Docker versus Podman from different angles, including architecture, security, and development points of view.

In the next chapter, we will go into a brief history of Kubernetes, how it works, and its architecture basics before we dive into OpenShift 4. We will see what makes OpenShift 4 special and how it differs from standard distributions, the way to install it, and key differences in comparison to its predecessor, OpenShift 3. Then, we will bring up our first OpenShift Local cluster on our desktop and finish the chapter with a quick quiz to ensure that you understood its main topics.

References

To learn more about the topics that were covered in this chapter, take a look at the following resources:

- [1] *VMware ESX Installation and Setup*: `https://techdocs.broadcom.com/us/en/vmware-cis/vsphere/vsphere/9-0/esx-installation-and-setup.html`
- [2] *Broadcom Support Documents and Downloads*: `https://docs.broadcom.com/`
- [3] *Enabling virtualization on AMD64 and Intel 64*: `https://docs.redhat.com/en/documentation/red_hat_enterprise_linux/9/html/configuring_and_managing_virtualization/assembly_enabling-virtualization-in-rhel-9_configuring-and-managing-virtualization#proc_enabling-virtualization-in-rhel-9_assembly_enabling-virtualization-in-rhel-9`
- [4] *Windows Server 2025 and FREE Hyper-V Dream*: `https://www.starwindsoftware.com/blog/windows-server-2025-and-free-hyper-v-dream/`
- [5] *Install Hyper-V*: `https://learn.microsoft.com/en-us/virtualization/hyper-v-on-windows/quick-start/enable-hyper-v`
- [6] Oracle VirtualBox: User Guide for Release 7.1 | *Chapter 2. Installation Details*: `https://www.virtualbox.org/manual/ch02.html`
- [7] *Download CentOS Stream*: `https://www.CentOS.org/download/`
- [8] Podman installation instructions: `https://podman.io/docs/installation`
- [9] *Vagrant Documentation*: `https://developer.hashicorp.com/vagrant/docs`
- [10] *The Almighty Pause Container:* `https://www.ianlewis.org/en/almighty-pause-container`
- [11] *Podman Desktop*: `https://podman-desktop.io/`
- [12] *Podman List Archives | Podman Swarm*: `https://lists.podman.io/archives/list/podman@lists.podman.io/thread/7NN6SFSBAF4553CXHKOFHWCSQ7IQR3M3/`

Quiz

Test your understanding of Podman with this quick quiz. Remember, some questions may have more than one correct answer!

1. Which of these statements accurately describes Podman's architecture?
    a. It relies on a long-running daemon process similar to Docker
    b. It utilizes a `fork/exec` model for managing containers and images
    c. It requires root privileges for all container operations
2. True or false? If you are already familiar with Docker commands, you'll feel right at home with most of Podman's basic usage.
    a. True
    b. False
3. Which of these tasks can Podman help you with? (Select all that apply.)
    a. Building container images
    b. Inspecting container images stored in remote registries
    c. Orchestrating large-scale, multi-container applications across a cluster
    d. Running a containerized database server
4. In a Podman context, what is a pod?
    a. A standalone container with its own network and storage resources
    b. A group of closely related containers sharing a network namespace and potentially storage
    c. A set of commands used to manage Podman from the command line
5. You want to run containers with the least possible privileges on your system. Is Podman or Docker likely the better default choice?
    a. Podman
    b. Docker
    c. They are equivalent in this regard

Answers

1. **b**. Unlike Docker, which operates on a client-server basis, Podman launches a child process using the `fork()` system call and then uses `exec()` to replace it with a container process, eliminating the need for a server and improving security.
2. **a**. Most Podman commands maintain backward compatibility with Docker, easing transition.
3. **a**, **b**, and **d**. To manage a complex application that consists of many interacting microservices running in containers, you will need an orchestrating engine, such as Kubernetes, or its derivatives (OpenShift being one of them).

4. **b.** Each pod contains one or more containers that share Linux kernel namespaces, for example, `network`, which means that processes inside the same pod can communicate with each other through the local network (localhost).
5. **a.** Due to its daemonless architecture and non-reliance on root access, Podman is a better choice when a better security posture is desired.

2

Kubernetes and OpenShift

The way we manage containerized applications has changed dramatically in recent years, and **Kubernetes** has been at the heart of that shift. In this chapter, we'll take a step back to look at how Kubernetes came to be, and the problems it set out to solve in the growing world of containers. Understanding its origin story helps explain why it has become such a crucial part of modern infrastructure.

In this chapter, we will break down the Kubernetes architecture and explain how Kubernetes components work together. The basics of Kubernetes are important for everyone who is looking into containerization and would like to adopt it in their environments, especially when it comes to performance, scaling, and high availability.

Later in this chapter, we will move forward to the main topic of this book (Red Hat OpenShift 4) and see the difference and what kind of broad ecosystem Red Hat prepared for platform engineers, developers, and architects – everyone who is looking for a reliable and standardized platform that would work for them on-premises and in the cloud. First, let's talk about Kubernetes itself, which is still the base for OpenShift and many other platforms.

To make all of this more tangible, you'll install and use **OpenShift Local** on your desktop. This hands-on setup gives you direct experience with a real Kubernetes environment, which is great for learning and trying things out in a safe, local space.

By the end of the chapter, you'll have a solid grasp of what Kubernetes is, how OpenShift 4 builds on it, and how to get started managing applications in a modern, container-based infrastructure.

We will cover the following main topics in this chapter:

- Brief history of Kubernetes
- Kubernetes distributions and managed solutions
- How Kubernetes functions
- OpenShift's differentiators
- What is new in OpenShift 4?

- Installing OpenShift Local
- Production considerations

Let's get started!

Technical requirements

In this chapter, you will need the following:

- Internet access
- Bash shell (other CLI shells work as well)
- Firefox (recommended) or any other browser
- Red Hat account

You can access this book's GitHub repository at `https://github.com/PacktPublishing/Learn-OpenShift-Second-Edition`.

Brief history of Kubernetes

Kubernetes was born out of Google's years of experience running containers at scale. Before Kubernetes, Google used an internal system called **Borg** to manage huge clusters of machines. Borg introduced ideas such as treating infrastructure as a shared pool of resources, using containers as the standard unit of deployment, and managing applications through declarative configuration. These core principles would later become central to Kubernetes.

Seeing the potential to bring these ideas to the wider tech community, Google open-sourced Kubernetes in mid-2014. Its focus on simplicity for developers, powerful orchestration, and strong community support quickly made it one of the fastest-growing open source projects in the infrastructure world.

The **Cloud Native Computing Foundation** (**CNCF**) was established to support Kubernetes and its ecosystem growth, so Kubernetes is the very first CNCF project. But the CNCF didn't just help Kubernetes gain traction; it built a thriving ecosystem around it. By bringing together tools, standards, and a global community, the CNCF made it much easier for organizations to adopt cloud-native practices. As more teams shifted toward **microservice architectures**, Kubernetes naturally became the platform of choice for managing these distributed, containerized applications.

Since its launch, Kubernetes has continued to evolve quickly. With each release, it adds features and improvements that make it more powerful, stable, and flexible. Some of the biggest improvements include the following:

- **Ease of use**: A focus on simplified installation, networking configuration, user-friendly tools, and a variety of interfaces eased the entry barrier.
- **Extensibility**: Mechanisms such as **Custom Resource Definitions** (**CRDs**) enabled seamless integration of new application types and management concepts. This stimulated Operator development, streamlining even complex application management.
- **Security**: **Role-Based Access Control** (**RBAC**), network policies, admission plugins, and integration with third-party security solutions helped mature the security posture of Kubernetes.

Kubernetes has become the leading platform for container orchestration. It's the standard choice for running cloud-native applications at scale, with strong support from all major cloud providers. Beyond managing containers, it also powers innovations in serverless computing, service meshes, and edge deployments.

Kubernetes distributions and managed solutions

The core Kubernetes project provides a strong foundation for container orchestration, but real-world use often calls for more, such as security hardening, easier upgrades, or integrations with existing infrastructure.

That's why a variety of **Kubernetes distributions** have emerged, each adding its own tools, features, and operational models on top of upstream Kubernetes.

These distributions generally fall into two main categories, depending on ownership, the level of control they provide, and the expertise required to operate them:

- **Cloud-managed:** Managed by cloud providers such as Google (GKE), Amazon (EKS), and Microsoft (AKS), these run directly on the provider's infrastructure and abstract much of the operational complexity. In most cases (as with Amazon EKS), cloud-managed solutions are managed according to the shared responsibility model; an enterprise manages its apps and data, while a cloud provider is in charge of the control plane (which is hidden from customers), security patching, maintenance, and availability.
- **Self-managed:** These are installed, fully owned, and operated by the organization itself, often (but not always) on-premises or in hybrid environments. Examples include Red Hat OpenShift, Rancher, and VMware Tanzu. These give you more control, but also more responsibility. They also require more in-house engineers and deeper involvement during upgrades, maintenance, and troubleshooting of the control plane.

We are not focusing here on all the pros and cons of every Kubernetes-based platform currently available, but it is important to clarify these main groups and also mention lightweight and easy-to-use K3s [1] and K0s [2]. These also allow you to spin up a little Kubernetes cluster very easily, but may be more suitable for edge deployments or some lab or home lab deployments.

Why distributions matter

The "vanilla" or upstream version of Kubernetes is like a box of Lego bricks; you get full flexibility, but you must assemble everything yourself. Setting it up typically involves manual steps such as configuring `kubeadm`, provisioning `etcd`, and managing core control plane components. Upgrades can be challenging and require careful planning to avoid disruptions.

Vanilla Kubernetes is often not the first choice for enterprises that need vendor support, integrated tooling, and hardened, production-ready features. However, in some cases, especially in the telecommunications sector (Telco), large organizations adopt and contribute directly to upstream Kubernetes. In fact, some Telcos have become significant contributors to the Kubernetes project, shaping its development to meet their large-scale, real-time infrastructure needs.

In contrast, Kubernetes distributions like OpenShift offer streamlined installation through tools such as **Installer-Provisioned Infrastructure** (IPI), which automates provisioning and deployment. These distributions often provide guided upgrades as well, making the process smoother and less error-prone.

When it comes to integrations, vanilla Kubernetes gives you the flexibility to choose tools, but it's up to you to wire them together. For example, adding monitoring (e.g., Prometheus), logging (e.g., Fluentd and Elasticsearch), or CI/CD tools (e.g., Jenkins, GitLab CI) must be done manually. This level of customization is powerful, but it can be time-consuming and prone to misconfigurations.

Distributions such as OpenShift simplify this by including a curated set of pre-integrated tools. You get a web-based console, built-in monitoring and logging dashboards, a container image registry, and CI/CD pipelines powered by Tekton or Jenkins, all out of the box.

Still, the most important difference is enterprise support. Vanilla Kubernetes is community-supported, which is great for learning and open collaboration, but it doesn't include formal support channels. Troubleshooting can require deep expertise. Distributions such as OpenShift come with vendor-backed support, making them a better fit for production environments that need stability and rapid issue resolution.

Let's summarize the advantages of enterprise-grade distributions:

- Simplified setup and management
- Integrated tools for CI/CD, logging, and monitoring
- Professional support and consulting
- Enhanced security, for example, projects and **SecurityContextConstraints** (**SCCs**) for multitenancy in large organizations
- Automated day-2 operations, such as backup/restore and automated cluster lifecycle management
- Extra vetting, testing, and certification. These are especially crucial for businesses with strict regulatory requirements, for example, handling of sensitive data or **Personally Identifiable Information** (**PII**)
- Professional training

Understanding these differences is crucial when choosing the right Kubernetes distribution for your organization. Whether you're a manager, administrator, or developer, this decision can directly impact your team's efficiency, security, and long-term success.

How Kubernetes functions

Most Kubernetes distributions follow the same basic architecture. They're made up of two main parts:

- **Control plane**: The brain of the system. Usually deployed across an odd number of nodes (1, 3, 5, etc.) for high availability. The control plane runs core services such as the Kubernetes API, scheduler, and `etcd`. Depending on the platform and deployment mode, the following configurations are supported:
    - All control plane components are packaged as images and run as Pods managed by Deployments and StatefulSets

- **Static Pods** (static pod is a pod not managed by the Kubernetes API but directly by the kubelet on its node. These pods are created by placing their manifests in a special directory on the node. They can be viewed using `kubectl/oc`, but they cannot be deleted through the API):
    - Traditional (control plane components run directly on a physical machine or VM as systemd services)
    - Managed (managed by a cloud provider, for example, EKS)
- **Worker nodes (data plane)**: These nodes run the actual applications. Developers use the web UI or CLI tooling to submit definitions of workloads to the API server, and the scheduler running on the control plane tries to find appropriate worker nodes for them.

OpenShift uses its own deployment mode, called **standalone**, where control plane components run as Pods managed by separate cluster Operators, while the kubelet and container runtime (CRI-O) run as systemd services on nodes. Another deployment mode is called **hosted**; it is distinguished by running the control plane on a separate cluster using HyperShift [3].

The following diagram serves as a visual representation of how different components of Kubernetes are distributed across a cluster:

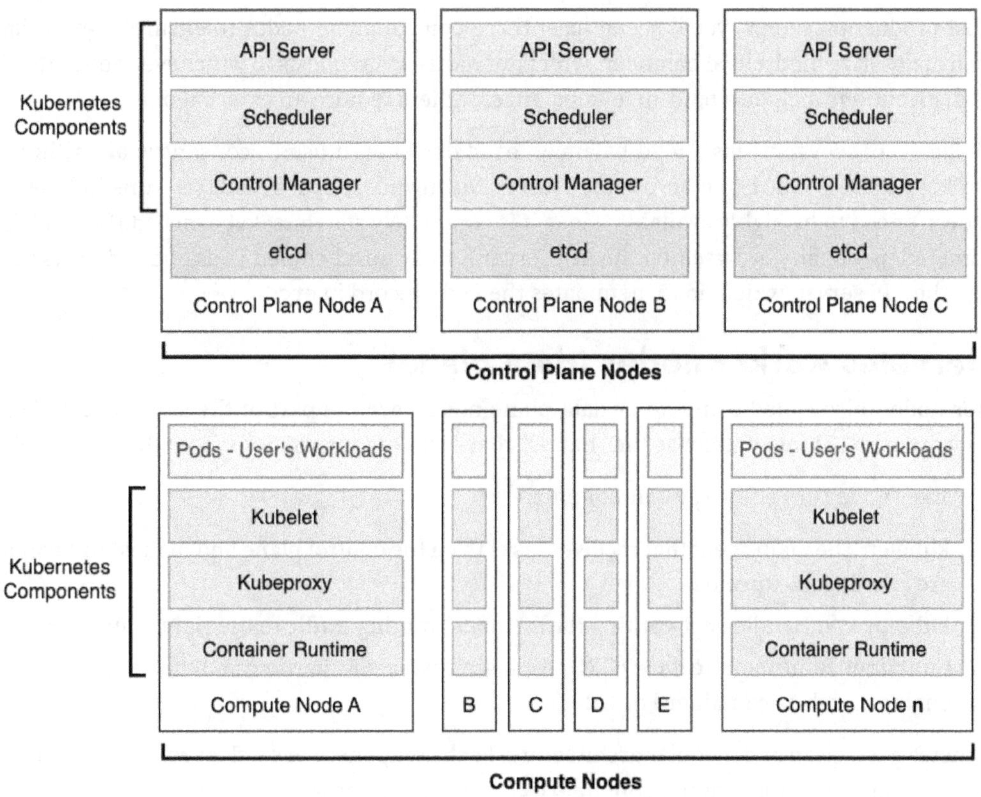

Figure 2.1: Kubernetes control plane and data plane

Let's explore them in detail.

Kubernetes control plane

The control plane is responsible for making decisions, scheduling workloads, and managing the overall state of the cluster. Its main components are as follows:

- `etcd`: A distributed key-value store used to save all cluster data and configurations.
- `kube-apiserver`: The entry point to the cluster. Every CLI command, API call, or UI interaction goes through this service. This is the only control plane component that interacts with `etcd` directly.
- `kube-scheduler`: Picks which worker node should run a new Pod based on the following factors:
    - Resource availability (capacity).
    - Node selectors, tolerations, and other placement rules, such as node affinity/anti-affinity and topology spread constraints. These will be covered in more detail later in this book.
- `kube-controller-manager`: Implements various controlling processes in a single binary. Through the API server, these controllers watch for changes to certain objects in `etcd`, such as Deployments, and take action, redeploying Pods from a new image or spinning up replacements for failed replicas, among others.

In most production setups, you'll see at least three control plane nodes to ensure high availability. These usually sit behind a **load balancer**, which forwards API requests to whichever node is available. Some distributions include a built-in load balancer; others require an external one.

While `kube-apiserver` needs a load balancer, `etcd` does not; it uses a consensus algorithm called Raft to keep its data consistent across the cluster. Meanwhile, `kube-scheduler` runs independently and doesn't need to be highly available, since it is completely stateless; `kube-scheduler` makes each decision independently by watching the API server for any unscheduled Pods and writes its decision back to the API server, which, in turn, updates the Pod's record in `etcd`.

Kubernetes worker nodes (data plane)

Worker nodes, also called compute or data plane nodes, are the part of the system that runs your actual workloads. Think of them as the "hands" that carry out instructions from the control plane.

Each worker node runs a few key components:

- **kubelet**: The main agent that receives tasks from the control plane and makes sure containers are running as expected
- **kube-proxy**: Handles networking for the node, routing traffic to the right container
- **Container Runtime Interface** (**CRI**): A plugin that lets Kubernetes talk to different container engines, such as containerd or CRI-O

Kubernetes has a clean and modular architecture. Each component has a clear role, and together they form a reliable system for running containerized applications at scale.

Distributions such as OpenShift build on this core architecture by adding more features, such as a web UI, built-in CI/CD tools, and advanced security controls. We'll dive into those enhancements later in this chapter.

OpenShift's differentiators

OpenShift is built on top of Kubernetes, adding features and tools that make it easier to run containerized applications in production. It extends core Kubernetes concepts to create a more complete, enterprise-ready platform.

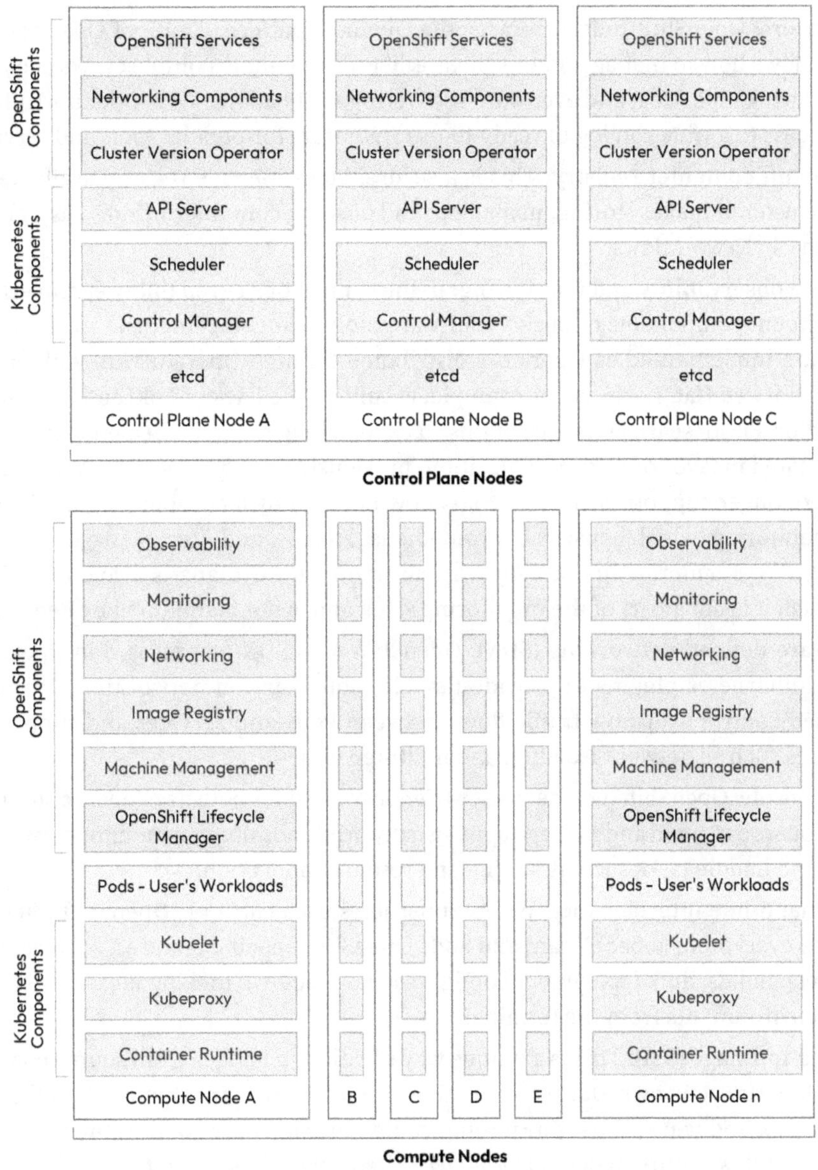

Figure 2.2: OpenShift components, Kubernetes control plane, and data plane

This section will examine OpenShift's architecture and how its components manage workloads and support developer workflows.

As mentioned earlier, all Kubernetes distributions, including OpenShift 4, are based on the same core architecture: a control plane (formerly called the "master") and a data plane (worker nodes). OpenShift follows this model but adds more services to enhance security, automation, and user experience.

OpenShift isn't just Kubernetes; it's Kubernetes with extra power. It builds on the core features and adds tools that improve security, streamline operations, and make life easier for developers and administrators alike. Here are a few standout features that set OpenShift apart:

- **Operators:** OpenShift fully embraces the Operator pattern. Think of Operators as software that knows how to manage other software. They can handle complex tasks such as installing, configuring, updating, and even auto-recovering applications. With OperatorHub built in, you get access to a wide catalog of ready-to-use Operators for popular tools and services.
- **OpenShift container registry:** This is a secure, built-in image registry available right inside your cluster. It makes storing, managing, and pushing container images easy, and plays a key role in CI/CD workflows.
- **Built-in observability and monitoring:** In the context of site reliability engineering, the main constituent components of observability are monitoring, logging, and tracing. In OpenShift, they are implemented as Operators distributed through OperatorHub with enterprise support from Red Hat. Logging, for example, is built on the back of Loki and the Cluster Logging Operator. Elasticsearch was part of this stack for a long time, until OpenShift 4.8, when it was deprecated in favor of Loki. Visualization, previously provided by Kibana (deprecated in 4.12 and no longer supported since 4.16), is now handled by a console plugin. The same is true for monitoring, which consists of Prometheus, Thanos, and Alert Manager. As we will see in *Chapter 13, Monitoring in OpenShift*, visualization with Grafana is also offered in OpenShift, although it is not a part of the monitoring stack and is not maintained by Red Hat.
- **Software-defined networking** (**SDN**): OpenShift uses SDN (deprecated in OpenShift 4.14) or OVN-Kubernetes plugins to provide flexible, policy-driven networking. This enables fine-grained control over how traffic flows between Pods and services and supports advanced features such as network isolation and multi-tenancy.
- **Web console:** OpenShift includes a user-friendly web UI for both developers and administrators. Developers can build and manage apps visually, while admins can monitor cluster health, view logs, and handle tasks such as scaling and resource allocation.
- **Command-line interface** (`oc`): While Kubernetes uses `kubectl`, OpenShift offers the oc CLI. It does everything `kubectl` can, and adds OpenShift-specific features, such as working with projects, builds, and deployment configs (see note below), making it easier to manage OpenShift environments from the terminal.
- **Source-to-Image (S2I):** This is a unique way of building images from source code; there is no need to write your own Dockerfile. It allows you to just point OpenShift to the source code repository, and you will have a running container with your application as a result; we will talk about this feature in detail in *Chapter 9, Developing for OpenShift*.

> The `DeploymentConfig` API was first introduced in OpenShift 3 and is now deprecated; however, it is still supported to ease migration. It is recommended to use Deployments, which are a part of the upstream Kubernetes project and compatible with all Kubernetes distributions.

OpenShift 4 is built on the same core Kubernetes architecture (control plane and compute nodes) but also adds a powerful layer of features and services on top. These include components such as Operators, the Operator Lifecycle Manager, machine management, an integrated container registry, and more (as shown in *Figure 2.2*).

Together, these enhancements make it easier for administrators to handle both Day 1 (initial setup) and Day 2 (ongoing operations) tasks efficiently. At the same time, developers benefit from a smoother experience for building and deploying applications, far simpler than working with a basic Kubernetes setup.

What is new in OpenShift 4?

OpenShift 4 introduces many new features that focus on operational efficiency, developer empowerment, and cloud-native best practices. Let's explore the essential changes driving this transformation.

OpenShift installation methods

Installing OpenShift isn't a one-size-fits-all process anymore. Red Hat offers several installation methods for OpenShift 4; each has its own pros and cons, but all of them are good to know and try at least once:

- User-provisioned infrastructure (UPI)
- Installer-provisioned infrastructure (IPI)
- Assisted Installer
- Agent-based Installer
- OpenShift Local

Let's take a look at them and see what the main differences would be.

UPI

The UPI installation method gives you full control over your environment. It's the most flexible option, but it does require a solid understanding of both your infrastructure and how OpenShift works.

With UPI, you manually set up everything: virtual machines (or bare-metal servers), networking (such as VLANs, firewall rules, etc.), and storage. Basically, the OpenShift UPI installer runs on top of the infrastructure that was prepared in advance and deploys the cluster components.

These are the advantages of this method:

- Great for complex or customized environments that don't fit standard provisioning models
- Allows you to reuse existing VMs or hardware without relying on OpenShift's automation tools
- Integrates well with existing automation and configuration management systems such as Ansible or Terraform

These are the limitations:

- You'll need deeper expertise in both your infrastructure stack and OpenShift itself, and/or a significant number of interactions with other teams, if we speak of enterprise environments
- Manual setup increases the chances of human error, especially in larger or more intricate environments
- Upgrades and changes may require more manual effort compared to fully automated methods

IPI

The IPI method changes the deployment approach toward automation, and for a long time, was the simplest and most robust way to deploy OpenShift on private or public cloud environments. The OpenShift IPI installer handles everything, from provisioning servers to configuring the cluster.

All you do is provide a few high-level details, such as your target cloud provider and desired cluster size. From there, the installer takes over: it spins up the virtual machines (or cloud resources), installs **Red Hat Enterprise Linux CoreOS (RHCOS)**, and sets up the Kubernetes control plane, networking, and OpenShift components.

These are the advantages of this method:

- Speeds up cluster deployment by automating most of the heavy lifting
- Creates standardized clusters with repeatable, predictable configurations
- Makes updates and scaling easier with minimal manual steps

These are the limitations:

- If you have complex or custom infrastructure needs, IPI might feel too rigid
- It works great on platforms such as AWS, Azure, and GCP, but using IPI in on-premises environments can be more involved

Assisted Installer

The Assisted Installer is designed to make on-premises OpenShift installations easier and more approachable. It strikes a balance between the control of UPI and the automation of IPI.

Instead of setting everything up manually, you use a web-based interface that walks you through the process. The Installer will check that all the prerequisites are met, generate config files, and allow you to observe the installation status and logs from the web UI.

These are the advantages of this method:

- Reduces the complexity of manual UPI setups
- Almost completely eliminates possible mistakes
- Covers most of the default configurations
- Allows easy enabling of additional functionality, for example, OpenShift virtualization

These are the limitations:

- It still requires some knowledge of your infrastructure (e.g., networking and storage)
- It doesn't offer as much deep customization as UPI

Agent-based Installer

The Agent-based Installer is a newer method introduced in OpenShift 4 to simplify deploying clusters in disconnected, air-gapped, or bare-metal environments, especially where automation and flexibility are needed. It builds on the principles of the Assisted Installer but adds more control and script capability.

Instead of a purely web-based flow, this method uses pre-generated ISO images that include all necessary configuration and agent services. You boot your machines using these ISO images, and they automatically join the cluster as configured.

It's especially useful when you need repeatable, unattended installations across distributed or resource-constrained environments.

These are the advantages of this method:

- Automates deployments across bare metal using bootable ISOs
- Supports disconnected (air-gapped) or restricted environments
- Easier to script and integrate into existing provisioning pipelines
- Offers more flexibility than Assisted Installer while retaining simplicity

These are the limitations:

- It is still relatively new, so it may lack the polish and maturity of IPI/UPI
- It requires generating the agent-based ISO in advance
- It is less interactive than Assisted Installer; better for users comfortable with automation and scripting

We will return to OpenShift installation methods and tackle the process itself in the next chapter, titled *Getting Started with OpenShift*.

OpenShift Local

OpenShift Local (previously known as **CodeReady Containers**, or **CRC**) is a tool that lets developers run a lightweight, self-contained OpenShift cluster on their local machine. It's not meant for production use, but it's perfect for learning, testing, and developing applications in a real OpenShift environment.

It runs inside a single VM on your laptop or desktop and includes everything you need to simulate a working OpenShift cluster with Kubernetes and the OpenShift API, web UI, and is accessible via the CLI.

We'll be using OpenShift Local throughout this book for hands-on labs and testing new concepts. At the end of this section, you'll find instructions on how to install it on your own system.

Operator-centric approach

OpenShift adopts an Operator-driven approach to managing both applications and platform services. Operators extend Kubernetes by embedding domain-specific operational knowledge directly into the platform. They are designed to automate complex lifecycle tasks, reducing the need for manual intervention and improving consistency in how software is deployed and maintained.

Operators provide several key capabilities:

- **Lifecycle automation:** An Operator can handle everything from installation and configuration to upgrades and recovery. It acts like a subject-matter expert built into the system, continually applying best practices for managing the target application.
- **State reconciliation:** Much like Kubernetes controllers, Operators continuously monitor the current state of a resource. If a change occurs, intended or not, the Operator can respond by adjusting the resource to match its desired state.
- **OperatorHub integration:** OpenShift includes OperatorHub, a built-in catalog offering a wide selection of Operators. Through this interface, users can easily discover and install Operators for various workloads, including databases, observability stacks, messaging systems, and more.

This model streamlines the management of complex services and encourages consistency across environments. It also supports community collaboration, as Operators can encode and share operational practices that others can adopt. For many use cases, such as running PostgreSQL or automating CI/CD pipelines, Operators significantly reduce the effort required to manage applications at scale.

CoreOS integration

With the release of OpenShift 4, Red Hat introduced **Red Hat CoreOS** as the default operating system for control planes and worker nodes. CoreOS is a container-optimized OS derived from **Container Linux by CoreOS**, which Red Hat acquired in 2018. This marked a significant shift toward a more streamlined, secure, and Kubernetes-native platform.

Red Hat CoreOS has the following specifics:

- **Immutability**: CoreOS uses an image-based update model. System updates are atomic and version-controlled, reducing configuration drift and making environments more predictable.
- **Minimal footprint**: The OS includes only the essential components needed to run containers and support Kubernetes. This smaller surface area lowers resource consumption and enhances security.
- **Kubernetes integration**: CoreOS is tightly integrated with OpenShift and Kubernetes. It supports automatic updates coordinated with the cluster lifecycle, simplifying Day 2 operations and reducing manual overhead.

By bringing CoreOS into the OpenShift architecture, Red Hat delivered a more robust and secure foundation for containerized workloads, one designed specifically for running at scale in modern, dynamic environments.

Focus on automation

OpenShift 4 brings automation into its DNA by allowing developers to build easy software development workflows with reliable and repeatable operations. Here's how:

- **CI/CD as a first-class citizen:** Build tools such as S2I and BuildConfig API offer native ways to build container images directly within the cluster. Deployments orchestrate robust releases. This tight integration simplifies a developer's journey from code to a running application. You can also install Tekton – an OpenShift-native solution for building complex CI/CD pipelines.
- **Embedded GitOps:** OpenShift provides tooling to support GitOps-style development approaches where all cluster state is managed in version control. This enhances auditability and enables streamlined, consistent infrastructure management.
- **Automated rollbacks:** In the event of failed deployments, OpenShift mechanisms empower swift rollbacks, ensuring operational stability and reducing downtime for critical applications.

Through its comprehensive automation capabilities and streamlined workflows, OpenShift 4 empowers developers to focus on building innovative applications with confidence, accelerating time-to-market, and mitigating risks in the ever-evolving landscape of software development.

Additional changes

It's worth briefly highlighting a few other important upgrades included with OpenShift 4:

- **Switch to the CRI-O container runtime:** Aligning with industry trends for better integration with the broader Kubernetes ecosystem
- **Enhanced web console:** Provides an even more intuitive experience for developers and administrators, visually managing workloads and infrastructure
- **Expanded networking and storage options:** Increased flexibility for configuring how Pods network and connect to diverse storage backends

Key differences between OpenShift 3 and OpenShift 4

If you work with OpenShift and had a chance to spend some time with OpenShift 3 back in the days, you should be aware that OpenShift 3.11 reached its end of maintenance in June 2022, and its extended life phase ended in June 2024 [4]. While OpenShift 3 served many organizations successfully, OpenShift 4 moved to a paradigm shift in architecture, container orchestration, and development approaches. It's crucial to understand these distinctions, both architecturally and practically.

The main difference is that OpenShift 4 is now Operator-based (core cluster components are now managed by cluster Operators). However, there are some other significant changes we will uncover in this book. Meanwhile, the following table provides a high-level summary of the differences between OpenShift 3 and OpenShift 4:

Area of Divergence	OpenShift 3	OpenShift 4	Potential Impacts
Networking	Primarily used its own SDN based on **Open vSwitch (OVS)**	Supports both SDN and the newer **Open Virtual Network (OVN)**. OVN is often chosen for advanced features, while SDN continues to enjoy official support and bug fixes from Red Hat, albeit only on existing clusters.	Network planning may change between versions. Network policies might need restructuring if relying on SDN-specific constructs.
Source-to-Image (S2I)	Core mechanism for building directly within the cluster	Remains crucial, but BuildConfigs become more prominent for customization, repeatability	Existing tooling built around S2I may need tweaking to function correctly in the OpenShift 4 context.
Project vs. Namespace	Projects in OpenShift 3 offered richer resource isolation options than standard Kubernetes namespaces	In OpenShift 4, projects largely behave like vanilla Kubernetes namespaces	Access control mechanisms and how applications are logically separated within a cluster might require re-evaluation.
Object Types	Some OpenShift-specific objects (such as `Route` for ingress or `DeploymentConfig` for managing workloads) existed outside core Kubernetes	Trend toward Kubernetes alignment; Deployments return, focus on standard objects where possible.	Custom scripts or third-party tools written heavily against OpenShift 3 APIs are more likely to break.
Image Handling	Docker-centric for pulling and managing container images	CRI-O integration means images must be OCI-compliant.	It may necessitate updates to low-level container build/push procedures if older CI/CD tooling relied on direct Docker manipulation.

Table 2.1: OpenShift version differences

With this foundational knowledge, let's move on to the installation part.

Installing OpenShift Local

As mentioned earlier in this chapter, Red Hat OpenShift Local brings a minimal OpenShift Container Platform 4 cluster and Podman container runtime to your local computer. It makes OpenShift Local ideal for learning and testing purposes.

This is the ideal setup as it runs on your local desktop, doesn't require any additional hardware, is quick and easy to install and deploy, and supports most of the desktop platforms. To run OpenShift locally on your laptop, you will need to satisfy basic hardware requirements:

- 4 physical CPU cores
- 9 GB of free memory
- 35 GB of storage space

These are the minimal requirements; for some of the tasks, you are going to need to bump up the CPU count to 8 and the memory to 32 GB.

To deploy OpenShift Local, you need to follow these steps:

1. Create an account at **Red Hat Hybrid Cloud Console** [5].
2. Once you create the account and your email is verified, you can log in to the portal and type `Clusters`, as shown in the following figure:

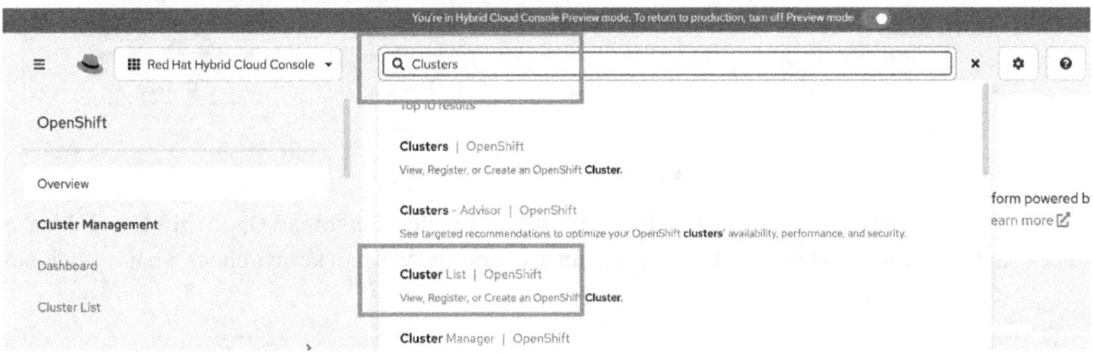

Figure 2.3: The console.redhat.com interface

3. Then, on the left menu, click **Cluster List**, and then click the **Create cluster** button:

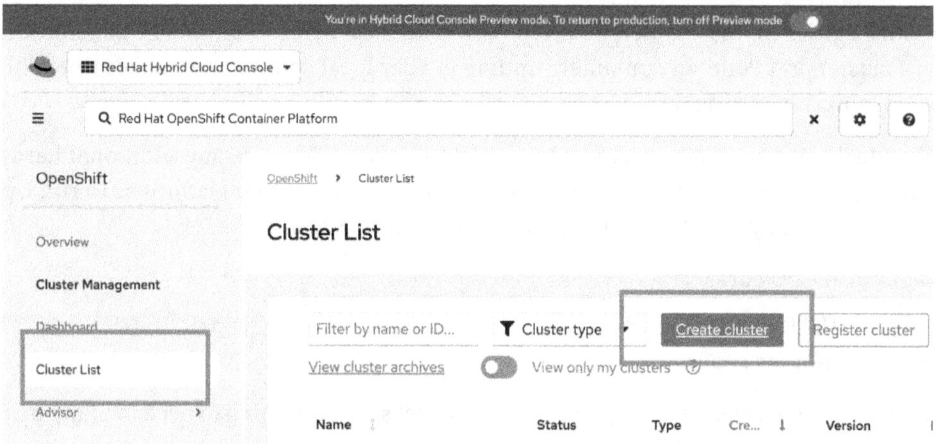

Figure 2.4: New cluster creation, step 1

4. Navigate to the **Local** installation tab:

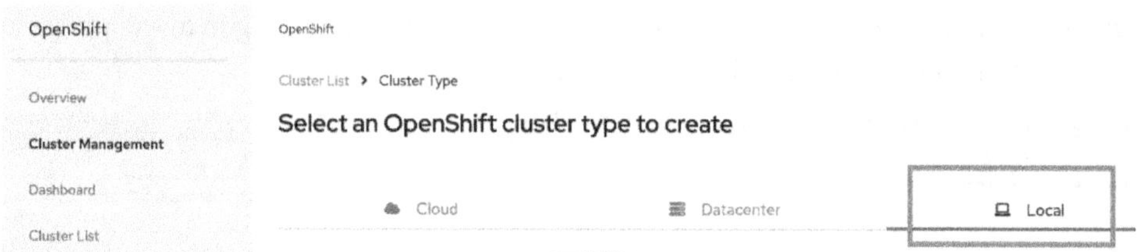

Figure 2.5: New cluster creation, step 2

5. Choose your desktop OS and architecture type and click **Download OpenShift Local**. Please note that the list of architectures may change over time; you can always check what is available directly on the mirror site [6]:

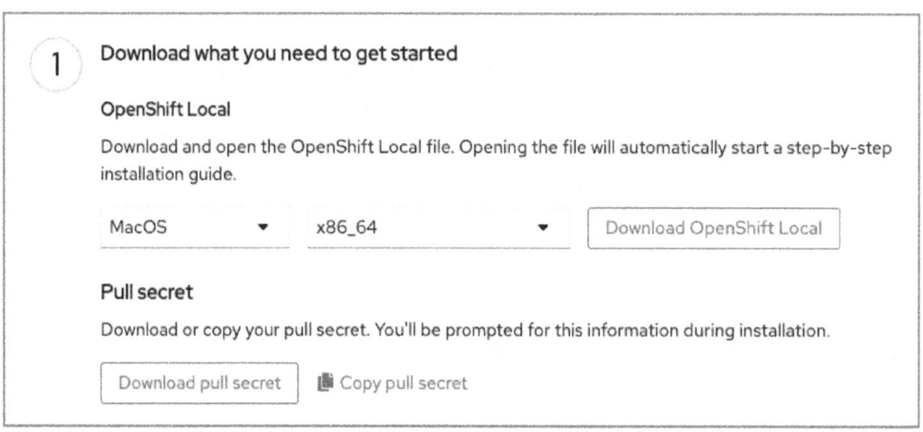

Figure 2.6: New cluster creation, step 3

6. Once you have downloaded the installation file, run it and go through the step-by-step installation process.
7. For every process, it looks a bit different, but the result of it is going to be that you have the `crc` utility available in your desktop OS CLI. In the next steps, we will show you what the process looks like for macOS.
8. Run the installation package you downloaded, and you will see the following window of the Installer:

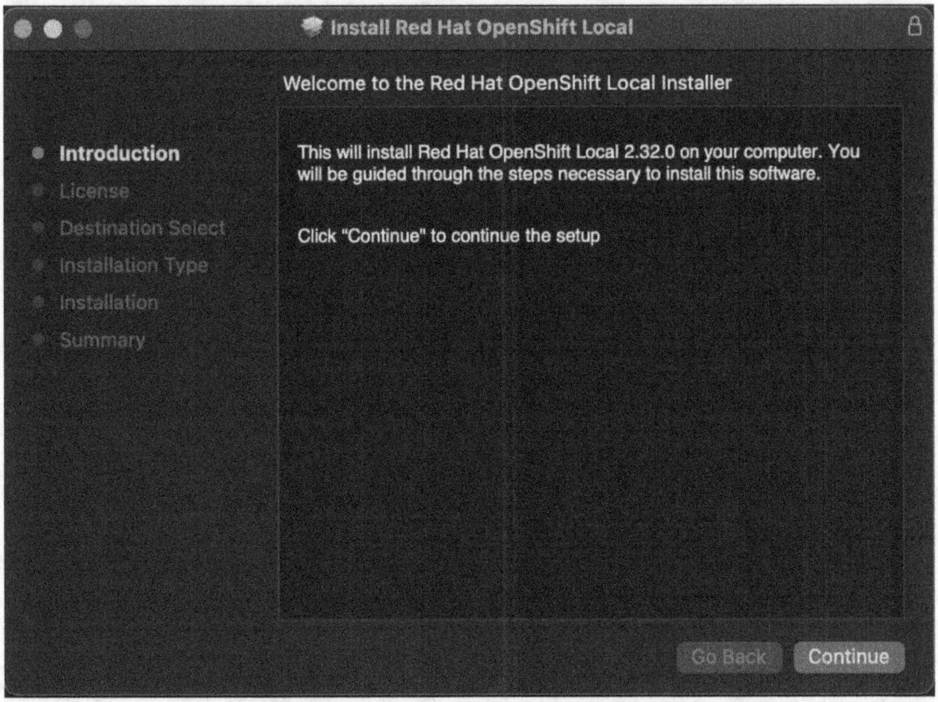

Figure 2.7: Installing OpenShift Local, step 1

9. Go through the step-by-step installation guide, and at the end, close the installation guide.

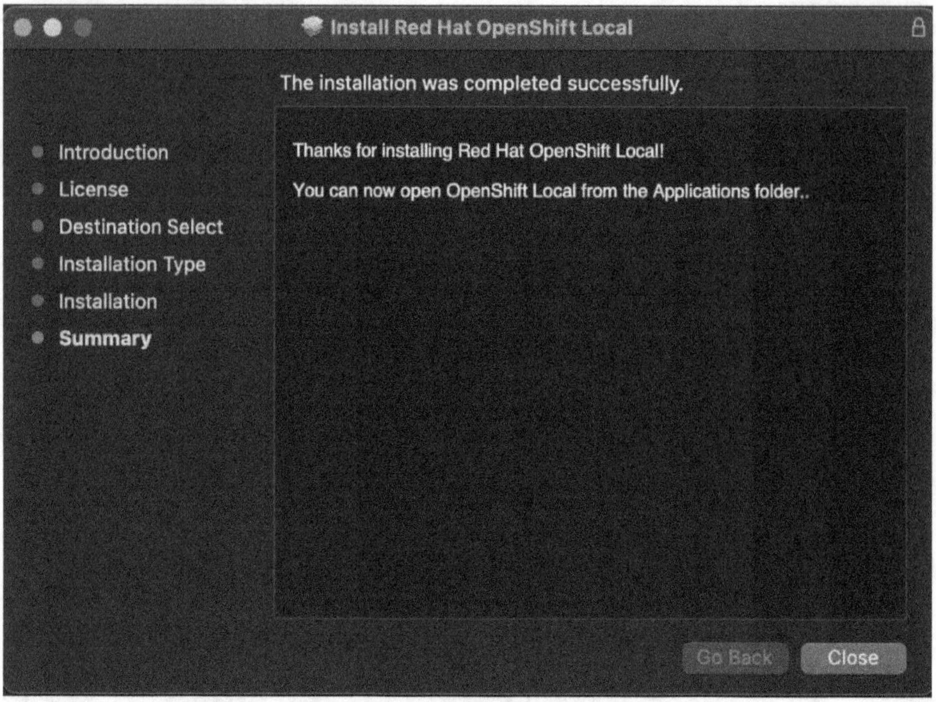

Figure 2.8: Installing OpenShift Local, step 2

10. Once the installation is complete, you should have a `crc` CLI command available. Open the CLI/terminal on your desktop and run the `crc setup` command, then go through the OpenShift Local instance's deployment process. On macOS, it should look like the following:

```
$ crc setup
```

The deployment process may take time, since it is downloading the VM image, where the whole OpenShift resides – the file's size is about 5.5 GB and the uncompressed size of the VM image is about 32 Gb. So, the process time may vary based on the network bandwidth and the workstation performance.

11. The installation has self-descriptive logging, and we will skip the unnecessary details. As soon as the installation is done, you will see the following:

```
INFO Checking if old launchd config for tray and/or daemon exists
INFO Checking if crc daemon plist file is present and loaded
INFO Adding crc daemon plist file and loading it
INFO Checking SSH port availability
Your system is correctly setup for using CRC. Use 'crc start' to start the instance
```

Figure 2.9: OpenShift Local setup command logs

> Please feel free to share the telemetry data if you would like to. Your OpenShift Local installation won't appear in the OpenShift Cluster Manager unless you enable cluster monitoring and telemetry, but you may keep it more private. From the personal experience of one of the authors, keeping telemetry disabled in OpenShift Local doesn't result in a worse experience. However, it is recommended to connect your production clusters to Red Hat, unless prohibited by your organization's policy. This helps Red Hat Support provide quicker and more relevant recommendations and helps with predictive analysis from Red Hat Insights.

12. Now, when you run the offered `crc start` command, you will again see the detailed startup logs. If you start it for the first time, it will ask you for a pull secret, which you can get from [7] (requires Red Hat account).

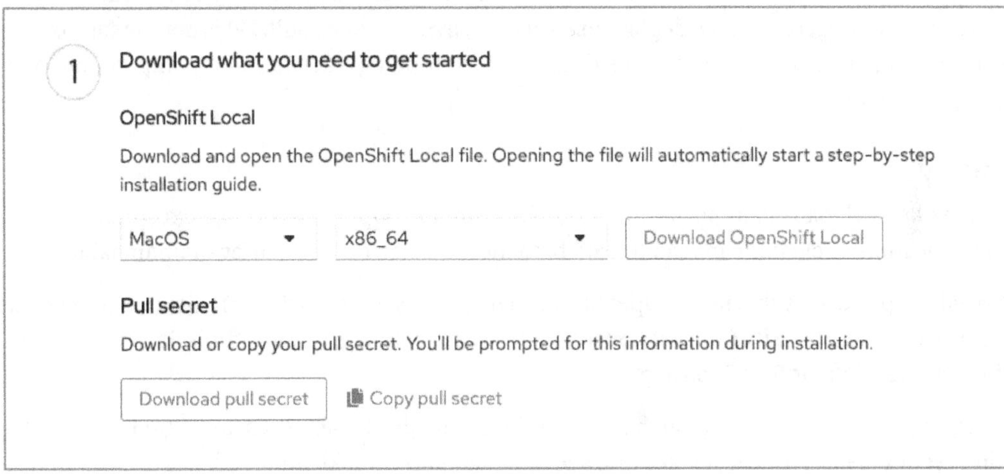

Figure 2.10: Pulling the OpenShift Local secret

13. If the startup process is successful, the output will be as follows:

```
Started the OpenShift cluster.

The server is accessible via web console at:
  https://console-openshift-console.apps-crc.testing

Log in as administrator:
  Username: kubeadmin
  Password: tRCNg-iIm2C-Dgg6V-w4eZF

Log in as user:
  Username: developer
  Password: developer

Use the 'oc' command line interface:
  $ eval $(crc oc-env)
  $ oc login -u developer https://api.crc.testing:6443
```

Figure 2.11: The OpenShift Local startup process's final message

Congratulations! You have installed OpenShift 4 Local on your laptop. You can use the provided links to open the web UI or connect to the cluster via the OC CLI.

Production considerations

OpenShift's architecture and the evolution from version 3 to 4 provide a solid foundation that allows us to translate that knowledge into actionable strategies for successfully deploying and managing OpenShift clusters in production.

Cluster installation and upgrades

Your journey toward a production-ready OpenShift 4 environment begins with solid planning and architecture, followed by installation and a well-thought-out upgrade strategy.

Currently, IPI can be considered a preferred installation mechanism. You will most likely use infrastructure provisioning, repeatable deployments across environments. Still, IPI is not a magic "one-click" solution. Appropriate pre-production testing, network topology design, and compute and storage planning remain essential.

Security

Securing your workloads is important for any platform, and OpenShift 4 is no exception. A compromised application or cluster can lead to data breaches, service outages, or even financial loss.

Compared to upstream Kubernetes, OpenShift provides stronger security defaults out of the box. For example, it enforces **Security Context Constraints** (SCCs), includes built-in admission controllers, and provides stricter default RBAC settings.

Later in this book, we'll walk through how to configure and use RBAC, SCCs, and other security layers to reduce your cluster's attack surface and secure production workloads.

You'll also learn how to define fine-grained network policies to control traffic between Pods, namespaces, and external services. This approach supports a defense-in-depth strategy by reducing the lateral movement available to attackers.

Finally, OpenShift can be integrated with external secrets management systems such as HashiCorp Vault or a cloud-native **key management service** (KMS), allowing you to avoid hardcoding sensitive information into Pod specs or config maps.

Resource management and scalability

Balancing performance, efficiency, and cost requires a solid understanding of how OpenShift 4 manages resources and supports scaling. An architect or platform owner should start by profiling the workloads. Are they CPU-bound, memory-intensive, I/O-heavy, or dependent on GPU acceleration? This information is essential for selecting appropriate node types and fine-tuning scheduler behavior.

For dynamic workloads, OpenShift allows combining a **Horizontal Pod Autoscaler** (HPA) based on resource metrics (CPU, memory, or custom metrics via the Metrics Server or Prometheus) with cluster autoscaling. The Cluster Autoscaler can automatically add or remove nodes through the Machine API to meet changing demand.

To ensure fair resource distribution across teams or projects, the architect can (or even must) define resource quotas and limit ranges at the namespace level. This helps prevent a single workload from consuming all available resources and negatively impacting others in a multi-tenant environment.

High availability and resiliency

Downtime directly impacts productivity and business continuity. Designing your OpenShift cluster for **high availability** (HA) and resiliency helps ensure that services remain accessible, even during failures.

Control plane (master) nodes should be deployed in an HA configuration with an odd number of nodes, typically at least three, to maintain `etcd` quorum and support fault tolerance. For worker nodes, distribute them across multiple **availability zones** (AZs), racks, **Power Distribution Units (PDUs)**, or even physical data centers (collectively referred to as **failure domains**) to improve resiliency and support disaster recovery objectives.

The `etcd` key-value store maintains your cluster's state, and is a critical dependency. A reliable backup and recovery strategy is non-negotiable. Use `etcdctl` to take regular snapshots and test disaster recovery procedures to ensure that you can restore the cluster if needed.

Consider introducing chaos engineering practices to deliberately simulate failures, such as killing Pods or nodes, to validate your HA design and identify weaknesses before they lead to real outages.

Monitoring and observability

Visibility is essential to understanding the health, performance, and stability of your OpenShift cluster.

OpenShift comes with an integrated monitoring stack based on Prometheus, AlertManager, and Thanos. While this built-in solution provides comprehensive metrics and alerting for cluster components and workloads, organizations with existing enterprise monitoring platforms should evaluate integration options. Consider whether the OpenShift monitoring stack alone can support business-critical applications, or whether it should be integrated with your company's centralized observability system. Monitoring will be discussed in more detail in *Chapter 13, Monitoring in OpenShift*.

Shipping logs to a log aggregation solution such as Elasticsearch, Loki, or another centralized logging backend enables cluster-wide log visibility. Correlating logs with metrics allows for faster root cause analysis and more effective incident response.

Avoid alert fatigue by focusing on meaningful, actionable alerts. Prioritize alerts tied to user-facing impact, such as elevated error rates or latency spikes, alongside infrastructure-level signals that provide early warnings to operations teams. We will take a closer look at the components of the logging stack in OpenShift, and Loki in particular, in *Chapter 12, Logging in OpenShift*.

CI/CD and developer enablement

A streamlined development workflow is essential for agility, consistency, and rapid innovation. CI/CD pipelines should build, test, and push container images to a registry, followed by committing declarative deployment artifacts (e.g., `DeploymentConfig`, Deployments, or Helm charts) to version control. This can trigger automated updates within OpenShift via tools such as webhooks, Argo CD, or Tekton pipelines.

Overall, adopting GitOps practices (where both the application and cluster states are defined in Git) enhances reproducibility and auditability and enables safe rollbacks. OpenShift Operators provide a powerful model for managing the full lifecycle of complex applications, such as databases, caches, and message queues.

Evaluate both certified Operators from Red Hat and those from the OperatorHub community to offload operational complexity, allowing developers to focus on writing application code rather than managing infrastructure.

Other important considerations

Cloud-managed OpenShift offerings, such as **Red Hat OpenShift Service on AWS (ROSA)**, **Azure Red Hat OpenShift (ARO)**, or **OpenShift Dedicated** simplify many operational tasks, but often at the cost of lower-level control. Please keep these options in mind.

Deploying and managing OpenShift 4 in production isn't trivial. However, by applying the principles outlined in this book and tailoring them to your environment, you'll be well-prepared to build a stable, secure, and scalable platform. OpenShift empowers development teams to deliver faster, but production readiness is not a one-time milestone; it's a continuous process of learning, adapting, and improving.

Summary

In this chapter, we explored a brief history of Kubernetes, its core concepts, and foundational architecture, setting the stage for understanding OpenShift 4. We looked at what makes OpenShift 4 unique, how it differs from upstream Kubernetes and older versions such as OpenShift 3, and how it can be installed. After covering these basics, we launched our first OpenShift Local instance on the desktop, and the chapter will close with a short quiz to reinforce the key takeaways.

In the next chapter, we'll get our hands dirty by performing a full OpenShift 4 installation using the UPI method in a VMware-based environment. We'll prepare the infrastructure and configure DNS, DHCP, and other critical services required for a successful deployment. We'll also dive into core OpenShift 4 concepts and its foundational APIs.

References

To learn more about the topics that were covered in this chapter, take a look at the following resources:

- [1] *K3s*: `https://k3s.io/`
- [2] *K0s*: `https://www.mirantis.com/software/k0s/`
- [3] *Hosted control planes*: `https://docs.redhat.com/en/documentation/openshift_container_platform/4.16/html/hosted_control_planes/index`
- [4] *Red Hat OpenShift Container Platform Life Cycle Policy (non-current versions)*: `https://access.redhat.com/support/policy/updates/openshift_noncurrent`
- [5] *Red Hat Hybrid Cloud Console*: `https://console.redhat.com/`

- [6] *OpenShift Local Mirror*: `https://mirror.openshift.com/pub/openshift-v4/clients/crc/latest/`
- [7] *Pull secret for a new OpenShift cluster*: `https://console.redhat.com/openshift/create/local`

Quiz

Test your understanding of Kubernetes and OpenShift with this quick quiz. Remember, some questions may have more than one correct answer!

1. Which of Google's internal systems heavily inspired the development of Kubernetes?
    a. Spanner
    b. Colossus
    c. Borg
    d. BigTable
2. What are the primary functions of the Kubernetes master node? (Choose all that apply.)
    a. Running application containers
    b. Storing cluster-wide state
    c. Scheduling Pods across nodes
    d. Providing a user-facing API
3. Operators are a key concept in OpenShift. What is their primary purpose?
    a. Managing low-level operating system updates
    b. Automating the lifecycle of complex applications
    c. Monitoring network traffic between Pods
    d. Orchestrating rolling deployments of Kubernetes itself
4. Which of these significant changes were introduced with OpenShift 4? (Choose all that apply.)
    a. Shift from Docker to CRI-O as the container runtime
    b. Built-in OperatorHub for managing applications
    c. IPI for streamlined deployment
    d. Removal of support for non-containerized workloads
5. When considering deploying a production OpenShift cluster, which of the following factors should be top of mind?
    a. The version of the browser that users will use to access the console
    b. Whether to deploy one large cluster or several smaller ones
    c. Selecting a backend database system for `etcd`
    d. The underlying Linux distribution for worker nodes

Answers

1. **c**. Kubernetes was directly inspired by Borg, Google's internal cluster management system. Borg was designed to manage Google's vast number of containers across data centers. Kubernetes borrows heavily from its architecture and concepts, including Pods, Services, and declarative configuration.
2. **b**, **c**, and **d**:
    - **b**: The `etcd` database runs on the master node and stores the entire cluster state
    - **c**: `kube-scheduler` decides which node should run a newly created Pod based on resources and constraints
    - **d**: `kube-apiserver` exposes the Kubernetes API, which users and other components interact with
3. **b**. Operators extend Kubernetes by using custom resources and controllers to automate tasks such as installation, upgrades, backups, and failure recovery for complex applications (e.g., databases and middleware). They encode operational knowledge and lifecycle management in software.
4. **a**, **b**, and **c**:
    - **a**: OpenShift 4 replaced Docker with CRI-O, a lightweight container runtime optimized for Kubernetes
    - **b**: OperatorHub was introduced as a central place to find and install Operators
    - **c**: Installer-Provisioned Infrastructure (IPI) automated cluster deployment, reducing manual steps
5. **b**. Deciding between a single large cluster or multiple smaller clusters affects resilience, fault isolation, and operational complexity.

Join us on Discord

For discussions around the book and to connect with your peers, join us on Discord at `http://packt.link/discordcloud` or scan the QR code below:

3

Getting Started with OpenShift

This is the most hands-on, intensive chapter of the book, as it deals with installing OpenShift on a virtualization platform. We will start with a discussion of the different platforms and installation methods that OpenShift supports. Although there is a common, consistent set of APIs and capabilities that OpenShift provides across all virtualization and cloud providers, different platforms enable their own additional features, which is why it is important to choose the provider that makes the most sense for you.

OpenShift is a complex container orchestrator with a lot of components performing different functions, and it supports all popular infrastructure providers. As such, it requires certain conditions to be met before installation can begin. Understanding these prerequisites is crucial for the successful installation of a properly functioning cluster.

Over the course of its development, OpenShift has matured enough to support automated and almost hands-off installation on platforms such as AWS, Azure, and VMware vSphere. The automated, or **installer-provided infrastructure** (IPI), method hides a lot of complexity under the hood, which makes it ideal for rapid deployments, but not particularly suitable for learning. This is why we chose a **user-provided infrastructure** (UPI) installation as a way to demonstrate what components are involved in the installation.

The OpenShift 4 base operating system, CoreOS, relies on Ignition as a system configuration tool. As such, it is important to understand how it works not only for manual installation but for any post-install configuration as well. Since Ignition can be used outside of OpenShift, this section carries an additional benefit of offering knowledge that has a broader area of application.

To facilitate the management of containerized workloads at scale, OpenShift provides a number of APIs that govern the behavior of various controllers – internal components that manage different types of workloads. Their complete understanding is vital for the ability to maintain OpenShift itself and manage business applications running on your cluster. This chapter will compare those APIs to more familiar concepts from the pre-container era so that it is easier for you to grasp their functions and where they apply.

This chapter concludes with a discussion of OpenShift API groups, their deprecation policies, and support terms. OpenShift is a dynamically evolving product with some APIs making it to the stable and fully supported phase, while others may remain in alpha/beta phases and eventually be deprecated. When you upgrade OpenShift, it is important to know whether your applications rely on any APIs that the new release of OpenShift no longer supports and, if so, migrate them to a newer version. If you would like to learn more about this process, please refer to *Chapter 17, Upgrading OpenShift* (the *Stage D – upgrading to the recommended minor version* section), where we explain how to check whether anything uses a particular API version.

We'll be covering the following topics in this chapter:

- Supported platforms
- Installation methods, including installation itself
- Post-installation validation
- Traditional concepts and OpenShift APIs
- API structure, versioning, and deprecation policy

The environment built in this chapter and the skills learned here will serve as a foundation for all chapters that follow. An understanding of OpenShift core constructs is necessary for successful progression through the rest of this book.

Technical requirements

In this chapter, we are going to use the following technologies and software:

- Bash shell
- VMware vSphere
- Firefox (recommended) or any other browser
- Red Hat account

You can access this book's GitHub repository at `https://github.com/PacktPublishing/Learn-OpenShift-Second-Edition`.

Supported platforms

One of the defining features of OpenShift that makes it so attractive for large enterprises is its platform-agnostic architecture inherited from Kubernetes. Whether your business has a presence in the cloud, on-premises, or both, OpenShift can fully integrate with the virtualization or cloud provider for the storage management and provisioning of new nodes, if native support is available. If it is not, OpenShift can still be run on it; however, you will have to set up the underlying infrastructure, including storage, yourself. Also, many features that rely on integration with the cloud API, such as dynamic volume provisioning, machine API, LB provisioning, and cluster autoscaling, may not be available.

OpenShift 4.16 supports the following platforms:

Platform	Installer-provisioned infrastructure	User-provisioned infrastructure
Alibaba Cloud	Yes	Yes
Amazon Web Services (AWS)	Yes	Yes
Bare metal (x86_64 and ARM)	Yes	Yes
Google Cloud Platform (GCP)	Yes	Yes
IBM Cloud	Yes	Yes
IBM Power (ppc64le)	Yes	Yes
IBM Z (s390x)/IBM LinuxONE	Yes	Yes
Microsoft Azure	Yes	Yes
Microsoft Azure Stack Hub	Yes	Yes
Nutanix AOS Storage	Yes	Yes
Oracle Cloud Infrastructure (OCI)	No	Yes
Red Hat OpenStack Platform (RHOSP)	Yes	Yes
VMware Cloud on AWS (VMC)	Yes	Yes
VMware vSphere	Yes	Yes
Bare metal	Yes	Yes

Table 3.1: Infrastructure providers supported by OpenShift

On bare metal, the IPI support is accomplished through the use of the Metal^3 (pronounced "metal cubed") operator and OpenStack Ironic, which use the out-of-band management interfaces of hardware nodes to configure them and manage their power cycle. That means the hardware baseboard is required to support the **Intelligent Platform Management Interface (IPMI)**, **iLo (Hewlett Packard Enterprise)**, **iDRAC (Dell Technologies)**, **Redfish**, or similar protocols/technologies.

Next, we will be talking about various installation methods that involve different degrees of manual labor and scenarios they are best suited for.

Installation methods

Depending on the level of control you want to have over the installation process and your infrastructure, the following methods for installing an OpenShift cluster are available to you:

- **Interactive via assisted installer:** The easiest and most "hands-off" way of installing OpenShift 4 in a connected environment. Implemented as a SaaS hosted by Red Hat [1], it provides you with a web UI where you choose a platform and configure the name, base domain, networking, and other parameters, including additional operators. Then it generates a discovery ISO (named after the standard 9660 for disk image files authored by the International Organization for Standardization) file that you are supposed to boot your machines from, and they will automatically register themselves with the service, showing up in the list of nodes. You can choose between the following images:
    - Full, self-contained ISO, about 1 GB in size, that contains everything required for nodes to bootstrap themselves.
    - Minimal ISO, about 100 MB in size, that downloads most dependencies on boot.
    - iPXE image for booting over HTTP. HTTPS is supported as well but is not recommended due to outdated ciphers.

  The assisted installer also performs various pre-flight checks to ensure that all requirements around networking and hardware have been met. Its primary benefits are the low entry barrier and the web UI, which may appeal to teams that prefer a web interface or newcomers.
- **Local agent-based:** A CLI-based approach to deploying a cluster that is particularly useful in disconnected and restrictive environments, such as banks. It is implemented with the `openshift-install agent` subcommand of the OpenShift installer CLI and combines the flexibility of the assisted installer with an option to run it offline. This method involves generating a bootable ISO from cluster configuration via the `openshift-install agent create image` command and using it to bootstrap machines.
- **Automated on IPI:** The OpenShift installer CLI interacts with the underlying cloud or virtualization platform to provision all necessary infrastructure resources, such as load balancers, storage, networking, and instances or VMs for the control and worker planes. For example, on AWS, it uses cloud credentials to create network load balancers for the API and ingress controller, route tables, VPC endpoints for private connectivity to the S3 object store used as the internal image registry, EBS volumes for block persistent storage, DNS records in Route 53, IAM roles, and EC2 instances. This method is often used for its relative simplicity and reduced risk of human errors; however, it may not always be available due to an unsupported platform or necessity for specific customization. It is well suited for scenarios when you want to configure the underlying cloud infrastructure across your organization in a repeatable manner without any manual involvement.

- **Full control on UPI:** This method has the steepest learning curve, as it relies on an understanding of the installation process and execution of steps in a specific order. However, it gives you the most freedom in how you can set up your cluster, for example, configuring hybrid networking, installing additional operators, or applying custom manifests. If you choose this way, you will have to prepare your environment for a new cluster by creating the necessary DNS records, setting up load balancers, as well as configuring persistent IP addresses for masters and workers. Then, you will have to manually boot your machines from a platform-specific or generic CoreOS image and monitor the progress as they join the cluster. The only phase where the installer CLI is used in this approach is for generating **Ignition configs**. Use it when you are installing on a platform that is not supported natively and/or customizations are required.

Realistically, we cannot cover all possible combinations of installation methods, platforms, and CPU architectures – the official documentation [2] is very thorough and can always be used as a reference. However, for the purpose of learning, we chose a CLI-based approach on user-provisioned infrastructure as the most involved way of deploying a new cluster. The intent is to have you perform the entire process step by step and see what is happening behind the scenes. With the exception of the initial bootstrap stage, internally, the process is the same regardless of the method selected.

Prerequisites

Any platform that OpenShift can be installed on has its own prerequisites that must be fulfilled for a successful installation and smooth operation. In particular, an account that is used for installation must have permission to manipulate certain provider-specific resources, such as load balancers (AWS) or datastores (vSphere). In this section, we will discuss the requirements of VMware vSphere as our platform of choice for this chapter. For this lab, we use an account that has full admin permissions; however, it is strongly recommended to have a dedicated account with only the necessary permissions granted. A full list of required permissions in vCenter is available at [6].

VMware vSphere

We chose VMware vSphere as an infrastructure provider for this chapter because it is still relatively common among businesses of various sizes (rivaled only by AWS and bare metal), and we, the authors of this book, are working on several projects that involve deploying OpenShift on vSphere using either UPI or IPI methods.

OpenShift 4 supports the following versions of VMware components:

Component	Version
Virtual hardware	15+
vSphere ESXi hosts	7.0 Update 2+ / 8.0 Update 1+
vCenter Server	7.0 Update 2+ / 8.0 Update 1+
NSX-T networking (optional)	7.0 Update 2+ / 8.0 Update 1+

Table 3.2: Versions of VMware vSphere components compatible with OpenShift 4.16

Networking

To be able to form a cluster, all components of OpenShift 4 must be able to communicate over the network, which means that routing/VLANs must be properly configured on your network devices, and the firewall, if used, must have rules to allow traffic to specific ports through. In certain organizations, particularly in the banking sector, there are strict security and compliance rules in place. Since obtaining all necessary exceptions can take time, it is recommended to begin planning and preparation in advance.

Listed in the following table are components of OpenShift and their corresponding ports that must be open:

Protocol	Port	Description	Direction
ICMP	N/A	Network reachability tests	All machines to all machines
TCP	`1936`	HAProxy metrics	
	`9000-9999`	Host-level services, including the node exporter (`9100`, `9101`) and Cluster Version Operator (`9099`)	
	`10250-10259`	Reserved by Kubernetes, including kubelet (`10250`)	
	`2379`, `2380`	etcd server and peer ports	Master to master
	`6443`	Kubernetes API	All to master
	`22623`	Machine Config Operator	
	`22624`	Machine Config Operator (bare metal)	
	`80`	Ingress controller HTTP	All machines to ingress machines External clients to ingress machines
	`443`	Ingress controller HTTPS	

Protocol	Port	Description	Direction
UDP	500	IPSec IKE packets	All to all
	4500	IPSec NAT-T packets	
	4789	VXLAN	
	6081	GENEVE	
	9000-9999	Host-level services, including the node exporter (9100, 9101) and Cluster Version Operator (9099)	
	CUSTOM_VXLAN_PORT	Hybrid networking for Windows workloads (explained later in this chapter)	
TCP/UDP	30000-32767	Default Kubernetes port range for NodePort services	
ESP	N/A	IPSec **Encapsulation Security Payload (ESP)**	

Table 3.3: Network requirements for OpenShift on VMware vSphere

IP assignment

There are two ways to assign IP addresses to the machines that will make up your cluster: statically or dynamically. Static allocation involves passing command-line arguments to machines at boot time, which for VMware means adding the `guestinfo.afterburn.initrd.network-kargs` property to each machine at creation time. The property's format is as follows:

```
ip=<IP>::<GATEWAY>:<NETMASK>:<HOSTNAME>:<INTERFACE>:<BOOT_PROTO>
nameserver=<NAMESERVER>
```

Here, `BOOT_PROTO` can be either `dhcp` (for dynamic assignment) or `none` (for static assignment).

Dynamic assignment is preferable for better scalability and predictability and involves mapping MAC (hardware) addresses of individual machines to desired IP addresses. DHCP is also a good way to pass additional parameters to machines, such as hostnames, nameservers, and NTP servers. On VMware vSphere, certain MAC address ranges must be used for installation to succeed:

- `00:05:69:00:00:00` - `00:05:69:FF:FF:FF`
- `00:0C:29:00:00:00` - `00:0C:29:FF:FF:FF`
- `00:1C:14:00:00:00` - `00:1C:14:FF:FF:FF`
- `00:50:56:00:00:00` - `00:50:56:3F:FF:FF` (used in this chapter)

For simplicity, we used `dhcpd` as a DHCP service for our lab. For your reference, a complete `dhcpd.conf` file is available in `chapters/3/snippets/dhcpd.conf` in this book's GitHub repository. If you decide to use it, make sure to replace the `example.com` domain placeholder with your environment's `domain-name` value and adjust other DHCP options, such as `domain-name-servers` and `ntp-servers`. Then, copy the file to `/etc/dhcp/dhcpd.conf` and run `sudo systemctl restart dhcpd` to apply it. If it fails to start for whatever reason and `journalctl -xeu dhcpd` doesn't show anything useful, you can try running it directly with `dhcpd -cf /etc/dhcp/dhcpd.conf` to see the errors.

> It is important to make sure there are no IP and MAC address collisions. Tools such as `arping` and `arp` can help with that. For example, this is how you can check whether any of the IP addresses you want to allocate to OpenShift are used:
>
> ```
> for i in 3 4 5 6 11 12 13 21 22 23 31 32 33; do
>     arping -c1 10.100.10.$i;
> done
> ```
>
> This is how to check the local ARP cache for assigned MAC addresses:
>
> ```
> $ arp -a
> ```

Name resolution

Another important prerequisite for OpenShift installation is a proper DNS configuration. You will need to create both forward (A) and reverse (PTR) records. If your infrastructure has IPv6 enabled, you'll also need AAAA records. PTRs are of particular importance because OpenShift uses them to set hostnames for nodes, unless they are being distributed via DHCP, and to create node **certificate signing requests** (CSRs) for kubelet agents running on nodes.

The following is a list of required records with their descriptions:

<table>
<tr><th>Component</th><th>Record</th><th>Record type(s)</th><th>Target(s)</th><th>Description</th></tr>
<tr><td rowspan="2">Kubernetes API</td><td><code>api.<CLUSTER_NAME>.<BASE_DOMAIN></code></td><td rowspan="2">A/AAAA, PTR</td><td rowspan="2">API LB(s)
It is sufficient to have a single LB instance/interface for both <code>api</code> and <code>api-int</code> records. However, in order to show that they are independent, we decided to set them up on separate machines. This approach has an added benefit of easier troubleshooting, since each instance's logs only list requests of a single type – external or internal.</td><td>Kubernetes API endpoint for external clients. Must be resolvable by both cluster nodes and external clients.</td></tr>
<tr><td><code>api-int.<CLUSTER_NAME>.<BASE_DOMAIN></code></td><td>Kubernetes API endpoint for internal communication. Must be resolvable by cluster nodes.</td></tr>
<tr><td>Ingress</td><td><code>*.apps.<CLUSTER_NAME>.<BASE_DOMAIN></code></td><td>A/AAAA</td><td>Ingress LB</td><td>A wildcard record that covers externally reachable addresses for OpenShift services, such as the web console and the OAuth server, as well as user applications. Must be resolvable by both cluster nodes and external clients.</td></tr>
</table>

Component	Record	Record type(s)	Target(s)	Description
Bootstrap node	bootstrap.<CLUSTER_NAME>.<BASE_DOMAIN>	A/AAAA, PTR	Bootstrap node's IP	Bootstrap machine. Must be resolvable by both cluster nodes and external clients.
Masters	master-<N>.<CLUSTER_NAME>.<BASE_DOMAIN>		Master IPs	Control plane machines. Must be resolvable by both cluster nodes and external clients.
Workers	worker-<N>.<CLUSTER_NAME>.<BASE_DOMAIN>		Worker IPs	Compute machines. Must be resolvable by both cluster nodes and external clients.

Table 3.4: DNS records required by OpenShift installed using UPI

For this book, we chose named (part of the BIND DNS software suite) as a relatively simple and common implementation of DNS. Refer to the chapters/3/snippets/example.com.fwd file in this book's GitHub repository for a full forward zone configuration, which we store in /etc/named/example.com.fwd in our lab.

Corresponding reverse zone configuration is provided in chapters/3/snippets/10.100.10.ptr. Adjusted for your environment, it is to be stored in /etc/named/10.100.10.ptr. Reverse record for the *.apps address is not required.

> It is important to include a dot (.) at the end of every PTR record; if it is named any other way, it will be interpreted as incomplete (not a **fully qualified domain name**, or **FQDN**) and extended with the domain to form an FQDN, which will lead to incorrect or failed name resolution. The trailing dot indicates an FQDN and is prescribed by RFC1035/1036.

You might have noticed that there are records for additional infra-{1,2,3} machines. Their purpose will be explained in *Chapter 4, Post-Install Configuration*. Also, feel free to choose another naming convention for your nodes.

If you too use named, run sudo systemctl restart named to apply the configuration.

You can use the following Bash one-liner to check whether all forward (A) records are in place:

```
$ for ep in api{,-int} *.apps bootstrap {mast,work}er-{1,2,3} infra-{1,2,3}; do
    dig +noall +answer $ep.ocp4.example.com;
done
```

The following is the expected output:

```
api.ocp4.example.com. 3600       IN      A       10.100.10.5
api-int.ocp4.example.com. 3600 IN        A       10.100.10.4
*.apps.ocp4.example.com. 3600 IN         A       10.100.10.6
bootstrap.ocp4.example.com.      3600 IN A       10.100.10.3
master-1.ocp4.example.com. 3600 IN       A       10.100.10.11
master-2.ocp4.example.com. 3600 IN       A       10.100.10.12
master-3.ocp4.example.com. 3600 IN       A       10.100.10.13
worker-1.ocp4.example.com. 3600 IN       A       10.100.10.21
worker-2.ocp4.example.com. 3600 IN       A       10.100.10.22
worker-3.ocp4.example.com. 3600 IN       A       10.100.10.23
infra-1.ocp4.example.com. 3600 IN        A       10.100.10.31
infra-2.ocp4.example.com. 3600 IN        A       10.100.10.32
infra-3.ocp4.example.com. 3600 IN        A       10.100.10.33
```

Figure 3.1: Forward (A) DNS records

Here is another one-liner for checking reverse (PTR) records:

```
$ for ip in 3 4 5 6 1{1,2,3} 2{1,2,3} 3{1,2,3}; do
    dig +noall +answer -x 10.100.10.$ip;
done
```

Your output should resemble the following:

```
3.10.100.10.in-addr.arpa. 3600  IN      PTR     bootstrap.ocp4.example.com.
4.10.100.10.in-addr.arpa. 3600  IN      PTR     api-int.ocp4.example.com.
5.10.100.10.in-addr.arpa. 3600  IN      PTR     api.ocp4.example.com.
11.10.100.10.in-addr.arpa. 3600 IN      PTR     master-1.ocp4.example.com.
12.10.100.10.in-addr.arpa. 3600 IN      PTR     master-2.ocp4.example.com.
13.10.100.10.in-addr.arpa. 3600 IN      PTR     master-3.ocp4.example.com.
21.10.100.10.in-addr.arpa. 3600 IN      PTR     worker-1.ocp4.example.com.
22.10.100.10.in-addr.arpa. 3600 IN      PTR     worker-2.ocp4.example.com.
23.10.100.10.in-addr.arpa. 3600 IN      PTR     worker-3.ocp4.example.com.
31.10.100.10.in-addr.arpa. 3600 IN      PTR     infra-1.ocp4.example.com.
32.10.100.10.in-addr.arpa. 3600 IN      PTR     infra-2.ocp4.example.com.
33.10.100.10.in-addr.arpa. 3600 IN      PTR     infra-3.ocp4.example.com.
```

Figure 3.2: Reverse (PTR) DNS records

Golang vSphere CLI

The OpenShift installation process on a UPI requires you to manually interact with vSphere when creating and booting VMs for your cluster. This is fine for small deployments, such as the one used for this lab; however, it does not scale well for large enterprise clusters that consist of dozens or even hundreds of nodes. This, and because its usage for modifying network parameters of VMs is not very well covered, is why we decided to use this chapter as an opportunity to introduce you to the **Golang vSphere CLI** (govc) – a command-line utility for interacting with vSphere. While it is not a strict requirement and using it may seem more complicated than using the UI, it is very useful for automating large-scale installations and when you have to repeatedly tear down and spin up clusters as part of experimenting and learning. Follow these steps to install and configure govc on your Bastion machine:

1. First, you have to download the govc binary, extract it, and place it into your `$PATH`:

```
$ curl -LO https://github.com/vmware/govmomi/releases/download/v0.36.2/
govc_Linux_x86_64.tar.gz
$ tar xzvf govc_Linux_x86_64.tar.gz
$ mv govc /usr/local/bin/
```

   We recommend you use the latest stable release of govc from [7].

2. Next, export the following `GOVC_*` environment variables into your shell so that govc knows the address of vCenter to connect to and access credentials, as well as other presets. You can use either the global `/etc/bash_profile` file or the user-specific `~/.bash_profile`:

```
$ export GOVC_URL=https://10.192.101.16
$ export GOVC_USERNAME=administrator@vsphere.local
$ export GOVC_PASSWORD=<MASKED>
$ export GOVC_DATACENTER=DC
$ export GOVC_DATASTORE=10.192.19.12-local-disk
$ export GOVC_FOLDER=learning-ocp4
$ export GOVC_NETWORK=pg-v3110-10.100.10.0%2f24
$ export GOVC_RESOURCE_POOL=learning-ocp4
```

   If any of your vSphere infrastructure components, such as the network, have / (forward slash) in their names, replace them with the URL encoding `%2f`; otherwise, govc commands that reference them, such as `vm.network.change`, will not be able to find them. For the network, the `govc find -type n` command shows the exact format that it expects.

3. To apply the changes, log out and log back in, or run `source ~/.bash_profile`.
4. Next, add vSphere's root CA to the trusted store of your machine by following these steps:

   1. Open the welcome page of your vSphere portal, located at `https://<IP_OR_HOST>`, and download the certificate bundle from **Download trusted root CA certificates** (`https://<VCENTER_IP_OR_HOST>/certs/download.zip`):

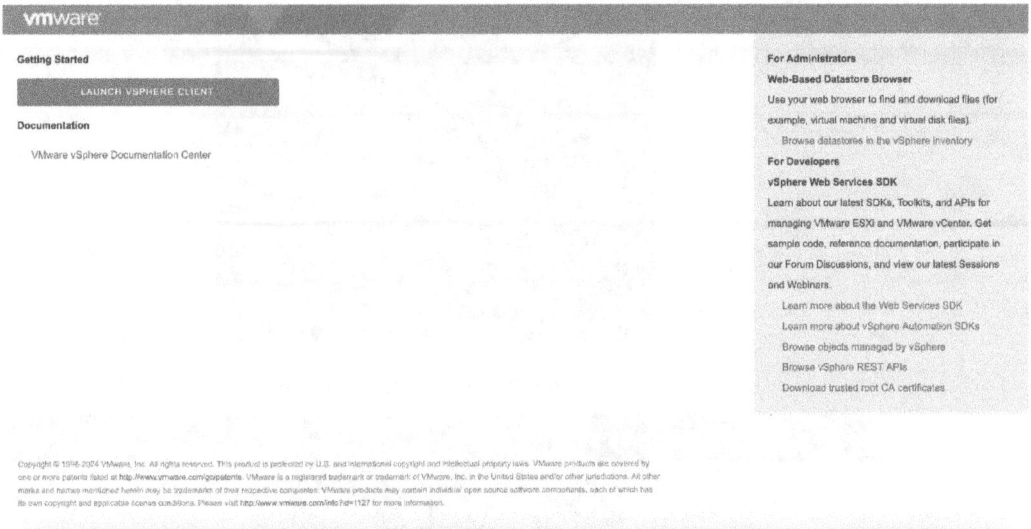

Figure 3.3: VMware vCenter landing page

2. Extract the bundle and add a file that corresponds to your operating system to the system's trust store (your filename may be different):

```
$ unzip download.zip
$ sudo cp certs/lin/dbad4059.0 /etc/pki/ca-trust/source/anchors/
```

Update the trust store database:

```
$ sudo update-ca-trust
```

Failure to perform the preceding steps will result in the following error when attempting to use govc:

```
govc: Post "https://10.192.101.16/sdk": tls: failed to verify
certificate: x509: certificate signed by unknown authority
```

The following are some simple commands you can run to check whether it is working and see some details about your vSphere cluster, such as networks (`n`), clusters (`r`), resource pools (`p`), datastores (`s`), ESXi hosts (`h`), and VM folders (`f`), that we will need later in this chapter:

```
$ govc find -type f
```

```
./vm
./host
./datastore
./network
./vm/VCF
./vm/dz3-ocp
./vm/Discovered virtual machine
./vm/dz2-ocp
./vm/infra
./vm/vCLS
./vm/learning-ocp4
./vm/Templates
```

Figure 3.4: Listing folders with govc

```
$ govc find -type h
```

```
./host/Cluster/10.192.19.12
./host/VCF/10.192.19.13
```

Figure 3.5: Listing ESXi hosts with govc

```
$ govc find -type n
```

```
./network/pg-uplinks
./network/pg-v3110-10.100.10.0%2f24
```

Figure 3.6: Listing networks with govc

```
$ govc find -type r
```

```
./host/Cluster
```

Figure 3.7: Listing clusters with govc

```
$ govc find -type p
```

```
./host/Cluster/Resources
./host/Cluster/Resources/dz2-ocp
./host/Cluster/Resources/learning-ocp4
./host/Cluster/Resources/infra
./host/Cluster/Resources/dz3-ocp
./host/Cluster/Resources/crc-test-01
./host/VCF/Resources
```

Figure 3.8: Listing resource pools with govc

```
$ govc find -type s
```

```
./datastore/10.192.19.12-local-disk-02
./datastore/10.192.19.12-local-disk
./datastore/iso-read-only
```

Figure 3.9: Listing datastores with govc

You may have noticed how all objects in vSphere form a hierarchy, at the top of which is the data center, specified in `GOVC_DATACENTER`. This is very similar to how most filesystems are organized.

In this chapter, we will be creating machines manually, using VMware vCenter.

OpenShift installer CLI

In order to generate the assets required for OpenShift installation, you will need the `openshift-install` binary, which can be obtained using these steps:

1. Go to `https://console.redhat.com/openshift/install/vsphere/user-provisioned`, select the correct platform (Linux, Windows, or Mac) for the OpenShift installer, and click **Download installer**:

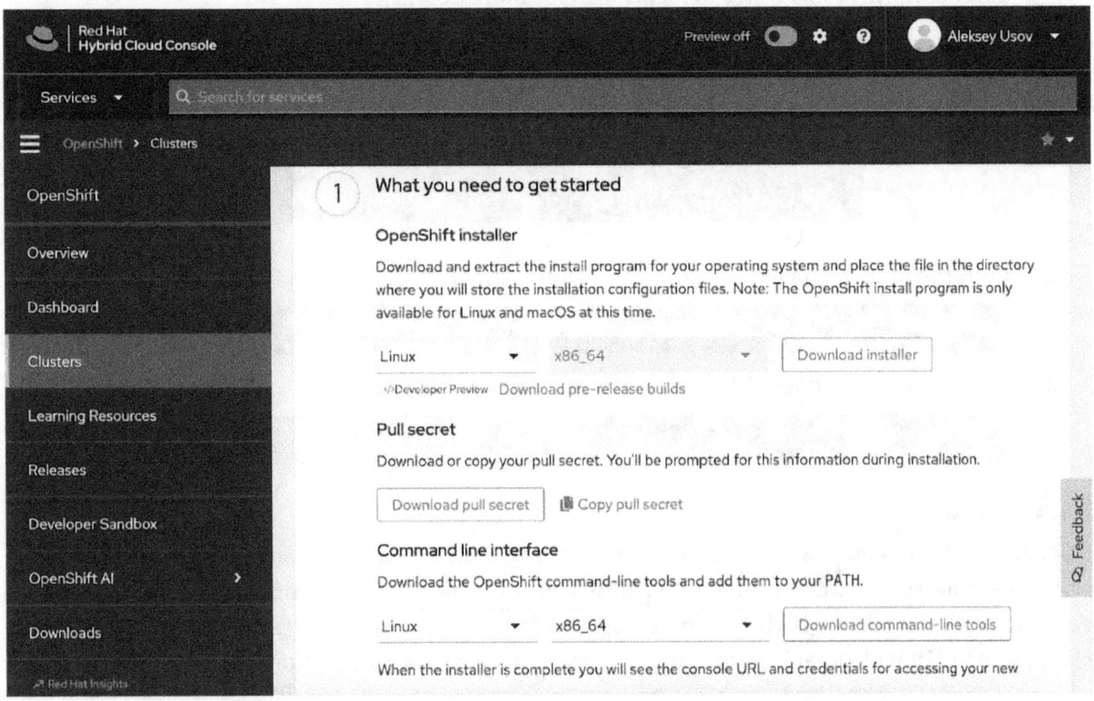

Figure 3.10: Obtaining the OpenShift installer from Red Hat Hybrid Cloud Console

> You can also use the following command to download it directly to your bastion host:
>
> ```
> $ curl -O https://mirror.openshift.com/pub/openshift-v4/
> x86_64/clients/ocp/stable/openshift-install-linux.tar.gz
> ```

2. Copy the archive to your bastion system and extract it:

```
$ tar xzvf openshift-install-linux.tar.gz
```

3. Copy the `openshift-install` binary into your `PATH`:

```
$ sudo mv openshift-install /usr/local/bin/
```

If you go one level up by clicking on **VMware vSphere** at the top of Hybrid Cloud Console, you will see direct links to the respective sections of the OpenShift docs that explain different installation methods.

OpenShift CLI

In order to interact with OpenShift, you will need the oc binary, which can be obtained using these steps:

1. Go to `https://console.redhat.com/openshift/install/vsphere/user-provisioned`, select the correct platform (Linux, Windows, or Mac) for the OpenShift installer, and click **Download command-line tools** (refer to *Figure 3.10* for more details).

   You can also use the following command to download it directly to your bastion host (just like you did in the previous section for the OpenShift installer):

   ```
   $ curl -O https://mirror.openshift.com/pub/openshift-v4/x86_64/clients/ocp/stable/openshift-client-linux.tar.gz
   ```

2. Copy the archive to your bastion system and extract it:

```
$ tar xzvf openshift-client-linux.tar.gz
```

3. Copy the `oc` and `kubectl` binaries into your `PATH`:

```
$ sudo mv -t /usr/local/bin kubectl oc
```

Pull secret

OpenShift requires access to numerous images provided through the `registry.redhat.io` and `registry.connect.redhat.io` image registries. You will need a JSON configuration that contains authentication details for both. It can be obtained through the same portal as the *OpenShift CLI* by clicking on the **Download pull secret** button. Store it in a separate file, for example, `pull-secret.json`.

Red Hat CoreOS OVA

All OpenShift nodes in this chapter will use CoreOS, which is distributed by Red Hat for all supported platforms, including vSphere. To obtain it, follow these steps:

1. Revisit the Red Hat Hybrid Cloud Console portal at `https://console.redhat.com/openshift/install/vsphere/user-provisioned`, right-click on **Download RHCOS OVA** (at the very bottom), and select **Copy link.** Or you can just use the URL [16] in the *References* section, which points directly to the release 4.16.0 instead of the latest.
2. Right-click on the folder in vSphere where you want to upload the OVA (Open Virtual Appliance – a compressed tar archive that contains all the files needed to run a VM), select **Deploy OVF Template...**, and provide the URL you copied in the previous step. You will likely be prompted with the **SSL certificate cannot be trusted** warning – click **Yes.**

3. Select the cluster, datastore, and VM network that you plan to use for your installation. For the purpose of this chapter, we chose thin storage provisioning, which means that disk space will be allocated on demand. This approach comes with a performance penalty, but it is fine for our lab, as it helps to save space. Do not customize hardware, including network interfaces and VM options – these will be done later for each individual machine that will be cloned from this OVA.
4. Select **Review** and then **Finish**. You will see two tasks running at the bottom: **Deploy OVF Template** and **Import OVF Package**. Wait until they're done.

If you are more comfortable working with the CLI, you can import OVA using govc; however, it requires some additional work, which you can find more details about at [17]:

1. First, obtain the OVA's spec manifest and store it in a file, for example, `options.json`:

```
$ govc import.spec https://mirror.openshift.com/pub/openshift-v4/x86_64/
dependencies/rhcos/4.16/4.16.0/rhcos-vmware.x86_64.ova | jq . > options.
json
```

2. Next, open the file with your favorite text editor and change your vCenter network name under `NetworkMapping[0].Network`. You can use the `chapters/3/snippets/options.json` file from this book's GitHub repository as a template.
3. Save the file and run the following command:

```
$ govc import.ova -options options.json -folder ./vm/Templates
https://mirror.openshift.com/pub/openshift-v4/x86_64/dependencies/
rhcos/4.16/4.16.0/rhcos-vmware.x86_64.ova
```

The import should complete in a few minutes:

```
[27-08-24 18:31:21] Uploading disk.vmdk... OK
```

Figure 3.11: CoreOS OVA is successfully imported into the datastore

SSH

In order to access nodes of your cluster, you will need an SSH key (it will be added to the user named `core` on each OpenShift node, including `masters`). Generate it using the following command:

```
$ ssh-keygen -t rsa -N '' -b 4096 -f ~/.ssh/id_rsa
```

In a real-life context, however, for example, in banking, it is very common not to generate SSH keys, thus disabling SSH access completely. This may be required for compliance or to discourage the direct manipulation of nodes, but it also means dependence on API availability (ability to run `oc debug no`) for access. Here's a quick summary of the pros and cons of this decision:

	SSH enabled	SSH disabled
Dependence on the API availability	No (we can access a node even if the API goes down)	Yes (`oc debug no` will not work without API).
Access control	SSH keys must be secured as part of a separate process	We can use RBAC to restrict the use of `oc debug no`. Specifically, we can restrict users' ability to invoke the `create` verb on the `node/exec` subresource. RBAC is discussed in *Chapter 5, Navigating Authentication and Authorization.*

Table 3.5: Long-term implications for having SSH enabled or disabled

In practice, when a node fails for whatever reason, it is faster and easier to just re-provision it than fix it manually. Another benefit of this approach is that it eliminates the risk of a configuration drift that may be introduced with manual changes. OpenShift 4 is built on a philosophy of immutable and disposable worker nodes managed by CoreOS, which was designed as an immutable OS where changes are introduced by an OpenShift configuration manager, **Machine Config Operator** (**MCO**), not manually. Before decommissioning a failed node, it is highly recommended to collect diagnostic data from the cluster with `oc adm must-gather`, from the node itself (if it can be accessed with `oc debug no`) with `sosreport`, and then open a case with Red Hat attaching generated archives.

Load balancers

Before you begin spinning up VMs for your cluster, you have to provision load-balancing infrastructure for API and ingress endpoints. There are a number of load-balancing solutions available, ranging from community-supported software such as **HAProxy**, used in this chapter, to enterprise-grade hardware appliances that offer L4 and L7 balancing, as well as TLS/SSL termination. Widely used examples include F5 BIG-IP, Citrix ADC (formerly NetScaler), and VMware Avi Load Balancer. Regardless of the implementation, they have to meet the conditions outlined in the following table:

DNS endpoint(s)	Port	Targets	Description	Protocol
`api` `api-int`	6443	**Control plane nodes**, including bootstrap. They expose the `/readyz` endpoint that must be used by an LB for health checks. The **bootstrap node** is removed after installation is complete. This should be L4 load balancing (raw TCP) without session persistence.	Kubernetes API	TCP
	22623		Machine Config server	
	22624			

DNS endpoint(s)	Port	Targets	Description	Protocol
`*.apps`	`80`	Nodes where the ingress controller is running. If no compute machines have been added, these are **master nodes.** Session persistence can be configured on a per-application basis.	Ingress controller HTTP	TCP
	`443`		Ingress controller HTTPS	

Table 3.6: Load balancer configuration for OpenShift

For this lab, we decided to use HAProxy because of its simplicity and popularity. Follow these steps to set it up:

1. Install HAProxy and `semanage`:

```
$ sudo yum -y install haproxy setroubleshoot-server
```

2. Copy the configuration from the `chapters/3/snippets/haproxy.cfg.api.pre-install` file in this book's GitHub repository to `/etc/haproxy/haproxy.cfg` on machines that you use for the `api` and `api-int` load balancers. Make sure to replace the `example.com` placeholder with the domain of your environment and set ownership of the config to the following:

```
$ sudo chown root:root /etc/haproxy/haproxy.cfg
```

3. Restore the correct SELinux label in case SELinux is in enforcing mode:

```
$ sudo restorecon -vRF /etc/haproxy
```

4. Allow connections to ports `6443` and `22623`:

```
$ sudo firewall-cmd --perm --add-po=6443/tcp --add-po=22623/tcp
$ sudo firewall-cmd --rel
```

5. Add API and MCP ports to the local SELinux policy:

```
$ sudo semanage port -a -p tcp -t http_port_t 6443
$ sudo semanage port -a -p tcp -t http_port_t 22623
```

6. Enable HAProxy on boot and start it immediately:

```
$ sudo systemctl enable haproxy --now
```

As mentioned earlier, a single LB instance can serve both the `api` and `api-int` endpoints; however, we felt that placing them on separate machines would be a learning opportunity and a good example of how traffic segregation can be used in production to simplify troubleshooting and traffic control.

As for the `*.apps` endpoint, the corresponding HAProxy configuration is available in the `chapters/3/snippets/haproxy.cfg.apps.pre-install` file – copy it to `/etc/haproxy/haproxy.cfg` on the machine that will serve the `*.apps` endpoint of your cluster. As before, replace the domain placeholder with what makes sense for your lab. Also, don't forget to allow connections to ports `80` and `443`:

```
$ sudo firewall-cmd --perm --add-se=http --add-se=https
$ sudo firewall-cmd --rel
```

When removing the bootstrap node from an HAProxy configuration – on `api` and `api-int` LBs, as you will be instructed at the end of installation – or making other changes, use `systemctl reload haproxy` (RHEL 7+) or `service haproxy reload` (RHEL 6 and older) to avoid service interruption.

Installing OpenShift on user-provided infrastructure

This section will guide you through the process of deploying OpenShift on an infrastructure provided and managed by you. We will begin by reviewing the architecture of a cluster we will build, then proceed to generate and customize the files required for bootstrapping nodes, and finally kickstart the installation process.

Architecture

While OpenShift 4 can be deployed on just a single node, the purpose of this book is to introduce readers to a configuration that can be used as a starting point for further expansion and resembles enterprise-grade installations as closely as possible. Therefore, for this chapter, our decision was to deploy OpenShift on a virtualization platform in a multi-master (HA) configuration with at least three workers that would host ingress (router) Pods. The following table contains CPU, memory, and storage details for our environment, including bastion VMs and VMs used as LBs:

Machine	vCPUs	Virtual RAM, GB	Persistent storage, GB	OS
Bootstrap	4	16	100	CoreOS 9.2
Masters	4	16	100	CoreOS 9.2
Workers	8	32	100	CoreOS 9.2 Unlike control plane nodes, compute machines can run RHEL 9.2, if a highly customized configuration for container runtime or greater control is required.
API LB	4	8	40	Rocky Linux 9.2
API LB (internal)	4	8	40	Rocky Linux 9.2

Machine	vCPUs	Virtual RAM, GB	Persistent storage, GB	OS
Ingress LB	4	8	40	Rocky Linux 9.2
Bastion	4	8	40	Rocky Linux 9.2

Table 3.7: Hardware configuration of the lab cluster

The following is a graphical representation of the lab used in this chapter. We will build OpenShift-related components in the sections that follow.

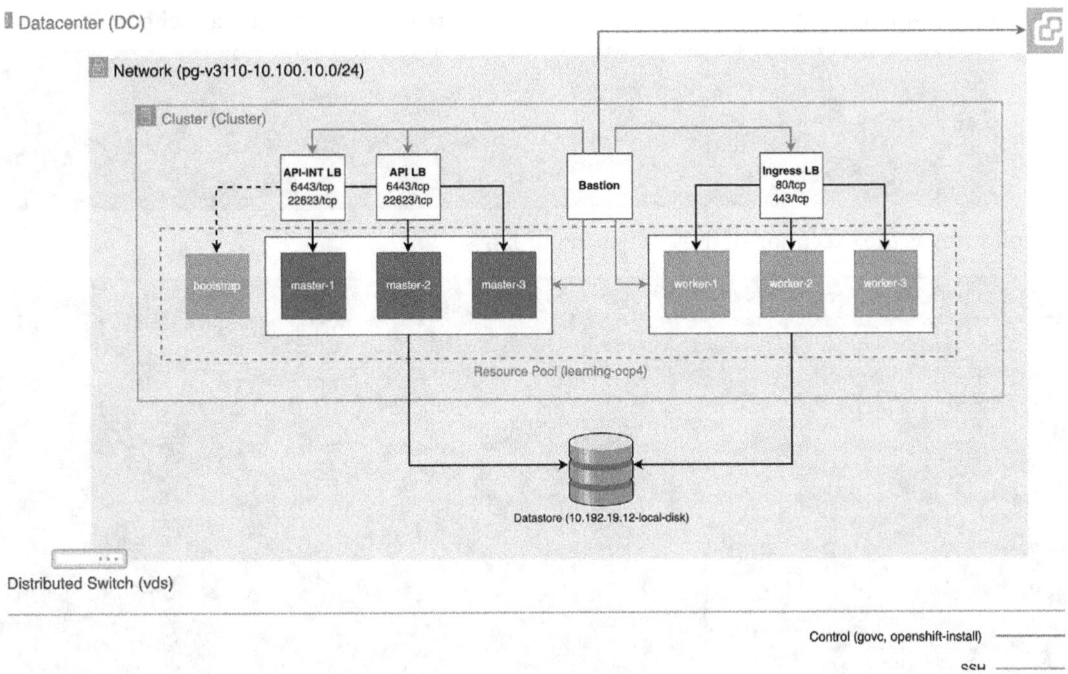

Figure 3.12: OpenShift on VMware

As the preceding figure illustrates, all nodes of our OpenShift cluster will reside in a single vCenter cluster and will use the same datastore. We will be running all our vCenter control commands (govc) and OpenShift CLI (oc) from the bastion host.

Configuring topology

OpenShift 4.16 can be installed in multiple clusters and even multiple data centers for better resilience and availability. So, the next step is to appropriately tag vSphere infrastructure resources that correspond to different failure domains to match the topology defined in our install config. This process involves the following steps (use the tag names that make sense for your physical topology):

1. Create tag categories named `openshift-region` and `openshift-zone`:

```
$ govc tags.category.create -d "OpenShift region" openshift-region
$ govc tags.category.create -d "OpenShift zone" openshift-zone
```

2. Create tags in those categories:

```
$ govc tags.create -c openshift-region us-ny
$ govc tags.create -c openshift-zone us-ny1
```

3. Attach the categories to the corresponding topology elements of VMware, such as data centers and clusters:

```
$ govc tags.attach -c openshift-region us-ny /DC
$ govc tags.attach -c openshift-zone us-ny1 /DC/host/Cluster
```

4. Check whether tag categories and tags have been created and properly attached:

```
$ govc tags.category.ls
$ govc tags.ls
$ govc tags.attached.ls us-ny
$ govc tags.attached.ls us-ny1
```

The following is the execution of these steps in our lab:

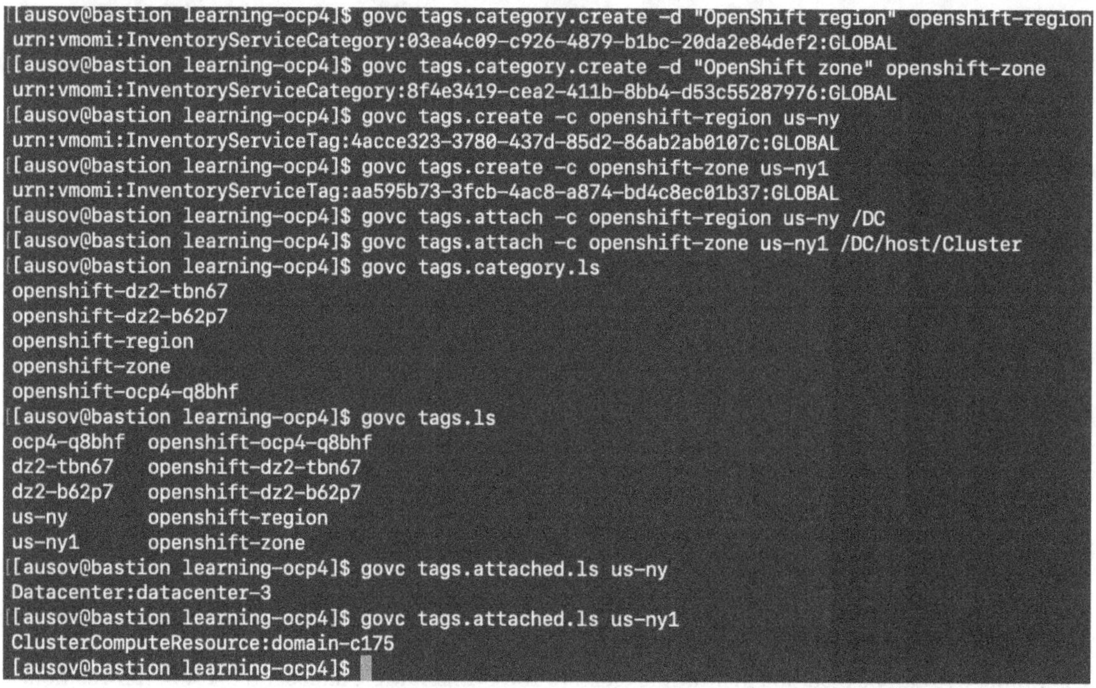

Figure 3.13: Tagging infrastructure failure domains in VMware vSphere

You may notice some extraneous tags – these are leftovers from other labs.

Even though our lab only consists of a single data center with one cluster, it is recommended to use the new install config format.

> Although descriptions of tag categories are arbitrary, the categories themselves must be named `openshift-region` and `openshift-zone`.

Generating install assets

Before installation can commence, a number of files have to be prepared. CoreOS machines use specially formatted files called **Ignition configs** to configure themselves (this process is explained in more detail close to the end of this chapter). Since OpenShift 4 is a complex distributed system made up of hundreds of components, putting together an Ignition config that can take care of each and every aspect of it manually is not practical. This is done via the `openshift-install` utility instead, which takes a much simpler configuration file called `install-config.yaml` and uses it to generate three Ignition config files – for bootstrap, master, and worker nodes. The install config defines the details of your environment, such as the following:

- The platform to install OpenShift on.
- The cluster name.
- The base domain.
- The SSH public keys to be added to the `core` user (optional).
- The pull secret for access to container images stored in the `registry.redhat.io` and `quay.io` registries.
- Whether to deploy a cluster in **Federal Information Processing Standard** (**FIPS**) mode, which changes cryptographic routines invoked by OpenShift from those provided by Kubernetes to CoreOS-provided ones that have been submitted to NIST for FIPS 140-2/140-3 validation on only the x86_64, ppc64le, and s390x architectures. If enabled in an install config, it must be enabled on a RHEL system where `openshift-install` is being run from as well.
- Hyperthreading for control plane and compute machines.
- Network customizations, such as IP address allocation ranges for Pods and services.

After the `install-config.yaml` file has been prepared, use `openshift-install` to generate install manifests that contain API resources that adjust the configuration of a cluster for a given platform. At this stage, custom configurations, such as hybrid networks or additional operators, can be added. Manifests are applied in lexicographical order.

The next step is to use `openshift-install` to consume the manifests and generate Ignition configs that configure machines according to their role – bootstrap, master, or worker.

This is what the overall process looks like:

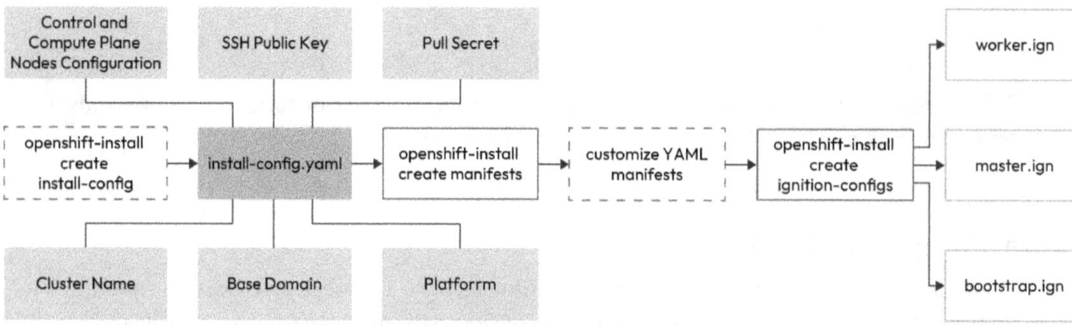

Figure 3.14: Generating install assets

Although you can create an install config by hand, there is a convenient interactive command, `openshift-install create install-config`, that asks you a series of questions about your platform and desired configuration and produces a ready-to-use `install-config.yaml` file that you can always customize further if you wish.

> It is a good practice to create (or recreate) a dedicated directory for all your install assets to keep everything organized and avoid dealing with issues that stem from using the wrong Ignition files or stale state. One particularly common error is the `x509: certificate signed by unknown authority` error in a VM console when trying to fetch an Ignition config from the control plane. This is caused by an X.509 certificate that was left over from a previous installation attempt.
>
> The OpenShift installer creates a hidden file called `.openshift_install_state.json` (notice the leading dot, `.`), which stores the contents of a newly generated `install-config.yaml` file, as well as other information, including certificates. If you run `openshift-install create ignition-config` again with this file present in the current directory, it will not prompt you for any details and will take them from the state file instead. You, however, can use this to your advantage if you forgot to back up your `install-config.yaml`. Make sure you delete the state file before making a new attempt if you want to keep it cleaner without spawning more directories.

Follow these steps to create an installation config:

1. First, create a directory for all your install-related files, for example, `learning-ocp4`, and change into it:

```
$ mkdir learning-ocp4
$ cd learning-ocp4
```

2. Next, use the following command to start the process of providing information for the config in an interactive mode:

```
$ openshift-install create install-config
```

3. Select an SSH public key that you created earlier:

```
[ausov@bastion learning-ocp4]$ openshift-install create install-config
? SSH Public Key  [Use arrows to move, type to filter, ? for more help]
> /home/ausov/.ssh/id_rsa.pub
  <none>
```

Figure 3.15: Selecting a public SSH key

4. Next, choose a platform. In our lab, this is vSphere:

```
[ausov@bastion learning-ocp4]$ openshift-install create install-config
? SSH Public Key /home/ausov/.ssh/id_rsa.pub
? Platform  [Use arrows to move, type to filter, ? for more help]
  baremetal
  gcp
  ibmcloud
  nutanix
  openstack
  powervs
> vsphere
```

Figure 3.16: Selecting the platform

5. Specify the `vCenter`, `Username`, and `Password` values:

```
[ausov@bastion learning-ocp4]$ openshift-install create install-config
? SSH Public Key /home/ausov/.ssh/id_rsa.pub
? Platform vsphere
? vCenter 10.192.101.16
? Username administrator@vsphere.local
? Password [? for help] **********
INFO Connecting to vCenter 10.192.101.16
INFO Defaulting to only available datacenter: DC
INFO Defaulting to only available cluster: /DC/host/Cluster
```

Figure 3.17: Specifying access credentials for the selected platform

6. Next, select a data center. In our lab, there is only one available, `DC`.
7. Next, you will be prompted for a datastore that will serve as a backend for the default storage class used for provisioning PersistentVolume objects:

```
? Default Datastore  [Use arrows to move, type to filter, ? for more help]
> /DC/datastore/10.192.19.12-local-disk
  /DC/datastore/10.192.19.12-local-disk-02
  /DC/datastore/iso-read-only
```

Figure 3.18: Selecting the datastore for the default storage class

8. Provide answers to the rest of the prompts, including the network, cluster name, base domain, and pull secret. You can specify any values for `Virtual IP Address for API` and `Virtual IP Address for Ingress` – we will remove them from the generated config later, as they are required only for IPI (fully automated) installations:

Figure 3.19: Specifying network, base domain, cluster name, and pull secret

A new `install-config.yaml` file will be created in the current directory:

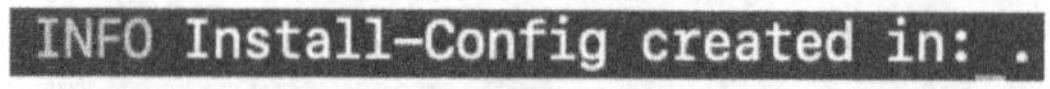

Figure 3.20: install-config.yaml has been created

9. Now, open the newly created file (if you generated it using the preceding approach) and adjust it using the `chapters/3/snippets/install-config.yaml` file from this book's GitHub repository as a reference (don't forget to replace placeholders and other details, including region and zone tags you created earlier, according to your environment). Also, make sure it has `.compute[].replicas: 0` for workers, as initially our cluster will be created with just one bootstrap and three master nodes. As for workers, we will be adding them later.
10. Back up your `install-config.yaml` file by copying it to a different location now, because the command that follows will delete it on consumption.
11. The next command will process the install config and generate several files containing Kubernetes and OpenShift API objects in the `manifests` and `openshift` subdirectories:

```
$ openshift-install create manifests
```

The command will generate an output similar to the following:

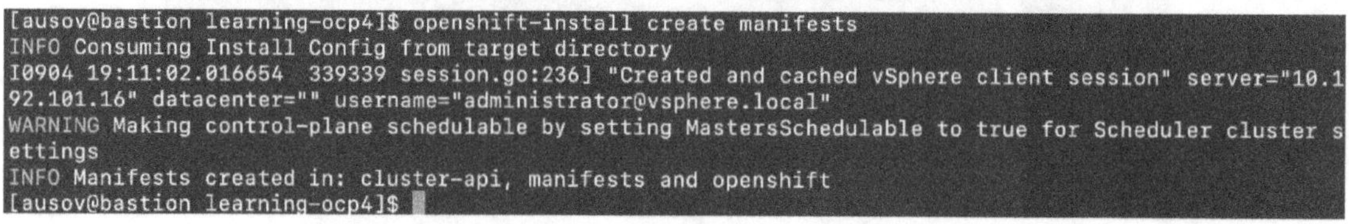

Figure 3.21: Generating manifests from the install config

12. Since we are provisioning VMs manually for now, we don't need master and worker MachineSets, as well as master machine manifests, so we are going to remove them:

```
$ rm -f openshift/99_openshift-cluster-api_master-machines-*.yaml
openshift/99_openshift-cluster-api_worker-machineset-*.yaml openshift/99_
openshift-machine-api_master-control-plane-machine-set.yaml
```

13. By default, control plane machines are marked as schedulable in case there are no worker nodes. Since we will be deploying three workers, we can mark masters as non-schedulable, which is recommended:

```
$ sed -i 's/mastersSchedulable: true/mastersSchedulable: false/'
manifests/cluster-scheduler-02-config.yml
```

Because we will be using Windows MCO later in this book, we need to define a hybrid network with a custom VXLAN port for traffic encapsulation. We prepared a manifest file for you in the `chapters/3/snippets/cluster-network-03-config.yml` file of this book's GitHub repository. Copy it into a file named `cluster-network-03-config.yml` in the `manifests` directory. The VXLAN port (`14789`) from the manifest was referred to as `CUSTOM_VXLAN_PORT` in the *Networking* section; make sure it's allowed through your firewall (if any) too.

> The hybrid network's CIDR must not overlap with `clusterNetwork` or `serviceNetwork` CIDRs defined in the `manifests/cluster-network-02-config.yml` file.

Now that all customizations have been applied, it is time to generate Ignition configs that will be used to bootstrap our VMs:

```
$ openshift-install create ignition-configs
```

The following is the expected output:

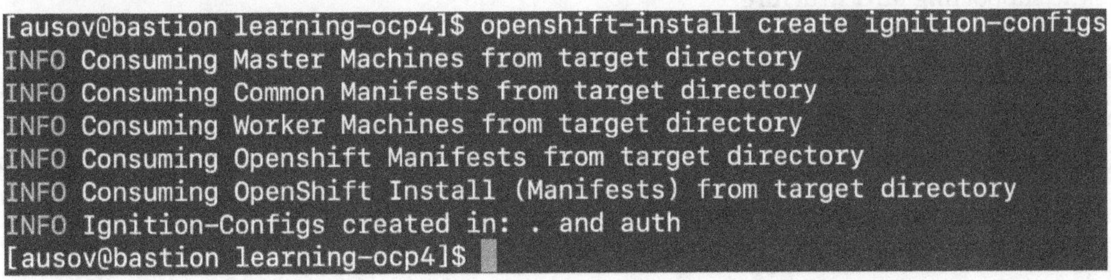

Figure 3.22: Using manifests to generate Ignition configuration files

The preceding step also deletes the `openshift` and `manifests` subdirectories and creates three Ignition configs and the `auth` subdirectory with the `kubeconfig` and `kubeadmin-password` files in it in their stead, as well as other internal manifests, which can be verified by viewing the structure of our current directory with `tree`:

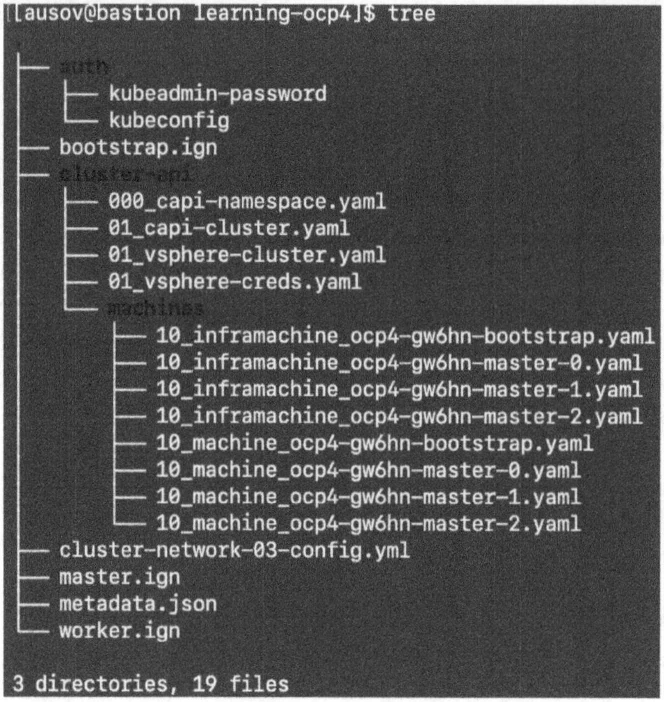

Figure 3.23: Final directory tree with all installation assets

Now that we have generated installation assets using the OpenShift installer, we can proceed to prepare the supporting infrastructure.

Serving Ignition configs over HTTP

Create a first-stage Ignition config file named `merge-bootstrap.ign` for your bootstrap machine, using `chapters/3/snippets/merge-bootstrap.ign` from this book's GitHub repository as a reference.

The config from the previous step references the `bootstrap.ign` file served by a web server installed on our bastion machine, which is what we will be setting up next:

```
$ sudo yum -y install httpd
$ sudo systemctl enable httpd --now
$ sudo cp bootstrap.ign /var/www/html/
$ chmod a+r /var/www/html/bootstrap.ign
```

If you have a firewall running (check with `systemctl is-active firewalld`), which is the default on RHEL and Rocky Linux 9, make sure to allow plain HTTP traffic (the first command adds it to the policy and the second one applies it):

```
$ firewall-cmd --perm --add-se http
$ firewall-cmd --rel
```

If SELinux is running in enforcing mode (check by executing `getenforce`), you will also need to set an appropriate SELinux file context (`httpd_sys_content_t`) on `bootstrap.ign`; otherwise, Apache will not be able to read the file:

```
$ restorecon -vRF /var/www/html
```

You can check whether the bootstrap machine will be able to access the file by issuing a simple `GET` request for `bootstrap.ign` to the web server (when the `-X <METHOD>` parameter is omitted, the `GET` method is assumed):

```
$ curl -I bastion.ocp4.example.com/bootstrap.ign
```

The following output indicates that the file is available, and the bootstrap machine will be able to obtain it:

```
[ausov@bastion learning-ocp4]$ curl -I bastion.ocp4.dz.vmw-nfv.rocks/bootstrap.ign
HTTP/1.1 200 OK
Date: Mon, 01 Apr 2024 03:41:27 GMT
Server: Apache/2.4.57 (Rocky Linux)
Last-Modified: Mon, 01 Apr 2024 03:40:03 GMT
ETag: "45445-61500beadbd14"
Accept-Ranges: bytes
Content-Length: 283717
Content-Type: application/vnd.coreos.ignition+json
```

Figure 3.24: Successful retrieval of the first-stage Ignition config

Finally, prepare Base64-encoded versions of three remaining Ignition configs – `master.ign`, `worker.ign`, and `merge-bootstrap.ign`. You can use the following Bash one-liner:

```
$ find . -type f -name '*.ign' ! -name bootstrap.ign -exec sh -c 'base64 -w0 {}
> $(basename {} .ign).b64' \;
```

Now we have everything to start rolling out our cluster.

Installation

Before we begin, let us take a closer look at how the install process works so that we know what is involved at every step:

1. The bootstrap machine uses the first-stage `merge-bootstrap.ign` Ignition configuration passed via VM properties to locate the second-stage Ignition config served by a web server and exposes the `https://api-int.CLUSTER_NAME.BASE_DOMAIN:22623/config/master` endpoint, which provides a complete Ignition configuration for control plane nodes.
2. A temporary single-node Kubernetes cluster backed by a single-node etcd cluster starts on the bootstrap node.
3. Each of the control plane machines boots from the `master.b64` Ignition config passed via a VM property. That config references a remote configuration endpoint exposed by the temporary API server. Both are merged and the resulting configuration is used to initialize a node.

4. The temporary control plane deploys the production control plane on control plane machines.
5. The Cluster Version Operator starts and deploys the etcd operator, which then schedules etcd onto control plane nodes.
6. The temporary control plane shuts down, passing control to the new control plane.
7. The new control plane exposes the `https://api-int.CLUSTER_NAME.BASE_DOMAIN:22623/config/worker` endpoint, which provides the complete Ignition configuration for compute nodes.
8. The bootstrap machine is shut down either automatically (IPI) or manually (UPI).
9. Much like control plane nodes, each of the worker machines boots from a `worker.b64` Ignition config passed via a VM property. That config references a remote configuration endpoint exposed by the API server (different from the one for masters). Both are merged, and the resulting configuration is used to initialize a node.
10. Additional services are deployed on the control plane by various operators.

The process is graphically depicted as follows with different colors and numbers used to indicate the sequence in which the bootstrap, masters, and workers initialize themselves, as well as traffic flow:

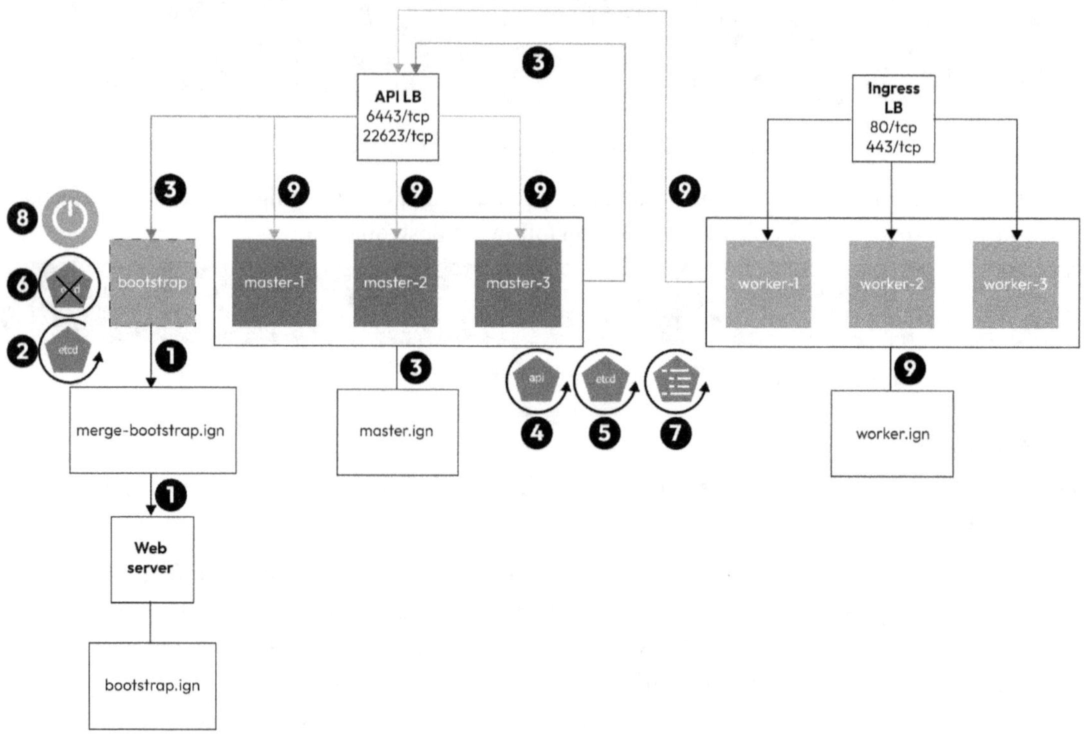

Figure 3.25: OpenShift installation sequence

Now that everything is ready, log in to your vCenter console and let's begin by creating the bootstrap VM:

1. First, click on the **VMs and Templates** view on the left side of the UI, then open the VM folder that you created earlier, right-click on the CoreOS template you downloaded, and select **Clone | Clone to Virtual Machine...**.

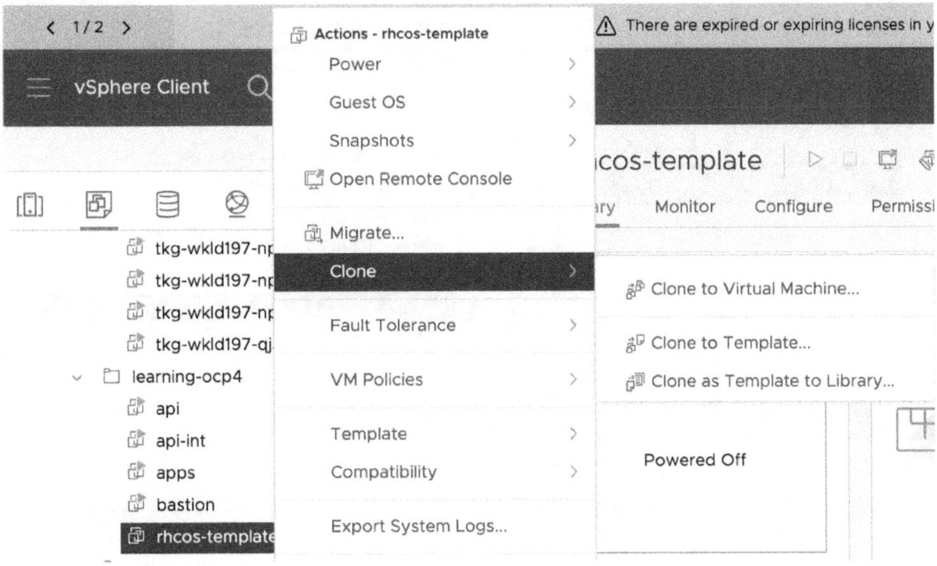

Figure 3.26: Cloning a VM from an OVA template

2. On the first screen, name your machine accordingly, then expand the data center node and select the VM folder for new machines:

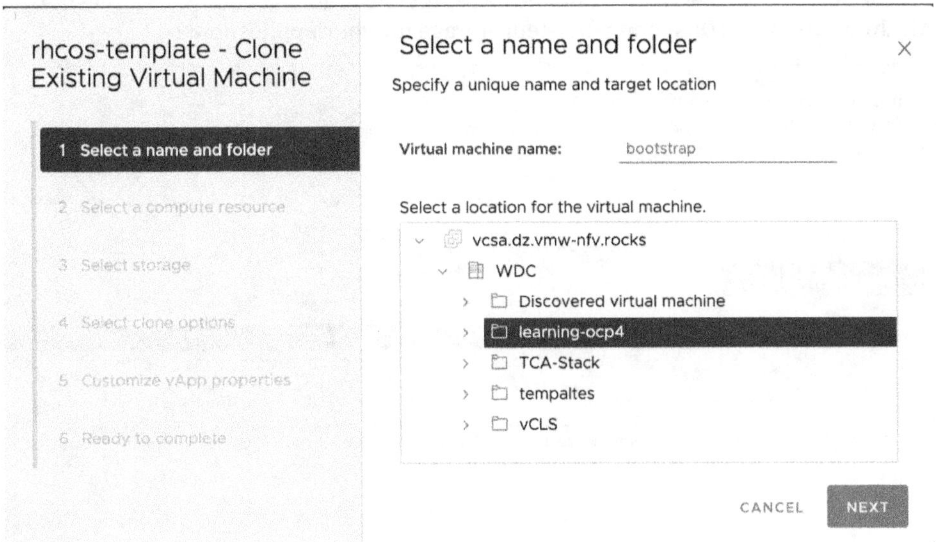

Figure 3.27: Cloning an existing VM – Select a name and folder

3. Next, select the resource pool you created when preparing your environment. While not strictly necessary, it is a good practice to create a dedicated resource pool for the nodes of your cluster for the more efficient management, reservation, and accounting of hardware resources, such as CPU shares:

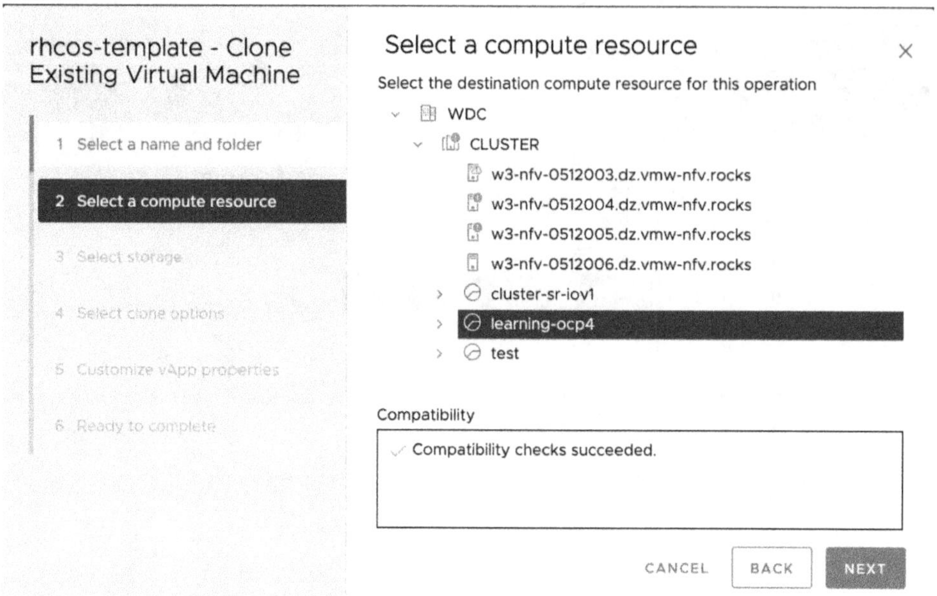

Figure 3.28: Cloning an existing VM – Select a compute resource

4. Proceed to the **Select storage** screen and select the datastore specified in your install config file. Make sure the datastore selected has sufficient capacity for all your machines' **Virtual Machine Disks (VMDKs)** and persistent storage for your applications:

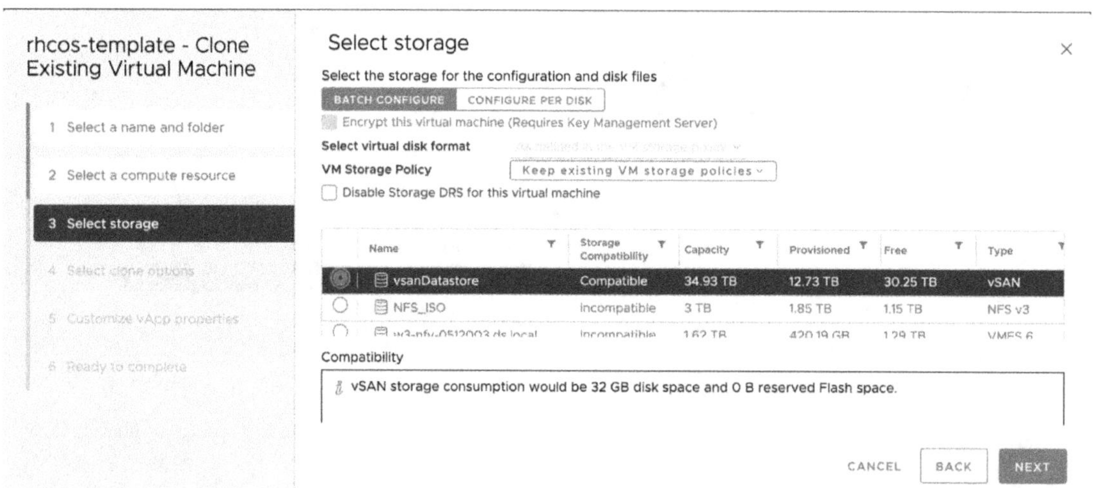

Figure 3.29: Cloning an existing VM – Select storage

You can also specify **Management Storage Policy - Thin**, if available.

5. Click **Next**, then select **Customize this virtual machine's hardware** and **Power on virtual machine after creation** (optional):

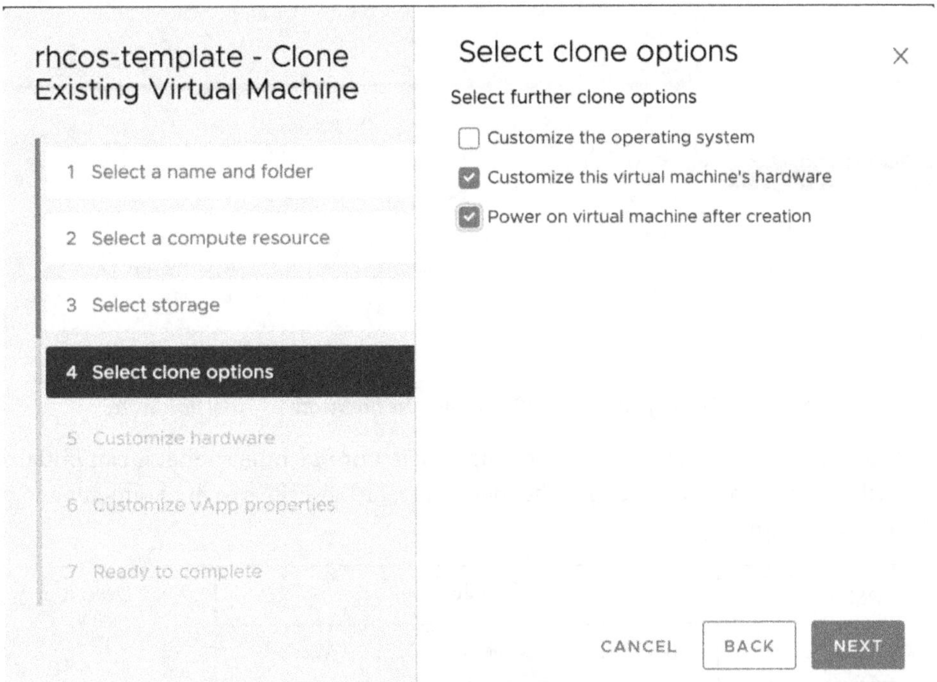

Figure 3.30: Cloning an existing VM – Select clone options

6. On the **Customize hardware** screen, set the desired number of vCPUs, the amount of RAM, and the disk size according to *Table 3.7* in the *Architecture* section. On the same screen, expand the **Network adapter 1** device, change the MAC address assignment to **Manual**, and specify a hardware address that is reserved for this machine in your DHCP configuration.

   It is recommended to use some form of numbering convention to simplify the management of IPs and hardware addresses. For example, in our lab, the `10.241.11.158` bootstrap machine IP maps to the `00:50:56:1a:bc:58` hardware address, which makes it easier to remember and spares us the need to constantly check with the DHCP config file. Also, make sure the interface is connected on boot:

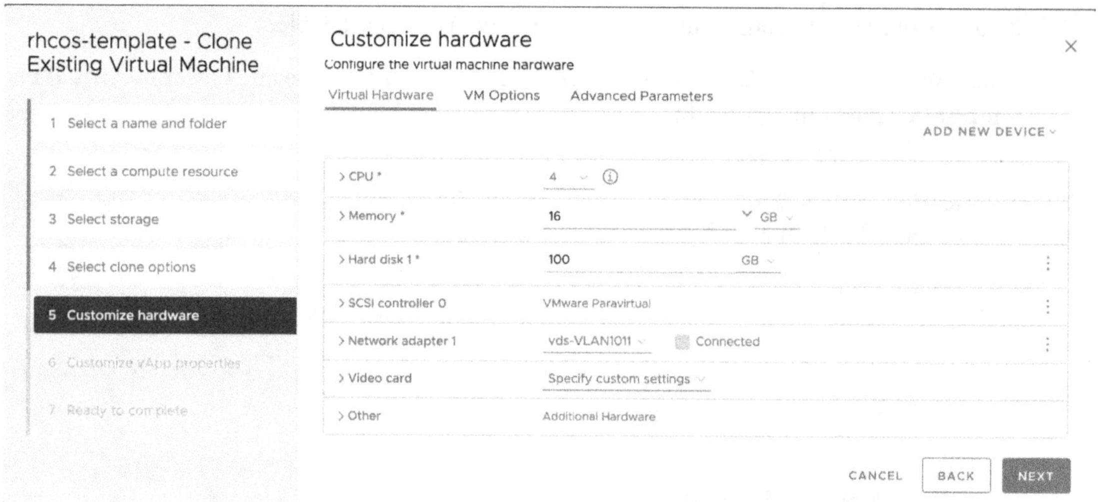

Figure 3.31: Cloning an existing VM – Customize hardware – virtual hardware

7. The next step is to pass the Ignition config data to our machine so that it can initialize itself, as well as some other parameters. The following table describes each parameter and its value for every machine type:

Key	Value			Description
	Bootstrap	Master	Worker	
`disk.EnableUUID`	`TRUE`	`TRUE`	`TRUE`	Needed so that the attached VMDKs present a consistent UUID to the VM, allowing the disk to be mounted properly.
`stealclock.enable`	`TRUE`	`TRUE`	Unset	Enables CPU steal time accounting of a VMware guest. Helpful for troubleshooting cluster performance issues.
`guestinfo.ignition.config.data`	The contents of `merge-bootstrap.b64`	The contents of `master.b64`	The contents of `worker.b64`	Ignition config from a corresponding `.b64` file encoded according to `guestinfo.igniton.config.data.encoding`.

Key	Value			Description
	Bootstrap	Master	Worker	
`guestinfo.ignition.config.data.encoding`	`base64`			Encoding of the Ignition config. Supported algorithms are `""` (empty), `base64`, and `gzip+base64`.

Table 3.8: Advanced parameters for different node types

The following is what these parameters should look like when set appropriately:

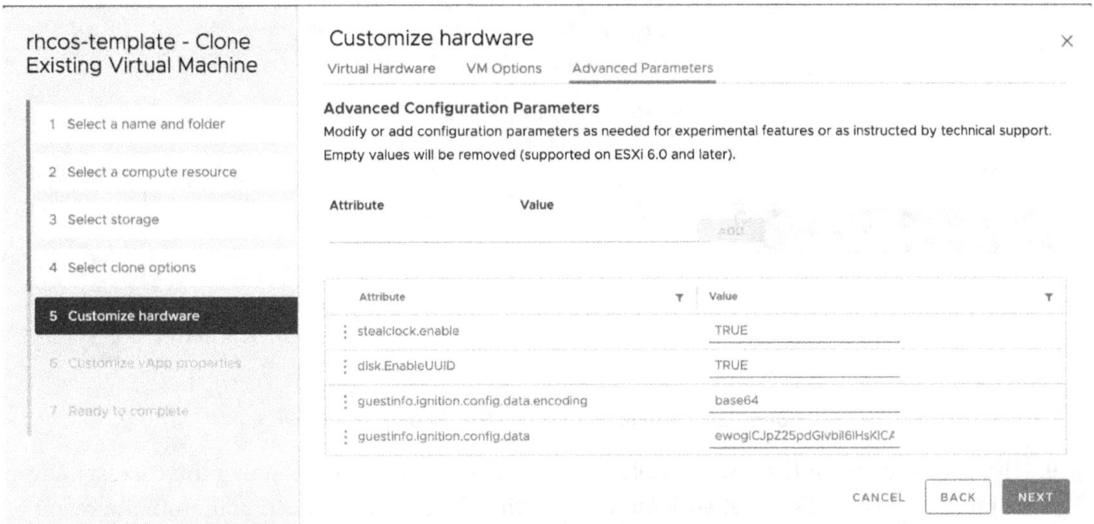

Figure 3.32: Cloning an existing VM – Customize hardware – advanced parameters

> Depending on your version of vCenter, the **Advanced Parameters** tab may not exist. If that is the case, go to **VM Options** | **Advanced** | **EDIT CONFIGURATION...**.

8. Now, click **Next**. There is nothing that needs to be added on the **Customize vApp properties** screen, so just click **Next** again, take one last look at the configuration to make sure everything is correct, and click **Finish**. If you selected **Power on virtual machine after creation** earlier, this will also start it.

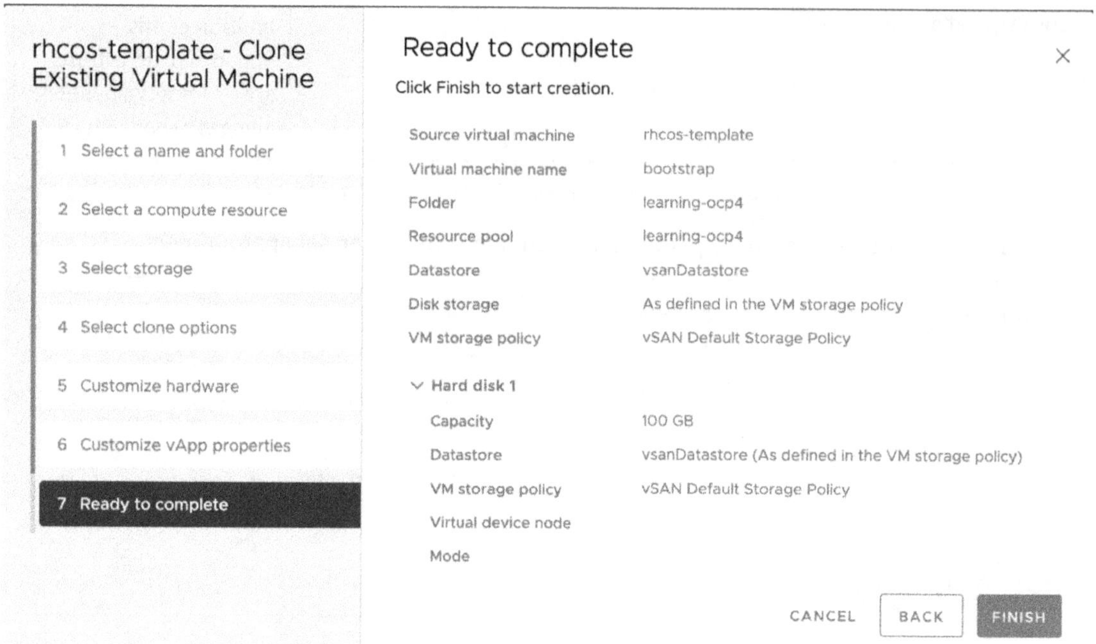

Figure 3.33: Cloning an existing VM – review and finish

9. Now, quickly open the VMs console by right-clicking on it and selecting the corresponding option. You should see **Network Manager** setting the machine's hostname from the result of a reverse DNS lookup, which is exactly why we created those PTR records. It also fetches the primary Ignition config from the web server, validates it, parses it, and finally uses it to initialize itself, as indicated by the following screenshot:

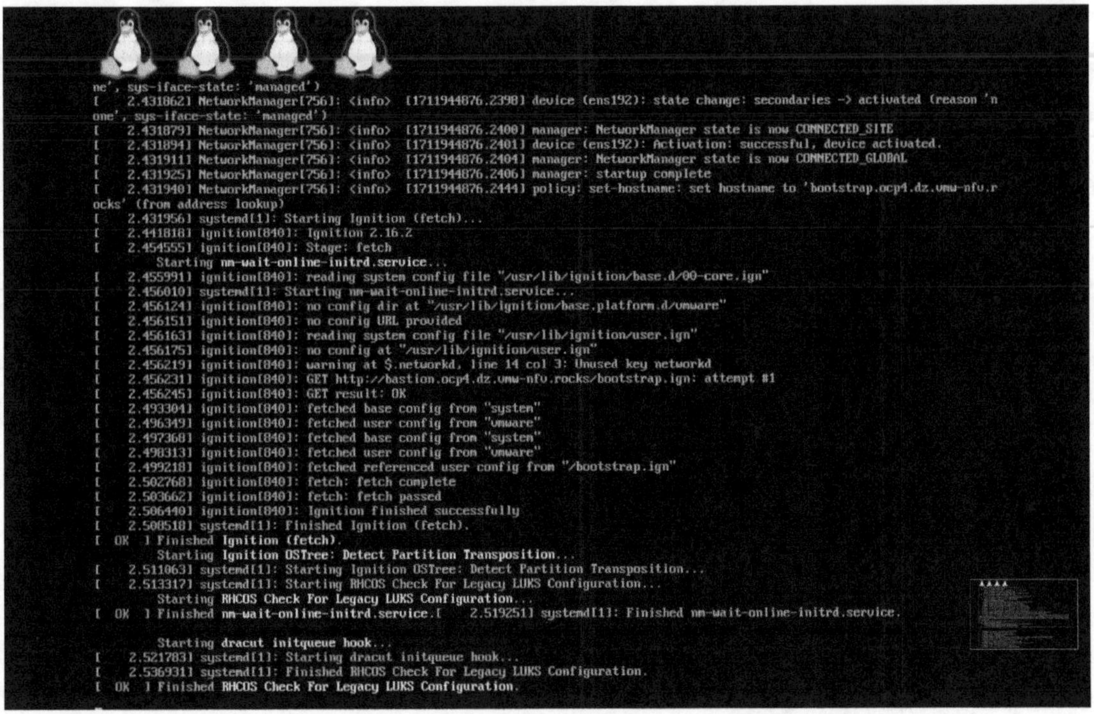

Figure 3.34: Bootstrap node applying its Ignition config

10. On the bastion host, where you prepared all your install assets, run the following command to monitor the progress and get notified when the bootstrap machine can be removed:

    ```
    $ openshift-install wait-for bootstrap-complete --log-level INFO
    ```

    You can run the preceding command at any point during the process, as it does not actually do anything except wait for the production control plane to become available. All the real work is happening behind the scenes and is driven purely by scripts encoded in the Ignition configs.

11. The next step is to start creating control plane machines. The process is identical to spinning up the bootstrap machine, except for the name, hardware address, and Ignition config passed via the `guestinfo.ignition.config.data` property. As before, open the machine's console to watch as it configures itself. You may notice that unlike the bootstrap node that had to be initialized from the config stored on a web server prepared by us, this machine gets its configuration from the temporary control plane created by the bootstrap machine. The endpoint is available at TCP port 22623, which is exposed by MCO – the internal configuration manager of OpenShift 4. The following is the console of a master node initializing itself:

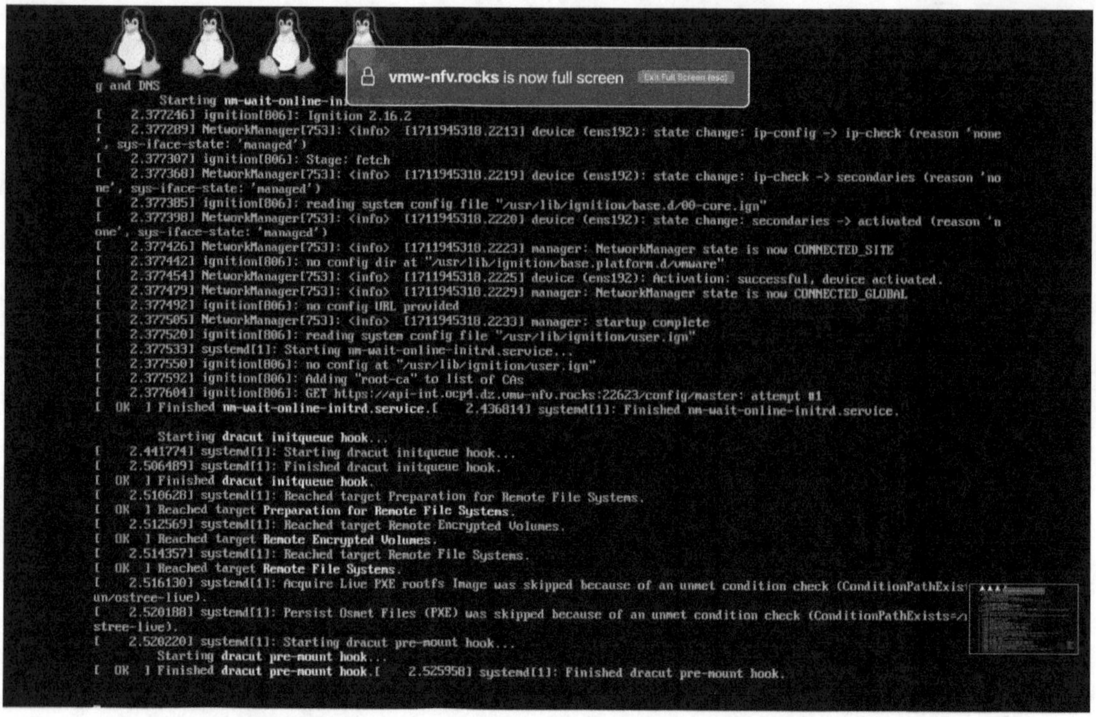

Figure 3.35: Master node fetching its Ignition config from the bootstrap node and applying it

The process finishes in mere seconds, and you should see a login prompt similar to what is shown in the following screenshot:

Figure 3.36: Master node received its network configuration over DHCP and successfully applied its Ignition config

12. In a few minutes (we suggest giving it at least 15), the `openshift-install wait-for bootstrap-complete` command from before should complete, indicating that the bootstrap machine can (and should) now be safely removed:

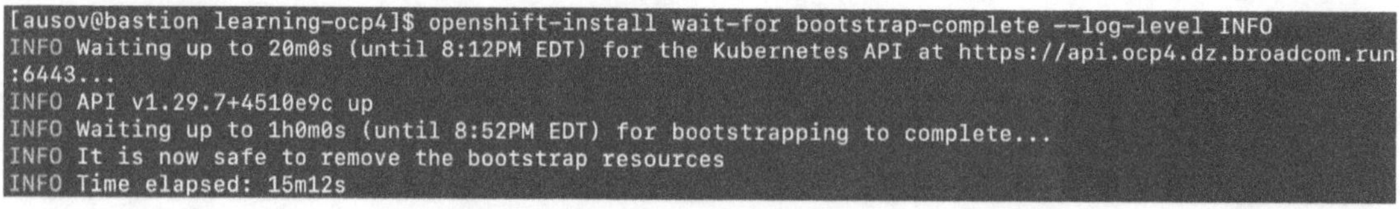

Figure 3.37: Bootstrap machine can be safely removed

At this stage, we log in to our `api` and `api-int` HAProxy machines, simply comment the bootstrap node out, and run `systemctl reload haproxy`.

> You may see some errors, such as failures to read certain API objects, in the preceding output. These are normal during bootstrap, as the installation program continuously polls for these resources until they become available. By default, it waits for up to one hour before giving up and returning an error, so you should be patient.

13. Now that the production control plane is up and running, we can go ahead and start provisioning workers, which will provide the CRI-O container runtime for cluster workloads. Again, the process is identical to creating the bootstrap and control plane machines, except for the VM names, hardware addresses, and Ignition config data. The screenshot that follows shows the process of booting up a worker machine:

Figure 3.38: Worker node fetching its Ignition config from one of the master nodes and applying it

As the boot messages flash through the screen, you may notice that worker machines initialize themselves from the production control plane that now serves the `https://api-int.CLUSTER_NAME.BASE_DOMAIN:22623/config/worker` endpoint. Notice that unlike with control plane machines, some of the initial attempts to fetch the Ignition config from the production control plane failed. This is because we booted that machine before the new control plane had enough time to come online. This is fine, as long as it does not take more than around 10 minutes. If you are curious, we encourage you to examine the config used by workers in more detail by running the following command:

```
$ curl -s https://api-int.CLUSTER_NAME.BASE_DOMAIN:22623/config/worker | jq -r .
```

If not available on your system, `jq` can be installed as easily as running `yum -y install jq` as root. If the respective repository is not configured, you should be able to use `python -m json.tool` instead.

You may recall that when we ran `openshift-install create ignition-configs`, aside from Ignition files themselves, it also generated a directory named `auth` with the `kubeconfig` and `kubeadmin-password` files inside. These are access credentials for your cluster that can be used to monitor its state as soon as the production control plane comes online. The recommended way is to export the `kubeconfig` file into the current shell by running `export KUBECONFIG=~/INSTALL_ASSETS_DIR/auth/kubeconfig` and use the oc subcommands to query and manage your cluster.

As workers apply the Ignition config, they begin starting the kubelet agent and generating kubelet CSRs for secure communication with the control plane. You can view them by running `oc get csr`. Use the following one-liner to approve them all:

```
$ oc get csr -o go-template='{{range .items}}{{if not .status}}{{.metadata.name}}{{"\n"}}{{end}}{{end}}' | xargs --no-run-if-empty oc adm certificate approve
```

Run `oc get csr` a few more times to make sure that no new CSRs are being generated. If they are, approve them as well as shown previously.

This output of the `oc get no` command was taken shortly after all worker machines had been provisioned and their CSRs were approved:

```
NAME                         STATUS    ROLES                 AGE  VERSION
master-1.ocp4.example.com    Ready     control-plane,master  24m  v1.29.7+4510e9c
master-2.ocp4.example.com    Ready     control-plane,master  20m  v1.29.7+4510e9c
master-3.ocp4.example.com    Ready     control-plane,master  11m  v1.29.7+4510e9c
worker-1.ocp4.example.com    NotReady  worker                52m  v1.29.7+4510e9c
worker-2.ocp4.example.com    NotReady  worker                48s  v1.29.7+4510e9c
worker-3.ocp4.example.com    NotReady  worker                48s  v1.29.7+4510e9c
```

Figure 3.39: OpenShift nodes initializing

At this point, it normally takes about five minutes for the machines to become ready. If they don't, check whether new CSRs have been generated with `oc get csr`, and if they have, approve them.

You may use the following command to monitor the progress and watch as the cluster brings itself to life:

```
$ watch -n1 oc get no,co
```

We are not providing its output in text here due to its large volume.

Finally, in 10–15 minutes, all nodes become available, and the cluster converges to a stable state:

```
NAME                              STATUS   ROLES                  AGE   VERSION
node/master-1.ocp4.example.com    Ready    control-plane,master   35m   v1.29.7+4510e9c
node/master-2.ocp4.example.com    Ready    control-plane,master   32m   v1.29.7+4510e9c
node/master-3.ocp4.example.com    Ready    control-plane,master   31m   v1.29.7+4510e9c
node/worker-1.ocp4.example.com    Ready    worker                 11m   v1.29.7+4510e9c
node/worker-2.ocp4.example.com    Ready    worker                 11m   v1.29.7+4510e9c
node/worker-3.ocp4.example.com    Ready    worker                 11m   v1.29.7+4510e9c

NAME                                                                        VERSION   AVAILABLE   PROGRESSING   DEGRADED   SINCE   MESSAGE
clusteroperator.config.openshift.io/authentication                          4.16.8    True        False         False      68s
clusteroperator.config.openshift.io/baremetal                               4.16.8    True        False         False      28m
clusteroperator.config.openshift.io/cloud-controller-manager                4.16.8    True        False         False      33m
clusteroperator.config.openshift.io/cloud-credential                        4.16.8    True        False         False      40m
clusteroperator.config.openshift.io/cluster-autoscaler                      4.16.8    True        False         False      28m
clusteroperator.config.openshift.io/config-operator                         4.16.8    True        False         False      28m
clusteroperator.config.openshift.io/console                                 4.16.8    True        False         False      6m58s
clusteroperator.config.openshift.io/control-plane-machine-set               4.16.8    True        False         False      28m
clusteroperator.config.openshift.io/csi-snapshot-controller                 4.16.8    True        False         False      28m
clusteroperator.config.openshift.io/dns                                     4.16.8    True        False         False      28m
clusteroperator.config.openshift.io/etcd                                    4.16.8    True        False         False      27m
clusteroperator.config.openshift.io/image-registry                          4.16.8    True        False         False      18m
clusteroperator.config.openshift.io/ingress                                 4.16.8    True        False         False      9m26s
clusteroperator.config.openshift.io/insights                                4.16.8    True        False         False      22m
clusteroperator.config.openshift.io/kube-apiserver                          4.16.8    True        False         False      23m
clusteroperator.config.openshift.io/kube-controller-manager                 4.16.8    True        False         False      26m
clusteroperator.config.openshift.io/kube-scheduler                          4.16.8    True        False         False      26m
clusteroperator.config.openshift.io/kube-storage-version-migrator           4.16.8    True        False         False      29m
clusteroperator.config.openshift.io/machine-api                             4.16.8    True        False         False      25m
clusteroperator.config.openshift.io/machine-approver                        4.16.8    True        False         False      28m
clusteroperator.config.openshift.io/machine-config                          4.16.8    True        False         False      28m
clusteroperator.config.openshift.io/marketplace                             4.16.8    True        False         False      28m
clusteroperator.config.openshift.io/monitoring                              4.16.8    True        False         False      6m10s
clusteroperator.config.openshift.io/network                                 4.16.8    True        False         False      29m
clusteroperator.config.openshift.io/node-tuning                             4.16.8    True        False         False      11m
clusteroperator.config.openshift.io/openshift-apiserver                     4.16.8    True        False         False      21m
clusteroperator.config.openshift.io/openshift-controller-manager            4.16.8    True        False         False      28m
clusteroperator.config.openshift.io/openshift-samples                       4.16.8    True        False         False      20m
clusteroperator.config.openshift.io/operator-lifecycle-manager              4.16.8    True        False         False      28m
clusteroperator.config.openshift.io/operator-lifecycle-manager-catalog      4.16.8    True        False         False      28m
clusteroperator.config.openshift.io/operator-lifecycle-manager-packageserver 4.16.8   True        False         False      21m
clusteroperator.config.openshift.io/service-ca                              4.16.8    True        False         False      29m
clusteroperator.config.openshift.io/storage                                 4.16.8    True        False         False      28m
```

Figure 3.40: OpenShift cluster is up and running – CLI

Now we have a minimal working cluster with control plane and worker nodes ready, as well as all cluster operators in a healthy state. We will do basic sanity checks in the section that follows, while post-installation steps will be a focus of the next chapter.

Post-install validation

First, let us confirm that everything is good by logging in to the web console with the `kubeadmin` user and the password from the `auth/kubeadmin-password` file. You can use the `oc whoami --show-console` command to obtain the URL of the console. This is what you should see if everything went well:

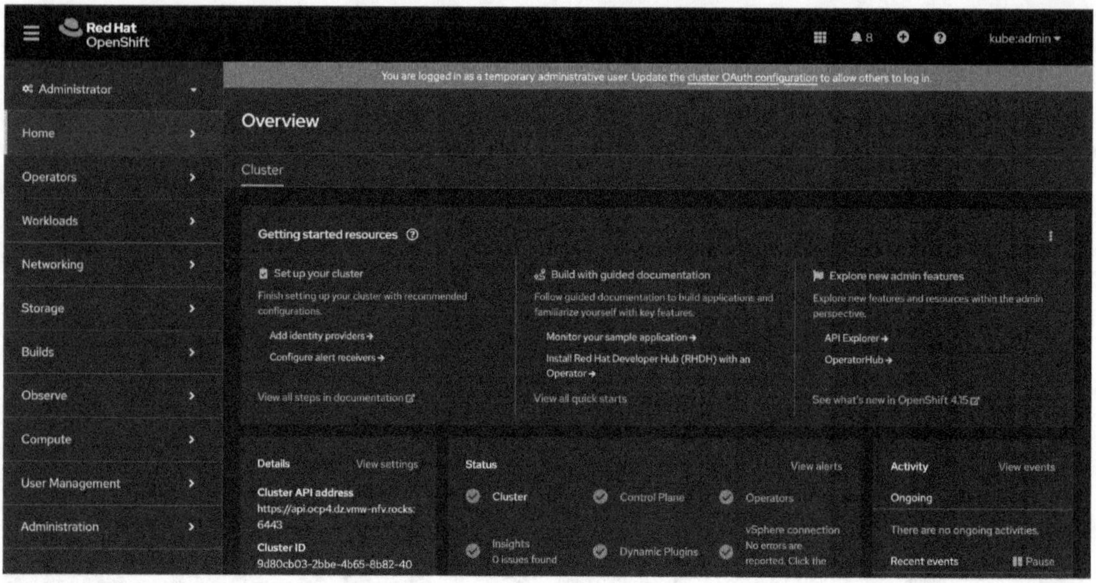

Figure 3.41: OpenShift cluster is up and running – web UI

Another useful sanity check is to run `oc get po -A` to see all Pods across all namespaces. Ideally, you want all of them to be either `Running` or `Completed`. You may, however, see a few failed installer Pods in the `openshift-kube-apiserver` namespace. As long as `apiserver` and other control plane Pods are running, these can be safely ignored.

Our new cluster still requires additional configuration, which we will tackle in the next chapter, *Chapter 4, Post-Install Configuration*.

Understanding Ignition, Afterburn, and Butane

Because **Ignition** governs all aspects of the initial configuration of CoreOS and is used when creating `MachineConfigs` for making changes to existing OpenShift 4 nodes, we felt that a short introduction to Ignition, as well as the auxiliary tools **Afterburn** and **Butane**, would be beneficial.

Ignition

Ignition is a bootstrapping tool used by CoreOS to configure itself at boot time – specifically, during `initramfs`, before it switches to the root filesystem. It works by looking up JSON-formatted configuration in a cloud- or hypervisor-specific location, such as the `userdata` instance (AWS) or the `guestinfo.ignition.config.data` VM property (VMware). Ignition can be used for everything that can be configured by manipulating the state of a disk, such as creating users, filesystems, files with arbitrary content, and systemd units. While being an integral part of CoreOS, Ignition is not OpenShift-specific but also used by systems such as Flatcar and SUSE Linux Enterprise Micro, which makes its understanding especially useful.

If you examine any of the Ignition config files created by `openshift-install`, you will see how complex they can be. For example, with OpenShift 4, Ignition is used to create bootstrapping scripts and certificates, as well as creating a *core* user that can be used to SSH into cluster nodes. As implied by the use of **JSON**, Ignition configurations are declarative and describe the desired state of a system, not a way to reach that state. It does not make any assumptions about your intentions, so all desired changes to your system should be specified explicitly. If it fails for any reason, the entire process is aborted. More information on Ignition can be found at [3].

Another useful tool that is worth mentioning is `ignition-validate`, which is a simple utility for validating the syntax of Ignition configs. Aside from syntax errors, it reports any unused fields too. Version 2.19.0, which is the latest at the moment of writing this chapter, can be obtained and installed on a Linux x86-64 system by executing the following commands:

```
$ curl -sLO https://github.com/coreos/ignition/releases/download/v2.19.0/
ignition-validate-x86_64-linux
$ sudo mv ignition-validate-x86_64-linux /usr/local/bin/ignition-validate
$ chmod a+x /usr/local/bin/ignition-validate
```

Now let's use it to validate the Ignition configs we generated earlier:

```
$ ignition-validate merge-bootstrap.ign
$ ignition-validate master.ign
$ ignition-validate worker.ign
```

Each of the preceding commands does not produce any output if no errors were found and exits with exit code `0`, as reported by `echo $?`.

> Ignition runs only once, on the first boot, so in order to re-provision a system from scratch, it is necessary to recreate it. For this reason, Ignition data does not need to be cleaned up from the machine's properties.

Afterburn

Afterburn is a complementary tool often used together with Ignition. It interacts with cloud- or hypervisor-specific endpoints to set hostnames, add SSH keys, or add command-line boot arguments (VMware). The latter is achieved by adding the `guestinfo.afterburn.initrd.network-kargs` property to a VM, as mentioned in the *IP assignment* subsection of the *Prerequisites* section. This is useful for static IP address allocation, in environments where DHCP is not available or additional parameters need to be configured. Afterburn accepts all `dracut` kernel options [13]. For other platforms, such as AWS, Afterburn can store cloud-specific metadata, such as public or private instance IP, hostname, instance type, availability zone, or region in environment variables in `/run/metadata/afterburn`, which can be consumed by systemd services or other applications.

Full (and rather short) documentation on Afterburn is available at [4].

Butane

Butane stands apart from Ignition and Afterburn in that it is not a service that runs during `initramfs` and brings a system into a desired state, but a helper tool used to generate Ignition configs. As can be seen in the Ignition files generated in this lab, they can be challenging to read, not to mention write by hand. This fact is exacerbated by JSON, which is considered less human-friendly than another popular serialization format, YAML. Butane provides its own syntax, which closely resembles Ignition, that allows you to define the configuration of an arbitrary complexity and then convert it to Ignition with a single command. While occasionally helpful, the use of Butane is not required. More on Butane can be found at [5].

Traditional concepts and OpenShift core APIs

From our training experience, one of the areas where people who encounter Kubernetes or OpenShift for the first time feel somewhat lost is how Kubernetes core APIs translate to familiar concepts, such as VMs and load balancers. Given the importance of this foundational subject for understanding more advanced concepts, we have decided to bring more clarity to the topic by investing some time into a brief discussion of Kubernetes core APIs and what goals they actually serve.

Before Kubernetes, and even before containers, applications used to be deployed on physical servers with real hardware or VMs with hardware or software load balancers distributing ingress traffic between instances of an application. It was not rare to have auxiliary services deployed alongside main applications – for example, for logging, monitoring, security, authentication, and so on. Shared libraries, language runtimes, and other dependencies required for applications to work were usually a part of a VM image, distributed as language-specific bundles (for example, Python `virtualenv`), or installed by a configuration management solution. For an application to be portable across environments (production/QA/etc.) without code changes, it has to rely on an external configuration, supplied by configuration files, environment variables, and/or a service discovery mechanism.

Some applications also required session persistence/stickiness; however, the general approach was the same – if traffic grows, do the following:

1. Spin up more machines ("scale out").
2. Deploy the same version of your application on each of them, whether manually or using configuration management tools, such as Puppet or Ansible.
3. Perform sanity checks on new instances to make sure they are ready to accept requests.
4. Add them to the load balancer's pool.

Since these steps must be performed to one degree or another every time we change the desired number of instances of our application, its configuration, or version of the application itself, we can define the **unit of deployment** as a unique combination of all three.

Similarly, when there is a need to change the application's configuration or update the application itself, we need a **deployment strategy** for rolling out these changes with as little impact on clients as possible. That strategy depends on a few factors:

- Whether an application is stateless or stateful, and, if it is the latter, whether it supports **n-1 compatibility** (an application's ability to run multiple versions at the same time without corrupting the shared state or losing data)
- Number of replicas (deployment size)
- Maximum rollout time that can be tolerated
- SLA

The following figure shows what such architecture might look like.

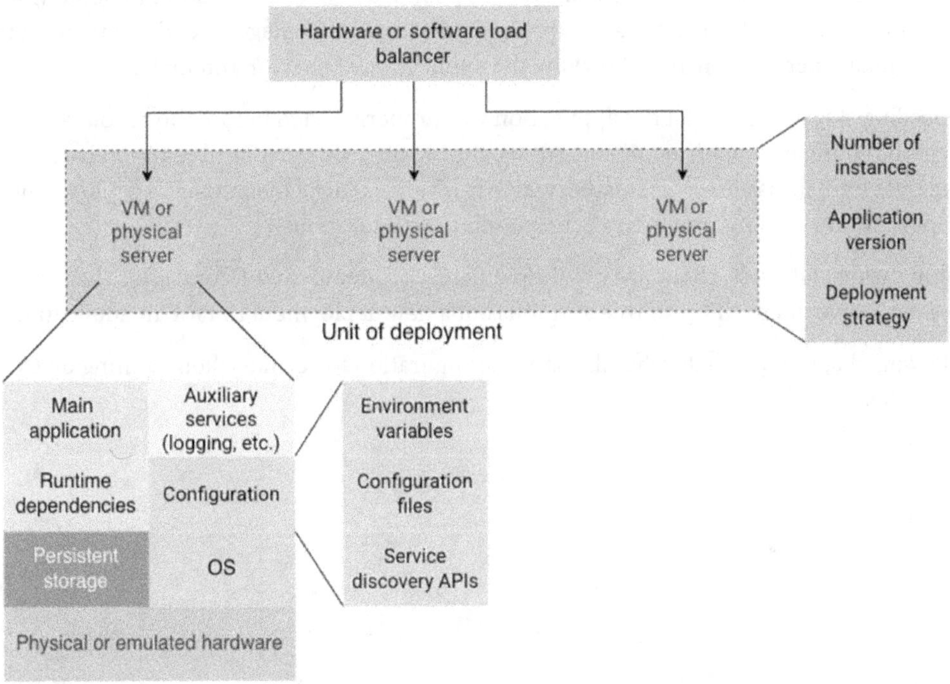

Figure 3.42: Traditional concepts

On the most basic level, there are two deployment strategies:

- **Rollout:** Gradually add new instances and remove old ones, making sure that health checks complete successfully every step of the way. This approach lends itself to production environments that require seamless transition with no loss of service or performance for clients.
- **Recreate:** Shut down all old instances at once and spin up new ones. This strategy has an obvious drawback of service interruption that potentially may take longer than expected if a new version of an application is unable to start for whatever reason. That said, it may be the only option if the application in question is not n-1-compatible.

Other, more advanced deployment strategies are explored in *Chapter 10, Deployment to OpenShift*.

Since the recreate strategy is relatively simple to understand, let us take a closer look at how rollouts work. If we think about how it is done in a traditional environment, whether manually or with the aid of automation, the following steps are necessary for each and every machine in a load balancer's pool, in this order:

1. Stop establishing new connections.
2. Wait until all currently open connections close.
3. Remove the machine from the pool.
4. Deploy a new version of the application on the machine with any updated dependencies and configuration changes, if necessary.
5. Perform sanity checks.
6. Add the machine back to the load balancer's pool. This can be done either by sending an equal share of traffic to that machine or exposing it to a small percentage of load as another safeguard, gradually increasing it and observing the application's behavior and metrics.

The preceding steps assume that the application was properly tested before the rollout and contains no defects or configuration errors. If something goes wrong, we must be able to roll back to the last working state until the issue is remediated, which is why it is crucial to maintain a deployment history of the application's versions and their corresponding configurations.

OpenShift tackles all these challenges by implementing a **deployment controller** that watches for changes to a Deployment API resource and rolls out a new deployment unit of an application.

The following diagram presents what the same configuration looks like when running on OpenShift or Kubernetes.

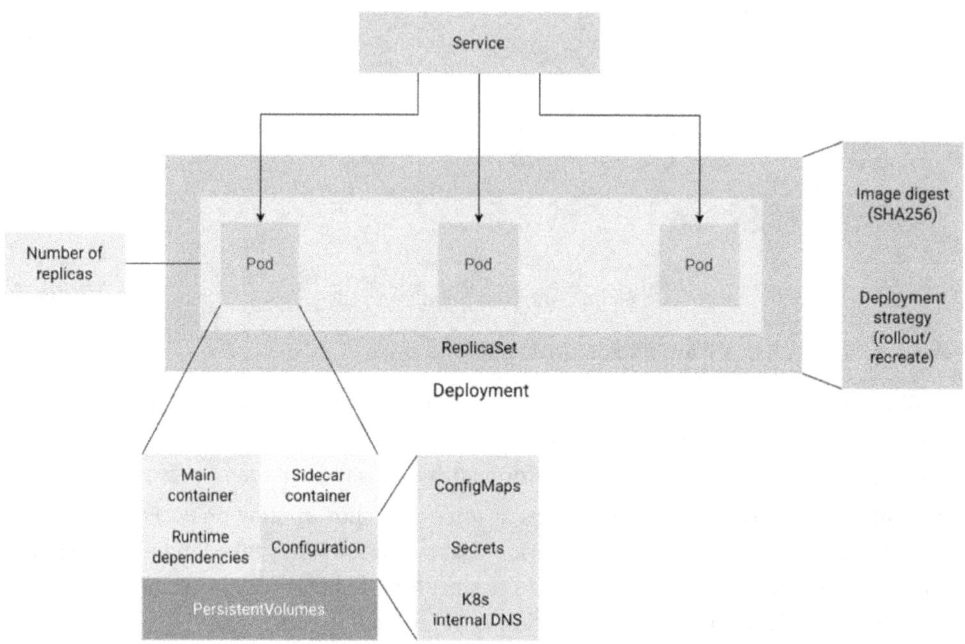

Figure 3.43: Kubernetes APIs

Let us examine it more closely and see how its components map to familiar concepts from the pre-containerization era:

- **Service:** A software load balancer, implemented as `iptables` rules on each node in a cluster. It serves as an integration point to connect to for an application's clients, which is necessitated by the ephemeral nature of containers as they constantly get recreated and their IP addresses change. By default, it spreads connection requests evenly (round-robin) across its backends; however, session persistence can be configured. OpenShift supports the following types of services:
    - **ClusterIP:** The most common type of service that is available only from within a cluster
    - **NodePort:** A service that builds on top of ClusterIP and, in addition, binds to a public IP and port of all nodes in a cluster. It is useful when an application that needs to be exposed communicates via a protocol not supported by an ingress controller or router.
    - **LoadBalancer:** Supported by cloud platforms such as AWS and Azure. It is implemented as a cloud load balancer, such as ALB or NLB (for AWS), that forwards traffic to a NodePort service, which, in turn, sends it to a ClusterIP service.
    - **ExternalName:** Creates an internal alias for an external service, such as a database or API. It is useful for bringing an externally hosted application to OpenShift by being able to send ingress traffic to both destinations during migration. When queried by an application, internal DNS returns a CNAME record pointing to the external address, which decouples your application's configuration from external addresses and provides consistent naming in case the external address ever changes.
- **Pod:** One or more containers that share a network namespace and volumes, which makes it equivalent to a physical or virtual host running multiple applications. Like a physical server or a VM, a Pod is a minimal unit of deployment that defines a container image with all runtime dependencies for every container it includes, a restart policy, volumes for storing persistent data or reading configuration from, health checks (aka *probes*), and the UID to run as, among other parameters.

  Running more than one container in the same Pod is referred to as the *sidecar pattern*, where the main container encapsulates all business logic and provides the actual application, while others provide supplemental services, such as augmenting logs with metadata and forwarding them to a remote location for long-term storage and indexing, monitoring, authentication proxy, or service mesh (covered in *Chapter 14, Understanding Service Mesh and Distributed Tracing*). A Pod can also include one or more init containers, which start before regular containers in the order they are defined and perform preparations for the main application, such as loading data from a remote database/inventory or initializing locally mounted storage. Although at any given time a Pod can run more than one regular container, `init` containers start and complete one by one, so only one such container may be running at a time.

- **Deployment:** A workload resource that defines the template for its Pods (including image tag or digest) that new replicas will be minted from, the number of replicas (propagated to a **ReplicaSet**), the deployment strategy, and how many configurations of previous deployments to keep for rollbacks. For every change to a deployment (usually that involves updating an image tag, environment variables, or `volumeMounts` of a Pod template), a new ReplicaSet is created that gradually or instantaneously (depending on the deployment strategy) supersedes the old one. For every Deployment, ten ReplicaSets, each with a corresponding Pod template, are maintained by default for the purpose of rollback (controlled by `.spec.revisionHistoryLimit`). There are some ways in which Deployment differs from an older OpenShift API, `DeploymentConfig`, which are explained in more detail at [12] and in *Chapter 10, Deployment to OpenShift*. We will explain how it controls application rollouts at the end of this list.
- **ConfigMap:** A resource that is used to pass configuration data to an application in the form of environment variables or entire configuration files. A ConfigMap is essentially a sequence of `key: value` pairs, where *value* can be either a simple string or the contents of an entire configuration file. An application can consume data from a ConfigMap in two ways: as environment variables (for simple configurations, such as database connection strings) or volumes with files mounted inside its container(s) (for complex configuration files, or X.509 certificate/key pairs).
- **Secret:** An object similar to ConfigMap intended to store sensitive and potentially non-text data, such as passwords, API tokens, binary license files, or Java keystores. Since different applications may accept different formats, not necessarily ASCII, all data in a Secret is encoded in Base64 format for serialization. Just like ConfigMaps, data from Secrets can be presented to an application as either environment variables or files mounted at a specific location inside its container(s). Secrets are designed to store only small amounts of data, and as such they are limited to the size of 1 MB.

  Ways to consume ConfigMaps and Secrets by Pods are discussed in *Chapter 9, Developing for OpenShift*.

  The name Secret is somewhat misleading, as it may lead one to believe that data in a Secret is protected by Base64 encoding. Encoding, however, should not be confused with encryption. The purpose of encoding is to serialize data for transmission or storage, and it can be easily reversed, as long as the encoding algorithm is known. Encryption, on the other hand, secures data by performing cryptographic operations on it and can be realistically reversed only with a decryption key. There are two types of encryption – symmetric and asymmetric. Symmetric encryption uses the same key for both encryption and decryption, while asymmetric one employs different keys, one (usually called public key) for encryption and another one (private) for decryption.

> It is possible to create a Secret with plain text data using the `stringData` field instead of `data`; however, internal representation is always Base64.

- **Kubernetes internal DNS**: By default, every Pod and every service created in a cluster registers itself with an internal DNS service that resolves names such as `integration-api-1.apis.svc.cluster.local` to internal IP addresses of corresponding services. The default format for DNS names of services is `SERVICE.PROJECT.svc.cluster.local`; however, due to the fact that Kubernetes injects the internal nameserver's service IP into `/etc/resolv.conf` in all new Pods, applications can find each other by short names, such as `integration-api-1`. Pods get internal DNS names as well, in the form of `POD_IP.PROJECT.pod.cluster.local`. Internal DNS support can be disabled via the `dnsPolicy` field of a Pod, if custom nameservers are desired, which can be configured via the `dnsConfig` field at the Pod or Pod template level.

The following is an illustration of how a rolling deployment in OpenShift progresses over time:

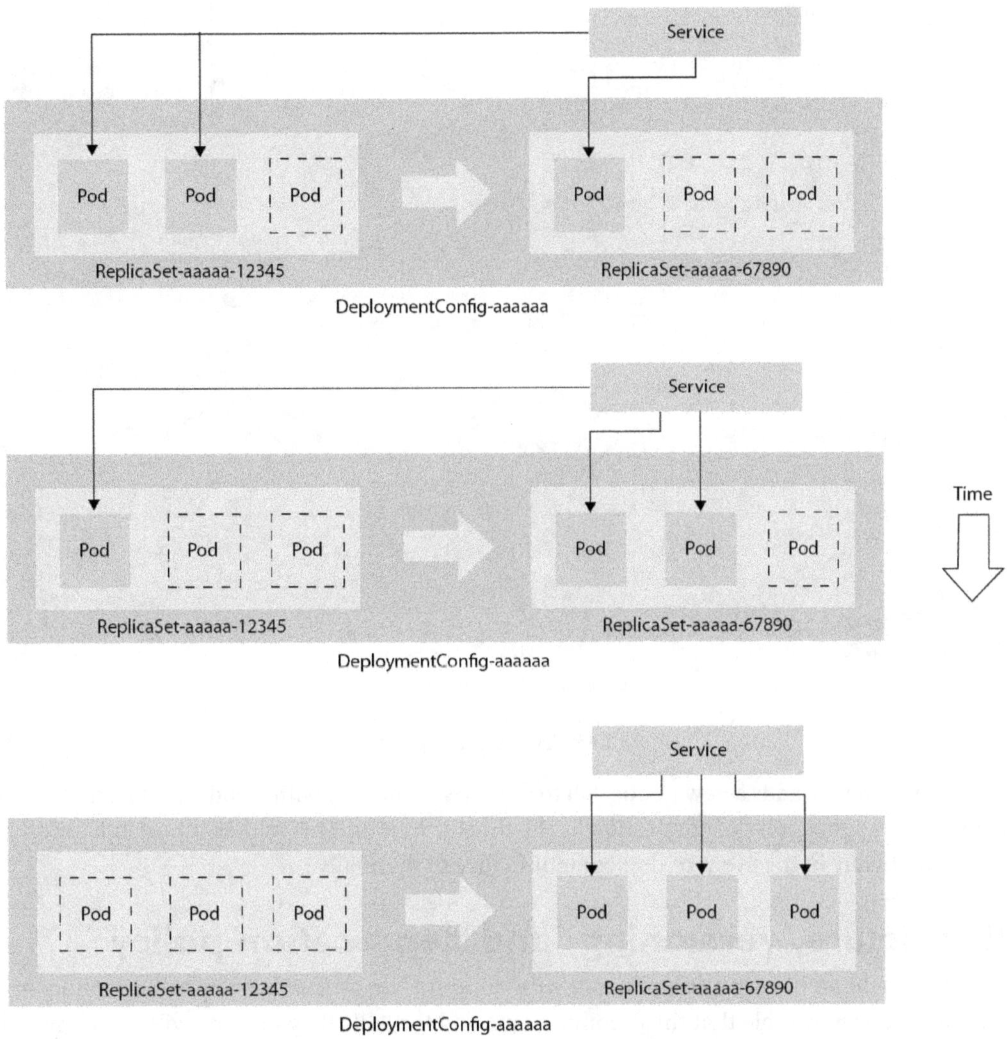

Figure 3.44: Progression of a deployment in OpenShift

As you can see, at no point does the service have fewer than three backends. A deployment resource supports configuration for the lower and upper boundaries of how many replicas can be running at the same time, to balance the need to guarantee a minimal level of performance and not to abuse the cluster's compute resources.

As applications evolve, they change versions, and their configuration needs to be updated as well – to take advantage of new features or to adjust their behavior in response to increasing traffic or external changes. The following is what a deployment may look like after a number of changes, introduced at either the application or configuration level.

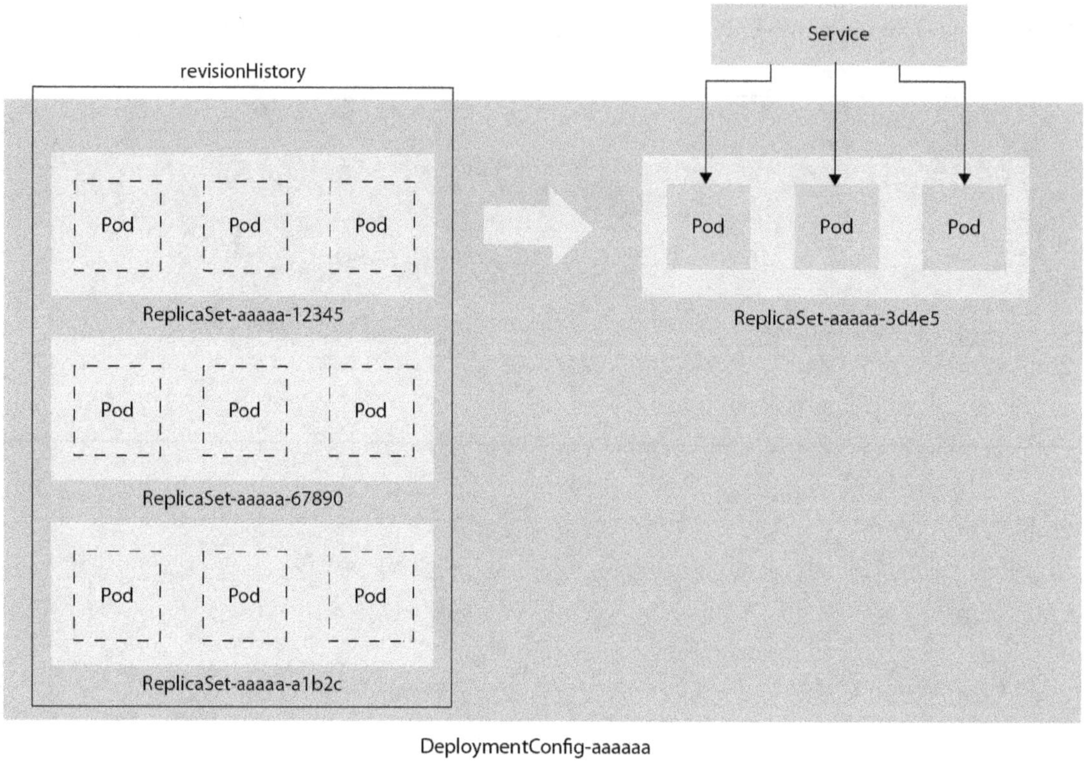

Figure 3.45: Revisions to deployment

As shown, each change adds a new ReplicaSet to the revision history with a Pod template that captures the state of the application's configuration at the time of rollout. This makes it possible to roll back either automatically in the event of deployment failure or manually.

API structure, versioning, and deprecation policy

OpenShift is made up of many components with different life cycles that depend on the upstream communities. It is inevitable that these components and the APIs they provide will evolve over time, adding new features and removing old ones to reduce the code base that needs to be maintained. New changes cannot always be introduced without losing compatibility with previous versions, which is why a reliable mechanism for deprecating old versions and a clear support contract are required.

In order to bring support to the end users of the platform, Red Hat assigns each component, API group, or feature to one of four support tiers that also map to Kubernetes API groups. A list of available tiers and their associated API groups is presented here:

OpenShift support tier	OpenShift API group	Monitoring APIs	Operator life cycle manager (OLM) API groups
Tier 1	`apps.openshift.io/v1`	`AlertManager.monitoring.coreos.com/v1`	`CatalogSource.operators.coreos.com/v1alpha1`
Tier 1	`authorization.openshift.io/v1`	`AlertManagerConfig.monitoring.coreos.com/v1beta1`	`ClusterServiceVersion.operators.coreos.com/v1alpha1`
Tier 1	`build.openshift.io/v1`	`ThanosRuler.monitoring.coreos.com/v1`	`InstallPlan.operators.coreos.com/v1alpha1`
Tier 1	`config.openshift.io/v1`	`ServiceMonitor.monitoring.coreos.com/v1`	`Subscription.operators.coreos.com/v1alpha1`
Tier 1	`image.openshift.io/v1`	`PodMonitor.monitoring.coreos.com/v1`	`OLMConfig.operators.coreos.com/v1alpha1`
Tier 1	`network.openshift.io/v1`	`Probe.monitoring.coreos.com/v1`	`Operator.operators.coreos.com/v1`
Tier 1	`network.operator.openshift.io/v1`	`Prometheus.monitoring.coreos.com/v1`	`OperatorGroup.operators.coreos.com/v1`
Tier 1	`outh.openshift.io/v1`	`PrometheusRule.monitoring.coreos.com/v1`	`PackageManifest.packages.operators.coreos.com/v1`
Tier 1	`project.openshift.io/v1`		`OperatorCondition.operators.coreos.com/v2`
Tier 1	`quota.openshift.io/v1`		
Tier 1	`route.openshift.io/v1`		
Tier 1	`imagecontentsourcepolicy.operator.openshift.io/v1alpha1`		

OpenShift support tier	OpenShift API group	Monitoring APIs	Operator life cycle manager (OLM) API groups
Tier 1	`template.openshift.io/v1`		
Tier 1	`security.openshift.io/v1`		
Tier 2	`console.openshift.io/v1`		
Tier 2	`PodSecurityPolicyReview.security.openshift.io/v1`		
Tier 2	`PodSecurityPolicySubjectReview.security.openshift.io/v1`		
Tier 2	`PodSecurityPolicySelfSubjectReview.security.openshift.io/v1`		
Tier 4	`RangeAllocation.security.openshift.io/v1`		

Table 3.9: OpenShift API's support tiers

The following table outlines support terms for different components, APIs, and their components (API objects, fields, annotations, and enumerated values).

Tier	Support terms
Tier 1	Stable within a major release. It may be deprecated within a major release but will not be removed until a subsequent major release. API objects, their fields, or annotations can only be removed by incrementing the group's version and API objects within a group support conversion without losing information, unless an object itself does not exist in a specific version. If a conversion is not possible, it is preserved in the form of annotations.
Tier 2	Supported for nine months or the releases from the announcement of deprecation, whichever is longer.
Tier 3	Follows component-specific cadence. This tier covers language runtimes, optional operators, and developer tools distributed through Operator Hub. Compatibility between minor versions is provided on a best-effort basis. This is a default tier for any component that does not explicitly specify the support tier.
Tier 4	No support guaranteed. If an application requires long-term support, it should not rely on components from this tier, as their APIs can change at any point.

Table 3.10: Support terms for different API tiers

The following is a graphical, color-coded representation of support tiers and separation of support responsibility for some of the most commonly used OpenShift and Kubernetes APIs.

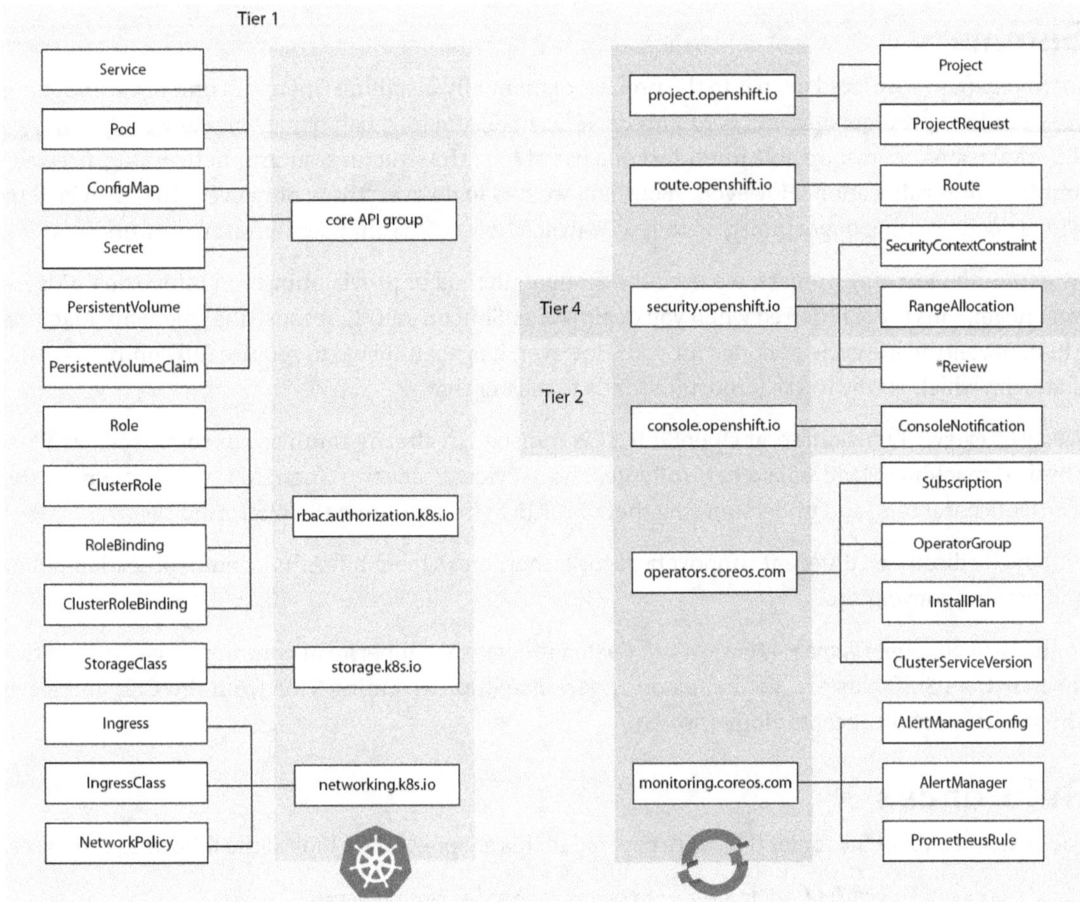

Figure 3.46: OpenShift APIs and their support tiers

As the preceding figure demonstrates, core APIs such as Pod, Secret, and Service enjoy the status of first-class citizens in the kingdom of OpenShift and Kubernetes APIs. They are the most stable and can only be removed in the next major release. Hypothetically speaking, if the Service API were to be deprecated in OpenShift 4.16, the closest release where it could be removed is 5.0, which gives customers plenty of time to plan their migration. It is important to keep track of OpenShift and Kubernetes release notes, as they always announce the deprecation of specific APIs.

> Remember that OpenShift releases follow semantic versioning, which is expressed as `major.minor.patch`, for example, 4.16.3.

A more detailed description of OpenShift API support tiers and API deprecation policy for Kubernetes is available at [8] and [9], respectively.

Summary

In this chapter, we delved deep into the process of manually installing OpenShift on VMware vSphere. We examined prerequisites and configured DHCP, DNS, and load balancing. In real-world scenarios, different teams are responsible for different parts of the infrastructure, such as networking, firewalls, and IP address allocation. However, in our lab, we had to do everything ourselves. That provided us with a good learning opportunity, so that we can see how OpenShift uses different network services.

As part of the learning process, we used the manual method of provisioning and initializing VMs for our cluster. This is not required when you deploy OpenShift on an IPI, because the OpenShift Machine API manages the life cycle of nodes for you. However, it is not unusual to require full control over the platform, which is why it was important for us to master that.

We also reviewed how different OpenShift APIs translate to already-familiar concepts, such as VMs/physical machines, load balancers, rollouts, and service discovery. OpenShift applies them to the world of containers, and understanding them is critical for operating the platform.

Finally, we discussed different support tiers for Kubernetes/OpenShift APIs, their deprecation policy, and naming convention.

In the next chapter, *Chapter 4, Post-Install Configuration*, we will perform common day-two activities for new OpenShift clusters, get hands-on experience in provisioning VMs from the CLI, and learn about a few useful concepts along the way.

References

To learn more about the topics that were covered in this chapter, take a look at the following resources:

- [1] *Red Hat Hybrid Cloud Console*: `https://console.redhat.com/`
- [2] *Installation overview*: `https://docs.redhat.com/en/documentation/openshift_container_platform/4.16/html/installation_overview/ocp-installation-overview`
- [3] *Ignition*: `https://coreos.github.io/ignition/`
- [4] *Afterburn*: `https://coreos.github.io/afterburn/`
- [5] *Butane* : `https://coreos.github.io/butane/getting-started/`
- [6] *vCenter requirements*: `https://docs.redhat.com/en/documentation/openshift_container_platform/4.16/html/installing_on_vsphere/user-provisioned-infrastructure#installation-vsphere-installer-infra-requirements_upi-vsphere-installation-reqs`
- [7] *govc*: `https://github.com/vmware/govmomi/releases`
- [8] *Understanding API support tiers*: `https://docs.redhat.com/en/documentation/openshift_container_platform/4.16/html/api_overview/understanding-api-support-tiers`
- [9] *Kubernetes Deprecation Policy*: `https://kubernetes.io/docs/reference/using-api/deprecation-policy/`

- [10] *Kubernetes ConfigMap design doc*: `https://github.com/rancher/migration-tools/blob/master/vendor/k8s.io/kubernetes/docs/design/configmap.md`
- [11] *Kubernetes Secret design doc*: `https://github.com/rancher/migration-tools/blob/master/vendor/k8s.io/kubernetes/docs/design/secrets.md`
- [12] *OpenShift deployments*: `https://docs.redhat.com/en/documentation/openshift_container_platform/4.16/html/building_applications/deployments#what-deployments-are`
- [13] *dracut kernel command-line options*: `https://www.man7.org/linux/man-pages/man7/dracut.cmdline.7.html`
- [14] *Kubernetes DaemonSet*: `https://kubernetes.io/docs/concepts/workloads/controllers/daemonset/`
- [15] *Navigating Kubernetes API deprecations and removals*: `https://access.redhat.com/articles/6955985`
- [16] *OpenShift mirror site*: `https://mirror.openshift.com/pub/openshift-v4/x86_64/dependencies/rhcos/4.16/4.16.0/rhcos-vmware.x86_64.ova`
- [17] *govc issue #1561: Host did not have any virtual network defined*: `https://github.com/vmware/govmomi/issues/1561`

Quiz

Test your understanding of OpenShift 4 foundations with this quick quiz. Remember, some questions may have more than one correct answer!

1. What is the name of the tool that CoreOS uses to bootstrap itself?
   a. Afterburn
   b. Butane
   c. Ignition
   d. Kickstart
2. What is the correct order of `openshift-install` commands when generating install assets?
   a. `create manifests > create install-config > create ignition-configs`
   b. `create install-config > create manifests > create ignition-configs`
   c. `create install-config > create ignition-configs > create manifests`
   d. `create ignition-configs > create manifests > create install-config`
3. What is the name of the VM property on VMware used to pass configuration data to a VM?
   a. `guestinfo.config`
   b. `vsphere.config.bootstrap`
   c. `guestinfo.ignition.config.data`
   d. `guestinfo.ignition.config.data.encoding`

4. Which type of Service can be used to expose an application to clients outside a cluster?
    a. ClusterIP
    b. NodePort
    c. LoadBalancer
    d. External
5. Which Kubernetes construct(s) provide an execution environment for your applications?
    a. CRI-O
    b. Container
    c. Pod
    d. Deployment

Answers

1. **a** and **c**. Although Ignition is the most commonly used, Afterburn can be leveraged to get additional metadata from cloud providers. Butane is not a provisioning tool per se, but rather a translator.
2. **b**. First, you need to create `install-config.yaml`, which will serve as a source of truth for the commands that follow. Next, you need to use it to generate the manifests that are to be applied to a cluster. Finally, you have to wrap them in Ignition configuration so that CoreOS machines can use them to bootstrap themselves.
3. **c**. The first two do not exist, while `guestinfo.ignition.config.data.encoding` is used to set the encoding of the data passed in `guestinfo.ignition.config.data`.
4. **b** and **c**. Let's examine the options one by one:
    a. ClusterIP services are accessible only from within a cluster's private network; therefore, they can't be used by external clients.
    b. NodePort services expose applications on all nodes in a cluster on a random or explicitly specified port allocated from a pre-configured range, so this would work.
    c. LoadBalancer services use NodePort behind the scenes and are backed by an external cloud load balancer, when OpenShift is deployed in a cloud provider, such as AWS, Azure, or GCP. It works as well.
    d. The `ExternalName` type of service is used to expose an external DNS name to applications in OpenShift under an alias, so it doesn't help us here.
5. **b** and **c**. Although technically your application always runs in a container on OpenShift, the container itself is wrapped in a Pod. CRI-O is a container runtime environment, which interfaces with lower-level OS primitives to provide isolated environments for processes, and Deployment is a higher-level workload resource that manages Pods.

Part 2

Post-Installation, Configuration, and Application Deployment

The goal of this chapter is to guide you through the process of configuring essential services of OpenShift, such as authentication and authorization, as well as deploying your first application. Upon completion, you will have your application up and running in a highly available and resilient configuration, adhering to best practices.

This part of the book includes the following chapters:

- *Chapter 4, Post-Install Configuration*
- *Chapter 5, Navigating Authentication and Authorization*
- *Chapter 6, Exploring Scalability with OpenShift*
- *Chapter 7, Application Security and Isolation*
- *Chapter 8, Working with Persistent Storage*
- *Chapter 9, Developing for OpenShift*
- *Chapter 10, Deployment to OpenShift*
- *Chapter 11, Deploying Applications with Helm and Kustomize*

4

Post-Install Configuration

Even though the cluster we set up in the previous chapter is up and healthy, there is still some work to be done before it becomes useful for business. For example, we need to create infra nodes for internal workloads, replace internally signed certificates for public endpoints with properly signed ones, and configure etcd encryption for extra security – these are just some of the topics that we will address in this chapter. Additional steps, such as configuring persistent storage, connecting to an external identity provider, and deploying centralized logging, are covered in their own chapters due to their complexity.

In particular, we'll cover the following topics:

- Adding infrastructure nodes
- Moving internal workloads to infra nodes
- Encrypting etcd
- Replacing default API and ingress certificates
- Considerations regarding iptables-alerter
- Disabling Keepalived (if enabled) on workers
- What to do about failing kube RBAC proxy CRIO pods (if any)

Technical requirements

In this chapter, you will need the following:

- The Bash shell
- The OpenShift cluster built in the previous chapter
- Firefox (recommended) or any other web browser
- An active Red Hat subscription to view Red Hat KB articles

You can access this book's GitHub repository at `https://github.com/PacktPublishing/Learn-OpenShift-Second-Edition`.

Adding infrastructure nodes

A multi-node OpenShift cluster requires at least two worker nodes; however, you can easily add more. OpenShift has a number of core critical components that run in their own pods – control plane services such as API servers and controller managers are scheduled on master nodes, while others, such as ingress and image registry, run on worker nodes. You can, however, allocate a subset of nodes called **infrastructure nodes** to OpenShift internal services and prohibit any business workloads from running on them. This approach has three benefits:

- **Clear separation of management and maintenance**: Custom configuration or maintenance of nodes no longer has to affect cluster services, aside from those that are scheduled on all nodes via DaemonSets. This also isolates disruptions that may be caused by misbehaving or misconfigured user applications.
- **Reduced subscription costs:** Red Hat recognizes certain types of workloads as internal to OpenShift and does not count the nodes that exclusively run these services towards subscription usage.
- **Resource allocation:** Certain optional components, such as storage, may require a considerable amount of RAM and/or CPU, and running them on separate nodes allows for better scalability and gives them more breathing room.

That being said, you have to be mindful about cost management: infra nodes need to be properly sized so that they're not overallocated and no capacity is wasted; otherwise, this may become very costly very quickly when implemented at an enterprise scale – for example, on dozens or hundreds of clusters. It is not uncommon for large organizations – for example, banks – to have 150-200 OpenShift clusters of 10-15 nodes each (including masters) for different environments and **lines of business (LOBs)**.

The process of preparing and making use of infrastructure nodes involves the following steps:

1. Deploying them either manually or automatically, using the Machine API (on supported cloud providers and virtualization platforms). In this chapter, we will focus on manual provisioning; the Machine API will be discussed in *Chapter 6, Exploring Scalability with OpenShift*.
2. Tainting them to prevent any pod that doesn't have matching toleration(s) from being scheduled on them and optionally evicting already running non-compliant workloads.
3. Labeling them with unique labels so that they can be exclusively targeted for scheduling.
4. Creating a dedicated MachineConfigPool to apply configuration changes to infra nodes independently from workers.
5. Adding matching node selectors and toleration(s) to the allowed workloads. Most cluster-critical workloads that provide node-level services and thus must run on all nodes already include tolerations that match any possible taint; however, there are exceptions, which we will get to later, in the *Moving internal workloads to infra nodes* section of this chapter.

The following subsections will walk you through these steps.

Provisioning infrastructure nodes

Infra nodes are dedicated machines that host only cluster-internal workloads, such as logging, monitoring, the router, and other optional services, such as storage. As far as OpenShift is concerned, infra nodes are configured and treated as regular worker nodes, with the only exception of not being schedulable for regular applications. They are created just like worker nodes – by spinning up VMs, provisioning them from the `worker.b64` ignition file, and then approving the CSRs generated by their kubelets so that they can join the cluster.

You have already seen how to create new machines with the vSphere web UI. That works fine for small clusters and a manual approach; however, it doesn't scale well and can't be easily automated. So, let us take this exercise one step further by provisioning new machines from the CLI – specifically, `govc`, which was briefly mentioned close to the beginning of the previous chapter. One of the biggest benefits of the CLI is that it can be used in automation pipelines, and with enough practice, you may even find it more comfortable than the web UI. A more common and enterprise-standard way of provisioning VMs is using an Infrastructure-as-a-Code tool, such as Terraform or Pulumi. We use `govc` here due to its relative simplicity, as IaC is outside the scope of this book. For example, older minor releases of the `openshift-install` utility even used to rely on Terraform as an embedded library for provisioning in IPI mode; however, starting from 4.16, provisioning on AWS, vSphere, and GCP is handled by the Cluster API. You can learn more in the OCP 4.16 release notes [1]. New nodes can also be provisioned using something called **Red Hat Advanced Cluster Management for Kubernetes (RHACM)**. We're not exploring this venue here, as RHACM is a whole different product that needs a book of its own.

As powerful as it is, `govc` does not provide a single command for configuring all aspects of a new VM, such as CPU, memory, storage, networking, and starting it, so this is going to be a multi-step process (use VM names and MAC addresses for your environment):

1. Clone a VM from the CoreOS template we used throughout the previous chapter (`govc vm.clone`):

```
$ govc vm.clone -vm rhcos-vmware.x86_64.ova -c=8 -m=32768 -on=false
infra-1
```

2. Increase the disk size (`govc vm.disk.change`):

```
$ govc vm.disk.change -vm infra-1 -disk.label 'Hard disk 1' -size 100G
```

3. Set the MAC address on the correct network interface (`govc vm.network.change`):

```
$ govc vm.network.change -vm infra-1 -net.address=00:50:56:1a:bc:31
ethernet-0
```

4. Add VM properties to the machine (`govc vm.change`):

```
$ govc vm.change -vm infra-1 -e guestinfo.ignition.config.data=$(cat
worker.b64) -e guestinfo.ignition.config.data.encoding=base64 -e disk.
EnableUUID=TRUE
```

5. Power the new VM on (`govc vm.power -on VM`):

```
$ govc vm.power -on infra-1
```

After repeating the preceding steps for the two remaining machines and approving their CSRs, as explained in the previous chapter (`oc adm certificate approve`), they join the cluster within a few minutes, as can be seen in the output of `watch -n1 oc get no` here:

```
Every 1.0s: oc get no

NAME                       STATUS   ROLES                  AGE    VERSION
infra-1.ocp4.example.com   Ready    worker                 2m3s   v1.29.7+4510e9c
infra-2.ocp4.example.com   Ready    worker                 43s    v1.29.7+4510e9c
infra-3.ocp4.example.com   Ready    worker                 43s    v1.29.7+4510e9c
master-1.ocp4.example.com  Ready    control-plane,master   79m    v1.29.7+4510e9c
master-2.ocp4.example.com  Ready    control-plane,master   77m    v1.29.7+4510e9c
master-3.ocp4.example.com  Ready    control-plane,master   75m    v1.29.7+4510e9c
worker-1.ocp4.example.com  Ready    worker                 55m    v1.29.7+4510e9c
worker-2.ocp4.example.com  Ready    worker                 55m    v1.29.7+4510e9c
worker-3.ocp4.example.com  Ready    worker                 55m    v1.29.7+4510e9c
```

Figure 4.1: Infra nodes successfully joining the cluster as workers

Notice that newly added nodes have the worker role due to the default `node-role.kubernetes.io/worker` label that is added to all new nodes – we will change it later. If you start monitoring the output of another command, `watch -n1 oc get co`, early on, you will notice that some cluster operators, such as cluster network operator, become degraded. This is because they run pods managed by the DaemonSet [2] controller on every node and they need time to start on the new nodes. They will recover shortly after they are able to start their pods.

We recommend waiting until the cluster fully settles down and none of the cluster operators are progressing or degraded. It is a good practice to move on to the next step only when a cluster is completely stable.

Tainting infrastructure nodes

The concept of a taint is not specific to infrastructure nodes. It is a general mechanism of reserving certain nodes for certain types of applications in Kubernetes. Taints are useful in the following scenarios:

- **Dedicating a set of nodes to specific workloads:** This is the case of infrastructure nodes used to host cluster-critical and supplemental services.
- **Running software with restrictive licensing terms:** Some applications, such as IBM Maximo Application Suite or similar **commercial-off-the-shelf (COTS)** software, may have special requirements and licensing policies that forbid co-locating them with other applications or restrict them to specific hardware.
- **Isolating applications that process sensitive data:** Government regulations that control the exposure of **Personally Identifiable Information (PII)** and other sensitive data often limit their exposure only to hardware servers that don't run any other applications with a lower clearance. Another example is **Personal Health Information (PHI)** regulated by the **Health Insurance Portability and Accountability Act (HIPAA)** of 1996.
- **Running certain applications in a DMZ** with a separate firewall policy.

- **Reserving a subset of nodes for applications that require special hardware:** Specialized hardware, such as GPUs or AI inference modules, is an expensive asset that should be consumed as efficiently as possible. Running other applications that may exhaust all available CPU or RAM will leave it underutilized.

Taints are a part of **NodeSpec** (specified under the `.spec.taints[]` field of a `Node` object) and have the format of `KEY=VALUE:EFFECT`. The following effects are supported:

- `NoSchedule`: Do not schedule workloads that don't tolerate this taint. Existing non-compliant pods keep running.
- `PreferNoSchedule`: Try not to schedule non-compliant pods if there are other nodes available. Existing non-compliant pods keep running.
- `NoExecute`: The same as `NoSchedule`, but also evict all non-compliant workloads.

A toleration is said to match a taint if one of the following applies:

- `KEY` and `EFFECT` are the same and the operator is `Exists`, in which case `VALUE` should be empty
- `KEY` and `EFFECT` are the same and the operator is `Equal`, in which case `VALUE` must match that of the taint

There is also a special case of so-called "blanket"/"catch-all" toleration that only specifies `operator: Exists` and matches all taints. This toleration is mostly used by DaemonSet-managed internal services that must be running on all nodes, such as **Container Network Interface** (**CNI**) agents that facilitate cluster-wide networking or **Container Storage Interface** (**CSI**) pods that mount storage volumes referenced by PVs to nodes.

To taint selected nodes for infrastructure use, execute the `oc adm taint` command as shown here:

```
$ oc adm taint no infra-1.ocp4.example.com node-role.kubernetes.io/
infra:NoExecute
$ oc adm taint no infra-2.ocp4.example.com node-role.kubernetes.io/
infra:NoExecute
$ oc adm taint no infra-3.ocp4.example.com node-role.kubernetes.io/
infra:NoExecute
```

We use the `NoExecute` effect here instead of `NoSchedule`, because the latter causes the DaemonSet that controls CoreDNS pods to lose ownership of pods that run on tainted nodes and a misleading alert about DNS pods "running where they are not supposed to run" firing. On the other hand, at the time of writing this chapter, `NoExecute` taints are known not to be tolerated by certain operators – for example, **Red Hat Advanced Cluster Management** (**RHACM**) for Kubernetes [3] and **Node Feature Discovery** (**NFD**) Operator [4]. One way to work around this is to use `NoSchedule` and manually evict all non-compliant workloads either individually or with `oc adm drain`.

Now that the nodes are properly tainted and no non-compliant applications are guaranteed to run on them, we can label them so that they can be selected by workloads for scheduling.

Warning!

Be careful applying taints with the `NoExecute` effect as they may cause unintended disruptions to your applications, unless they are protected by `PodDisruptionBudgets`. To ensure a smooth experience for your users, we recommend following this procedure:

1. Apply a `NoSchedule` taint first, to prevent new applications from running on the tainted node.
2. Schedule a maintenance window and trigger a rollout of an application you're evicting with `oc rollout restart`. This will cause the application to re-deploy in accordance with its rollout strategy, `RollingUpdate` being the least disruptive.
3. Repeat *step 2* for all non-compliant critical applications.
4. Change the taint's effect to `NoExecute` to evict any remaining non-mission-critical workloads.

Labeling infrastructure nodes

In order to be able to schedule certain workloads exclusively on new nodes, you need to label them with a unique label or labels:

```
$ oc label no/infra-1.ocp4.example.com node-role.kubernetes.io/infra=
$ oc label no/infra-2.ocp4.example.com node-role.kubernetes.io/infra=
$ oc label no/infra-3.ocp4.example.com node-role.kubernetes.io/infra=
```

Note = at the end of every command. This is no typo – when set like this, a label is assigned an empty string as value; however, you can also use `"true"`, which is pretty common too, or any other non-empty string. Just remember to use the exact same label as a selector for workloads and infra MachineConfigPool, which is covered next.

The following command will remove (note - at the end) the default label assigned to new workers from our infra nodes, so that they are no longer managed by the worker MachineConfigPool:

```
$ oc label no -l node-role.kubernetes.io/infra node-role.kubernetes.io/worker-
```

Now let's talk about what MachineConfigPools are and how to create a dedicated one just for infra nodes.

Creating an infra MachineConfigPool

All updates and configuration changes to OpenShift nodes are managed by the **Machine Config Operator** (**MCO**). It provides the following APIs from the `machineconfiguration.openshift.io` group:

- **MachineConfig (MC):** A wrapper for an encoded Ignition configuration – for example, `chrony` (time synchronization daemon) configuration.
- **KubeletConfig:** Contains Kubelet configuration, such as the maximum number of pods a node can run or the maximum size of a single log file kept for each container before it is rotated.

- **ContainerRuntimeConfig**: Contains CRI-O configuration.
- **MachineConfigPool (MCP)**: Binds the preceding entities, which represent configuration changes to different components of a node, to one or more machines via label selectors.

MachineConfigPools serve the purpose of applying different configurations to different classes of nodes – for example, configuring hardware modules present only on a subset of hosts, increasing the number of pods allowed by Kubelet for certain machines (we will cover this use case in *Chapter 18, Troubleshooting and Maintenance*), and so on. In a production-grade OpenShift cluster, it is recommended to set aside at least three infrastructure nodes for hosting OpenShift internal workloads, such as the image registry, storage, monitoring, logging, and ingress. Being a separate class of nodes that run only specific workloads, it is a good practice to create a dedicated MCP for infrastructure nodes, so that custom configuration can be applied to them exclusively if and when necessary.

Let's take a look at a typical MCP manifest used for infra nodes. Open the `chapters/4/snippets/mcp-infra.yml` file of this book's GitHub repository. Notice in the preceding manifest that the MCP selects not just infra, but worker MachineConfigs too, indicated by `.spec.machineConfigSelector`. This is necessary to make sure that all worker-specific configuration changes and cluster upgrades are applied to infra nodes as well, since infra nodes are just a specialized type of worker. Now create the MCP and watch as MCO updates its status:

```
$ oc create -f chapters/4/snippets/mcp-infra.yml
$ watch -n1 oc get mcp
```

The whole process shouldn't take more than a minute before the new MCP becomes available. Ideally, every MCP should have `True/False/False` for its `UPDATED/UPDATING/DEGRADED` columns, respectively:

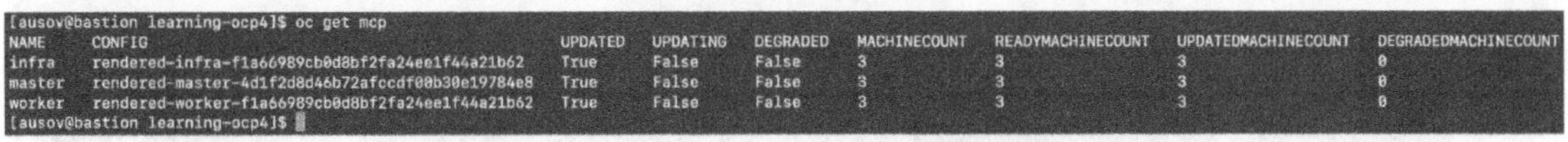

Figure 4.2: Infra MCP initialized and ready to apply updates

By default, MCO updates one node at a time, which may lead to a long update time for large clusters. You can set the `.spec.maxUnavailable` field to a value larger than `1` to enable MCO to update and reboot multiple nodes in parallel. Be mindful of the following caveats, though:

- `.spec.maxUnavailable` specifies the number of nodes that can be unavailable at any time for any reason. That includes any drained or failed nodes.
- Make sure your workloads and their **PodDisruptionBudgets** (**PDBs**) can tolerate the number of nodes that you specified going down; otherwise, MCO will get stuck trying to drain a node if that would violate a PDB.

> A **PodDisruptionBudget (PDB)** is an object that limits the number of an application's pods that can be down due to voluntary (not node failures) disruptions, such as node drains. PDBs and how they come into play with cluster upgrades are discussed in more detail in *Chapter 17, Upgrading OpenShift*.

Use the `oc explain mcp.spec` command for more details on MCP configuration.

Now that we have infra nodes ready and configured, we can start migrating workloads to them. This process involves adding tolerations to workloads and varies from component to component, so let's discuss them separately in the sections that follow.

Moving internal workloads to infra nodes

OpenShift 4 is an operator-centric platform, which means that all cluster-level subsystems are managed by their own operators that expose their configuration via different means. We will discuss operators in general and cluster operators in particular in more detail in *Chapter 16, Understanding Operators and the Operator Framework*. For now, we will explore the configuration of certain important cluster components only as far as their placement is concerned.

Ingress controller

Every multinode OpenShift cluster requires at least two worker nodes to run a router – the default implementation of Ingress in OpenShift. Routers run containerized HAProxy instances in the `openshift-ingress` namespace. Each router runs as a privileged container that binds to TCP ports `80` and `443` on its resident node's public IP address(es) to allow external clients to connect to applications running on OpenShift, including its web console and authentication server. Follow these steps to move router pods to infrastructure nodes:

1. First, examine the `chapters/4/snippets/ingresscontroller-default.yml` file from this book's GitHub repository. It contains a node selector that tells the default scheduler to put routers on matching nodes and a toleration that permits them to be scheduled on those nodes.
2. Apply the manifest as a `patch` (`oc apply` will have the same desired effect):

   ```
   $ oc patch --patch-file chapters/4/snippets/ingresscontroller-default.yml
   --type merge ingresscontroller/default -n openshift-ingress-operator
   ```

3. Wait until the ingress controller re-deploys routers:

   ```
   $ oc get po -o wide -n openshift-ingress
   ```

   After 1-2 minutes, all pods should be running on infrastructure nodes:

```
NAME                             READY   STATUS    RESTARTS   AGE   IP             NODE
router-default-bbd5cf896-gp9xl   1/1     Running   0          56s   10.100.10.31   infra-1.ocp4.example.com
router-default-bbd5cf896-b759s   1/1     Running   0          91s   10.100.10.32   infra-2.ocp4.example.com
router-default-bbd5cf896-kc6zx   1/1     Running   0          2m    10.100.10.33   infra-3.ocp4.example.com
```

Figure 4.3: Ingress pods successfully migrated to infra nodes

   If they get stuck in the `Pending` phase, check local events with `oc get ev -n openshift-ingress` for any scheduling errors and double-check whether node selectors and tolerations match infrastructure nodes.

Before deploying our cluster in the previous chapter, we configured the ingress load balancer on a separate VM to forward ingress traffic to worker nodes, because this is where router pods get initially deployed. Now that we have moved them, you may notice that the authentication operator has become

`Degraded`, indicating that it can't reach ingress pods anymore. To fix that, you have to change backend servers on the machine that you use as a load balancer for the `*.apps` endpoint in the `/etc/haproxy/haproxy.cfg` file from workers to infra nodes to restore connectivity. Use the `chapters/4/snippets/haproxy.cfg.apps.post-install` file from this book's GitHub repository as a reference. Don't forget to reload the HAProxy configuration with `sudo systemctl reload haproxy` to apply the change. In a few seconds, the authentication operator and web console will become available again.

Other workloads

There are other cluster services that qualify as infrastructure workloads. Since they are discussed in their own chapters, we felt that the topics of migrating each of them to infra nodes belong in their corresponding chapters and would create a better flow of narrative:

1. For this book, we chose **OpenShift Data Foundation** (**ODF**) as a software-defined storage provider. It is recognized by Red Hat as an infrastructure service, which means it can be moved to infrastructure nodes without disqualifying them from subscription exemption. ODF installation and configuration, including running it on specific nodes, are discussed in *Chapter 8, Working with Persistent Storage*.
2. When deploying a centralized logging solution for our cluster, we will also configure it to run on the infrastructure nodes that we have created. This is explored in detail in *Chapter 12, Logging in OpenShift*.
3. A cluster monitoring stack managed by the **Cluster Monitoring Operator** (**CMO**) is another component that is best to be moved to dedicated nodes. Because of the importance of this component, we discuss it in a separate chapter. As part of its configuration, we will migrate it to infrastructure nodes. Please refer to *Chapter 13, Monitoring in OpenShift*, for more details.
4. Due to how the Image Registry Operator manages registry pods, they can be created only when storage (persistent or ephemeral) is configured, which will be addressed in *Chapter 15, Exploring Additional Services in OpenShift*.

Enabling a DNS DaemonSet on infra nodes

As mentioned earlier, almost all DaemonSet-managed core workloads of OpenShift include a toleration that tolerates all taints, with CoreDNS being one exception. If you list pods and their resident nodes in the `openshift-dns` namespace via `oc get po -o wide -n openshift-dns`, you will notice that they are running on all nodes, except infrastructure nodes:

```
NAME                  READY   STATUS    RESTARTS   AGE   IP             NODE
dns-default-f6gqd     2/2     Running   0          51m   10.128.2.36    worker-2.ocp4.example.com
dns-default-fphjn     2/2     Running   0          53m   10.129.2.26    worker-3.ocp4.example.com
dns-default-nc4kp     2/2     Running   0          53m   10.128.0.85    master-1.ocp4.example.com
dns-default-npxln     2/2     Running   0          51m   10.130.0.135   master-3.ocp4.example.com
dns-default-vl7pw     2/2     Running   0          51m   10.131.0.15    worker-1.ocp4.example.com
dns-default-x8rh9     2/2     Running   0          52m   10.129.0.72    master-2.ocp4.example.com
```

Figure 4.4: CoreDNS pods are not running on infra nodes due to a missing toleration

The problem and remediation steps are described in the KB article [6]. Examine the `chapters/4/snippets/dns.operator-default.yml` manifest file from this book's GitHub repository. Notice the `operator: Exists` catch-all toleration. It allows CoreDNS pods to run on all nodes. Apply the manifest:

```
$ oc apply -f chapters/4/snippets/dns.operator-default.yml
```

Then wait until all DNS pods are re-deployed with `watch -n1 oc get po -o wide -n openshift-dns`. Additional pods should now be running on infrastructure nodes:

```
NAME                 READY   STATUS    RESTARTS   AGE   IP             NODE
dns-default-f6gqd    2/2     Running   0          53m   10.128.2.36    worker-2.ocp4.example.com
dns-default-fphjn    2/2     Running   0          55m   10.129.2.26    worker-3.ocp4.example.com
dns-default-fwznw    2/2     Running   0          54m   10.130.2.31    infra-1.ocp4.example.com
dns-default-kz9tt    2/2     Running   0          55m   10.131.2.32    infra-2.ocp4.example.com
dns-default-nc4kp    2/2     Running   0          54m   10.128.0.85    master-1.ocp4.example.com
dns-default-npxln    2/2     Running   0          53m   10.130.0.135   master-3.ocp4.example.com
dns-default-phbhs    2/2     Running   0          53m   10.128.4.26    infra-3.ocp4.example.com
dns-default-vl7pw    2/2     Running   0          52m   10.131.0.15    worker-1.ocp4.example.com
dns-default-x8rh9    2/2     Running   0          54m   10.129.0.72    master-2.ocp4.example.com
```

Figure 4.5: CoreDNS pods successfully restart on infra nodes after a toleration is added

This concludes the subject of enabling internal cluster workloads to run on infrastructure nodes. Other components not covered by this book, such as third-party CNI/CSI plugins, expose their configuration, including placement settings, in different ways. Consult the documentation from a specific vendor for details.

Encrypting etcd

etcd is a distributed key-value database where the OpenShift API server stores the desired state of all resources and updates to their status. You can improve the security posture of your OpenShift environment by encrypting the etcd database. This is useful to protect any potentially sensitive information that might be stored in Secrets or ConfigMaps from exposure if someone obtains unauthorized access to your cluster's backups. Etcd encryption only protects Secrets, ConfigMaps, routes, OAuth access tokens, and OAuth authorization tokens (explained in the next chapter).

Open the file called `chapters/4/snippets/apiserver-cluster.yml` in this book's GitHub repository. It's very simple and only specifies the encryption algorithm. Supported types are listed here:

- `aescbc`: **AES Chain Block Encryption** (**AES-CBC**) with PKCS#7 padding and a 32-byte encryption key. An older encryption method, discouraged for use due to its vulnerability to padding oracle attacks.
- `aesgcm`: **AES Galois Counter Mode** (**AES-GCM**) with random nonce and a 32-byte encryption key. More resistant to attacks and less vulnerable than CBC.
- `identity`: No encryption.
- `"" (unset)`: The same as `identity`; however, this behavior may change in future releases of OpenShift.

All keys have a length of 32 bytes and are rotated weekly.

Next, apply the manifest:

```
$ oc apply -f chapters/4/snippets/apiserver-cluster.yml
```

The process takes about 20 minutes on average, depending on the size of your etcd database. You can use the following command to check the encryption status for different resource types from time to time:

```
$ oc get openshiftapiserver -o=jsonpath='{range .items[0].status.
conditions[?(@.type=="Encrypted")]}{.reason}{"\n"}{.message}{"\n"}'
$ oc get kubeapiserver -o=jsonpath='{range .items[0].status.conditions[?(@.
type=="Encrypted")]}{.reason}{"\n"}{.message}{"\n"}'
$ oc get authentication.operator.openshift.io -o=jsonpath='{range .items[0].
status.conditions[?(@.type=="Encrypted")]}{.reason}{"\n"}{.message}{"\n"}'
```

The following is what you will see after the encryption has just started:

```
[ausov@bastion learning-ocp4]$ oc get openshiftapiserver -o=jsonpath='{range .items[0].status.conditio
ns[?(@.type=="Encrypted")]}{.reason}{"\n"}{.message}{"\n"}'
EncryptionInProgress
Resource routes.route.openshift.io is not encrypted


[ausov@bastion learning-ocp4]$ oc get kubeapiserver -o=jsonpath='{range .items[0].status.conditions[?(
@.type=="Encrypted")]}{.reason}{"\n"}{.message}{"\n"}'
EncryptionInProgress
Resource secrets is not encrypted


[ausov@bastion learning-ocp4]$ oc get authentication.operator.openshift.io -o=jsonpath='{range .items[
0].status.conditions[?(@.type=="Encrypted")]}{.reason}{"\n"}{.message}{"\n"}'
EncryptionInProgress
Resource oauthaccesstokens.oauth.openshift.io is not encrypted
```

Figure 4.6: Encryption has started

As objects are being encrypted, API server pods will re-deploy, which you can see with the `oc get po -n openshift-apiserver` command:

```
[ausov@bastion learning-ocp4]$ oc get po -n openshift-apiserver
NAME                          READY   STATUS        RESTARTS   AGE
apiserver-7d769bf795-gqzzs    2/2     Running       0          47h
apiserver-7d769bf795-knpq9    2/2     Terminating   0          47h
apiserver-b48b4dd45-kfgc6     0/2     Pending       0          2s
apiserver-b48b4dd45-m47z8     2/2     Running       0          92s
[ausov@bastion learning-ocp4]$
```

Figure 4.7: API pods' rollout in progress

If you check the pods after encryption has been completed, you will see them all running, as if nothing happened, which may lead you to believe that no change was applied. You can always check the `AGE` column to determine whether a pod (or another object) was created recently. When deployment undergoes a rollout, its pods are **re-created**, not **restarted**, meaning that their age is reset.

You may also use the `oc get po -n openshift-oauth-apiserver` command to monitor OAuth api-server pods as they encrypt OAuth tokens:

```
[ausov@bastion learning-ocp4]$ oc get po -n openshift-oauth-apiserver
NAME                          READY   STATUS        RESTARTS   AGE
apiserver-668f59d79-2vqkn     0/1     Pending       0          12s
apiserver-668f59d79-gnqjc     1/1     Running       0          36s
apiserver-668f59d79-hrqpx     1/1     Running       0          58s
apiserver-69fdfcd74-vwl4n     0/1     Terminating   0          2m15s
[ausov@bastion learning-ocp4]$
```

Figure 4.8: Rollout of OAuth API server pods in progress

Encrypting etcd has a certain security implication for etcd backups. Every etcd backup consists of two files: `snapshot_TIMESTAMP.db` and `static_kuberesources_TIMESTAMP.tar.gz` (etcd snapshot and resource manifests, respectively). If etcd encryption is enabled, the latter file also contains encryption keys. It is recommended to store it in a secure location – for example, a local vault. Restoring from a backup requires both files. Also, keep in mind that only values of fields in objects are encrypted, not keys, so resource types and metadata, including names, namespaces, labels, and annotations will remain unencrypted. Similarly, use the `oc get po -n openshift-kube-apiserver` command to track the status of Kubernetes API pods.

Eventually, encryption will be complete:

```
[ausov@bastion learning-ocp4]$ oc get openshiftapiserver -o=jsonpath='{range .items[0].status.conditio
ns[?(@.type=="Encrypted")]}{.reason}{"\n"}{.message}{"\n"}'
EncryptionCompleted
All resources encrypted: routes.route.openshift.io


[ausov@bastion learning-ocp4]$ oc get kubeapiserver -o=jsonpath='{range .items[0].status.conditions[?(
@.type=="Encrypted")]}{.reason}{"\n"}{.message}{"\n"}'
EncryptionCompleted
All resources encrypted: secrets, configmaps


[ausov@bastion learning-ocp4]$ oc get authentication.operator.openshift.io -o=jsonpath='{range .items[
0].status.conditions[?(@.type=="Encrypted")]}{.reason}{"\n"}{.message}{"\n"}'
EncryptionCompleted
All resources encrypted: oauthaccesstokens.oauth.openshift.io, oauthauthorizetokens.oauth.openshift.io
```

Figure 4.9: Encryption complete

Etcd encryption is not irreversible; you can restore etcd back to an unencrypted state by changing `.spec.encryption.type` of the `cluster` APIServer instance to `identity`, which will kick off a decryption process.

Replacing default API and ingress certificates

OpenShift uses TLS to secure communications between its internal components, such as kubelets, controller managers, etcd, and API servers. They are signed by an OpenShift internal **Certificate Authority** (CA), and while technically doable, there is no officially supported procedure for replacing them. You can, however, change certificates used by public API and Ingress endpoints to those signed by your corporate CA, which is very common. The procedure can be broken down into the following steps:

1. Create a CA. This step is not necessary if you already have an enterprise-grade CA.
2. Generate a **Certificate Signing Request** (CSR) for a particular endpoint, submit it to your CA, and retrieve a certificate bundle that includes the entire certificate chain, all the way down to your new certificate and key.
3. Add the CA root certificate or an entire certificate chain, including all intermediate certificates, to the cluster-wide proxy resource called `cluster`, which configures OpenShift's cluster-wide egress proxy used by OpenShift components when they connect to external endpoints – for example, an LDAP server or ingress public endpoint. This step is necessary so that components of OpenShift that connect to public API and ingress endpoints trust the new certificates. The content of the ConfigMap referenced in the object is copied into the `trusted-ca-bundle` ConfigMap in the `openshift-config-managed` namespace. The certificate chain is also merged into the trust bundle on all nodes and injected into the trust bundles of all components that make egress calls.
4. Create a secret from the certificate and key of the endpoint.
5. Point the API server or ingress controller to the secret by configuring a respective operator.

For this exercise, we will use a self-signed CA to sign our API and ingress certificates. In the real world, you would submit CSRs to your company's CA, such as Venafi, Dogtag, or Microsoft CA. Another reason for using a self-signed CA for this exercise is that our lab can only be accessed through VPN, making it impossible for public CAs such as GoDaddy to verify our ownership of the domain where the cluster is deployed. Overall, using a self-signed certificate proved to be much easier.

Setting up a custom CA

As mentioned in the previous section, before replacing default API and ingress certificates, we need to generate a self-signed CA first (again, only necessary in this lab since we don't have an enterprise CA):

1. First, let's use OpenSSL to generate a 4,096-bit private key and a certificate:

```
$ openssl genrsa -out ocp4.example.com.key 4096
$ openssl req -x509 -new -nodes -key ocp4.example.com.key -sha256 -days
365 -out ocp4.example.com.crt -subj '/CN=Learning OCP4 Lab CA/C=US/ST=AZ/
L=Phoenix/O=Packt'
```

2. Use the following command to decode the certificate and view it in plain text for verification:

```
$ openssl x509 -in ocp4.example.com.crt -noout -text
```

3. The next step is to put the certificate in a ConfigMap for the internal proxy:

```
$ oc create cm learning-ocp4-ca --from-file ca-bundle.crt=ocp4.example.
com.crt -n openshift-config
```

4. Update the proxy to use the ConfigMap:

```
$ oc patch proxy/cluster -p '{"spec": {"trustedCA": {"name": "learning-ocp4-ca"}}}' --type merge
```

   Applying the change will cause the MCO to reboot nodes. Among other scenarios, when OpenShift needs to establish a secure connection to external systems, this step is also required if you intend to add an external identity provider, such as AD or LDAP (discussed in the next chapter), whose certificates were signed by their own CA. In reality, however, all secure endpoints in a company's intranet typically use certificates signed by the same root CA or its intermediaries, so doing it only once should be enough, as long as you include the complete chain.

5. Add the certificate to your system's trust store and update the local trust database so that `curl`, `wget`, `openssl`, and other utilities that rely on the store don't fail certificate verification:

```
$ sudo cp ocp4.example.com.crt /etc/pki/ca-trust/source/anchors/
$ sudo update-ca-trust
```

Now that the CA is created and added to OpenShift, we can move on to configuring individual endpoints.

Replacing the default API certificate

Replacing the default external API certificate for the `api.ocp4.example.com` endpoint is a relatively straightforward process. Before you update the `APIServer` resource as directed in one of the following steps, however, make sure that all external clients that use the `api.ocp4.example.com` external API endpoint have the CA in their trust stores.

> If you replace the public API certificate, you will have to replace the ingress certificate as well; otherwise, `oc login` will fail with `error: x509 certificate signed by unknown authority`. This is because `oc login` reaches out to two endpoints: `api.ocp4.example.com` and `openshift-oauth.apps.ocp4.example.com`. The latter is served by the ingress controller, which means it has to be secured with a certificate signed by a trusted CA too. Read more at [5].

The procedure involves the following steps:

1. Generate a CSR to be signed by your CA and a private key:

```
$ openssl req -new -nodes -out api.ocp4.example.com.csr -newkey rsa:4096
-keyout api.ocp4.example.com.key -subj '/CN=api.ocp4.example.com'
```

   A random seed will be generated, as indicated by a long sequence of `+` and `.` (dot) characters.

2. Examine the `chapters/4/snippets/api.ocp4.example.com.v3.ext` OpenSSL configuration file from this book's GitHub repository. This file is required to add the API endpoint's address to the `subjectAltNames` field of the CSR. We will use it in the next step to generate a certificate.

3. Sign the certificate using our CA and the extension configuration from the previous step:

```
$ openssl x509 -req -in api.ocp4.example.com.csr -CA ocp4.example.com.crt
-CAkey ocp4.example.com.key -CAcreateserial -out api.ocp4.example.com.
crt -days 365 -sha256 -extfile chapters/4/snippets/api.ocp4.example.com.
v3.ext
```

4. Create a certificate chain by appending the CA certificate to the API certificate (be careful to use >>, **not** >, as the latter will overwrite the file!):

```
$ cat ocp4.example.com.crt >> api.ocp4.example.com.crt
```

5. Create a secret for the certificate and its key:

```
$ oc create secret tls learning-ocp4-api-cert --cert api.ocp4.example.
com.crt --key api.ocp4.example.com.key -n openshift-config
```

6. Point the `APIServer` object to the secret:

```
$ oc patch -p '{"spec": {"servingCerts": {"namedCertificates": [{"names":
["api.ocp4.example.com"], "servingCertificate": {"name": "learning-ocp4-
api-cert"}}]}}}' --type merge apiserver/cluster
```

API server pods will re-deploy to apply the change, which will take between 5 and 10 minutes. There may be a delay of up to 5 mins before the rollout starts in the `openshift-kube-apiserver` namespace. If you continuously run an oc command that uses the API – for example, `watch -n1 oc get no`, you will notice how it starts intermittently returning the `x509: certificate signed by unknown authority` error until it stops working completely. This is because the API now uses a different certificate signed by a CA that is not trusted by your oc client, which uses the `certificate-authority-data` field in its kubeconfig, pointed to by the `KUBECONFIG` environment variable, to verify the API certificate. We will rectify this in the next step.

7. You can manually encode your CA certificate in base64 and put it in the `certificate-authority-data` of your kubeconfig; however, there is a way to do that with just one simple command:

```
$ oc config refresh-ca-bundle --insecure-skip-tls-verify
```

This command grabs the certificate from ConfigMap called `serviceaccount-ca` in the `openshift-kube-controller-manager` namespace. The `--insecure-skip-tls-verify` option is required only once in order to connect to the API server to obtain the new certificate.

If it doesn't work and you're still getting the x509 error, do this:

```
$ oc config get-clusters
NAME
<CLUSTER_NAME>
$ oc config set-cluster <CLUSTER_NAME> --certificate-authority ocp4.
example.com.crt --embed-certs
```

8. As a verification, use OpenSSL to check the API's certificate:

```
$ openssl s_client -connect api.ocp4.example.com:6443
```

Check the subject and issuer fields for each certificate in the chain. Look for `Verification: OK` and `Verify return code: 0 (ok)` in the output of the preceding command (we updated the local trust store, so verification should pass). We don't provide output here due to its size.

Now all that's left for us to do is replace the ingress certificate.

Replacing the default ingress certificate

Replacing the default ingress certificate is performed similarly to updating the public API endpoint. Before you update the ingress resource as directed in one of the following steps, however, make sure that all external clients that use the `*.apps.ocp4.example.com` ingress endpoint have the CA in their trust stores. Follow these steps to replace the ingress certificate:

1. Generate a CSR to be signed by your CA and a private key:

```
$ openssl req -new -nodes -out apps.ocp4.example.com.csr -newkey rsa:4096
-keyout apps.ocp4.example.com.key -subj '/CN=*.apps.ocp4.example.com'
```

2. Open the `chapters/4/snippets/apps.ocp4.example.com.v3.ext` OpenSSL configuration file from this book's GitHub repository. Similar to the public API's part, this file is required to add the ingress endpoint's address to the `subjectAltNames` field of the CSR. We will use it in the next step to generate a certificate.
3. Sign the certificate using our CA and the extension configuration from the previous step:

```
$ openssl x509 -req -in apps.ocp4.example.com.csr -CA ocp4.example.com.
crt -CAkey ocp4.example.com.key -CAcreateserial -out apps.ocp4.example.
com.crt -days 365 -sha256 -extfile chapters/4/snippets/apps.ocp4.example.
com.v3.ext
```

4. Create a certificate chain by appending the CA certificate to the ingress certificate:

```
$ cat ocp4.example.com.crt >> apps.ocp4.example.com.crt
```

5. Create a secret for the certificate and its key:

```
$ oc create secret tls learning-ocp-ingress-cert --cert apps.ocp4.
example.com.crt --key apps.ocp4.example.com.key -n openshift-ingress
```

6. Point the `IngressController` object to the secret:

```
$ oc patch ingresscontroller/default -p '{"spec": {"defaultCertificate":
{"name": "learning-ocp-ingress-cert"}}}' --type merge -n openshift-
ingress-operator
```

After you apply the patch, router pods in the `openshift-ingress` namespace will re-deploy, which you can observe with the following command:

```
$ watch -n1 oc get po -n openshift-ingress
```

This process normally takes 3-5 minutes, during which the authentication cluster operator may become temporarily unavailable, which you may notice if you run `oc get co/authentication`.

7. As a verification, use OpenSSL to check the ingress certificate:

```
$ openssl s_client -connect console-openshift-console.apps.ocp4.example.
com:443
```

   Check the subject and issuer fields for each certificate in the chain. Look for `Verification: OK` and `Verify return code: 0 (ok)` in the preceding output (we updated the local trust store, so verification should pass). As before, we don't provide output here due to its size.

The procedure is now complete on OpenShift's side; however, if we try to open its web console, we will still get a security warning about a self-signed certificate. In a real scenario, a CA certificate would be included in our local trust store as part of the image from which developers' machines are initialized, or included with the browser itself, if it's a public CA. All modern browsers are distributed with certificates of all public CAs. In this lab, however, we will have to do this ourselves, which may be tedious, but presents a good learning opportunity. We will demonstrate how to add a custom CA to Firefox; however, the procedure is similar for Chrome:

1. Click on the hamburger menu icon in the upper-right corner > **Settings** > **Privacy & Security** > **Certificates** > **View Certificates** > **Authorities** > **Import** > select the root certificate or chain file > **Trust this CA to identify websites.** You should now see your CA in the list of CAs trusted by Firefox:

Figure 4.10: A certificate added to Certificate Manager in Firefox

2. Go to `https://console-openshift-console.apps.ocp4.example.com` and verify that the ingress certificate is now trusted by your browser:

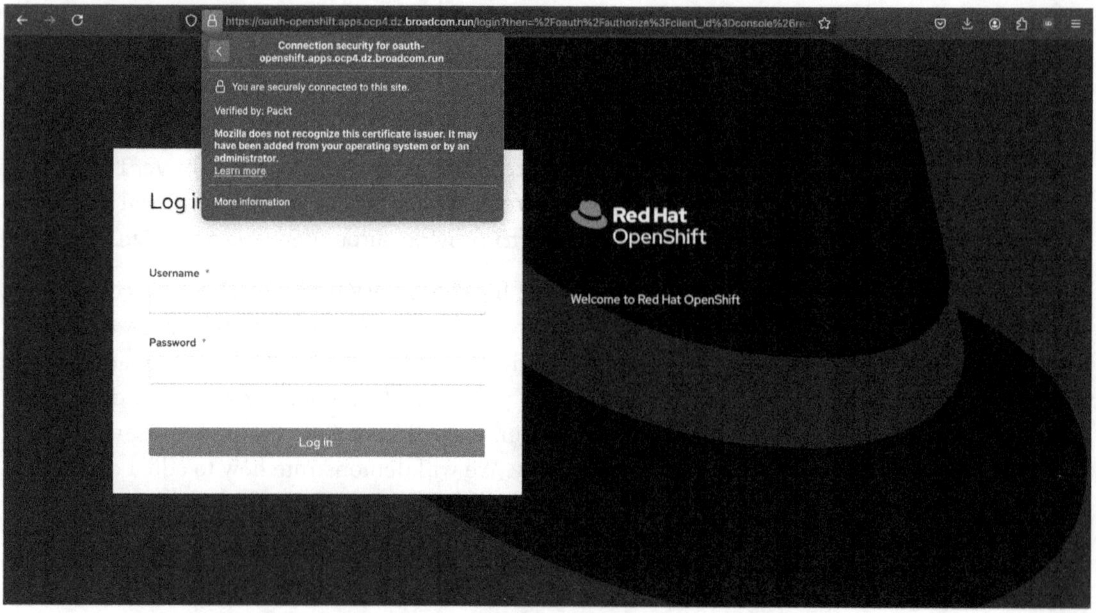

Figure 4.11: Ingress certificate is trusted by Firefox

We have just successfully replaced the default API and ingress certificate to comply with internal security regulations, which is a common procedure among businesses of all sizes.

Considerations regarding iptables-alerter

Starting from 4.16, OpenShift includes a DaemonSet called `iptables-alerter` that tries to detect if customers are using iptables in any of their pods. If so, it logs events warning them that iptables is going away in RHEL 10 in 2025. Like CoreDNS pods, `iptables-alerter` pods also fail to start on nodes with custom taints; however, adding tolerations to this DaemonSet is not supported. This does not affect operations, only logging. Read more at [7].

You can check whether you are affected with `oc get po -o wide -n openshift-network-operator`:

```
NAME                      READY   STATUS    RESTARTS        AGE     IP             NODE
iptables-alerter-bgznp    1/1     Running   1               6h52m   10.100.10.11   master-1.ocp4.example.com
iptables-alerter-kjmvw    1/1     Running   4 (102m ago)    6h31m   10.100.10.22   worker-2.ocp4.example.com
iptables-alerter-nqfbv    1/1     Running   4               6h52m   10.100.10.12   master-2.ocp4.example.com
iptables-alerter-rqc4x    1/1     Running   3 (14m ago)     6h31m   10.100.10.23   worker-3.ocp4.example.com
iptables-alerter-svhqf    1/1     Running   2 (36m ago)     44m     10.100.10.21   worker-1.ocp4.example.com
iptables-alerter-wglsl    1/1     Running   3               6h52m   10.100.10.13   master-3.ocp4.example.com
```

Figure 4.12: iptables-alerter pods are not running on infra nodes

As you can see, there are no such pods running on our infra nodes. This is a known issue that is being tracked in [8]. At the time of writing this chapter, there is no supported fix for this. An unsupported solution would be to change the Network CR to **Unmanaged**, so that it doesn't reset DaemonSet configuration, and add a toleration directly to the DaemonSet. It only checks for iptables being used in user pods, and since no user pods are supposed to run on infrastructure nodes, there is no impact on observability either.

Another reason is that these pods use system resources and running them on all nodes would contribute to that, taking resources away from business applications.

Disabling keepalived on workers

If you deploy OpenShift on VMware vSphere using the IPI method, there will be an additional namespace called `openshift-vsphere-infra` with one `keepalived` pod per node. Keepalived uses the **Virtual Router Redundancy Protocol (VRRP)** to share a single virtual IP address between multiple nodes with only one (leader) owning it at any given time. Each node can also serve as a load balancer thanks to the HAProxy instance running on that node. Together, keepalived and HAProxy implement a load balancing mechanism that provides connectivity to a cluster in the absence of an external load balancer. If you moved router pods to infra nodes, keepalived is not required to run on other worker nodes and can be safely disabled. The procedure is explained in the KB article [9]. You can also read more details about keepalived in OpenShift IPI in [10].

Kube RBAC proxy CRIO pods failing

You may see one or more `kube-rbac-proxy-crio-<NODE_NAME>` pods in the `openshift-machine-config-operator` namespace fail with a `CrashLoopBackOff` status. Check its logs with the following command:

```
$ oc logs po/kube-rbac-proxy-crio-<NODE_NAME> -n openshift-machine-config-operator
```

You should see an error similar to the following:

```
Defaulted container "kube-rbac-proxy-crio" out of: kube-rbac-proxy-crio, setup (init)
W0303 06:49:03.713160       1 deprecated.go:66]
==== Removed Flag Warning ======================

logtostderr is removed in the k8s upstream and has no effect any more.

===============================================

I0303 06:49:03.713265       1 kube-rbac-proxy.go:530] Reading config file: /etc/kubernetes/crio-metrics-proxy.cfg
I0303 06:49:03.714686       1 kube-rbac-proxy.go:233] Valid token audiences:
I0303 06:49:03.714876       1 kube-rbac-proxy.go:347] Reading certificate files
E0303 06:49:03.714915       1 run.go:74] "command failed" err="failed to initialize certificate reloader: error loading certificates: error loading certificate: open /var/lib/kubelet/pki/kubelet-server-current.pem: no such file or directory"
```

Figure 4.13: Node's kubelet is missing a certificate due to a pending CSR

If that happens, check for any pending kubelet CSRs from the failing pod's resident node and approve them, just like during installation:

```
$ oc get csr -o go-template='{{range .items}}{{if not .status}}{{.metadata.
name}}{{"\n"}}{{end}}{{end}}' | xargs --no-run-if-empty oc adm certificate
approve
```

Failed pod(s) may take a few minutes to restart and become running.

This concludes the topic of post-install configuration. Depending on your business's requirements, there may be other steps that need to be taken before opening a cluster up to users, such as deploying a networking solution or specialized agents; however, the items we have covered here are the most common.

Summary

By this point, you should have a solid understanding of basic day-2 configuration items that are typically completed for new clusters.

We have learned how infra nodes can be used to separate special and cluster-internal workloads from regular applications, about licensing implications, and how to configure these nodes with a dedicated MachineConfigPool. We also moved ingress pods to infra nodes and provided you with references to other parts of this book where migration procedures for other components are covered.

Another item that we tackled in this chapter was the encryption of some of the most sensitive API resources in etcd, which is very common in security-conscious environments.

We also practiced replacing default API and ingress certificates with the ones signed by our self-signed CA, which is probably one of the most common day-2 steps across all organizations.

Lastly, we covered some of the items that you may encounter due to bugs, deprecation, or when deploying OpenShift with IPI.

The procedures we discussed here are by no means exhaustive, as they depend on an organization and some of them may require extra steps, such as installing Compliance Operator, connecting to an external log collection service, deploying monitoring agents, and so on. However, from our experience, they serve as a good starting point and provide a good learning opportunity.

We will now proceed to explore how authentication and authorization work in OpenShift in the next chapter.

References

To learn more about the topics that were covered in this chapter, take a look at the following resources:

- [1] *OpenShift Container Platform 4.16 release notes*: `https://docs.redhat.com/en/documentation/openshift_container_platform/4.16/html/release_notes/ocp-4-16-release-notes`
- [2] *DaemonSet*: `https://kubernetes.io/docs/concepts/workloads/controllers/daemonset/`
- [3] *klusterlet add-ons does not tolerate Infra taints NoExecute*: `https://access.redhat.com/solutions/7063198`

- [4] *nfd-worker DaemonSet to tolerate NoExecute*: `https://issues.redhat.com/browse/RFE-4727`
- [5] `error: x509 certificate signed by unknown authority` *when logging in OpenShift 4 after replacing API certificate*: `https://access.redhat.com/solutions/4878721`
- [6] *Openshift-dns daemonsets doesn't include toleration to run on nodes with taints*: `https://access.redhat.com/solutions/6592171`
- [7] *Deprecation of iptables in OpenShift version 4.16 and onwards*: `https://access.redhat.com/solutions/7080183`
- [8] `iptables-alerter` *causes DaemonSetMisScheduled alerts in clusters with infra nodes*: `https://issues.redhat.com/browse/OCPBUGS-38367`
- [9] *How to disable keepalived on nodes that are not dedicated infra nodes*: `https://access.redhat.com/solutions/7026132`
- [10] *Load Balancing and DNS with OpenShift IPI in VMware & On-Premise (Part I)*: `https://rcarrata.com/openshift/ocp4_ipi_vmware_deep_dive/`

Quiz

Test your understanding of post-installation steps with this quick quiz. Remember, some questions may have more than one correct answer!

1. Which label(s) can be used to add the infra role to a node?
   a. `node-role.kubernetes.io/infra="anything"`
   b. `role.kubernetes.io/infra`
   c. `node-role.kubernetes.io/infra=""`
   d. `node-role.kubernetes.io/infra="true"`
2. What labels must be listed in `machineConfigSelector` for an infra MachineConfigPool?
   a. `["infra"]`
   b. `["worker"]`
   c. `["worker", "infra"]`
   d. `["*"]`
3. Which resource types are encrypted when etcd encryption is enabled?
   a. ConfigMaps, Secrets, routes, OAuth access tokens, and OAuth authorization tokens
   b. OAuth access tokens and OAuth authorization tokens
   c. ConfigMaps and Secrets
   d. All
4. Which resource must be updated with a reference to the ConfigMap containing a certificate chain for validating secure connections to a proxy or any external endpoint?
   a. `ingresscontroller/default`
   b. `apiserver/cluster`
   c. `proxy/cluster`
   d. `cm/cloud-provider-config -n openshift-config`

5. Which resource must be updated with a reference to the Secret containing a certificate and a key for the public API endpoint?
    a. `ingresscontroller/default`
    b. `apiserver/cluster`
    c. `proxy/cluster`
    d. `cm/cloud-provider-config -n openshift-config`
6. Which resource must be updated with a reference to the Secret containing a certificate and a key for the ingress endpoint?
    a. `ingresscontroller/default`
    b. `apiserver/cluster`
    c. `proxy/cluster`
    d. `cm/cloud-provider-config -n openshift-config`

Answers

1. **a**, **c**, and **d**. Although setting the value to "true" or an empty string is more common, any non-empty string will work.
2. **c**. When infra nodes of your cluster are labeled with an additional `node-role.kubernetes.io/infra` key, their MachineConfigPool must use both `worker` and `infra` MachineConfig selectors. This is necessary so that changes intended for workers are applied to infra nodes as well; otherwise, they will not get updated during an upgrade.
3. **a**. Not all resources are encrypted, so D is incorrect. B and C are only partially correct, which leaves A.
4. **c**. `proxy/cluster` references a certificate chain that validates external endpoints for connections made by OpenShift components. That chain is added to the trusted bundle on all CoreOS nodes.
5. **b**. The correct resource to update when configuring a public API certificate is `apiserver/cluster`.
6. **a**. The correct resource to update when configuring a public ingress certificate is `ingresscontroller/default`.

Join us on Discord

For discussions around the book and to connect with your peers, join us on Discord at `http://packt.link/discordcloud` or scan the QR code below:

5

Navigating Authentication and Authorization

In today's digital world, security is crucial, and controlling who can access and act within your systems is key to keeping them safe. Authentication and authorization are important security concepts, and grasping them is necessary for securing your OpenShift cluster. **Authentication** makes sure that only the right users and services can get in, while **authorization** controls what they can do once inside. Together, these processes protect your applications and infrastructure from unauthorized access and potential threats.

This chapter will walk you through the basics of authentication and authorization in OpenShift. We'll cover different ways to authenticate users, including how to connect with external identity providers, and explore how to manage access and permissions within your cluster. By the end, you'll know how to secure your OpenShift environment, making sure only the right people and processes have the right access.

We are going to cover the following topics in this chapter:

- Authentication and authorization as concepts
- OpenShift OAuth and its components
- Authentication providers in OCP
- RBAC, users, groups, and service accounts

Technical requirements

In this chapter, you will need the following:

- Bash shell
- OpenShift 4.16
- LDAP or AD server, if you want to set up LDAP authentication

You can access this book's GitHub repository at `https://github.com/PacktPublishing/Learn-OpenShift-Second-Edition`.

Authentication and authorization

In any secure system, knowing who is accessing your environment and what they are allowed to do is crucial. In OpenShift, this is managed through authentication and authorization processes. Authentication ensures that only legitimate users can access the cluster, while authorization determines what actions those users can perform once authenticated. Together, these mechanisms protect your OpenShift environment from unauthorized access and potential security threats. Let's talk about authentication and authorization to ensure we are on the same page.

Authentication

Authentication controls initial access to the Red Hat **OpenShift Container Platform** (OCP) cluster by verifying the identity of the client that sends a request to the API server. Only clients who can prove their identity are allowed to proceed to the authorization phase.

OCP's built-in OAuth server issues bearer access tokens, and the API server also accepts X.509 client certificates (commonly used by controllers and automation). A request that carries a valid token in an `Authorization: Bearer <token>` header or presents a trusted certificate is mapped to a user or service account; all others are rejected with a `401 Unauthorized` response.

You can plug in many identity providers (LDAP, GitHub, OpenID Connect, htpasswd, and more), but once authentication succeeds, the API server handles only the resolved username and group memberships.

Authorization

Authorization decides whether the authenticated identity (user, group, or service account) may perform a particular action (verb + resource + namespace). The layer works only with identity information passed from authentication.

We are going to talk about the concept of **role-based access control** (RBAC) in detail further in this chapter, but let's quickly enumerate the key objects of the OCP RBAC:

- **Role:** List of permission rules valid inside one project
- **ClusterRole:** The same as `Role`, but cluster-wide
- **RoleBinding:** Attaches a `Role/ClusterRole` to subjects in one project
- **ClusterRoleBinding:** Attaches a `ClusterRole` cluster-wide

Together with the projects (objects in OpenShift created over namespaces), they make access control in OpenShift extremely powerful and flexible. The following sections describe the most important components and processes in detail.

OAuth and components

Controlling who can access your OpenShift cluster and how they authenticate is crucial for security. In this section, we'll cover the basics of OAuth, identity management, and user accounts in OpenShift. By understanding these, you'll be able to manage access effectively, ensuring that only the right users can interact with the necessary resources.

Introduction to OAuth in OpenShift

As mentioned previously, the OCP has its own built-in OAuth server, one of the default and main system components deployed on the cluster. The OAuth server implements the OAuth 2.0 authorization framework (RFC 6749), an open standard for delegated authorization. The component is responsible for issuing access tokens, allowing the user to authenticate themselves against an API server.

When a user initiates a request for a new OAuth token, the OAuth server communicates with the configured identity provider to determine the requester's identity. Then, the OAuth server establishes the corresponding user identity, generates an access token for that user, and provides the token for further use.

So, the overall process looks like this:

1. The user requests a new OAuth token.
2. The OAuth server receives the request.
3. OAuth verifies the credentials with the **identity provider** (**IdP**).
4. The OAuth server maps that IdP account to (or creates) the corresponding OpenShift `User` and `Identity` objects.
5. Once verified, the OAuth server generates a unique access token.
6. Then, the OAuth token is sent back to the user.
7. The user can interact with the OCP API server.

Next, let's discuss the components of OAuth in OpenShift: identity, users, and groups.

Identity

Before we dive into users and groups, let's cover one more logical component: identity. An identity does not require you to create a separate resource in YAML; instead, it is created automatically by OpenShift after you configure an external IdP in the cluster's `OAuth` configuration and a user successfully logs in.

In OpenShift, an identity is linked to a `User` object and records details returned by the IdP, such as provider name, provider-specific username, and optional attributes such as email. RBAC roles and permissions are applied later to the user or its groups, not stored on the identity itself.

The most common IdPs in enterprise environments are Microsoft Entra ID (formerly Azure AD), Microsoft Active Directory, LDAP, and **OpenID Connect** (**OIDC**) servers. OpenShift supports eight built-in IdP types; we will look at the most widely used ones in the *Integrating external IdPs* section later in this chapter.

Users

In the section about authorization, we referenced *the user* as the entity making requests to the OCP, which is then authenticated and authorized by the OAuth server. Let's clarify what a *user* means in the context of the OCP.

A **user** in OpenShift is an entity that can perform actions or make API requests within the OpenShift environment. This is represented within OpenShift as a `User` object, which acts as a placeholder for an individual's permission in the system. These permissions are defined by the roles assigned directly to the user or to the groups the user is a part of.

Typically, a user represents someone such as a developer or administrator who interacts with the OCP, carrying out tasks ranging from deploying applications to managing the system's configuration.

There are a few types of users that may be defined:

<table>
<tr><th>User type</th><th>Description</th></tr>
<tr><td>Regular users</td><td>Regular users may be created on the IdP side and then automatically created in the OCP. Regular users can also be created via the API or CLI. Regular users are represented with the <code>User</code> object. Examples are <code>alex</code> and <code>dan</code>.</td></tr>
<tr><td>System users</td><td>System users are automatically created during the OpenShift deployment process; most exist to allow the platform components to interact securely with the OpenShift API. A cluster administrator (root-level user) is one of them.

Most OpenShift cluster operators and components have their own system users, such as the following:
• <code>system:admin</code>
• <code>system:openshift-registry</code>
• <code>system:node:node1.example.com</code>

There is also an anonymous system user, which is used for unauthenticated requests.</td></tr>
<tr><td>Service accounts</td><td>Every OpenShift project has its own special users, called service accounts (SAs). Some are created automatically, but nothing limits the project or platform administrator's ability to create more.

Service accounts are represented with the <code>ServiceAccount</code> object, such as these examples:
• <code>system:serviceaccount:default:deployer</code>
• <code>system:serviceaccount:foo:builder</code>

More details on the service account are covered in the Service accounts for automated access section.</td></tr>
</table>

Table 5.1: Types of users in OpenShift

Every user must authenticate to access the OCP. API requests that lack authentication or contain invalid authentication credentials are processed as if made by an anonymous system user. Once a user successfully authenticates, the platform's policies dictate the range of actions the user can perform.

Groups

A user may belong to one or several groups, each encapsulating a specific cohort of users. Utilizing groups simplifies the administration of authorization policies by enabling permissions to be assigned collectively to several users, such as providing access rights to resources within a project rather than assigning permissions individually.

The administrator can create specific groups if needed, but some groups will also be predefined, using the same logic as with users; these groups will be `System` or `Virtual` groups. The most important virtual groups are described in the following table:

Virtual group	Description
`system:authenticated`	Automatically associated with all authenticated users
`system:authenticated:oauth`	Automatically associated with all users authenticated with an OAuth access token
`system:unauthenticated`	Automatically associated with all unauthenticated users

Table 5.2: Virtual groups in OpenShift

By mastering OAuth, identity management, and user accounts, you lay the groundwork for secure and efficient access control in your OpenShift cluster. With these fundamentals in place, we can now move on to the next section, where we'll dive into the details of clients, tokens, and grants. These elements are key to how users and applications interact securely with your cluster.

Clients, tokens, grants

In this section, we'll delve into the role of OAuth clients in OpenShift, exploring the various types of tokens they use and how these tokens facilitate secure interactions with the cluster. We'll also cover the best practices for managing OAuth clients and tokens to ensure your environment remains both accessible and secure. Let's dive deeper into these essential components.

OAuth clients

OAuth clients are any application, service, or CLI toolset that requests the OpenShift API on behalf of the user. The most familiar example is the oc OpenShift console utility, which sends many API calls under the hood and still requires user information to authenticate and authorize against the OCP.

OpenShift has a few different types of OAuth clients out of the box; for version 4.16 and above, the following clients will be created at deployment time:

OAuth client	Usage
`openshift-browser-client`	Requests tokens at `<namespace_route>/oauth/token/request` with a user agent that can handle interactive logins. To get `namespace_route`, you can execute the following: `$ oc get route oauth-openshift -n openshift-authentication -o json | jq .spec.host`
`openshift-challenging-client`	Requests tokens with a user agent that can handle WWW-Authenticate challenges.
`openshift-cli-client`	Requests tokens by using a local HTTP server, fetching an authorization code grant.

Table 5.3: Default OAuth clients in OpenShift

To get detailed output for the available OAuth clients, you can run the following command:

```
$ oc get oauthclient -o custom-columns=NAME:.metadata.name,REDIRECT-URIS:.
redirectURIs[]
```

The output you are expecting to see is the following:

```
$ oc get oauthclient -o custom-columns=NAME:.metadata.name,REDIRECT-URIS:.redirectURIs[]
NAME                           REDIRECT-URIS
console                        https://console-openshift-console.apps.cluster.example.com/auth/callback
openshift-browser-client       https://oauth-openshift.apps.cluster.example.com/oauth/token/display
openshift-challenging-client   https://oauth-openshift.apps.cluster.example.com/oauth/token/implicit
openshift-cli-client           http://127.0.0.1/callback
```

Figure 5.1: The list of available OAuth clients

Please note, we are running a command with the `custom-columns` flag to make the screenshot more suitable for the book; feel free to run the same command without it, and see the complete output.

In the preceding output, you may also see the `console` OAuth client, which exists for console authentication. Let's take a look at the `console` OAuth client structure by executing the following:

```
$ oc get oauthclient console -o yaml
```

Here is the example output of the preceding command:

```
$ oc get oauthclient console -o yaml
apiVersion: oauth.openshift.io/v1
grantMethod: auto
kind: OAuthClient
metadata:
  annotations:
    capability.openshift.io/name: Console
    include.release.openshift.io/hypershift: "true"
    include.release.openshift.io/ibm-cloud-managed: "true"
    include.release.openshift.io/self-managed-high-availability: "true"
    include.release.openshift.io/single-node-developer: "true"
    release.openshift.io/create-only: "true"
  creationTimestamp: "2025-07-28T13:13:37Z"
  name: console
  ownerReferences:
  - apiVersion: config.openshift.io/v1
    kind: ClusterVersion
    name: version
    uid: c14358b4-242f-4e61-9273-b16286471e42
  resourceVersion: "14119"
  uid: 0e6dbf5b-29c1-414f-b449-40507facbd12
redirectURIs:
- https://console-openshift-console.apps.cluster.example.com/auth/callback
secret: Jx-fLz5ea2By4XY2oD84RxjuDm5uny2dNyYe3iFQJ-k
```

Figure 5.2: The OAuth client's details

Now that you are familiar with OAuth clients, let's talk about how you can create a custom OAuth client.

Custom OAuth client

The platform administrator can define a new, custom OAuth client. To create a new OAuth client, the following prerequisites should be prepared:

- **Callback URLs (also known as redirect URIs)**: These are endpoints where the OAuth server sends the user after a successful authentication. They must be pre-registered to prevent redirection attacks. For example, if your application is hosted at `https://myapp.example.com`, you might have a callback URL such as `https://myapp.example.com/oauth/callback`.
- **Client secret**: OAuth clients will use this secret to authenticate with the OAuth server. These secrets must be securely stored on the client side. OpenShift allows you to specify a client secret when registering the `OAuthClient` object. It's crucial to protect this secret to prevent unauthorized access.
- **Grant method**: `grantMethod` determines what action to take when the OAuth client requests tokens and has not yet been granted access by the user:
    - `auto`: Automatically approve the grant and retry the request
    - `prompt`: Prompt the user to approve or deny the grant

Here is an example of the definition of a custom OAuth client:

```
apiVersion: oauth.openshift.io/v1
kind: OAuthClient
metadata:
  name: <name>
secret: "<client secret name>" # Client Secret name
redirectURIs:
  - "http://www.example.com/" # Callback URL
grantMethod: prompt
```

After registering the OAuth client, it's essential to test the authentication flow thoroughly. This ensures that the redirections are correctly configured, and the client can request and receive access tokens.

OAuth tokens

OAuth tokens ensure that only authorized users can access the platform's features and resources. These tokens act as digital keys, allowing users to prove their identity and permissions. Effective management of these tokens is critical, not just for security but also for maintaining a smooth operation within OpenShift environments.

Managing OAuth tokens

The user can access the list and details of their OAuth tokens by running the following command:

```
$ oc get useroauthaccesstokens
```

```
$  oc get useroauthaccesstokens -o custom-columns=NAME:.metadata.name,CLIENT_NAME:.clientName
NAME                                                CLIENT_NAME
sha256~7SwcQW8_d2hwY7P5tGN7Xnh9tnXzxpN3MWGWCGWpQ24   openshift-browser-client
sha256~EdT6P2TmT0_fkbRB53zF0rIjsWgMl3iTG4AVWKHRMCQ   openshift-browser-client
sha256~xuldDJbQs5sx3e2LHWsgIbkS3wZZC5ezkja2xY-HQmA   console
```

Figure 5.3: The list of OAuth tokens

The command will return a full list of available tokens for each OAuth client, such as `console` or `openshift-challenging-client`, which were mentioned in previous sections. Every token could be described via the `oc describe` command as any other object in OpenShift or Kubernetes. Keep the following in mind:

- Users can see only their own tokens.
- The output will be empty for system users (such as the default `system:admin` user) and service accounts, as they don't have OAuth-issued tokens. However, if you log in as a regular user, such as `kubeadmin`, you will be granted a token and will be able to view it with the preceding command.

For example, the following token originated by the OpenShift `console` component was created when the `kubeadmin` user accessed the OpenShift web UI; see the `Client Name` and `User Name` fields:

```
$ oc describe useroauthaccesstokens sha256~7SwcQW8_d2hwY7P5tGN7Xnh9tnXzxpN3MWGWCGWpQ24
Name:               sha256~7SwcQW8_d2hwY7P5tGN7Xnh9tnXzxpN3MWGWCGWpQ24
Namespace:
Labels:             <none>
Annotations:        <none>
API Version:        oauth.openshift.io/v1
Authorize Token:    sha256~1w3UY08zQD0bLBd-i42-ltl4gU3jXD2tM_MWzBCKcKQ
Client Name:        openshift-browser-client
Expires In:         86400
Kind:               UserOAuthAccessToken
Metadata:
  Creation Timestamp:  2025-07-28T23:34:26Z
  Resource Version:    109550
  UID:                 0992baed-686c-44c3-98d2-dc7e16c4add7
Redirect URI:          https://oauth-openshift.apps.cluster.example.com/oauth/token/display
Scopes:
  user:full
User Name:  kube:admin
User UID:   UWAqBd3KOWw446ynIhIg8EuL1A2_zfVSwv0EvwLuzssEDTlb1E5ghgAe4fZjMEhlIRfLvS1_Fy5ifIiOd4-HkA
Events:     <none>
```

Figure 5.4: The OAuth token's details

You can also delete a token in the same way as you usually delete other Kubernetes objects – by running `oc delete useroauthaccesstokens <token-name>` – but it is unnecessary for now, so please skip it.

OAuth token configuration

A few additional parameters can be assigned to OAuth tokens; these parameters can be configured via an object we mentioned before: `OAuthClient`. These parameters may need to be configured according to the company's security policies or just to align the OCP cluster with your architecture ideas:

- `accessTokenInactivityTimeoutSeconds`: This parameter sets a custom inactivity timeout for tokens linked to this client, overriding the default timeout. This value is the maximum time allowed between uses of the token. The token will expire if not used within this timeframe, and the user must then obtain a new one. Possible settings include the following:
    - `0`: The client's tokens do not expire due to inactivity.
    - `X`: The client's tokens expire after *X* seconds of inactivity. The minimum value is 300 seconds.
- `accessTokenMaxAgeSeconds`: This parameter changes the default maximum age (which is 24 hours) for access tokens issued to this client. Possible settings include the following:
    - `0`: The client's tokens never expire
    - `X`: The client's tokens expire after *X* seconds

Please note that reducing the value affects only new tokens; existing tokens keep the limits they were issued with.

Grants

A grant records that a user has consented for a specific OAuth client to obtain tokens on their behalf. In OpenShift, this is stored as an `OAuthClientAuthorization` object and is unique to a user-client pair.

A grant is created when a client completes the login flow, so the OAuth server evaluates the `grantMethod` of the OAuthClient:

- `deny`: Never approve. No grant is created, and the flow fails.
- `prompt`: Show a consent page. On approval, a grant is stored.
- `auto`: Approve automatically. A grant is stored.

Once present, the grant allows the client to receive tokens for that user without asking for consent again, until the grant is removed.

Grants are standard API resources (`OAuthClientAuthorization`); you can list, inspect, and delete them like other cluster objects. Removing a grant revokes the client's ability to obtain new tokens for that user.

Integrating external IdPs

By default, only the `kubeadmin` user exists in the OCP cluster (CRC also provides a "developer" user). This is a root-like bootstrap account with the `cluster-admin` role. It's meant for the initial setup, and it should be removed **after** you configure and verify an external IdP (the exact command to remove it is in the *Cheat sheet* section of the chapter).

> **Warning!**
>
> Do not remove `kubeadmin` until at least one external IdP is configured and a replacement user has been created, tested, and has `cluster-admin` privileges. **The operation is irreversible, and you could lose access to the cluster entirely.**

OpenShift supports multiple IdPs (`htpasswd`, `keystone`, `ldap`, `basic-authentication`, and `request-header`) and multiple OIDC providers (for example, GitHub, GitLab, Google, Keycloak, Microsoft Entra ID, Okta, and PingID).

The full list changes and grows, so for the details, please take a look at the official Red Hat documentation; see [1] for the complete list of supported IdPs and [2] for configuration details on each of them.

So, why would we need to remove the convenient `kubeadmin` and configure the IdP? The real clusters have many users, and the IdP gives you centralized identity, SSO/MFA, and a secure way to onboard/offboard and manage users; the IdP is the essential component for the production and enterprise environment.

There are a lot of IdPs that are currently popular, but there are two that are most common:

- `htpasswd`: The most popular Authentication provider among small and testing deployments, where the admin may need a few different users and teams
- `ldap`: The most popular among large enterprises, especially for the on-premises OpenShift deployments – VMware-based, or bare metal

Of course, you may encounter other providers being used, but the following two are the main ones you will probably see and configure in your lab (`htpasswd`) or enterprise environment (`ldap`).

Before we move on to the configuration, here is what OpenShift uses for the `user.openshift.io` authentication:

- **Identity**: Created by the IdP integration. It holds provider-specific details (`providerName`, `providerUserName`, and optional extras such as LDAP attributes).
- **User**: The subject RBAC evaluates, and you bind in `RoleBindings` and `ClusterRoleBindings` (`kind: User`). A single user can have multiple identities.
- **Group** (optional but common): A collection of users. RBAC is often granted to groups. Groups can be synced from your directory or managed in-cluster.

The mapping would look like this:

- Each **identity** maps to exactly one **user**
- One **user** may have many **identities** (e.g., LDAP + GitHub), so the same person stays one RBAC subject

This is why it all matters (we spoke about it, but let's recap quickly):

- Authentication (IdP: identity) proves who the user is
- Authorization (RBAC on user/group) decides what they can do

With that model in mind, we're ready to configure and enable the first IdP.

htpasswd

`htpasswd` is a utility that creates and updates flat files to store usernames and **hashed** passwords for basic authentication of HTTP users. The `htpasswd` IdP in OpenShift allows users to be managed using such a plain text file. Historically, this `cli` tool was used to manage Apache servers, but it is available as an independent and standalone binary. It is provided by the `httpd-tools` package and should already be installed on most Linux distributions we recommended earlier in this book, including Rocky Linux 9.4. In case it is not installed for you, use the following command to rectify this:

```
# yum -y install httpd-tools
```

To enable an `htpasswd`-based IdP, follow the next steps:

1. Create or update a flat file:

   ```
   $ htpasswd -c -B -b </path/to/users.htpasswd> <username> <password>
   ```

   In the preceding command, the `-B` flag indicates Bcrypt hashing, which is based on the Blowfish cipher and is considered particularly resistant to brute-force attacks.

Here is what you are expecting to see from the preceding command. Let's say we create a user, `alice`, then the output:

```
$ htpasswd -c -B -b users.htpasswd alice AlicePassword!
Adding password for user alice
```

Figure 5.5: The password file update example

2. Add more users to the flat file – in this case, the only difference with the previous command is that you omit the `-c` option (`-c` stands for *create* and would truncate and create a new file):

> **Warning!**
>
> If you accidentally include the `-c` option in your following command, `htpasswd` will overwrite the file, and you will lose all existing entities.

```
$ htpasswd -B -b </path/to/users.htpasswd> <username> <password>
```

3. Let's say your password file's name is `users.htpasswd` and contains a few users – now, we can create a secret from the file in the `openshift-config` namespace, the command would look like this:

```
$ oc create secret generic htpass-secret --from-file=htpasswd=<path_to_
users.htpasswd> -n openshift-config
```

We expect the following response from the command – nothing special:

```
$ oc create secret generic htpass-secret --from-file=htpasswd=users.htpasswd -n openshift-config
secret/htpass-secret created
```

Figure 5.6: The secret creation output

4. Create an OAuth configuration that will make the OAuth server use the secret:

```
apiVersion: config.openshift.io/v1
kind: OAuth
metadata:
  name: cluster
spec:
  identityProviders:
  - name: my_htpasswd_provider
    mappingMethod: claim
    type: HTPasswd
    htpasswd:
      fileData:
        name: htpass-secret
```

5. Now, we can create a provider from the preceding snippet. Use the following command to apply the manifest:

   ```
   $ oc apply -f </path/to/file.yaml>
   ```

   This operation will trigger a new rollout of the OAuth deployment in the `openshift-authentication` namespace. Progress can be monitored with the following command:

   ```
   $ watch -n1 oc get po -n openshift-authentication
   ```

The authentication operator usually picks up changes within 1–1.5 minutes after applying them to the OAuth resource and may take 3–5 minutes total to complete the rollout on a cluster with 3 master nodes. Changes to the secret with the `htpasswd` file, however, are picked up almost instantly.

> **Warning!**
>
> Be careful executing this in a cluster with already configured IdPs. Because of how `apply` works, it will replace the entire list, erasing all preexisting IdPs. So, if you already have IdPs configured, you should copy their configuration to the file first.

When there are other IdPs configured already, other ways to add an extra provider involve the use of `oc edit` for interactive editing or a more elegant and advanced solution using a JSON patch to modify the resource. Here's what such a patch might look like:

```
[
 {
   "op": "add",
   "path": "/spec/identityProviders/-",
   "value": {
     "name": "my_htpasswd_provider",
     "type": "HTPasswd",
     "mappingMethod": "claim",
     "htpasswd": {
       "fileData": {
         "name": "htpass-secret"
       }
     }
   }
 }
]
```

The preceding patch will append the `HTPasswd` provider's configuration to the end of the `identityProviders[]` list, as indicated by "-" in the path. If you didn't have another IdP configured or have already merged them, feel free to skip the following `oc patch` command. Otherwise, save it in a file, for example, `oauth-patch.yml`, and apply it with the following command (which will fail if the `identityProviders[]` list is empty):

```
$ oc patch --type json --patch-file oauth-patch.yml oauth/cluster
```

Now, assuming we have added a user named `alice` to the `htpasswd` file, let's do the following:

1. Log in to our cluster as `alice`:

   ```
   $ oc login https://API_SERVER_ENDPOINT:6443 -u alice
   ```

2. List identities with `oc get identities`. You are expecting to see the following:

```
NAME                          IDP NAME              IDP USER NAME   USER NAME   USER UID
my_htpasswd_provider:alice    my_htpasswd_provider  alice           alice       dd48aace-16d1-4066-ad2b-22961b56ed4e
```

Figure 5.7: The oc get identities command's output

3. List users with `oc get user`:

```
NAME    UID                                    FULL NAME   IDENTITIES
alice   dd48aace-16d1-4066-ad2b-22961b56ed4e               my_htpasswd_provider:alice
```

Figure 5.8: The oc get user output example

   Note that the user ID is the same as in the details of the identity, which establishes their relationship.

4. Lastly, let's look at the YAML manifest of our user with `oc get -o yaml user/alice`:

```
apiVersion: user.openshift.io/v1
groups: null
identities:
- my_htpasswd_provider:alice
kind: User
metadata:
  creationTimestamp: "2025-06-27T03:56:52Z"
  name: alice
  resourceVersion: "79244903"
  uid: dd48aace-16d1-4066-ad2b-22961b56ed4e
```

Figure 5.9: The user's details

   You may notice that `identities[]` is a list, which means that a single user can be mapped to (or claimed by) multiple identities.

`HTPasswd` is a very basic IdP and is rarely used by large organizations in production due to its poor scalability, challenges around management, and "flat" structure, which doesn't provide any user attributes. Let's look at another IdP that is much more common in enterprises.

LDAP

The LDAP identity provider is the most common across enterprise environments; in most cases, MS Active Directory plays the role of the LDAP server. In general, any LDAPv3 server could be used.

To configure the LDAP provider, you must make sure that a few prerequisites are met:

- The `bind` password for the LDAP server is available
- The OpenShift cluster (control plane) can reach the LDAP server ports:
    - LDAP: `389`
    - LDAPS: `636`
- The LDAP URL is created in alignment with the RFC 2255 URL:
    - `ldap://host:port/basedn?attribute?scope?filter`, broken down as follows:
        - `ldap`: `ldap` or `ldaps`
        - `host:port`: `<ldap-server-fqdn or IP>:<389 or 636>`
        - `basedn`: **Distinguished Name (DN)** of a node in LDAP hierarchy to start the search from
        - `attribute`: Default is `uid`, but can be configured
        - `scope`: one or sub
        - `filter`: LDAP search filter

It is a good practice to plan the AD structure accordingly and try to scope `basedn` on some specific AD group where the OpenShift users will reside. The rule is simple: the more precise the group and filter, the faster authentication will happen. It is extremely important for large enterprises where AD may have a very complex structure, and LDAP search may take a long time.

The following best practices are essential to keep in mind:

- Use a dedicated service account for bind operations
- Implement secure connections; use LDAPS when possible
- Optimize LDAP queries; filter attributes and use pagination

You may need to work with your LDAP team very closely, depending on the size of the environment and AD/LDAP structure.

To enable an LDAP-based identity provider, follow the next steps:

1. Create a Secret with a `bind` password:

```
$ oc create secret generic ldap-secret \
--from-literal=bindPassword=<secret> \
-n openshift-config
```

2. Create a ConfigMap with the certificate authority (`ca`) bundle (not necessary if the CA that issues the LDAP certificate is already a part of the trust bundle configured in the `proxy/cluster` resource, as explained in the previous chapter's *Setting up a custom CA* section):

```
$ oc create configmap ca-config-map \
--from-file=ca.crt=/path/to/ca \
-n openshift-config
```

3. Create an OAuth configuration that will make the OAuth server use the Secret and `ConfigMap` (if you didn't create a CA `ConfigMap` in *step 2*, drop the `ca.name` field from the following snippet):

```
apiVersion: config.openshift.io/v1
kind: OAuth
metadata:
  name: cluster
spec:
  identityProviders:
  - name: ldapidp
    mappingMethod: claim
    type: LDAP
    ldap:
      attributes:
        id:
        - dn
        email:
        - mail
        name:
        - cn
        preferredUsername:
        - uid
      bindDN: ""
      bindPassword:
        name: ldap-secret
      ca:
        name: ca-config-map
      insecure: false
      url: "ldaps://ldaps.example.com/ou=users,dc=acme,dc=com?uid"
```

4. Create a provider from the file you just made:

```
$ oc apply -f </path/to/file.yaml>
```

When LDAP is used, it's a standard practice to sync LDAP groups so that roles and cluster roles can be assigned to them instead of individual users. Consult [3] for doing it ad hoc or automatically.

Multiple IdPs

OpenShift supports using multiple IdPs simultaneously, which may be helpful for a number of reasons, such as the following:

- **Redundancy and reliability:** Relying on a single IdP can be a single point of failure in your system. If the IdP experiences downtime or an outage, it could prevent all users from logging in to OpenShift.
- **Diverse user bases:** Different groups of users may require different authentication mechanisms based on their roles, geographic locations, or specific security requirements.
- **Compliance and security requirements:** Different industries and projects may have specific regulatory or security requirements that dictate how authentication must be handled.
- **Integration with legacy systems:** In many cases, organizations undergoing digital transformation are required to maintain legacy systems alongside new platforms.
- **User choice and flexibility:** Offering multiple authentication options can improve user satisfaction and accessibility. Users can choose the login method that they prefer.
- **Specialized access control:** Different IdPs may offer different levels of control and capabilities concerning user access management.
- **Seamless migration from one IdP to another:** If both IdPs are configured with a completely identical set of users, you can use `mappingMethod: add` for them for the duration of migration so that users are added to existing identities when they log in through the new IdP. Then, you would remove the old IdP and clean up leftover users and identities.

So, the possible logical relationship between users and identities is *one-to-many*, as shown in the following diagram:

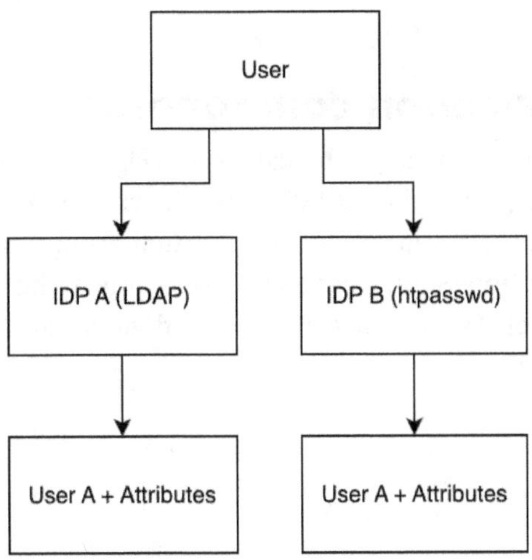

Figure 5.10: User and identities relationship

Due to this flexibility, there is a high possibility that the user's identities may overlap. To handle this, the IdP configuration has a special parameter: `mappingMethod`. It defines how new identities will be mapped to users when they log in; the following parameters are supported:

- `claim`: Assigns a user their preferred username but fails if it is already mapped to another identity.
- `lookup`: Checks for existing identity mappings and users without automatic provisioning. This method requires a manual user setup.
- `add`: Links a user to their chosen username and merges mappings if the username already exists. This method is useful when multiple IdPs are configured, as explained earlier.

> When you have two IdPs configured with `mappingMethod: claim` and there is an overlap between them (some or all users are present in both providers), whichever IdP creates an identity will claim it and another provider will not be able to link a user to it on login. The issue is indicated by a message such as the following in the authentication operator's logs:
>
> ```
> AuthenticationError: user "bob" cannot be claimed by
> identity "my_htpasswd_provider:bob" because it is already
> mapped to [my_htpasswd_provider_new:bob]
> ```
>
> The problem and solution are described in [4].

If you try logging in with any of the users provided through the IdP(s) you configured, you will notice that they have a very limited view. By default, new users are assigned a `basic-user` ClusterRole, which allows limited read-only access. In the following section, we will discuss how to grant them additional privileges.

RBAC and authorization components

RBAC is the most common way to manage who can access certain parts of systems or data. Instead of giving each user individual permission, RBAC assigns permissions to roles. These roles are then given to users, service accounts, groups of users, or virtual groups. So, RBAC controls what users can do based on their role. In OpenShift, it restricts access only to the API, which is but one layer of security. Guardrails on the level of namespace, pod, and individual containers are explored in *Chapter 7, Application Security and Isolation*.

Fundamentals of RBAC

In OpenShift, using RBAC helps ensure that users (or applications) have the proper access to do their jobs without unnecessary extra permissions. This is key to keeping OpenShift secure and organized.

As mentioned before, OpenShift operates rules, cluster- and namespace-level roles, and bindings. This section will describe the main RBAC components and how to control access using them.

OpenShift also operates two levels of RBAC (cluster RBAC and local RBAC), as follows:

- **Cluster RBAC:** `ClusterRole` and `ClusterRoleBinding` objects that are at the cluster level
- **Local RBAC:** `Role` and `RoleBinding` objects that are at the namespace level

In most cases, cluster RBAC would be used by administrators, cluster operators, and other operators requiring access across all the namespaces. In some cases, roles would be assigned to groups or users, and in others, to service accounts. Service accounts are described in the last section of this chapter: *Service accounts for automated access.*

Understanding rules, roles, and role bindings

In OpenShift, controlling who can do what within your cluster is essential for maintaining security and order. This is where rules, roles, and role bindings come into play. **Rules** define specific actions that can be performed, **roles** group these rules together, and **role bindings** assign these roles to users, groups, or service accounts. Understanding these concepts is crucial because they form the backbone of OpenShift's access control system.

These rules enable you to finely tune permissions within your cluster, ensuring that users have just the right level of access they need – no more, no less. This hierarchy and how it ties in with multiple IdPs are depicted in the following diagram:

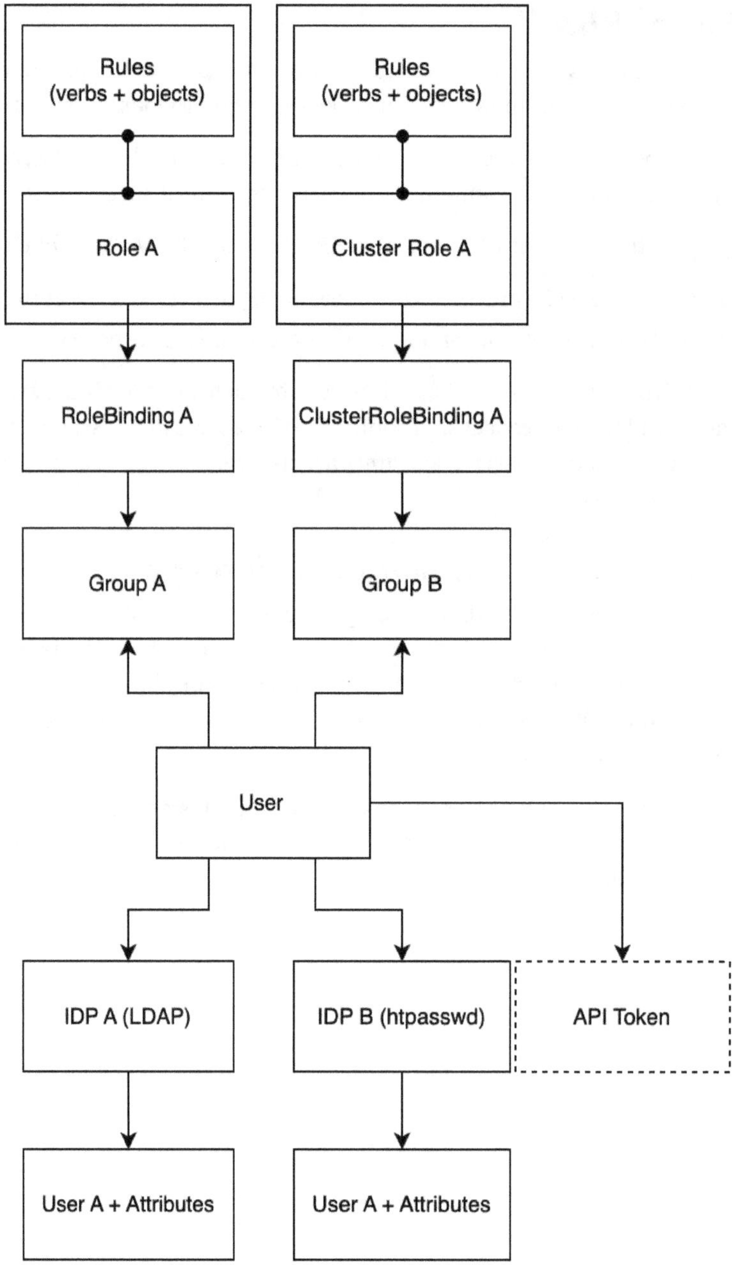

Figure 5.11: RBAC structure

Let's learn more about each of the RBAC logical components.

Rules

Rules are sets of permitted actions or *verbs*; verbs can be performed against core Kubernetes objects, custom resources, and non-resource URLs (API endpoints). For example, *create a Pod or delete a namespace*. You can even scope a rule to specific resources via the `resourceNames` field.

There are no deny rules in OpenShift and Kubernetes RBAC – everything is forbidden by default. So, rules are evaluated in the following order:

- Cluster-level (cluster-wide) rules (allow only)
- Namespace-level (locally bound) rules (allow only)
- Deny by default

To be more precise and not make it difficult, rules are always a part of some Role or ClusterRole, and you can't define a rule by itself, as there is no API object for it. Let's figure out how we define a Role and ClusterRole.

Roles and ClusterRoles

Both types of roles can be created by either `oc-cli` or a raw manifest file; let's look at the process and check the resulting manifests.

Roles

Here is an example of how you would create a Role via the oc CLI. You can define roles imperatively (via the CLI) or declaratively (by applying a YAML manifest), like almost everything in OpenShift and Kubernetes. This is how to do it via the oc client:

```
$ oc create role <name> --verb=<verb> --resource=<resource> -n <project>
```

Here is what the different elements in the code refer to:

- `name`: Role name
- `verb`: List of API verbs (actions) taken against a resource. They can be categorized like this:
    - **View:** `get`, `list`, and `watch`
    - **Create:** `create`
    - **Modify:** `update` and `patch`
    - **Delete:** `delete` (single resource by name) and `deletecollection` (multiple resources either explicitly or by their labels)
    - **Virtual verbs (supported only by certain resources):** `use` (SCC), `impersonate` (user, group, or service account), `bind`, and `escalate`
- `resource`: A comma-separated list of resource types without spaces, such as `pod,namespace`

- `project`: Namespace/project name

> There is no definitive list of supported verbs in Kubernetes or OpenShift, beyond those supported by core and some other standard APIs, such as `apps` or `jobs.batch`. You can use `oc auth can-i --list` as the cluster admin; however, even that wouldn't give you a complete picture, because that command only displays verbs that are allowed explicitly and through a wildcard (*), which isn't always the case for `cluster-admin`. Technically, you can even allow a non-existent verb on any resource, and OpenShift won't throw any errors; however, this will be incomplete without a controller that would map that verb to an HTTP method. This is an advanced topic, but if you're curious, you can read more at [5].

So, let's create a role that will allow `create` pods in a specific namespace:

```
$ oc create role myrole --verb=create --resource=pod -n myproject
```

Let's look at the role we made:

```
$ oc get role myrole -n myproject -o yaml
```

```
apiVersion: rbac.authorization.k8s.io/v1
kind: Role
metadata:
  creationTimestamp: "2024-04-05T20:50:23Z"
  name: myrole
  namespace: myproject
  resourceVersion: "182001"
  uid: 7a9e05a0-cbf1-44b2-9424-5a48e98363ed
rules:
- apiGroups:
  - ""
  resources:
  - pods
  verbs:
  - create
```

As described previously, the role consists of rules (see the `rules` section):

```
rules:
- apiGroups: # here a specific API the Role can use can be specified
  - ""
  resources: # here a specific Resource(s) the Role can use can be specified
  - pods
  verbs:     # here a specific Verbs the Role can use can be specified
  - create
```

The `apiGroups` field scopes a role or ClusterRole to a specific API group. Every resource in OpenShift has the `apiVersion: <GROUP>/<VERSION>` field, so while it may seem obvious, `apiGroups` must include only `<GROUP>` without `<VERSION>` (for example, `apps` for Deployments, StatefulSets, and DaemonSets, not `apps/v1`). For the core API group (`apiVersion: v1`), however, `apiGroups` must be an empty string (`""`).

Other important fields include `kind` and `namespace` (roles are namespace resources):

```
apiVersion: rbac.authorization.k8s.io/v1
kind: Role # kind defines a type of the object
metadata:
  creationTimestamp: "2024-04-05T20:50:23Z"
  name: myrole
  namespace: myproject # the project where the Role is created
  resourceVersion: "182001"
```

ClusterRoles

Now, let's see how you create a ClusterRole:

```
$ oc create clusterrole <name> --verb=<verb> --resource=<resource>
```

Here is what the different elements in the code refer to:

- `name`: Role name
- `verb`: `get`, `create`, and others
- `resource`: Pod, namespace, and so on

So, let's create a ClusterRole that will allow `create verb` on pods in any namespace:

```
$ oc create clusterrole myclusterrole --verb=create --resource=pod
```

The only difference would be the type of resource (`role` and `clusterrole`) and the presence of the `-n <project>` key for the role since the role is a namespace-level object or namespaced.

Let's take a look now at the role we made:

```
apiVersion: rbac.authorization.k8s.io/v1
kind: ClusterRole
metadata:
  creationTimestamp: "2024-04-05T21:14:02Z"
  name: myclusterrole
  resourceVersion: "185258"
  uid: 33b9ae1e-753d-47e5-b54c-75517e1f46be
rules:
- apiGroups:
  - ""
```

```
resources:
- pods
verbs:
- create
```

`ClusterRole` looks very similar to `Role`; the main differences are `kind: ClusterRole` and the lack of a namespace in the definition, since `ClusterRole` is a cluster-level or cluster-wide object.

Let's quickly summarize the differences between `Role` and `ClusterRole`:

- Roles are namespace-scoped and can be referenced only by `RoleBindings` in the same namespace.
- ClusterRoles are cluster-scoped and can be referenced by both `ClusterRoleBindings` (which are cluster-wide as well) and `RoleBindings` in any namespace. This is useful not only for granting access to cluster-level resources, such as nodes, but also for reusing common permissions across groups of users.

Roles and ClusterRoles by themselves don't grant any permissions; to make them work, we need `RoleBindings` and `ClusterRoleBindings` that tie them with subjects. Let's discuss them in more detail.

RoleBindings and ClusterRoleBindings

To make a role work and assign it to a group or user, another object type should be created: `Binding`. Bindings can also be namespace-level or cluster-level: `RoleBinding` and `ClusterRoleBinding`, respectively. Both types can be made via the `oc-cli` command or the Kubernetes manifest.

RoleBindings

As mentioned previously, `RoleBinding` can be created inside a project (since it is a namespaced resource) and will attach a Role or a ClusterRole to a user, group, or service account:

```
$ oc adm policy add-role-to-user <role-name> <user> --role-namespace=<role-namespace> -n <namespace> --rolebinding-name=<rolebinding-name>
```

Here are the details:

- `role-name`: Role name
- `user`: User name
- `role-namespace`: Namespace where the role is located
- `namespace`: Namespace where the `RoleBinding` object will be created
- `rolebinding-name`: The `RoleBinding` name

To assign roles to a group, a very similar command could be used:

```
$ oc adm policy add-role-to-group <role-name> <group> --role-namespace=<role-namespace> -n <namespace> --rolebinding-name=<rolebinding-name>
```

The parameters include the following:

- `role-name`: Role name
- `group`: Group name
- `role-namespace`: Namespace where the role is located
- `namespace`: Namespace where the `RoleBinding` object will be created
- `rolebinding-name`: The `RoleBinding` name

Here is an example of a `RoleBinding` definition, with two sections present – `roleRef` and `subjects`:

```
apiVersion: rbac.authorization.k8s.io/v1
kind: RoleBinding
metadata:
  name: myrole
  namespace: myproject
roleRef:
  apiGroup: rbac.authorization.k8s.io
  kind: Role
  name: myrole
subjects:
- apiGroup: rbac.authorization.k8s.io
  kind: Group
  name: mygroup
```

In the preceding manifest, `roleRef` points to just one and only one role or `ClusterRole`; `subjects` is a list of users, groups, and/or service accounts. Thus, `Roles` and `ClusterRoles` form a "one-to-many" type of relationship with their subjects.

ClusterRoleBindings

Unlike their namespace-bound counterparts, `ClusterRoleBindings` exist at the cluster level. They can be created similarly; the commands would just be slightly different:

```
$ oc adm policy add-cluster-role-to-user <cluster-role-name> <user>
--rolebinding-name=<cluster-rolebinding-name>
```

- `cluster-role-name`: The `ClusterRole` name
- `user`: User name
- `cluster-rolebinding-name`: The `ClusterRoleBinding` name

To assign `ClusterRoles` to groups, a very similar command is used:

```
$ oc adm policy add-cluster-role-to-group <cluster-role-name> <group>
--rolebinding-name=<cluster-rolebinding-name>
```

- `cluster-role-name`: Role name
- `group`: Group name
- `cluster-rolebinding-name`: The `ClusterRoleBinding` name

Here, `oc adm policy` is the most comfortable way to start working with RBAC resources. It also has a few other commands; `add-scc-to-group` and `add-scc-to-user` are among them – we will use them in *Chapter 7, Application Security and Isolation*.

OpenShift doesn't prevent you from creating `RoleBindings` and `ClusterRoleBindings` that reference non-existent roles, `ClusterRoles`, or subjects. For example, if you try to bind a non-existent user to a non-existent `ClusterRole` imperatively (via `oc adm policy`), you will get the following warning:

```
Warning: role 'nonexistent' not found
Warning: User 'bob' not found
clusterrole.rbac.authorization.k8s.io/nonexistent added: "bob"
```

This message is somewhat misleading because no `ClusterRole` was actually created, only `ClusterRoleBinding` (which can be verified with `oc get clusterrole,clusterrolebinding | grep nonexistent`). Note that the binding was created even though both the `ClusterRole` with the name `nonexistent` and the user `bob` don't exist. This is by design, so as to avoid strong coupling and interdependency on RBAC objects and subjects. With that, we can pre-create a binding to a group that will be synced from LDAP later or to a `ClusterRole` that will be created later, and when the group or `ClusterRole` is removed, permissions will be automatically revoked. However, that also means that if you make a typo in the subject or `ClusterRole` name, you won't know about it until a subject with the correct name is created, but without the necessary permissions.

The following is a representation of the scopes at which RBAC objects are evaluated and how they affect access rights:

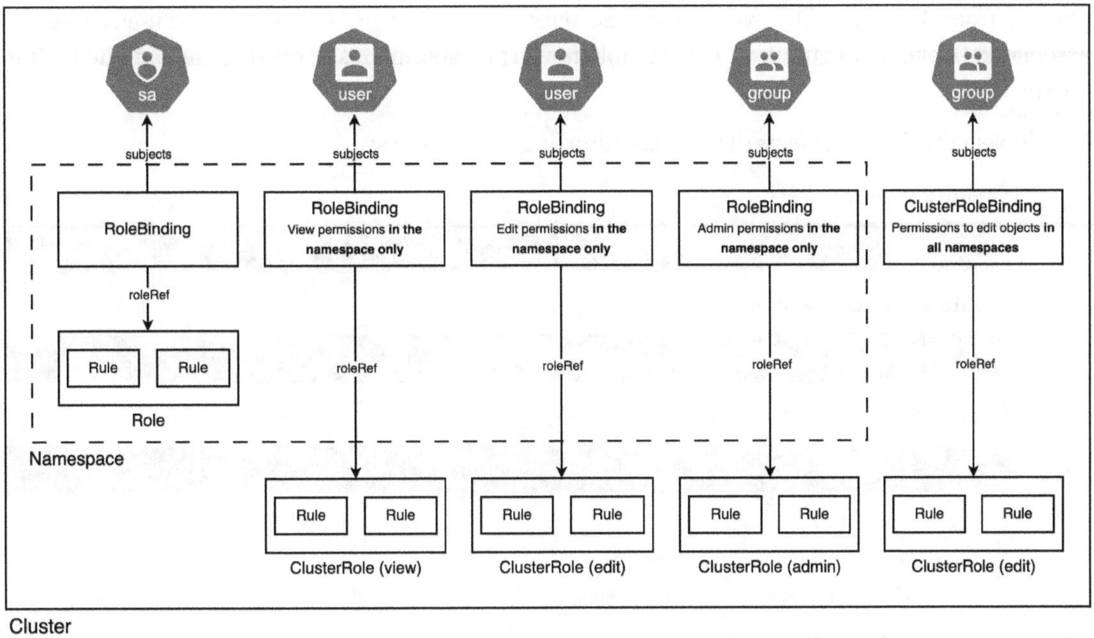

Figure 5.12: RBAC scopes

We already discussed two types of subjects – users and groups. Now, let's tackle the last one – service accounts.

Service accounts for automated access

Another crucial component of Red Hat OpenShift's RBAC is service accounts; they are vital for automating tasks and keeping the cluster secure. The service account concept is generally standard for enterprises and is built into Kubernetes by design.

So, service accounts are intended for use by applications, services, operators, and automation in OpenShift. A service account in OpenShift and Kubernetes is a namespaced resource. By default, it cannot access resources or perform actions in other namespaces unless explicitly allowed through roles or policies that span multiple namespaces.

Service account specifics

Each of the service accounts on the platform is also a member of two default groups:

- `system:serviceaccounts`: A group that includes all service accounts
- `system:serviceaccounts:<project>`: A group that consists of all service accounts in the namespace/project

As you may have noticed, for OpenShift version 4.15 and below, creating a service account automatically generates two secrets: an API token and a Docker configuration. This behavior is specific to the underlying version of Kubernetes that OpenShift used.

Starting from OpenShift 4.16, every service account in OpenShift has only one predefined secret: an associated Docker configuration. The API token won't be automatically created and assigned to the SA anymore.

Let's look at the default objects that the creation of a SA generates:

1. Create a project:

```
$ oc new-project test-sa-project
```

2. Create a service account:

```
$ oc create sa test-service-account
```

3. Check the available secrets:

```
$ oc get sa test-service-account -o yaml
```


```
apiVersion: v1
imagePullSecrets:
- name: test-service-account-dockercfg-ln5zq
kind: ServiceAccount
metadata:
  annotations:
    openshift.io/internal-registry-pull-secret-ref: test-service-account-
dockercfg-ln5zq
  creationTimestamp: "2024-09-16T23:36:54Z"
  name: test-service-account
  namespace: test-sa-project
  resourceVersion: "30493"
  uid: d9e44097-6a1e-4500-bd6e-e3f28e6d1f54
secrets:
- name: test-service-account-dockercfg-ln5zq
```


As you see, there is only one secret, `test-service-account-dockercfg-ln5zq`, which allows the SA to interact with the internal OpenShift registry. The internal OpenShift registry uses the `dockercfg` format of Docker registry authentication files, so the secret consists of the following:

- `Data`: It contains a file in the `.dockercfg` or `.docker/config.json` format, which includes the authentication data needed to pull or push images to a Docker registry. This configuration file is crucial for the build process, allowing the builder service account to interact with private image registries securely.
- It might also include an authentication token that can be used instead of username and password-based authentication. This token represents the logged-in user session and grants permission to access the registry.

> An image pull secret won't be generated for each service account if you do not enable the `ImageRegistry` capability or disable the integrated OpenShift image registry in the cluster image registry operator's configuration, as explained in *Chapter 15, Exploring Additional Services in OpenShift*.

The registry secret is pretty transparent, but what about an API token?

> **Warning!**
>
> When the integrated OpenShift image registry is disabled on a previously enabled cluster, the previously generated image pull secrets are deleted automatically.

What if I need my SA to authenticate against the Kubernetes API? There are two options for your service:

- The preferred option is to go with `oc create token`, which will use the `TokenRequest` API; it will immediately print a token for you, as in this example:

```
$ oc create token test-service-account
```

```
eyJhbGciOiJSUzI1NiIsImtpZCI6Ik1nZTNZZEg4QnJHajlibnlqMWcyY2RWMy15SjFIeFk1c
Tc1Mzc1NDMxOCwiaWF0IjoxNzUzNzUwNzE4LCJpc3MiOiJodHRwczovL2t1YmVybmV0ZXMuZG
nZpY2VhY2NvdW50Ijp7Im5hbWUiOiJ0ZXN0LXNlcnZpY2UtYWNjb3VudCIsInVpZCI6ImMxOG
XN0ZW06c2VydmljZWFjY291bnQ6dGVzdC1zYS1wcm9qZWN0OnRlc3Qtc2VydmljZS1hY2NvdW
m-ZPmwPMEE-bpZ2FmvUyGAnsnbZhis5ge_BxNXnqTB_OQ7Ng95l7MMeHV2LA2FAHyMIxtr6wt
fZ8PLxpv1oQQyf9apfnySWMpVJco7SscVHzgjkb4k2GtCQ_nt6kGk50CijpbDbIUmFvzlWvmC_
nlVSWYs7Q-BLmLlgkQdhitZmG_yqJ7BWvCVNm7wlLHTbKI0uD2Dhgq6YhH8IAtVSVTC3YCDum
ve_rzIK702lXaHVyV9v7tmrztsJPnAzvO_-usbCiV1VNqJkIpvzTWIwo1IT1F5xBykyU1Vy9N
```


Figure 5.13: The token creation output

See the details in the following *Automated access* section.

- An alternative option is the long-living token. You do this by creating a secret of the `kubernetes.io/service-account-token` type. The secret contains no data at creation time; you set only the required annotation, and the API server later injects the token:

```
apiVersion: v1
kind: Secret
type: kubernetes.io/service-account-token
metadata:
  name: test-service-account-token
  namespace: test-sa-project
  annotations:
    kubernetes.io/service-account.name: test-service-account
```

You can create a token for testing purposes and check its definition via `oc get secret test-service-account-token -o yaml`. We won't provide the complete output of the command, since there is a lot of data; instead, we will run the following command to print only the available fields in the `data` section of the YAML:

```
$ oc get secret test-service-account-token -o jsonpath='{.data}{"\n"}' | jq 'keys'

[
  "ca.crt",
  "namespace",
  "service-ca.crt",
  "token"
]
```

Figure 5.14: The secret fields structure

There are a few essential sections to notice:

- `ca.crt`: This is the certificate of the CA that signed the API server's certificate, allowing the client (the application using the token) to verify the server's identity.
- `namespace`: If the user/administrator uses `base64 -d` on the value, it will return the decoded name of this secret's namespace.
- **`service-ca.crt`**: This is the CA for in-cluster services, managed by OpenShift's `service-ca controller`.
- **`token`**: This is the authentication token used in HTTP requests to the OpenShift API. The token authenticates the request as coming from the service account and, by extension, any pods running under that service account.

Plus, if you run the same `-o jsonpath` command, you will see an annotation (`kubernetes.io/service-account.name: my-sa-test`) that points to the SA that the token belongs to.

The "alternative" long-living token is not preferred and may generate significant security risks. This is why it is being deprecated, and modern best practices want you to avoid using it.

The `oc get secrets -o wide` command shows that there are a few more tokens and Docker configuration sets; these objects belong to the default service accounts, which are created automatically when a new project/namespace is created. The next section describes these SAs in detail.

Default service account

The OpenShift cluster operators follow this methodology, and every project will have a set of predefined service accounts.

When a new namespace or project gets created, a few service accounts are created automatically; these service accounts are the following:

- `default`:
    - **Purpose:** The `default` service account is automatically used to run pods if no specific service account is chosen. It also supports processes within these pods when they don't have a specified service account.
    - **Permissions:** This account comes with only the essential permissions required for basic operations within the cluster. It typically doesn't have extensive access to the OpenShift API, making it suitable for applications that don't interact directly with the API.
- `builder`:
    - **Purpose:** The `builder` service account is created to build container images from source code. It's used by the build pods to convert source code into runnable images within OpenShift.
    - **Permissions:** This account has broader permissions than the `default` service account, allowing it to access source code, interact with the integrated image registry to upload or download images, and manage related resources needed for building images.
- `deployer`:
    - **Purpose:** OpenShift utilizes the `deployer` service account to handle the deployment process. It operates within deployment pods to manage and orchestrate the release of new application versions.
    - **Permissions:** This account has the necessary permissions to alter pods and other relevant deployment resources, which allows it to control the stopping and starting of application instances as part of the deployment process.

Automated access

Service accounts may be very useful for authenticating an automation entity against OAuth and working with the API, which is extremely useful for building auto-provisioning processes or when you don't want to provide direct access to the cluster console or UI. Both scenarios are common among enterprises and help maintain adequate resource consumption and planning, and prevent operational mistakes.

So, every service account has a default token, which may be recreated, but there are a few more options to obtain tokens, scope them, and refresh them if needed. To create a token for your service account from the command line, please use the following command:

```
$ oc create token <service-account-name> --namespace <namespace>
```

The command will send a `POST` request to the following API endpoint:

```
https://api.<OCP_CLUSTER_FQDN>:6443/api/v1/namespaces/<NAMESPACE>/
serviceaccounts/<SERVICEACCOUNT>/token
```

The response will consist of a new token you may use for the service account.

> If you have experience with the previous version of OpenShift, you are familiar with the `oc sa get-token` command. This will be deprecated, so please avoid using it when possible.

This concludes the topic of authentication and authorization in OpenShift. As a wrap-up on this chapter, let's summarize some of the commands that you may find useful when working with RBAC in OpenShift.

Cheat sheet

In this section, you'll find a handy collection of commands that can be incredibly useful in your day-to-day work with OpenShift. Practicing and memorizing these commands can save you time and streamline your workflow, making your real-life work situations more efficient and effective:

```
Create a user:
$ oc create user <username>

Create a group:
$ oc adm groups new <group-name>

Create a group and add a user to it:
$ oc adm groups new <group-name> <username>

Remove a user from a group:
$ oc adm groups remove-users <group-name> <username>

Synchronize a group with the LDAP IdP info:
$ oc adm groups sync --sync-config=/path/to/ldap-sync-config.yaml --confirm

Create an SA:
$ oc create serviceaccount <sa-name>  [-n <namespace>]

Create a Role:
$ oc create role <role-name> --verb=<list> --resource=<list>  [-n <namespace>]

Create a ClusterRole:
$ oc create clusterrole <role-name> --verb=<list> --resource=<list>

Create RoleBinding for User:
$ oc create rolebinding admin --clusterrole= <role-name> --user=<user-name>
```

```
--group=<group-name>

Create RoleBinding for Service Account:
$ oc create rolebinding admin-binding --role=admin
--serviceaccount=<namespace>:<sa-name>

Get RoleBindings, Users, Groups, and Service Accounts for them:

$ oc get rolebindings -owide  [-n <namespace>]

Check who can do specific actions, for example:
$ oc adm policy who-can <verb> <resource> [-n <namespace>]

Remove the kubeadmin user:
$ oc delete secret kubeadmin -n kube-system
```

Summary

In this chapter, we explored the critical concepts of authentication and authorization in OpenShift. We began by understanding the importance of these security mechanisms and how they form the foundation of protecting your cluster. We then delved into OpenShift's OAuth system, covering its key components and how they interact with authentication providers. We also examined RBAC, including how users, groups, and service accounts are managed to enforce security policies.

Additionally, we discussed service accounts in more detail – what they are in general and the default one in particular. At this point, you should have a solid grasp of how to implement and manage authentication and authorization in your OpenShift environment.

In the next chapter, we'll move from security to performance, exploring how to scale your applications and infrastructure with OpenShift. You'll learn how to keep your environment responsive and efficient as demand grows.

References

To learn more about the topics that were covered in this chapter, take a look at the following resources:

- [1] *Supported identity providers*: `https://docs.redhat.com/en/documentation/openshift_container_platform/4.16/html/authentication_and_authorization/understanding-identity-provider#supported-identity-providers`
- [2] *Configuring identity providers*: `https://docs.redhat.com/en/documentation/openshift_container_platform/4.16/html/authentication_and_authorization/configuring-identity-providers`
- [3] *Automatically syncing LDAP groups*: `https://docs.redhat.com/en/documentation/openshift_container_platform/4.16/html/authentication_and_authorization/ldap-syncing#ldap-auto-syncing_ldap-syncing-groups`

- [4] *OAuth authentication error in RHOCP 4: users cannot be claimed by an identity as it is already mapped*: `https://access.redhat.com/solutions/4814461`
- [5] *RBAC Virtual Verbs – Teaching Kubernetes to Educate Dolphins*: `https://www.aquasec.com/blog/kubernetes-verbs/`

Questions

Let's test your knowledge with a few simple questions about the topics covered in this chapter:

1. In the RBAC model in OpenShift, what is the difference between `Role` and `ClusterRole`?
    a. `Role` is used for cluster-wide permissions, while `ClusterRole` is used for specific namespaces
    b. `Role` is used within a specific namespace, while `ClusterRole` can be applied across all namespaces
    c. `Role` and `ClusterRole` are the same; the terminology is used differently in different documents
    d. `Role` is used for node-level permissions, while `ClusterRole` is used for pod-level permissions
2. What is the primary function of `RoleBindings` in OpenShift's RBAC?
    a. To define permissions that can be granted
    b. To assign a role to users, groups, or service accounts within a specific namespace
    c. To manage container runtime behaviors
    d. To control pod scheduling across nodes
3. In OpenShift RBAC, what does a role define?
    a. A collection of permissions that can be assigned to a user within a namespace
    b. The assignment of a user to a particular operational task
    c. A security policy that all users in a namespace must adhere to
    d. A list of users who can log in to the cluster
4. You need to grant a pod in OpenShift the ability to pull images from a private registry. Which service account's secret should you use?
    a. `default`
    b. `builder`
    c. `deployer`
    d. `kube-system`

5. When a user logs in to OpenShift via `oc login`, what component is primarily responsible for verifying their credentials?
    a. OAuth server
    b. Kubelet
    c. API server
    d. etcd

Answers

The answers to the questions are as follows:

1. **b.** `Role` is namespace-specific, granting permissions within that namespace, whereas `ClusterRole` grants permissions across all namespaces.
2. **b.** `RoleBindings` link or bind roles to users, groups, or service accounts, assigning the permissions defined in the role to those users, groups, or service accounts within a specific namespace.
3. **a.** In RBAC, a role defines a set of permissions that can be assigned to users, groups, or service accounts within a specific namespace.
4. **b.** The `builder` service account is typically configured with secrets that allow pulling images from the internal registry as part of the build process.
5. **b.** The OAuth server handles authentication in OpenShift. It accepts a username/password, token, or external IdP (LDAP, GitHub, or SSO) and issues OAuth access tokens if credentials are valid.

6

Exploring Scalability with OpenShift

Today's world challenges businesses more than ever – increased competition for customers requires companies to be flexible and responsive to feedback, and to react fast to changing demand. That means that user-facing applications run by modern companies must be able to handle a sudden increase in traffic, and at the same time, use hardware resources efficiently to avoid unnecessary expenses. In the context of OpenShift, that implies the ability of applications to scale automatically based on user demand. Eventually, OpenShift's capacity must be expanded to accommodate extra replicas of business applications. Doing this manually takes time and human resources, scales poorly, and carries the risk of human error. Another problem is that when extra capacity is no longer needed, idle hardware keeps incurring costs without any value to the business. To circumvent that, we need a mechanism that scales our cluster out automatically when it starts running out of capacity and scales it in when the load is back to normal, which is the subject of this chapter.

This chapter teaches you how to prepare to add new worker nodes to an existing cluster, provides guidance around their compute capacity and capabilities, and explains how to drain them of running workloads for maintenance. You will also learn how a cluster can scale out and in automatically in cloud environments. Understanding these concepts is important for extending the capacity of OpenShift when business demands it.

We'll cover the following topics:

- Scaling via MachineSets
- Autoscaling

Let's get started!

Technical requirements

In this chapter, we are going to use the following technologies and software:

- The Bash shell
- The OpenShift 4.16 cluster built in *Chapter 3, Getting Started with OpenShift*
- Firefox (recommended) or any other browser

You can access this book's GitHub repository at `https://github.com/PacktPublishing/Learn-OpenShift-Second-Edition`.

Scaling via MachineSets

Before we get to technical details, it is important to understand why scaling is important, what types of scaling exist, and when to use which. We will begin by discussing the concepts of performance and availability and what they mean in the context of this chapter.

Performance and availability

Once we have created a cluster – for example, using the method outlined in *Chapter 3, Getting Started with OpenShift*, and deployed an application on it, it starts performing its business functions. But that alone is not enough – it has to perform them with certain levels of *performance* and *availability*. These concepts may seem self-explanatory, but it is important to understand them, as they are the drivers behind the subject of this chapter:

- **Performance** is defined as a system's ability to perform its business functions within certain quantitative boundaries, such as response time, throughput, bandwidth, or IOPS. Performance is a function of resources available to the system, such as CPU, RAM, network, or storage.
- **Availability** is a system's ability to produce results in the event of a failure in one or multiple of its components or dependent systems, or resource contention. It can be calculated using the following formula:

  $$\text{Availability} = \text{Uptime}/(\text{Uptime}+\text{Downtime})$$

  For example, if a system was in operation for 365 x 24 x 60 = *525,600* minutes (1 year), of which it was unavailable for 30 minutes for any reason, then its availability is approximately *0.99994292563* or *99.994292563%*. For comparison, some AWS S3 storage classes have availability of "*11 9*'s" or *99.999999999%*.

Performance and availability can be (and often are) connected. For example, when a system is not performing with a required level of quality, it may become unavailable soon due to resource contention, which may be caused by bad planning and insufficient allocation of resources or a **(Distributed) Denial-of-Service** (**(D)DOS**) attack. Therefore, it is important to consider both of these factors together when planning for a distributed system, such as OpenShift, that will run your applications. Let us take a closer look at how these problems are dealt with by OpenShift.

Vertical versus horizontal scaling

When your application is underperforming due to a lack of compute resources, the logical step is to add more CPU, RAM, or better storage. But one can only scale a single machine so far - even though you can find servers with terabytes (TB) of RAM, with a theoretical addressable limit of 4 petabytes (PB) for modern CPUs, this is a hard limit that has to be considered nonetheless (while 64-bit CPU architecture theoretically allows for 16 million PBs of addressable memory, modern processors only use 52 bits). As history has taught us, the *640 KB should be enough for everybody* approach is not a commercially sound strategy. The number of CPUs supported by a single motherboard is limited too - by such factors as technological process (commonly expressed in nanometers, *nm*) and packaging.

In other words, increasing compute and storage resources on a single machine provides only short-term benefits for performance, merely delaying the inevitable - the moment when your system has no more capacity for additional users that keep coming (assuming your business is doing well and expanding, of course).

There is also another important consideration. When you keep investing all your resources in a single machine, it becomes more valuable and less replaceable. The more hardware you add to it in order to keep up with the demands of the business, the greater the likelihood that a piece of hardware will eventually fail. Fixing the problem may be risky and may result in downtime for maintenance, which will mean loss of money for the business. Mathematically, this can be expressed with the following formula:

$$P(\bar{X}) = 1 - \prod_{i=1}^{n} p_n$$

where P(X) is the probability of failure of an entire system/machine, p_n is the probability that a single component will not fail, and i=1∏n (product). As you can see, the more components we "plug" in, each posing a certain risk of failure, the greater the probability of failure for the entire system. This approach is used to analyze the resilience of electric circuits - for example, if we plug multiple elements sequentially, what is the risk that the current will not be able to complete the circuit at some point? Even though it has been historically applied to electric circuits, the underlying problem is still the same - when the resilience of a system depends on the resilience of *all* components, what is the risk that it will fail?

The approach we just discussed is called *scaling up* or *vertical scaling*, as opposed to *scaling out* or *horizontal scaling* - the alternate and preferred way of dealing with the problem of limited resources and low availability. As we established in *Chapter 3*, in the *Traditional concepts and OpenShift core APIs* section, this means adding more servers running copies of your application to your fleet to keep up with increasing demand. Not only that, but scaling out has other extra benefits compared to scaling up:

- **Increased availability**: When one machine fails, others can take over so that end users are unaffected. Ideally, different machines have to be placed in different *failure domains* to reduce the risk of simultaneous failures. This will be discussed in more detail later in this section.
- **Easier maintenance:** When we need to upgrade hardware or the OS, or introduce a change, we can safely take one server down as long as there is at least one more to serve clients' requests.

- **Locality:** For example, if you're running OpenShift in a public cloud provider, such as AWS, and you have an application that needs to access an external (to OpenShift) service running in the same **availability zone** (**AZ**), you may want to schedule it on a node in the same AZ to lower latency and avoid inter-AZ traffic charges.
- **Safer releases:** When all you have is a single server running your application, you have very little room for mistakes, assuming the application in question can even be updated live without interruption of service. If an update is unsuccessful, you have to roll back – all while your clients are using the application. When you have multiple servers, you can safely remove your machines from a load balancer's pool and update them one by one or in batches. See *Chapter 3*, in the *Traditional concepts and OpenShift core APIs* section, for more details on various deployment strategies.

Let us take a closer look at availability since it bears the most relevance to this book.

Having more machines means higher availability because they work in parallel, analogous to how an electric circuit with multiple elements connected in parallel is complete as long as there is at least one element through which a current can flow. Contrary to the example of sequentially connected elements, a mathematical representation of this problem is expressed here:

$$Q(\bar{X}) = \prod_{i=1}^{n} q_n$$

where Q(X) is the probability of failure for a system with components connected in parallel and q_n is the risk of failure of a single element. Notice that Q(X) diminishes as *n* increases (since each q < 1, their product will be less than the smallest of operands), meaning that the more paths there are for the current, the less likelihood that all of them will fail, which is quite evident from everyday experience. Putting this in the context of this book means that a service becomes more resilient to failures and more available the more separate servers/application replicas serving user requests we have.

The law we have just established is only relevant for *completely independent* components, which is not the case in reality. Even if you spin up another server/VM/container running your application, it will still share some underlying infrastructure with its ilk – be it an ESXi host (in the case of VMware), network, datacenter, or region. These are collectively referred to as *failure domains*, as they represent an interdependency between contained systems that can lead to their simultaneous failure. There is no such thing as *completely* independent failure domains, only *sufficiently* independent. For our discussion of OpenShift on VMware, that means spreading cluster nodes across multiple failure domains on different levels, such as the following:

- Datacenters or regions (supported since OpenShift 4.13)
- Clusters or availability zones (supported since OpenShift 4.13)
- **Power Distribution Units** (**PDUs**) that power a set of server racks
- Individual server racks
- Hypervisors or ESXi hosts

Again, it does not always make sense financially or may not be technically possible to implement all the levels above, so plan based on the requirements of your organization and risks that you're willing to accept.

Scaling out and scaling in in OpenShift

Depending on the platform where OpenShift is installed, one or two scaling methods are supported:

- **Manual**, which follows the same steps as when adding worker machines during installation. It involves using the same ignition file, `worker.ign`, and therefore is not covered here. Please refer to *Chapter 3, Getting Started with OpenShift*, for more details.
- **Automated**, which relies on the Machine API. It is supported only for clusters installed with platform-specific (not *platform: none*) configuration in `install-config.yaml`. For the UPI installation approach used for this book, this method requires additional configuration.

Let us examine the automated approach in more detail.

Creating a MachineSet

1. First, export the kubeconfig for your cluster into your shell. If you followed the installation procedure from *Chapter 3*, the following command would do it:

```
$ export KUBECONFIG=~/learning-ocp4/auth/kubeconfig
```

2. To interact with vSphere and manage the lifecycle of VMs, the machine controller needs vSphere credentials. They are stored in the `vsphere-cloud-credentials` secret in the `openshift-machine-api` namespace and can be extracted with the following command:

```
$ oc get secret/vsphere-cloud-credentials -o go-template='{{range
$k,$v := .data}}{{printf "%s: " $k}}{{if not $v}}{{$v}}{{else}}{{$v |
base64decode}}{{end}}{{"\n"}}{{end}}' -n openshift-machine-api
```

Here is what the expected output looks like:

```
REDACTED.password: REDACTED
REDACTED.username: REDACTED
[ausov@bastion learning-ocp4]$
```

Figure 6.1: Base64-encoded vSphere access credentials

> Part of the preceding command, enclosed in '' (single quotes), is not an OpenShift CLI command, but a special construct called a Go template. It is used to present the output in a custom format and is considered an advanced way of manipulating data.

3. Another component required by the Machine API for provisioning new nodes is an ignition configuration that you are already familiar with from *Chapter 3*. It contains a link to the endpoint on the **Machine Config Server** (**MCS**), where worker ignition configuration can be obtained and the certificate bundle required to validate the certificate presented by MCS. It is stored in

the worker-user-data secret in the openshift-machine-api namespace:

```
$ oc get secret/worker-user-data -o go-template='{{range $k,$v := .data}}
{{printf "%s: " $k}}{{if not $v}}{{$v}}{{else}}{{$v | base64decode}}
{{end}}{{"\n"}}{{end}}' -n openshift-machine-api
```

This is what it looks like:


```
disableTemplating: true

userData: {"ignition":{"config":{"merge":[{"source":"https://api-int.ocp4.example.com:22623/config/worker"
]},"security":{"tls":{"certificateAuthorities":[{"source":"data:text/plain;charset=utf-8;base64,LS0tLS1CRU
JTiBDRVJUSUZJQ0FURS0tLS0tCk1JSURFRENDQWZpZ0F3SUJBZ01JRUtjR2dJZUdmZ293RFFZSktvWklodmNOQVFFTEJRQXdKakVTTUJBR
ExVUUKQ3hNSmIzQmxibk5vYVdaME1SQXdEZ1lEVlFRREV3ZHliMjkwTFdOaE1CNFhEVEkxTURnd016QTJNVGN3TVZvWApEVE0xTURnd01U
TJNVGN3TVZvd0pqRVNNQkFHQTFVRUN4TUpiM0JsYm5Ob2FXWjBNUkF3RGdZRFZRUURFd2R5CmIyOTBMV05oTUlJQklqQU5CZ2txaGtpRzl
MEJBUUVGQUFPQ0FROEFNSUlCQ2dLQ0FRRUF1WHhxUCt1Y2Vnb24KSzVpNm9QamhubFFnOUxESkw5dDRSYUU3VG1RVy9jSXNqYStMQXJ6Y0
wd09FNlZIY3BxZ0RQbHUvWGdVUnYwNgp3MElhclFybWV6aGVhb1RYQjBpakhpekE2TUdEYjg3ZWVPSFBHdmxwc05YNzBhTWQvVksxTFVNR
JkNjMzQktSCmw4SUVsYjVWVDNKZVJ0SExGdDlNdHdiOC9paXFXTkljNWpkeUpmbWYwNWtBYW4xTlQ4KzlMdmtZNHFmcVFGUWEKaEtMRWtJ
WFwdG5mcW1DSTNLL2dnWFBlMlVMNVp1U0hDbDdyQkR2eUNmNldnRFNHVitLYUJibyt2MmNrbkx6dgo0RFZVZ01HNjBaU1ZUTUlheHlPYjc
azVkUU44RFVTTEN2bnBKZDg1aW9USHFHZndObE1iRjZ1VlIxRHJibXZqCkV3dXY5SmJYOHdJREFRQUJvME13UURBT0JnTlZIUThCQWY4RU
BTUNBcVF3RHdZRFZSMFRBUUgvQkFVd0F3RUIKL3pBZEJnTlZIUTRFRmdRVXNsZFpZNFJFQ3ZHQ3VoVXVBbXZkSGhqYXg4NHdEUVlKS29aS
h2Y05BUUVMQlFBRApnZ0VCQUg0aEtrTW1ieUVmc1lWeW1QSnp3M25jTGlkWVdZQ3ZjVTFNczlBbnBkaW96enlDeWhzMitrVlp1NlkrCmZY
zA5eWZheDUzKzRtdmRTTytNZjczdGhuRGR1dWMxck1pSEVRY3lUVmxNVElEWlZoaUQzbVpScHdscTZidWMKNStBZXZrWk80bGh3cUJEYTJ
cDlGZG9vS3FHUmZJV0RUTlNSMFl3TDBTZ0VnN1ptVmxYS1VyTm5HVFhDSkpYMAprbnV2TG9IRUNFNnhYbVdWY25wcWN2ZzRJSklmL2lCa2
mUU8vMGRjbDNCSGwzU3dsS0xPTC9CSW1nNHJCVWZNCkhrQkp6Vm5xUmdGc2JLVlJ3b3ZlbWNvTHV4SEdVcGFEN0NNR1BnVW1FZFVOa2QrQ
l5ZUs4SGpMMGFhVTZ1MjQKZ2k1TmY2aVl1VXJWaHVNOEM4MEJpT3ZPY3BzPQotLS0tLUVORCBDRVJUSUZJQ0FURS0tLS0tCg=="}]}},"ve
rsion":"3.2.0"}}
```


Figure 6.2: Worker ignition configuration

4. The last missing piece is a MachineSet itself that will instruct the Machine API on which OVA template to use for new nodes, as well as where to deploy them in vSphere. The chapters/6/snippets/machineset-infra.yml file in this book's GitHub repository provides the manifest.

   While the names of most placeholders are self-explanatory, CLUSTER_INFRA_ID is unique to every cluster and must be the same across all MachineSets of a given cluster. It can be extracted with the following command:

   ```
   $ oc get -o jsonpath='{.status.infrastructureName}{"\n"}' infrastructure
   cluster
   ```

   Replace CLUSTER_INFRA_ID with the value from the output, as well as other placeholders with what makes sense for your infrastructure, and create the MachineSet:

   ```
   $ oc create -f chapters/6/snippets/machineset-infra.yml
   ```

> You may see the `Warning: providerSpec.diskGiB: 100 is missing or less than the recommended minimum (120): nodes may fail to start if disk size is too low` message, because we have chosen to use a 100 GB disk for consistency, which is less than the recommended 120 GB. Since this is a lab and not a production environment, this warning can be safely ignored. In enterprise clusters, however, it's common to have a 200 GB disk per node.

5. Now, let us make sure the MachineSet was created successfully:

```
$ oc get machine,machineset -n openshift-machine-api
```

As you can see, it has already begun provisioning one machine, as specified in the `spec.replicas` field:

```
NAME                                                  PHASE          TYPE   REGION   ZONE   AGE
machine.machine.openshift.io/ocp4-q8bhf-infra-jrrk6   Provisioning                          3s

NAME                                             DESIRED   CURRENT   READY   AVAILABLE   AGE
machineset.machine.openshift.io/ocp4-q8bhf-infra   1         1                             3s
```

Figure 6.3: Machine provisioning in progress

Machines managed by the Machine API go through the following stages during their lifecycle: *Provisioning* > *Provisioned* > *Running* > *Deleting*. If something goes wrong on the cloud or virtualization provider's side, you will see a `Failed` status, in which case you should examine the conditions of the machine itself or the machine controller's logs in the `openshift-machine-api` namespace:

```
$ oc logs -f machine-api-controllers-xxxxxxxxxx-xxxxx -n openshift-
machine-api
$ oc get -o yaml machine/<MACHINE> -n openshift-machine-api
```

6. Use the following command to list cluster nodes every second:

```
$ watch -n1 oc get no
```

Shortly after a machine enters the `Running` state, the corresponding node is created and joins the cluster (from here on out, the output is abbreviated; we're not showing the three initial infra nodes we created back in *Chapter 4, Post-Install Configuration*):

```
NAME                         STATUS   ROLES                  AGE   VERSION
master-1.ocp4.example.com    Ready    control-plane,master   56m   v1.29.7+4510e9c
master-2.ocp4.example.com    Ready    control-plane,master   54m   v1.29.7+4510e9c
master-3.ocp4.example.com    Ready    control-plane,master   50m   v1.29.7+4510e9c
ocp4-q8bhf-infra-jrrk6       Ready    infra,worker           62s   v1.29.7+4510e9c
worker-1.ocp4.example.com    Ready    worker                 38m   v1.29.7+4510e9c
worker-2.ocp4.example.com    Ready    worker                 38m   v1.29.7+4510e9c
worker-3.ocp4.example.com    Ready    worker                 38m   v1.29.7+4510e9c
```

Figure 6.4: Provisioned node joined the cluster

In our lab, it took a machine about 2 minutes to provision a VM and less than a minute to join the cluster. If a new node is not showing up, but the corresponding machine is provisioned, check its console logs in vCenter – perhaps, there is a problem with IP address assignment, and it can't fetch an ignition config from the API.

7. Let's check whether the corresponding machine has been created:

```
$ oc get machine,machineset -n openshift-machine-api
```

A new machine should appear:

```
NAME                                                  PHASE     TYPE   REGION   ZONE   AGE
machine.machine.openshift.io/ocp4-q8bhf-infra-jrrk6   Running                          3m37s

NAME                                             DESIRED   CURRENT   READY   AVAILABLE   AGE
machineset.machine.openshift.io/ocp4-q8bhf-infra   1         1         1       1           3m37s
```

Figure 6.5: Machine provisioning complete

Adding worker nodes

1. Now that we have a MachineSet, adding more workers is as easy as executing a simple command to scale the MachineSet:

```
$ oc scale machineset/ocp4-q8bhf-infra --replicas 3 -n openshift-machine-api
```

2. If you run `oc get no` again in a couple of minutes, two more nodes will show up in the list after their corresponding machines are provisioned:

```
NAME                       STATUS   ROLES                  AGE   VERSION
master-1.ocp4.example.com  Ready    control-plane,master   80m   v1.29.7+4510e9c
master-2.ocp4.example.com  Ready    control-plane,master   78m   v1.29.7+4510e9c
master-3.ocp4.example.com  Ready    control-plane,master   75m   v1.29.7+4510e9c
ocp4-q8bhf-infra-gt658     Ready    infra,worker           49s   v1.29.7+4510e9c
ocp4-q8bhf-infra-jrrk6     Ready    infra,worker           24m   v1.29.7+4510e9c
ocp4-q8bhf-infra-ksdkf     Ready    infra,worker           51s   v1.29.7+4510e9c
worker-1.ocp4.example.com  Ready    worker                 63m   v1.29.7+4510e9c
worker-2.ocp4.example.com  Ready    worker                 62m   v1.29.7+4510e9c
worker-3.ocp4.example.com  Ready    worker                 63m   v1.29.7+4510e9c
```

Figure 6.6: Two more nodes are added by scaling the MachineSet

This is similar to how you add more instances of your application by scaling the corresponding **ReplicaSet** or **Deployment**.

3. Now list the machines again:

```
$ oc get machine -n openshift-machine-api
```

As always, there is a one-to-one relationship between machines and nodes:

```
[ausov@bastion learning-ocp4]$ KUBECONFIG=auth/kubeconfig oc get machine -n openshift-machine-api
NAME                     PHASE     TYPE   REGION   ZONE   AGE
ocp4-q8bhf-infra-gt658   Running                          109m
ocp4-q8bhf-infra-jrrk6   Running                          113m
ocp4-q8bhf-infra-ksdkf   Running                          109m
```

Figure 6.7: Each node corresponds to a running machine

4. Now, let us suppose we need to scale our MachineSet down. The question is, which machines will be removed, and more generally, in which order are the machines removed? This is governed by MachineSet's `.spec.deletePolicy` field, which defaults to `Random`, meaning that a random machine will be randomly selected. This is not always what we want, because this may require extra rescheduling of workloads, if a node selected has been running since the cluster was installed and is already at capacity. We can override this behavior by adding a special annotation to the machine that we want to be removed first:

```
$ oc annotate machine/ocp4-q8bhf-infra-ksdkf machine.openshift.io/delete-machine="true" -n openshift-machine-api
```

5. Now let us scale our MachineSet down to two instances:

```
$ oc scale machineset/ocp4-q8bhf-infra --replicas 2 -n openshift-machine-api
$ oc get machine -n openshift-machine-api
```

Indeed, the annotated machine was deleted:

```
[ausov@bastion learning-ocp4]$ KUBECONFIG=auth/kubeconfig oc get machine -n openshift-machine-api
NAME                       PHASE     TYPE   REGION   ZONE   AGE
ocp4-q8bhf-infra-gt658     Running                          110m
ocp4-q8bhf-infra-jrrk6     Running                          114m
```

Figure 6.8: Marking a machine for a prioritized removal

> If you set the annotation on a machine before it reaches the `Running` phase, it will be deleted shortly thereafter.
>
> If the annotation is set on more than one machine, they will be deleted in the reverse creation order, which is analogous to `.spec.deletePolicy: Newest`, discussed next in this section.

When a MachineSet scales in, a decision has to be made: in which order to delete machines and corresponding nodes. On the surface, this may not seem like an important consideration – after all, machines are supposed to be easily replaceable and identical to each other. In reality, however, there are different factors influencing this decision. For example, machines that were created last typically have fewer pods running on them if they were added recently. In this case, removing them takes less time because each node is drained of all pods before removal, and a lot of pods take longer to evict.

Let us see how different delete policies work.

Machine delete policies

The MachineSet API supports several delete policies that determine the order in which machines are removed when scale-in is triggered. Let's examine them one by one:

1. First, set `.spec.deletePolicy` to `Newest` in your MachineSet:

```
$ oc patch -p '{"spec": {"deletePolicy": "Newest"}}' --type=merge
machineset/ocp4-q8bhf-infra -n openshift-machine-api
```

2. Now let us scale our MachineSet to 4 nodes in order to have a more representative dataset to work with:

```
$ oc scale machineset/ocp4-q8bhf-infra --replicas 4 -n openshift-machine-
api
```

3. Wait until all machines have finished provisioning and list them:

```
$ oc get machine -n openshift-machine-api
```

Note the order in which they were created:

```
[ausov@bastion learning-ocp4]$ KUBECONFIG=auth/kubeconfig oc get machine -n openshift-machine-api
NAME                      PHASE     TYPE   REGION   ZONE   AGE
ocp4-q8bhf-infra-47977    Running                          2m12s
ocp4-q8bhf-infra-gt658    Running                          121m
ocp4-q8bhf-infra-jrrk6    Running                          125m
ocp4-q8bhf-infra-zqxk2    Running                          2m13s
[ausov@bastion learning-ocp4]$
```

Figure 6.9: MachineSet scaled to four replicas

You can run this command with `--sort-by .metadata.creationTimestamp` to display objects in the order they were created for easier tracking.

4. Next, scale the MachineSet down to 2 instances:

```
$ oc scale machineset/ocp4-q8bhf-infra --replicas 2 -n openshift-machine-
api
$ oc get machine -n openshift-machine-api
```

As expected, the two most recently created machines were deleted:

```
[ausov@bastion learning-ocp4]$ KUBECONFIG=auth/kubeconfig oc get machine -n openshift-machine-api
NAME                      PHASE     TYPE   REGION   ZONE   AGE
ocp4-q8bhf-infra-gt658    Running                          123m
ocp4-q8bhf-infra-jrrk6    Running                          127m
[ausov@bastion learning-ocp4]$
```

Figure 6.10: Only the oldest machines remain with deletePolicy set to Newest after an automatic scale-in

5. Moving on to the next `deletePolicy`, `Oldest`, scale the MachineSet to 4 machines again:

```
$ oc scale machineset/ocp4-q8bhf-infra --replicas 4 -n openshift-machine-
api
```

6. Again, wait until all machines have finished provisioning and list them:

```
$ oc get machine -n openshift-machine-api
```

   Note the order in which they were created:

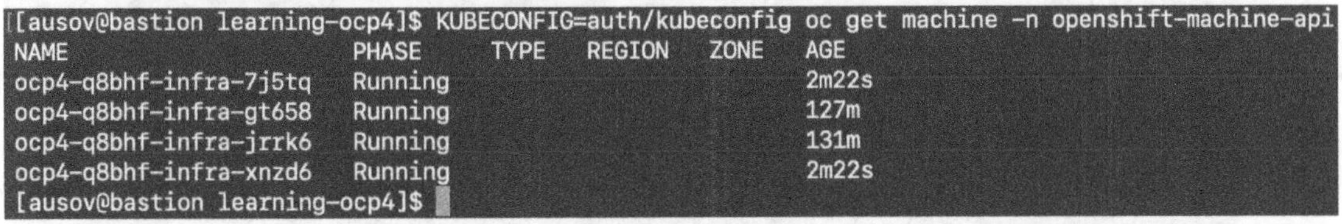

Figure 6.11: Scaling out to four replicas again for another test; the 7j5tq and xnzd6 machines are the newest

7. Next, change the MachineSet's `deletePolicy` to `Oldest`:

```
$ oc patch -p '{"spec": {"deletePolicy": "Oldest"}}' --type=merge
machineset/ocp4-q8bhf-infra -n openshift-machine-api
```

8. Scale the MachineSet down again to 2 nodes:

```
$ oc scale machineset/ocp4-q8bhf-infra --replicas 2 -n openshift-machine-
api
$ oc get machine -n openshift-machine-api
```

   In accordance with the new policy, the 2 oldest machines were removed:

Figure 6.12: The oldest machines were removed; only the ones added recently remain

9. To prepare for the last test, restore the number of replicas of your MachineSet:

```
$ oc scale machineset/ocp4-q8bhf-infra --replicas 4 -n openshift-machine-
api
```

10. As before, wait until all machines have finished provisioning and list them with the following command:

```
$ oc get machine -n openshift-machine-api
```

   Once again, note the order in which they were created:

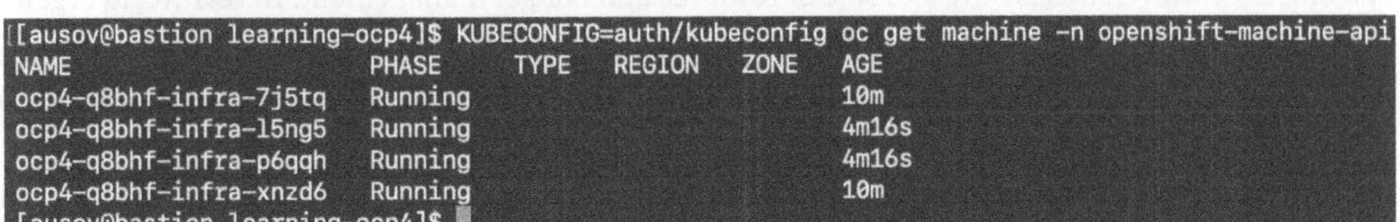

Figure 6.13: Restoring the MachineSet to four replicas for the final test

11. Now we will remove the `.spec.deletePolicy` field altogether so that it falls back to the default, `Random`:

```
$ oc patch -p '[{"path": "/spec/deletePolicy", "op": "remove"}]' --type
json machineset/ocp4-q8bhf-infra -n openshift-machine-api
```

12. Let us see what happens when we scale back into 2 replicas:

```
$ oc scale machineset/ocp4-q8bhf-infra --replicas 2 -n openshift-machine-
api
$ oc get machine -n openshift-machine-api
```

This time, no particular order was used, and machines to delete were selected randomly, as expected:

```
[ausov@bastion learning-ocp4]$ KUBECONFIG=auth/kubeconfig oc get machine -n openshift-machine-api
NAME                       PHASE     TYPE   REGION   ZONE   AGE
ocp4-q8bhf-infra-p6qqh     Running                          5m46s
ocp4-q8bhf-infra-xnzd6     Running                          11m
[ausov@bastion learning-ocp4]$
```

Figure 6.14: Two machines were picked randomly for deletion

If you are quick and list the nodes of your cluster right after you initiate a scale down, you may notice that the nodes being deleted briefly transition into the `SchedulingDisabled` phase. This is by design – in order to gracefully migrate all workloads that may have been scheduled on a node since its creation elsewhere in a cluster, the machine controller cordons it off and initiates the drain operation (more on it in the next section). Sometimes this may not be required, or something, such as a misconfigured `PodDisruptionBudget` (more on it in the next section), may block the operation, in which case it will never succeed, and the node will not be removed. In such scenarios, you may use the following annotation to skip draining (provided it is safe for the application in question):

```
$ oc annotate machine/<MACHINE> machine.openshift.io/exclude-node-
draining="true" -n openshift-machine-api
```

Now that we have mastered the process of adding and removing nodes using the Machine API, let's explore the topic of removing them manually, which is something you may be required to do when the Machine API is not available, such as on bare-metal clusters.

Removing workers manually

Scaling out is necessary when your business expands, launching new products and attracting new customers. However, this is only one side of resource and budget management. In real-world organizations, you may encounter the following scenarios:

- New products don't always make it to the general availability phase, and old projects are decommissioned to free up compute resources and reduce costs.
- Downsizing applications' requests (capacity reserved for successful scheduling) to match their usage pattern more closely and cut costs by reclaiming excess capacity.

- Moving from one datacenter to another, when you gradually reduce the capacity of your old cluster while increasing the capacity of the new one.
- When a node becomes inoperative due to a hardware failure. Performing maintenance on a node is not always worth the time and effort, especially in cloud environments – a better approach is to replace the faulty node completely.

All of these scenarios involve *scaling in* or removing nodes from your cluster.

Contrary to adding nodes, removing them is much easier and comes down to the following steps:

1. Draining all workloads from the node, allowing them to complete gracefully and restart on other nodes:

   ```
   $ oc adm drain <NODE> --ignore-daemonsets --delete-emptydir-data --force
   ```

   Draining may not be able to be completed within the timeout due to an API resource called `PodDisruptionBudget`, whose job is to make sure that a certain number of an application's replicas are running at any time. More on it in *Chapter 10, Deployment to OpenShift.*

2. Removing the node:

   ```
   $ oc delete no/<NODE>
   ```

   At this point, we can still change our minds and get the node back. If SSH is enabled, connect to the node as the `core` user and restart the kubelet: `sudo systemctl restart kubelet`. The node will immediately re-join the cluster. If SSH is not enabled, you can simply power-cycle the node; when it reboots, it'll re-join the cluster just the same.

   After the node re-joins the cluster, its MachineConfigPool may switch to infinitely `UPDATING`, which you may notice if you run `oc get mcp`:

```
NAME     CONFIG                                             UPDATED   UPDATING   DEGRADED
infra    rendered-infra-dcf7cf9b8965a7e2520d84dd55940fe9    True      False      False
master   rendered-master-48c100ec1f76e308d737729bdfb4a112   True      False      False
worker   rendered-worker-dcf7cf9b8965a7e2520d84dd55940fe9   False     True       False
```

Figure 6.15: A node's MCP switches to UPDATING when the node is removed

   If you run `oc describe no/NODE` on the node that just re-joined, you will see the following message in its annotations:

   ```
   missing MachineConfig \nmachineconfig.machineconfiguration.openshift.io
   \"\" not found"
   ```

   If this happens, you will need to restart the `MachineConfigDaemon` pod running on that node:

   ```
   $ MCD_POD=$(oc get po -l k8s-app=machine-config-daemon -o wide -n
   openshift-machine-config-operator | grep <NODE> | cut -d' ' -f1)
   $ oc delete po/$MCD_POD -n openshift-machine-config-operator
   ```

That should fix the problem and the MCP should be back to `UPDATED`:

```
NAME     CONFIG                                              UPDATED   UPDATING   DEGRADED
infra    rendered-infra-dcf7cf9b8965a7e2520d84dd55940fe9     True      False      False
master   rendered-master-48c100ec1f76e308d737729bdfb4a112    True      False      False
worker   rendered-worker-dcf7cf9b8965a7e2520d84dd55940fe9    True      False      False
```

Figure 6.16: The MCP of a re-added node is restored back to normal after re-creating its MCD pod

3. Decommissioning the node: This step may involve wiping off the OS and using whatever means are mandated by a given organization to destroy all remaining data on the node's storage devices.

Autoscaling

Being able to scale a cluster manually or using the OpenShift API is certainly useful, however, it is not always possible to predict the load that your cluster will experience and when, so in order to achieve true elasticity, we need a mechanism that can scale our clusters automatically for us based on certain rules. OpenShift provides two APIs for autoscaling:

- **ClusterAutoscaler**: Defines the lower and upper limits for autoscaling, expressed in the number of CPU cores, amount of memory, and number of nodes, which include master nodes as well, even though they are not managed by an autoscaler. It also has fields for various rules regarding scale down, such as `delayAfterAdd` (how long to wait before deleting a node, after a node has been added) or `utilizationThreshold` (percentage of combined resource requests relative to the total capacity of a node, below which a node triggers scale down operation).
- **MachineAutoscaler**: Governs the size of a specific MachineSet that it references by specifying the lower and upper boundaries for the number of machines.

Keep in mind the following when using the autoscaling feature:

- Specify resource requests (usually CPU and memory) for your workloads, as they are used by the autoscaler to determine whether your cluster has reached its capacity and a new node is required.
- Do not use any autoscaling features provided by the underlying cloud or virtualization platform, such as AWS EC2 Auto Scaling, as it may conflict with the OpenShift autoscaler.
- Make sure your underlying platform can support the maximum number of nodes that may be provisioned by the autoscaler. Depending on your platform, this can be either your total hardware capacity or a cloud provider's quota.

Configuring autoscaling

Now that we have learned the basics, it is time to practice.

1. Start by using the `chapters/6/snippets/clusterautoscaler-default.yml` file from this book's GitHub repository to create a ClusterAutoscaler:

```
$ oc create -f chapters/6/snippets/clusterautoscaler-default.yml
```

2. Next, we will need to create a `MachineAutoscaler` resource that references the MachineSet we prepared earlier. Use the `chapters/6/snippets/machineautoscaler-CLUSTER_INFRA_ID-infra.yml` file from the same repository (replace the placeholder with the name of your MachineSet):

```
$ oc create -f chapters/6/snippets/machineautoscaler-CLUSTER_INFRA_ID-
infra.yml
```

3. If you use the `describe` operation on the newly created `MachineAutoscaler`, you will notice that it was correctly linked to our MachineSet:

```
$ oc describe machineautoscaler -n openshift-machine-api
```

As you can see, your ClusterAutoscaler now references the desired MachineSet that it is supposed to scale:

```
Events:
  Type    Reason             Age                From                           Message
  ----    ------             ----               ----                           -------
  Normal  SuccessfulUpdate   19s (x3 over 19s)  machine_autoscaler_controller  Updated MachineAutoscaler target: openshift-machine-api/ocp4-q8bhf-infra
```

Figure 6.17: ClusterAutoscaler was successfully linked to a MachineAutoscaler

4. Let us take a closer look at the internals of that MachineSet:

```
$ oc get -o yaml machineset/ocp4-q8bhf-infra -n openshift-machine-api
```

As you can see, it was annotated by the autoscaling controller with the minimum and maximum number of nodes:

```
apiVersion: machine.openshift.io/v1beta1
kind: MachineSet
metadata:
  annotations:
    autoscaling.openshift.io/machineautoscaler: openshift-machine-api/ocp4-q8bhf-infra
    capacity.cluster-autoscaler.kubernetes.io/cpu: "8"
    capacity.cluster-autoscaler.kubernetes.io/memory: "34359738368"
    machine.openshift.io/cluster-api-autoscaler-node-group-max-size: "3"
    machine.openshift.io/cluster-api-autoscaler-node-group-min-size: "1"
```

Figure 6.18: ClusterAutoscaler-specific annotations on the MachineSet

5. If we list the machines about 5 minutes after creating both `ClusterAutoscaler` and `MachineAutoscaler`, we will see that one of the machines we created earlier has been removed, as it was not needed, as specified in `.spec.scaleDown.unneededTime` of the `ClusterAutoscaler` and `.spec.minReplicas` of the `MachineAutoscaler`:

```
$ oc get machine -n openshift-machine-api
```

As expected, there is only one machine running now:

```
[ausov@bastion learning-ocp4]$ KUBECONFIG=auth/kubeconfig oc get machine -n openshift-machine-api
NAME                     PHASE     TYPE   REGION   ZONE   AGE
ocp4-q8bhf-infra-p6qqh   Running                          4h2m
[ausov@bastion learning-ocp4]$
```

Figure 6.19: ClusterAutoscaler removed all nodes but one in the absence of demand

Now let's see autoscaling in action.

Triggering autoscaling

In order to see how autoscaling works, we need to create a situation where our cluster cannot satisfy a workload's requests and is forced to spin up one or more nodes. To that end, we will create a number of pods with containers launched from a `busybox` image. They will not do anything, except wait for 1 hour (3,600 seconds) before completing:

1. Use the `chapters/6/snippets/deploy-busybox-autoscale.yml` file from this book's GitHub repository to create a deployment in a new project named `test`:

```
$ oc new-project test
$ oc create -f chapters/6/snippets/deploy-busybox-autoscale.yml
```

> As you may recall, we specified the `spec.template.spec.taints` field in our MachineSet to mimic how infrastructure nodes are created. Therefore, in order to be able to use these nodes, we needed to configure the corresponding toleration in the preceding deployment.

If you examine the YAML manifest, you will see that the deployment starts a single replica of a pod with only one container that requests 6 vCPUs and 16 Gi of RAM. Requests are required for this test to work because the cluster autoscaler uses them to determine whether a cluster has enough capacity to start a pod.

2. We are starting with just one replica for now, so that you can see how it consumes the node's resources:

```
$ oc get po -o wide
```

As the following output demonstrates, the pod successfully started on the second worker (the node may be different in your lab):

Figure 6.20: One replica of a test application is running

3. Let us examine the node on which that replica was scheduled more closely:

```
$ oc describe no/worker-2.ocp4.example.com
```

As you will notice, the pod's requests for CPU and memory contribute to the node's allocated resources. These are reserved resources, which means that even though they may not necessarily be used by the pod, they are now non-allocatable to other workloads:

```
  Namespace                                 Name                                                         CPU Requests  CPU Limits  Memory Requests
  ---------                                 ----                                                         ------------  ----------  ---------------
  openshift-cluster-csi-drivers             vmware-vsphere-csi-driver-node-dbqpw                         30m (0%)      0 (0%)      150Mi (0%)
  openshift-cluster-node-tuning-operator    tuned-vj8jr                                                  10m (0%)      0 (0%)      50Mi (0%)
  openshift-dns                             dns-default-kkfzm                                            60m (0%)      0 (0%)      110Mi (0%)
  openshift-dns                             node-resolver-m4rmd                                          5m (0%)       0 (0%)      21Mi (0%)
  openshift-image-registry                  node-ca-bqt6l                                                10m (0%)      0 (0%)      10Mi (0%)
  openshift-ingress-canary                  ingress-canary-6cqd4                                         10m (0%)      0 (0%)      20Mi (0%)
  openshift-ingress                         router-default-674d7977b8-7mk27                              100m (1%)     0 (0%)      256Mi (0%)
  openshift-machine-config-operator         kube-rbac-proxy-crio-worker-2.ocp4.                          20m (0%)      0 (0%)      50Mi (0%)
  openshift-machine-config-operator         machine-config-daemon-pck4w                                  40m (0%)      0 (0%)      100Mi (0%)
  openshift-monitoring                      monitoring-plugin-76ff987cd7-bzhmn                           10m (0%)      0 (0%)      50Mi (0%)
  openshift-monitoring                      node-exporter-tz2qm                                          9m (0%)       0 (0%)      47Mi (0%)
  openshift-monitoring                      prometheus-adapter-5cd6db788-2vqb2                           1m (0%)       0 (0%)      40Mi (0%)
  openshift-monitoring                      prometheus-operator-admission-webhook-77bbf6ddf7-cr9m9       5m (0%)       0 (0%)      30Mi (0%)
  openshift-monitoring                      telemeter-client-58dc76bf8d-httrk                            3m (0%)       0 (0%)      70Mi (0%)
  openshift-multus                          multus-4b161                                                 10m (0%)      0 (0%)      65Mi (0%)
  openshift-multus                          multus-additional-cni-plugins-dtx44                          10m (0%)      0 (0%)      10Mi (0%)
  openshift-multus                          network-metrics-daemon-d8t7v                                 20m (0%)      0 (0%)      120Mi (0%)
  openshift-network-diagnostics             network-check-source-5cdb6bfcbf-t6mb5                        10m (0%)      0 (0%)      40Mi (0%)
  openshift-network-diagnostics             network-check-target-ggdmn                                   10m (0%)      0 (0%)      15Mi (0%)
  openshift-ovn-kubernetes                  ovnkube-node-9bnw7                                           80m (1%)      0 (0%)      1630Mi (5%)
  test                                      test-7969df6998-27x5v                                        6 (80%)       0 (0%)      16Gi (52%)
Allocated resources:
  (Total limits may be over 100 percent, i.e., overcommitted.)
  Resource           Requests        Limits
  --------           --------        ------
  cpu                6453m (86%)     0 (0%)
  memory             19268Mi (62%)   0 (0%)
```

Figure 6.21: CPU and memory reserved for the pod as per its resource requests

4. Given the node's capacity of 8 vCPUs and 32 GB RAM, it cannot accommodate another replica, as doing so would put combined memory requests on that node over 100%, but combined requests cannot exceed the capacity of a node. That means that even under ideal circumstances (no other applications requesting resources), we can run one replica of our deployment at most, and we have only three schedulable nodes (masters are unschedulable, and all four infra nodes are tainted). Let us scale our deployment to 8 replicas (one per worker node + one per original infra node + one for the infra node created by the MachineSet + one more in excess) to exhaust what little capacity our cluster has and trigger autoscaling:

```
$ oc scale deploy/test --replicas=8
```

5. Use the following command to check where your pods were scheduled:

```
$ oc get po -o wide
```

Notice that while the scheduler was able to find nodes for 6 more pods, one remains in the `Pending` phase:

```
test-7969df6998-pxjdd   0/1     Pending   0          2s    <none>        <none>
```

Figure 6.22: One replica couldn't be scheduled due to insufficient capacity

6. Now, in order to accommodate the remaining replica, we need to add at least 1 more node, which is exactly what the machine autoscaler will do. Check the machines in your cluster:

```
$ oc get machine -n openshift-machine-api
```

Once the autoscaler kicks in (it should take no more than a few seconds), you should see one more node provisioning:

```
[ausov@bastion learning-ocp4]$ KUBECONFIG=auth/kubeconfig oc get machine -n openshift-machine-api
NAME                        PHASE          TYPE   REGION   ZONE   AGE
ocp4-q8bhf-infra-p6qqh      Running                               14h
ocp4-q8bhf-infra-wfwnc      Provisioning                          27s
```

Figure 6.23: An extra node is being provisioned to provide the required capacity

In our lab, it takes 2 minutes for a machine to become `Running`:

```
[ausov@bastion learning-ocp4]$ KUBECONFIG=auth/kubeconfig oc get machine -n openshift-machine-api
NAME                        PHASE     TYPE   REGION   ZONE   AGE
ocp4-q8bhf-infra-p6qqh      Running                          14h
ocp4-q8bhf-infra-wfwnc      Running                          2m24s
[ausov@bastion learning-ocp4]$
```

Figure 6.24: Provisioning of the node is complete

Now that we have tested scaling out, let us test scaling in.

Scaling in automatically

Follow these steps to have your cluster scale back in:

1. Delete one replica from our deployment and observe how the autoscaler removes one machine about 5 mins after that replica terminates, in accordance with the ClusterAutoscaler's `.spec.scaleDown.unneededTime`:

   ```
   $ oc scale deploy/test --replicas=7
   $ oc get machine -n openshift-machine-api
   ```

   As expected, now that the machine is no longer necessary, the autoscaler removes it:

```
[ausov@bastion learning-ocp4]$ KUBECONFIG=auth/kubeconfig oc get machine -n openshift-machine-api
NAME                        PHASE     TYPE   REGION   ZONE   AGE
ocp4-q8bhf-infra-p6qqh      Running                          14h
[ausov@bastion learning-ocp4]$
```

Figure 6.25: Redundant machines are removed by the cluster autoscaler

2. One problem that you may encounter is when a pod requests an amount of resources that exceeds the node's capacity – for example, when it requests 48 Gi of memory and your MachineSet is configured to create machines with only 32 Gi. No matter how many nodes the autoscaler spawns, that pod will not be able to run, because a pod represents a minimal unit of scheduling. This problem manifests itself as the following event, if you run `oc describe` on the pod:

```
Events:
  Type     Reason              Age                From                Message
  ----     ------              ----               ----                -------
  Warning  FailedScheduling    66s                default-scheduler   0/7 nodes are available: 3 node(s) had untolerated taint {node-role.kubernetes.io/master: }, 4 Insufficient cpu, 4 Insufficient memory.
preemption: 0/7 nodes are available: 3 Preemption is not helpful for scheduling, 4 No preemption victims found for incoming pod..
  Normal   NotTriggerScaleUp   3s (x6 over 62s)   cluster-autoscaler  pod didn't trigger scale-up: 1 Insufficient cpu, 1 Insufficient memory
[ausov@bastion learning-ocp4]$
```

Figure 6.26: Pod requests an unsatisfiable amount of resources

To solve the problem, you have to either reduce the amount of requested resources for the pod's workload controller (for example, deployment) or increase the capacity of machines in the MachineSet.

As a wrap-up, let's clean everything up:

```
$ oc delete -f chapters/6/snippets/deploy-busybox-autoscale.yml
$ oc delete -f chapters/6/snippets/machineautoscaler-CLUSTER_INFRA_ID-infra.yml
$ oc delete -f chapters/6/snippets/clusterautoscaler-default.yml
$ oc delete -f chapters/6/snippets/machineset-infra.yml
```

Check whether the remaining node that was provisioned via the Machine API is now gone: `oc get machine,no -n openshift-machine-api`.

This concludes the topic of cluster scalability and the Machine API in OpenShift.

Summary

Now that this chapter is over, it is time to reflect on what we have learned. We discussed why scaling is important and what goals it tries to achieve, as well as different methods of scaling your cluster – manual and automatic. We saw firsthand how different options affect the behavior of autoscaling and what caveats you have to be aware of when scaling your cluster. In the next chapter, we will move up one layer, from infrastructure to logical partitioning. You will learn how multitenancy works in OpenShift and what guardrails exist to ensure safe and disruption-free work for everyone. In particular, we will discuss the basic unit of multitenancy in OpenShift – projects, their relationship with Kubernetes namespaces, as well as ResourceQuotas, LimitRanges, NetworkPolicies, and SecurityContextConstraints.

References

To learn more about the topics that were covered in this chapter, take a look at the following resources:

- [1] *Overview of machine management*: `https://docs.redhat.com/en/documentation/openshift_container_platform/4.16/html/machine_management/overview-of-machine-management`
- [2] *Creating a compute machine set on vSphere*: `https://docs.redhat.com/en/documentation/openshift_container_platform/4.16/html/machine_management/managing-compute-machines-with-the-machine-api#creating-machineset-vsphere`
- [3] *Manually scaling a compute machine set*: `https://docs.redhat.com/en/documentation/openshift_container_platform/4.16/html/machine_management/manually-scaling-machineset`
- [4] *Modifying a compute machine set*: `https://docs.redhat.com/en/documentation/openshift_container_platform/4.16/html/machine_management/modifying-machineset`
- [5] *Machine phases and lifecycle*: `https://docs.redhat.com/en/documentation/openshift_container_platform/4.16/html/machine_management/machine-phases-lifecycle`
- [6] *Deleting a machine*: `https://docs.redhat.com/en/documentation/openshift_container_platform/4.16/html/machine_management/deleting-machine`

- [7] *Applying autoscaling to an OpenShift Container Platform cluster*: `https://docs.redhat.com/en/documentation/openshift_container_platform/4.16/html/machine_management/applying-autoscaling`
- [8] *Creating infrastructure machine sets*: `https://docs.redhat.com/en/documentation/openshift_container_platform/4.16/html/machine_management/creating-infrastructure-machinesets`
- [9] *Adding compute machines to vSphere manually*: `https://docs.redhat.com/en/documentation/openshift_container_platform/4.16/html/machine_management/managing-user-provisioned-infrastructure-manually#adding-vsphere-compute-user-infra`
- [10] *Deleting nodes from a bare-metal cluster*: `https://docs.redhat.com/en/documentation/openshift_container_platform/4.16/html/nodes/working-with-nodes#nodes-nodes-working-deleting-bare-metal_nodes-nodes-working`

Quiz

Test your understanding of OpenShift 4 scalability with this quick quiz. Remember, some questions may have more than one correct answer!

1. If a system was in operation for 3 years, of which it was down for 1 hour, what is its availability?
   a. 99.5%
   b. 95%
   c. 99.99%
   d. 66.66%
2. When manually removing a node, what is the correct sequence of steps
   a. Remove, drain, decommission
   b. Drain, remove, decommission
   c. Drain, decommission, remove
   d. Decommission, drain, remove
3. Which of the following scenarios warrants complete node removal?
   a. Failure of a Host Bus Adapter (HBA) controller on a bare-metal node
   b. Hypervisor failure in a cloud provider
   c. Consolidating applications to reduce costs and environmental footprint
   d. Memory upgrade
4. Which Machine API object represents a single node?
   a. Replica
   b. Machine
   c. ReplicaSet
   d. MachineSet

5. What annotation on a machine can be used to prioritize node deletion over its MachineSet's `deletePolicy`?
   a. `openshift.machine.io/delete-machine="true"`
   b. `openshift.machine.io/delete="true"`
   c. `machine.openshift.io/delete="true"`
   d. `machine.openshift.io/delete-machine="true"`
6. What is the default `deletePolicy` of a MachineSet?
   a. Newest
   b. Oldest
   c. Random
   d. MostRecent
7. What is required and sufficient in a pod's definition for it to trigger an autoscaling event?
   a. Requests
   b. Limits
   c. Requests and limits
   d. None of the above
8. Suppose 4 nodes were created in the order A, B, C, and D, `deletePolicy` is set to `Oldest`, and the `machine.openshift.io/delete-machine="true"` annotation is set on node D. Which nodes will be removed when the MachineSet that owns them is scaled down to 2?
   a. C and D
   b. A and C
   c. A and B
   d. None of the above

Answers

1. **c**. Refer to the formula from page 2. If we plug the numbers into it, we will get 365 × 3 × 24/(365 × 3 × 24 + 1) = 0.9999619496975001, or approximately 99.99% when rounded down.
2. **b**. First, you have to block all new workloads from scheduling on a node (cordon). Then, remove all workloads that are already running on it (drain). The next step is to remove the node itself from your cluster. Lastly, decommission the node according to your company's policies. Note that both cordon and drain operations can be performed with a single command: `oc adm drain`.
3. **b** and **c**. Failure of an HBA controller that provides a storage interface does not necessitate node removal, only maintenance, which requires cordoning and draining the node. A failed hypervisor, on the other hand, may result in a node not being recoverable, which means it will have to be replaced. The goal of consolidation is to free up some of the nodes in a cluster so that they can be removed. Finally, when upgrading memory or other hardware, maintenance is sufficient.

4. **b.** In the Machine API, each node's configuration is represented by a `Machine` resource.
5. **d.** The correct annotation that needs to be set on a machine to preempt its MachineSet's `deletePolicy` is `machine.openshift.io/delete-machine="true"`.
6. **c.** The default is `Random` and the `MostRecent` policy does not exist.
7. **a.** Requests are used by the OpenShift autoscaler to determine whether a cluster has enough capacity to run a new pod.
8. **d.** The correct answer is A and D, which was not listed. The annotation overrides the MachineSet's `deletePolicy`, so node D is eligible for deletion; the rest of the nodes are treated in accordance with the policy, which means A will be deleted too, as the oldest node.

Join us on Discord

For discussions around the book and to connect with your peers, join us on Discord at `http://packt.link/discordcloud` or scan the QR code below:

7

Application Security and Isolation

In this chapter, we will learn about the concepts essential for securing access to our applications in a multitenant environment and setting up guardrails around them in production. We will also discuss how to further harden our applications and improve their security posture by limiting the actions they are allowed to perform. Understanding the concepts laid out here is important for ensuring the security and stability of applications deployed on your OpenShift cluster.

Projects are the implementation of logical partitioning within OpenShift, which makes them critical to understand for tackling more advanced topics. This chapter starts by explaining what OpenShift projects are, their relationship with Kubernetes **namespaces**, and how they implement multitenancy in a shared environment.

In multitenant environments that involve many **lines of business (LOBs)** and different teams working within those LOBs, ensuring an equal playing field for everyone is of paramount importance. This chapter will help you understand how **ResourceQuotas** and **LimitRanges** can be used to set up guardrails around projects so that no one can consume all resources, starving others.

Even though different tenants may share the same OpenShift cluster, they shouldn't necessarily be allowed to interact with each other. A classic example is an environment shared by multiple independent customers, where their projects must be isolated from each other at the network level. In this chapter, we will talk about how network policies can be used to restrict communication between different applications within the same project or separate projects.

Next, we will move on to **Security Context Constraints (SCCs)**, which exist to help you harden your applications by restricting the actions they can perform. The benefit of that approach is multilayered security, where in addition to network security, you also decide which OpenShift resources applications on your cluster are permitted to use and their privileges.

This chapter concludes with a discussion of **Pod Security Standards (PSSs)**, which represent different security profiles with predefined security context settings for different classes of applications.

In summary, we'll cover the following topics:

- Understanding OpenShift projects
- ResourceQuotas
- LimitRanges
- Network policies
- Security context constraints
- Pod Security Standards

Let's get started!

Technical requirements

In this chapter, you will need the following:

- Bash shell
- OpenShift 4.16
- An active Red Hat subscription to view Red Hat KB articles

You can access this book's GitHub repository at `https://github.com/PacktPublishing/Learn-OpenShift-Second-Edition`.

Understanding OpenShift projects

Projects are the mechanism that facilitates multitenancy in OpenShift by allowing multiple tenants, such as individuals or entire teams, to work on their applications without having to worry about object name collisions or unintended interaction with applications of other tenants. As an added benefit, **role-based access control** (RBAC) rules can be scoped only to specific projects, providing granular access only to objects in those projects, and quotas can be used to control resource consumption. OpenShift projects are built on Kubernetes namespaces and essentially serve the same function. As such, an understanding of both concepts is crucial for grasping more advanced topics, including cluster-wide and namespace-scoped API objects, as well as Roles and ClusterRoles.

OpenShift projects versus Kubernetes namespaces

One of the most defining features of platforms such as Kubernetes and OpenShift is multitenancy – a collective name for a set of mechanisms that provide isolation between different users or teams running their own workloads. Kubernetes implements this concept by means of namespaces, which are exactly what the name suggests – independent, logical partitions within a cluster that enforce unique names of objects of the same type. For example, a namespace can contain a Pod and a Service with the same name, but not multiple Pods. Different namespaces, however, can have objects of the same type under the same name, so different teams don't have to worry about name conflicts and can work as if each of them were a sole user (or tenant) of a cluster.

Another rationale behind namespaces is the necessity to limit resource consumption for different applications. As will become clear in the following section, you can implement quotas and resource limits on a per-namespace basis to prevent applications from using up all resources in a cluster or to enforce CPU and/or memory requests.

Namespaces also let you configure RBAC to grant different levels of access to different users and groups. We discussed this in more detail in *Chapter 5, Navigating Authentication and Authorization.*

OpenShift takes the concept of namespaces further by wrapping them in a Project API entity. Most users use projects in the same way as namespaces; however, projects can have additional annotations and present more controls. For example, the OpenShift 4 API allows you to customize the default project template, which defines the content of the projects and the level of permissions users have within them. In this book, we use the terms "namespace" and "project" interchangeably, unless a distinction needs to be emphasized.

Getting ready

This section will provide several exercises around listing, creating, and deleting projects, mostly focused on the use of the CLI for better learning outcomes. Before we start, run the following command to export the `kubeconfig` file for your cluster into your shell. For the cluster built in *Chapter 3, Getting Started with OpenShift*, the following command will do it:

```
$ export KUBECONFIG=~/learning-ocp4/auth/kubeconfig
```

Now your environment is ready for the exercises in this chapter.

Viewing projects

To see which projects are available to you, use the following command:

```
$ oc projects
```

The list of projects presented to you depends on your permissions:

```
You have access to the following projects and can switch between them with ' project <projectname>':

    default
    kube-node-lease
    kube-public
    kube-system
    openshift
    openshift-apiserver
    openshift-apiserver-operator
    openshift-authentication
```

Figure 7.1: Listing the names of available projects

Another way to list available projects, along with their descriptions and states, is as follows:

```
$ oc get projects
```

Unlike the first command, this one gives a bit more information about the projects available to you, for example, their status, which is particularly useful when you have just deleted a project and are waiting for OpenShift to clean it of all resources and delete it (in which case it is displayed as **Terminating**):

```
NAME                              DISPLAY NAME   STATUS
default                                          Active
kube-node-lease                                  Active
kube-public                                      Active
kube-system                                      Active
openshift                                        Active
openshift-apiserver                              Active
openshift-apiserver-operator                     Active
openshift-authentication                         Active
```

Figure 7.2: Obtaining extended information about available projects

Creating projects

Now that we know how to view projects on a cluster, let's get to more practical examples of creating and manipulating them.

The first step is to create a project:

```
$ oc new-project chapter-7-project-1
```

> The preceding command assumes your user has the `self-provisioners` role assigned. If you're logged in as `kubeadmin`, you don't have to worry about that.

The preceding command creates a `ProjectRequest` object, which is then fulfilled by the OpenShift API, and the project itself is created (more on their differences in [5]). Then, you are immediately switched to it:

```
Now using project "chapter-7-project-1" on server "https://api.ocp4.example.com:6443".

You can add applications to this project with the 'new-app' command. For example, try:

    oc new-app rails-postgresql-example

to build a new example application in Ruby. Or use kubectl to deploy a simple Kubernetes application:

    kubectl create deployment hello-node --image=registry.k8s.io/e2e-test-images/agnhost:2.43 -- /agnhost serve-hostname
```

Figure 7.3: Creating a project

Let us have a closer look at the project's metadata:

```
$ oc get -o yaml project/chapter-7-project-1
```

You should see an output similar to the following:

```
apiVersion: project.openshift.io/v1
kind: Project
metadata:
  annotations:
    openshift.io/description: ""
    openshift.io/display-name: ""
    openshift.io/requester: system:admin
    openshift.io/sa.scc.mcs: s0:c27,c4
    openshift.io/sa.scc.supplemental-groups: 1000710000/10000
    openshift.io/sa.scc.uid-range: 1000710000/10000
  creationTimestamp: "2025-08-04T03:52:21Z"
  labels:
    kubernetes.io/metadata.name: chapter-7-project-1
    pod-security.kubernetes.io/audit: restricted
    pod-security.kubernetes.io/audit-version: v1.24
    pod-security.kubernetes.io/warn: restricted
    pod-security.kubernetes.io/warn-version: v1.24
  name: chapter-7-project-1
  resourceVersion: "566149"
  uid: cae4f865-d4d2-4d5a-a6f8-5afe1fc4a2f7
spec:
  finalizers:
  - kubernetes
status:
  phase: Active
```

Figure 7.4: YAML definition of a project

The numbers in your output may be different. Adjust the manifests in the exercises that follow accordingly.

All parameters of a project are specified in its annotations, which can be categorized into two groups:

- Provided via a project template (discussed later in this section):

Annotation	Description	Project template parameter
`openshift.io/description`	Project description.	`PROJECT_DESCRIPTION`
`openshift.io/display-name`	Project name, displayed in the output of `oc get projects`.	`PROJECT_DISPLAYNAME`
`openshift.io/requester`	User who requested the project. By default, this user is assigned an admin role for the project.	`PROJECT_REQUESTING_USER`

Table 7.1: Project annotations and their corresponding project template parameters

- Filled in by one of OpenShift's controllers:

Annotation	Description
`openshift.io/sa.scc.mcs`	SELinux multi-category security (MCS) level and category. MCS is an additional guardrail of SELinux that is applied after discretionary access control (DAC) and type enforcement (TE) rules, further enhancing security and process isolation.
`openshift.io/sa.scc.supplemental-groups`	Supplemental groups that are assigned to containerized processes, running within a project. Takes the form `START/NUMBER`, where `START` is the initial group for the first process and `NUMBER` is the total number of groups supported by that namespace.
`openshift.io/sa.scc.uid-range`	User IDs (UIDs) assigned to containerized processes, running within a project. Takes the form `START/NUMBER`, where `START` is the initial UID for the first process and `NUMBER` is the total number of UIDs supported by that namespace.

Table 7.2: Security annotations of a project

As you can see from the labels, every project also has the `restricted` PSS enabled for its workloads in `audit` (violations are recorded in the audit log) and `warn` (user-facing warnings are generated) modes, as indicated by its labels. They were not introduced by OpenShift but inherited from Kubernetes. Read more about PSSs in [31] and [32]. We will also briefly discuss them at the end of this chapter.

Now, let us create a workload and see which UID and groups its process is assigned. Open the `chapters/7/snippets/deploy-busybox.yml` manifest from this book's GitHub repository and examine its content. Use the oc client to submit it to the OpenShift API and verify its creation:

```
$ oc create -f chapters/7/snippets/deploy-busybox.yml
$ oc get po
```

The deployment controller should create a single Pod:

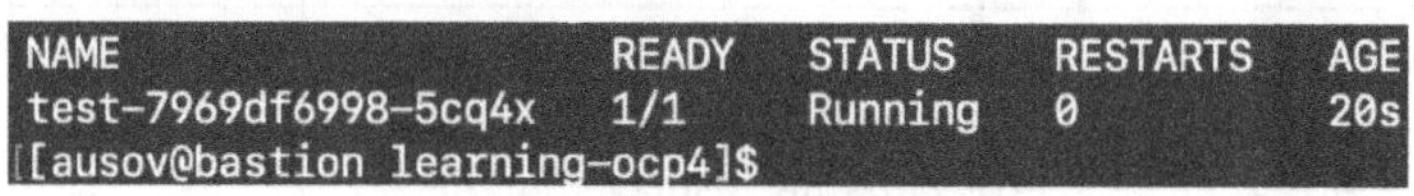

Figure 7.5: Listing Pods in a project

Run the following command to get a UID of the process running inside that Pod's only container:

```
$ oc exec deploy/test -- id
```

As evidenced by the following screenshot, the process was assigned the first UID and first supplemental **group ID (GID)** from the ranges specified in the project's respective annotations:

```
uid=1000710000(1000710000) gid=0(root) groups=0(root),1000710000
```

Figure 7.6: Containerized process' ID and groups

We could've accomplished the same by using `exec` on the Pod directly with `oc exec po/<POD> -- id`.

In the preceding step, we relied on OpenShift to assign the UID and a supplementary group to our workload automatically. Now, let's take this exercise a bit further by specifying them and SELinux MCS categories explicitly. Open another file, `chapters/7/snippets/deploy-busybox-chapter-7-projects.yml`, and note the `securityContext` at the container and Pod levels. Update `runAsUser`, `supplementalGroups`, and `seLinuxOptions` to align with ranges and values set in the project's annotations. Create the defined workload:

```
$ oc create -f chapters/7/snippets/deploy-busybox-chapter-7-projects.yml
```

Now use the following command to check whether the workload was created correctly with assigned parameters:

```
$ oc get po -o jsonpath='{range .items[*]}{@.metadata.name}{" runAsUser: "}
{@.spec.containers[*].securityContext.runAsUser}{" seLinuxOptions: "}{@.spec.
securityContext.seLinuxOptions.level}{"\n"} {" supplementalGroups: "}{@.spec.
securityContext.supplementalGroups[*]}{"\n"}{end}'
```

> The preceding construct uses JSONPath – a language for querying complex JSON structures, which is very useful for extracting specific fields from a large number of objects of the same type. More on JSONPath can be found at [28].

The output confirms that the parameters were indeed applied correctly:

```
test-599cc6cdcd-5kz9f runAsUser: 1000710000 seLinuxOptions: s0:c27,c4
  supplementalGroups:
test-chapter-7-projects-5dcfdc7d64-2kvfg runAsUser: 1000710001 seLinuxOptions: s0:c27,c4
  supplementalGroups: 1000710001
```

Figure 7.7: Checking UID and SELinux

Now use the already-familiar command below to find out the UID and supplemental groups of the process in your Pod:

```
$ oc exec deploy/test-chapter-7-projects -- id
```

As you can see, the process was assigned a UID and supplemental group `1000710001` – exactly as we specified (as a reminder, your numbers will likely be different):

```
uid=1000710001(1000710001) gid=0(root) groups=0(root),1000710000,1000710001
```

Figure 7.8: ID and groups of a process with an extra supplemental group

Now, let us see what happens when we specify a UID and a supplemental group outside of the range prescribed by the namespace. In the `chapters/7/snippets/deploy-busybox-out-of-range.yml` file, note that we've changed the values of the `supplementalGroups` and `runAsUser` fields to fall outside the range of allowed GIDs (as before, make sure to update `seLinuxOptions` to match your namespace and `runAsUser` to fall outside the project's range). Create the object:

```
$ oc create -f chapters/7/snippets/deploy-busybox-out-of-range.yml
```

You will get the following warning, but the deployment will be created nonetheless:

```
Warning: would violate PodSecurity "restricted:v1.24": allowPrivilegeEscalation != false (conta
iner "busybox" must set securityContext.allowPrivilegeEscalation=false), unrestricted capabilit
ies (container "busybox" must set securityContext.capabilities.drop=["ALL"]), runAsNonRoot != t
rue (pod or container "busybox" must set securityContext.runAsNonRoot=true), seccompProfile (po
d or container "busybox" must set securityContext.seccompProfile.type to "RuntimeDefault" or "L
ocalhost")
deployment.apps/test-out-of-range created
```

Figure 7.9: Creating a deployment to test an out-of-range UID assignment

We will explain what that is at the end of this chapter.

Now, let's list deployments in the current project:

```
$ oc get deploy
```

Even though the output says that the deployment was created, it was unable to start a new Pod:

```
NAME                      READY   UP-TO-DATE   AVAILABLE   AGE
test                      1/1     1            1           30m
test-chapter-7-projects   1/1     1            1           22m
test-out-of-range         0/1     0            0           11s
```

Figure 7.10: Test deployment is unable to complete a rollout

The reason is the default `SecurityContextConstraint` object (`restricted-v2`) that defines allowed UID and supplemental group ranges, among other things, prohibits creation of a Pod that would violate these constraints, and the Pod was not granted permission to use any other SCC. You can find a more descriptive message by examining the events of the deployment:

```
$ oc get -o yaml deploy/test-out-of-range
```

From the output, you can see that the allowed UIDs should fall within the range **[1000710000, 1000719999]**:

```
- lastTransitionTime: "2025-08-04T04:30:56Z"
  lastUpdateTime: "2025-08-04T04:30:56Z"
  message: 'pods "test-out-of-range-855b899474-" is forbidden: unable to validate
    against any security context constraint: [provider "anyuid": Forbidden: not
    usable by user or serviceaccount, provider restricted-v2: .containers[0].runAsUser:
    Invalid value: 1000700001: must be in the ranges: [1000710000, 1000719999],
    provider "restricted": Forbidden: not usable by user or serviceaccount, provider
    "nonroot-v2": Forbidden: not usable by user or serviceaccount, provider "nonroot":
    Forbidden: not usable by user or serviceaccount, provider "hostmount-anyuid":
    Forbidden: not usable by user or serviceaccount, provider "machine-api-termination-handler":
    Forbidden: not usable by user or serviceaccount, provider "hostnetwork-v2":
    Forbidden: not usable by user or serviceaccount, provider "hostnetwork": Forbidden:
    not usable by user or serviceaccount, provider "hostaccess": Forbidden: not
    usable by user or serviceaccount, provider "node-exporter": Forbidden: not usable
    by user or serviceaccount, provider "privileged": Forbidden: not usable by user
    or serviceaccount]'
  reason: FailedCreate
  status: "True"
  type: ReplicaFailure
```

Figure 7.11: Error message indicating an incorrect UID that violates the default SCC, restricted-v2

In order to allow the workload, you will have to do two things:

1. Assign a less restrictive SCC to it that has the value `type: RunAsAny` for the `runAsUser` field.
2. Grant the `ServiceAccount` that the Pod is executed under permission to use that SCC.

First, run the following command to assign the `anyuid` SCC to the Pod's template inside your deployment by placing a special annotation on it:

> **Warning!**
>
> The `anyuid` SCC is the least restrictive and allows workloads under any UID, including 0 (root). Use it with caution. We are using it in this book only for demonstration.

```
$ oc patch --type=merge -p '{"spec": {"template": {"metadata": {"annotations":
{"openshift.io/required-scc": "anyuid"}}}}}' deploy/test-out-of-range
```

> We can't use the more convenient `oc annotate` command because it would annotate the deployment itself (`.metadata.annotations`), and we need to place the annotation on its Pod's template (`.spec.template.metadata.annotations`).

Use the following command to check whether your deployment spawned any Pods:

```
$ oc get po -l app=test-out-of-range
```

Evidently, a Pod still fails to create:

```
No resources found in chapter-7-project-1 namespace.
```

Figure 7.12: No Pods were created

Let's look at events with `oc get ev` or `oc events` (automatically sorts events by creation timestamp). You can see that the Pod is still not allowed to use this SCC:

```
2m10s (x19 over 13m)   Warning   FailedCreate        ReplicaSet/test-out-of-range-855b899474
Error creating: pods "test-out-of-range-855b899474-" is forbidden: unable to validate against any sec
urity context constraint: [provider "anyuid": Forbidden: not usable by user or serviceaccount, provid
er restricted-v2: .containers[0].runAsUser: Invalid value: 1000700001: must be in the ranges: [100071
0000, 1000719999], provider "restricted": Forbidden: not usable by user or serviceaccount, provider "
nonroot-v2": Forbidden: not usable by user or serviceaccount, provider "nonroot": Forbidden: not usab
le by user or serviceaccount, provider "hostmount-anyuid": Forbidden: not usable by user or serviceac
count, provider "machine-api-termination-handler": Forbidden: not usable by user or serviceaccount, p
rovider "hostnetwork-v2": Forbidden: not usable by user or serviceaccount, provider "hostnetwork": Fo
rbidden: not usable by user or serviceaccount, provider "hostaccess": Forbidden: not usable by user o
r serviceaccount, provider "node-exporter": Forbidden: not usable by user or serviceaccount, provider
 "privileged": Forbidden: not usable by user or serviceaccount]
51s (x15 over 2m13s)   Warning   FailedCreate        ReplicaSet/test-out-of-range-68f87965c7
Error creating: pods "test-out-of-range-68f87965c7-" is forbidden: unable to validate against any sec
urity context constraint: provider "anyuid": Forbidden: not usable by user or serviceaccount
```

Figure 7.13: ServiceAccount is prohibited from using all SCCs except restricted-v2, which is too restrictive

So, just assigning an SCC is not enough. Now we must allow the default `ServiceAccount` to use that SCC:

```
$ oc adm policy add-scc-to-user anyuid -z default
```

In a few seconds, the Pod is successfully created:

```
NAME                                READY   STATUS    RESTARTS   AGE
test-out-of-range-84f9c4bcf-4cr6d   1/1     Running   0          36s
```

Figure 7.14: A Pod is created after its ServiceAccount is allowed to use an SCC

If it's taking too long, you can force the creation of a new Pod by restarting the deployment with this command:

```
$ oc rollout restart deploy/test-out-of-range
```

We will discuss SCCs in greater detail later in this chapter.

Now it is time for another exercise. Try to create a project whose name starts with `openshift-`:

```
$ oc new-project openshift-test
```

The command fails:

```
Error from server (Forbidden): project.project.openshift.io "openshift-test" is forbidden:
 cannot request a project starting with "openshift-"
```

Figure 7.15: Regular user CLI command fails to create a project whose name starts with openshift-

This is by design. Since openshift-* and kube-* projects are used by OpenShift internal components and operators, it has been decided to delegate the capability of creating such privileged projects to a separate command:

```
$ oc adm new-project openshift-test
```

This time, it works:

Figure 7.16: Using the admin CLI command to create a project whose name starts with openshift-

Notice that unlike its less privileged counterpart, oc new-project, this command doesn't automatically switch our context to the new project.

Since we will not be using this project, let us delete it before moving on to the next topic:

```
$ oc delete project openshift-test
```

> The shell prompt may not return immediately after initiating a project deletion - this is expected, as the cluster needs to do a proper cleanup of project-scoped resources. In some situations, if you run oc get project <YOUR_PROJECT> shortly thereafter, you may see it in the Terminating state. If it is stuck in this phase for more than a few minutes, this usually indicates a problem with the cleanup - some resources inside the project cannot be deleted.

Customizing project roles

First, we need to go to the web console of our cluster. You can use the following command to obtain its URL:

```
$ oc whoami --show-console
```

Log in with the user kubeadmin and the password from the auth/kubeadmin-password file. To learn how to configure additional identity providers so that other users can log in and the kubeadmin account can be safely disabled, consult *Chapter 5, Navigating Authentication and Authorization.*

When you create a new project, by default, you can assign users or service accounts three ClusterRoles:

- **Admin**
- **Edit**
- **View**

This can be easily seen in the web console, under **Developer** | **Project**, when you select a project at the top:

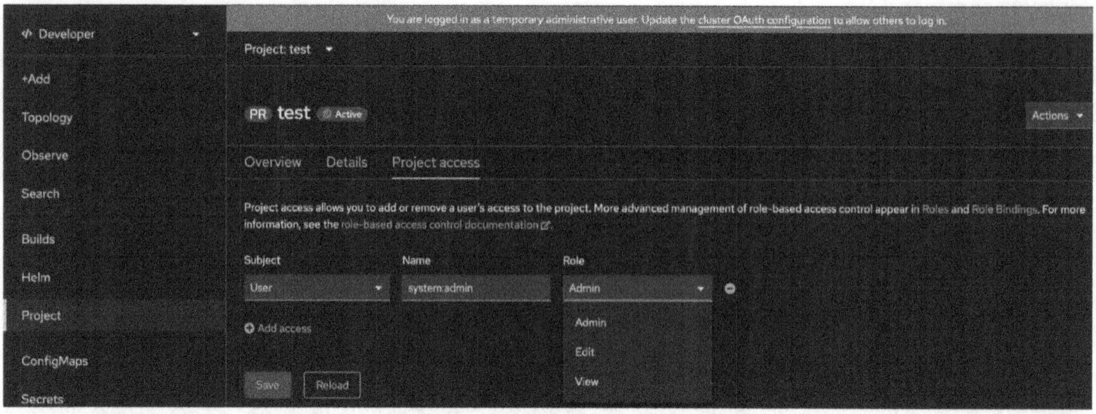

Figure 7.17: Default cluster roles for a project

Roles available for assignment are exposed to cluster administrators via the Console API resource from the `operator.openshift.io` API group. By default, the list of roles is not set, which essentially means that all roles are available for use. Execute the following command to set it to a single role, `view`:

```
$ oc patch -p '{"spec": {"customization": {"projectAccess":
{"availableClusterRoles": ["view"]}}}}' --type merge console.operator/cluster
```

The following command will show you whether your modifications were applied successfully:

```
$ oc get -o yaml console.operator/cluster
```

Look for this section of the output:

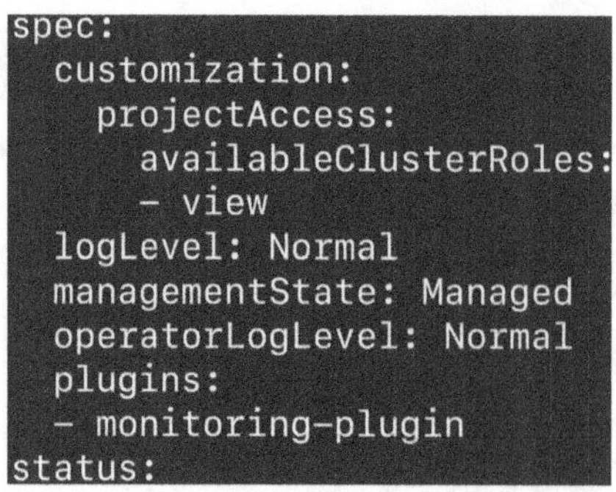

```
spec:
  customization:
    projectAccess:
      availableClusterRoles:
      - view
  logLevel: Normal
  managementState: Managed
  operatorLogLevel: Normal
  plugins:
  - monitoring-plugin
status:
```

Figure 7.18: Using the CLI to verify customized roles available for assignment in a project

Now, refresh the web console in your browser, then click **Add access** and then on the **Role** drop-down list. You should see only the **view** role:

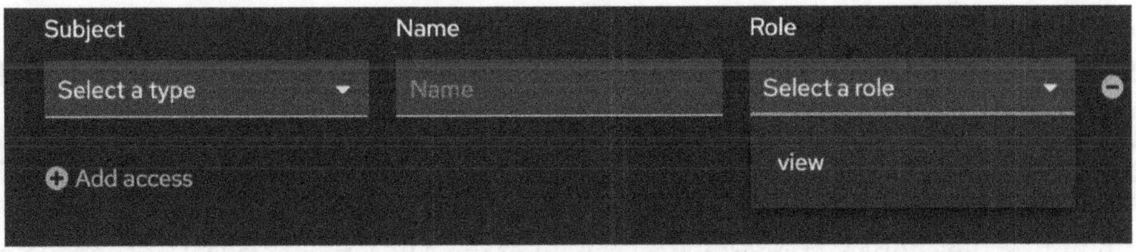

Figure 7.19: Only explicitly configured roles show up in the drop-down list

This may be useful for preventing any new users from obtaining **admin** and **edit** privileges – for example, during an audit.

Now that you have completed this exercise, reset the `Console` object to its original state:

```
$ oc patch -p '[{"path": "/spec/customization", "op": "remove"}]' --type json console.operator/cluster
```

The preceding command simply removes the `/spec/customization` node and all of its descendants. You may have to wait for a few minutes until the API server completes the rollout and the change is reflected in the web UI.

Customizing a default project template

When a user requests a new project, the OpenShift API passes the provided details, including the name of the requesting user, to a default template that generates the project's definition and a `RoleBinding` object that assigns the requesting user the `admin` role for that project. That template can be customized to include any objects that may make sense for a specific organization or department. In the example that follows, we will customize the template so that every new project comes with an object called `LimitRange` that restricts CPU and memory resources that can be assigned to workloads in that project, as well as making sure that workloads with undefined resources are assigned default resource requests. We will examine the structure and usage of `LimitRanges` in a subsequent section of this chapter. For now, just follow these steps:

1. Normally, you would use the `oc adm create-bootstrap-project-template -o yaml > project-template.yml` command to extract the default project template and then modify it according to your needs. But to save you time, we already prepared a ready-to-use template in `chapters/7/snippets/project-template.yml` of this book's GitHub repository. Inspect it and note a `LimitRange` object in the list of objects, then create it:

   ```
   $ oc create -f chapters/7/snippets/project-template.yml
   ```

   > The template must be created in the `openshift-config` project. We included the name of the namespace in the template's definition to reduce the risk of human error.

2. Just creating a template is not enough; we must also tell OpenShift how to find it. This is done by modifying the project resource named `cluster` from the `config.openshift.io` API group:

```
$ oc patch -p '{"spec": {"projectRequestTemplate": {"name": "project-request"}}}' --type merge project.config/cluster
```

3. Submitting the changes triggers a new rollout of the API server's Pods. Use the following command to monitor the process in near-real time:

```
$ watch -n1 oc get po -n openshift-apiserver
```

   The `watch` command will keep executing whatever command that follows every second (as indicated by `-n1`), giving you a near-real-time view of the rollout in progress:

```
NAME                              READY   STATUS        RESTARTS   AGE
apiserver-7b9c7f9c9f-p95xx        0/2     Pending       0          11s
apiserver-86c58bd999-2xjd5        2/2     Running       0          19h
apiserver-86c58bd999-8jgf8        1/2     Terminating   0          19h
apiserver-86c58bd999-mh8pd        2/2     Running       0          19h
```

   Figure 7.20: Deployment rollout in progress

   The rollout should be complete in a few minutes.

4. Now it is time to test our changes. Create a new project, `chapter-7-project-2`:

```
$ oc new-project chapter-7-project-2
```

5. Let us see whether LimitRange was created with `oc get limitrange` or `oc get limits`. As you can see, we now have a project with a pre-configured LimitRange object:

```
NAME                    CREATED AT
chapter-7-limitrange    2025-08-04T05:28:38Z
```

   Figure 7.21: Listing LimitRange resources in the current namespace

This is a very simple yet convenient way of making sure that all projects come with a default set of guardrails or other objects for every user or team.

> Adding resources to a project template is not the only way of supplying all projects with specific content. Another approach that will be explored later in this book is the use of an operator – a **CustomResourceDefinition** (**CRD**) that accepts parameters for configuring resources and a controller that applies those changes and constantly monitors the CRD for updates. This is particularly useful if you have different classes of projects, each with its own required objects or configuration of objects – for example, different quotas for different tenants. You can also use GitOps to ensure the presence of certain resources in every project and of the project itself. We will briefly touch on the topic of GitOps in *Chapter 15, Exploring Additional Services in OpenShift*.

Now that we have completed this exercise, let us clean things up:

1. Remove the modifications to the `project.config/cluster` resource:

   ```
   $ oc patch -p '[{"path": "/spec/projectRequestTemplate", "op":
   "remove"}]' --type json project.config/cluster
   ```

   Just like before, the API server's Pods will begin a new rollout to apply the changes.

2. Next, delete the template, as it is no longer being used:

   ```
   $ oc delete -f chapters/7/snippets/project-template.yml
   ```

3. Finally, delete the project itself:

   ```
   $ oc delete project chapter-7-project-2
   ```

   If you try to create another project before the API server's Pods finish rolling out, you may get the following error:

```
Error from server (NotFound): templates.template.openshift.io "project-request" not found
[ausov@bastion learning-ocp4]$
```

Figure 7.22: Trying to create another project too early

   Simply wait until the rollout is over and retry.

Also, please keep in mind that the default project template applies *only* when you request a new project with `oc new-project`, not with `oc adm new-project`.

> If you create a project *declaratively*, for example, using a GitOps process or from a YAML/JSON manifest with `oc create/apply`, as opposed to imperatively (with `oc new-project`), you may notice that it doesn't include resources specified in the project template. This is also true if you create just a namespace imperatively with `oc create ns`. This is by design; a project template applies only when you create a `ProjectRequest` object first, which is exactly what `oc new-project` does behind the scenes. Consequently, the necessary RoleBinding that makes a project requester the admin of the project is not created either. You also can't specify a requester in the `ProjectRequest` itself, as it is derived from the token submitted as part of an API call. In that case, you will have to create those objects explicitly; one way of doing this is creating a list of objects using the default project template directly with `oc process project-request -n openshift-config -p PROJECT_REQUESTING_USER=<REQUESTER> -p ...` and then either applying it with `oc create/apply` or storing it in a file and pushing it to a Git repository, from where it will presumably be picked up by a GitOps server. We also do not recommend creating a `ProjectRequest` object using GitOps, as it is deleted almost immediately after a corresponding project is created, leading to a reconciliation failure on the GitOps side. This is largely because the `ProjectRequest` API was introduced before the idea of GitOps, essentially making it a remnant from OpenShift 3. We will discuss GitOps in more detail in *Chapter 15, Exploring Additional Services in OpenShift*.

Now that we know what projects are and how they can be customized, for example, to come with default guardrails, it is time to take a closer look at the guardrails themselves.

ResourceQuotas

One of the major concerns of all multitenant platforms, including Kubernetes and OpenShift, is unfair distribution of available compute and storage resources, when a small number of "bad actors" use up all cluster capacity. To mitigate this problem, `ResourceQuota` (project-scoped) and `ClusterResourceQuota` (cluster-wide) API objects are used.

The following is a list of all compute resources that can be constrained by `ResourceQuota` and `ClusterResourceQuota`:

- `cpu` (same as `requests.cpu`)
- `memory` (same as `requests.memory`)
- `limits.cpu`
- `limits.memory`

Quotas track *combined* requests and limits across *all* Pods and containers in a given project.

> Compute resources are tracked by quotas only for Pods in a non-terminal state that is not in the `Succeeded` (corresponds to the `Completed` state, as returned by `oc get po`) or `Failed` phase.
>
> If your quota includes constraints around CPU or RAM requests/limits, they must be specified in your Pods – either directly, including them in the workload controller's (deployment, etc.) manifest, or indirectly, specifying defaults in a `LimitRange` object in the same namespace; otherwise, your Pod will be rejected.

LimitRanges are discussed in the next section.

As for the storage resources that can be limited by quotas, optionally on a per-storage-class basis, they are as follows:

- In any state:
  - `requests.storage`
  - `<STORAGECLASS>.storageclass.storage.k8s.io/requests.storage`
  - `<STORAGECLASS>.storageclass.storage.k8s.io/persistentvolumeclaims`
- In a non-terminal state:
  - `limits.ephemeral-storage`
  - `ephemeral-storage` (same as `requests.ephemeral-storage`)

Aside from compute and storage resources, both objects can also limit the number of objects of various types:

- `pods`
- `replicationcontrollers`
- `services`
- `services.nodeports`
- `services.loadbalancers`
- `configmaps`
- `secrets`
- `openshift.io/imagestreams`
- `persistentvolumeclaims`
- `resourcequotas`

Other API resources are also supported through the `count/RESOURCE_TYPE.API_GROUP` format, for example, `count/deployments.apps` or `count/statefulsets.apps`.

Working with quotas

Now let us use what we have learned about quotas in this exercise:

1. First, create a project named `chapter-7-quota-1`:

```
$ oc new-project chapter-7-quota-1
```

2. Next, create a quota from the `chapters/7/snippets/resourcequota.yml` definition from this book's GitHub repository:

```
$ oc create -f chapters/7/snippets/resourcequota.yml
```

3. The next step is to create a workload that will consume some of the resources limited by the quota. The deployment is stored in `chapters/7/snippets/deploy-busybox-quotas.yml` of this book's GitHub repository. Create the workload and list the Pods it created:

```
$ oc create -f chapters/7/snippets/deploy-busybox-quotas.yml
$ oc get po
```

Notice that only 2 out of 3 replicas were created:

```
NAME                    READY   STATUS    RESTARTS   AGE
test-5b54c846bd-cv87h   1/1     Running   0          5s
test-5b54c846bd-jvq7f   1/1     Running   0          5s
```

Figure 7.23: Quota limiting creation of a Pod

4. Let us take a look at the events to determine what went wrong by running `oc get ev`. The following message clearly indicates that the quota, specifically the number of allowed Pods, was exceeded:

```
3m8s        Normal    SuccessfulCreate    replicaset/test-5b54c846bd   Created pod: test-5b54c846bd-cv87h
3m8s        Warning   FailedCreate        replicaset/test-5b54c846bd   Error creating: pods "test-5b54c846b
d-p959g" is forbidden: exceeded quota: chapter-7-quota, requested: pods=1, used: pods=2, limited: pods=2
3m8s        Normal    SuccessfulCreate    replicaset/test-5b54c846bd   Created pod: test-5b54c846bd-jvq7f
```

Figure 7.24: Pod quota exceeded for the chapter-7-quota-1 project

5. Use the following command to obtain your quota's usage summary:

```
$ oc describe quota
```

As expected, we have already exhausted our already-small allowance:

```
Name:                   chapter-7-quota
Namespace:              chapter-7-quota-1
Resource                Used  Hard
--------                ----  ----
configmaps              2     10
persistentvolumeclaims  0     4
pods                    2     2
replicationcontrollers  0     20
secrets                 0     10
services                0     10
```

Figure 7.25: ResourceQuota summary for the chapter-7-quota-1 project

6. Finally, let us clean things up:

```
$ oc delete -f chapters/7/snippets/resourcequota.yml
```

> You can also create quotas imperatively using the CLI:
>
> ```
> $ oc create quota chapter-7-quota-1
> --hard=configmaps=10,persistentvolumeclaims=4,replicat
> ioncontrollers=20,secrets=10,services=10,pods=2
> $ oc delete quota chapter-7-quota-1
> ```

Now let's turn our attention to applying quotas at scale.

Applying quotas at scale using ClusterResourceQuota resources

Since the `ResourceQuota` object is project-scoped (or namespaced), it must be created for every project independently, which does not scale very well. Of course, this problem can be solved with automation, but a much simpler solution is to use a `ClusterResourceQuota` resource that is applied to multiple projects based on labels and annotations. Let us see how this works:

1. First, we must label and/or annotate the projects we wish to be constrained by our quota:

   ```
   $ oc annotate ns/chapter-7-quota-1 openshift.io/description=restricted-by-cluster-quota --overwrite
   $ oc label ns/chapter-7-quota-1 tier=minimal
   ```

   You can use either labels or annotations or both, but if they are both specified, only projects that have matching labels and annotations will be selected.

2. Now create another project, `chapter-7-quota-2`, with the same description as the value of the `openshift.io/description` annotation for the `chapter-7-quota-1` project and label it the same way:

   ```
   $ oc new-project chapter-7-quota-2 --description=restricted-by-cluster-quota
   $ oc label ns/chapter-7-quota-2 tier=minimal
   ```

   When you provide the `--description` parameter to the `oc new-project` command, the description is stored in the `openshift.io/description` annotation of the project. The reason why we didn't set this description on the `chapter-7-quota-1` project's creation is to avoid confusion.

3. Now that labels and annotations are in place, examine the `chapters/7/snippets/clusterresourcequota.yml` file from this book's GitHub repository and use it to create a quota:

   ```
   $ oc create -f chapters/7/snippets/clusterresourcequota.yml
   ```

   The `.spec.selector` substructure determines what projects the restrictions from `.spec.quota.hard` will be applied to.

4. Now let us examine its effect on namespaces. Use the following command to see the summary of your new quota and what namespaces it was applied to based on its selector:

   ```
   $ oc describe clusterresourcequota
   ```

   As the following screenshot demonstrates, the quota was applied to two namespaces, tracking resource consumption for them individually:

```
Name:             chapter-7-cluster-quota
Created:          2 seconds ago
Labels:           <none>
Annotations:      <none>
Namespace Selector: ["chapter-7-quota-2" "chapter-7-quota-1"]
Label Selector: tier=minimal
AnnotationSelector: map[openshift.io/description:restricted-by-cluster-quota]
Resource                  Used    Hard
--------                  ----    ----
count/deployments.apps    1       1
pods                      3       1
```

Figure 7.26: ClusterResourceQuota applied to multiple projects

> According to the preceding screenshot, three Pods are running in one of the namespaces controlled by this cluster quota. These are actually the Pods we created earlier through a deployment in the `chapter-7-quota-1` namespace, but only two of them were able to start. However, after we removed the ResourceQuota resource as part of the cleanup, the corresponding ReplicaSet was free to create a third one, which is what we're seeing here. If, for example, you created the `ClusterResourceQuota` resource shortly or immediately after the cleanup, you would see two Pods in the `Used` column.

5. Let us take this exercise a little further by creating another `ClusterResourceQuota` resource. First, add another label to the `chapter-7-quota-1` project:

```
$ oc label ns/chapter-7-quota-1 no-sts=true
```

6. We prepared a manifest file in `chapters/7/snippets/clusterresourcequota-statefulsets.yml` of this book's GitHub repository. Examine it and then use it to create a new cluster quota:

```
$ oc create -f chapters/7/snippets/clusterresourcequota-statefulsets.yml
```

The preceding quota will limit the number of `StatefulSet` objects to one, which is not very practical but serves the purpose of our experiment.

7. If you run the `oc describe` command on your cluster quotas again, you will see both objects – the one created earlier and the one you just created, as expected:

```
$ oc describe clusterresourcequota
```

As you might expect, the cluster quota was applied only to a single project with a matching label:

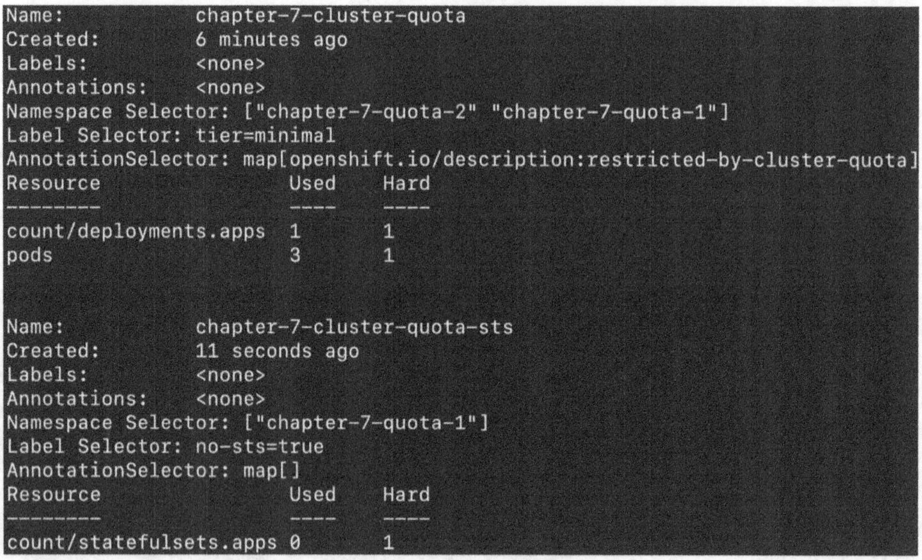

Figure 7.27: ClusterResourceQuota applied to a single project

8. From the output in the previous step, you can tell pretty easily what quotas were set on each project. But what if you have tens or even hundreds of namespaces? This is where an API resource called `AppliedClusterResourceQuota` comes in. Being a namespaced object, it allows you to see only the cluster quotas that were applied to a specific project. Run the following command to see what effective restrictions were set on the `chapter-7-quota-2` project, which wasn't assigned any additional labels or annotations and thus wasn't selected by the most recent cluster quota:

```
$ oc describe appliedclusterresourcequota -n chapter-7-quota-2
```

As you can see, there is only one `AppliedClusterResourceQuota` resource that corresponds to a single `ClusterResourceQuota` that was applied to this project, although the cluster quota is mapped to the total of two projects by its selector (the `Namespace Selector` field):

```
Name:               chapter-7-cluster-quota
Created:            9 minutes ago
Labels:             <none>
Annotations:        <none>
Namespace Selector: ["chapter-7-quota-2" "chapter-7-quota-1"]
Label Selector: tier=minimal
AnnotationSelector: map[openshift.io/description:restricted-by-cluster-quota]
Resource                  Used    Hard
--------                  ----    ----
count/deployments.apps    1       1
pods                      3       1
```

Figure 7.28: AppliedClusterResourceQuota for a single project selected by a ClusterResourceQuota resource

9. Now do the same for `chapter-7-quota-1`:

```
$ oc describe appliedclusterresourcequota -n chapter-7-quota-1
```

As you can see, the view for that project is different, because it was selected by the last cluster quota as well:

```
Name:               chapter-7-cluster-quota
Created:            10 minutes ago
Labels:             <none>
Annotations:        <none>
Namespace Selector: ["chapter-7-quota-2" "chapter-7-quota-1"]
Label Selector: tier=minimal
AnnotationSelector: map[openshift.io/description:restricted-by-cluster-quota]
Resource                  Used    Hard
--------                  ----    ----
count/deployments.apps    1       1
pods                      3       1


Name:               chapter-7-cluster-quota-sts
Created:            4 minutes ago
Labels:             <none>
Annotations:        <none>
Namespace Selector: ["chapter-7-quota-1"]
Label Selector: no-sts=true
AnnotationSelector: map[]
Resource                  Used    Hard
--------                  ----    ----
count/statefulsets.apps 0         1
```

Figure 7.29: AppliedClusterResourceQuota for multiple projects selected by ClusterResourceQuota(s)

One thing that might have caught your attention before is that the number of Pods in the `chapter-7-quota-1` project exceeds the quota, which doesn't seem to make sense. The reason is that namespaced and cluster-wide quotas are only applied at the admission stage of the API pipeline, so pre-existing resources continue to exist without OpenShift retroactively deleting them. Let's see how this works in practice:

1. Scale your deployment from `chapter-7-quota-1` down to 1 to satisfy the quota:

```
$ oc scale deploy/test --replicas=1 -n chapter-7-quota-1
```

2. Now try to scale it back up to 2 and examine events in the project:

```
$ oc scale deploy/test --replicas=2 -n chapter-7-quota-1
$ oc get ev -n chapter-7-quota-1
```

The operation failed, which makes perfect sense because otherwise, the quota would be violated:

```
7s          Warning   FailedCreate          replicaset/test-5b54c846bd
Error creating: pods "test-5b54c846bd-lwsdp" is forbidden: exceeded quo
ta: chapter-7-cluster-quota, requested: pods=1, used: pods=1, limited:
pods=1
```

Figure 7.30: Quotas are evaluated only at the admission stage

The lesson is that only the creation of new resources gets constrained. Another way to say it is that quotas are enforced only at the admission stage. If you need quotas to apply to pre-existing objects as well, then you need a controller that would constantly *watch* (this is an actual API verb in Kubernetes and OpenShift used exactly for this purpose) for new resources and delete those that violate the quota. That would require some sort of prioritization, based on which objects are to be removed, but this is outside the scope of this book.

Both ResourceQuotas and ClusterResourceQuotas are enforced on the namespace level. For more granular control, they are often paired with another type of guardrail – LimitRanges – which are the focus of the next section.

LimitRanges

In the previous section, we briefly mentioned the necessity of constraining the number of resources that different tenants are allowed to consume. By default, when a Pod is created, the amount of CPU, RAM, or persistent storage it can use is not restricted. That means that a single tenant can exhaust all available quota within a namespace. LimitRange has three purposes:

- Enforce default requests and limits for CPU and memory for the workloads that neglect to set them explicitly.
- Constrain requests and limits for CPU and memory within certain ranges that individual workloads are allowed to specify.
- Enforce a ratio between requests and limits.

Both `ResourceQuota` and `LimitRange` objects serve a similar purpose of keeping the resource usage of all tenants in check, but they do so on different levels. The following are the main differences between the two:

	ResourceQuota	**LimitRange**
Scope	Namespace	Pod or container
Resources that can be constrained	• CPU • Memory • Persistent storage • Persistent storage for a specific storage class • Ephemeral storage • Number of API objects	• CPU • Memory • Persistent storage • Maximum allowed size of images that can be pushed into the internal registry • Number of tags and image references for ImageStreams
Enforcement of defaults	No	Can enforce default requests and limits, as well as the maximum ratio between them

Table 7.3: Comparison of ResourceQuotas and LimitRanges

It is considered good practice to create both ResourceQuota/`ClusterResourceQuota` and LimitRange in order to set up guardrails on all levels – namespaces, Pods, and containers.

Working with LimitRanges

Now it is time to see how LimitRanges work in practice:

1. First, create a new project for this exercise:

```
$ oc new-project chapter-7-limits
```

2. We prepared a LimitRange manifest in a file named `chapters/7/snippets/limitrange.yml` in this book's GitHub repository. Examine it and then create the LimitRange:

```
$ oc create -f chapters/7/snippets/limitrange.yml
```

3. Now we need a workload to test the LimitRange we have just created. We have prepared a file named `chapters/7/snippets/busybox-limitranges-no-requests.yml` in this book's GitHub repository with a deployment manifest. It doesn't specify any requests or limits; therefore, it should be subject to the defaults set in the LimitRange. Create the deployment:

```
$ oc create -f chapters/7/snippets/busybox-limitranges-no-requests.yml
```

4. Now, list the Pods in the current project with oc get po. The Pod was created successfully:

```
NAME                     READY   STATUS    RESTARTS   AGE
test-599cc6cdcd-dpqwc    1/1     Running   0          25s
```

Figure 7.31: Pod successfully admitted

5. Use the following command to examine the YAML representation of the Pod:

```
$ oc get -o yaml po -l app=test
```

As you can see in the following screenshot, the LimitRange configured the API admission controller to add default requests and limits for both CPU and RAM:

```
spec:
  containers:
  - command:
    - /bin/sh
    - -c
    - sleep 3600
    image: busybox
    imagePullPolicy: Always
    name: busybox
    resources:
      limits:
        cpu: 500m
        memory: 300Mi
      requests:
        cpu: 200m
        memory: 100Mi
```

Figure 7.32: Default limits and requests for CPU and memory added to the Pod

6. Delete the deployment to prepare for the next exercise:

```
$ oc delete -f chapters/7/snippets/busybox-limitranges-no-requests.yml
```

7. Now, let's create another workload, this time with CPU and memory requests set. Open the `chapters/7/snippets/busybox-limitranges-requests.yml` file from this book's GitHub repository and note that it is the same deployment as the one from the previous step, with CPU and memory requests added under `.spec.template.spec.containers`. Create the deployment:

```
$ oc create -f chapters/7/snippets/busybox-limitranges-requests.yml
```

8. List the Pods again with oc get po. This time, no Pod was created:

```
No resources found in chapter-7-limits namespace.
```

Figure 7.33: No Pod was created by the Deployment

9. Why? As before, let's examine the namespace's events to find out why the Pod wasn't accepted:

```
$ oc get ev
```

You should see the following message indicating the reason for our Pod not being allowed:

```
112s        Warning   FailedCreate        replicaset/test-558cb67574
Error creating: Pod "test-558cb67574-64fpr" is invalid: [spec.container
s[0].resources.requests: Invalid value: "3": must be less than or equal
 to cpu limit of 500m, spec.containers[0].resources.requests: Invalid v
alue: "1Gi": must be less than or equal to memory limit of 300Mi]
```

Figure 7.34: Pod was rejected due to requests and limits being out of alignment

Let's take a closer look at what that message actually says. Since we didn't specify limits, just requests, they were set to the default values configured in the LimitRange, which are 500 millicores for CPU and 300 Mi for memory. These values are lower than requests from the Pod's manifest – 3 full cores and 1 Gi, respectively. API admission controller rejects all Pods with improperly set ranges, where requests are higher than limits.

10. Let's clean things up before the next exercise:

```
$ oc delete project/chapter-7-limits
```

In a similar fashion, you can set limits, requests, and their defaults on a Pod level (`type: Pod`).

ResourceQuotas, `ClusterResourceQuota` resources, and LimitRanges are admission-stage guardrails; that is, they are enforced only on creating or updating resources. We will now discuss network policies, which are used to enforce rules on Pod-to-Pod communication, making them runtime-stage guardrails.

Network policies

By default, all Pods in all namespaces can communicate with each other – directly or via Service primitives. While convenient, this is not always desirable, especially when a cluster is shared by many different companies and namespaces are provided as part of a subscription. In order to mitigate this problem, the `NetworkPolicy` object was introduced in Kubernetes, which allows you to do the following:

- Allow access to all Pods in specific namespaces, while blocking other traffic.
- Selectively allow access to specific Pods inside selected namespaces, while blocking access to all other resources inside those namespaces.
- Selectively block ingress, egress, or both connections.
- Allow access to entire CIDRs while blocking access to specific IP addresses.

Network policies are subject to the following limitations:

- The underlying network plugin must support network policies; otherwise, they will have no effect. For example, both OpenShift SDN and OVN-Kubernetes (used in our lab) meet this condition.
- Network policies cannot block access between Pods and the nodes they are running on.

- Only the TCP, UDP, and SCTP protocols are supported, which means no layer 7 (based on HTTP methods, paths, or headers) rules.
- No added SSL/TLS encryption/termination.
- Pods and namespaces cannot be targeted by their names, only labels.
- Network policies do not support routing or redirection; so, for example, you cannot use them to force traffic to go through a common gateway.

> This feature is commonly found in various service mesh implementations, such as Istio and Solo, in which case routing is performed by an Envoy proxy. The concept of service mesh is discussed in more detail in *Chapter 14, Understanding Service Mesh and Distributed Tracing*.

- Network policies deny traffic by default, so you need to formulate rules to allow the communication you need. As such, no explicit deny rules are supported.
- Unlike `ResourceQuota` and `ClusterResourceQuota`, there is no cluster-wide counterpart for `NetworkPolicy`, so rules must be defined independently for each project.

There are a couple more things to keep in mind when working with network policies:

- Network policies are additive, so you can use simple policies as building blocks for more complex scenarios.
- Network policies are independent, which means that if you want to allow communication between two parties, A and B, where A initiates a connection, you have to allow egress traffic from A and ingress traffic to B. There is no need, however, to allow the return traffic, as it is done automatically (meaning that they are stateful, which makes them similar to AWS security groups in this regard).

Network policies in action

In this section, we will demonstrate how simple policies work using three namespaces:

- `chapter-7-netpol-1`
- `chapter-7-netpol-2`
- `chapter-7-netpol-3`

Each scenario will be accompanied by a diagram showing the direction of traffic and Pods inside each namespace so that it is easier for you to understand different use cases.

Let's set up our environment before we start experimenting with access controls:

1. First, create a new namespace, `chapter-7-netpol-1`:

```
$ oc new-project chapter-7-netpol-1
```

2. One thing we must do before we create a workload in that namespace is to allow its UID. The container image we are going to use for this exercise starts a process under UID 0, which is prohibited by a default SCC (discussed in the next section). The easiest, albeit strongly discour-

aged in production, way to circumvent that is to assign another, less restrictive SCC, `anyuid`, to the service account named `default`, which is used by default to run all workloads:

```
$ oc adm policy add-scc-to-user anyuid -z default
```

3. Now we can create a deployment that will spawn test Pods. Open the file named `chapters/7/snippets/deploy-nginx-netpol-1.yml` from this book's GitHub repository and examine it. The deployment creates two Pods that start a single nginx container each. Create the object:

```
$ oc create -f chapters/7/snippets/deploy-nginx-netpol-1.yml
```

4. Now wait until both replicas are running. For this exercise, it doesn't matter if they end up on the same or different nodes. The following is an expected output of `oc get po -o wide`:

```
NAME                         READY   STATUS    RESTARTS   AGE   IP
netpol-1-5cdf79d999-64sqj    1/1     Running   0          13s   10.131.0.118
netpol-1-5cdf79d999-g4k9d    1/1     Running   0          13s   10.129.2.42
```

Figure 7.35: Creating a two-replica deployment

The `-o wide` option displays the resident node of each Pod, as well as Pods' IP addresses, which we will use shortly.

5. In order to test cross-namespace communications, we need at least one more namespace. Let's add it with the following:

```
$ oc new-project chapter-7-netpol-2
```

6. As before, in our lab, we must grant its default service account the necessary capabilities by assigning it the `anyuid` SCC:

```
$ oc adm policy add-scc-to-user anyuid -z default
```

7. This namespace also requires its own workload, which we will create from the same image. Use the file named `chapters/7/snippets/deploy-nginx-netpol-2.yml` from this book's GitHub repository:

```
$ oc create -f chapters/7/snippets/deploy-nginx-netpol-2.yml
```

A new Pod should start successfully, as evident by the output of `oc get po -o wide`:

```
NAME                         READY   STATUS    RESTARTS   AGE   IP
netpol-2-69796474c4-sx8dk    1/1     Running   0          2s    10.131.0.120
```

Figure 7.36: Creating a Pod in another test project

> Since both deployments are meant to reside in separate namespaces, it is not strictly necessary to use a different name, labels, and selectors. We do it only so that it is easier for you to tell what namespace you are currently in without checking it with `oc project`.

8. Now we will use this setup to simulate communication between two participants that reside in different namespaces. Use the following commands to establish a connection from the Pod in the `chapter-7-netpol-2` namespace to one of the Pods in the `chapter-7-netpol-1` namespace (don't forget to replace the source Pod's name and the destination Pod's IP address):

```
$ oc exec netpol-2-69796474c4-sx8dk -- curl -so /dev/null -w "%{response_
code}\n%header{Server}\n%{remote_ip}\n" 10.131.0.118
```

The connection was established successfully:

```
200
nginx/1.29.0
10.131.0.118
```

Figure 7.37: Connection attempt from the Pod in chapter-7-netpol-2 to one of the Pods in chapter-7-netpol-1

9. Now let's test connectivity to another Pod in the `chapter-7-netpol-1` namespace:

```
$ oc exec netpol-2-69796474c4-sx8dk -- curl -so /dev/null -w "%{response_
code}\n%header{Server}\n%{remote_ip}\n" 10.129.2.42
```

The connection attempt succeeds for that Pod as well:

```
200
nginx/1.29.0
10.129.2.42
```

Figure 7.38: Connection attempt from the Pod in chapter-7-netpol-2 to another Pod in chapter-7-netpol-1

10. As expected, in the absence of network policies, communication between namespaces is unrestricted. To complete the experiment, we need to check whether communication in the opposite direction works as well. Switch back to the `chapter-7-netpol-1` project:

```
$ oc project chapter-7-netpol-1
```

11. Now let's use the oc exec command from before to check whether we can reach the Pod in `chapter-7-netpol-2`:

```
$ oc exec netpol-1-5cdf79d999-64sqj -- curl -so /dev/null -w "%{response_
code}\n%header{Server}\n%{remote_ip}\n" 10.131.0.120
```

The server responds, which indicates success:

```
200
nginx/1.29.0
10.131.0.120
```

Figure 7.39: Successful connection from a Pod in chapter-7-netpol-1 to a Pod in chapter-7-netpol-2

12. Since we already know that there are no network policies involved yet and we already tested communication between one of the Pods in `chapter-7-netpol-1` and the only Pod in `chapter-7-netpol-2`, it is certain that the connection from the second Pod is going to work too. Instead, let's try to reach the Pod in the same namespace – this is exactly why we spun up two of them:

```
$ oc exec netpol-1-5cdf79d999-64sqj -- curl -so /dev/null -w "%{response_
code}\n%header{Server}\n%{remote_ip}\n" 10.129.2.42
```

Again, the connection was successful:

```
200
nginx/1.29.0
10.129.2.42
```

Figure 7.40: Successful connection between Pods in the chapter-7-netpol-1 namespace

It likely didn't come as a surprise at this point; however, the scientific approach dictates that we should establish a good baseline before introducing any changes.

The following diagram illustrates the configuration we have just created:

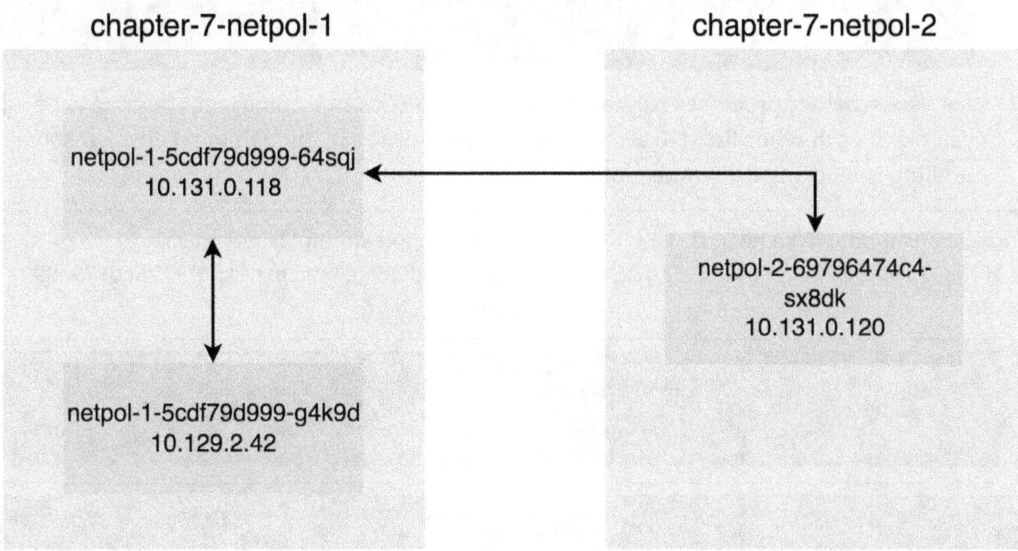

Figure 7.41: Namespace-bound and cross-namespace connection attempts succeed without network policies involved

Now let us examine a few common network policies that should give you an idea of how they may be used to restrict communication in certain scenarios.

Deny all

In this exercise, we are going to create a very simple network policy that blocks all ingress traffic from Pods in all namespaces to all Pods in the current namespace.

Let's open the file named `chapters/7/snippets/netpol-deny-all.yml` in this book's GitHub repository and look at the manifest inside. In order to be able to create correct policies, you must first understand how they are applied to workloads and traffic origins/destinations:

- The `podSelector: {}` field selects *all* Pods within the current namespace, so all Pods will be subject to whatever confines are set by the policy.
- The `ingress: []` construct configures no rules for ingress traffic, which means that no traffic will be allowed. The way network policies work is that when at least one exists, it blocks all ingress or egress traffic or both, as long as there are no rules that explicitly allow exceptions.

Now it's time for practice:

1. Let's make sure we are in the correct project and create our first policy:

```
$ oc project chapter-7-netpol-1
$ oc create -f chapters/7/snippets/netpol-deny-all.yml
```

2. Let's see whether processes running inside our two Pods in the `project-7-netpol-1` project can reach each other first (10 seconds should be more than enough to receive a response, if nothing is blocking the connection):

Connection attempt from `netpol-1-5cdf79d999-64sqj` to `netpol-1-5cdf79d999-g4k9d`	Connection attempt from `netpol-1-5cdf79d999-g4k9d` to `netpol-1-5cdf79d999-64sqj`
`$ oc exec netpol-1-5cdf79d999-64sqj -- curl -sv 10.129.2.42 --connect-timeout 10`	`$ oc exec netpol-1-5cdf79d999-g4k9d -- curl -sv 10.131.0.118 --connect-timeout 10`

`*   Trying 10.129.2.42:80...`
`* ipv4 connect timeout after 10000ms, move on!`
`* Failed to connect to 10.129.2.42 port 80 after 10001 ms: Timeout was reached`
`* Closing connection 0`
`command terminated with exit code 28`
	`*   Trying 10.131.0.118:80...`
	`* ipv4 connect timeout after 10000ms, move on!`
	`* Failed to connect to 10.131.0.118 port 80 after 10001 ms: Timeout was reached`
	`* Closing connection 0`
	`command terminated with exit code 28`

Table 7.4: Namespace-bound communication blocked

As the preceding screenshots show, each Pod is now inaccessible from any other in the same namespace.

3. Now let's try and reach the Pod running in the `chapter-7-netpol-2` namespace:

```
$ oc exec netpol-1-5cdf79d999-64sqj -- curl -so /dev/null -w "%{response_code}\n%header{Server}\n%{remote_ip}\n" 10.131.0.120
```

The connection is successful:

```
200
nginx/1.29.0
10.131.0.120
```

Figure 7.42: Cross-namespace communication allowed

This worked for two reasons:

- The policy we created in `chapter-7-netpol-1` didn't specify the egress stanza at all, which means that all egress traffic is unrestricted. The situation is different for ingress – by mentioning `ingress: []`, we blocked all ingress traffic, and to allow any exceptions, we must specify them in `[]`.
- We haven't created any network policies in `chapter-7-netpol-2` yet, so all traffic in both directions is allowed to pass. As we said before, with network policies, there are always two of them involved at both ends of a conversation.

4. Now let's switch to `chapter-7-netpol-2` with `oc project chapter-7-netpol-2` and use the following commands to test connectivity to Pods in `chapter-7-netpol-1`:

Connection attempt from `netpol-2-69796474c4-sx8dk` to `netpol-1-5cdf79d999-g4k9d`	Connection attempt from `netpol-2-69796474c4-sx8dk` to `netpol-1-5cdf79d999-64sqj`
`$ oc exec netpol-2-69796474c4-sx8dk -- curl -sv 10.129.2.42 --connect-timeout 10`	`$ oc exec netpol-2-69796474c4-sx8dk -- curl -sv 10.131.0.118 --connect-timeout 10`

`*   Trying 10.129.2.42:80...`
`* ipv4 connect timeout after 10000ms, move on!`
`* Failed to connect to 10.129.2.42 port 80 after 10001 ms: Timeout was reached`
`* Closing connection 0`
`command terminated with exit code 28`
	`*   Trying 10.131.0.118:80...`
	`* ipv4 connect timeout after 10000ms, move on!`
	`* Failed to connect to 10.131.0.118 port 80 after 10001 ms: Timeout was reached`
	`* Closing connection 0`
	`command terminated with exit code 28`

Table 7.5: Deny-all policy blocks ingress connections

As you would expect, connections from that namespace are not allowed either – because our deny-all policy doesn't have any exceptions for specific namespaces.

The following diagram highlights the communication paths we tested in this exercise:

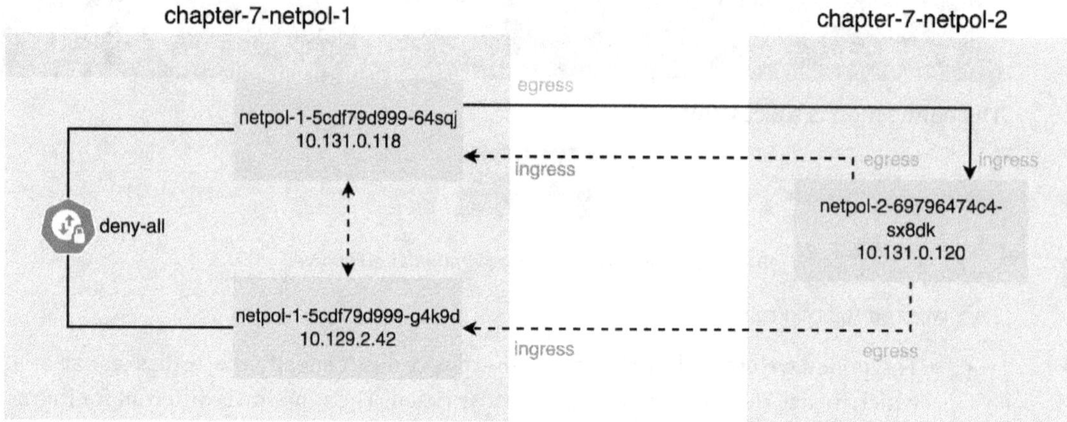

Figure 7.43: Deny-all blocking ingress communications regardless of origin

To conclude this exercise, switch to the `chapter-7-netpol-1` namespace and delete the deny-all policy:

```
$ oc project chapter-7-netpol-1
$ oc delete -f chapters/7/snippets/netpol-deny-all.yml
```

Allow selected namespaces

In this scenario, we will expand on the previous policy to make it allow communications from a specifically labeled namespace:

1. Let's go ahead and create a new project, `chapter-7-netpol-3`:

   ```
   $ oc new-project chapter-7-netpol-3
   ```

2. Again, we need to add the `anyuid` SCC to the `default` service account that our workload will use:

   ```
   $ oc adm policy add-scc-to-user anyuid -z default
   ```

3. Next, examine the manifest for a test workload stored in `chapters/7/snippets/deploy-nginx-netpol-3.yml` of this book's GitHub repository and create the deployment:

   ```
   $ oc create -f chapters/7/snippets/deploy-nginx-netpol-3.yml
   ```

4. The next step is to configure a network policy for our project. The policy manifest is stored in the `chapters/7/snippets/netpol-pod-ns.yml` file of this book's GitHub repository. Open it and notice that unlike the deny-all policy from the previous exercise, this one has an explicit allow rule in the ingress field, which permits traffic from Pods in any namespace labeled as `allowed="true"`. So, in order for the preceding policy to work as expected, let's label the `chapter-7-netpol-2` namespace accordingly:

   ```
   $ oc label ns/chapter-7-netpol-2 allowed=true
   ```

> You may ask, why label the namespace and not the project as a native OpenShift construct? The reason is that projects are immutable in OpenShift, and if you try doing it with `oc label project/chapter-7-netpol-2 allowed=true`, you will get an error:
>
> ```
> The Project "chapter-7-netpol-2" is invalid: metadata.
> labels[allowed]: Invalid value: "true": field is immutable,
> try updating the namespace
> ```

5. Now that we have properly labeled our namespace, let's create the network policy:

```
$ oc create -f chapters/7/snippets/netpol-pod-ns.yml
```

6. Use the following command to see the private IP address that your Pod was assigned:

```
$ oc get po -o wide
```

7. In our lab, it is `10.131.0.125`, but for you, it will likely be different. Remember that we applied the necessary label only to the `chapter-7-netpol-2` namespace. Switch to the `chapter-7-netpol-1` namespace and from one of the Pods there, try to reach the Pod running in `chapter-7-netpol-3`:

```
$ oc project chapter-7-netpol-1
$ oc exec netpol-1-5cdf79d999-64sqj -- curl -sv 10.131.0.125 --connect-timeout 10
```

As you might have expected, it didn't work, because our policy allows only specifically labeled namespaces:

```
*   Trying 10.131.0.125:80...
* ipv4 connect timeout after 10000ms, move on!
* Failed to connect to 10.131.0.125 port 80 after 10002 ms:
 Timeout was reached
* Closing connection 0
command terminated with exit code 28
```

Figure 7.44: Network policy blocking ingress connections from an unlabeled project

8. Let's change our current namespace to `chapter-7-netpol-2` and try the same check:

```
$ oc project chapter-7-netpol-2
$ oc exec netpol-2-69796474c4-sx8dk -- curl -so /dev/null -w "%{response_code}\n%header{Server}\n%{remote_ip}\n" 10.131.0.125
```

This time it worked, because the `chapter-7-netpol-2` namespace has a proper label that is permitted by the policy:

```
200
nginx/1.29.0
10.131.0.125
```

Figure 7.45: Communications from a properly labeled project are allowed

The following diagram depicts the scenario we just considered:

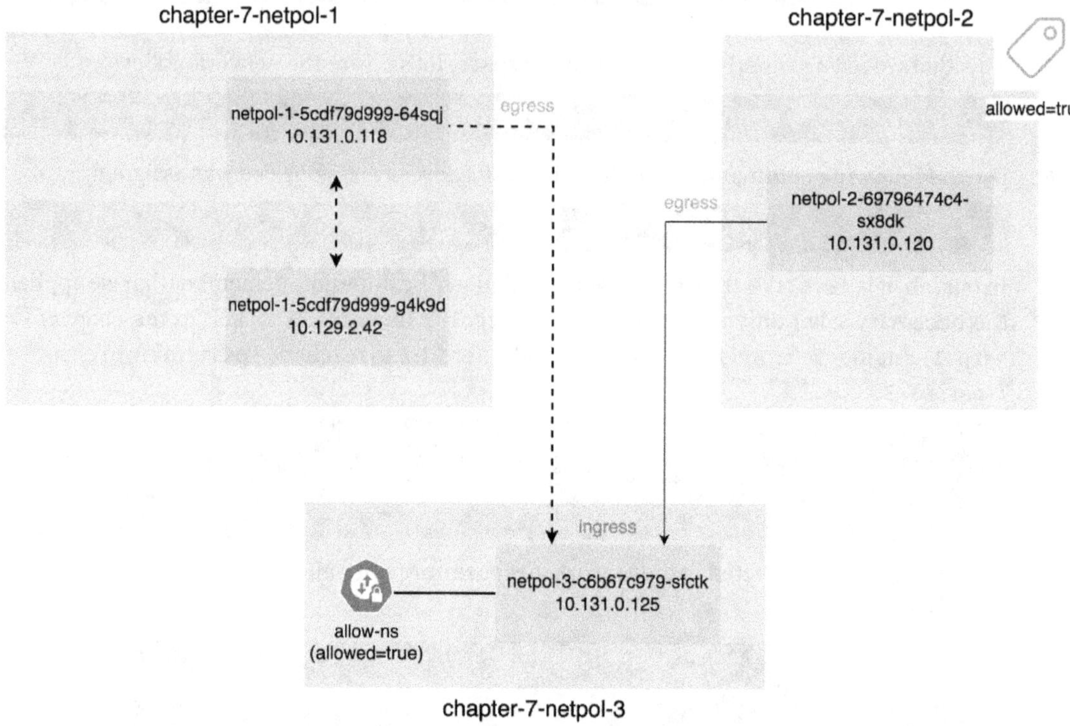

Figure 7.46: Network policy restricting communications from projects based on their labels

We couldn't explore every possible situation within the scope of this chapter; however, we believe that the basic policies you have seen will set you on the right path. Network policies in enterprise clusters can be very complex; for example, they may include multiple criteria, such as `podSelector` and/or `ipBlock` in the `from` node, and permit connections only to certain ports via `spec.ingress.ports[]` or `spec.egress.ports[]`. In general, be aware of the following caveats:

- When analyzing how a network policy you are about to add will impact traffic for a Pod, remember to account for *all* network policies that apply to that Pod via the `spec.podSelector` field, including the ones that may already exist.
- Pay attention to indentations in your policy's YAML manifest. One mistake can lead to an interruption of service and have a negative impact on your SLA. For example, consider the following policy excerpts:

<table>
<tr><th>AND logic</th><th>OR logic</th></tr>
<tr><td><pre>
ingress:
  - from:
    - namespaceSelector:
        matchLabels:
          allowed: "true"
      podSelector:
        matchLabels:
          role: "frontend"
</pre></td><td><pre>
ingress:
  - from:
    - namespaceSelector:
        matchLabels:
          allowed: "true"
    - podSelector:
        matchLabels:
          role: "frontend"
</pre></td></tr>
</table>

Table 7.6: The presence of - makes a difference in how network policies are interpreted

They may look the same at first glance, but the first policy permits traffic only from Pods that both reside in namespaces labeled as `allowed="true"` *and* labeled as `role="frontend"`, while the latter applies `OR` logic when evaluating the rules, allowing a connection attempt as long as at least one rule matches. The leading - (hyphen) in front of `podSelector` makes all the difference.

If you need to match against multiple labels, consolidate them under `matchExpressions[]` instead of using multiple rules with different `matchLabels`. Not only does this improve readability and spare you the need to check for each and every policy in a namespace to assess their collective impact, but it also improves performance for large numbers of policies. This is also useful when you want to allow access from namespaces or Pods that *do not* have specific labels, as follows:

```
ingress:
  - from:
    - namespaceSelector:
        - key: "role"
          operator: NotIn
          values: ["frontend", "backend"]
```

We encourage you to read the detailed explanation of how network policies are evaluated at [17]. Another useful source of information is the `oc explain` command, which provides you with an offline guide to most Kubernetes and OpenShift API objects. For example, to obtain a list of fields and their types supported by the `spec.ingress.from` field, use the following command:

```
$ oc explain networkpolicy.spec.ingress.from
```

Now that we're done with network policies, let's clean things up before moving on to the next section:

```
$ oc delete project/chapter-7-netpol-1 project/chapter-7-netpol-2 project/
chapter-7-netpol-3
```

Now that we have covered network policies and other basic elements, it is time to discuss SCCs, which serve as guardrails around what processes running inside containers can do on a node.

Security context constraints

Kubernetes and OpenShift rely on multiple levels of security. For example, Role and ClusterRole objects control the ability of users, groups, and service accounts to invoke specific API verbs, such as get, create, or delete, on other API objects. Another layer of protection that we already know about is network policies that allow us to selectively enable certain projects to communicate with each other or allow our applications to access external services identified by their IP addresses. These, however, do not offer any protection in situations where a malicious application exploits a vulnerability in the Linux kernel on its resident node in order to gain elevated privileges or perform actions that are not part of its business functionality, because these kinds of exploits do not involve the use of API or Pod networking. When you create a Pod (either directly or through a controller, such as a Deployment), you can configure the **security context** for all its containers (at the Pod level) or individually (with the container level always taking precedence). Available parameters include (but are not limited to) the following:

Security Context Setting	Pod Level	Container Level	Description
`runAsUser`	✓	✓	UID
`runAsGroup`	✓	✓	GID. Defaults to `0` (root).
`runAsNonRoot`	✓	✓	A Boolean that requires a container to run with a non-root (other than `0`) UID. If an image contains the `USER 0` instruction or `runAsUser` is set to `0`, the container will fail to start.
`supplementalGroups`	✓	✕	A list of supplemental groups for providing group-level access to files inside containers.
`fsGroup`	✓	✕	A filesystem group that owns files on mounted persistent volumes. It is added to the list of supplemental groups. When specified, the container runtime will recursively change group ownership of the mount point to match, set the `SETGID` bit on it (so that new files are owned by the same group), and set `OR` permissions with `660` (`rw-rw----`) to produce effective UNIX permissions. If you're using NetApp NAS (NFS) for persistent storage, make sure that the corresponding storage class includes `fsType: nfs` (or any other non-null value) in its `parameters` and the `accessModes` parameter of your PVC includes `ReadWriteOnce`, or it won't be honored.

Security Context Setting	Pod Level	Container Level	Description
`privileged`	✗	✓	A Boolean that controls whether a container is privileged or not. Privileged containers are allowed to bind to privileged ports (`0-1024`) and mount host volumes, among other things.
`allowPrivilegeEscalation`	✗	✓	A Boolean that allows a containerized process to acquire more privileges than its parent process. Implied to be true when `privileged: true` or `capabilities.add[]` includes `CAP_SYS_ADMIN`.
`capabilities.add`	✗	✓	A list of capabilities that a container can (but isn't required to) acquire. For example, the `CAP_NET_BIND_SERVICE` capability permits binding to privileged ports, and `CAP_NET_RAW` allows an application to capture traffic on its container's NICs. You can think of capabilities as controls or flags of the Linux kernel that are necessary for certain actions.
`capabilities.drop`	✗	✓	A list of capabilities that a container is required to drop.
`seLinuxOptions`	✓	✓	SELinux options. SCCs let you control the `user`, `role`, and `type` labels of the process and files inside a Pod, as well as its level of clearance. For example, you may use these options to set the following SELinux metadata on a file: `unconfined_u:object_r:home_user_t:s0`. A level is a multi-layer security (MLS) concept that goes way back to the US government's classification system with a total of 16 levels – `s0` being the lowest clearance and `s15` being the highest. SELinux MLS implements the Bell-LaPadula model, which follows the principle "no read up, no write down." That means that a process cannot read the data that requires a higher level of clearance and cannot pass data to lower clearance levels. SELinux MLS, however, makes it even stricter by limiting write access only to the same level. You can find out more about how MLS is implemented in SELinux at [30].

Security Context Setting	Pod Level	Container Level	Description
`seccompProfile`	✓	✓	Secure computing is a mechanism that controls access to Linux kernel system calls. This is useful when you know the execution profile of your application and want to harden it against potential attackers by reducing its attack surface. This, however, requires close collaboration between operations, development, and security teams in order to make security a part of the delivery pipeline. This modus operandi is known as **DevSecOps**.
`readOnlyRootFilesystem`	✕	✓	A Boolean that determines whether the root filesystem of a container is in read-only mode.
`sysctls`	✓	✕	List of namespaced and safe sysctl parameters set for all containers in a Pod. Note that CRI-O does not support all parameters. There are certain caveats to which namespaced sysctl knobs are considered safe, so please refer to [33] for additional guidance.

Table 7.7: Security context settings

When no capabilities are dropped or added, the container gets a default list of capabilities determined by the container runtime, which for CRI-O is as follows: `CHOWN`, `DAC_OVERRIDE`, `FSETID`, `FOWNER`, `SETUID`, `SETGID`, `SETPCAP`, `NET_BIND_SERVICE`, and `KILL`. However, the effective set of capabilities is determined by an assigned SCC. See [34] for more details.

OpenShift, by design, enforces many of the best practices that other containerization platforms do not; it makes OpenShift a very reliable and good choice for enterprise environments, where the proper guardrails help to maintain a higher level of security. In particular, it offers a way to control what capabilities and actions are allowed on a container's side – SCCs. Despite its name, this API is not just for constraining allowed security context settings, but it is also backed by its own admission controller that can set values for fields such as `runAsUser`, `supplementalGroups`, `fsGroup`, and `seLinuxContext` if unspecified or drop capabilities of a container (`requiredDropCapabilities`). It controls the following, among other aspects:

- Capabilities that will be dropped and those that can be acquired
- Range of allowed UIDs, supplementary groups, and filesystem groups for containerized processes
- Allowed seccomp profiles

- Volume types, such as **PersistentVolumeClaims** (**PVCs**), Secrets, or ConfigMaps, among others
- Priority, if multiple SCCs with the same restrictions exist
- Allowed SELinux options
- Privileged flag
- Privilege escalation
- Sysctl controls that can be set on a node

For example, an attempt to run a privileged process and/or with UID 0 (root) will fail by default, forcing users to use unprivileged containers with non-root UIDs. A full list of controls supported by SCCs can be obtained by executing `oc explain scc`.

> While access to SCCs is regulated by RBAC, as we will see in the hands-on part of this section, SCCs themselves are not a part of the authorization process. RBAC objects control granular access to the OpenShift API based on actions (verbs), subjects (service accounts, users, or groups), resource types (kinds), and, optionally, resource names. SCCs, on the other hand, are evaluated *after* authorization, at the **admission** stage, and control OS-level access for workloads. For example, while your user or service account may be allowed to create Pods, the OpenShift admission controller may not allow it if its security context violates an assigned (either implicitly or explicitly) SCC.

Enforcement of core OS-level security policies via SCCs is one of the most defining features of OpenShift, which emphasizes security by default and makes it different from many other Kubernetes platforms, such as **Tanzu Kubernetes Grid Integrator** (**TKGI**) or **Pivotal Cloud Foundry** (**PCF**). For this reason, developers often find it challenging to migrate to, and they will rely on your help to guide them.

Let's get down to business and see what SCCs we have available on our system with `oc get scc`. You will see the following list of pre-configured SCCs:

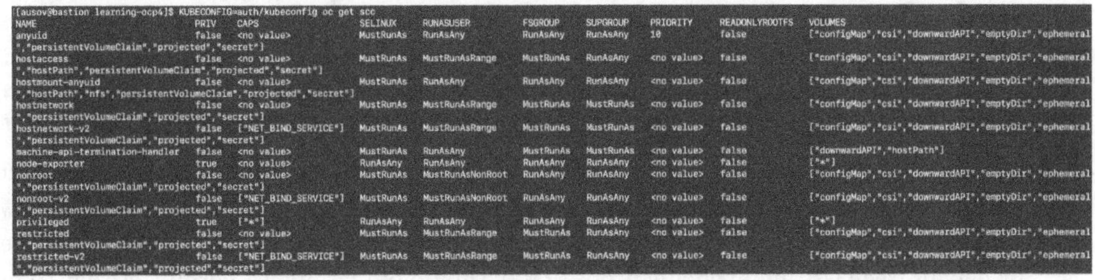

```
[ausov@bastion learning-ocp4]$ KUBECONFIG=auth/kubeconfig oc get scc
NAME                              PRIV    CAPS                    SELINUX     RUNASUSER          FSGROUP     SUPGROUP    PRIORITY     READONLYROOTFS   VOLUMES
anyuid                            false   <no value>              MustRunAs   RunAsAny           RunAsAny    RunAsAny    10           false            ["configMap","csi","downwardAPI","emptyDir","ephemeral
","persistentVolumeClaim","projected","secret"]
hostaccess                        false   <no value>              MustRunAs   MustRunAsRange     MustRunAs   RunAsAny    <no value>   false            ["configMap","csi","downwardAPI","emptyDir","ephemeral
","hostPath","persistentVolumeClaim","projected","secret"]
hostmount-anyuid                  false   <no value>              MustRunAs   RunAsAny           RunAsAny    RunAsAny    <no value>   false            ["configMap","csi","downwardAPI","emptyDir","ephemeral
","hostPath","nfs","persistentVolumeClaim","projected","secret"]
hostnetwork                       false   <no value>              MustRunAs   MustRunAsRange     MustRunAs   MustRunAs   <no value>   false            ["configMap","csi","downwardAPI","emptyDir","ephemeral
","persistentVolumeClaim","projected","secret"]
hostnetwork-v2                    false   ["NET_BIND_SERVICE"]    MustRunAs   MustRunAsRange     MustRunAs   MustRunAs   <no value>   false            ["configMap","csi","downwardAPI","emptyDir","ephemeral
","persistentVolumeClaim","projected","secret"]
machine-api-termination-handler   false   <no value>              MustRunAs   RunAsAny           MustRunAs   MustRunAs   <no value>   false            ["downwardAPI","hostPath"]
node-exporter                     true    <no value>              RunAsAny    RunAsAny           RunAsAny    RunAsAny    <no value>   false            ["*"]
nonroot                           false   <no value>              MustRunAs   MustRunAsNonRoot   RunAsAny    RunAsAny    <no value>   false            ["configMap","csi","downwardAPI","emptyDir","ephemeral
","persistentVolumeClaim","projected","secret"]
nonroot-v2                        false   ["NET_BIND_SERVICE"]    MustRunAs   MustRunAsNonRoot   RunAsAny    RunAsAny    <no value>   false            ["configMap","csi","downwardAPI","emptyDir","ephemeral
","persistentVolumeClaim","projected","secret"]
privileged                        true    ["*"]                   RunAsAny    RunAsAny           RunAsAny    RunAsAny    <no value>   false            ["*"]
restricted                        false   <no value>              MustRunAs   MustRunAsRange     MustRunAs   RunAsAny    <no value>   false            ["configMap","csi","downwardAPI","emptyDir","ephemeral
","persistentVolumeClaim","projected","secret"]
restricted-v2                     false   ["NET_BIND_SERVICE"]    MustRunAs   MustRunAsRange     MustRunAs   RunAsAny    <no value>   false            ["configMap","csi","downwardAPI","emptyDir","ephemeral
","persistentVolumeClaim","projected","secret"]
```

Figure 7.47: Default SCCs

There are a few SCCs provided in every installation of OpenShift, each with different restrictions and designed for different needs. For example, the `anyuid` SCC, which you are already briefly familiar with, allows an application to run under any UID (as the name implies), including 0. This is useful when you wish to run an application that wasn't containerized for OpenShift with best practices in mind, such as changing the UID of the `ENTRYPOINT` process inside the container's image via the `USER` instruction. The default SCC is `restricted-v2`, which imposes a number of constraints on a process, forcing it, for example, to run under a UID that falls within the range specified in an annotation of the controlled Pod's namespace. To simplify things, the following is a table that explains where certain SCC controls take their values from if they are not specified in the SCC itself, as is the case for the `restricted-v2` SCC:

SCC Control	Strategy	Namespace Annotation
`RunAsUser`	`MustRunAsRange`	`openshift.io/sa.scc.uid-range`
`SELinuxContext`	`MustRunAs`	`openshift.io/sa.scc.mcs`
`FSGroup`	`MustRunAs`	`openshift.io/sa.scc.supplemental-groups`
`SupplementalGroups`	`MustRunAs`	`openshift.io/sa.scc.supplemental-groups`

Table 7.8: SCC identity settings

Let's examine pre-existing SCCs in more detail.

Default SCCs and their use cases

The official documentation describes SCCs in detail, but let's discuss why administrators may need them and their high-level definitions and differences. OpenShift has 11 SCCs pre-configured out of the box:

- `restricted`: This is the legacy SCC that used to be used by default, which is still available for backward compatibility. It is superseded by `restricted-v2` as of OpenShift 4.11. The UID, SE-Linux context, and filesystem group are allocated from the namespace of a Pod it is assigned to. The `KILL`, `MKNOD`, `SETUID`, and `SETGID` capabilities are dropped from containers, and none are explicitly allowed or added. While it allows escalation of privileges, privileged containers are blocked.
- `restricted-v2`: This is the default SCC starting from OpenShift 4.11 and is available for all OCP users – privileged or not. It is built on `restricted`; however, it doesn't allow privilege escalation and drops all capabilities, except for an explicitly allowed `NET_BIND_SERVICE`. It is the least permissive SCC intended for most applications that do not require any special permissions. It is also useful when you want to enforce a seccomp profile to `runtime/default` and disallow any others.
- `anyuid`: This is the most frequently used non-default SCC, which, unlike `restricted-v2`, allows containers to run under any UID and in any filesystem group. However, it doesn't allow containers to request any extra capabilities beyond those provided by the container runtime by default (see [34]) and explicitly drops `MKNOD`. On top of that, it also permits escalation of privileges. It may be required in cases when a Docker image wasn't built for OpenShift and fixing it isn't practical. It is also often used as a base for custom SCCs. Refer to [35] for guidance on how to build images that do not require this SCC and can run under UIDs generated by OpenShift (the `openshift.io/sa.scc.uid-range` annotation on the namespace). No seccomp profiles are allowed.

- `hostaccess`: This is similar to `restricted` but allows a Pod and its containers to access the host OS' network, IPC, and PID namespaces, as well as binding to ports directly on the host system. It is usually required by some observability, security, and **software-defined storage (SDS)** solutions. It also allows the use of `hostPath` volumes used for direct access to the host's filesystem. No seccomp profiles are allowed.
- `hostmount-anyuid`: Compared to restricted SCC, it allows containers to run with any UID and filesystem group and drops only `MKNOD` capability. Additionally, it permits containers to mount `hostPath` and `nfs` volumes. Although primarily used by the persistent volume recycler, this SCC may also be used by SDS solutions and monitoring agents, and in cases when host mounts are needed for some reason.
- `hostnetwork`: It may seem similar to `restricted`, but there are some key differences – this SCC allows a container to run in the network namespace of its host and bind to its ports, while still mandating that it must operate under a UID and SELinux context assigned to its Kubernetes namespace. Aside from that, it also requires a container process to run with supplementary group(s) allocated from the range specified in the `openshift.io/sa.scc.supplemental-groups` annotation of its project.
- `hostnetwork-v2`: This is a new version of the `hostnetwork` SCC. The difference from `hostnetwork` is the same as between `restricted-v2` and `restricted` – access to the host's network namespace, ports, and restrictions on supplementary groups.
- `privileged`: This is the least recommended SCC, as it allows completely unrestricted access to a host – a container can access all of the host's namespaces, acquire elevated privileges, request all capabilities, mount all types of volumes, use any seccomp profile, set any unsafe sysctls, as well as run as any user and under any groups and SELinux contexts. It may be used for system-level operators and applications. It is not uncommon to use it for regular applications *as a last resort*; however, we highly recommend encouraging developers not to rely on it and to design their software/build their images according to the principle of least privilege. One example when one of the authors of this book had to use it is getting Kaniko (project discontinued) image builds to work.
- `node-exporter`: This is a very specific SCC that is used by Prometheus Node Exporter. Essentially, it's a "tuned down" version of privileged SCC, with two differences – it supports only the `runtime/default` seccomp profile and doesn't allow the use of the host's IPC namespace.
- `nonroot`: This is similar to `restricted` but allows containers to run under any UID (except for 0) and filesystem group.
- `nonroot-v2`: Like other updated SCCs, this introduces the following changes compared to its predecessor: forbids escalation of privileges, supports only `runtime/default` seccomp profiles, drops all privileges, and allows only `NET_BIND_SERVICE`.

We encourage you to inspect them more closely with `oc get -o yaml scc/<SCC>`. Now that we're aware of the SCCs provided out of the box and what parameters are supported by this API, it's time to put this knowledge into practice and create an SCC of our own.

Working with SCCs

While OpenShift provides several default SCCs to cover common use cases, there might be situations where you need to define custom SCCs tailored to the specific requirements of your applications. This section guides you through creating and managing these custom SCCs. Let's take a quick look at the key parameters that make up an SCC.

Available key parameters

When configuring SCCs in OpenShift, understanding each parameter's role is crucial for securing your Pods. Here are some of the most commonly used controls:

- `allowPrivilegeEscalation`: A Boolean that determines whether a container can escalate its privileges.
- `allowPrivilegedContainer`: A Boolean parameter that controls whether a container can run in privileged mode. Privileged containers have all the capabilities of the host machine; thus, this should be set to `false` unless necessary for the application's function.
- `readOnlyRootFilesystem`: This determines whether the container's root filesystem can be modified. Setting this to `true` enhances security by preventing changes to the root filesystem, which can protect against malicious modifications; however, that means that the application can store all its data, including logs, only on a persistent (PV/PVC) or ephemeral (`emptyDir`) storage.
- `requiredDropCapabilities`: This lists the Linux capabilities that will be dropped from the container. Dropping unnecessary capabilities reduces the risk of privilege escalation attacks. Standard capabilities to drop include `NET_RAW` and `MKNOD`.
- `runAsUser`: This defines the policy for controlling the UID with which the container runs. Its `type` (aka strategy) can be set to the following values:
    - `RunAsAny` for no restrictions.
    - `MustRunAs` with a single allowed value (`uid` field).
    - `MustRunAsNonRoot` to make sure that a Pod is not assigned UID 0.
    - `MustRunAsRange` with a range of allowed UIDs (`uidRangeMin`/`uidRangeMax`), enhancing control over container privileges. As noted in *Table 7.8*, if this allocation strategy is used and no range is specified, a value will be allocated from the range specified in the `openshift.io/sa.scc.uid-range` annotation of the project.
- `fsGroup`: This specifies the filesystem group ID that owns the container's volumes. This parameter controls access to the volumes by ensuring that a specific group owns all volume mounts.
- `supplementalGroups`: This controls the range of supplemental group IDs that can be assigned to a Pod.
- `volumes`: This lists the types of volumes that are allowed to be mounted into a container. Restricting volumes to certain types, such as `emptyDir` or `secret`, helps minimize the risk of sensitive data exposure or unauthorized data access.

You can learn more about each of these settings and others with `oc explain scc`. Also, refer to [38] for a more detailed explanation of how values for the `runAsUser`, `supplementalGroups`, `fsGroup`, and `seLinuxContext` fields are allocated for different strategies, if not specified.

The following section provides an example of an SCC definition and a set of steps to assign that SCC to a specific service account.

Creating and using a custom SCC

While OpenShift offers SCCs that cover a wide spectrum of common scenarios, sometimes your environment requires a custom approach. For example, you may have a **commercial off-the-shelf** (**COTS**) application that needs to run as root (UID 0) or with privileged access. Such requirements are neither inherently bad nor are they necessarily indicative of any malicious intent. In fact, certain processes, such as device drivers or monitoring agents, require this level of access to function, so each application's requirements must be evaluated by a company's security team individually. Also, a lot of operators, such as ODF (which will be discussed in the next chapter) and Trident (the NetApp integration layer), bring their own SCCs.

In this exercise, we'll guide you through creating a custom SCC to align security policies with your application's specific needs. This will give you greater control over Pod operations, enhancing security while ensuring your application works as intended:

1. Let's start a new exercise by creating a project named `chapter-7-scc`:

   ```
   $ oc new-project chapter-7-scc
   ```

2. Use the following command to reveal the project's YAML manifest:

   ```
   $ oc get -o yaml project/chapter-7-scc
   ```

   What we are interested in is the list of security annotations:


```
apiVersion: project.openshift.io/v1
kind: Project
metadata:
  annotations:
    openshift.io/description: ""
    openshift.io/display-name: ""
    openshift.io/requester: system:admin
    openshift.io/sa.scc.mcs: s0:c29,c19
    openshift.io/sa.scc.supplemental-groups: 1000850000/10000
    openshift.io/sa.scc.uid-range: 1000850000/10000
  creationTimestamp: "2025-08-04T08:26:03Z"
  labels:
    kubernetes.io/metadata.name: chapter-7-scc
    pod-security.kubernetes.io/audit: restricted
    pod-security.kubernetes.io/audit-version: v1.24
    pod-security.kubernetes.io/warn: restricted
    pod-security.kubernetes.io/warn-version: v1.24
  name: chapter-7-scc
  resourceVersion: "683494"
  uid: 1d2d73f6-4cfe-4188-920f-f949f8d827d3
spec:
  finalizers:
  - kubernetes
status:
  phase: Active
```


Figure 7.48: Project's PSS annotations

Take note of the `openshift.io/sa.scc.uid-range` annotation. It specifies the starting UID as `1000850000`, and the total number of unique UIDs supported per namespace is `10000`. Keep in mind, though, that your numbers will likely be different, so you may need to adjust the code snippets that follow accordingly.

3. Now we will create our own SCC that we will use to observe the effect it has on the customized security context of the workload we will create right after. We have prepared an SCC manifest that is based on the `restricted-v2` SCC. It is provided in `chapters/7/snippets/scc-chapter-7.yml` in this book's GitHub repository. Examine it and create the SCC:

```
$ oc create -f chapters/7/snippets/scc-chapter-7.yml
```

4. The next step is to permit the default service account to use that SCC, as it will be used to run our test application:

```
$ oc adm policy add-scc-to-user chapter-7-scc -z default
```

In older releases of OpenShift, the `add-scc-to-user` subcommand was used to update the `users` field in an SCC. However, in OpenShift 4.5+, it instead creates a ClusterRoleBinding that binds a service account in a specific namespace to a pre-existing ClusterRole that permits the `use` verb on the SCC; see [36] and [37] for details. If this is a custom SCC for which there is no ClusterRole, the ClusterRole is created behind the scenes. You can replicate this setup using the following steps (*not necessary here; these are provided purely for educational purposes*):

1. Create a Role or ClusterRole that allows the `use` API verb on that specific SCC. The following is the CLI command that can be used to accomplish this:

```
$ oc create role chapter-7-scc-use --verb use
--resource scc --resource-name chapter-7-scc -n
chapter-7-scc
```

Creating a Role means that it will be visible only to service accounts in the same namespace. If you want it to be visible cluster wide, create a ClusterRole instead.

2. Create a RoleBinding or ClusterRoleBinding that binds a previously created Role or ClusterRole, respectively, to that SCC. You can use the following command to establish this relationship:

```
$ oc create rolebinding chapter-7-scc-use --role
chapter-7-scc-use --serviceaccount chapter-7-
scc:default
```

5. Now we need a test workload. Examine the deployment manifest stored in the file named `chapters/7/snippets/deploy-busybox-scc.yml` in this book's GitHub repository. You will need to pick a value that is outside the range `[1000700000,1000710000]` of allowed UIDs in

the SCC, but within the range [1000850000,1000859999] allowed by the namespace, and put it in runAsUser. In our example, 1000850001 will work. However, you may need to adjust the deployment according to the numbers of your namespace. Another detail is the openshift.io/required-scc annotation, which prevents our SCC from being preempted by another SCC. Let's create the deployment and see what happens:

```
$ oc create -f chapters/7/snippets/deploy-busybox-scc.yml
```

6. If you try to get the list of Pods with oc get po now, you will notice that there are none. Let's take a look at the events of our deployment, recorded in the status field:

```
$ oc get -o yaml deploy/test
```

You should see an error about the improper UID of our process:

```
- lastTransitionTime: "2025-08-04T09:06:30Z"
  lastUpdateTime: "2025-08-04T09:06:30Z"
  message: 'pods "test-968cc8d8-" is forbidden: unable to validate against any security
    context constraint: provider chapter-7-scc: .containers[0].runAsUser: Invalid
    value: 1000850001: must be in the ranges: [1000700000, 1000710000]'
  reason: FailedCreate
  status: "True"
  type: ReplicaFailure
```

Figure 7.49: UID specified in the workload controller violates the assigned SCC

The preceding message unequivocally tells us that the workload was denied because of an incorrect UID that violates the restrictions set in our SCC.

7. Let's delete that deployment before proceeding:

```
$ oc delete deploy/test
```

8. Now let's move on to customizing our SCC's settings. Examine the chapters/7/snippets/scc-chapter-7-caps.yml file. This time, we relax the condition on the UID, but require workloads bound to that SCC to drop the NET_BIND_SERVICE capability in order to prevent them from binding to privileged ports.

> In the Linux kernel, full names of capabilities have the CAP_ prefix; however, in SCCs, they are specified without it.

9. Apply the file from the previous step to the existing SCC we created before:

```
$ oc apply -f chapters/7/snippets/scc-chapter-7-caps.yml
```

10. Now create an nginx-based workload from the chapters/7/snippets/deploy-nginx-no-bind.yml manifest stored in this book's GitHub repository:

```
$ oc create -f chapters/7/snippets/deploy-nginx-no-bind.yml
```

11. The name of your Pod will most likely be different, but you should see the following status with `oc get po`:

```
NAME                    READY   STATUS   RESTARTS     AGE
test-86ccb8c69c-r4nz8   0/1     Error    1 (1s ago)   2s
```

Figure 7.50: Pod was allowed by the SCC, but still failed to start

This time, the Pod passed the SCC admission stage; however, it was unable to start because the `NET_BIND_SERVICE` capability is required for binding to privileged ports (`0-1024`), as evidenced by the output of the `oc logs -l app=test` command:

```
/docker-entrypoint.sh: Looking for shell scripts in /docker-entrypoint.d/
/docker-entrypoint.sh: Launching /docker-entrypoint.d/10-listen-on-ipv6-by-default.sh
10-listen-on-ipv6-by-default.sh: info: Getting the checksum of /etc/nginx/conf.d/default.conf
10-listen-on-ipv6-by-default.sh: info: Enabled listen on IPv6 in /etc/nginx/conf.d/default.conf
/docker-entrypoint.sh: Sourcing /docker-entrypoint.d/15-local-resolvers.envsh
/docker-entrypoint.sh: Launching /docker-entrypoint.d/20-envsubst-on-templates.sh
/docker-entrypoint.sh: Launching /docker-entrypoint.d/30-tune-worker-processes.sh
/docker-entrypoint.sh: Configuration complete; ready for start up
2025/08/04 09:15:39 [emerg] 1#1: bind() to 0.0.0.0:80 failed (13: Permission denied)
nginx: [emerg] bind() to 0.0.0.0:80 failed (13: Permission denied)
```

Figure 7.51: Pod fails to start due to missing capability

We have seen before that granting the `anyuid` SCC to the workload based on the same nginx image allows it to start; therefore, we are not repeating it here. The goal here was to demonstrate how different SCC settings can affect your application. It is not very common to see `NET_BIND_SERVICE` dropped, as a lot of applications require network access and businesses often just don't bother writing finely tuned SCCs that prohibit binding to privileged ports for apps that are supposed to use unprivileged ports. However, it is a good example of how you can restrict the networking capabilities of your application and reduce its attack surface. As a final recommendation on the topic of SCCs, write your custom SCCs following the principle of least privilege. Only grant the permissions necessary for your application to function correctly.

Now it's time to move on to the final OpenShift security concept we're going to discuss in this book – PSSs.

Pod Security Standards

PSSs replace the older **Pod Security Policy** (**PSP**) type of objects, providing a more streamlined and manageable approach to securing Pod operations. One of the main differences is that PSPs apply cluster wide and require careful configuration of roles and ClusterRoleBindings to associate policies with specific users, groups, or service accounts. PSSs, on the other hand, can just be attached as labels to target namespaces.

PSSs are essential for running Kubernetes Pods safely. They help apply uniform security measures across all Pods in a cluster. Using these standards in OpenShift helps avoid potential security risks by enforcing safe configurations and practices.

PSS levels and modes

PSSs are categorized into three levels, aka "profiles," each providing a different degree of security:

- **Privileged:** This level provides no restrictions, allowing Pods broad permissions. It's typically used for workloads that require extensive system capabilities, for example, components of OpenShift itself.
- **Baseline:** Often set as the default, this level offers a good balance by applying a moderate security profile that allows enough freedom for most common applications to operate effectively.
- **Restricted:** This is the most stringent level that enforces the tightest security constraints on Pod operations by encapsulating restrictions from the baseline policy plus additional guardrails. It is best suited for highly sensitive workloads where the principle of least privilege must be rigorously enforced.

Each level can be applied to a namespace in three different modes; here is a detailed description and some use case examples:

- `enforce`: This mode strictly enforces security standards. If a Pod doesn't meet the required security settings (privileged, baseline, or restricted), its creation or modification is blocked by **Pod security admission (PSA)**.

  Use case: Best for production environments where strict adherence to security standards is critical to ensure all Pods comply without exceptions.

- `audit`: This mode does not block Pods that don't meet security standards; instead, it records an audit log showing which Pods failed to comply. This lets administrators track potential issues without disrupting the Pods.

  Use case: Useful for evaluating the effects of new security policies on existing and new Pods, helping to refine policies without impacting current operations.

- `warn`: In this mode, the PSA controller issues user-facing warnings for non-compliant Pod requests but doesn't stop them.

  Use case: Ideal during the development phase as it provides immediate feedback to developers on security requirements without blocking Pod deployment, encouraging security integration from the early stages.

To apply a PSS with a specific mode to a namespace, you must label a namespace in the format `pod-security.kubernetes.io/<MODE>: "<LEVEL>"`, as follows:

```
metadata:
  labels:
    pod-security.kubernetes.io/enforce: "baseline"
    pod-security.kubernetes.io/warn: "restricted"
```

With the preceding labels, the PSA controller will enforce the baseline profile and produce warnings when the restricted profile is violated. This is useful when hardening your application's security context, as it allows you to see which settings would be blocked in enforce mode. You can also use the pod-security.kubernetes.io/<MODE>-version: "<VERSION>" label to "pin" a policy to a specific version of the Kubernetes API. This helps to ensure consistent enforcement of policies in case they are changed with OpenShift upgrades.

As you saw at the beginning of this chapter, when we created a project and examined its metadata, new projects receive the following labels on OpenShift 4.16 (based on Kubernetes v1.29):

```
metadata:
  labels:
    pod-security.kubernetes.io/audit: restricted
    pod-security.kubernetes.io/audit-version: v1.24
    pod-security.kubernetes.io/warn: restricted
    pod-security.kubernetes.io/warn-version: v1.24
```

If, for example, we create another project and try to run an nginx deployment with runAsUser: 0 in its Pod or container's security context, we will see the following:

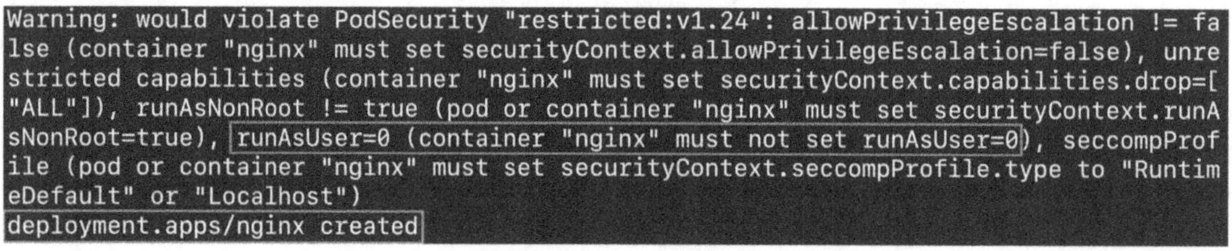

```
Warning: would violate PodSecurity "restricted:v1.24": allowPrivilegeEscalation != fa
lse (container "nginx" must set securityContext.allowPrivilegeEscalation=false), unre
stricted capabilities (container "nginx" must set securityContext.capabilities.drop=[
"ALL"]), runAsNonRoot != true (pod or container "nginx" must set securityContext.runA
sNonRoot=true), runAsUser=0 (container "nginx" must not set runAsUser=0), seccompProf
ile (pod or container "nginx" must set securityContext.seccompProfile.type to "Runtim
eDefault" or "Localhost")
deployment.apps/nginx created
```

Figure 7.52: PSA in action

Notice that the PSA controller warned us about a potential violation, because the restricted PSS doesn't allow runAsUser: 0, but admitted the Pod anyway.

> Please note that neither SCCs nor PSA prevent workload controllers, such as Deployments, from creation. When you create a Deployment, your user must pass an authorization check (RBAC) first, but the Pod is created by a controller that runs under its own service account and, as such, is subject to SCC and PSA admission checks, in addition to RBAC. So, even though you may be allowed to create a Deployment, it may not necessarily be able to spawn any Pods, depending on its security context, PSA labels on its namespace, and SCCs allowed for the Deployment's service account. Always check for Pods directly.

Still, the warning was both presented to us and recorded in the audit log, which leaves a clear trail of a user attempting a potentially insecure setting. You may have seen a similar warning earlier, when doing exercises in this chapter. Now you know what's causing it.

> If you check the Pod with `oc get po`, you will notice that it's still missing. Can you guess why? As you may recall, the `restricted-v2` SCC, which is assigned to workloads by default, doesn't allow containers running as root (UID 0). Since we didn't allow the service account of our Pod (default) to use the `anyuid` SCC, it fails SCC admission check, and the following event is emitted (`oc get ev`):
>
> ```
> provider restricted-v2: .containers[0].runAsUser: Invalid value:
> 0: must be in the ranges: [1000860000, 1000869999]
> ```
>
> `provider` in this context means the SCC. By now, you should know how to fix this problem (hint: `anyuid`).

Now that we're done with PSSs, it's time to look back and summarize what we have learned.

Summary

In this chapter, we have discussed projects – the most basic unit of logical partitioning within OpenShift, as well as differences and similarities between them and Kubernetes namespaces. We acquired first-hand experience working with `ResourceQuotas` and `LimitRanges` – primary guardrails that make multitenancy practical. We also examined network policies, discussed how they can be used to limit traffic between applications in your cluster, and created two simple policies with the goal of obtaining hands-on experience. Finally, we created a custom `SecurityContextConstraint` to see how it limits the capabilities of new workloads and discussed how PSSs can be used to enforce security context policies.

In the next chapter, you will learn how to provide your applications with persistent storage, as well as about different types of access modes, differences between stateful and stateless applications, and OpenShift Data Foundation – an SDS solution that stands on the shoulders of giants – Rook's Ceph and NooBaa projects, which offer different types of storage interfaces for a wide variety of use cases – block, object, and file.

References

To learn more about the topics that were covered in this chapter, take a look at the following resources:

- [1] *Working with projects*: `https://docs.redhat.com/en/documentation/openshift_container_platform/4.16/html/building_applications/projects#working-with-projects`
- [2] *A Guide to OpenShift and UIDs*: `https://www.redhat.com/en/blog/a-guide-to-openshift-and-uids`
- [3] *Creating a project as another user*: `https://docs.redhat.com/en/documentation/openshift_container_platform/4.16/html/building_applications/projects#creating-project-other-user`
- [4] *Configuring project creation*: `https://docs.redhat.com/en/documentation/openshift_container_platform/4.16/html/building_applications/projects#configuring-project-creation`

- [5] *Differences between "Project" and "ProjectRequest" objects on OpenShift*: https://access.redhat.com/solutions/6616071
- [6] *How to create a project/namespace through a YAML file or API call in OpenShift 4.x?*: https://access.redhat.com/solutions/5135211
- [7] *Resource quotas per project*: https://docs.redhat.com/en/documentation/openshift_container_platform/4.16/html/building_applications/quotas#quotas-setting-per-project
- [8] *Resource quotas across multiple projects*: https://docs.redhat.com/en/documentation/openshift_container_platform/4.16/html/building_applications/quotas#setting-quotas-across-multiple-projects
- [9] *Resource Quotas*: https://kubernetes.io/docs/concepts/policy/resource-quotas/
- [10] *Restrict resource consumption with limit ranges*: https://docs.redhat.com/en/documentation/openshift_container_platform/4.16/html/nodes/working-with-clusters#nodes-cluster-limit-ranges
- [11] *Limit Ranges*: https://kubernetes.io/docs/concepts/policy/limit-range/
- [12] *About network policy*: https://docs.redhat.com/en/documentation/openshift_container_platform/4.16/html/networking/network-security#network-policy
- [13] *Creating a network policy*: https://docs.redhat.com/en/documentation/openshift_container_platform/4.16/html/networking/network-security#creating-network-policy
- [14] *Viewing a network policy*: https://docs.redhat.com/en/documentation/openshift_container_platform/4.16/html/networking/network-security#viewing-network-policy
- [15] *Editing a network policy*: https://docs.redhat.com/en/documentation/openshift_container_platform/4.16/html/networking/network-security#editing-network-policy
- [16] *Deleting a network policy*: https://docs.redhat.com/en/documentation/openshift_container_platform/4.16/html/networking/network-security#deleting-network-policy
- [17] *Defining a default network policy for projects*: https://docs.redhat.com/en/documentation/openshift_container_platform/4.16/html/networking/network-security#default-network-policy
- [18] *Configuring multitenant isolation with network policy*: https://docs.redhat.com/en/documentation/openshift_container_platform/4.16/html/networking/network-security#multitenant-network-policy
- [19] *Network Policies*: https://kubernetes.io/docs/concepts/services-networking/network-policies/
- [20] *Network Policy Editor by Isovalent*: https://editor.networkpolicy.io
- [21] *Managing security context constraints*: https://docs.redhat.com/en/documentation/openshift_container_platform/4.16/html/authentication_and_authorization/managing-pod-security-policies#managing-pod-security-policies
- [22] *Security Profiles Operator overview*: https://docs.redhat.com/en/documentation/openshift_container_platform/4.16/html/security_and_compliance/security-profiles-operator#spo-overview

- [23] *Managing SELinux profiles*: `https://docs.redhat.com/en/documentation/openshift_container_platform/4.16/html/security_and_compliance/security-profiles-operator#spo-selinux`
- [24] *Managing seccomp profiles*: `https://docs.redhat.com/en/documentation/openshift_container_platform/4.16/html/security_and_compliance/security-profiles-operator#spo-seccomp`
- [25] *Configuring seccomp profiles*: `https://docs.redhat.com/en/documentation/openshift_container_platform/4.16/html/security_and_compliance/seccomp-profiles`
- [26] *Restrict a Container's Syscalls with seccomp*: `https://kubernetes.io/docs/tutorials/security/seccomp/`
- [27] *Toolkit for hardening container images and reducing their attack surface*: `https://github.com/slimtoolkit/slim`
- [28] *JSONPath Support*: `https://kubernetes.io/docs/reference/kubectl/jsonpath/`
- [29] *capabilities(7) – Linux manual page*: `https://man7.org/linux/man-pages/man7/capabilities.7.html`
- [30] *Using Multi-Level Security (MLS)*: `https://docs.redhat.com/en/documentation/red_hat_enterprise_linux/9/html/using_selinux/using-multi-level-security-mls_using-selinux#multi-level-security-mls_using-multi-level-security-mls`
- [31] *Pod Security Admission*: `https://kubernetes.io/docs/concepts/security/pod-security-admission/`
- [32] *Pod Security Standards*: `https://kubernetes.io/docs/concepts/security/pod-security-standards/`
- [33] *Using sysctls in containers*: `https://docs.redhat.com/en/documentation/openshift_container_platform/4.16/html/nodes/working-with-containers#nodes-containers-sysctls`
- [34] *CRI-O configuration file reference*: `https://github.com/cri-o/cri-o/blob/main/docs/crio.conf.5.md#crioruntime-table`
- [35] *OpenShift 4.16 Documentation | Creating images | Support arbitrary user ids*: `https://docs.redhat.com/en/documentation/openshift_container_platform/4.16/html/images/creating-images#use-uid_create-images`
- [36] *`oc adm policy add-scc-to-user` behavior / implementation changes from editing SCC object to creating a cluster role binfing in Red Hat OpenShift Container Platform 4.x*: `https://access.redhat.com/solutions/5529581`
- [37] *Red Hat Bugzilla – Bug 1906375 | scc missing users with correct clusterrolebinding*: `https://bugzilla.redhat.com/show_bug.cgi?id=1906375`
- [38] *About pre-allocated security context constraints values*: `https://docs.redhat.com/en/documentation/openshift_container_platform/4.16/html/authentication_and_authorization/managing-pod-security-policies#security-context-constraints-pre-allocated-values_configuring-internal-oauth`

Quiz

Test your understanding of OpenShift 4 security and isolation concepts with this quick quiz. Remember, some questions may have more than one correct answer!

1. In what project must a customized project template be saved in order to be used by OpenShift?
    a. `openshift-templates`
    b. `openshift-config`
    c. `default`
    d. `kube-system`
2. Which resource must be edited in order to change the default roles that can be assigned to users in a project?
    a. `console.config/cluster`
    b. `console.config.openshift.io/cluster`
    c. `console.operator/cluster`
    d. `console.operator.openshift.io/cluster`
3. What API object tracks all applied quotas on a per-project basis?
    a. `ClusterResourceQuota`
    b. `NamespaceResourceQuota`
    c. `AppliedClusterResourceQuota`
    d. There is no such resource. All quotas must be examined either manually or automatically to determine which projects they apply to.
4. Consider the following LimitRange and resource requests/limits from a workload's PodSpec:

<table>
<tr><th>LimitRange</th><th>PodSpec</th></tr>
<tr><td><pre>- type: Container
  max:
    cpu: "2"
    memory: 4Gi
  min:
    cpu: 100m
    memory: 100Mi
  default:
    cpu: "1"
    memory: 2Gi
  defaultRequest:
    cpu: 200m
    memory: 100Mi</pre></td><td><pre>resources:
  requests:
    cpu: 2500m
    memory: 1Gi</pre></td></tr>
</table>

Table 7.9: LimitRange and PodSpec

What will happen when we create the LimitRange followed by a Pod?

a. The Pod will be accepted
b. The Pod will be accepted with `limits` set to `2` for `cpu` and `1Gi` for memory
c. The Pod will be rejected due to missing limits in its PodSpec
d. The Pod will be rejected due to incorrect relative values of requests and limits

5. Given the following requirements for a REST API application:

- Accepts connections on TCP ports `80` (HTTP) and `443` (HTTPS)
- Must be available only for applications or entire projects labeled with `api-consumer="true"`
- Applies only to Pods labeled with `tier="api"`
- The principle of least privilege must be adhered to

Choose the correct network policy:

<table>
<tr><th>A</th><th>B</th></tr>
<tr><td><pre>podSelector:
  matchLabels:
    tier: api
ingress:
- from:
  - namespaceSelector:
      matchLabels:
        api-consumer: "true"
    podSelector:
      matchLabels:
        api-consumer: "true"
  ports:
  - port: 80
    protocol: TCP
  - port: 443
    protocol: TCP</pre></td><td><pre>podSelector:
  matchLabels:
    tier: api
ingress:
- from:
  - namespaceSelector:
      matchLabels:
        api-consumer: "true"
  - podSelector:
      matchLabels:
        api-consumer: "true"
  ports:
  - port: 80
    endPort: 443
    protocol: TCP</pre></td></tr>
</table>

<table>
<tr><th>C</th><th>D</th></tr>
<tr><td><pre>podSelector:
  matchLabels:
    tier: api
ingress:
- from:
  - namespaceSelector:
      matchLabels:
        api-consumer: "true"
  - podSelector:
      matchLabels:
        api-consumer: "true"</pre></td><td><pre>podSelector:
  matchLabels:
    tier: api
ingress:
- from:
  - namespaceSelector:
      matchLabels:
        api-consumer: "true"
  - podSelector:
      matchLabels:
        api-consumer: "true"
  ports:
  - port: 80
    protocol: TCP
  - port: 443
    protocol: TCP</pre></td></tr>
</table>

Table 7.10: Sample network policies

6. What is the correct annotation for "pinning" an SCC to a Pod:
    a. `security.openshift.io/required-scc`
    b. `openshift.io/required-scc`
    c. `security.openshift.io/scc-required`
    d. `openshift.io/scc-required`
7. Which statement best describes Pod Security Standards in OpenShift?
    a. They are optional recommendations for securing Pods
    b. They enforce security settings at the cluster level
    c. They offer predefined security levels to enforce Pod isolation and privileges
8. If you want to prohibit privileged containers, which PSS level is *sufficient*?
    a. Privileged
    b. Baseline
    c. Restricted

Answers

1. **b.** Make sure that you save your project template in the `openshift-config` namespace.
2. **c.** and **d.** `console.operator.openshift.io` is a fully qualified name of the `console.operator` resource.
3. **c.** You can use `AppliedClusterResourceQuota` to see the effective quota on a specific project.
4. **d.** Because we didn't specify limits in the PodSpec, they will be set to 1 CPU core and 2 Gi of RAM (`LimitRange.spec.limits[].default`), which violates the CPU request of 2,500 millicores (2.5 cores) from the PodSpec, because requests cannot be higher than limits. That leads to the Pod getting rejected by an admission controller.
5. **d.** Let's examine the choices more closely:

   a. Notice the missing - in front of `.spec.ingress[].from[].podSelector`. That indicates `AND` logic, meaning that for this rule to match, a connection attempt must originate from a Pod labeled with `api-consumer="true"` `AND` from a namespace that has the same label, while the original requirement is less strict.

   b. The `port` and `endPort` fields at the end of the manifest indicate a range between `80` and `443`, which opens additional ports not required by the task, violating the principle of least privilege.

   c. The policy doesn't specify any ports at all, which means that ingress connections are accepted on all ports instead of just two, which violates the principle of least privilege even more than B.

   d. This is the correct policy that meets all requirements without granting any extra permissions.

6. **b.** Don't forget that the `openshift.io/required-scc` annotation must be set in a Pod template's metadata inside a Deployment, ReplicaSet, DaemonSet, or StatefulSet and *not* on the latter's metadata.
7. **c.** Pod Security Standards provide predefined security levels (privileged, baseline, and restricted) that help enforce specific security practices and configurations for Pods.
8. **b.** The privileged level enforces no restrictions, so it's not the right answer. Although both the baseline and restricted levels require the `privileged` field in the security context of all containers to be either undefined or set to `false`, the restricted level adds additional restrictions on top of that, which makes baseline sufficient.

8

Working with Persistent Storage

In this chapter, we will take a look at the foundation of OpenShift 4 storage components, such as PersistentVolumes, PersistentVolumeClaims, and StorageClasses. We will then turn our attention to the Container Storage Interface and move on to **OpenShift Data Foundation** (ODF) fundamentals, its architecture, and lots of practical tasks, which will allow us to understand how to operate ODF to support application needs.

In this chapter, we'll cover the following topics:

- The foundation of data persistence in OpenShift 4
- Stateful versus stateless workloads
- OpenShift and Kubernetes persistent volume framework
- Container Storage Interface (CSI)
- OpenShift Data Foundation (ODF)

Let's get started!

Technical requirements

In this chapter, you will need the following:

- Internet access
- Bash shell (other shells work as well)
- OpenShift Local
- OpenShift on vSphere, built in *Chapter 3, Getting Started with OpenShift*
- Infra nodes, added and configured as directed in *Chapter 4, Post-Install Configuration*
- Firefox (recommended) or any other web browser

You can access this book's GitHub repository at `https://github.com/PacktPublishing/Learn-OpenShift-Second-Edition`.

The foundation of data persistence in OpenShift 4

In the dynamic world of cloud-native applications, the concept of "state" often takes center stage. While some applications can operate seamlessly without retaining information between sessions, others critically depend on preserving data, configurations, and user-specific details. This is where persistent storage emerges as a fundamental building block.

Imagine a database housing critical customer records, or a messaging queue ensuring reliable communication between services. Losing this data due to a pod restart or node failure would be catastrophic. OpenShift 4, Red Hat's enterprise Kubernetes platform, recognizes this and offers a comprehensive framework to manage persistent storage, ensuring your applications remain resilient and your data remains secure.

Unlike traditional infrastructure, OpenShift doesn't provide a production-ready persistent storage solution out of the box. It acts as an intelligent orchestrator, integrating with a wide array of storage providers, from **network-attached storage (NAS)** solutions such as NFS to cloud-based offerings such as AWS **Elastic Block Store (EBS)**. This flexibility allows you to tailor your storage choices to the specific needs of your applications, optimizing cost, performance, or specific features.

In this chapter, we'll embark on a journey through OpenShift's storage ecosystem. We'll begin by demystifying the distinction between stateful and stateless applications, understanding why persistent storage is indispensable for certain workloads. Then, we'll delve into the core storage APIs provided by Kubernetes and OpenShift, learning how to provision and manage storage volumes for your applications.

As we progress, we will explore the **Container Storage Interface** (CSI), a powerful standard that has revolutionized the way storage providers integrate with Kubernetes. We'll examine the advantages of CSI and how OpenShift leverages it to provide seamless integration with a multitude of storage solutions.

To equip you with the knowledge to make informed decisions, we'll survey the landscape of supported storage providers in OpenShift. We'll compare their strengths and weaknesses, guiding you towards the best fit for your unique requirements.

By the end of this chapter, you'll have a firm grasp of OpenShift's storage capabilities, enabling you to confidently deploy and manage stateful applications with the assurance that your data remains accessible regardless of the state of your application. Whether you're building a simple database-backed application or a complex distributed system, the knowledge you gain here will be essential to managing data persistence in OpenShift.

Stateful versus stateless workloads

In the realm of cloud-native applications, the terms "stateful" and "stateless" represent fundamental differences that show how applications interact with data and shape their architectural design. Understanding this distinction is crucial when working with OpenShift, as it directly impacts how you approach storage and data management.

Stateless applications, as the name suggests, operate without any inherent memory of past interactions. Each request they receive is treated as an independent event, requiring no knowledge of previous requests or user sessions. This makes them incredibly scalable, as multiple instances can be spun up or down to handle varying workloads without worrying about data synchronization. Examples of stateless applications include web servers delivering static content, API endpoints processing individual requests, or batch processing jobs that operate on discrete chunks of data.

On the other side of the spectrum lie stateful applications. These applications maintain and rely on information about their past interactions. This state can take various forms, from session data that tracks a user's activity to database records that store critical business information. Stateful applications are often the backbone of complex systems, managing persistent connections, maintaining user preferences, and coordinating workflows. Think of databases such as PostgreSQL or MySQL, message queues such as Kafka or RabbitMQ, or even simple key-value stores such as Redis.

The challenge with stateful applications is that their state needs to be preserved even when the underlying infrastructure changes. If a pod crashes or a node fails, the application must be able to recover its state seamlessly to continue functioning correctly. This is where OpenShift's storage mechanisms come into play. By providing persistent volumes that outlive the lifespan of individual pods, OpenShift enables stateful applications to reliably store and retrieve their data, ensuring uninterrupted operation even in the face of disruptions.

In this chapter, we will focus on stateful applications and Kubernetes/OpenShift APIs that support them. To that end, the next section will familiarize you with types of persistent volumes, how to create them, and the procedure of presenting them to applications.

OpenShift and Kubernetes persistent volume framework

OpenShift Container Platform leverages the Kubernetes **PersistentVolume (PV)** framework, enabling cluster administrators to allocate persistent storage resources efficiently. Developers, in turn, can employ **PersistentVolumeClaims (PVCs)** to request these resources without requiring in-depth knowledge of the underlying storage infrastructure.

Provisioning storage

Two primary methods for provisioning storage in OpenShift 4 exist: static and dynamic.

- **Static provisioning**: Requires administrators to manually create persistent volumes beforehand.
- **Dynamic provisioning**: Utilizes storage classes to generate persistent volumes on demand, aligning with the specific requirements of applications.

Types of persistent volumes

Here are just some of the many types of persistent volumes supported by OpenShift 4:

- `hostPath`: Mounts files/directories from the host node, primarily for development and testing in single-node clusters.
- `iSCSI`: Provides block-level access to storage devices through an IP-based standard.

- `local`: Grants access to local storage devices such as disks or partitions, with the caveat of being tied to node availability.
- `NFS`: Enables shared data access among multiple pods concurrently.

For the full list, see [1].

PersistentVolumes (PVs)

PVs define storage plugin-specific details, such as NFS server address and export path, iSCSI target and portal, host path directory, or Amazon EBS volume ID. When you provision storage statically by creating PVs manually, you normally specify those parameters yourself, as opposed to dynamic provisioning, which we will cover later in this chapter.

PersistentVolumeClaims (PVCs)

PVCs represent storage requests from applications, specifying minimum requirements such as capacity and access mode. Kubernetes then matches PVCs to suitable PVs based on these requirements.

This is what the relationship between containers, PVs, and PVCs looks like:

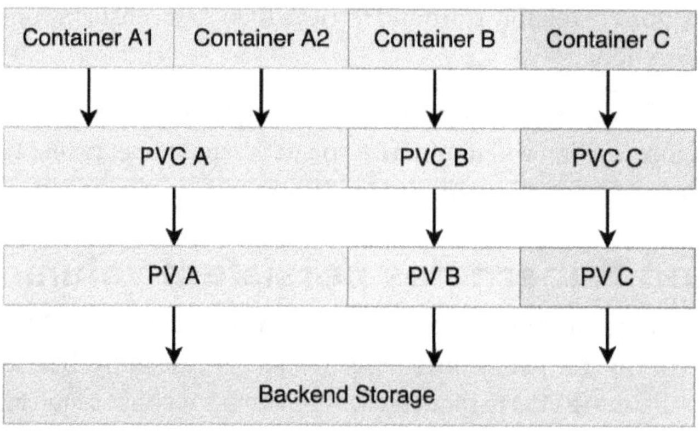

Figure 8.1: Mapping between PVs, PVCs, and containers

Volume access modes

Volume access modes dictate how a PV can be mounted and accessed by applications. OpenShift 4 defines four distinct access modes that can be specified in both PVs and PVCs:

- **ReadWriteOnce (RWO)**: The volume can be mounted by a single node in read/write mode. This mode is suitable for applications that require exclusive access to the data.
- **ReadOnlyMany (ROX)**: The volume can be mounted by multiple nodes simultaneously in read-only mode. This mode is ideal for sharing static data such as configuration files or reference datasets across multiple pods.
- **ReadWriteMany (RWX)**: The volume can be mounted by multiple nodes simultaneously in read/write mode. This mode is necessary for applications that need shared write access to the data, such as collaborative editing tools or databases.

- **ReadWriteOncePod (RWOP):** The volume can be mounted in read-write mode by a single pod. If the pod is deleted, the underlying PersistentVolume is also deleted. This mode is specifically for ephemeral storage that is tied to the lifetime of a pod.

> Access modes do not directly represent actual capabilities of the underlying storage and are only used to match PVs with PVCs. That is, OpenShift itself doesn't enforce them on the level of storage. For example, it is possible to define an NFS-backed PV as RWO even though an NFS share technically can be mounted on multiple machines simultaneously. This gives cluster administrators extra flexibility in controlling access to different storage backends to satisfy company policies or other non-technical requirements. That being said, you must be careful specifying only access modes supported by a given volume type. For example, you can mount an NFS share as RWO, RWX, ROX, or RWOP, and it won't do any harm, since NFS supports all of them; however, iSCSI or Amazon EBS only support RWO and ROX, otherwise data corruption may occur.

Since we have a certain degree of freedom in defining access modes for our PVs and PVCs, the logical question would be which modes make sense for different classes of applications and volume types.

Choosing the right access mode

Selecting the appropriate access mode depends entirely on the specific requirements of your application. For instance, a single-instance database would typically utilize RWO, while a shared content repository might leverage ROX or RWX, depending on whether write access from multiple nodes is necessary.

Volume Type	RWO	ROX	RWX	RWOP
hostPath	Y	N	N	Y
iSCSI	Y	Y	N	N
local	Y	N	N	Y
NFS	Y	Y	Y	Y

Table 8.1: PersistentVolume types

You can refer to the official documentation listed in the *Further reading* section [2] to find out which access modes are supported for different types of PVs.

Volume modes

OpenShift 4 supports two volume modes for persistent volumes:

- **Filesystem:** The default mode, where data is organized within a file system hierarchy. This mode is suitable for most applications that interact with files and directories.

- **Block:** Provides raw block device access, bypassing the file system layer. This mode can offer performance advantages for applications that directly manipulate data blocks, such as databases or storage systems.

Block volume support

OpenShift Container Platform enables provisioning raw block volumes, which don't have a file system and can enhance performance for specific applications. These volumes are typically utilized by databases, storage services, or applications that perform direct disk writes. To provision a block volume, you need to specify `.spec.volumeMode: Block` in both the PV and PVC specifications.

The following table shows block volume support by plugin type:

Volume Plugin	Manually Provisioned	Dynamically Provisioned	Fully Supported
AWS EBS (Block)	Y	Y	Y
Azure Disk	Y	Y	Y
GCP	Y	Y	Y
Fibre Channel	Y	N	Y
iSCSI	Y	N	Y
Local volume	Y	N	Y
VMware vSphere	Y	Y	Y

Table 8.2: Volume modes

Using any of the block volumes that can be provisioned manually, but are not provided as fully supported, is a Technology Preview feature only, meaning that they are not recommended to be used in production, as the functionality is not complete.

Please refer to [3] if you want to know about block volume support details for other volume types.

Provisioning a local block volume device

Since most of the block volumes require external storage, we are going to use a local volume plugin that requires just creating an additional block device on our local PC.

We will create a virtual block device (loop) on our OpenShift Local node, and use it to create a PV:

1. First, install the oc utility on your laptop or desktop if you're going to proceed with CRC. *Chapter 3, Getting Started with OpenShift*, in the **Installation Methods** > **Prerequisites** > **OpenShift CLI** section, provides instructions.
2. Run `crc setup` and `crc start`, unless CRC is already up and running on your system.
3. Log in to the OpenShift Local node:

```
$ oc debug node/crc
```

```
Starting pod/crc-debug-z55fz ...
To use host binaries, run `chroot /host`
Pod IP: 192.168.126.11
```

Figure 8.2: Starting a debug session on an OpenShift Local node

If you don't see a command prompt, try pressing *Enter* (or *return* on Mac):

```
sh-4.4# chroot /host
sh-5.1# bash
```

Your prompt should change as follows:

```
[systemd]
Failed Units: 1
  qemu-guest-agent.service
[root@crc /]#
```

Figure 8.3: qemu-guest-agent.service may be in the failed state

The warning about the failed `qemu-guest-agent.service` unit may not always show up, but can be safely disregarded if it does.

4. Create a 100 MB file and fill it with zeroes:

```
[root@crc /]# cd /root/
[root@crc /]# dd if=/dev/zero of=block1.img bs=100M count=1
```

```
1+0 records in
1+0 records out
104857600 bytes (105 MB, 100 MiB) copied, 0.17577 s, 597 MB/s
```

Figure 8.4: Loop device file was created successfully

As you can see here, the file was successfully created:

```
[root@crc ~]# ls -lah block1.img
```

```
-rw-r--r--. 1 root root 100M Jun 14 02:45 block1.img
```

Figure 8.5: Confirming that the file exists

5. Create a virtual block device from that file:

```
[root@crc ~]# losetup  -fP block1.img
[root@crc ~]# losetup -a
```

```
/dev/loop0: [64516]:2616958 (/var/roothome/block1.img)
```

Figure 8.6: Local loop device was set up successfully

Now let's use that loop device to create a PV.

Creating a PersistentVolume

Now we can use that block file to create a PV. PVs can be manually created using a PV manifest file, defining attributes such as capacity, access modes, volume mode, and storage-specific details. Alternatively, the OpenShift web console provides a user-friendly interface for PV creation. For a better experience, we will go with the first option:

1. Exit from the OpenShift local node back to your laptop by typing `exit` (or pressing *Ctrl* + *D*) three times:

```
[root@crc /]# exit
exit
sh-5.1# exit
exit
sh-4.4# exit
exit
Removing debug pod ...
$
```

2. Create a PV manifest from the `chapters/8/snippets/local-block-pv.yml` file of this book's GitHub repository:

```
$ oc create -f chapters/8/snippets/local-block-pv.yml
```

Let's examine the specification contained therein:

- `.spec.capacity`: Specifies the storage capacity of the volume (`100Mi` in our example).
- `.spec.accessModes`: Uses `ReadWriteOncePod` for exclusive access by a single pod, with the volume being deleted when the pod is deleted.
- `.spec.volumeMode`: Sets the mode to `Block` for raw block device access.
- `.spec.local.path`: Points to the path of the local block device on the OpenShift node.
- `.spec.nodeAffinity`: Restricts the PV's availability and placement of the pod that mounts this PV only to a specified node (`crc` in our example).

3. Verify that the PV was created:

```
$ oc get pv local-block-pv
```

The new PV should show up as `Available`:

```
NAME             CAPACITY   ACCESS MODES   RECLAIM POLICY   STATUS
local-block-pv   100Mi      RWOP           Delete           Available
```

Figure 8.7: PV for the loop device is created and available for binding

> `STATUS` shows as `Available`, meaning there are no PVCs associated with this PV yet.

Now we will create a PVC and associate it with the PV we just created:

1. Create a PVC from the `chapters/8/snippets/local-block-pvc.yml` manifest:

```
$ oc create -f chapters/8/snippets/local-block-pvc.yml
```

In this manifest, there is the following:

- `.spec.accessModes`: Must be a subset or a complete match of the PV's access modes (`ReadWriteOncePod`).
- `.spec.volumeMode`: Must match the PV's volume mode (`Block`).
- `.spec.resources.requests.storage`: Specifies the desired storage capacity (100Mi in this example). You can request less, and the PV controller will try to find a PV of the same size or bigger.

2. Verify that the PVC was created and bound to the PV created earlier:

```
$ oc get pvc
```

`Bound` indicates successful binding:

```
NAME              STATUS   VOLUME           CAPACITY   ACCESS MODES
local-block-pvc   Bound    local-block-pv   100Mi      RWOP
```

Figure 8.8: PVC was created and successfully bound to the PV

If you see your PVC not bound due to *Cannot bind to requested volume "local-block-pv": storageClassName does not match* when you run `oc describe pvc local-block-pv`, you might need to patch the default StorageClass resource with the following command:

```
$ oc patch storageclass crc-csi-hostpath-provisioner -p
'{"metadata": {"annotations":{"storageclass.kubernetes.io/
is-default-class":"false"}}}'
```

Then, recreate the PVC. First, delete the existing PVC with `oc delete pvc local-block-pvc`, and then rerun the command from *step 1* to recreate it.

Another way to fix that is to set `.spec.storageClassName: ""` and recreate the PVC.

The final part is to create a pod that uses our PVC:

1. Create a pod manifest from `chapters/8/snippets/pod-httpd.yml`:

```
$ oc create -f chapters/8/snippets/pod-httpd.yml
```

In this manifest, there are the following fields:

- `.spec.volumes[].name`: The name of the volume within the pod.
- `.spec.volumes[].persistentVolumeClaim.claimName`: The name of the PVC to use.

2. Verify that the pod was created:

```
$ oc get pods
```

There should be one pod running:

```
NAME     READY   STATUS    RESTARTS   AGE
httpd    1/1     Running   0          22s
```

Figure 8.9: A test httpd pod is running

Depending on your internet connection, the creation of a pod may take some time. If you see a different state other than `Running`, run `oc describe pods httpd` to see the error explaining why your pod is having trouble starting.

3. Because we are using a block device, it is going to be shown as the same block device in our node. Verify that with the following command:

```
$ oc exec -it httpd -- lsblk | grep loop
```

You should see the attached block device in the container:

```
loop0    7:0    0  100M  0 loop
```

Figure 8.10: Loop device that backs the PV is mounted inside the test pod

> All PVCs and pods that we create in this chapter do not specify a namespace for simplicity, which means that they will be created in the current namespace/project, which is `default`, unless you change it with `oc project <PROJECT>`. In a production environment, however, it is recommended to always specify the project where you want a given resource to exist to ensure consistency.

Now that we know how volumes backed by block devices are provisioned, let's see how it works for volumes formatted with filesystems.

Filesystem storage

On the other hand, filesystem storage is the default and most common mode for persistent volumes in OpenShift 4. It provides a familiar hierarchical structure for storing and organizing files and directories, making it suitable for a wide range of applications.

OpenShift 4 offers support for filesystem storage through various storage backends, including the following:

- **Network Filesystem (NFS)**: A popular network file system that allows multiple clients to access and share files over a network.
- **CephFS**: A highly scalable and fault-tolerant distributed file system designed for object storage, block storage, and file system services.
- **GlusterFS**: Another distributed file system known for its flexibility, scalability, and performance.
- **OpenShift Data Foundation (ODF)**: A software-defined storage solution integrated with OpenShift that provides block, file, and object storage using Ceph technology.
- **HostPath**: HostPath volumes directly mount a directory or file from the worker node's filesystem into a pod.

Provisioning a hostPath volume

In this exercise, we are going to use a `hostPath` volume, as most of the other supported filesystem volumes are external and require additional setup:

1. Create a PV manifest from `chapters/8/snippets/hostpath-pv.yml`:

```
$ oc create -f chapters/8/snippets/hostpath-pv.yml
```

2. Verify that the PV was created:

```
$ oc get pv hostpath-pv
```

You should see a single available PV:

```
NAME          CAPACITY   ACCESS MODES   RECLAIM POLICY   STATUS
hostpath-pv   100Mi      RWO            Delete           Available
```

Figure 8.11: A hostPath PV is created and available for binding

The following is in the PV's manifest:

- `.spec.hostPath.path`: Specifies the absolute path on the node's filesystem.
- `.spec.hostPath.type`: Defines how the path should be handled. In our case, we are creating a directory if it doesn't exist.

3. Create a PVC manifest from another file, `chapters/8/snippets/hostpath-pvc.yml`:

```
$ oc create -f chapters/8/snippets/hostpath-pvc.yml
```

> If you didn't patch the default StorageClass as instructed in the previous exercise, the PVC will be stuck in the `Pending` phase, and you will see the same StorageClass-related error in the events, as in the previous exercise. If that happens, go ahead and make the modifications now or set `.spec.storageClassName: ""` in the PVC, recreating it afterwards.

4. Verify that the PVC is created and bound to the PV we just created:

```
$ oc get pvc hostpath-pvc
```

A single PVC bound to the previously created PV is expected:

```
NAME           STATUS   VOLUME        CAPACITY   ACCESS MODES
hostpath-pvc   Bound    hostpath-pv   100Mi      RWO
```

Figure 8.12: A PVC is created and bound to the hostPath PV

5. Deploy a pod using the `chapters/8/snippets/hostpath-pod.yml` manifest from this book's GitHub repository, which uses the previously created PVC:

```
$ oc create -f chapters/8/snippets/hostpath-pod.yml
```

6. Verify that `hostpath-pod` is created and is in the `Running` state:

```
$ oc get pods hostpath-pod
```

The pod is expected to start successfully:

```
NAME           READY   STATUS    RESTARTS   AGE
hostpath-pod   1/1     Running   0          36s
```

Figure 8.13: A test httpd pod is up and running

> We must create a privileged pod using `privileged: true` in order to access the underlying node's filesystem on `/mnt`. Otherwise, we won't be able to access that directory from inside the pod, because OpenShift security guardrails prevent this level of access by default.

7. Create a test file inside the pod in `/mnt` and verify that it exists:

```
$ oc exec -it hostpath-pod -- touch /mnt/persistent_data
$ oc exec -it hostpath-pod -- ls /mnt
```

The second command is expected to display the created file:

```
$ oc exec -it hostpath-pod -- ls /mnt
persistent_data
```

Figure 8.14: A test file is created on the mounted volume

Now we are going to delete and recreate the same pod to make sure that the `persistent_data` we have just created persists through pod deletion:

1. Delete and recreate the pod:

```
$ oc delete pod hostpath-pod
$ oc create -f chapters/8/snippets/hostpath-pod.yml
```

2. Verify that the `persistent_file` still exists in the pod:

```
$ oc exec -it hostpath-pod -- ls /mnt
```

The command is expected to return the following output:

```
$ oc exec -it hostpath-pod -- ls /mnt
persistent_data
```

Figure 8.15: The test file still exists on the volume after the test pod is re-created

As you can see, the file exists independently of our pod's lifecycle.

> Please note that `hostPath` volumes are not recommended for production use for various reasons:
>
> - Each `hostPath` volume exists directly on a node, thus limiting where its consuming pods can run.
> - When you lose a node where such a volume resides, you lose all of its data.
>
> That being said, `hostPath` volumes are good for learning, which is exactly what we're using them for in this chapter.

Next, we will discuss how different vendors can implement support for their storage products using a reliable interface provided by OpenShift.

Container Storage Interface (CSI)

As Kubernetes and OpenShift gained popularity and the ecosystem of storage providers expanded, a new challenge emerged: the limitations of the traditional "in-tree" storage plugins. These plugins were tightly coupled with the Kubernetes code base, making it difficult to add support for new storage providers without modifying the core Kubernetes code. This tight coupling also posed challenges in terms of upgrades and maintenance, as any changes to the storage plugins required a corresponding Kubernetes upgrade.

To address these limitations and foster a more flexible and scalable storage ecosystem, the **Container Storage Interface (CSI)** was born. CSI is a standard specification that defines a set of APIs for interacting with storage systems. It acts as a bridge between container orchestrators such as Kubernetes and OpenShift and the underlying storage providers, enabling seamless integration and management of a wide range of storage solutions.

The beauty of CSI lies in its standardized approach. Storage vendors can develop CSI drivers for their specific storage systems, adhering to the CSI specification. These drivers are then deployed as separate components within the Kubernetes cluster, independent of the core Kubernetes code. This separation of concerns brings numerous advantages:

- **Flexibility**: CSI enables third-party storage providers to easily integrate their products with Kubernetes and OpenShift without requiring any changes to the core code base. This opens up a vast array of storage options for users, allowing them to choose the best fit for their specific needs.
- **Simplified development, testing, and maintenance**: CSI drivers are developed and maintained independently of Kubernetes, making it easier for storage vendors to release updates and bug fixes without impacting the Kubernetes upgrade cycle. This also simplifies the development and testing processes (integration and unit testing in particular) for storage vendors, as they only need to focus on implementing the CSI specification.
- **Improved security and stability**: By running CSI drivers as separate components, any potential issues or vulnerabilities within a driver are isolated, minimizing the risk of impacting the entire Kubernetes cluster. This also enhances the stability of the overall system, as updates to CSI drivers can be rolled out independently without requiring a full Kubernetes upgrade.

OpenShift has embraced the CSI standard wholeheartedly, recognizing its transformative potential in the storage landscape. By leveraging CSI, OpenShift provides a robust and extensible storage framework that seamlessly integrates with a multitude of storage providers. This enables you to choose from a wide range of storage options, from on-premises solutions such as Ceph and NFS to cloud-based offerings such as AWS EBS and Azure Disk Storage, all while enjoying the benefits of a standardized interface.

In this section, we'll dive into the details of CSI. We'll explore how CSI works, its architecture, and the key components involved in the communication between Kubernetes, OpenShift, and the storage providers. We'll examine the advantages of CSI over traditional in-tree plugins and discuss how OpenShift leverages CSI to deliver a seamless storage experience for your applications.

What is CSI?

CSI is a standard interface designed to streamline the way storage systems interact with container orchestration platforms such as Kubernetes and, by extension, OpenShift. It provides a uniform mechanism for exposing storage resources to containerized applications, abstracting away the complexities of different storage backends.

CSI architecture

CSI operates in a client-server model that consists of the following components:

- **CSI driver:** The CSI driver is a vendor-specific component responsible for managing the underlying storage system. It runs as a container within the OpenShift cluster.
- **CSI node plugin:** This component runs on each node and communicates with the CSI driver to handle volume operations such as attaching, detaching, mounting, and unmounting volumes.
- **CSI controller plugin:** The controller plugin is responsible for managing the lifecycle of volumes across the cluster. It handles tasks such as volume provisioning, snapshotting, and cloning.
- **Kubernetes/OpenShift components:** These components interact with the CSI driver to manage storage requests from applications (via persistent volume claims) and to orchestrate volume operations.

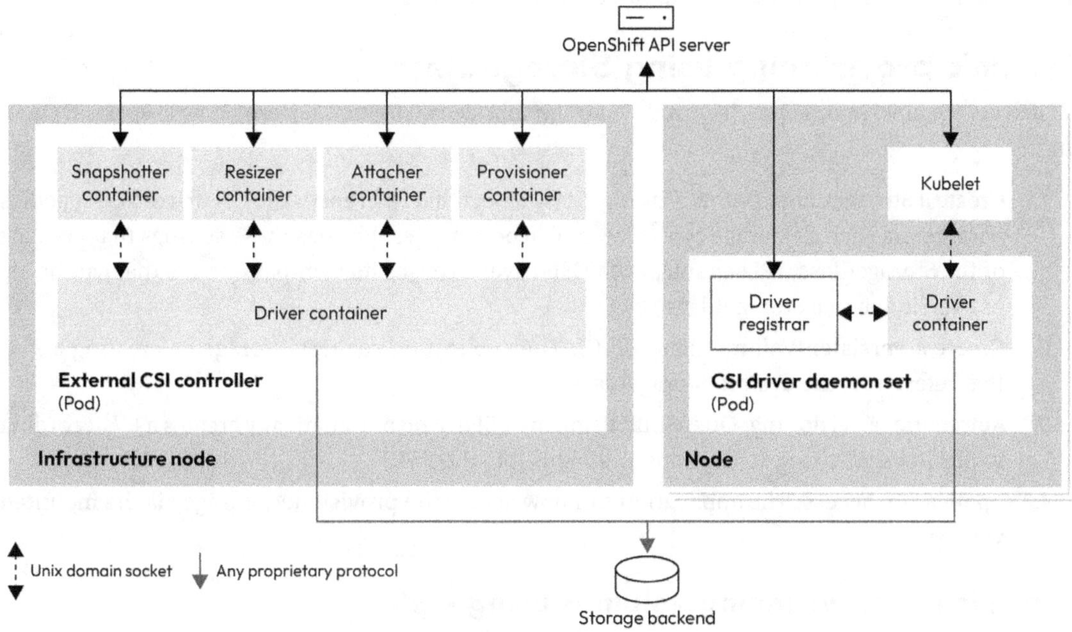

Figure 8.16: CSI architecture

CSI drivers supported by OpenShift Container Platform

OpenShift supports a wide range of CSI drivers, both from storage vendors and the open source community. Some popular CSI drivers include, but are not limited to the following:

CSI driver	CSI volume snapshots	CSI cloning	CSI resizing
AWS EBS	Y	N	Y
GCP PD	Y	Y	Y
MS Azure Disk	Y	Y	Y
OpenShift ODF	Y	Y	Y
VMware vSphere	Y	N	Y

Table 8.3: OpenShift-supported CSI drivers

This is not an exhaustive list, and new CSI drivers are continually being developed. Refer to the OpenShift documentation [4] for the most up-to-date list of supported drivers.

Dynamic provisioning using StorageClass

CSI drivers enable dynamic provisioning of storage volumes on demand. Here's how it works in OpenShift:

1. **Create a StorageClass:** Define a StorageClass object that references the CSI driver and specifies parameters such as storage type, size, and access modes. Besides these settings that are part of the StorageClass API schema, each CSI driver exposes its own parameters that can be set or overridden in a StorageClass.
2. **Create a PersistentVolumeClaim (PVC):** The application requests storage by creating a PVC that references the desired StorageClass.
3. **Automatic provisioning:** OpenShift, using the CSI driver, automatically creates a PV according to the StorageClass specifications and binds it to the PVC.
4. **Application access:** The application can now access the provisioned storage via the mounted volume.

Dynamically provisioning volumes using CSI

Let's see how this works in practice. Our OpenShift installation with OpenShift Local comes with a default StorageClass that uses the `hostpath` provisioner, similar to what we used earlier in this chapter:

1. Verify that you have a single storage class in your OpenShift setup created on installation:

```
$ oc get sc
```

You should see a single entry in the output:

```
NAME                           PROVISIONER
crc-csi-hostpath-provisioner   kubevirt.io.hostpath-provisioner
```

Figure 8.17: OpenShift Local StorageClass

2. Create a PVC from the `chapters/8/snippets/sc-hostpath-pvc.yml` manifest that uses the preceding StorageClass:

```
$ oc create -f chapters/8/snippets/sc-hostpath-pvc.yml
```

3. Verify that the PVC was created:

```
$ oc get pvc sc-hostpath-pvc
```

```
NAME              STATUS
sc-hostpath-pvc   Pending
```

Figure 8.18: A PVC that references a StorageClass with volumeBindingMode: WaitForFirstConsumer is Pending until a consuming pod is created

> `STATUS` may be `Pending` until we create a pod that uses that PVC. It happens when the value of `.spec.volumeBindingMode` of its StorageClass is set to `WaitForFirstConsumer`.

4. Create a pod from the `chapters/8/snippets/sc-hostpath-pod.yml` manifest that uses the PVC we just created:

```
$ oc create -f chapters/8/snippets/sc-hostpath-pod.yml
```

5. Verify that both the POD and PVC were created:

```
$ oc get pods sc-hostpath-pod
```

The pod should start quickly:

```
NAME              READY   STATUS    RESTARTS   AGE
sc-hostpath-pod   1/1     Running   0          9s
```

Figure 8.19: A test httpd pod is up and running

```
$ oc get pvc sc-hostpath-pvc
```

The PVC should be present as well:

```
NAME              STATUS   VOLUME                                     CAPACITY   ACCESS MODES
sc-hostpath-pvc   Bound    pvc-53464f25-7f6a-4626-b868-21aac6510127   30Gi       RWO
```

Figure 8.20: Now that the consuming pod is created, a PV is provisioned, and the PVC is Bound

> The volume's allocated capacity depends on the system where CRC is installed, but a PVC is always matched with a PV of the same size or bigger. In our case, it was 30Gi, but it may be different for you.

Now that we have learned the basics of OpenShift storage APIs, it's time to dive into something more challenging. We mentioned that `hostPath` volumes are not a path forward in enterprise, so in the next section, we will discuss OpenShift Data Foundation – enterprise-grade **software-defined storage** (SDS) for a variety of use cases and types of applications.

OpenShift Data Foundation (ODF)

Red Hat OpenShift Data Foundation (ODF) provides a comprehensive, cloud-native data services platform for **OpenShift Container Platform (OCP)** and other infrastructures. It addresses common storage challenges such as limited portability, complex deployment, and vendor lock-in by integrating seamlessly with OpenShift. ODF delivers file, block, and object storage powered by Ceph, making it suitable for diverse workloads such as the following:

- Databases and data warehouses (data at rest)
- Pipelines and data processing (data in motion)
- Continuous deployment, analytics, AI/ML (data in action)

Additionally, ODF incorporates the **Multicloud Object Gateway** (MCG) service based on the NooBaa project. MCG provides a unified object storage interface (S3 API) that can be backed by local or cloud-native storage, ensuring a consistent experience across environments. Rook-Ceph further enhances ODF by orchestrating persistent volume claims and enabling dynamic storage provisioning.

ODF advantages over traditional storage solutions

Compared to traditional solutions such as NFS, EBS, or vSphere volumes, ODF offers significant advantages:

- **High availability and scalability**: ODF's multi-site availability and Ceph-based replication ensure data resilience and eliminate single points of failure.
- **Simplified management**: ODF streamlines storage administration, eliminating manual tasks and easing operational overhead.
- **Multi-cloud flexibility**: ODF supports various cloud providers and deployment models, providing flexibility and avoiding vendor lock-in.
- **Advanced features**: ODF offers features such as snapshotting, cloning, and data tiering that are not always available in traditional storage solutions.

ODF architecture

ODF is comprised of three key operators:

- **OpenShift Container Storage (OCS) operator:** Acts as a meta-operator that orchestrates the installation and management of Rook-Ceph and NooBaa operators and triggers the creation of CRs that they reconcile. It depends on CRs provided by these two operators, as specified in its ClusterServiceVersion.
- **Rook-Ceph storage operator:** Backed by the Rook upstream project, it delivers the core storage capabilities, including block, file, and object storage powered by a containerized Ceph cluster. The Ceph cluster itself is managed by corresponding CRDs, such as CephCluster and CephBlockPool.
- **NooBaa operator:** Based on the Noobaa community project, it represents a **MultiCluster Object Gateway (MCG)** – an API layer that abstracts access to different cloud providers, such as Amazon S3 or Azure Blob Storage. When OpenShift is deployed on-premise (as in our lab), MCG uses the **RADOS Gateway (RGW)** object store provided by the Rook Ceph operator by default; otherwise, it connects to the cloud provider's object store. There's more information in the *Further reading* section at [5].

The ODF architecture, including the preceding constituent operators, is presented in the following diagram:

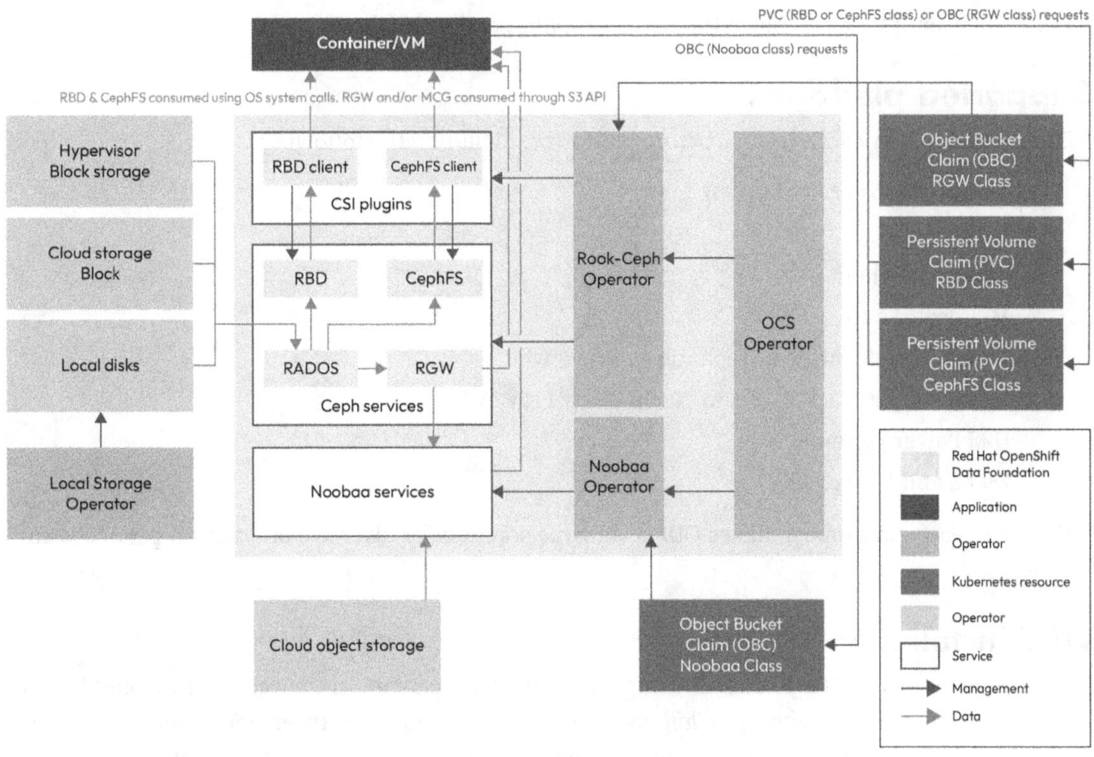

Figure 8.21: ODF architecture

This modular architecture ensures flexibility and scalability, allowing you to tailor ODF to your specific storage needs.

Deployment modes

ODF offers both internal (within the OpenShift cluster) and external (external Ceph cluster) deployment modes:

- **Internal**: Suitable for smaller deployments or when consolidating infrastructure. It leverages local storage or portable storage such as EBS or vSphere volumes.
- **External**: Recommended for large-scale deployments or when storage is managed separately. It utilizes an external Red Hat Ceph Storage cluster.

Subscriptions

Red Hat offers two editions of ODF:

- **Essentials**: Included with Red Hat OpenShift Platform Plus
- **Advanced**: Contact Red Hat for an upgrade

On top of what is offered in Essentials, such as block/file/object storage, cluster-wide encryption, and VolumeSnapshots, the Advanced edition includes support for Metro- and Regional-DR, as well as volume-level encryption, integration with an external KMS, and external cluster mode. More information on their differences is available in the *Further reading* section at [6].

Supported platforms

ODF is available on various infrastructure platforms, including the following:

- Amazon Web Services (AWS)
- Bare metal
- VMware vSphere
- Microsoft Azure
- Google Cloud Platform (Technology Preview)
- Red Hat OpenStack Platform (Technology Preview)
- IBM Power Systems
- IBM Z and LinuxONE

This broad platform support makes ODF a versatile solution for diverse cloud and on-premises environments.

ODF installation

We are going to install ODF in our lab using the OpenShift 4 cluster on VMware that we built back in *Chapter 3, Getting Started with OpenShift*, as it requires a minimum of three nodes and a significant amount of compute resources. It is recommended to have dedicated nodes to run ODF components and infra nodes that we added in *Chapter 4, Post-Install Configuration*, are well-suited for this.

The following table provides requirements for infra nodes if they are to be used for ODF too:

Node Type	CPU per node	RAM per node	Additional Storage Per Node	disk.EnableUUID Advanced parameter
Infra	8	32	0.5TB	TRUE

Table 8.4: Specifications of additional nodes required for ODF

There are several things to note here:

- We already have a cluster installed and infra nodes added, so if you do not have the required number of CPU/RAM per node, you need to drain infra nodes, power them off, adjust the resources, and uncordon them one by one.
- Master nodes don't need to be adjusted as they don't run any ODF components.
- `disk.EnableUUID` needs to be set in the advanced properties of a VM in vCenter. It was described in *Chapter 3, Getting Started with OpenShift*, and we also set it for infra nodes in *Chapter 4, Post-Install Configuration*.
- Required additional storage per node is going to be created dynamically during the ODF installation by the ODF operator using the default `thin-csi` StorageClass, so there is no need to do that manually.
- You are not required to actually have 1.5 TB free in your datastore since we are using thin provisioning, when storage is allocated on demand.

If you followed the two previous chapters, you should already have all the resources you need for this exercise. Follow these steps to install the ODF operator and create a storage stack:

1. First, we need to create a project for ODF and override the project's default node selector:

```
$ oc adm new-project openshift-storage
$ oc annotate ns openshift-storage openshift.io/node-selector=
```

2. Now we can go to the OperatorHub, type `ODF` in the search box, and click on the **OpenShift Data Foundation** operator's tile, at which point we will be taken through a series of steps in order to configure it. Click **Install**, keep the default project (`openshift-storage`) on the next screen, set the approval strategy to **Manual**, and begin the installation.
3. Now, go to the list of installed operators and switch to the `openshift-storage` project in the drop-down menu at the top to monitor the progress (you will need to enable the **Show default projects** toggle to see the project). You may notice that the status switches from **Unknown** to **UpgradePending**, and then to **Upgrade available** shortly after. Since we chose the **Manual** approval strategy to have more control over upgrading the operator, we now have to manually approve the installation. Click on **Upgrade available** > **Preview InstallPlan** > **Approve** to complete the process. The installation will finish shortly, and you will see a popup in the top-right corner of the screen, prompting you with **Refresh web console**.

4. ODF also installs the **OpenShift Data Foundation Client** operator as a dependency. On the **Installed Operators** screen, click on the operator and enable its console plugin on the right-hand side (or click **Plugin available** > **View operator details** > click on **Disabled** under **Console plugin**). It may take 3-5 minutes for both operators to report **Succeeded**.

> In case you want to use a declarative approach to installing ODF for extra learning, we prepared the `chapters/8/snippets/og-odf.yml` and `chapters/8/snippets/sub-odf.yml` files for ODF `OperatorGroup` and `Subscription`, respectively. Don't forget to approve the InstallPlan!

The ODF operator and its dependent operators provide a number of APIs, of which the following are of particular interest to us:

- **OCSInitialization**, which encapsulates high-level operations on the level of `ocs-operator`. In particular, it triggers initialization tasks for deploying ODF and makes sure that necessary SCCs exist. If necessary, these tasks can be triggered again by deleting the `OCCSInitialization` instance.
- **StorageSystem**, which is a high-level resource provided by `odf-operator`. It ensures the existence of a **Subscription** instance for the storage backend of a type defined in its specification.
- **StorageCluster**, which represents configurations for CephCluster and the Noobaa object store. Currently, only one instance per cluster is supported. In order to create a storage stack, only an instance of StorageCluster is required.
- **CephCluster**, which represents a Ceph cluster that includes **monitors (MONs)** for cluster maps, **Object Storage Device Daemons (OSDs)** for storage, **MetaData Services (MDSs)** for managing CephFS metadata, **RADOS Gateway (RGW)** for object store, and **Managers (MGRs)** for monitoring.
- **Noobaa**, which represents a MultiCloud Object Gateway that can interface with RGW or object storage provided by a public cloud platform – for example, Amazon S3.

5. After the ODF operator is successfully installed, we will need to configure a `StorageCluster` object that will use the `thin-csi` StorageClass (created by default if a cluster was installed following the instructions in *Chapter 3, Getting Started with OpenShift*) to provision underlying storage, from which secondary storage classes will be created. From the list of installed operators, click on the ODF operator and then on **Create StorageSystem**. That will open a wizard that will ask you to provide information on how to provision the underlying storage and select nodes for the storage cluster, among others.

   On top of using an existing StorageClass, the ODF operator can be configured to use locally attached devices configured by the **Local Storage Operator (LSO)** or a remote Ceph cluster; however, for the sake of simplicity, we will go with **Use an existing StorageClass**:

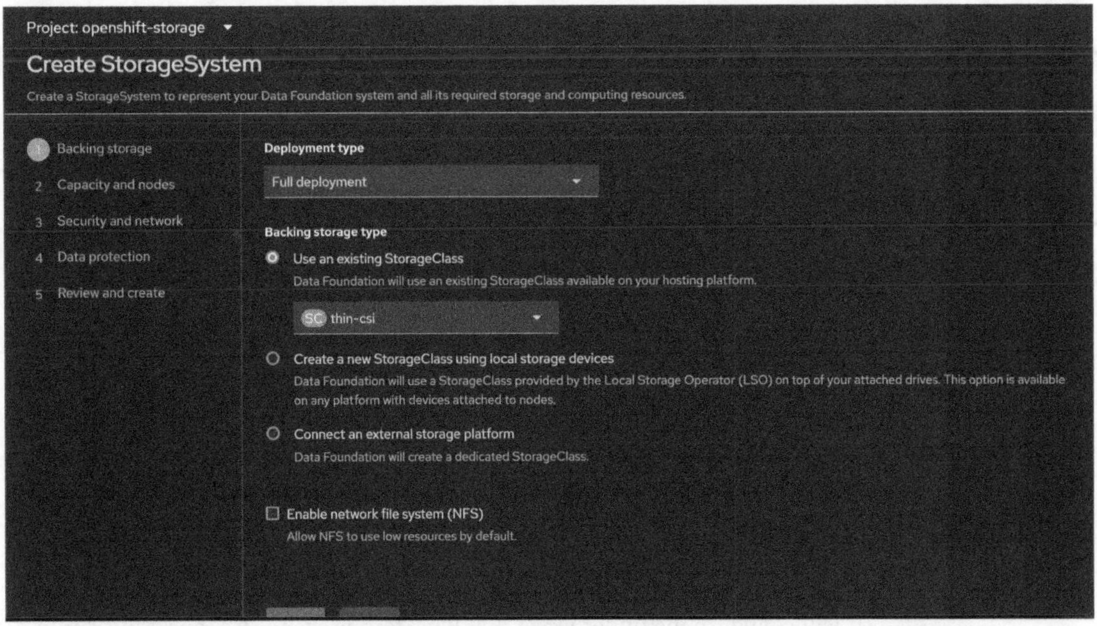

Figure 8.22: Creating a StorageSystem for ODF

6. Click **Next** and you will be presented with a screen where you get to select storage nodes for the StorageCluster:

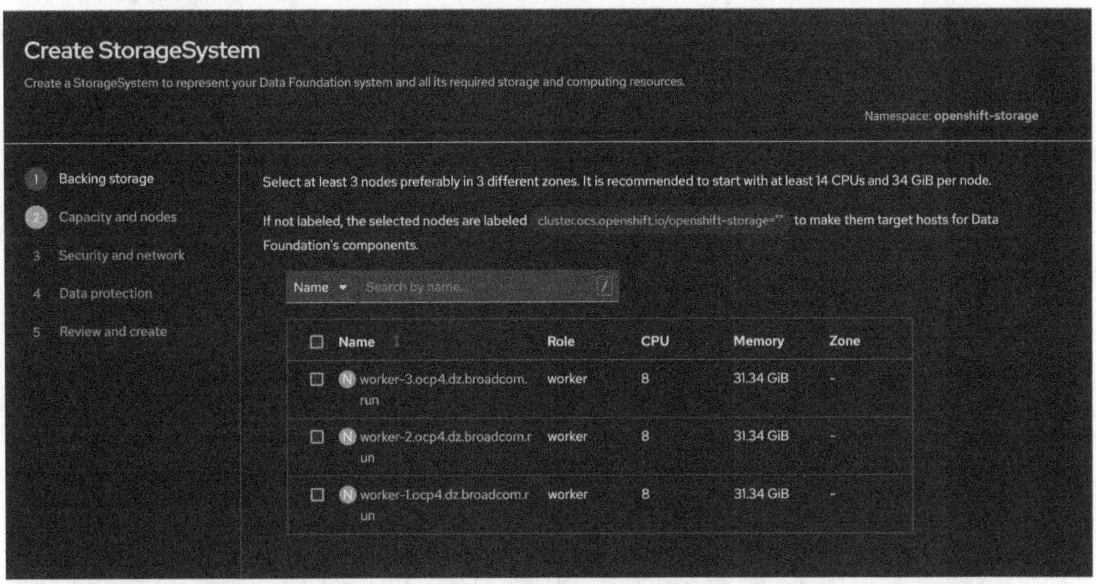

Figure 8.23: Selecting nodes for ODF

As you can see, only three worker nodes are available, despite the fact that we created three more infra nodes specifically for infrastructure workloads, such as ODF. As you may recall from *Chapter 4, Post-Install Configuration*, we tainted those nodes so that only workloads that have corresponding tolerations can be run on them. The UI wizard for creating a StorageCluster doesn't provide a way to add those tolerations to ODF components, so we will create a StorageCluster using the YAML manifest provided in `chapters/8/snippets/ocs-storagecluster.yml` of this book's GitHub repository. Just examine its structure for now and notice that tolerations for various components match the ones we created in *Chapter 4, Post-Install Configuration*. It also requests 0.5 TB of storage per storage node from our StorageClass.

> When creating a StorageCluster in the UI, you can choose to configure it for **Disaster Recovery (DR)**. Although not explored in this book due to the dependency on **Advanced Cluster Management (ACM)** for Kubernetes and limitations of our lab environment, you can enable it in your YAML manifest by adding the following annotation:
>
> `ocs.openshift.io/clusterIsDisasterRecoveryTarget: "true"`
>
> It will configure the underlying Ceph BlueStore backend to support mirroring, which is required for DR.

7. One of the ODF components is a DaemonSet that deploys CSI plugins on all nodes where storage consumers are expected to run. Assuming we will run such workloads on all nodes except for masters, we will need to patch the ConfigMap named `rook-ceph-operator-config`. Examine the `chapters/8/snippets/cm-rook-ceph-operator-config.yml` manifest from this book's repository and apply it:

```
$ oc apply -f chapters/8/snippets/cm-rook-ceph-operator-config.yml
```

The ConfigMap already exists, so we used `apply` instead of `create`. You can safely disregard the warning about the `kubectl.kubernetes.io/last-applied-configuration` annotation.

8. Next, label the `openshift-storage` namespace so that ODF exports usage metrics to the OpenShift monitoring stack:

```
$ oc label ns/openshift-storage openshift.io/cluster-monitoring="true"
```

9. Now we can create the StorageCluster:

```
$ oc create -f chapters/8/snippets/ocs-storagecluster.yml
```

You can use the following command to monitor the progress:

```
$ watch -n1 oc get
storagecluster,cephcluster,ocsinitialization,noobaa,po,pdb,sc,pvc -o wide
-n openshift-storage
```

You will see a number of pods get created; some of them may fail and restart a few times. This happens because ODF is made up of several interdependent components, and if some start earlier than their dependencies, they will keep failing and restarting until the dependencies are up and running. The entire process may take 5-10 minutes. This is what you should see when the operator rolls everything out:

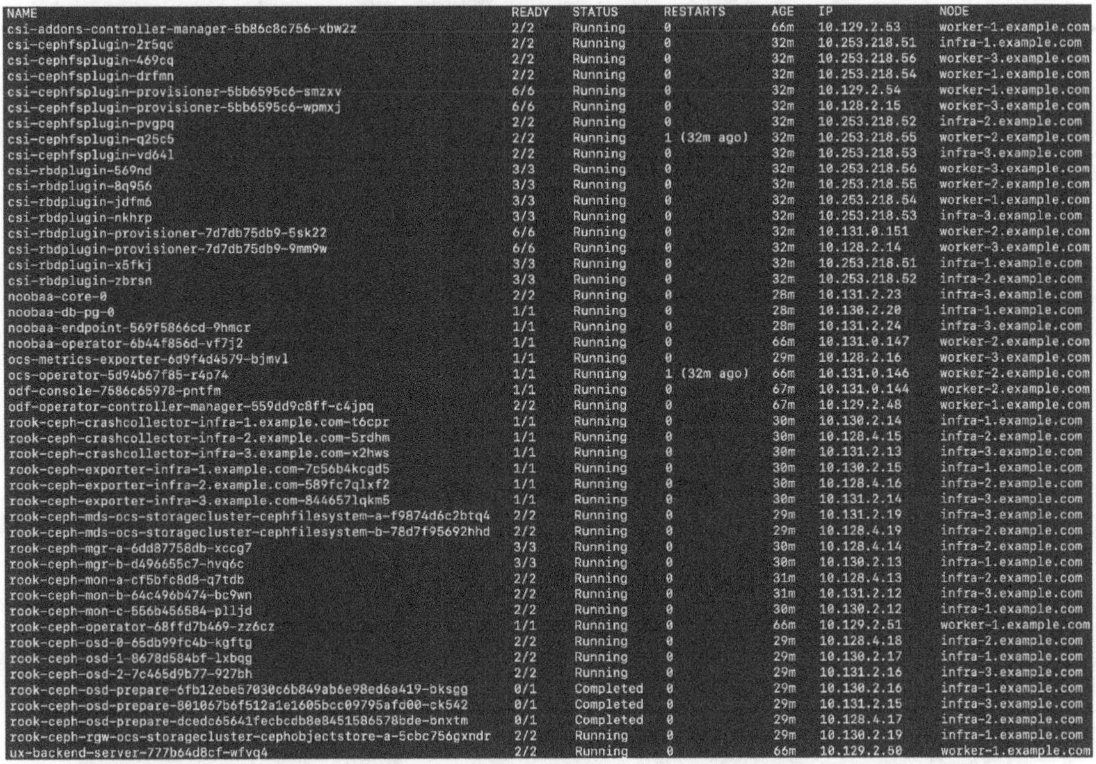

NAME	READY	STATUS	RESTARTS	AGE	IP	NODE
csi-addons-controller-manager-5b86c8c756-xbw2z	2/2	Running	0	66m	10.129.2.53	worker-1.example.com
csi-cephfsplugin-2r5qc	2/2	Running	0	32m	10.253.218.51	infra-1.example.com
csi-cephfsplugin-469cq	2/2	Running	0	32m	10.253.218.56	worker-3.example.com
csi-cephfsplugin-drfmn	2/2	Running	0	32m	10.253.218.54	worker-1.example.com
csi-cephfsplugin-provisioner-5bb6595c6-smzxv	6/6	Running	0	32m	10.129.2.54	worker-1.example.com
csi-cephfsplugin-provisioner-5bb6595c6-wpmxj	6/6	Running	0	32m	10.128.2.15	worker-3.example.com
csi-cephfsplugin-pvgpq	2/2	Running	0	32m	10.253.218.52	infra-2.example.com
csi-cephfsplugin-q25c5	2/2	Running	1 (32m ago)	32m	10.253.218.55	worker-2.example.com
csi-cephfsplugin-vd641	2/2	Running	0	32m	10.253.218.53	infra-3.example.com
csi-rbdplugin-569nd	3/3	Running	0	32m	10.253.218.56	worker-3.example.com
csi-rbdplugin-8q956	3/3	Running	0	32m	10.253.218.55	worker-2.example.com
csi-rbdplugin-jdfm6	3/3	Running	0	32m	10.253.218.54	worker-1.example.com
csi-rbdplugin-nkhrp	3/3	Running	0	32m	10.253.218.53	infra-3.example.com
csi-rbdplugin-provisioner-7d7db75db9-5sk22	6/6	Running	0	32m	10.131.0.151	worker-2.example.com
csi-rbdplugin-provisioner-7d7db75db9-9mm9w	6/6	Running	0	32m	10.128.2.14	worker-3.example.com
csi-rbdplugin-x5fkj	3/3	Running	0	32m	10.253.218.51	infra-1.example.com
csi-rbdplugin-zbrsn	3/3	Running	0	32m	10.253.218.52	infra-2.example.com
noobaa-core-0	2/2	Running	0	28m	10.131.2.23	infra-3.example.com
noobaa-db-pg-0	1/1	Running	0	28m	10.130.2.20	infra-1.example.com
noobaa-endpoint-569f5866cd-9hmcr	1/1	Running	0	28m	10.131.2.24	infra-3.example.com
noobaa-operator-6b44f856d-vf7j2	1/1	Running	0	66m	10.131.0.147	worker-2.example.com
ocs-metrics-exporter-6d9f4d4579-bjmvl	1/1	Running	0	29m	10.128.2.16	worker-3.example.com
ocs-operator-5d94b67f85-r4p74	1/1	Running	1 (32m ago)	66m	10.131.0.146	worker-2.example.com
odf-console-7586c65978-pntfm	1/1	Running	0	67m	10.131.0.144	worker-2.example.com
odf-operator-controller-manager-559dd9c8ff-c4jpq	2/2	Running	0	67m	10.129.2.48	worker-1.example.com
rook-ceph-crashcollector-infra-1.example.com-t6cpr	1/1	Running	0	30m	10.130.2.14	infra-1.example.com
rook-ceph-crashcollector-infra-2.example.com-5rdhm	1/1	Running	0	30m	10.128.4.15	infra-2.example.com
rook-ceph-crashcollector-infra-3.example.com-x2hws	1/1	Running	0	30m	10.131.2.13	infra-3.example.com
rook-ceph-exporter-infra-1.example.com-7c56b4kcgd5	1/1	Running	0	30m	10.130.2.15	infra-1.example.com
rook-ceph-exporter-infra-2.example.com-589fc7qlxf2	1/1	Running	0	30m	10.128.4.16	infra-2.example.com
rook-ceph-exporter-infra-3.example.com-844657lqkm5	1/1	Running	0	30m	10.131.2.14	infra-3.example.com
rook-ceph-mds-ocs-storagecluster-cephfilesystem-a-f9874d6c2btq4	2/2	Running	0	29m	10.131.2.19	infra-3.example.com
rook-ceph-mds-ocs-storagecluster-cephfilesystem-b-78d7f95692hhd	2/2	Running	0	29m	10.128.4.19	infra-2.example.com
rook-ceph-mgr-a-6dd87758db-xccg7	3/3	Running	0	30m	10.128.4.14	infra-2.example.com
rook-ceph-mgr-b-d496655c7-hvq6c	3/3	Running	0	30m	10.130.2.13	infra-1.example.com
rook-ceph-mon-a-cf5bfc8d8-q7tdb	2/2	Running	0	31m	10.128.4.13	infra-2.example.com
rook-ceph-mon-b-64c496b474-bc9wn	2/2	Running	0	31m	10.131.2.12	infra-3.example.com
rook-ceph-mon-c-556b456584-plljd	2/2	Running	0	30m	10.130.2.12	infra-1.example.com
rook-ceph-operator-68ffd7b469-zz6cz	1/1	Running	0	66m	10.129.2.51	worker-1.example.com
rook-ceph-osd-0-65db99fc4b-kgftg	2/2	Running	0	29m	10.128.4.18	infra-2.example.com
rook-ceph-osd-1-8678d584bf-lxbqg	2/2	Running	0	29m	10.130.2.17	infra-1.example.com
rook-ceph-osd-2-7c465d9b77-927bh	2/2	Running	0	29m	10.131.2.16	infra-3.example.com
rook-ceph-osd-prepare-6fb12ebe57030c6b849ab6e98ed6a419-bksgg	0/1	Completed	0	29m	10.130.2.16	infra-1.example.com
rook-ceph-osd-prepare-801067b6f512a1e1605bcc09795afd00-ck542	0/1	Completed	0	29m	10.131.2.15	infra-3.example.com
rook-ceph-osd-prepare-dcedc65641fecbcdb8e8451586578bde-bnxtm	0/1	Completed	0	29m	10.128.4.17	infra-2.example.com
rook-ceph-rgw-ocs-storagecluster-cephobjectstore-a-5cbc756gxndr	2/2	Running	0	29m	10.130.2.19	infra-1.example.com
ux-backend-server-777b64d8cf-wfvq4	2/2	Running	0	66m	10.129.2.50	worker-1.example.com

Figure 8.24: ODF is successfully deployed – CLI

You don't need to examine each and every pod in the preceding screenshot. Just see if they're all showing as `Running` or `Completed`, and the `READY/TOTAL` numbers are the same for each running pod.

The author of this chapter particularly likes this command for its comprehensiveness, although its output may be intimidating to fresh users:

```
$ oc get storagecluster,cephcluster,cephobjectstore,cephobjectstoreuser,
cephfilesystem,cephblockpool,ocsinitialization,noobaa,bucketclasses,
backingstore,po,pdb,sc,pvc -o wide -n openshift-storage
```

For a healthy ODF cluster, you're supposed to see only `Ready`, `Replicated`, and `HEALTH_OK`.

In your environment, pod names most likely will be different. What matters here is the number of pods and that all of them should be running.

> vSphere can take a minute or two to provision PVCs as large as in this demo (512 Gi). If you check namespace events via `oc get ev` during that time, you may notice messages like this:
>
> ```
> Waiting for a volume to be created either by the external
> provisioner 'csi.vsphere.vmware.com' or manually by the
> system administrator. If volume creation is delayed, please
> verify that the provisioner is running and correctly
> registered.
> ```
>
> If you see this, no action should be necessary – volumes will be provisioned shortly.

Notice that only CSI (storage drivers) and operator pods run on both worker and infra nodes; everything else (Noobaa, Ceph monitors/managers/metadata servers, and OSDs) was scheduled on infra nodes. This is because CSI pods are managed by DaemonSets that schedule them on all nodes where storage consumers are expected to run.

As an extra check, go to **Storage** > **Data Foundation** and check whether everything is green across the board:

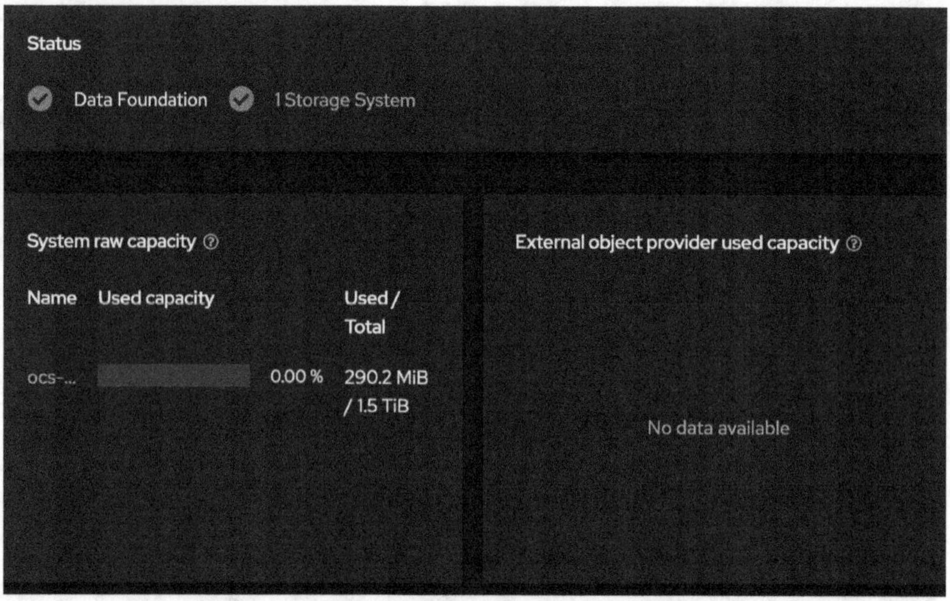

Figure 8.25: ODF is successfully deployed and healthy – Web UI

10. Finally, let's take a look at what StorageClasses have been provisioned by the ODF operator by running `oc get sc`:

```
NAME                          PROVISIONER
ocs-storagecluster-ceph-rbd   openshift-storage.rbd.csi.ceph.com
ocs-storagecluster-ceph-rgw   openshift-storage.ceph.rook.io/bucket
ocs-storagecluster-cephfs     openshift-storage.cephfs.csi.ceph.com
openshift-storage.noobaa.io   openshift-storage.noobaa.io/obc
thin-csi (default)            csi.vsphere.vmware.com
```

Figure 8.26: StorageClasses created by ODF

We're showing only two columns in the preceding screenshot to save space, so here's what you're expected to see for the rest of them:

- **RECLAIMPOLICY:** `Delete`
- **VOLUMEBINDINGMODE:** `Immediate`
- **ALLOWVOLUMEEXPANSION:** `true` for RBD- and CephFS-backed StorageClasses and `false` for the other two

As a cherry on top, we can even move the ODF operator's controller manager pod to one of the infra nodes:

1. Open an interactive editor to edit the ODF `Subscription` resource:

```
$ oc edit sub/odf-operator -n openshift-storage
```

2. Add the following under `.spec` (on the same level as name, channel, etc):

```
  config:
    nodeSelector:
      node-role.kubernetes.io/infra: ""
    tolerations:
    - key: node-role.kubernetes.io/infra
      operator: Exists
```

3. Save and close (`:x` if your default editor is vim).
4. Run the following command and watch how the controller pod terminates and then restarts on an infra node:

```
$ watch -n1 'oc get po -n openshift-storage -o wide | grep operator'
```

This is a feature of the **Operator Lifecycle Manager (OLM)** that manages all add-on operators on OpenShift 4, so it's not exclusive to ODF. We will discuss OLM and operators in general in more detail in *Chapter 16, Understanding Operators and the Operator Framework*.

Now that we have successfully installed ODF on our cluster, we can use it to provision PersistentVolumes for applications and cluster subsystems. In particular, we will use it to configure storage for the Image Registry Operator in *Chapter 15, Exploring Additional Services in OpenShift*.

Here's an interesting fact we discovered while working on this chapter:

Tolerations can be added to `noobaa-core-0` and `noobaa-endpoint-xxxxxxxxx-xxxxx` pods directly, and they won't be removed by the operator, which technically is a bug.

In this section, we configured an enterprise-grade storage backend offering block, filesystem, and object types of storage for our cluster and we will use it to provide persistent storage for the integrated image registry later in this book. ODF is a complex product with a lot of interacting components and options, so we encourage you to familiarize yourself with it more closely using the official documentation at [7].

Ceph architecture

As mentioned earlier in this chapter, the ODF storage architecture utilizes Ceph as an underlying storage solution, which has been proven over the years to be a reliable, enterprise-ready software-defined storage solution that can scale horizontally and provide the required redundancy, reliability, and performance.

Ceph has a modular and distributed architecture that contains the following elements:

- An object storage backend known as **RADOS** (**Reliable Autonomic Distributed Object Store**). RADOS is a self-healing and self-managing software-based object store.
- A variety of access methods to interact with RADOS.

See the following diagram for a visual representation of all Ceph components:

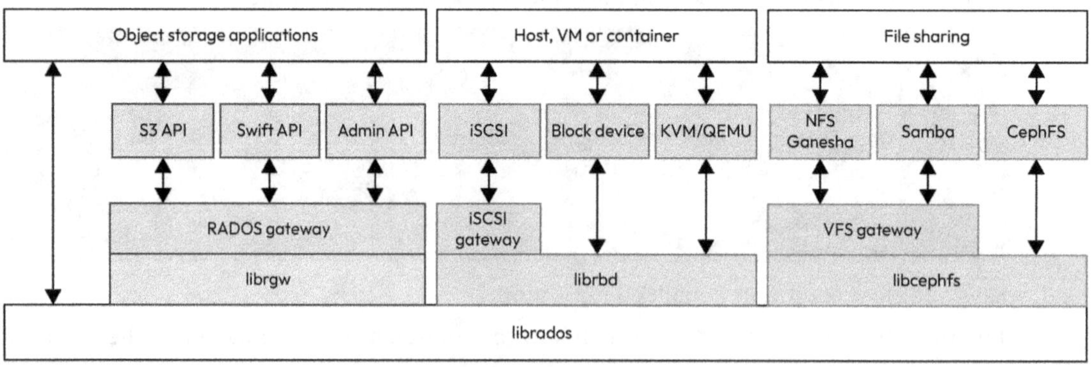

Figure 8.27: Ceph architecture

As part of the creation of a `SystemStorage` object, ODF's Rook-Ceph operator creates several PVs using the Local Storage Operator we have installed before, alongside the ODF operator.

Let's see what it looks like using the CLI:

```
$ oc get pv
```

You can see that we have three 512Gi PVs for Ceph OSDs (storage devices), three 50Gi PVs for Ceph monitors, and one 50Gi PV for the object store (Noobaa):

```
NAME                                       CAPACITY   STATUS   CLAIM                                    STORAGECLASS
pvc-56843f99-3f7b-4f18-aab6-525b8a36dea1   512Gi      Bound    ocs-deviceset-thin-csi-2-data-05kw5t     thin-csi
pvc-57e8b2b8-64f0-4e4a-8a5a-3d5c24481138   50Gi       Bound    db-noobaa-db-pg-0                        ocs-storagecluster-ceph-rbd
pvc-749f8dfe-06c3-4259-94d0-0c6c835d73ce   512Gi      Bound    ocs-deviceset-thin-csi-0-data-0pkk64     thin-csi
pvc-a98c07ff-d700-4d97-a581-d8c655b3b54b   512Gi      Bound    ocs-deviceset-thin-csi-1-data-0sm8s9     thin-csi
pvc-c72eca4a-469f-4b8b-8a15-47cebcce6012   50Gi       Bound    rook-ceph-mon-c                          thin-csi
pvc-df6b2991-a5b1-4aba-bdfc-127f395cf3da   50Gi       Bound    rook-ceph-mon-b                          thin-csi
pvc-f3900861-181d-4230-b7fb-a5672c93f2a1   50Gi       Bound    rook-ceph-mon-a                          thin-csi
```

Figure 8.28: Block devices used by ODF

The preceding output is actually the result of a more complex command that we used to print only columns of interest. We only used it to fit the layout constraints of this book:

```
$ oc get pv -o custom-columns=NAME:.metadata.name,CAPACITY:.spec.capacity.
storage,STATUS:.status.phase,CLAIM:.spec.claimRef.name,STORAGECLASS:.spec.
storageClassName
```

All PVs, except for the one for Noobaa, should have been provisioned by the `thin-csi` StorageClass, if running on vSphere. They are created and managed by the ODF operator – in particular, the `rook-ceph` operator we installed in the `openshift-storage` namespace.

Check the status of the Ceph cluster using the following commands:

```
$ ROOK_CEPH_OPERATOR_POD=$(oc get po -l app=rook-ceph-operator -n openshift-
storage -o name)
$ oc exec $ROOK_CEPH_OPERATOR_POD -c rook-ceph-operator -n openshift-storage --
ceph -c /var/lib/rook/openshift-storage/openshift-storage.config -s
```

You should see something like this:

```
cluster:
  id:     7b801992-6feb-42dd-b8db-cbd30c7be5e1
  health: HEALTH_OK

services:
  mon: 3 daemons, quorum a,b,c (age 82m)
  mgr: a(active, since 41m), standbys: b
  mds: 1/1 daemons up, 1 hot standby
  osd: 3 osds: 3 up (since 81m), 3 in (since 82m)
  rgw: 1 daemon active (1 hosts, 1 zones)

data:
  volumes: 1/1 healthy
  pools:   12 pools, 169 pgs
  objects: 455 objects, 150 MiB
  usage:   430 MiB used, 1.5 TiB / 1.5 TiB avail
  pgs:     169 active+clean

io:
  client:   853 B/s rd, 8.7 KiB/s wr, 1 op/s rd, 0 op/s wr
```

Figure 8.29: Ceph status is HEALTH_OK, which is the desired state

Here is how to check the Ceph cluster's storage usage:

```
$ oc exec $ROOK_CEPH_OPERATOR_POD -c rook-ceph-operator -n openshift-storage --
ceph -c /var/lib/rook/openshift-storage/openshift-storage.config df
```

This is what you're expected to see (actual numbers will likely differ):

```
--- RAW STORAGE ---
CLASS     SIZE    AVAIL     USED  RAW USED  %RAW USED
ssd    1.5 TiB  1.5 TiB  430 MiB   430 MiB       0.03
TOTAL  1.5 TiB  1.5 TiB  430 MiB   430 MiB       0.03

--- POOLS ---
POOL                                                 ID  PGS   STORED  OBJECTS     USED  %USED  MAX AVAIL
ocs-storagecluster-cephblockpool                      1   32   91 MiB       72  273 MiB   0.02    435 GiB
.rgw.root                                             2    8  5.7 KiB       17  192 KiB      0    435 GiB
ocs-storagecluster-cephobjectstore.rgw.log            3    8   23 KiB      308  1.9 MiB      0    435 GiB
ocs-storagecluster-cephobjectstore.rgw.meta           4    8  2.8 KiB       14  144 KiB      0    435 GiB
ocs-storagecluster-cephobjectstore.rgw.otp            5    8      0 B        0      0 B      0    435 GiB
ocs-storagecluster-cephobjectstore.rgw.control        6    8      0 B        8      0 B      0    435 GiB
ocs-storagecluster-cephobjectstore.rgw.buckets.index  7    8      0 B       11      0 B      0    435 GiB
ocs-storagecluster-cephobjectstore.rgw.buckets.non-ec 8    8      0 B        0      0 B      0    435 GiB
ocs-storagecluster-cephfilesystem-metadata            9   16   47 KiB       22  228 KiB      0    435 GiB
.mgr                                                 10    1  577 KiB        2  1.7 MiB      0    435 GiB
ocs-storagecluster-cephfilesystem-data0              11   32      0 B        0      0 B      0    435 GiB
ocs-storagecluster-cephobjectstore.rgw.buckets.data  12   32    1 KiB        1   12 KiB      0    435 GiB
```

Figure 8.30: Storage usage on a newly created Ceph cluster

We have already practiced static storage provisioning when you created PVs manually. Now that we have ODF, we can see how dynamic provisioning works.

Dynamically provisioning volumes using ODF file storage

As we mentioned before, ODF comes with multiple components out of the box, one of which is file storage with the Rook-Ceph operator provided by the CephFS client. This is what file storage provisioning looks like using CephFS at a high level:

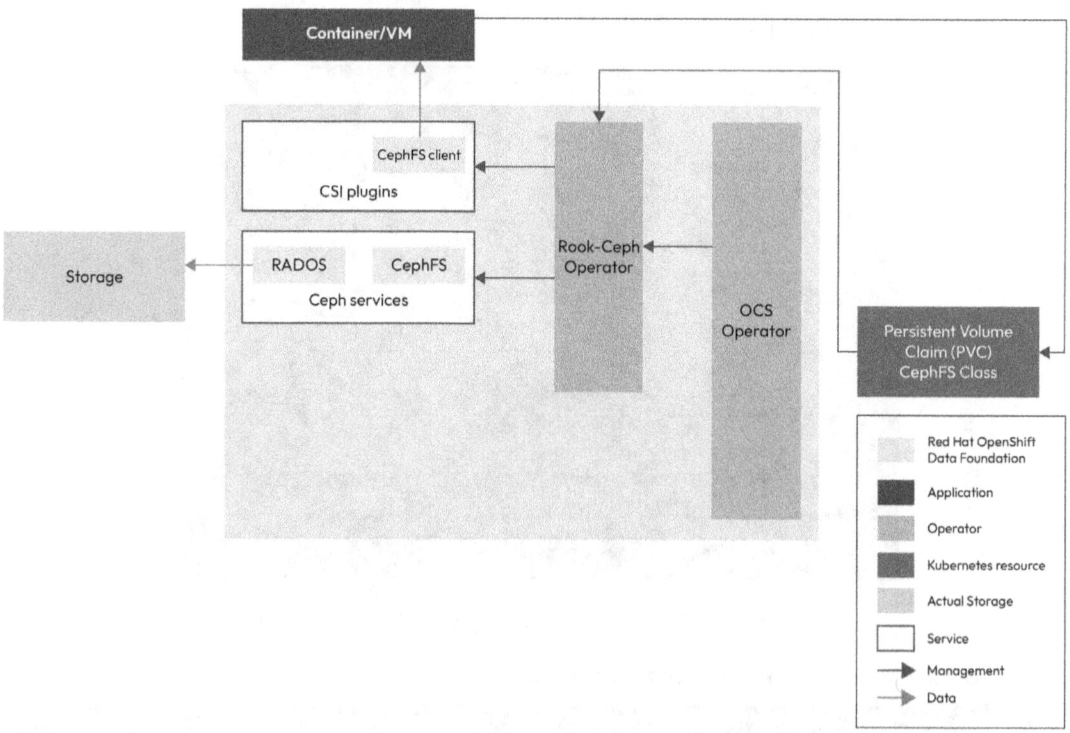

Figure 8.31: ODF components involved in provisioning filesystem-based storage

You can learn more about the architecture of ODF at [7].

Let's see how it works in action by using code snippets from this book's GitHub repository. First, create a PVC that uses the `ocs-storagecluster-cephfs` StorageClass:

```
$ oc apply -f chapters/8/snippets/ceph-pvc.yml
```

Verify that the PVC was created:

```
$ oc get pvc
```

```
NAME       STATUS   VOLUME                                     CAPACITY   ACCESS MODES   STORAGECLASS
ceph-pvc   Bound    pvc-f9a8e5eb-ba96-47cc-b551-732c2d28e2fc   10Gi       RWX            ocs-storagecluster-cephfs
```

Figure 8.32: A PVC is created and bound to a CephFS-backed PV

Create a pod that consumes this PVC:

```
$ oc apply -f chapters/8/snippets/pod-busybox.yml
```

Verify it is running and using our PVC:

```
$ oc get pods busybox
```

You should see a single pod running:

```
NAME      READY   STATUS    RESTARTS   AGE
busybox   1/1     Running   0          10s
```

Figure 8.33: A test busybox pod that uses the CephFS PV is up and running

Let's execute the `df -h /mnt` command inside our pod's container to see how the PVC is mounted:

```
$ oc exec busybox -- df -h /mnt
```

As you can see, it's provided by CephFS:

```
Filesystem                Size      Used Available Use% Mounted on
172.30.66.233:3300,172.30.249.47:3300,172.30.142.140:3300:/volumes/csi/csi-vol
-1e5a80b6-9d67-4a38-8c92-db2895325590/c5661e55-35f9-4e73-83d4-1dcd12159ead
                          10.0G         0     10.0G   0% /mnt
```

Figure 8.34: CephFS volume is successfully mounted via CSI

Before we proceed to the next section, let's clean up the lab and delete the pod and PVC we created (the pod takes a bit more time to be deleted, so you may want to run the first command with `--force`, which skips waiting for the pod to complete):

```
$ oc delete po/busybox
$ oc delete pvc/ceph-pvc
```

Now that we've tackled static provisioning of PVs, it's time to move on to dynamic volume provisioning with ODF.

Dynamically provisioning volumes using ODF block storage

Another storage provider that comes with ODF out of the box is block storage with the Rook-Ceph operator provided by the **RADOS Block Device** (**RBD**) client. This is what file storage provisioning looks like using RBD at a high level:

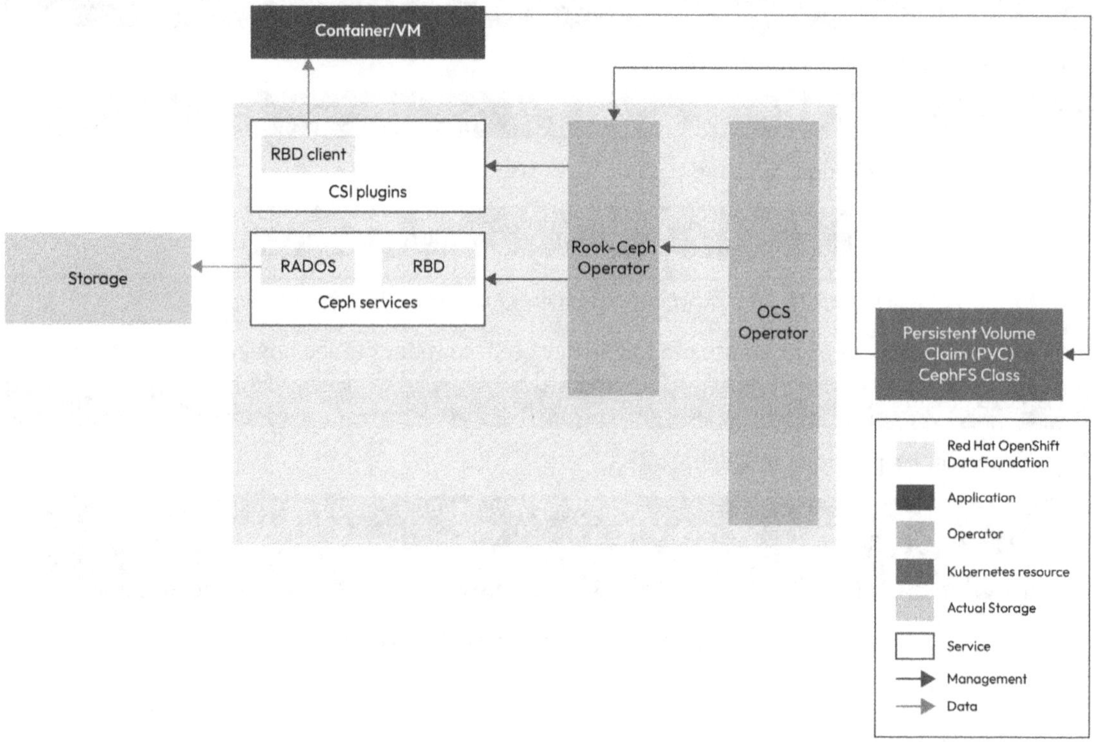

Figure 8.35: ODF components involved in provisioning block storage

Let's see how it works in action. First, create a PVC that uses the `ocs-storagecluster-ceph-rbd` storageclass, using the OpenShift UI this time. Log in to your OpenShift web console, navigate to **Storage** > **PersistentVolumeClaims**, > click on **Create PersistentVolumeClaim**, fill in the following parameters as you see them in the following screenshot, and click **Create**:

- **Project: default**
- **StorageClass: ocs-storagecluster-ceph-rbd**
- **PersistentVolumeClaim name: ceph-rbd-pvc**
- **Access mode: Single user (RWO)**
- **Size: 10 GiB**
- **Volume mode: Block**

This is what it looks like in the UI:

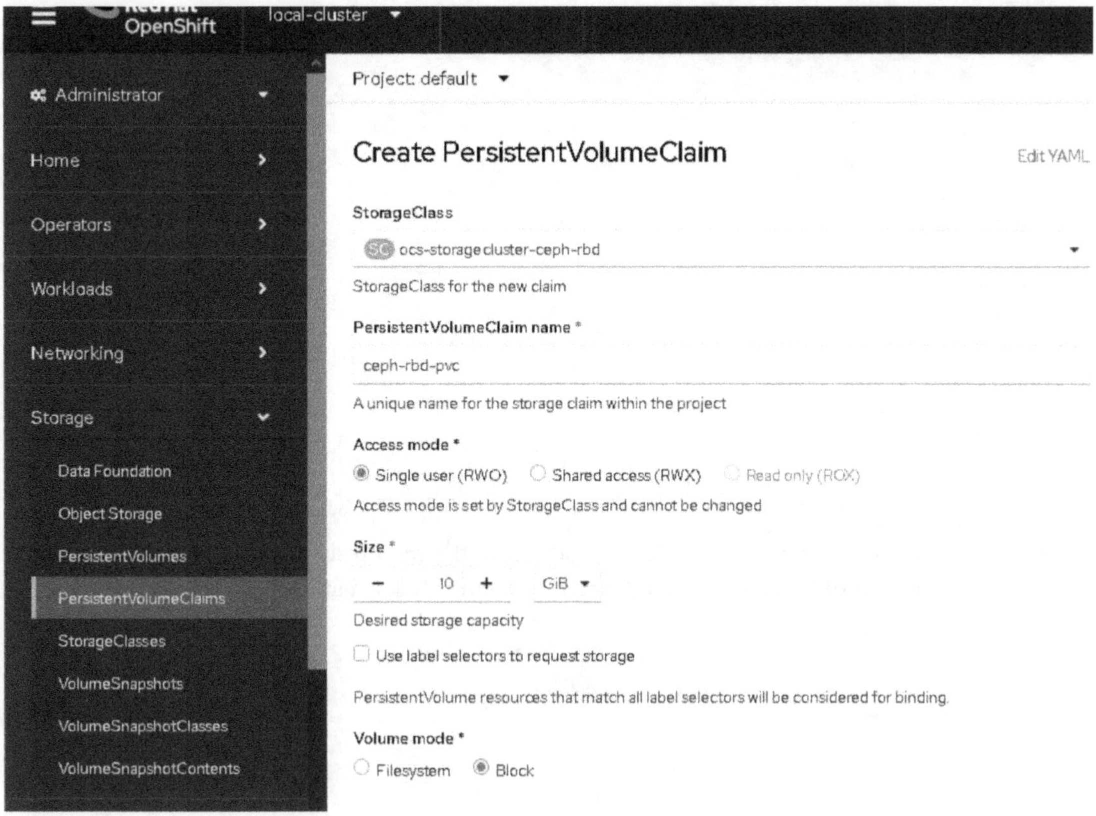

Figure 8.36: Creating a PVC in the OpenShift web UI

On the following screen, you should see the confirmation that the PVC was created:

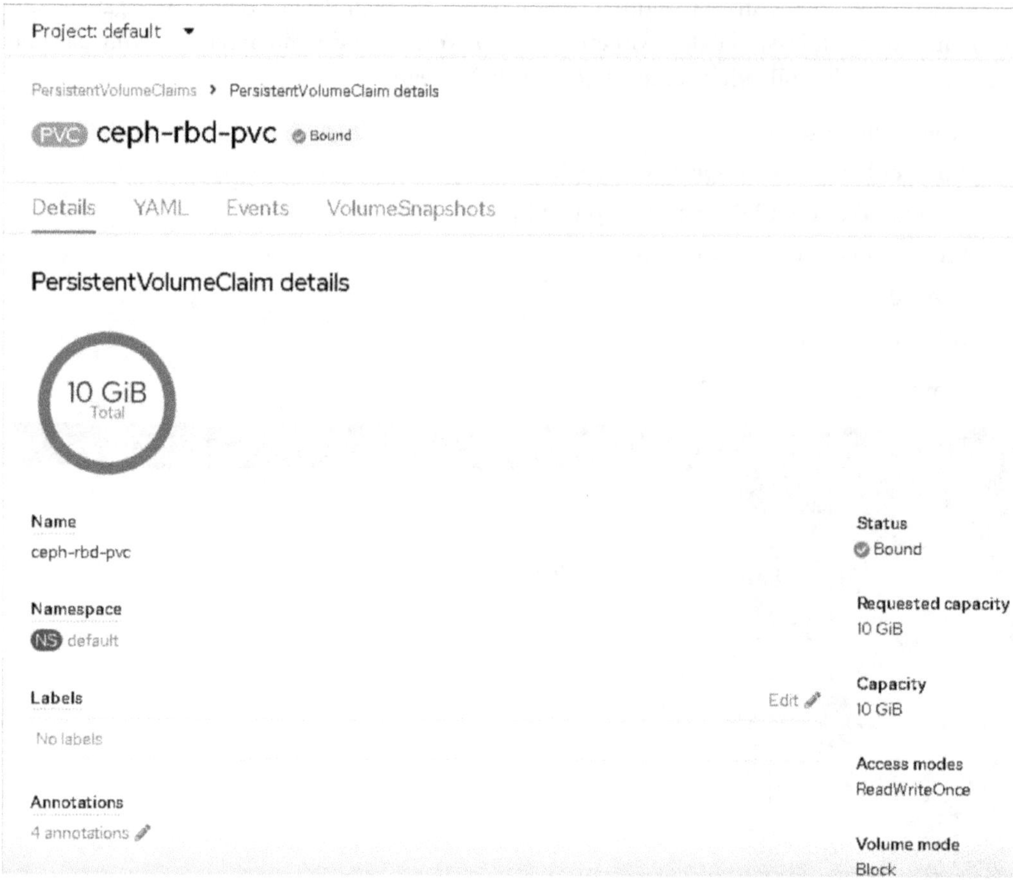

Figure 8.37: Verifying that a PVC was created

Then navigate to **Workloads** > **Pods** > **Create Pod**, paste the manifest from `chapters/8/snippets/pod-busybox-rbd.yml` of this book's GitHub repository, and click **Create**:

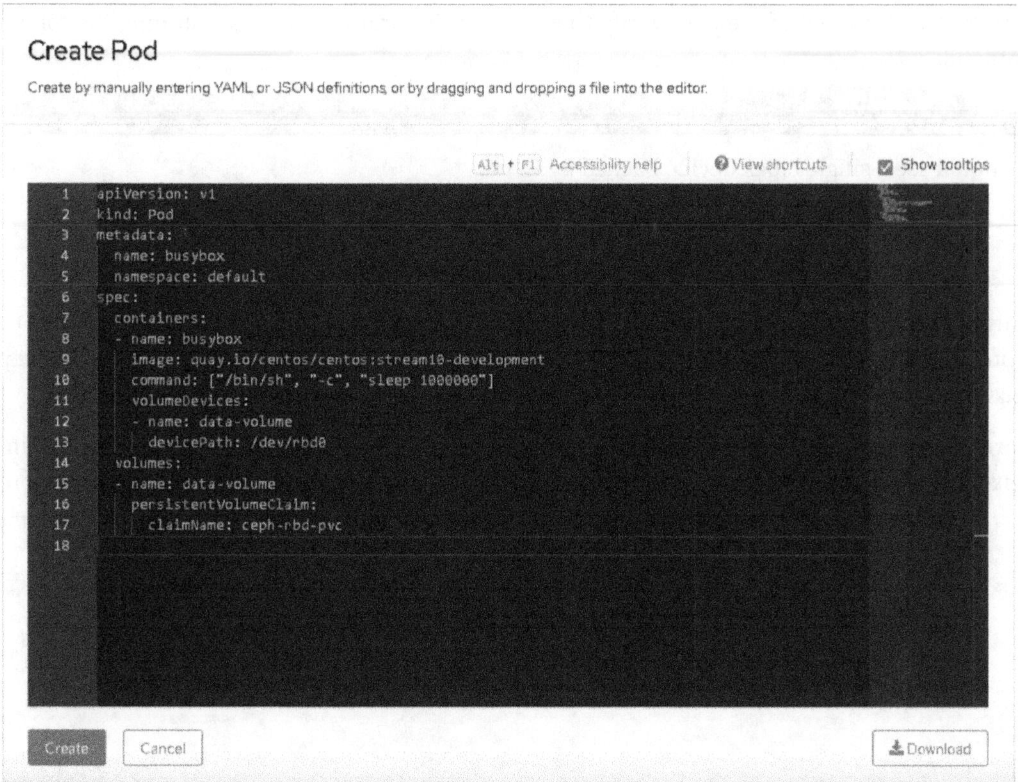

Figure 8.38: Creating a busybox pod from a manifest

Wait for the pod to be in the running state, then go to the **Terminal** tab to access the shell of the pod we have just created:

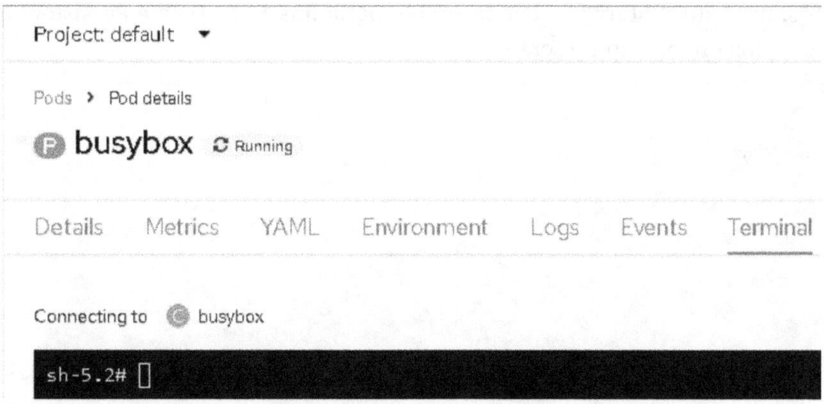

Figure 8.39: Accessing the terminal of a busybox pod

From the web terminal of the pod, verify that our PVC is connected to it by running the following command:

```
# ls -la /dev/rbd0
```

You should see a single block device backed by Ceph:

```
brw-rw-rw-. 1 root disk 252, 0 Aug  4 09:47 /dev/rbd0
```

Figure 8.40: RBD-backed device is successfully provisioned and mounted inside the pod

Creating partitions, formatting, and placing files on this block device is outside of the scope of this chapter, but if you are eager to learn more, make sure that you are running this container in the privileged mode with `.spec.containers[].securityContext.privileged: true`.

Before we proceed, let's clean up your environment and delete both the pod and PVC we created in the lab exercise. Navigate to **Workloads** > **Pods** > **...** > **Delete Pod** and confirm deletion on the pop-up screen:

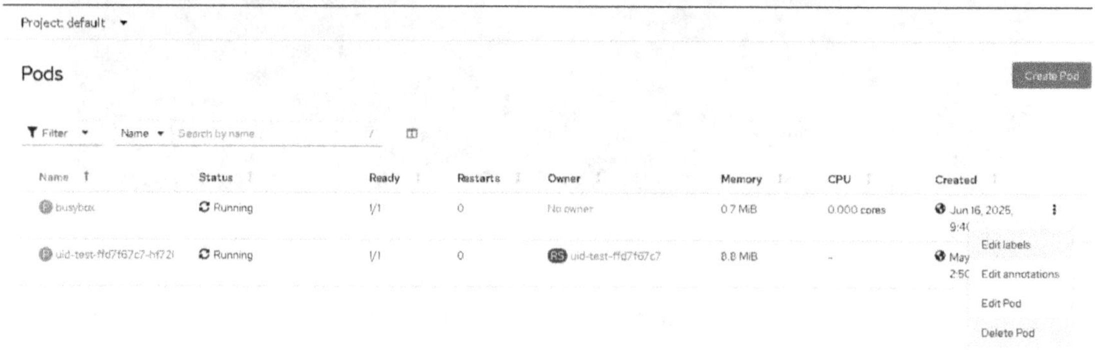

Figure 8.41: Deleting a pod from the OpenShift web UI

To delete a PVC, navigate to **Storage** > **PeristentVolumeClaims** > **...** > **Delete PersistentVolumeClaim** and confirm deletion on the pop-up screen:

Figure 8.42: Deleting a PVC from the OpenShift web UI

This concludes our lab exercises for this chapter, and we are ready to move on to the next one.

Summary

In this chapter, we looked at the foundation of OpenShift 4 storage APIs such as PersistentVolumes, PersistentVolumeClaims, and StorageClasses. We then took a look at the Container Storage Interface and moved on to OpenShift Data Foundation fundamentals, its architecture, and lots of practical tasks, which allowed us to understand how to operate ODF to support application needs. In the following chapter, we will deep dive into the application development process and discuss different tools and methods on how to properly develop and deploy applications on OpenShift 4.

References

To learn more about the topics that were covered in this chapter, take a look at the following resources:

- [1] *Types of PVs*: `https://docs.redhat.com/en/documentation/openshift_container_platform/4.16/html/storage/understanding-persistent-storage#types-of-persistent-volumes_understanding-persistent-storage`
- [2] *Access modes*: `https://docs.redhat.com/en/documentation/openshift_container_platform/4.16/html/storage/understanding-persistent-storage#pv-access-modes_understanding-persistent-storage`
- [3] *Block volume support*: `https://docs.redhat.com/en/documentation/openshift_container_platform/4.16/html/storage/understanding-persistent-storage#block-volume-support_understanding-persistent-storage`
- [4] *CSI drivers supported by OpenShift Container Platform*: `https://docs.redhat.com/en/documentation/openshift_container_platform/4.16/html/storage/using-container-storage-interface-csi#csi-drivers-supported_persistent-storage-csi`
- [5] *ODF: MCG or RGW*: `https://learn.redhat.com/t5/Containers-DevOps-OpenShift/ODF-MCG-or-RGW/td-p/22413`
- [6] *Red Hat OpenShift Data Foundation editions*: `https://www.redhat.com/en/resources/add-capabilities-enterprise-deployments-datasheet`
- [7] *Red Hat OpenShift Data Foundation Architecture*: `https://docs.redhat.com/en/documentation/red_hat_openshift_data_foundation/4.16/html/red_hat_openshift_data_foundation_architecture/index`

Quiz

Test your understanding of OpenShift persistent storage with this quick quiz. Remember, some questions may have more than one correct answer!

1. Which of the following are *not* core components of the Kubernetes storage model?

    a. Persistent Volume (PV)

    b. Persistent Volume Claim (PVC)

    c. Storage Node

    d. Storage Class

2. The **Container Storage Interface (CSI)** is tightly coupled with the Kubernetes code base, requiring modifications to the core Kubernetes code to add support for new storage providers.
    a. True
    b. False
3. Which volume can be mounted on multiple nodes?
    a. Amazon EBS
    b. Local
    c. hostPath
    d. NFS
4. NFS is a popular choice for providing block storage in OpenShift environments.
    a. True
    b. False
5. Which of the following protocols is commonly used for connecting to iSCSI SAN storage?
    a. TCP/IP
    b. Fibre Channel
    c. NFS
    d. SMB

Answers

1. **c.** Only PV, PVC, and StorageClass APIs are involved in the lifecycle of a storage volume. While technically volumes are always mounted to nodes, node objects themselves are not a part of the Kubernetes storage model.
2. **b.** The benefit of CSI is that it allows storage vendors to develop and maintain storage plugins without touching the core code base of Kubernetes.
3. **d.** Of the listed PV types, only NFS supports multiple clients.
4. **b.** NFS is used for providing shared filesystem storage, not block volumes.
5. **a.** iSCSI relies on TCP/IP for transport, with iSCSI commands encapsulated in IP packets routable through standard IP networks and TCP, being a connection-oriented protocol, providing reliability.

Join us on Discord

For discussions around the book and to connect with your peers, join us on Discord at `http://packt.link/discordcloud` or scan the QR code below:

9

Developing for OpenShift

Developing applications on OpenShift is about more than just writing code; it's about understanding the developer-focused tools and workflows that make the platform more straightforward to use daily. While previous chapters introduced OpenShift's architecture and platform capabilities, this chapter takes a closer look at the developer's perspective.

Here, we'll focus on how you, as a developer, can interact with OpenShift in practical ways. We'll begin by exploring access methods, including the oc CLI, the developer-oriented odo CLI, and the web-based Developer Console. From there, we'll look at the image ecosystem – registries, image streams, and builds – that form the foundation of application development and deployment.

We'll also explore how **Source-to-Image** (**S2I**) accelerates your workflow by turning source code directly into runnable container images, and how **ConfigMaps** and **Secrets** objects give you a clean and secure way to manage configuration parameters and sensitive information.

By the end of this chapter, you'll have not only a technical understanding of these tools but also the confidence to set up your environment, build applications, and securely manage their configurations. This is the developer's toolkit inside OpenShift – everything you need to take your application from source code to running workload.

We'll cover the following main topics:

- Introduction to OpenShift 4 development
- Setting up your development environment
- Image ecosystem in OpenShift
- Managing configurations and secrets

Before we dive into the hands-on workflows, let's take a step back and briefly revisit what OpenShift 4 brings to the table for developers.

Technical requirements

In this chapter, you will need the following:

- Internet access
- A shell (Bash, Zsh, or similar)
- Access to an OpenShift 4.16 cluster
- A modern web browser (Firefox or Chrome recommended)
- Git installed and the Git repository (on Quay.io, for example)
- The Go toolchain

You can access this book's GitHub repository at `https://github.com/PacktPublishing/Learn-OpenShift-Second-Edition`.

Introduction to OpenShift 4 development

OpenShift 4 is a significant leap in container orchestration and development. It offers developers a comprehensive platform to build, deploy, and manage applications efficiently. OpenShift brings flexibility, security, and scalability to modern cloud-native environments.

The most crucial change in OpenShift 4 for those planning a development or application migration is that it is based on Kubernetes and provides many OpenShift-specific concepts that help speed up and automate the development and delivery of applications and solutions.

OpenShift 4 brings the following new features:

- **Automated updates**: OpenShift 4's automated update system ensures that clusters stay updated with the latest security patches and improvements, reducing the operational burden on developers and administrators.
- **Operator framework**: Operators in OpenShift 4 automate the management of complex applications, providing self-healing, scaling, and monitoring capabilities.
- **S2I**: S2I simplifies the process of building and deploying containerized applications. It automates the creation of Docker images directly from source code using customizable builder images, streamlining the development and deployment pipeline.
- **Developer console**: The Developer console provides a user-friendly interface tailored for application developers, enabling them to visualize, deploy, and monitor their applications easily.
- **Serverless**: Knative integration enables developers to build serverless applications that scale on demand, reducing resource consumption and improving responsiveness.
- **Service mesh**: Built-in Istio support provides a service mesh that improves traffic management, security, and observability between microservices.
- **CI/CD integration**: Tekton Pipelines allow for flexible CI/CD workflows, making it easier to build, test, and deploy applications directly on OpenShift.
- **GitOps integration**: The GitOps Operator with ArgoCD under the hood helps automate and streamline application delivery and ensures that it is healthy and running.

This is why OpenShift 4 may be a good standard for your environment:

- **Unified platform:** OpenShift 4 integrates multiple tools and frameworks, offering developers a single, unified platform for coding, testing, building, and deploying applications.
- **Security and compliance:** Built-in security features and compliance options ensure that your applications meet the most stringent security requirements. The functionality helps to secure the cluster and applications on a basic level. Still, since OpenShift uses the Kubernetes model, it allows you to use any security tools for Kubernetes (including Sysdig, Aqua, and Palo Alto), bring OSS security tooling such as Falco, or use Red Hat **Advanced Cluster Security** (**ACS**) to protect the cluster.
- **Multi-cloud and hybrid:** OpenShift 4 supports hybrid and multi-cloud deployments, allowing applications to run consistently across on-premises and public cloud environments. It offers a standard approach and a set of objects that can be used across any public or private cloud.

As you learned from previous chapters, OpenShift introduces a significant number of objects on top of the Kubernetes default APIs; in this chapter, we will discuss a few additional concepts and specifics that are required for successful application development and deployment in the OpenShift environment.

From a developer's perspective, OpenShift offers several convenient features:

- Rich API, CLI tools (Kubernetes and OCP-focused), and a web UI.
- Projects that allow you to isolate and manage applications.
- Image building and maintaining an ecosystem with registry, image streams, and builds.
- Simplified ways to deploy your applications using the S2I approach.
- Examples and templates for most of the common programming languages and frameworks.
- OpenShift Pipelines Operator based on Tekton – a powerful CI/CD solution **out of the box** (**OOTB**).
- Kubernetes-native Deployments and `DeploymentConfigs` with their specifics; please note, `DeploymentConfigs` are deprecated.
- Serverless, provided through the Knative Operator, available in OperatorHub from the Red Hat Operators catalog.
- Kubernetes-native Secrets and ConfigMaps to maintain your application's configurations.
- **Horizontal Pod Autoscaler** (**HPA**) and **Vertical Pod Autoscaler** (**VPA**), nodeSelector-based node selection, and taint- and toleration-based scheduling controls.
- Resource management and enforcement through ResourceQuotas, and container-level CPU and memory requests and limits.
- Broad and flexible RBAC with OOTB support for multiple authentication providers.

There are also dozens of enterprise-ready operators from the Red Hat and Partners ecosystem, which allow your developers or you to focus on development and spend less time maintaining applications.

This chapter will guide you through setting up your development environment, building your first application, and leveraging OpenShift 4's features to automate deployment and management. You will learn how to use OpenShift's advanced capabilities to create flexible, resilient, high-performing applications that scale with your organization's needs.

Whether you're new to OpenShift or migrating from a previous version, this chapter provides valuable insights and practical steps for developing using the OpenShift 4 platform.

Setting up your development environment

A development environment usually includes toolsets to improve your performance and experience working with the platform, allowing you to leverage the target platform specifics and emulate the environment. We could say the same about OpenShift.

Red Hat thought about the developers and supplied the community and OpenShift users with specific CLI tools, such as the following:

- **oc**: The OpenShift CLI utility, which you already encountered in chapters before.
- **odo**: The developer CLI for OpenShift, which is specifically created for developers.

Red Hat also supplies you with a subset of Microsoft code extensions that help developers interact with OpenShift (and Kubernetes) clusters, deploy applications, control them, and check their status. There are currently multiple official extensions by Red Hat, such as OpenShift Toolkit, OpenShift Extension Pack, OpenShift Extension Pack for Java, Tekton Pipelines, and Knative. **OpenShift Toolkit** is the best place to start with since it includes all necessary modules to work with application deployment processes in general, Helm, Tekton, and Knative.

But what OpenShift environment do you need for development? The most comprehensive way to explore OpenShift, its Operators, and platform features is a full, production-style deployment with multiple control plane and worker nodes. In reality, however, most development work happens on a laptop.

This is where **OpenShift Local** (formerly **CodeReady Containers**, or CRC) becomes useful. **OpenShift Local** provides a lightweight, single-node OpenShift cluster that runs locally and is well suited for learning, experimentation, and application development.

The installation of OpenShift Local was covered in *Chapter 2, Kubernetes and OpenShift*, in the *Installing OpenShift Local* section. The installation of a production-grade OpenShift cluster was covered in *Chapter 3, Getting Started with OpenShift*.

Getting familiar with the oc and odo CLI tools

Before we start building applications, let's ensure you have the basic CLI tools installed on your workstation. These will be your primary way of interacting with OpenShift from day to day:

- **The oc CLI, or oc**: This is the main instrument for interacting with the cluster; it is the main utility you must have on your workstation, bastion host, or laptop. You can use either Red Hat's portal to obtain the oc CLI, as mentioned in *Chapter 3*, or download it from `mirror.redhat.com` [1]. There are multiple files available; as usual, you need to pick the most suitable one for your operating system and architecture, for example [2]. The archive will include two binaries, `oc` and `kubectl`. It also contains a `README.md` file that explains how to add `oc` and `kubectl` to your `$PATH`.

- **odo (OpenShift Do)**: This is a lightweight CLI built for developers. Instead of managing resources with oc or `kubectl`, you describe your app in a `Devfile` and let odo handle the "build-run-iterate" cycle: start a dev session, sync changes, inspect logs, and expose ports. It's especially convenient if you're focusing on OpenShift. Get it from [3].

The packaging for odo and oc is similar, with one small convenience: you can grab a standalone binary directly from the mirror (not just a compressed archive). For either format, checksum files are provided – verify them before installing. On macOS, you can use the following one-liner to validate the SHA-256 and add the binary to your `$PATH`:

```
% if [ $(sha256sum --quiet ~/Downloads/odo-darwin-amd64) = $(cat ~/Downloads/
sha256sum.txt | grep odo-darwin-arm64 | grep -v gz | cut -d' ' -f1) ]; then
echo OK; sudo mv ~/Downloads/odo-darwin-amd64 /usr/local/bin/odo; sudo chmod
a+x /usr/local/bin/odo; else echo FAIL; fi
```

Now that you have the key CLIs, let's put them to work. We'll spin up an OpenShift Local cluster and connect to it using oc, odo, and the web console.

Accessing OpenShift

OpenShift gives you three primary ways to work:

- OpenShift CLI (oc): Cluster and project administration, and day-to-day ops.
- Developer CLI (odo): App-centric workflows (create, run, and iterate).
- Web console with two perspectives:
    - The Administrator perspective: Manage clusters, workloads, storage, networking, and platform settings, with some actions requiring elevated privileges.
    - The Developer perspective: Build and connect application components, configure services, and monitor application health.

In the following sections, we will try the available options and see how they fit into the development journey. Please follow the next sections sequentially to see the specifics, create your first project, and access it via oc, odo, and the web UI.

Accessing with the oc CLI

As mentioned before, oc will be your main utility for interacting with OpenShift daily, especially when it comes to the development environment.

> If you are using OpenShift deployed on VMware or somewhere else, please feel free to skip *Steps 1* and *2*; you will have the `kubeadmin` and password credentials for it, or maybe you already have the IdP configured.

It is essential to understand a few options of the CLI (we will use OpenShift Local as an example):

1. Initialize and start OpenShift Local, unless you have already done so:

```
$ crc setup
$ crc start
```

   The `crc start` command will generate and print a significant number of logs, and at the end, print the access credentials for the `kubeadmin` and `developer` users, as well as the API endpoint address.

2. If you still need access credentials, retrieve them from OpenShift Local (or use your credentials from a regular deployment – in this case, make sure you have a default `developer` user) with this command:

```
$ crc console --credentials
To login as a regular user, run 'oc login -u developer -p developer
https://api.crc.testing:6443'.
To login as an admin, run 'oc login -u kubeadmin -p H97ew-sn2Y2-rTTtX-
b5f5g https://api.crc.testing:6443'
```

3. You will have a default `developer` user that emulates regular `developer` access and cluster admin (`kubeadmin`) with full privileges in your OpenShift instance. Let's use `developer` access:

```
$ oc login -u developer https://api.crc.testing:6443
Logged into "https://api.crc.testing:6443" as "developer" using existing
credentials.
```

4. Please note the CLI tells you that you have no projects, and it will offer to create one; if you just run some command, such as `oc get pods`, you will get an error:

```
$ oc get pods
Error from server (Forbidden): pods is forbidden: User "developer" cannot
list resource "pods" in API group "" in the namespace "default"
```

   Well, it is expected. You are not an administrator and have no privileges on the cluster level or in namespaces that do not belong to you. If you logged in as `kubeadmin` or another user with cluster-admin privileges, you wouldn't have this error.

5. Let's create a project as the CLI offered, using the following:

```
$ oc new-project my-awesome-project-01
```

   You expect output such as the following:

```
$ oc new-project my-awesome-project-01
Now using project "my-awesome-project-01" on server "https://api.cluster.example.com:6443".

You can add applications to this project with the 'new-app' command. For example, try:

    oc new-app rails-postgresql-example

to build a new example application in Ruby. Or use kubectl to deploy a simple Kubernetes application:

    kubectl create deployment hello-node --image=registry.k8s.io/e2e-test-images/agnhost:2.43 -- /agnhost serve-hostname
```

Figure 9.1: The oc new-project command's output

You can always create a project by running `oc create ns <namespace-name>`, but in this case, OpenShift won't supply you with the tips on how to start the application, as shown in the preceding screenshot. We learned more about how projects are created in *Chapter 7, Application Security and Isolation*.

So, the OpenShift CLI and some OpenShift API objects are designed to help you with the onboarding, but let's skip application creation for now and talk about odo.

While the oc CLI gives you full access to OpenShift resources, developers often need a simpler tool tailored to day-to-day workflows. That's where the odo CLI comes in; it abstracts Kubernetes complexity and focuses on fast application development.

Accessing with odo

When you get your project and namespace, you have full control of what you will do in this project. We decided to go with the `developer` user and its privileges since developers and operations teams typically have access only to the specific namespaces in real environments.

Look at this from a cluster administrator's perspective. It will all make sense; you don't want somebody accidentally deploying applications in the wrong namespace or deleting one of the cluster operators.

Now, let's proceed and see what odo will allow the developer to do:

1. Let's start by retrieving the credentials:
    - If you are using OpenShift Local: `crc console --credentials`
    - If you are using OCP Cluster, use `kubeadmin` or your user credentials
2. Now, let's log in using odo; the syntax is slightly different from oc:

    ```
    $ odo login -u kubeadmin
    ```

    When you run odo for the first time, it will show you a warning and offer you to send telemetry; it is up to you whether you want to share information (`Y/y`) or not (`n`):

```
$ odo login -u kubeadmin
? Help odo improve by allowing it to collect usage data. Read about our privacy statement: https://developers.redhat.com/article/too
? Help odo improve by allowing it to collect usage data. Read about our privacy statement: https://developers.redhat.com/article/too
l-data-collection. You can change your preference later by changing the ConsentTelemetry preference. No
Connecting to the OpenShift cluster

Authentication required for https://api.cluster.example.com:6443 (openshift)
Username: kubeadmin
Password:
Login successful.

You have access to 74 projects, the list has been suppressed. You can list all projects with 'odo list project'

Using project "my-awesome-project-01".
```

Figure 9.2: The odo login command's output

It automatically points you to the project/namespace you just created.

> Parameters will be written in `~/.odo/preference.yaml`, so you can change them later if needed. If you want to start anew, simply delete the file with `rm ~/.odo/preference.yaml`.

3. If you run the odo `help` command, the utility will show you a detailed guide and many additional parameters. So, what can odo do? It can do a lot:
   - Initialize and develop an application
   - Build, push, and deploy applications
   - Run a standalone Podman instance

odo also provides extensions for Visual Studio Code (VS Code). While odo is a powerful CLI tool and we will explore its usage in detail, not every developer prefers to work exclusively in the terminal. For those who favor a graphical approach, OpenShift includes the Developer console – a web-based interface that exposes many of the same capabilities in an accessible, visual environment. Let's now look at how to access the web console.

Accessing the Developer console

One of the most common approaches to working with OpenShift for developers is by accessing the OpenShift web UI. The web UI has two views (or **perspectives**) available for users: **Administrator** and **Developer**. Let's try both.

First, we need to get the web UI URL; usually, you will know it from the installation logs or from the `crc` output, but let's imagine you've got only a CLI address via, say, `kubeconfig` that the cluster owners shared with you. How would you get this URL? Let's obtain it and jump into the web UI:

1. To get the address, you can execute one of the following commands:

```
$ oc whoami --show-console
$ oc get console cluster -o jsonpath='{.status.consoleURL}{"\n"}'
```

   These commands will give you the same output as follows:
   - For CRC, the URL will be like this: `https://console-openshift-console.apps-crc.testing/`
   - For the regular OpenShift cluster, the web console URL will be like this: https://console-openshift-console.apps.<cluster-name>.<your-domain>
2. Take the URL from the preceding step, copy it to your browser, and log in to the web UI (OpenShift web console) with `developer/developer`, which is the default development user for CRC.
3. As soon as you are logged in, the console will offer you a tour. Click **Get started**, and it will explain the main concepts you will need to know. In the next section, we will discuss the available menu items and see how we use them to deploy and control applications.

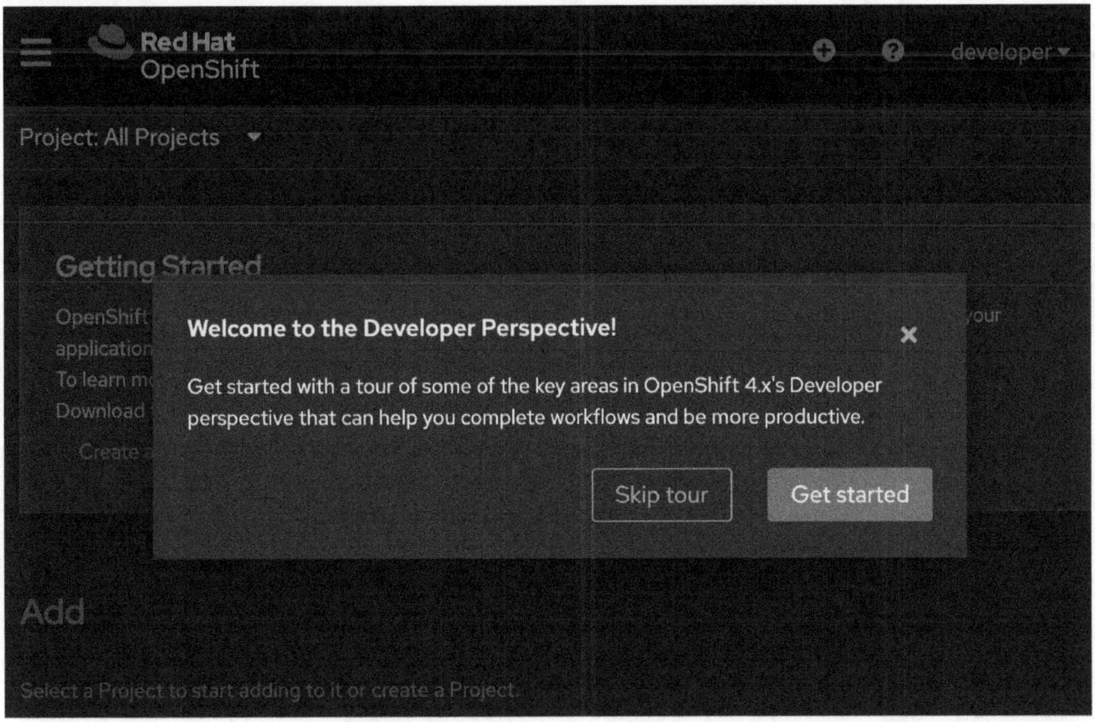

Figure 9.3: Web UI Developer perspective guide

Now that you know all the main ways to access the cluster and spin up a local development environment, it is time to create a "Hello World" application and deploy it. The following section describes how to quickly start with odo. We will see how to develop and deploy your application to the OpenShift cluster.

Developer CLI (odo)

Now that you know how to access the cluster with odo, let's see what it looks like to actually build and run an application using it.

Development with ODO

As previously discussed, odo is an excellent open source tool for creating, developing, and managing applications for the OpenShift and Kubernetes platforms. It provides built-in logic for spinning up an application and starting development.

The overall specifics are described in the official documentation [4], but let's quickly initialize an application and see how simple it is. The following section is based on a Golang example from the documentation.

Before you proceed, follow these steps:

1. Ensure that you have Go available; please refer to the Golang documentation [5] to install it. When the installation is done, ensure it works by running the following:

```
$ go version
```

You should see an output like this:

```
go version go1.22.3 darwin/arm64
```

2. If you plan to run the next steps on CRC, ensure it has enough memory. In the following example, we set the memory to 16 GB of RAM and disk space to 50 GB:

```
$ crc config set memory 16384 && crc stop && crc start
$ crc config set disk-size 50
```

> Allocating sufficient resources to your OpenShift Local VM is important for the examples from this chapter and the following one (*Chapter 10*) to work. If your workstation doesn't have enough resources, please use the lab setup described in *Chapter 3*.

Now that Golang is available and the memory is configured, let's go ahead and proceed with the application initialization with odo:

1. Create a working directory where you will do the development and change to it:

```
$ mkdir ~/my-awesome-app-01 && cd ~/my-awesome-app-01
```

2. Copy the following `main.go` file to your directory from the book's repo: `chapters/9/code/main.go`.
3. Initialize the `go.mod` file:

```
$ go mod init my.awesome.app.01
$ go mod tidy
```

The last command is not expected to produce any output.

Before you proceed with odo, please make sure your Go version in the `mod` file looks like `X.YY`; the notation `X.YY.ZZ` will cause an error on one of the next steps. You can simply open it with a text editor and remove the `.ZZ` part. This is what the `go.mod` file should look like after the change:

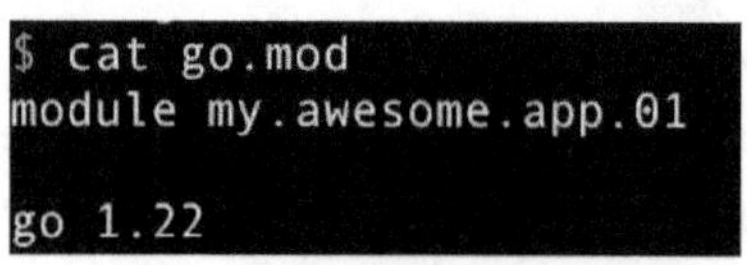

Figure 9.4: The go.mod file

4. Log in to the OpenShift cluster using odo, unless you have already done so in an earlier part of this chapter:

```
$ odo login https://api.crc.testing:6443 --username=developer
--password=developer
```

Again, if you're using the cluster from *Chapter 3, Getting Started with OpenShift*, you can just log in with `kubeadmin` or any non-privileged user.

5. Let's initialize a new application and see how odo does its magic; run odo `init`:

```
$ odo init
  __
 /  \__     Initializing a new component
 \__/  \    Files: Source code detected, a Devfile will be determined based upon source code autodetection
 /  \__/    odo version: v3.15.0 (10b5e8a8f)
 \__/

Interactive mode enabled, please answer the following questions:
 ✓  Determining a Devfile for the current directory [456ms]
Based on the files in the current directory odo detected
Supported architectures: all
Language: Go
Project type: Go
Application ports: 8080
The devfile "go:1.2.1" from the registry "DefaultDevfileRegistry" will be downloaded.
? Is this correct? (Y/n) _
```

Figure 9.5: The odo init Devfile selection

6. So, odo got everything you need. It detected the language and the TCP port that it will use, and even offered a base image for our application; all you need to do here is type `Y` or `y` and hit *Enter*:

```
? Is this correct? Yes
 ✓  Downloading devfile "go:1.2.1" from registry "DefaultDevfileRegistry" [416ms]

↪ Container Configuration "runtime":
  OPEN PORTS:
    - 8080
    - 5858
  ENVIRONMENT VARIABLES:
    - DEBUG_PORT = 5858

? Select container for which you want to change configuration?  [Use arrows to move, type to filter]
  runtime
> NONE - configuration is correct
```

Figure 9.6: The odo init container selection for a configuration change

7. Now, we need to hit *Enter* again to choose `NONE` for no configuration change. The console will ask you for the name of your component, but we can just hit *Enter* one more time, so odo will finish the initialization process and show you the command you can run next time to skip the interactive shell interaction:

```
? Enter component name: my-awesome-app-01

You can automate this command by executing:
   odo init --name my-awesome-app-01 --devfile go --devfile-registry DefaultDevfileRegistry --devfile-version 1.2.1

Your new component 'my-awesome-app-01' is ready in the current directory.
To start editing your component, use 'odo dev' and open this folder in your favorite IDE.
Changes will be directly reflected on the cluster.

---
A newer version of odo (v3.16.1) is available,
visit https://github.com/redhat-developer/odo/releases to update.
If you wish to disable this notification, run:
odo preference set UpdateNotification false
---
```

Figure 9.7: odo init providing a component name

8. Now, let's execute odo dev:

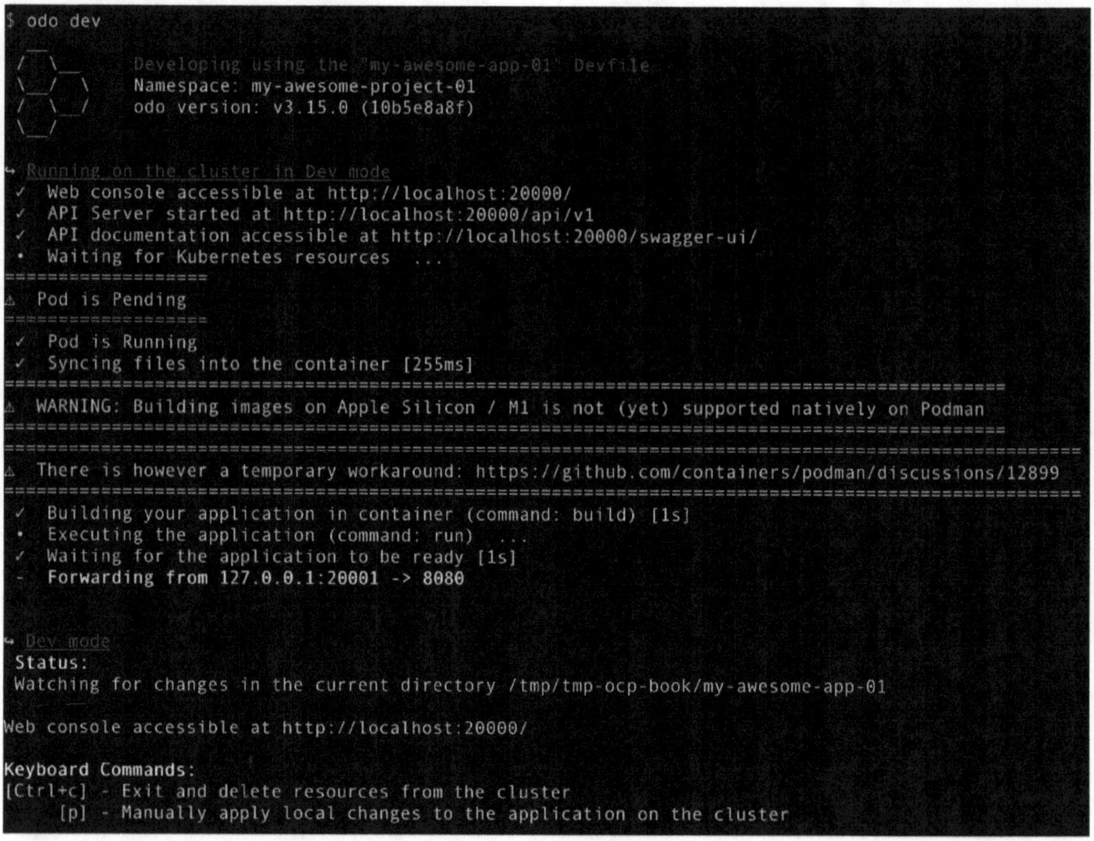

Figure 9.8: Running odo dev

Please do not confuse the web console mentioned in the output with your application's endpoint. The web console allows you to review the current odo and environment parameters and change them on the fly. The application console will be on TCP port `20001`, according to the output: `Forwarding from 127.0.0.1:20001 -> 8080`.

> **Warning!**
>
> Do not close the terminal session with odo – it is interactive, and the application runs while it is running.

That is it: your first version of a new Golang application is running and exposed via port forwarding on your local machine. The application will be available via port `20001`. You can open the following URL in your browser to access it: `http://localhost:20001`.

Figure 9.9: Accessing the application via the web browser – initial output

Or, if you're running everything on a Linux box without a GUI, you can simply open another SSH session and run the following:

```
$ curl localhost:20001
```

odo will track all the local changes and synchronize them with the currently running development environment. It will automatically detect changes and make an updated application version available via `http://localhost:20001`.

Try to change the output of the application by editing `main.go`; just change the output to something like this:

```
fmt.Fprintf(w, "Update! The request time is %s.", currentTime)
```

If you do it in another smaller terminal window overlayed on top of the one where you have odo `dev` running, you will notice how even the smallest updates trigger a new build, making this a near-real-time experience.

Then, save the file, wait a bit, and then refresh your browser (or run `curl localhost:20001` again):

Figure 9.10: Accessing the application via the web browser – updated output

That is it! You just updated an application, and odo made an update for the running copy of it; no Git involved, nothing. It is super convenient for local development, so you may suggest it to your developers or use it yourself.

Okay, you are doing great! Now, before we move forward, let's press *Ctrl* + *C* to stop the odo loop and check what files it created in the directory with `ls -la`:

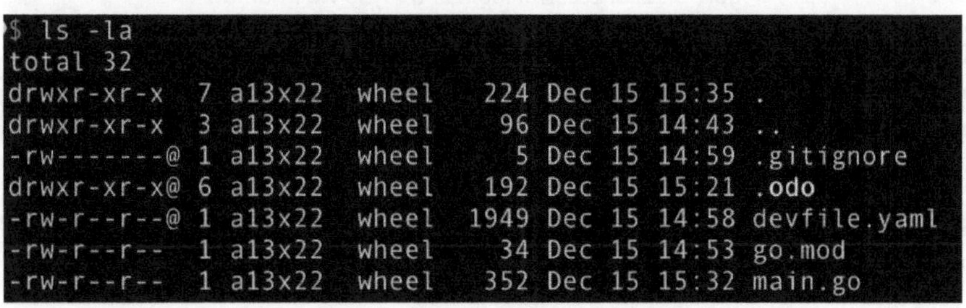

```
$ ls -la
total 32
drwxr-xr-x   7 a13x22  wheel   224 Dec 15 15:35 .
drwxr-xr-x   3 a13x22  wheel    96 Dec 15 14:43 ..
-rw-------@  1 a13x22  wheel     5 Dec 15 14:59 .gitignore
drwxr-xr-x@  6 a13x22  wheel   192 Dec 15 15:21 .odo
-rw-r--r--@  1 a13x22  wheel  1949 Dec 15 14:58 devfile.yaml
-rw-r--r--   1 a13x22  wheel    34 Dec 15 14:53 go.mod
-rw-r--r--   1 a13x22  wheel   352 Dec 15 15:32 main.go
```

Figure 9.11: Files created by odo

So, here's what you will see:

- `.gitignore`: Git will ignore the `.odo` directory
- `.odo`: The service folder where odo tracks the app metadata
- `devfile.yaml`: A YAML definition of the desired application's environment
- `main.go` and `go.mod`: The application itself and its mod file, respectively

We'll focus on `devfile.yaml` now and talk about how we could move from development to deployment using odo. You can learn more about the development approach in the official *ODO Quickstart Guide* [6].

Deployment with odo

As you can see, odo is a very convenient tool that allows you to develop and quickly test your application. Now that your application is ready, you can use odo to deploy it to your OpenShift cluster. Let's quickly go through the process together.

Before we proceed, let's ensure you have a Docker registry you could use to keep your artifacts (i.e., an application container image you will build); it could be any registry. For this example, we will use Quay [7], one of the Red Hat products.

Ensure you have a registry, image repository, and service account with read/write permissions (a **robot account** in Quay terminology). If you go with `quay.io`, please read [8] to [10] before moving forward.

The easiest way to complete the following exercise is to make your Quay repository public so that OpenShift can pull the image that you'll build. Getting it to work with a private repo will require some extra steps that we will mention along the way.

Let's proceed and execute the test deployment with odo:

1. Configure the registry by running the following command:

```
$ odo preference set ImageRegistry quay.io
```

2. Log in to the registry with `podman login quay.io` and make sure the login is successful:

```
$ podman login quay.io
Username: a13x22+ocprbt
Password:
Login Succeeded!
```

Figure 9.12: Successful login to quay.io via Podman

3. Define the building platform, as in this example:

```
$ export ODO_IMAGE_BUILD_ARGS="--platform=linux/arm64"
```

In this particular case, we are using `linux/arm64` since, in our lab, OpenShift Local is running on a MacBook Pro M3, but you may need to set it to `linux/amd64`, depending on where you are running OpenShift Local or deploying your lab environment.

4. Create a Dockerfile:
   - Make sure you're in the odo application directory, if you moved around after the previous exercise:

   ```
   $ cd ~/my-awesome-app-01
   ```

   - Create a Dockerfile by copying the following file: `chapters/9/snippets/Dockerfile`.
5. Back up your `devfile.yaml` file:

```
$ cp devfile.yaml devfile.yaml.bkp
```

6. Update your `devfile.yaml` file:
   - You can use the following example if you created a public repository: `chapters/9/snippets/devfile-deploy.yaml`. If your repository is private, use the `chapters/9/snippets/devfile-deploy-private.yaml` file. Overwrite your original `devfile.yaml` file:

   ```
   $ mv devfile{-deploy,}.yaml
   ```

   - Or, for a private repo, use the following:

   ```
   $ mv devfile{-deploy-private,}.yaml
   ```

   - For a private repo, you will need to create an image pull secret referenced by `chapters/9/snippets/devfile-deploy-private.yaml`. On Rocky Linux 9.5, when you run `podman login`, it stores access credentials in `/run/user/<YOUR_UID>/containers/auth.json`. On macOS X, the location is `/Users/<USERNAME>/.config/containers/auth.json`. We will use that file to create a `docker-registry` secret:

   ```
   $ oc create secret docker-registry quay-secret --from-file=.
   dockerconfigjson=/run/user/<YOUR_UID>/containers/auth.json
   ```

   - Or, for macOS X, use the following:

   ```
   $ oc create secret docker-registry quay-secret --from-file=.
   dockerconfigjson=/Users/<YOUR_USERNAME>/.config/containers/auth.
   json
   ```

   - On Linux, the value of `YOUR_UID` can be obtained simply by running `id`.
   - Please ensure that you have updated the `IMAGE_NAME` variable and pointed it to your registry, where we expect odo to keep your builds.

7. It's time to deploy it. Execute `odo deploy` to do so; the application will generate a lot of logs, but basically, it does the following:
    1. Builds your application
    2. Creates an image
    3. Pushes it to the registry
    4. Creates a deployment on your cluster

    We are expecting the following output:

```
 ✓  Building image locally [1s]
 •  Pushing image to container registry  ...
Getting image source signatures
Copying blob sha256:ecae9ce95163af9f8bfdf5eca043dfa6b219e4ed24438f4fb79ab7fa907a1a01
Copying blob sha256:b2895e270b92553486aeac91787556e826ded154226489d50361ff14fba3d42f
Copying blob sha256:ec8cbb2796aec1c16ac52437c37b9b7449112fe9267edf10c4aa7596e7059605
Copying config sha256:15c28d851c46076622bb02222848af6dc0645ac0327ccab9216eb25b6d9e418c
Writing manifest to image destination
 ✓  Pushing image to container registry [13s]

↪ Deploying Kubernetes Component: my-awesome-app-01
 ✓  Creating resource Deployment/my-awesome-app-01

↪ Deploying Kubernetes Component: my-awesome-app-01
 ✓  Creating resource Service/my-awesome-app-01

↪ Deploying Kubernetes Component: my-awesome-app-01
 ✓  Creating resource Route/my-awesome-app-01

Your Devfile has been successfully deployed
```

Figure 9.13: Running odo deploy

> If the build fails with errors such as `E: The repository 'http://deb.debian.org/debian ... Release' does not have a Release file`, that means the Debian release that is used by base images in the Dockerfile has been archived and is no longer supported.
>
> To fix this, you'll have to find the most recent stable tag for each image in `https://hub.docker.com/_/golang/tags` and `https://hub.docker.com/_/debian/tags` and update both `FROM` instructions.

8. Congratulations! Your first application is deployed. Let's quickly confirm what objects are available on the cluster:
    - Ensure that your current project is `my-awesome-project-01`:

    ```
    $ oc project my-awesome-project-01
    ```

    - Now, let's get the list of objects by running `oc get all`:

```
$ oc get all
Warning: apps.openshift.io/v1 DeploymentConfig is deprecated in v4.14+, unavailable in v4.10000+
Warning: kubevirt.io/v1 VirtualMachineInstancePresets is now deprecated and will be removed in v2.
NAME                                         READY   STATUS             RESTARTS        AGE
pod/my-awesome-app-01-58899cd57b-vm9bq       0/1     CrashLoopBackOff   7 (61s ago)     12m

NAME                         TYPE       CLUSTER-IP      EXTERNAL-IP   PORT(S)           AGE
service/my-awesome-app-01    NodePort   172.30.10.193   <none>        8080:32030/TCP    12m

NAME                                  READY   UP-TO-DATE   AVAILABLE   AGE
deployment.apps/my-awesome-app-01     0/1     1            0           12m

NAME                                            DESIRED   CURRENT   READY   AGE
replicaset.apps/my-awesome-app-01-58899cd57b    1         1         0       12m

NAME                                            HOST/PORT
route.route.openshift.io/my-awesome-app-01      my-awesome-app-01-my-awesome-project-01.apps.cluster.example.com
```

Figure 9.14: Listing all objects generated by odo deploy

- So, in the `my-awesome-project-01` project/namespace, odo created the following resources:
    - Deployment (which in turn, created a ReplicaSet and a Pod)
    - Service
    - Route
- We can even invoke our app with `curl my-awesome-app-01-my-awesome-project-01.apps.cluster.example.com` and get the same response as before.

9. Let's clean this up and remove our application:

```
$ odo delete component
```

```
$ odo delete component
Searching resources to delete, please wait...
This will delete "my-awesome-app-01" from the namespace "my-awesome-project-01".
 •  The following resources will get deleted from cluster:
 •      - Deployment: my-awesome-app-01
 •      - Service: my-awesome-app-01
 •      - Route: my-awesome-app-01

? Are you sure you want to delete "my-awesome-app-01" and all its resources? (y/N) _
```

Figure 9.15: Deleting the odo component

Type `Y` or `y` and then *Enter*, so odo will clean up the project. You can then move forward and deploy a new application using the next, not less exciting methods.

It also makes sense to review the official Devfile documentation, to better understand its purpose, structure, and ways to use; the main resource would be `https://devfile.io/`, in particular the materials at [11].

odo not only streamlines local development, but also helps package and deploy applications on OpenShift with minimal friction. It bridges the gap between coding on your laptop and running workloads in the cluster. So, odo is focused on the inner development loop (development in a local environment), rather than the external development loop (external CI/CD pipelines).

However, it allows you to standardize the processes in the inner loop, as you or your DevOps team would do for the external loop: the order and the governance from the beginning.

With the basics of interacting with OpenShift covered, let's turn to one of the most critical aspects of development on the platform: container images. OpenShift's image ecosystem powers how your code is built, stored, and deployed.

Image ecosystem in OpenShift

Container images are crucial to running applications in OpenShift, packaging everything needed for consistency across environments. The OpenShift integrated registry stores and manages these images, making them available for deployment. OpenShift also uses image streams, which help automate updates and track versions, ensuring apps always use the necessary and most secure images. This simplifies image management and supports collaboration between teams. In the following sections, we'll examine how OpenShift handles images, image streams, and the integrated registry to streamline and secure the application life cycle.

Container images

Container images are lightweight, standalone, and executable software packages that include everything needed to run an application, such as code, runtime, and libraries. Settings, on the other hand, are supposed to be provided externally at runtime via volumes and environment variables to avoid tight coupling between an image and the environment it runs in. In the OpenShift environment, these container images are fundamental building blocks for deploying applications. OpenShift manages containers based on OCI- and Docker-formatted images, ensuring compatibility and flexibility in the deployment process.

There are a few core concepts you will face while working with containers; let's cover them here:

- **Image layers**: Image layers are the building blocks of a container image. Each layer represents a set of filesystem changes, such as adding, modifying, or deleting files. These layers are stacked on top of each other to form the complete container image. Here is an example of a container image with layers:

```
FROM ubuntu:latest  # Base Layer
RUN apt-get update  # New Layer
COPY . /app         # New Layer
```

- **Image registry**: An image registry is a storage and distribution system for container images. It allows users to store, manage, and retrieve container images.
- **Image repository**: An image repository is a specific location within an image registry where container images are stored and organized. It serves as a collection point for related images, often grouped by application, project, or organization.
- **Image tags**: Image tags are identifiers that mark specific versions of container images within an image repository. They play a crucial role in managing, deploying, and maintaining containerized applications.

- **Image digests:** Image digests are unique identifiers assigned to each container image in a registry. Unlike tags, which are human-readable and can be changed or reused, image digests are immutable and provide a definitive reference to a specific image. Here are a couple of examples:
    - Complete image digest: `sha256:4d6bce7a4bce769283ec43d3e5780ed621c706fc0d921c40972b4d5cdbb65d53`
    - Shortened image digest: `4d6bce7a4bce`

OpenShift and Kubernetes, in general, run containers from images inside pods. Pods can be bare (standalone) or managed by controllers such as Deployments, DaemonSets, StatefulSets, or Jobs/CronJobs.

Let's move forward and discuss the OpenShift image ecosystem, including what components it brings and how they help you.

Image ecosystem components in OpenShift

If you've used Kubernetes or other container platforms, images, containers, and pods before, then you are already in familiar territory. Red Hat OpenShift adds a few opinionated building blocks around images that are worth learning because they make day-to-day development and delivery smoother – and enterprise operation safer.

In the following sections, we'll cover three OpenShift-specific pieces of the image puzzle:

- **Cluster Samples Operator:** Seeds your cluster with curated, ready-to-use language/runtime templates so you can scaffold apps fast without hunting for base images.
- **Integrated registry:** A built-in, cluster-native container registry that simplifies pushing/pulling, image retention, and on-cluster image promotion – especially useful in regulated or disconnected environments.
- **Image streams (ImageStream / is):** OpenShift's metadata layer that tracks image tags across registries and triggers builds/deployments when images change (think: safer tag indirection, traceability, and automated rollouts).

This is why this ecosystem is essential for you:

- **Faster inner loop development:** Samples and image streams reduce boilerplate and let you iterate on code, build, and deploy with fewer moving parts.
- **Safer deployments:** Image streams decouple what your app runs from where the image lives, enabling controlled rollouts, rollbacks, and auditability.
- **Enterprise governance:** The integrated registry and image streams make it easier to enforce image sources, sign/verify artifacts, and meet compliance needs.
- **Air-gapped/disconnected friendly:** Cluster-local mirroring and promotion flows work even without external registries.
- **Operational simplicity:** Fewer external dependencies, first-class integration with OpenShift builds/pipelines, and clear image lineage.

So, let's dive in. We will start with the Cluster Samples Operator.

Cluster Samples Operator

The Cluster Samples Operator is a component that manages the life cycle of sample image streams and templates. These samples provide a starting point for developers, helping them quickly create applications and services on OpenShift.

The Cluster Samples Operator will always be aligned with the OpenShift version you use and supply you with S2I images and templates, including the most popular ones such as Ruby, Python, Node.js, Perl, HTTPD, NGINX, EAP, Java, .NET, and Go.

Before we move forward, let's make sure that this operator is available; it will be a great source of examples for this and the following sections. The operator is available OOTB, after OpenShift deployment. In some cases, it may be in a `Removed` state; this usually happens when it can't reach `registry.redhat.io`, detects that it is running on an IPv6 network, or there are some specific `image.config.openshift.io/cluster` configuration parameters in use.

Let's make sure it is up and running:

1. Log in to the cluster with `kubeadmin` (here is the example with CRC):

```
$ oc login -u kubeadmin -p <PASSWORD> https://api.crc.testing:6443
```

2. Check whether the Operator is available:

```
$ oc get configs.samples.operator.openshift.io/cluster -o yaml
```

The operator is expected to be in the `Managed` state, according to the following screenshot:

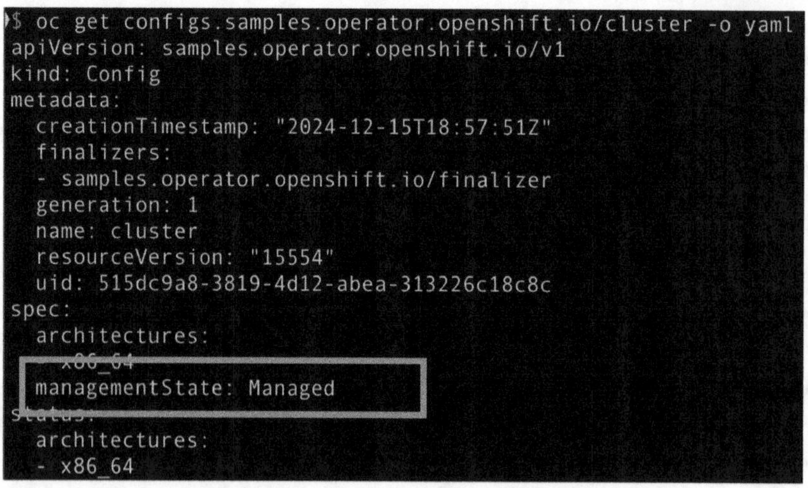

Figure 9.16: Cluster Samples Operator configuration

When the Cluster Samples Operator is enabled, it seeds the `openshift` namespace with a curated set of image streams (and related templates). These image streams are readable cluster-wide by default, so developers can reference them from any project as builder or base images. You can browse what's available with these simple commands:

- `oc get is -n openshift`
- `oc describe is <is name> -n openshift`

In the next sections, we will discuss how to consume these image streams in your own projects. For configuration and customization details (which samples to install, registry mapping for disconnected clusters, and policy controls), see the official OpenShift documentation at [12] and [13].

Integrated registry

In the section that follows, we will be discussing images and image streams. Both can use the same system component – the integrated registry. The integrated registry is available as the default OCP component and is managed by the Image Registry Operator.

This registry runs on the cluster, allowing users to manage their images easily without needing extra infrastructure. It scales like other workloads and integrates with the cluster's user authentication and authorization, controlling access based on user permissions.

The registry stores images built on the cluster and provides images for workloads running on the cluster. When a new image is added, the cluster is notified, and other components can use the updated image. As mentioned previously, it is often used as the target for image streams.

Image data is stored in two places:

- The image data is kept in a configurable storage, such as cloud storage or a filesystem volume.
- The image metadata, used for access control, is stored as standard API resources called images and image streams.

> To access the internal registry, you need the `cluster-admin` cluster role. To consume images, a user needs `registry-viewer` or `registry-editor` roles. Please make sure you have at least one or another or log in to the cluster with the `kubeadmin` user.

The integrated registry may be published outside of the cluster and consumed by external systems. However, in enterprise environments, it is recommended to use a dedicated solution instead, which may consume fewer resources and provide better control, as well as all necessary RBAC functionality and integration of authentication providers. The details on the way you can expose the integrated registry can be found at [14].

If you're using a VMware-based lab, the Image Registry Operator starts in the `Removed` state. This is because the environment usually lacks a **ReadWriteMany** (**RWX**) storage class required for the default persistent registry deployment.

To enable the integrated registry, you can run the following oc `patch` commands:

```
$ oc patch configs.imageregistry.operator.openshift.io cluster --type merge
--patch '{"spec":{"storage":{"emptyDir":{}}}}'
$ oc patch configs.imageregistry.operator.openshift.io cluster --type merge -p
'{"spec": {"managementState": "Managed"}}'
```

The second command will trigger a deployment of registry pods. You can monitor the progress with the following command:

```
$ watch -n1 oc get po -n openshift-image-registry
```

This step is also necessary for the S2I build samples provided by the Samples operator to work. We will show you a working example in the *S2I discovery* section.

> **Warning!**
>
> The preceding example is acceptable only for non-production environments. If you would like to configure it according to best practices and make it useful for something more than a sandbox, please follow the documentation page at [15].

For CRC, the integrated registry is in the `Managed` state, but `.spec.storage.managementState` is `Unmanaged`, so the Operator uses a local PVC; if you lose it, you'll lose all your images.

There is nothing you need to configure additionally. Let's just check the registry and operator status:

```
$ oc get pods -n openshift-image-registry
NAME                                              READY   STATUS      RESTARTS   AGE
cluster-image-registry-operator-7b9d6f6749-xcqtk  1/1     Running     0          29h
image-pruner-28905120-9vv8k                       0/1     Completed   0          23h
image-registry-75d79fb89b-b9hlq                   1/1     Running     0          25h
node-ca-dnbjn                                     1/1     Running     0          28h
```

Figure 9.17: Integrated registry's pods

With the operator healthy and the pods running, the integrated registry is ready for on-cluster use. At this point, note that the OpenShift registry supports two consumption models:

- **Internal:** Used by workloads and builds inside the cluster
- **External:** Optionally accessible from outside the cluster

For organization-wide distribution and multi-cluster sharing, a dedicated registry – such as **Red Hat Quay/Quay.io** – is usually a better fit. Making the integrated registry your primary **external** registry shifts storage, network, and CPU load onto the cluster (large blobs, garbage collection, and concurrent pushes/pulls), which can get costly and resource-intensive.

If you choose to expose it externally, plan for the following:

- **Capacity:** IOPS/throughput, storage sizing, and GC windows
- **Security:** TLS, `authn/z`, and access policy
- **Operations:** Backup/retention and life cycle management

We will return to the integrated registry in *Chapter 15, Exploring Additional Services in OpenShift*, for additional configuration.

Image streams

An image stream is OpenShift's metadata layer that tracks where an image tag lives and when it changes. Think of it as a virtual pointer to one or more container image tags (from the integrated registry or any external registry such as Quay). Because the pointer is a first-class API, OpenShift can trigger builds and deployments when the underlying image updates, while giving you indirection for rollbacks and provenance.

This is why image streams are useful:

- **Traceability**: Decouple what you run from where the image is stored
- **Automation:** Image changes can trigger builds/deployments
- **Governance:** Centralized policy on which image sources/tags are allowed

So, an image stream is an OpenShift API resource that maps and tracks image tags across registries, enabling automated reactions (builds/deploys), safer rollouts, and clear image lineage.

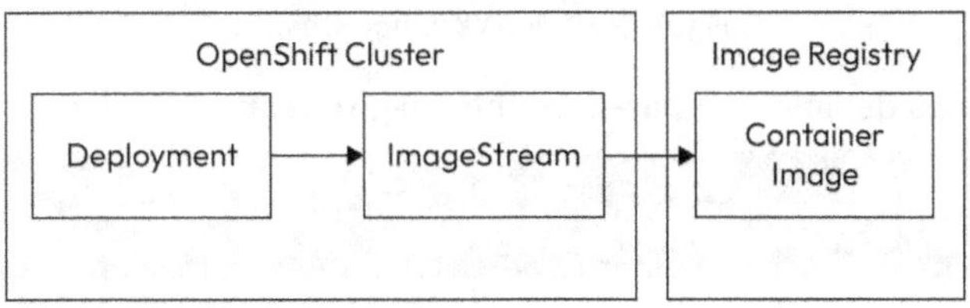

Figure 9.18: Image stream

One of the biggest wins with image streams is controlled automation. When a referenced image changes, OpenShift can react via triggers – most commonly `ImageChange` triggers on `DeploymentConfig` or builds. This enables hands-off updates when you want them, while keeping the safety of tag indirection.

Please note, a vanilla Kubernetes Deployment does not watch image streams by itself. For auto-rollouts on OpenShift, you typically use `DeploymentConfig` and `ImageChangeTrigger`, or an external controller/pipeline that reacts to `ImageStream` updates.

So, let's describe some of the benefits of using image streams:

- **Safe indirection and rollbacks:** You can retag to promote/roll back without re-pushes. Your workloads track tags you control (e.g., `stable`) rather than whatever happens upstream.
- **Event-driven automation:** Image stream updates can trigger builds and `DeploymentConfigs` (`ImageChange` triggers), enabling continuous delivery when a new image arrives.
- **Scheduled imports (auto-tracking):** Tags can be set to import on a schedule to track external registries; when the source tag moves, the image stream updates and can fire triggers.
- **Known-good pinning:** Even if the upstream image changes, your `ImageStreamTag` can remain pinned to a digest you trust. You choose when to retag to a newer image.

- **Access control and sharing:** Image streams live in projects (namespaces) and respect OpenShift RBAC, enabling fine-grained sharing across teams without granting broad, cluster-level image permissions.
- **Traceability and provenance:** Image stream history records where an image came from and which digest/tag was used – useful for audits, **Software Bill of Materials** (**SBOM**)/attestation workflows, and reproducibility.
- **Cleaner promotion flows:** You can promote images across environments (`dev`, `stage`, and `prod`) by retagging within or across namespaces/registries, instead of copying blobs.

Let's try to create a deployment using an image stream. Follow these steps:

1. Log in to the cluster and ensure you are in the proper namespace, as usual, by using `oc login`.
2. Get a list of available image streams (provided by the Samples Operator) with the following:

```
$ oc get is -n openshift | grep nginx:
```

```
$ oc get is -n openshift | grep nginx | awk '{print $2}'
image-registry.openshift-image-registry.svc:5000/openshift/nginx
```

Figure 9.19: NGINX image stream

3. Now, let's create a deployment based on the image stream:

```
$ oc create deploy nginx --image=image-registry.openshift-image-registry.
svc:5000/openshift/nginx -- sleep infinity
```

The `sleep infinity` command is required to keep the pod running – being an S2I build image, it doesn't have an NGINX startup command in its entrypoint.

> Depending on the type of your OpenShift deployment, the image name may be different; please keep it in mind.

4. Let's review what objects we have in the project by using `oc get all`:

```
$ oc get all
Warning: apps.openshift.io/v1 DeploymentConfig is deprecated in v4.14+, unavailable in v4.10000+
Warning: kubevirt.io/v1 VirtualMachineInstancePresets is now deprecated and will be removed in v2.
NAME                         READY   STATUS              RESTARTS   AGE
pod/nginx-5b797cc4bf-dld2h   0/1     ContainerCreating   0          6s

NAME                    READY   UP-TO-DATE   AVAILABLE   AGE
deployment.apps/nginx   0/1     1            0           6s

NAME                               DESIRED   CURRENT   READY   AGE
replicaset.apps/nginx-5b797cc4bf   1         1         0       6s
```

Figure 9.20: Listing NGINX deployment, replicaset, and pod

We have `deployment`, `replicaset`, and `pod`. Please note the warning; we will talk about this later in this chapter.

Warning!

As you may recall, we generated a self-signed CA and configured the cluster-wide proxy to use it back in *Chapter 4, Post-Install Configuration*. Sometimes the change doesn't fully propagate, which may result in the preceding deployment failing and the following error showing up in the events:

```
Failed to pull image "image-registry.openshift-image-
registry.svc:5000/openshift/nginx": pinging container
registry image-registry.openshift-image-registry.svc:5000:
Get "https://image-registry.openshift-image-registry.
svc:5000/v2/": tls: failed to verify certificate: x509:
certificate signed by unknown authority
```

If you see this on your cluster that you built in vSphere, you'll need to copy your CA certificate and manually add it to the trust chain in the `serviceaccount-ca` ConfigMap in the `openshift-kube-controller-manager` namespace. A simple way of doing that is by using `oc edit cm/serviceaccount-ca -n openshift-kube-controller-manager`. Add your CA at the very bottom on the same level as the chain. Then, delete and recreate the `nginx` deployment.

That's it, you have a deployment that uses an image from the internal registry, which is bound to the image stream and tagged by the `latest` tag. Image streams track changes to images, triggering automated workflows such as builds and deployments when new images are pushed to the registry.

You can create an image stream and point it to an existing image stream tag, image, or to the custom image registry. Next, you will find simple commands that allow you to do so.

First, let's create an image stream from an existing image. Please note the first command we use: - `oc get is -n openshift`. This is so we list all the image streams available from the Cluster Samples Operator. Then, let's `grep` for `cli` and create your own image stream based on the image from the output:

```
$ oc get is -n openshift | grep cli
$ oc create is my-cli
$ oc import-image my-cli --from=image-registry.openshift-image-registry.
svc:5000/openshift/cli
```

Here is the visual record of these steps:

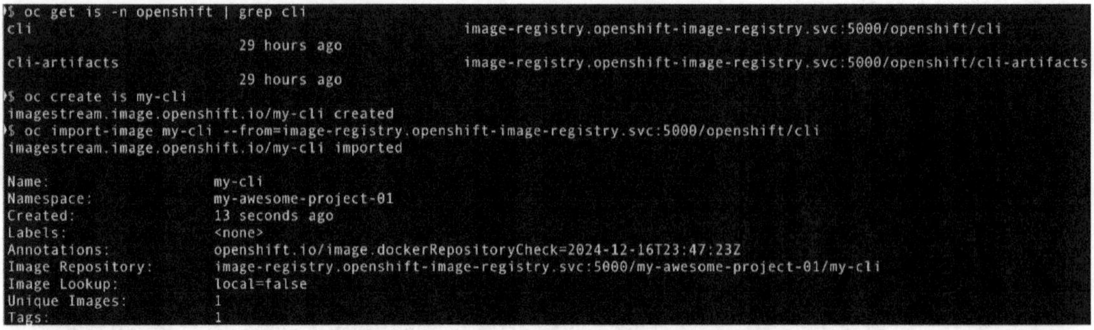

Figure 9.21: The oc create and oc import outputs

Now, let's quickly create an image stream using an external image registry and simplify a command, so we don't need to create an image stream first. We can *import* an image and create the image stream in a similar way by using oc `import-image`:

```
$ oc create is my-memcached
$ oc import-image my-memcached --from=memcached:latest --confirm
```

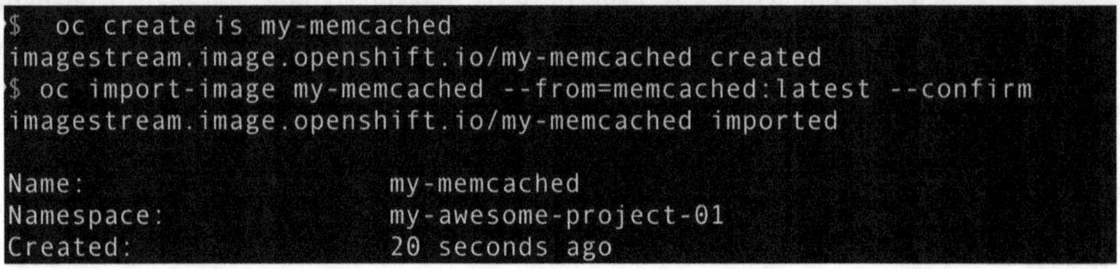

Figure 9.22: Creating an image stream and importing an image

Done! Now, you have two image streams:

- `my-cli` points to the internal image stream in the `openshift` namespace/project, and uses the latest image available for the built-in image, `cli`, which has OpenShift CLI and many other useful tools.
- `my-memcached` points to the external registry (Docker Hub, in this case); it also uses the `latest` tag.

Let's remove both image streams and our NGINX deployment, and move forward:

```
$ oc delete is my-memcached my-cli -n my-awesome-project-01
$ oc delete deploy/nginx
```

The detailed configuration options for image streams are described in the official OpenShift documentation [16].

Image controller configuration

For Enterprise environments, some policies and additional control of the container images in the infrastructure, in general, and among Kubernetes clusters are required.

OpenShift solves this problem OOTB by allowing administrators to configure trusted registries, custom CAs, and other parameters. For example, to configure a list of trusted registries, you can use the `.spec.registrySources.allowedRegistries` parameter in the `image.config.openshift.io/cluster` object; please follow the official documentation [17] to fine-tune your cluster.

You've now seen how OpenShift organizes, stores, and tracks images. But wouldn't it be easier if OpenShift could create those images for you directly from your source code? That's exactly what S2I provides.

S2I discovery

As we discussed in the previous section, odo is a very useful utility that basically helps you to go through the full application development cycle: initialize it, develop and run while you are making changes, and then deploy it to the target cluster using your favorite image registry. You may like and use it, and make it standard in your organization. But of course, it is up to you – there are plenty of other options, and we'll cover them next. First, let's talk about S2I, a toolkit highly recommended by Red Hat.

> S2I image samples are available from the Cluster Samples Operator, and basically, this is the only type of images this Operator will support starting OpenShift 4.16, so it will stop managing non-S2I image streams and templates.

S2I builds

S2I lets you turn source code into a production-ready container image without writing a Dockerfile. It injects your code into a builder image (with the right binaries and libraries), runs build/assemble scripts, and outputs a runnable image. Developers spend less time on image structure and more time shipping features.

> The next steps are done using the `developer` user on OpenShift Local. If you are using your lab environment, you can either create a new unprivileged user or use `kubeadmin`, but switch to the Developer perspective to better understand how a developer would see the UI.

S2I builder images are available for .NET, Java, Go, Node.js, Perl, PHP, Python, and Ruby. When the Cluster Samples Operator is enabled, the corresponding image streams are created in the `openshift` namespace. You can browse them in two ways:

1. The oc CLI (we mentioned it already, but just in case):
    - `oc get is -n openshift`
    - `oc describe is <name> -n openshift`

2. Web console:

    - **Developer perspective** > **Add** > **Developer Catalog**, then filter for builder images (or search for a runtime such as Python or Node.js).
    - **Administrator perspective** > **Workloads** > **ImageStreams**, and set the project to `openshift` to view the seeded streams.

Let's try to do it with the web console, by using the Developer perspective:

1. Log in to the cluster console via the web UI, using your `developer` user.
2. Ensure you are in the `my-awesome-project-01` project and click **+Add** on the left menu:

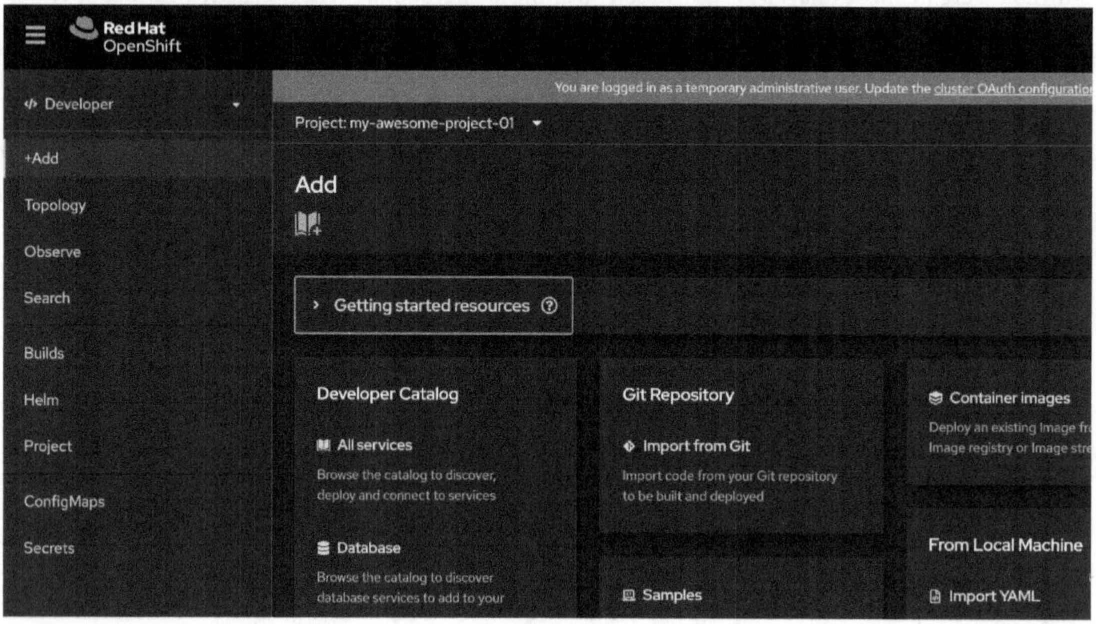

Figure 9.23: Web UI Add page

You will see the following panes:

- **Getting started resources**: Orientation tiles with short tutorials, docs links, and quick starts (including S2I examples such as Quarkus). Use this to onboard new developers to OpenShift concepts and workflows.
- **Developer Catalog**: A curated marketplace of deployables: Helm charts, templates, operators, databases, and Devfiles. Start here when you want a known-good stack (e.g., Postgres, Keycloak, Kafka) or a framework scaffold with sensible defaults.
- **Git Repository**: Builds an app directly from your code. Supports three flows:
    - From Git (detects language and builds)
    - From Devfile (uses devfile instructions)
    - From Dockerfile (uses your image recipe)

- **Container images:** Deploy from an existing image (internal `ImageStream` tag or external registry reference). Ideal when the image is already built by your pipeline and you just need to run it.
- **From Local Machine:** Create resources from local files: apply YAML/JSON manifests or upload an artifact (e.g., a JAR) that a template/operator can consume. Useful for quick experiments or when Git isn't ready yet.
- **Sharing:** Project/namespace access control. Invite teammates, assign roles, and scope permissions so the right people can view, deploy, or operate your app.
- **Samples:** Shortcuts to content seeded by the Cluster Samples Operator (e.g., S2I builder image streams and example templates). Use this to spin up example apps or base images without hunting registries.

You may also see **Serverless** and **Pipelines** options if Tekton and Knative are available on the cluster.

> For S2I builds to work, the integrated registry must be enabled, as explained in the *Integrated registry* section of this chapter. If you have done it already, you can move forward; otherwise, please ensure the integrated registry is ready.

3. Let's select **Samples** and pick **Basic Go**:

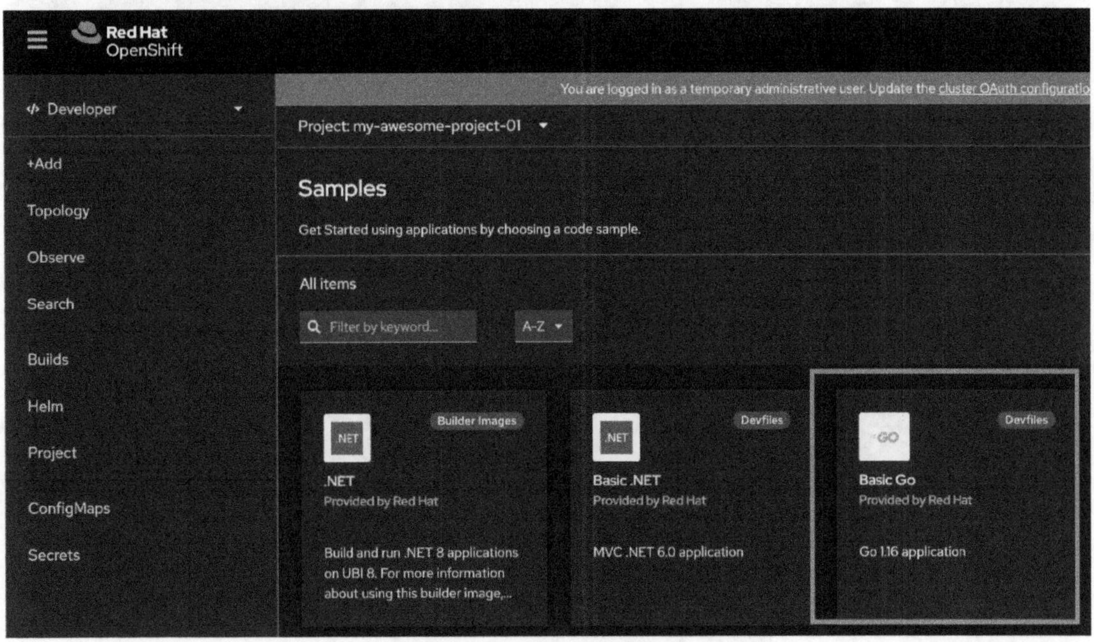

Figure 9.24: Web UI Samples

4. It will show you a few parameters:
   - Git:
     - **Git Repo URL:** A link to the Git repo with the sample application code and dependencies: `https://github.com/devfile-samples/devfile-sample-go-basic.git`
   - General:
     - **Name:** The application name you can redefine
     - **Security:** Router configuration, TLS termination, and certificates

   For now, let's disable TLS (deselect **Secure Route** under the **Security** section) and click **Create**:

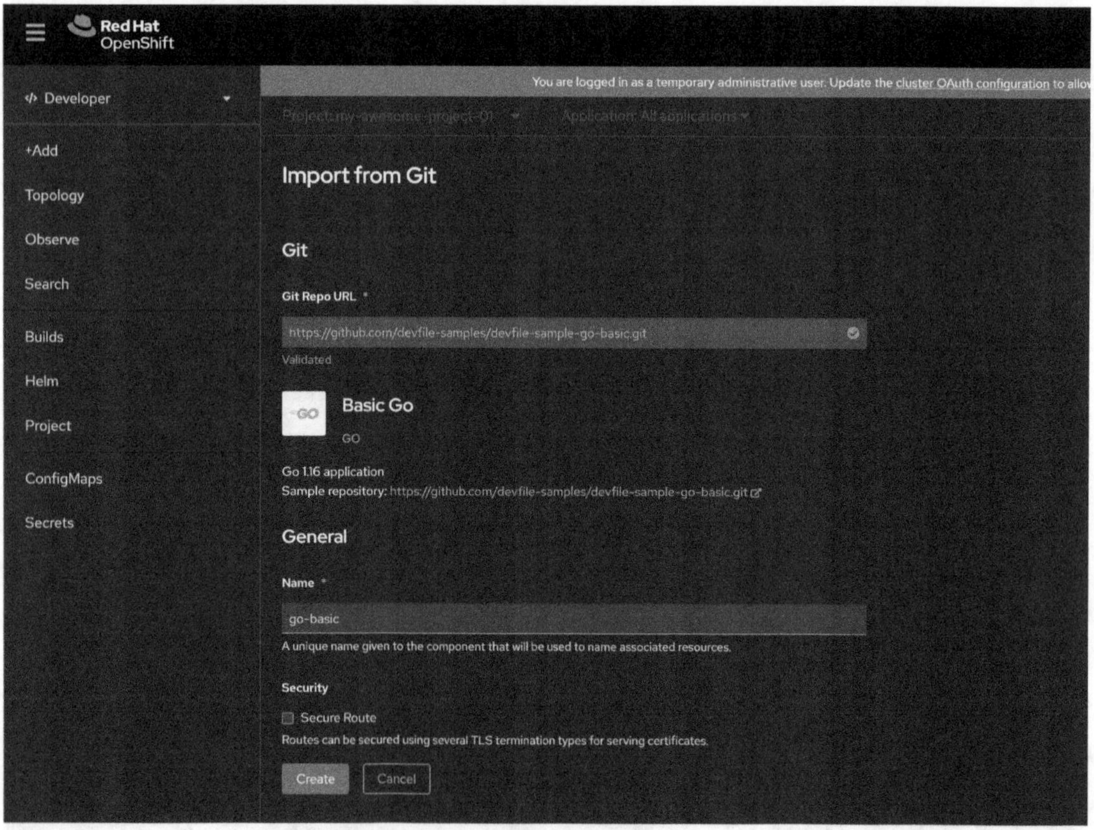

Figure 9.25: Web UI import from Git

5. The web UI will forward you to the **Topology** view, where you will see the sample application; you can click on the application pictogram to see its current status – the same view you used to check the application you were developing with odo:

Figure 9.26: Web UI application status

6. Click on your application and scroll down the application's details pane to the **Routes** section and click on the routes **Location** link:

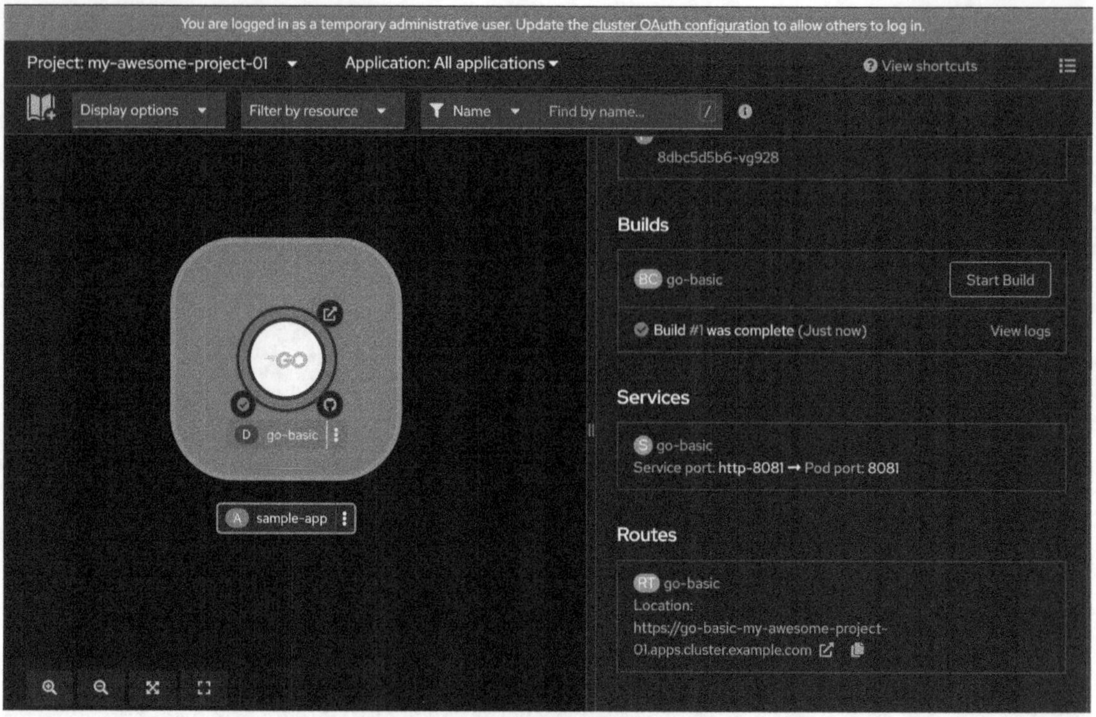

Figure 9.27: Web UI application details

7. That is it! Your application is deployed via S2I, so if you go to the **Routes** link, you will see the following:

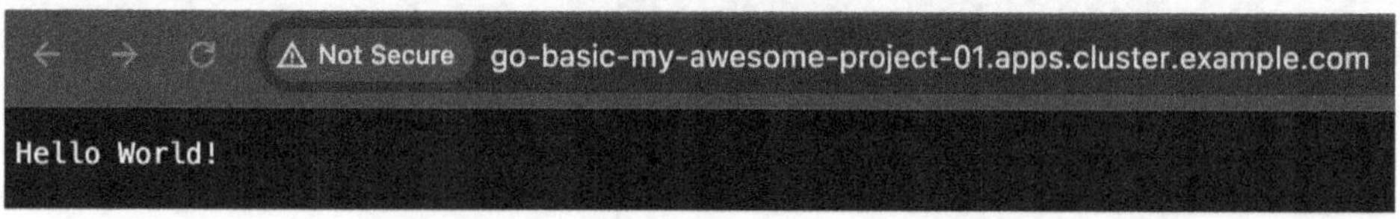

Figure 9.28: Web UI application web page

Now, let's take a look at the artifacts and understand the S2I process better. Let's start from the CLI. Log in to the CLI as `developer` and check what objects the S2I process created for us with the familiar `oc get all` command:

```
$ oc get all
Warning: apps.openshift.io/v1 DeploymentConfig is deprecated in v4.14+, unavailable in v4.10000+
Warning: kubevirt.io/v1 VirtualMachineInstancePresets is now deprecated and will be removed in v2.
NAME                          READY   STATUS      RESTARTS   AGE
pod/go-basic-1-build          0/1     Completed   0          23m
pod/go-basic-6f67d7c4d-g76rf  1/1     Running     0          23m

NAME               TYPE        CLUSTER-IP      EXTERNAL-IP   PORT(S)    AGE
service/go-basic   ClusterIP   172.30.121.67   <none>        8081/TCP   23m

NAME                       READY   UP-TO-DATE   AVAILABLE   AGE
deployment.apps/go-basic   1/1     1            1           23m

NAME                                 DESIRED   CURRENT   READY   AGE
replicaset.apps/go-basic-6f67d7c4d   1         1         1       23m

NAME                                       TYPE     FROM   LATEST
buildconfig.build.openshift.io/go-basic    Docker   Git    1

NAME                                    TYPE     FROM          STATUS     STARTED          DURATION
build.build.openshift.io/go-basic-1     Docker   Git@cff4cde   Complete   23 minutes ago   24s

NAME                                      IMAGE REPOSITORY
imagestream.image.openshift.io/go-basic   image-registry.openshift-image-registry.svc:5000/my-aweson

NAME                                  HOST/PORT                                               PATH
route.route.openshift.io/go-basic    go-basic-my-awesome-project-01.apps.cluster.example.com
```

Figure 9.29: Application status via the oc CLI

We now have all the expected objects: `BuildConfig`, `ImageStream`, Deployment (which creates a ReplicaSet and Pod), Service, and route. There's also a secret, but note that `oc get all` does not list secrets (and `ConfigMaps` too) – use `oc get secret` to see it.

Okay, if you look at the console output or *Figure 9.29*, you will notice that there are two pods. Why are there two pods?

- `go-basic-1-build`: This is the build pod created by the S2I `BuildConfig`. It runs a builder image, assembles your source into a runnable image, and then pushes that image to the integrated registry. This pod is ephemeral and exits when the build finishes (`Succeeded/Failed`).
- `go-basic-6f67d7c4d-g76rf`: This is the application pod created by the Deployment. Its container uses the image that S2I just produced and tagged in your image stream. This pod should be in a `Running` state once the rollout completes.

The overall S2I flow at a glance is as follows:

1. **Commit**: A developer pushes code to a Git repo.
2. **Build**: An S2I `BuildConfig` pulls the repo, runs the builder image's assembly steps, resolves deps, and (if needed) compiles the code.
3. **Image**: The build produces a new container image and pushes it to the integrated registry, updating the target `ImageStreamTag`.
4. **Trigger**: The `ImageStreamTag` update can trigger a rollout (e.g., `DeploymentConfig` with an `ImageChange` trigger), or your pipeline can deploy manually.
5. **Run and expose**: The application Pod starts (via `Deployment/DeploymentConfig`) and is reachable through a Service and, if created, a route.

You can delete the project now:

```
$ oc project default && oc delete ns my-awesome-project-01
```

Building and deploying applications is just one part of the story. Once your workloads are running, they require configuration data and sometimes sensitive information, such as passwords, TLS certificates, key stores, service account tokens, and API keys. OpenShift provides first-class support for managing these through `ConfigMaps` and Secrets.

Managing Configurations and Secrets

Deployments handle rollout and lifecycle management for your workloads. Next, we'll tackle application configuration and sensitive data. OpenShift/Kubernetes provides two purpose-built resources: **ConfigMaps** for non-secret settings (flags, URLs, and templates) and **Secrets** for credentials and other sensitive values. Using these keeps configuration out of images, avoids hardcoding, and enables safe, repeatable upgrades – improving both security and operational efficiency.

Up next, a detailed look at Secrets and `ConfigMaps` – what they store, how they differ, and how to mount or inject them into your apps.

ConfigMaps

In OpenShift and Kubernetes, the way to store non-sensitive configuration data is `ConfigMaps`; the information will be stored in key-value pairs:

- **Usage:** Can be used to define environment variables, command-line arguments, and configuration files that are injected into your application pods.
- **Advantages:** Centralized configuration management, allowing updates without rebuilding images or redeploying applications.

Create `ConfigMaps` alongside your deployments and Secrets (discussed shortly). In a mature setup, manage all three with GitOps so changes are reviewed, versioned, and promoted across environments. Knowing how to define `ConfigMaps` and Secrets is essential for declarative deployments. The `ConfigMap` structure is straightforward – see the example in the repo at `chapters/9/snippets/ConfigMap.yaml`.

The applications would consume the `ConfigMaps` according to the definition of your Deployment, Pod, and so on, with one of the following options:

- **Environment variables:** Simple flags, URLs, and feature toggles.
- **Mounted files:** Larger configs (INI/YAML/JSON), templates, and so on, when environment variables aren't practical.

While you can inline plain-text values directly in a Deployment, prefer `ConfigMaps` for better reuse, auditability, and GitOps workflows.

Here is an example of a Pod that uses the `ConfigMap` defined in the previous paragraph. To keep the chapter concise, the complete definition has been added to the Git repository, where you can view it in a more detailed and accurate format.

```
$ cat PodWithConfig.yaml
apiVersion: v1
kind: Pod
metadata:
  name: example-pod
  namespace: my-awesome-project-01
spec:
  containers:
    - name: example-container
      image: registry.access.redhat.com/ubi9/ubi:latest
      command: ["sleep", "3600"]
      env:
        - name: LOG_LEVEL
          valueFrom:
            configMapKeyRef:
              name: example-configmap
              key: log.level
      volumeMounts:
        - name: config-volume
          mountPath: /etc/config
  volumes:
    - name: config-volume
      configMap:
        name: example-configmap
```

Figure 9.30: Pod definition

The `ConfigMap` is mounted to the Pod as a Volume:

- The `log.level` parameter will be added as an environment variable (`LOG_LEVEL`).
- The contents of `example-configmap` will be available as two files under `/etc/config` – `app.properties` and `log.level`.

The source of the object is available in Git: `chapters/9/snippets/PodWithConfig.yaml`.

Secrets

A Secret stores sensitive data (passwords, API keys, and tokens) separate from Pods and images. Kubernetes/OpenShift can mount Secrets into containers as files or inject them as environment variables; some system components also use Secrets (e.g., image pull credentials):

- **Usage:** Can be used to inject sensitive data into pods as environment variables or mounted as files.
- **Advantages:** Enhances security by keeping sensitive data out of the application code and image.

There is a common misconception that Kubernetes/OpenShift users have that Secrets make data secure. Secrets keep encoded but not encrypted data, so you can encode it and decode it with the `base64` CLI tool. This is why it is **extremely important** to keep the `etcd` data encrypted and properly configure RBAC for your cluster. Eventually, you will need to try to move all sensitive data to a specialized solution, such as HashiCorp Vault.

Currently, OpenShift has seven types of Secrets, all of which are standardized in a specific way and validated on creation, so OpenShift will check whether the Secret is defined correctly or not. The only exception is `Opaque`, which is the default and can be used for all your applications' sensitive data.

Secret Type	Description
`Opaque`	Default type, arbitrary key-value pairs
`basic-auth`	Basic authentication
`dockercfg`	Image pull secret (old format)
`dockerconfigjson`	Image pull secret (modern format)
`service-account-token`	Legacy service account API token
`ssh-auth`	SSH key authentication
`tls`	TLS certificate authorities

Table 9.1: Types of secrets in OpenShift 4

The following examples are available on Git for convenience. For real-world use, ensure you use a proper secrets management solution (such as HashiCorp Vault) and never store sensitive information directly in Git.

Let's review a simple secret (which is available in Git, `chapters/9/snippets/Secret.yaml`) and see how we could define it via the CLI. So, if you open the link or download the file, you will see this:

```
apiVersion: v1
kind: Secret
metadata:
  name: example-secret
  namespace: my-awesome-project-01
type: Opaque
data:
  username: dXNlcm5hbWU=     # Base64-encoded 'username'
  password: cGFzc3dvcmQ=     # Base64-encoded 'password'
```

Figure 9.31: Secret definition

As the Secret definition's comments stated, if you take `username` or `password` values and decode them via `base64 -d`, you will immediately see their value, as in this example:

```
$ echo dXNlcm5hbWU= | base64 -d
username
```

So, the value of `username` is the word `username` with no newline character. You can create such encoded values as follows:

```
$ echo "hello world" | base64 -w 0
aGVsbG8gd29ybGQ=
```

If you run it on an older version of the base64 utility, you may need to use the following command instead:

```
$ echo "hello world" | tr -d \\n | base64
aGVsbG8gd29ybGQ=
```

To create a secret from the CLI, you can run the following command:

```
$ oc create secret generic my-super-secret --from-literal=key1=hello123
```

The `hello123` value will be encoded in `base64`, and you will have a very similar definition as we just discussed. You are welcome to create other types of secrets and investigate other options the oc CLI gives you by using the `oc create secret -h` command.

As well as the `ConfigMap`, the Secret value could be consumed the same way as an environment variable to pass it to your application, or can be mounted as a file. You can get the Pod definition from Git and review it: `chapters/9/snippets/PodWithSecret.yaml`.

```
apiVersion: v1
kind: Pod
metadata:
  name: example-pod-secret
  namespace: my-awesome-project-01
spec:
  containers:
    - name: example-container
      image: registry.access.redhat.com/ubi9/ubi:latest
      command: ["sleep", "3600"]

      # Consume secret as environment variables
      env:
        - name: SECRET_USERNAME
          valueFrom:
            secretKeyRef:
              name: example-secret
              key: username
        - name: SECRET_PASSWORD
          valueFrom:
            secretKeyRef:
              name: example-secret
              key: password

      # Consume secret as mounted files
      volumeMounts:
        - name: secret-volume
          mountPath: "/etc/secret"
          readOnly: true

  volumes:
    - name: secret-volume
      secret:
        secretName: example-secret
```

Figure 9.32: Pod with Secret definition

You've seen how to define and consume Secrets and `ConfigMaps`. Next, let's step back and turn those mechanics into day-to-day habits with a few best practices.

Best practices

Here are some high-level best practices to help you plan your application using Secrets and `ConfigMaps`:

- **Separate config from code**: Keep configuration and sensitive data out of images and source repos.
- **Use an external secrets manager**: In production, source credentials from HashiCorp Vault (or similar) and sync them into Kubernetes only when needed.
- **Enforce least privilege (RBAC)**: Limit who can get/list/watch Secrets and `ConfigMaps`; scope access per namespace/app.
- **Rotate regularly**: Change credentials on a schedule and on demand after incidents; automate when possible.
- **Prefer files for highly sensitive data**: Mount Secrets as files instead of environment variables to reduce accidental exposure.
- **Encrypt etcd at rest**: Ensure that cluster-level encryption is enabled and monitored.
- **Audit and monitor**: Log Secret/`ConfigMap` access and watch for anomalous reads or changes.
- **Use GitOps with safeguards**: If you manage manifests in Git, use sealed/external Secrets and avoid committing raw secrets.

This concludes our discussion of managing the configuration of applications in OpenShift and brings us to the end of this chapter. Now that we are familiar with key concepts around developing applications with OpenShift, it is time to take a look at what we have learned before moving forward.

Summary

This chapter centered around the developer experience in OpenShift: how to reach the cluster, build images, and configure applications safely. We began with access methods – `oc`, the developer-oriented `odo`, and the web Developer console – so you can choose the interface that best fits your workflow. We then mapped the image ecosystem: how container images flow through image streams, how the integrated registry supports in-cluster builds and promotion, and how the Cluster Samples Operator seeds ready-to-use builder image streams and examples.

A major focus was S2I, which turns source code and a builder image into a runnable container image without a Dockerfile, integrating cleanly with OpenShift CI/CD and GitOps. Finally, we covered configuration and credentials: `ConfigMaps` for non-secret settings and Secrets for sensitive values, keeping both out of source code and images while enabling RBAC, as well as ensuring rotation and auditability.

Taken together, these pieces show how OpenShift smooths day-to-day development on top of Kubernetes, reducing boilerplate without sacrificing control. With these foundations, you can build, update, and operate applications on OpenShift securely, efficiently, and at scale.

To wrap up this chapter, let's reinforce the key concepts with a quick quiz. This will help you check your understanding of the development workflows and tools we've explored.

In the next chapter, we shift from development workflows to application delivery, exploring how OpenShift supports building, deploying, and scaling applications reliably. You'll learn how source code becomes runnable images, how deployments are rolled out across clusters, and how OpenShift helps balance speed, stability, and operational control.

References

To learn more about the topics that were covered in this chapter, take a look at the following resources:

- [1] OpenShift 4 latest client binaries: `https://mirror.openshift.com/pub/openshift-v4/clients/ocp/latest/`
- [2] OpenShift 4 latest macOS ARM64 oc client: `https://mirror.openshift.com/pub/openshift-v4/clients/ocp/latest/openshift-client-mac-arm64.tar.gz`
- [3] OpenShift 4 latest odo binaries: `https://mirror.openshift.com/pub/openshift-v4/clients/odo/latest`
- [4] Odo documentation: `https://odo.dev/docs/introduction`
- [5] Go documentation > *Download and Install*: `https://go.dev/doc/install`
- [6] Odo Quickstart Guide: `https://odo.dev/docs/user-guides/quickstart/`
- [7] Red Hat Quay: `https://quay.io/`
- [8] Red Hat Quay > *Creating a repository*: `https://docs.quay.io/guides/create-repo.html`
- [9] Red Hat Quay > *Repository permissions*: `https://docs.quay.io/guides/repo-permissions.html`
- [10] Red Hat Quay > *Robot accounts*: `https://docs.quay.io/glossary/robot-accounts.html`
- [11] *What is a devfile*: `https://devfile.io/docs/2.3.0/what-is-a-devfile`
- [12] *Configuring the Cluster Samples Operator*: `https://docs.redhat.com/en/documentation/openshift_container_platform/4.16/html/images/configuring-samples-operator`
- [13] *Using the Cluster Samples Operator with an alternate registry*: `https://docs.redhat.com/en/documentation/openshift_container_platform/4.16/html/images/samples-operator-alt-registry`
- [14] *Exposing the registry*: `https://docs.redhat.com/en/documentation/openshift_container_platform/4.16/html/registry/securing-exposing-registry`
- [15] *Configuring the registry for vSphere*: `https://docs.redhat.com/en/documentation/openshift_container_platform/4.16/html/registry/setting-up-and-configuring-the-registry#configuring-registry-storage-vsphere`
- [16] *Managing image streams*: `https://docs.openshift.com/container-platform/4.16/openshift_images/image-streams-manage.html`
- [17] *Image configuration resources*: `https://docs.redhat.com/en/documentation/openshift_container_platform/4.16/html/images/image-configuration`

Quiz

Let's test your understanding of OpenShift 4 development-focused tools with this quick quiz:

1. What is the purpose of the Cluster Samples Operator in OpenShift?
   a. To provide a mechanism for monitoring application performance
   b. To manage and automate the delivery of default sample images
   c. To automate the scaling of the OpenShift cluster
   d. To manage network policies for secure communication between pods
2. Which CLI tool is designed specifically for fast application development in OpenShift?
   a. `kubectl`
   b. `oc`
   c. `odo`
   d. `helm`
3. When using S2I in OpenShift, what is the primary purpose of this process?
   a. To create custom operating system images
   b. To convert source code into an OCI-compatible image
   c. To build Docker images without writing a Dockerfile
   d. To manage Kubernetes deployments
4. In OpenShift, how are `ConfigMaps` primarily used?
   a. To store sensitive data such as passwords
   b. To store non-sensitive configuration data for applications
   c. To manage user permissions within the cluster
   d. To provide network routing information
5. What is the role of an image stream in OpenShift?
   a. To create a network connection between nodes
   b. To manage container image builds from the source
   c. To track changes and updates to a specific container image
   d. To replicate data between persistent storage volumes

Answers

1. **b**. The Cluster Samples Operator in OpenShift manages and automates the distribution and configuration of default sample images, which can be used as a base for application development or testing.
2. **c**. odo is a command-line tool for developers to build, test, and manage applications quickly in OpenShift. It's designed for simplicity, specifically for application development, while oc is more general-purpose.
3. **c**. **Source-to-Image (S2I)** is an OpenShift build process that takes application source code, compiles it using a predefined builder image, and produces a runnable container image without requiring a Dockerfile. The resulting image can then be deployed in OpenShift.
4. **b**. `ConfigMaps` store non-sensitive configuration data, such as environment variables and settings, that can be consumed by containers in OpenShift. Sensitive data should be stored in Secrets instead.
5. **c**. Image streams in OpenShift provide an abstraction layer that allows developers to track image changes and updates. This helps ensure that applications automatically update when a new version of an image is available.

10

Deployment to OpenShift

In this chapter, we will focus on how OpenShift enables the reliable and flexible deployment of applications. While previous chapters examined development workflows and tools, this chapter turns to the delivery side – building, packaging, and rolling out applications across clusters. Deployment in OpenShift combines Kubernetes-native primitives with OpenShift-specific extensions, giving you more control over automation, rollout strategies, and scaling.

We will start by looking at templates, which allow developers to quickly instantiate common applications and standardize configurations. From there, we will move on to builds, examining both the traditional `BuildConfig` objects and the newer Shipwright-based Builds Operator. Together, these illustrate how OpenShift transforms source code and artifacts into runnable images.

Next, we'll introduce OpenShift Pipelines, based on Tekton, which extends builds into complete CI/CD workflows. Then, we'll compare `DeploymentConfig` objects with Kubernetes Deployments, explaining their history and differences, and why Red Hat is deprecating `DeploymentConfig` objects. With this foundation in place, we'll explore deployment strategies such as recreating, rolling, blue-green, canary, A/B testing, and shadow deployments, looking at when it makes sense to use each one.

Finally, we'll cover scaling and placement, including **HorizontalPodAutoscaler** (**HPA**) and **VerticalPodAutoscaler** (**VPA**), node selectors, and affinity rules – all of which help ensure that applications run efficiently and resiliently across the cluster.

By the end of this chapter, you will have a complete view of how OpenShift manages application builds, deployments, and scaling. You'll be ready to design rollout processes that balance speed, stability, and flexibility.

We'll cover the following topics:

- Deploying applications
- Deployments versus `DeploymentConfig` objects
- Deployment strategies
- Scaling and managing applications

Let's get started!

Technical requirements

To follow along with the exercises in this chapter, you will need the following:

- Internet access
- A CLI with Bash or Zsh
- Access to an OpenShift 4.16 cluster
- A modern web browser (Firefox or Chrome recommended)

You can access this book's GitHub repository at `https://github.com/PacktPublishing/Learn-OpenShift-Second-Edition`.

Deploying applications

OpenShift provides Kubernetes-native and OpenShift-specific objects (see *Chapter 3*, the *Traditional concepts and OpenShift core APIs* section) to roll out and manage applications. Multiple approaches, such as using odo and its objects, **Source-to-Image** (**S2I**), or templates, can be used to build and deploy an application quickly.

Let's discuss the objects and tools that facilitate deployment and standardization. We will review some features crucial to understanding and exploring additional aspects of OpenShift.

Application delivery

OpenShift provides powerful tools to streamline application building and delivery. In the following sections, we will briefly introduce the key components that make this process efficient and effective. Before looking at builds and operators, let's begin with templates – a simple yet powerful way to package and reuse application definitions.

Templates

Before we look deeper into the objects we are planning to discuss, let's take a look at templates. A template in OpenShift describes a set of objects that can be customized and processed to create resources such as services, build configurations, and deployments. We can also apply a set of labels to all objects defined in a template. We can create objects from templates using the CLI and web UI.

You can consider templates to be a manifest or a set of manifests with parameters that could be overridden. Let's look at an example together. Run the following command in the terminal:

```
oc get template httpd-example -n openshift -o yaml
```

It will print pretty long YAML output. You are welcome to check out this output on the console, or, as usual, you can go to GitHub (`chapters/10/snippets/template-httpd-example.yaml`) and find a snippet there.

You will notice variables defined as `${VALUE}`, for example `${MEMORY_LIMIT}`, and the `parameters` section of the definition. These variables are designed to help you redefine them at the instantiation stage – the logic of the object is similar to any other templating solutions for Kubernetes, such as Helm.

As you can see, a template consists of a list of object definitions, such as `Deployment`, `Service`, and `Route`. Some values in these objects are replaced with placeholders such as `${VALUE}`, which can be parameterized, as we mentioned previously.

Parameters are defined in a separate section called `parameters` and usually include a name, description, and value. The `value` field describes a default variable value that will be used if no alternative values are provided.

> The `openshift` namespace contains many predefined templates, which you can use as examples if you want to create a custom template or create an application from them.

You can *instantiate* templates via the CLI and web UI. Let's use the oc CLI, as we want you to become comfortable and familiar with using it. We will use the same `httpd-example` that we just reviewed. To achieve this, you need to run these two commands:

- We run this to ensure that we are in the namespace where templates will be instantiated:

```
$ oc new-project my-awesome-project-01
```

- This is how we process the template. The `oc process` command renders manifests from the template using default values for variables and passes them to the standard input of the `oc create` command, as indicated by the - character after `-f`:

```
$ oc process httpd-example -n openshift | oc create -f-
```

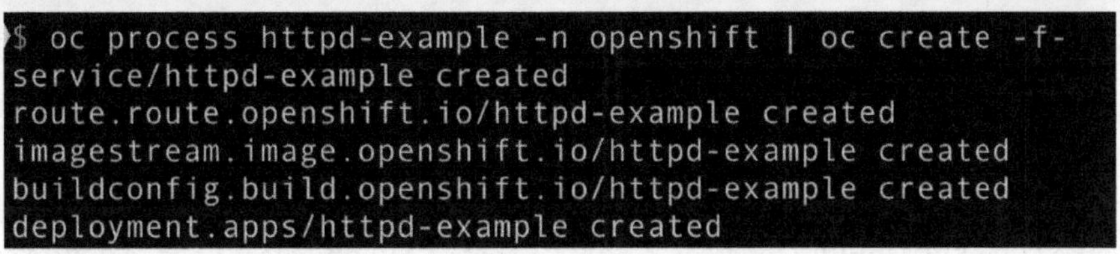

Figure 10.1: Template processing output

That's it! OpenShift will build an example using S2I images and process all the objects and parameters, and you will have an Apache server with an example page when all the processes are done. You can view information about the application and its route on the **Topology** page in the web UI.

Please don't hesitate to drill down into the topic and read the official documentation on templates [1].

> **Warning!**
>
> One of the main downsides of using **out-of-the-box** (**OOTB**) templates is that most of them still use the `DeploymentConfig` API, which has been deprecated since OpenShift 4.14.

Templates help you quickly create and standardize application resources, but deploying real workloads also requires building container images. OpenShift offers several build types designed for different needs – let's explore them.

Build types

A build is the process of transforming input parameters (such as source code) into a resulting artifact, typically a runnable image. OpenShift supports many build strategies to turn your source code into deployable container images. The most common are the following:

- **S2I:** Automatically converts source code into a deployable image, streamlining the build process.
- **Docker builds:** Uses Dockerfiles to create images, offering greater control over the build steps.
- **Custom builds:** Allows advanced users to define bespoke build processes for specialized needs.

The build process can be defined using a `BuildConfig` object or implemented through the OpenShift Builds Operator, which is based on Shipwright (see the next section). While both approaches are supported and described here, starting with the Builds Operator often makes more sense if you are new to OpenShift or already familiar with Kubernetes.

Using the traditional `BuildConfig`-based approach, the following Kubernetes `Build` API objects are involved in defining and tracking the build process (note the API – `build.openshift.io/v1`):

Object	API	Description
`BuildConfig`	`kind: BuildConfig` `apiVersion: build.openshift.io/v1`	Defines what to build, how, and where to store the result
`Build`	`kind: Build` `apiVersion: build.openshift.io/v1`	An object that represents the status of the build

Table 10.1: BuildConfig-based Build API objects and their roles

When using the OpenShift Builds Operator, a different set of API objects is used to define and execute builds (note the API – `shipwright.io/v1beta1`):

Object	API	Description
`Build`	`apiVersion: shipwright.io/v1beta1` `kind: Build`	Defines what to build, how, and where to store the result
`BuildRun`	`apiVersion: shipwright.io/v1beta1` `kind: BuildRun`	An object that represents the status of the build

Table 10.2: Builds Operator (Shipwright) API objects and their roles

Note the APIs and origins of these objects. The "default" `Build` object, along with `BuildConfig`, comes from `build.openshift.io/v1` and has been a part of OpenShift for quite some time. On the other hand, `Build` and `BuildRun` are part of Shipwright, a newer component. In the next section, we will explore examples of these artifacts and discuss their specific features. With the main strategies introduced, let's dive into how `BuildConfig` objects and `Build` objects work together in practice.

BuildConfig and Build

`BuildConfig` in OpenShift is a resource configuration that defines how builds are executed and managed within the platform. It specifies the source code, the strategy for building the application, and the triggers that initiate builds.

Historically, `BuildConfig` objects were often paired with `DeploymentConfig` objects to trigger deployments when new images became available. `DeploymentConfig` objects are now deprecated but remain available and continue to support image change triggers. In modern OpenShift environments, application rollout is typically handled using Kubernetes Deployments, with image updates driven by CI/CD or GitOps workflows.

`ImageStream` objects track container image versions produced by builds and make them available for downstream consumers. Historically, they were commonly used to connect `BuildConfig` objects with `DeploymentConfig`-based deployments.

A `DeploymentConfig` object can automatically roll out a new image when an `ImageStreamTag` changes. To enable this, add an `ImageChange` trigger to your `DeploymentConfig` object and set the `automatic` parameter to `true` in `imageChangeParams`. When `automatic` is `true`, OpenShift immediately rolls out the new image. When set to `false`, image changes do not trigger deployments - you must start the rollout manually (for example, using `oc rollout latest`).

Best practice: Avoid using the `latest` tag, as it can introduce ambiguity, instability, and security risks in build and deployment workflows.

Okay, now let's get back to builds. They involve the following steps:

1. **Input evaluation:** Source code, dependencies, and so on are evaluated.
2. **Build execution:** The process transforms the inputs into a runnable image.
3. **Logging:** The build process is logged.
4. **Image publishing:** Successful builds are pushed to the integrated image registry.
5. **Final status:** The build status is published.

Builds can specify resource limitations such as CPU, memory (`.spec.resources.requests` and `.spec.resources.limits`), and a maximum build duration (`.spec. completionDeadlineSeconds`). Additionally, as we already mentioned, OpenShift supports Docker, S2I, and custom build strategies.

Earlier OpenShift versions included a Jenkins-based pipeline build strategy, which has since been deprecated. Modern CI/CD workflows in OpenShift are implemented using OpenShift Pipelines, based on Tekton, and are covered later in this chapter.

To better understand `BuildConfig` objects, let's examine the `BuildConfig` manifest. If you instantiated the Apache HTTP Server template in your `my-awesome-project-01` namespace, you can run the following command and review the output:

```
$ oc -n my-awesome-project-01 get bc -o yaml
```

For your convenience, the output is also available in the book's Git repository at `chapters/10/snippets/buildconfig-example.yaml`.

As you can see, the main parameters define the source to use, where the resulting image is stored, and the **build strategy** – an `ImageStreamTag` in this case. Once the `BuildConfig` is created, a corresponding `Build` object is generated. You can verify this by running the following command.

```
$ oc -n my-awesome-project-01 get builds
```

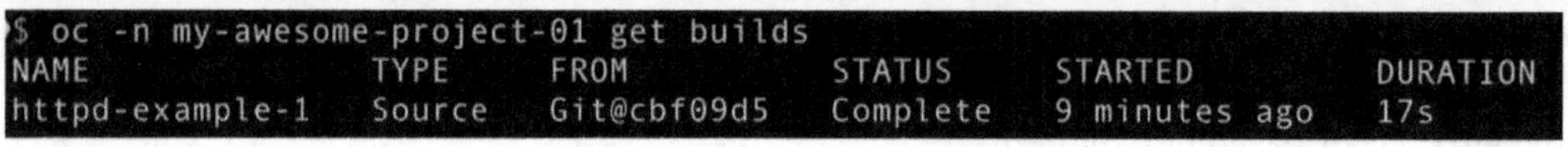

Figure 10.2: Build status – oc CLI

We expect the build to be completed successfully and its status to be `Complete`. You can review the status details by running `oc -n my-awesome-project-01 get build httpd-example-1 -o yaml`, or review it in the UI – click on the build name (`httpd-example` in the following screenshot):

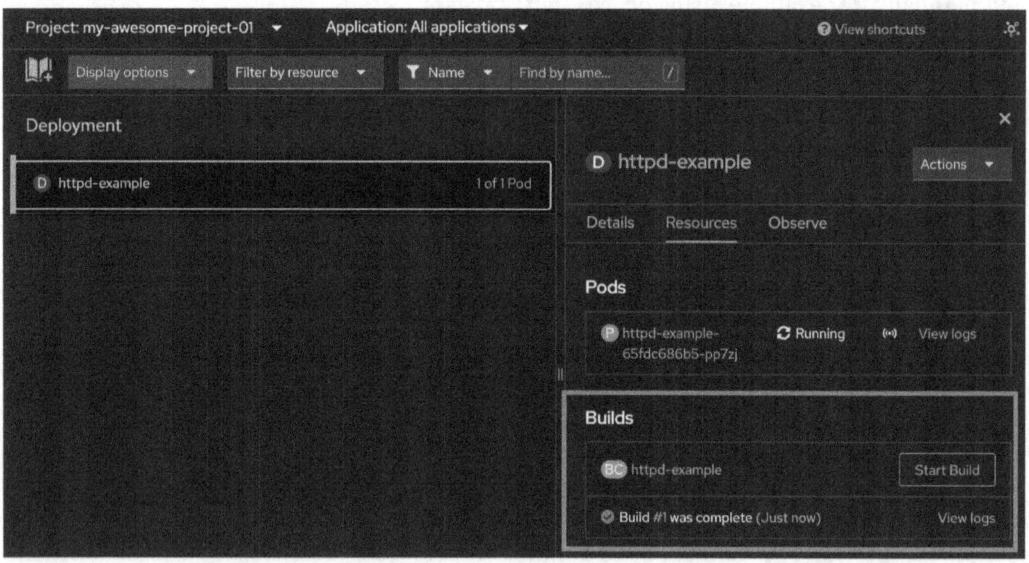

Figure 10.3: Build status – web UI

For more details on OpenShift `BuildConfig` objects and their usage, please refer to the official documentation – [2] and [3].

`BuildConfig` objects have served OpenShift well since its early days, but the platform is evolving. With OpenShift 4.14, Red Hat introduced the Shipwright-based Builds Operator, offering a more flexible and extensible model for managing container builds. The rationale for this evolution is outlined next.

Although Docker, S2I, and custom builds have been reliable for many years, each has inherent constraints:

- Docker requires ongoing Dockerfile maintenance and can encounter friction with cluster security policies.
- S2I accelerates builds for common language stacks, but is limited by the capabilities and opinions of its builder images.
- Custom builds provide maximum flexibility but typically increase governance requirements and operational overhead.

The Shipwright-based Builds Operator addresses these limitations by decoupling build intent (`Build/BuildRun`) from build implementation (strategies defined via `BuildStrategy/ClusterBuildStrategy`). This separation allows teams to use the following:

- Kaniko for Dockerfile/Containerfile-based builds without requiring a Docker daemon.
- Buildah for builds that do not rely on a Docker daemon.
- Buildpacks, when they want to avoid maintaining Dockerfiles/Containerfiles.
- S2I when curated builder images are preferred.

In practice, retain existing `BuildConfig` objects when they already meet requirements. Adopt Shipwright with Buildpacks for mainstream runtimes and minimal configuration. Prefer Shipwright with Buildah or Kaniko when precise Dockerfile control is required under restrictive policies. Use a custom Shipwright strategy for non-standard toolchains that benefit from reusable guardrails.

Let's now move on and discuss the OpenShift Pipelines Operator as the prerequisite for the Builds Operator. We will also discuss the Builds Operator itself, as well as how to deploy both of these. Please note that we will be using the following:

- Red Hat OpenShift Pipelines 1.20.0
- Builds for Red Hat OpenShift Operator – 1.5.0

Red Hat OpenShift Pipelines

Red Hat OpenShift Pipelines is Red Hat's distribution of Tekton, a Kubernetes-native CI/CD framework. It installs and manages Tekton components on OpenShift, allowing you to define CI/CD as Kubernetes objects and run each task in its own Pod with a service account-scoped security context. In practice, you compose tasks into pipelines and execute them by creating `TaskRun` and `PipelineRun` resources. Triggers can turn incoming webhooks (for example, from GitHub) into new `PipelineRun` resources with parameters derived from the event.

Builds for Red Hat OpenShift (alternatively, the Builds Operator) is an extensible image-building framework based on Shipwright. Because it relies on Tekton components, Red Hat documentation lists the **OpenShift Pipelines Operator** as a prerequisite for installing it. When both operators are installed, you can define `ShipwrightBuild` resources and execute them through `BuildRun` objects.

Pipelines and Builds are independent operators, but they are designed to work together: Pipelines Operator orchestrates workflows, while Builds handles image builds using tools such as S2I and Buildah. You can invoke builds from a pipeline – for example, by adding a task that creates a `BuildRun` object (or otherwise calls the Shipwright API) as part of the pipeline flow.

Together, Pipelines Operator and Builds Operator provide a strong, Red Hat-supported foundation for day-to-day CI/CD on OpenShift (orchestration and image builds). Many enterprises pair them with additional components (e.g., GitOps for progressive delivery), but you can cover a large portion of typical CI/CD needs with these two operators.

The following list explains how Tekton (via the OpenShift Pipelines Operator) works in practice and introduces the primary resources you will use:

- **Pipeline:** A *definition* of a CI/CD workflow as an ordered set of tasks. A pipeline can declare parameters, workspaces, and simple control flow (for example, *when* expressions and *finally* tasks). A pipeline describes what should happen, not when it happens.
- **Task:** A reusable unit of work within a pipeline. A task is composed of one or more steps and declares its inputs (parameters and workspaces), outputs (artifacts/results), and runtime requirements.
- **Step:** A single command executed in a container as part of a task. When a task runs, its steps execute **sequentially** within the same task execution environment and can share mounted volumes (for example, workspaces, secrets, and ConfigMaps).
- **PipelineRun:** A single execution of a pipeline using concrete parameter values and workspace bindings. Creating a `PipelineRun` is what *actually starts work*: Tekton uses it to create the required `TaskRun` to execute the pipeline.
- **TaskRun:** A single execution of a task with specific inputs, parameters, and workspace bindings. A `TaskRun` executes the task's steps and reports success or failure (and typically exposes results, logs, and status).
- **Workspace:** A named, shared filesystem that a task or pipeline requires at runtime (for example, source checkout, build artifacts, and caches). You declare a workspace in the pipeline/task, then you **bind** it to a concrete volume when creating a `PipelineRun` (or `TaskRun`).
- **Triggers:** Let external systems (for example, a GitHub webhook) start pipelines automatically and pass event data into them.

Let's look at how all these resources are used in practice:

1. A webhook request arrives over HTTP (headers + JSON body).
2. A `TriggerBinding` extracts values from headers and/or JSON fields using `$(...)` expressions (for example, event type headers such as `X-GitHub-Event`, signature headers such as `X-Hub-Signature-256`, and body fields such as `repository.full_name`, `pull_request.number`, or `ref`).

3. Those extracted values are passed into a `TriggerTemplate`, which renders Kubernetes resources – most commonly, a `PipelineRun` with parameters and workspace bindings populated from the event.
4. **Interceptors** (for example, CEL or GitHub interceptors) can optionally verify signatures and filter/validate events *before* the binding/template step.
5. If the sender uses `CloudEvents`, useful context values can also arrive via HTTP headers (for example, `Ce-Type` or `Ce-Id`) and can be bound the same way.

The best places to learn more about the OpenShift Pipelines Operator are the following documentation – [6] and [7].

Let's deploy the OpenShift Pipelines Operator and ensure that it is up and running; to do so, take the following steps:

1. Go to the web UI and navigate to the **Operators | OperatorHub** menu, then search for `OpenShift Pipelines` and click on the **Red Hat OpenShift Pipelines** option:

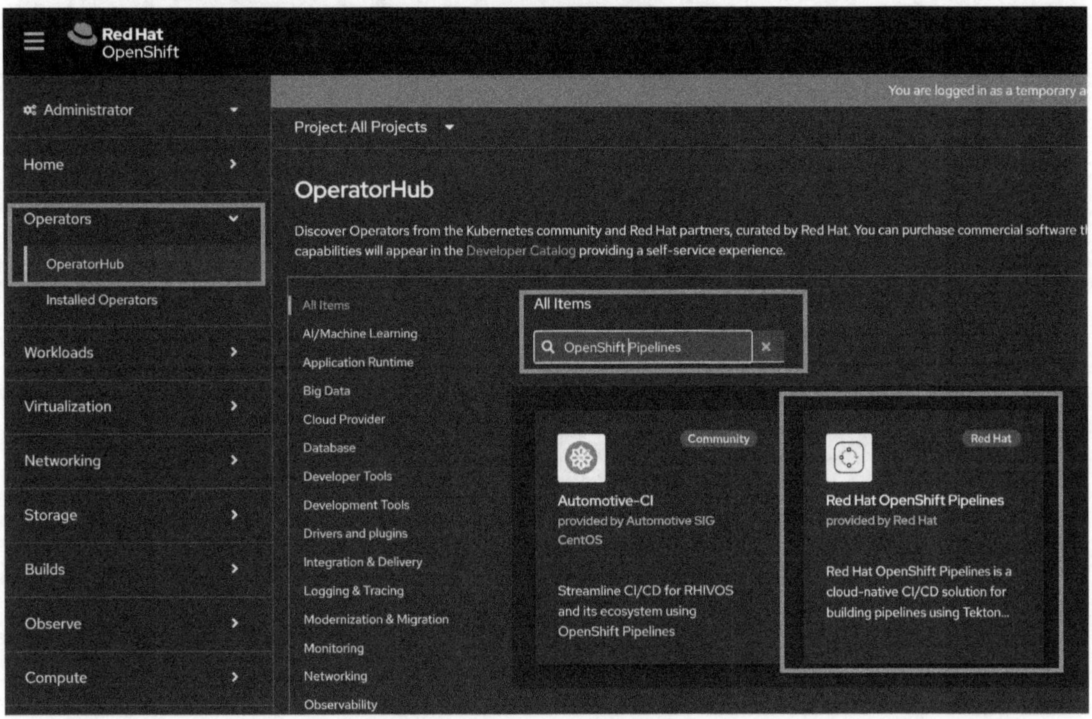

Figure 10.4: OpenShift Pipelines in OperatorHub

2. The installation page will appear – please read the documentation on the page, and ensure that you follow all the recommended links and documentation. When you are done with the provided materials, click the **Install** button. There are multiple versions available, but please use **1.20.0**, so that it is compatible with the next operator we are going to deploy.

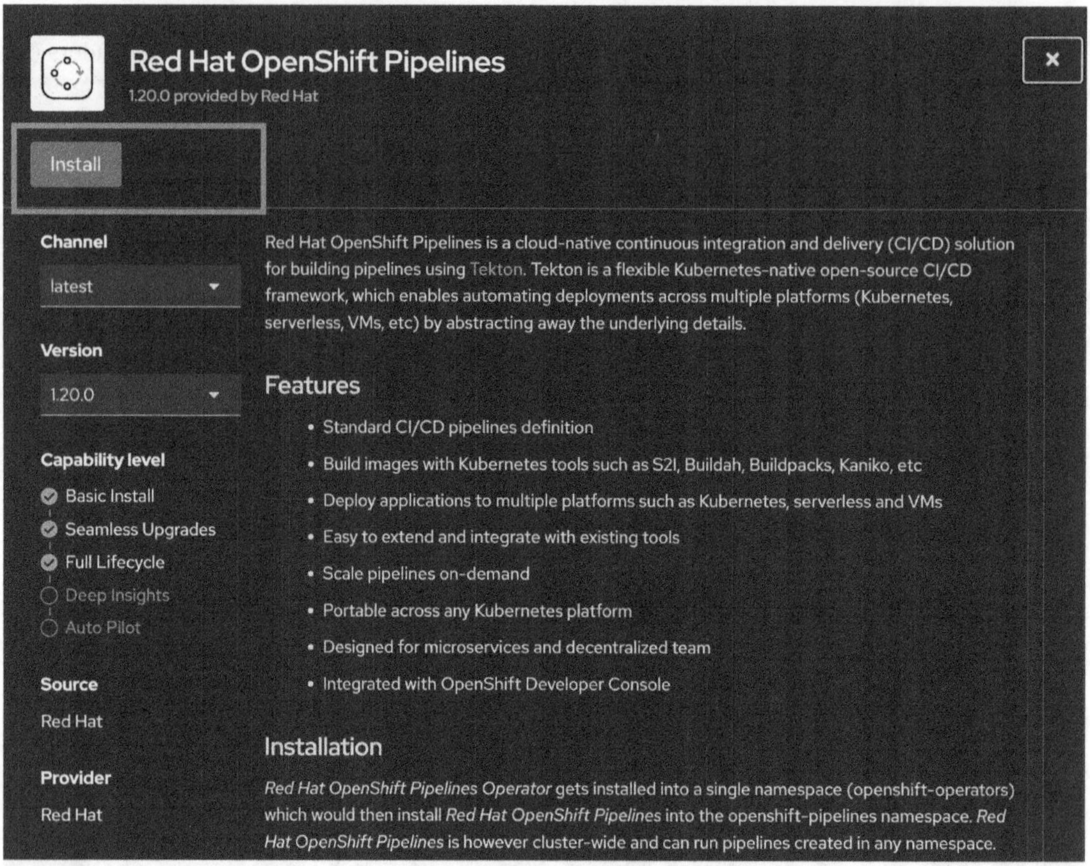

Figure 10.5: OpenShift Pipelines Operator details page

3. On the next screen, you need to click **Install** once again and then wait for the operator to be ready. To find the **Install** button, scroll all the way down the page.

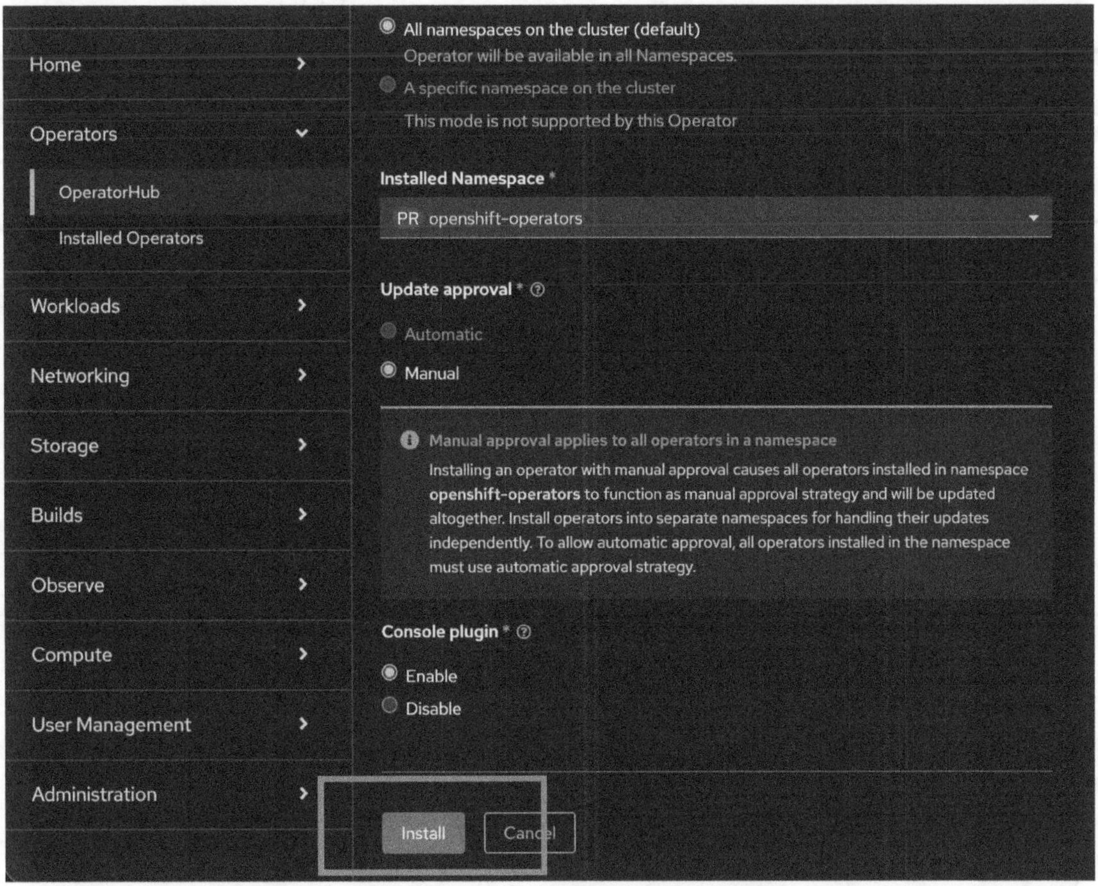

Figure 10.6: OpenShift Pipelines Operator installation parameters

Here is how the page will look when the installation process is done:

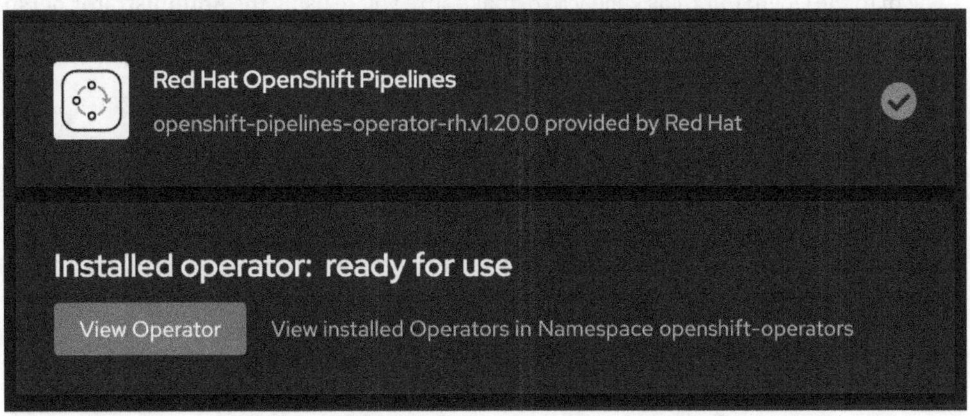

Figure 10.7: OpenShift Pipelines Operator – installation status

Click the **View Operator** button or click on any of the other menu buttons to see the Operator status.

Okay, the operator is installed and ready. It is important to mention once again that you can always use the Pipelines Operator on its own, but in this chapter, we won't go through the details of doing so and will move on to the Builds Operator.

Builds for Red Hat OpenShift Operator

The OpenShift Builds Operator became available as GA starting with OpenShift 4.14. The operator is based on the OSS Shipwright framework (see the official Git repository [4]) and enables easy migration from other Kubernetes platforms, standardizing the entire environment.

The Builds Operator can work on the same OpenShift cluster where you use "default" `BuildConfig` objects.

The operator has the following capabilities:

- Kubernetes-native API for building container images from source code and Dockerfiles/Containerfiles.
- Build strategies, such as S2I and Buildah, which are installed cluster-wide by the operator.
- Extensible strategies that allow for adding **Custom Resources** (**CRs**), such as `BuildStrategy/ClusterBuildStrategy`.
- Local directory builds, so you can execute builds from a local working directory (in addition to Git, etc.).
- The Shipwright CLI (`shp`), which allows you to manage builds and view logs from the CLI.
- Developer perspective integration in the OpenShift web console.

Let's deploy the operator and see what it looks like. To do so, we can go to the UI and use OperatorHub. Let's begin:

1. Log in to the OpenShift UI as `kubeadmin`, make sure you're using the **Administrator** perspective, and click on **Operators | OperatorHub**.
2. Search for `builds` and click on the option for the operator:

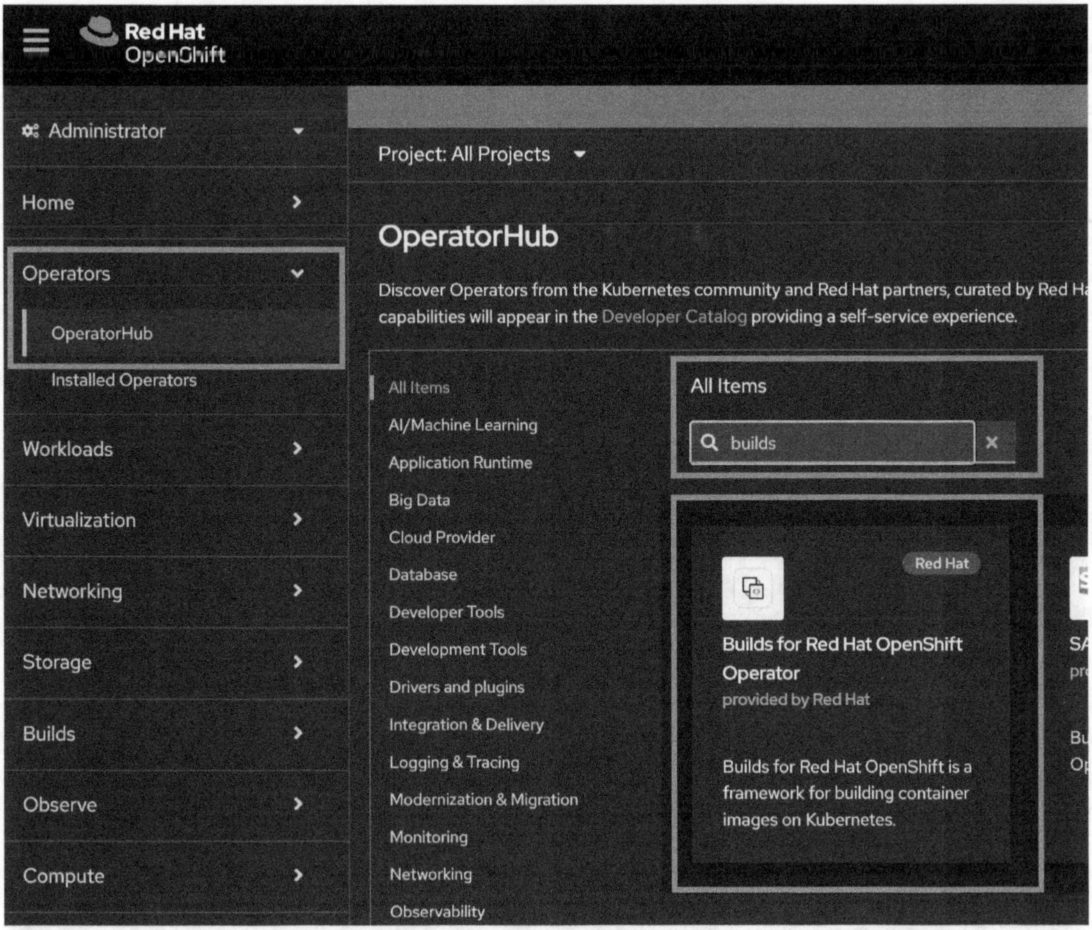

Figure 10.8: Builds Operator option

3. Read the description and ensure that you meet the prerequisites – the Pipelines Operator must be installed first. If you missed this step for some reason, please refer to the previous section to install it. So, if the Pipelines Operator is already available, please pick version **1.5.0** of the Builds for Red Hat OpenShift Operator, and click **Install**:

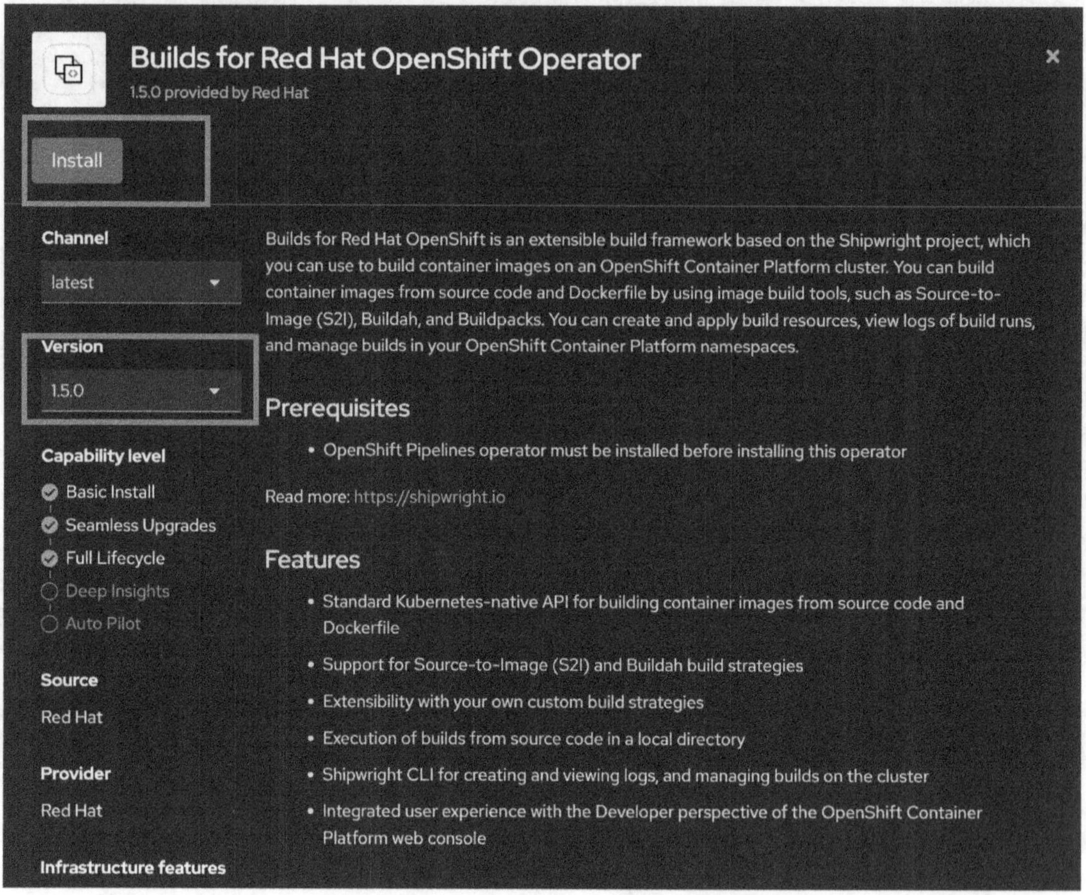

Figure 10.9: Builds Operator installation page

4. On the next screen, click the **Install** button again to invoke the installation process and make the operator available. Scroll all the way down the page to find the **Install** button. No additional configuration is needed at this point.

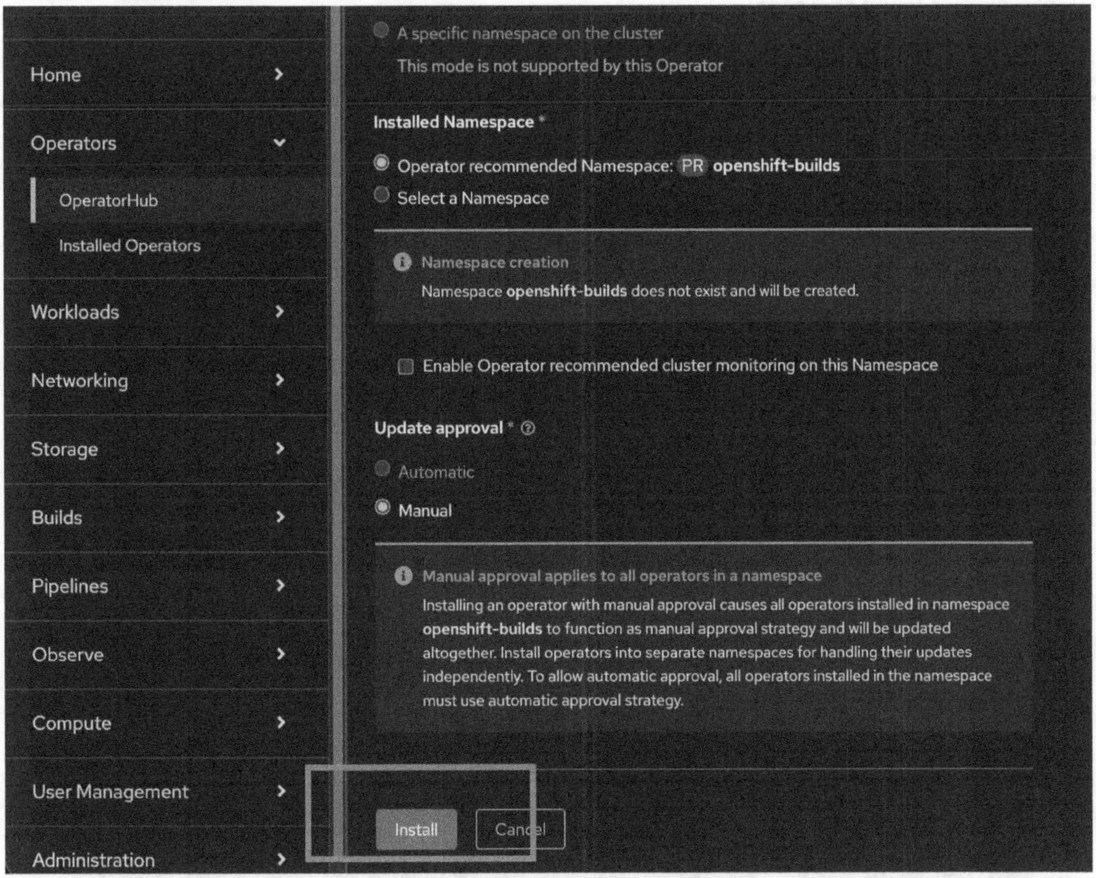

Figure 10.10: Builds Operator installation parameters

The **Operator Lifecycle Manager (OLM)** will handle deploying the operator and ensuring that it is running. The deployment process for OpenShift Local can take some time; please wait until the deployment is done.

The console shows a **Manual approval required** banner – that's expected. The Builds for Red Hat OpenShift Operator declares a dependency on the OpenShift Pipelines Operator, so the OLM creates an installation plan that lists both. Because the subscription uses manual approval, the OLM pauses until you approve it.

5. Click **Approve** to continue. You could install in the opposite order and let the Builds Operator pull pipelines as a dependency; we installed them separately here for clarity and learning purposes. If the OpenShift Pipelines Operator is already at a compatible version, the OLM just verifies it and proceeds.

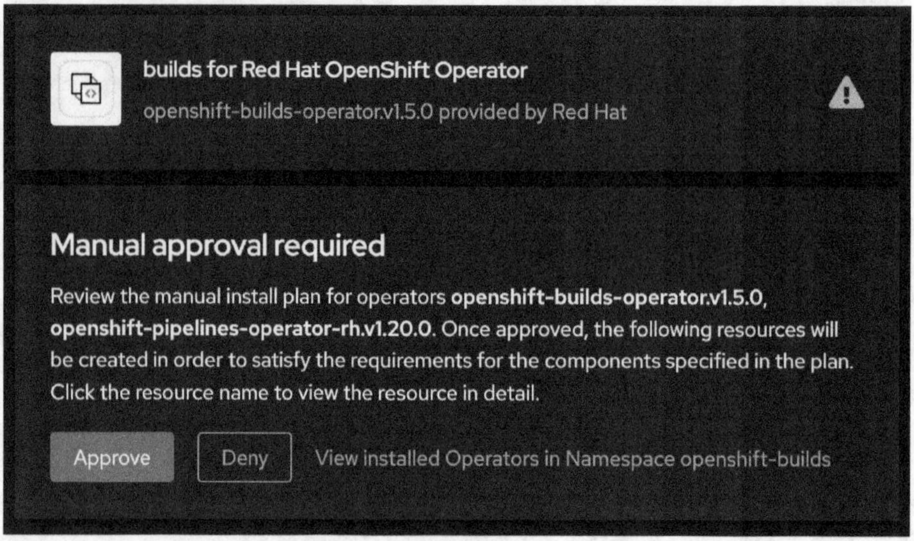

Figure 10.11: Builds Operator installation plan approval warning

6. When the installation is done, you can go to the **Operators** | **Installed Operators** menu, select **Projects** | **All Projects**, and check the operator's status.

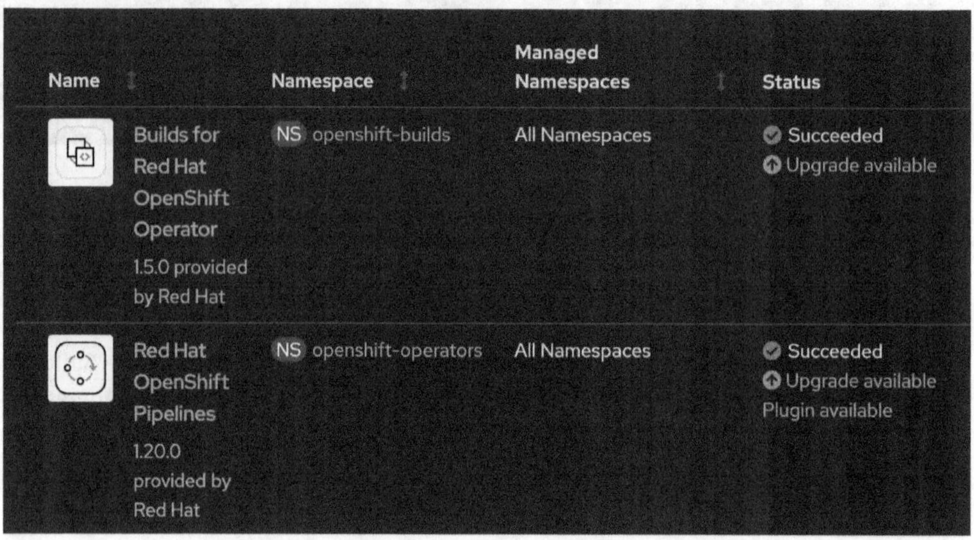

Figure 10.12: Installed Operators status page

The complete Builds Operator documentation is available at [5]. Now, we will briefly go over the terminology to ensure that we are on the same page (there are too many definitions of "build" floating around):

- **Builds Operator:** The operator managing Shipwright controllers and CRDs
- **Build/BuildRun:** Shipwright CRDs that declare and execute a build
- **BuildStrategy/ClusterBuildStrategy:** Shipwright CRDs that define how a build runs
- **BuildConfigs:** The legacy OpenShift build API (`build.openshift.io/v1`)
- **Builds (generic):** The act of producing a container image

A full list of CRDs provided by the operator can be obtained with any of the following commands:

```
$ oc get crd | grep ship
$ oc api-resources | grep ship
$ oc api-resources --api-group shipwright.io
```

The Builds Operator operates a few CRDs and abstractions, which we mentioned before:

- **Build:** Declares the *what* and *where* of a build – the source inputs (e.g., Git or Dockerfile), the intended image/output, and a reference to a `BuildStrategy` or `ClusterBuildStrategy` resource that will perform the build. It does not embed the build steps itself.
- **BuildRun:** Creates and executes a specific build (the *when*). Each `BuildRun` resource triggers a Pod to carry out the work and records the execution status and results, similar to a Kubernetes Job or Tekton `TaskRun` resource.
- **BuildStrategy:** A namespace-scoped strategy that defines the *how* – the steps and tooling used to assemble the image (e.g., Buildah, Buildpacks, or S2I). It is reusable by `Build` resources within the same namespace.
- **ClusterBuildStrategy:** A cluster-scoped variant of `BuildStrategy` that provides the same *how* definition but is available cluster-wide to all namespaces (for example, the curated `buildah` strategy installed by the operator).

Basically, `Build` = *what/where*, `BuildRun` = *when*, and `(Cluster)BuildStrategy` = *how*.

So, with the introduction of the `shipwright.io` API group, there are now three `Build` objects in our cluster from three different groups:

- `builds.build.openshift.io`
- `builds.config.openshift.io`
- `builds.shipwright.io`

If you run `oc get build`, you'll get the list of `Build` objects from the first group (`build.openshift.io`). Suppose you want to see other resources, for example, `builds.shipwright.io`; you'll need to use their fully qualified names, or at least add enough characters after the dot (`.`) for unambiguous identification:

- `oc get build.shipwright.io`
- `oc get build.s`

Now, let's create a build and review its outcomes. Create a file from the definition available in the Git repository: `chapters/10/snippets/shipwright-build.yaml`.

When the object is created, it is time to review some of the most critical parameters and tune them if needed – see the following table, which outlines these parameters:

Field	Value
`source`	`https://github.com/shipwright-io/sample-go`
`output`	`image-registry.openshift-image-registry.svc:5000/my-awesome-project-01/sample-go-app`
`strategy`	`ClusterBuildStrategy`

Table 10.3: Shipwright build definition parameters

Pull the Git repository or copy the definition to a file, name the file `shipwright-build.yaml`, and execute the following well-known command:

```
$ oc create -f shipwright-build.yaml
```

Wait for a minute and run another command:

```
$ oc get build.shipwright.io/buildah-golang-build
```

You will see the status of Shipwright's build, where we expect the `REASON` field to be `Succeeded`.

Now, you can trigger the building process by creating another object – `BuildRun`. The definition, as usual, is available on GitHub: `chapters/10/snippets/shipwright-buildrun.yaml`.

Please download or create this file and create a `BuildRun` by running the following command:

```
$ oc create -f shipwright-buildrun.yaml
```

You may need to wait about three minutes for the build process to be successfully finished, and then you can check the build status by running the following:

```
$ oc get buildrun buildah-golang-buildrun
```

As usual, we are looking for `SUCCEEDED: True` or `REASON: Succeeded`.

So, to execute a build, you create a `BuildRun`. Of course, you can create it by leveraging the web console. Go to **Builds** | **Shipwright Builds**, locate the `buildah-golang-build` build, open the actions menu (⋮), and click **Start**. This creates a `BuildRun` for that build and kicks off the process.

Alternatively, you can use the Shipwright CLI (`shp`) to start runs and view logs from the terminal. Install `shp` from the official Shipwright releases page: `https://developers.redhat.com/content-gateway/rest/browse/pub/openshift-v4/clients/openshift-builds/1.0.1-222/`.

Note that we are using version 1.0.1-222 only as an example; please refer to the documentation for the latest version at the time of reading this book.

Please refer to the official Builds for Red Hat OpenShift documentation for details on how to configure all the objects further and use different build strategies with the Builds Operator [5].

To wrap up on the topic of builds, let's do a cleanup and remove our namespace:

```
$ oc project default && oc delete ns my-awesome-project-01
```

Once you have images and CI/CD pipelines in place, the next step is to start rolling them out. Well, you already know the answer to the question of *how* – OpenShift historically introduced `DeploymentConfig` objects, but Kubernetes-native Deployments have since become the standard. Let's compare the two.

Deployments versus DeploymentConfig objects

If you have experience with Kubernetes and regularly work with Kubernetes-based platforms, you might have noticed that in the previous chapter, when we deployed an application from a template, OCP created a `DeploymentConfig` object. But what exactly is `DeploymentConfig`, and how does it differ from a standard Deployment object? In this section, we will explore the differences between Deployments and `DeploymentConfig` objects to help you understand their distinct roles and functionalities.

DeploymentConfig

In June 2015, OpenShift 3.0 introduced `DeploymentConfig`, which users quickly adopted for their advanced deployment capabilities specific to OpenShift. `DeploymentConfig` evolved with OpenShift, significantly expanding deployment lifecycle management by integrating triggers, lifecycle hooks, and custom strategies.

`DeploymentConfig` provided OpenShift platform users with the following features:

- **Triggers for automated deployments**: Supports triggers that automatically start new deployments in response to events (notably, configuration changes and image stream tag updates).
- **User-configurable deployment strategies**: Supports strategies to transition between versions, including the common rolling (default) and recreating approaches, plus custom strategies.
- **Lifecycle hooks (deployment hooks)**: Supports lifecycle hooks to run custom behavior at defined points in the deployment process (commonly pre/mid/post hooks depending on the strategy).
- **Versioning and rollbacks**: Maintains deployment revisions and supports rollbacks (manually, and OpenShift docs also describe rollback support in failure scenarios).
- **Scaling and autoscaling**: Supports manual replica scaling and autoscaling (via external autoscalers).

Historically, `DeploymentConfig` objects have been a core part of OpenShift, offering features that standard Kubernetes Deployments did not initially support. This includes defining complex deployment triggers based on changes in configurations or image streams and incorporating hooks to run custom scripts at various stages of the deployment process.

`DeploymentConfig` works in tandem with `ReplicationController` to manage the lifecycle of application pods. `DeploymentConfig` defines the deployment strategy and other deployment-related configurations, while `ReplicationController` handles the actual replication and scaling of pods to ensure that the desired number of pod replicas are running at any time.

This partnership between `DeploymentConfig` and `ReplicationController` is detailed in the *Deployments* section of the official OpenShift documentation [12]. It enhances OpenShift's deployment management by ensuring the following:

- **Robustness:** Ensuring that the desired state of applications is maintained, even during node failures or pod restarts.
- **Flexibility:** Allowing various deployment strategies and customizations to suit different application needs.
- **Scalability:** Facilitating easy scaling of applications both manually and automatically.
- **Resilience:** Providing mechanisms for rolling back to previous stable versions in case of failures.

`DeploymentConfig` and `ReplicationController` enable robust and flexible application deployment workflows, making OpenShift a powerful platform for managing complex application lifecycles.

The `DeploymentConfigs` API was deprecated in OpenShift version 4.14; as the official Red Hat KB article states [13], the main reason is as follows:

The current implementation of DeploymentConfigs is based on management of ReplicationController objects. However development of ReplicationController has ceased and upstream recommends to use ReplicaSet objects instead.

In addition, the DeploymentConfig API is a Red Hat OpenShift Container Platform specific API that is not available in other Kubernetes distribution and in fact has been superset with Kubernetes Deployments that are available in all Kubernetes distributions.

Let's examine what Deployments are and when they appeared.

Deployments

In March 2016, a new concept called **Deployment** was introduced in Kubernetes 1.2 (see Kubernetes 1.2 Changelog [14]). Kubernetes quickly gained popularity, with many companies adopting it and building their own solutions.

In June 2019, OpenShift 4.1 was released, where Kubernetes served as the base platform, incorporating all the great OpenShift concepts and adopting all the Kubernetes specifics. Consequently, Deployments have become the default across many platforms and are now the standard way to manage applications. For more information about OpenShift 4.1, you can refer to the official documentation [8].

Deployments use ReplicaSets to manage pods, replacing the ReplicationControllers used by `DeploymentConfigs`. This means all the components have modern, Kubernetes-native alternatives.

Deployments offer the following high-level features:

- **Declarative updates:** Maintain the desired state of applications, ensuring that the correct number of replicas are running.
- **Automated rollbacks:** Support automated rollbacks to previous versions in case of deployment failures.
- **Horizontal scaling:** Integrate well with HPA based on metrics.
- **Pause and resume:** Allow pausing and resuming deployments, which is useful for making multiple changes before rolling them out.
- **Advanced deployment strategies:** Support advanced deployment strategies, such as canary and blue-green deployments, through additional tools such as Argo Rollouts.
- **Proportional scaling:** Handle proportional scaling during rollouts to ensure smooth transitions between versions.

Deployments are the upstream Kubernetes standard for managing stateless applications, which makes them portable across Kubernetes distributions and cloud providers (including OpenShift and Amazon EKS). With that context – and having introduced both resources – let's compare OpenShift's `DeploymentConfig` with the Kubernetes Deployment side by side. Please review this table:

Feature	DeploymentConfig	Deployment
Underlying object	`ReplicationController`	`ReplicaSet`
Triggers	Supports config and image change triggers	Implicit config change trigger, image change via manual updates
Lifecycle hooks	Supports pre- and post-deployment hooks	Not supported natively
Custom strategies	Supports custom deployment strategies	Limited to built-in strategies (e.g., rolling or recreating)
Automated rollbacks	Not automated, but supports manual rollback	Supports automated rollbacks
Pause and resume	Not supported	Supported
Horizontal scaling	Supported, manual	Supported, integrates with HPA
Advanced deployment strategies	Limited, requires custom strategies	Supported through additional tools such as Argo Rollouts

Feature	DeploymentConfig	Deployment
Portability	Specific to OpenShift	Portable across Kubernetes environments
Use cases	Complex deployment logic, OpenShift-specific features	Standard deployments, Kubernetes-native features

Table 10.4: DeploymentConfig and Deployment high-level comparison

Another key difference in the overall Deployment and `DeploymentConfig` logic is the rollout process design:

- `DeploymentConfig`: Prioritizes consistency. If a node with a deployer pod fails, it waits for the node to recover or be manually deleted, affecting rollout progress.
- `Deployment`: Prioritizes availability. Managed by a controller manager that runs in high-availability mode on multiple masters. It can handle failures by allowing other masters to take over quickly, though this may cause temporary inconsistencies.

As of OpenShift 4.14, the `DeploymentConfigs` API has been deprecated to align more closely with Kubernetes-native resources. Originally, `DeploymentConfigs` offered advanced features such as custom deployment strategies, lifecycle hooks, and triggers. However, Kubernetes Deployments have evolved to provide these capabilities, including automated rollbacks, horizontal scaling, and advanced deployment strategies, making them the preferred choice.

While `DeploymentConfig` objects are still supported for backward compatibility, new applications should use Deployments for better integration and future-proofing. This shift simplifies the deployment process and ensures compatibility with the latest Kubernetes advancements, providing a more unified and efficient platform for managing containerized applications.

With the key objects clarified, let's now explore the strategies you can use to roll out applications in your environments.

Deployment strategies

A Kubernetes Deployment (which is now also adopted by OpenShift) is a resource that allows administrators to manage updates to applications declaratively. By defining specific images and the desired number of pods, the Kubernetes backend automates the entire update process without user intervention.

Deployments support declarative configuration and a GitOps development style, where the desired state is defined, and Kubernetes ensures that this state is achieved. This automation reduces the need for manual updates and minimizes human error.

Deployments natively support basic strategies such as "recreate" and "rolling update," but there are several other popular approaches that can be more suitable for your application or its workload profile. Let's review these types and highlight specific details to help you determine which strategy will work best for you:

- **Recreate strategy**: The recreate strategy stops all current pod instances and then creates new ones with the latest version. It's often used in development environments where downtime is acceptable. The main benefit of this strategy is speed. It's also used when an application doesn't support running both new and old image versions simultaneously. This strategy causes downtime and interrupts current operations, so it is not recommended for production environments.
- **Rolling update strategy**: The rolling update deployment strategy gradually updates an application by replacing old pods with new ones one at a time. The new version of the application runs alongside the old version until the update is complete. Rolling updates offer a safe and controlled way to transition between versions, but the process can take time. It can also be challenging to roll back or stop the update if issues arise during the transition.
- **Blue-green deployment**: The blue/green strategy allows for a quick switch between application versions. The "green" version (new) is deployed alongside the "blue" version (old). Once the green version is tested and works well, traffic is switched from the blue to the green version. Traffic can be switched back to the blue version if any issues arise. If the green version is stable, it becomes the new blue version.

  The main drawback is that it requires double the resources during the transition period.

  Please keep in mind that the blue-green deployment is not an OOTB approach – there are no functions of OpenShift that will just let you use it; you would need to use some external tooling, such as Argo CD or OpenShift GitOps Operator (Argo CD-based).

- **Canary deployment**: In a canary deployment, a small group of users is directed to the new version of the application, running on a limited number of pods. If there are no significant issues and users are happy, the new application's version is gradually rolled out to all users, eventually replacing the old version.

  Canary deployments are useful for testing new features with a small user group and can be easily rolled back if needed. They help determine the impact of new code on the system and user experience.

  The downside is that the application must support running two versions simultaneously, which many legacy applications do not. An effective canary strategy also requires a service mesh or network gateway to split traffic between the current and canary versions.

- **A/B testing**: A/B testing distributes traffic between different versions of an application based on specific parameters. Unlike canary deployments, which gradually phase out the old version, A/B testing keeps both versions running continuously.

  It allows you to test different features and only roll out the most successful ones to all users. A/B testing helps compare options, but it is complex and often requires a service mesh for precise traffic control.

- **Shadow deployment:** A shadow deployment tests a new application version under real production loads without affecting users. It runs a copy of the production environment, but users don't interact with it. This allows testing in a realistic setting. If the new version is stable and performs well, it can then be rolled out to users. Shadow deployments are ideal for assessing performance impacts without user disruption. They require more resources than regular deployments but can sometimes use fewer resources than a full blue/green deployment, making them more cost-effective.

The native Kubernetes Deployment object supports only the `RollingUpdate` and `Recreate` strategies. `Recreate` causes application downtime, while `RollingUpdate` provides basic safety guarantees but has several limitations.

`RollingUpdate` offers limited control over rollout speed, cannot manage traffic flow to the new version, is unsuitable for stress tests, cannot verify updates with external metrics, and cannot easily abort and roll back updates.

For mission-critical production environments, `RollingUpdate` is often inadequate. It lacks control over change impacts, may roll out changes too quickly, and has no automated rollback option. These limitations have led to the development of dedicated tools for more advanced deployment options in Kubernetes clusters, such as Argo CD and OpenShift GitOps Operator.

Both are great tools and time-tested. The great advantage of the OpenShift GitOps Operator is its enhanced integration with OpenShift, as well as the fact that it provides Red Hat's support, which can be crucial in the enterprise environment. The GitOps Operator will be briefly discussed in *Chapter 15, Exploring Additional Services in OpenShift*.

Here is a table that summarizes all the deployment strategies together so you can see which may be more suitable for your cases and what advantages and disadvantages these strategies bring:

Deployment strategy	Available OOTB	Description	Advantages	Disadvantages	Use cases
Recreate	Yes	Stops all current pods and creates new ones	Quick, simple to implement	Causes downtime and interrupts operations	Development environments where downtime is acceptable
Rolling update	Yes	Gradually replaces old pods with new ones	Zero downtime, controlled transition	Can be slow; difficult to roll back mid-transition	Most production environments

Deployment strategy	Available OOTB	Description	Advantages	Disadvantages	Use cases
Blue/green	No	Runs the new version alongside the old version; switches traffic to the new version once tested	Quick switch; allows testing in production	Requires double resources during transition	Production environments that need quick rollbacks and thorough testing
Canary	No	Routes a small percentage of users to a new version, gradually increasing	Allows you to test new features with real users; easy to roll back	Needs to support running two versions; requires traffic management	Testing new features with minimal risk
A/B testing	No	Distributes traffic based on parameters to different versions	Compares features; keeps both versions running	Complex setup; needs traffic control	Feature comparison and user experience testing
Shadow	No	Runs the new version alongside the old version without user interaction	Tests in the production environment without affecting users	Requires extra resources, but can be cost-effective if using a subset of resources	Performance testing and non-functional impact assessment

Table 10.5: Deployment strategies summary

Rolling out an application is just part of the journey. To stay resilient and efficient, workloads must also scale on demand and run in the right place. Let's see how OpenShift handles scaling and placement.

Scaling and managing applications

Now that we understand how to use the OpenShift CLI and work with Deployments, templates, and other essential concepts, we can move on to application scaling and deployment placement across cluster nodes. This involves discussing Kubernetes architecture, microservices, node selectors, and scaling approaches.

Architecture

Before we talk about scaling and operating applications, it's worth understanding the architecture of Kubernetes and how OpenShift extends it. A clear mental model of the platform makes day-to-day microservices work much easier.

Kubernetes architecture

As you already know, OpenShift is based on Kubernetes, and Kubernetes is a container orchestration system that automates deployment, scaling, and lifecycle management of workloads. At a high level, it consists of the following components:

- **Control plane**:
    - **API server:** The front door to the cluster; all reads/writes go through the Kubernetes API.
    - **Controller manager**: Runs built-in controllers that drive the actual state toward the desired state.
    - **Cloud controller manager (optional)**: Integrates Kubernetes with a cloud provider, managing cloud resources such as load balancers, nodes, routes, and so on.
    - **Scheduler**: Assigns pods to nodes based on resource requests and constraints.
    - **etcd**: The strongly consistent key-value store for cluster state.
- **Worker nodes**:
    - **kubelet**: Node agent that ensures that the containers for each scheduled Pod are running and healthy.
    - **Container runtime** (CRI): Starts/stops containers; commonly `containerd` or CRI-O (`dockershim` is long gone).
    - **kube-proxy**: Implements Kubernetes Service virtual IP behavior and basic load balancing on many clusters. In OpenShift, this depends on the network provider – for example, OVN-Kubernetes can provide Service handling without the traditional kube-proxy data plane.
- **Core workload primitives**:
    - **Pod**: The smallest deployable unit (one or more tightly coupled containers).
    - **Deployment**: Declarative rollout/rollback and horizontal scaling for stateless Pods (manages a ReplicaSet for you).
    - **ReplicaSet**: Keeps a specified number of identical Pods running (which you don't manage directly).
    - **StatefulSet**: Stable network IDs and storage per replica; ordered start/stop/updates for stateful or identity-sensitive services (often with a headless Service and `volumeClaimTemplate`).
    - **DaemonSet**: Ensures one (or *N*) Pod per selected node; ideal for node-level agents (logging, CNI, CSI, or monitoring).

- **Job** (`batch/v1`): Run-to-completion tasks with completions, parallelism, and `backoffLimit`.
- **CronJob** (`batch/v1`): Time-based jobs on a schedule (`crontab` syntax).

To simplify your onboarding to the OCP, we would like to share a simple diagram. You have encountered other diagrams in the book; they are provided to simplify onboarding to Kubernetes and OpenShift for visual learners.

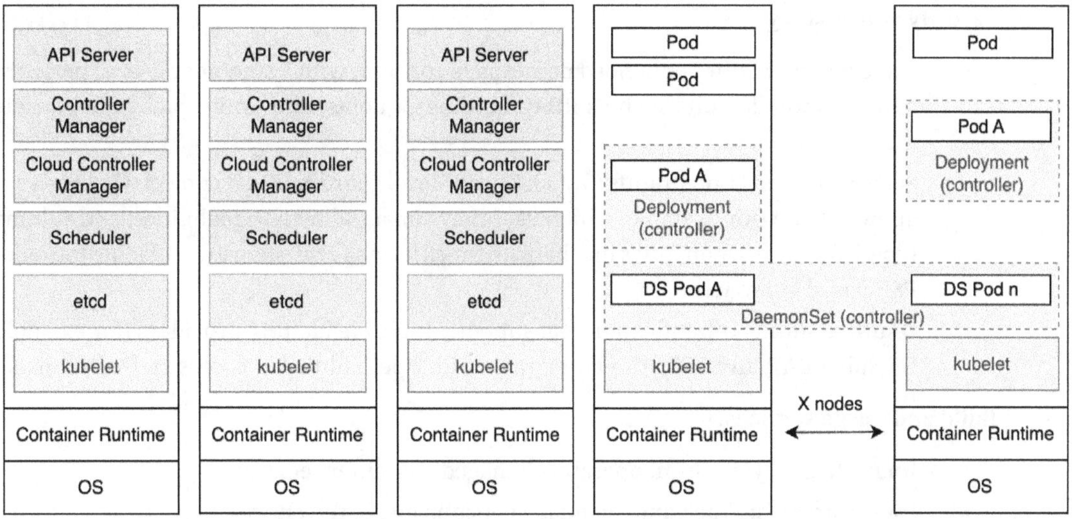

Figure 10.13: Kubernetes components high-level diagram

To keep the diagram simple, networking and storage details are not shown (e.g., **services/EndpointSlice, kube-proxy, CNI plugins**, and **CSI drivers**). The goal is to highlight the primitives you'll use when planning your application lifecycle on OpenShift/Kubernetes and briefly describe core components of the control plane.

OpenShift architecture

So, OpenShift is Kubernetes with a supported, opinionated stack of operators, security defaults, and developer tooling. It adds the following features to Kubernetes:

- **Control plane extensions:**
  - OpenShift API server and OpenShift controller manager: Add OpenShift-specific APIs/logic (projects, builds, routes, etc.):
    - **OLM**: Installs and upgrades user-installed operators.
    - **Cluster Version Operator** (CVO): Orchestrates platform upgrades and manages cluster operators.
  - Machine API: Manages nodes as cloud "machines" (CRDs: `Machine`, `MachineSet`, and `MachineAutoscaler`).

- **Networking:**
    - OVN-Kubernetes is the default OpenShift 4 network provider and implements Service handling in the OVN/OVS data plane, so `kube-proxy`'s traditional configuration is not used.
    - Ingress/routes via the ingress controller (`HAProxy`) expose services at the edge with TLS and host/path routing.
- **Security and tenancy:**
    - **Projects:** OpenShift's enhanced namespace concept, with a smoother user experience and common defaults such as RBAC bindings, quotas, and limits, plus tight console integration.
    - **Security Context Constraints (SCCs):** Cluster-level guardrails that control what Pods are allowed to do (for example, which user they run as, allowed capabilities, and volume types). SCCs are OpenShift's mechanism for enforcing Pod security, replacing the older PSP-based approach.
    - **OAuth:** Built-in authentication that supports multiple identity providers (for example, GitHub, LDAP, and OIDC) and integrates with OpenShift's API access and web console.
- **Build and image services:**
    - **Image Registry:** Built-in, operator-managed container registry.
    - **Image streams:** Track and tag image versions inside the cluster.
    - **BuildConfigs/DeploymentConfigs:** OpenShift-native build/deploy primitives (fully supported); many teams also use standard Deployments
    - **S2I:** Repeatable builds from source into runnable images.
- **Host/node operating system: Red Hat CoreOS (RHCOS)** is the default node operating system in OpenShift. It's designed to be immutable and managed through the platform, which helps keep both control plane and worker nodes consistent and easy to update. In some environments, you may also see RHEL-based worker nodes – typically chosen when you need OS-level customization or third-party tooling that isn't a good fit for RHCOS.

OpenShift and Kubernetes clusters typically scale out (by adding nodes) rather than scaling up a single node. In practice, the number of Pods you can run on a node is limited by several factors:

- kubelet settings (e.g., `maxPods`)
- CPU and memory requests
- CNI/IPAM address space
- Node resources and kernel limits (CPU, memory, PIDs, and file descriptors)
- Workload characteristics (I/O, network, huge pages, etc.)

On OpenShift, a common pattern is to dedicate infra nodes – using labels/taints with matching tolerations – for platform workloads such as ingress controllers, the internal registry, and core observability components (logging and monitoring). This keeps application worker nodes focused on business workloads.

For elasticity, you typically scale out through MachineSets (and, when appropriate, Cluster Autoscaler with the machine autoscaler) so the cluster can add or remove capacity in a controlled, predictable way.

This separation maps cleanly to a microservices model: lightweight, horizontally scalable application Pods run on worker pools; platform "plumbing" runs on infra pools; and a small, highly available control plane steers the cluster. Next, we'll briefly review microservices and how they translate into OpenShift/Kubernetes primitives – because this is where application scaling starts.

Microservices in OpenShift

Microservices decompose an application into small, independently deployable services with well-defined APIs. On OpenShift (Kubernetes), services typically communicate over HTTP/HTTPS or gRPC, and many teams also use async messaging (Kafka or AMQP) for decoupling.

So, what does OpenShift give you OOTB to make day-to-day development and operations easier? Here are the core platform capabilities that map directly to common microservices needs:

- **Service discovery**: A Kubernetes Service provides a stable virtual IP and DNS name (for example, `svc.ns.svc.cluster.local`) that routes to a set of backing Pods. For workloads that need direct Pod identities (common with stateful patterns), use a headless Service.
- **Load balancing and exposure**: Inside the cluster, Services spread traffic across ready Pods. For external access, OpenShift typically exposes applications using routes (via the OpenShift router) or standard Kubernetes Ingress. Both support host/path routing and can be configured to terminate TLS or pass it through, depending on the use case.
- **Traffic management patterns**: Circuit breaking, retries, timeouts, mTLS, and progressive delivery patterns (for example, canary) are typically provided by Red Hat OpenShift Service Mesh (Istio) rather than core Kubernetes Services. In practice, these behaviors are configured through mesh resources (for example, `VirtualService` and `DestinationRule`).
- **API gateway**: When you require cross-cutting API concerns – rate limiting, authentication integration, key management, analytics, and developer portals – use **Red Hat 3scale API Management (APIcast)** or a third-party gateway.
- **Security and tenancy**: Projects (namespaces with OpenShift UX and defaults), RBAC, SCCs, and network policies help you constrain each service's blast radius and enforce least privilege.

The familiar microservice characteristics – scalability, resilience, and flexibility – aren't abstract ideals on OpenShift; they map to concrete resources and patterns you enable per service. Think of each service as a self-contained unit you can scale horizontally, harden against failures, and implement in the stack of your choice – the following list describes the native constructs that make this practical:

- **Scalability**: You can scale each service independently with Deployments and HPA.
- **Resilience**: You can fail one service without impacting the rest – use readiness/liveness/startup probes, **Pod Disruption Budgets (PDBs)**, and graceful shutdown (`preStop` hooks and `terminationGracePeriodSeconds` definitions).
- **Flexibility**: Each service ships as its own container image with (potentially) its own CI/CD process.

Great, now let's try to answer the next question that may come up – how can we scale our microservices out in OpenShift? There are multiple levels of scaling, which you may combine depending on where your OpenShift cluster is running – on-premises or in the cloud – and what virtualization platform is in use, what features of the cloud providers your organization uses, and so on. Let's discuss your options for scaling at a high level:

- **HPA (built-in)**: Allows you to adjust the replica count based on metrics (CPU, memory, or custom/external metrics if you wire those in).
- **Event-driven autoscaling (optional)**: For example, KEDA Operator allows you to scale on queue depth, HTTP concurrency, and so on. You can always use KEDA when HPA is not flexible enough. To read more about KEDA, please see [9].
- **Cluster capacity is also scalable**: You can pair workload auto-scaling with Cluster Autoscaler and the machine autoscaler, so the OpenShift platform will add or remove nodes when the workload increases and replicas are scaling out.

When the application developers and platform team (those who are responsible for the OpenShift clusters) have good communication channels and coordination between them, the organization can reach a good state where the entire platform scales seamlessly and scalers, quotas, taints, and tolerations work together.

What can be crucial to define for your microservices to get the maximum benefits from OCP? Here is a checklist that may be helpful in your journey:

- **Set resource requests and limits intentionally**: Define CPU/memory requests to drive scheduling and autoscaling decisions, and use limits carefully – especially CPU limits, which can introduce throttling under load.
- **Make health signaling explicit**: Use readiness probes to gate traffic, startup probes to protect slow-starting services, and liveness probes only when a process truly can't self-recover.
- **Add application-level resiliency**: Define timeouts, retries, and backoff in clients and servers. Don't rely on the platform alone to prevent cascading failures.
- **Protect availability during disruptions**: Use PDBs to preserve a minimum number (or percentage) of replicas during voluntary disruptions such as node drains and upgrades.
- **Keep Pods stateless, externalize state**: Put durable state in managed services (databases, object storage, or queues/streams). Treat Pods as replaceable.
- **Instrument and observe by default**: Emit structured logs, metrics, and traces. Define SLOs and alerts so you can detect and act on real user impact, not just infrastructure symptoms.
- **Choose a rollout strategy up front**: Decide how you'll ship changes – rolling updates, blue/green, or canary (via routes, Ingress, or Service Mesh) – and what your rollback path is.
- **Isolate and constrain blast radius**: Use projects, RBAC, network policies, and resource quotas/limit ranges to enforce tenancy boundaries and prevent noisy-neighbor issues.

With all these details in mind, let's move forward and talk about how we use autoscaling and what workload placement mechanisms we have. In the next section, we will briefly discuss HPA, VPA, node selectors, and other entities you may encounter.

Autoscaling and placement

In modern cloud-native environments, efficient resource management is crucial for maintaining performance and cost-effectiveness. OpenShift provides robust features for autoscaling and workload placement, ensuring that applications run efficiently while meeting performance requirements.

Autoscaling is a fundamental capability in OpenShift that allows applications to dynamically adjust their resource usage based on demand. OpenShift supports several autoscaling mechanisms, with the most commonly used being HPA.

We will look at HPA, VPA, node selectors, and affinity rules, which are essential tools for managing workloads in OpenShift.

HPA

As a developer, you can use an HPA in OpenShift to automatically adjust the number of Pods for a workload based on observed metrics. You can create an HPA for common scalable controllers such as `Deployment`, `DeploymentConfig`, `ReplicaSet`, `ReplicationController`, and `StatefulSet`. You configure the minimum and maximum replica counts and set targets such as CPU or memory utilization.

Once an HPA is created, OpenShift periodically evaluates resource metrics for the Pods in the target workload (CPU utilization is a common default). A key detail is that utilization is calculated relative to resource requests. In other words, if your Pods do not define CPU/memory requests, the HPA cannot make reliable scaling decisions. Based on the measured utilization, the HPA increases or decreases the replica count to reach the target. Because this loop runs on a schedule, scaling changes are not instantaneous, and you may see a short delay before the new replica count is visible.

For `ReplicationController` and `DeploymentConfig` objects, manual scaling changes the replica count directly. With `DeploymentConfig`, autoscaling affects only the most recent deployment `ReplicationController` managed by that `DeploymentConfig` object (not older rollout revisions), after that deployment has reached the `Complete` state.

To avoid unstable scaling decisions during transient conditions (for example, startup spikes), the HPA relies on Pod readiness and metric availability. Pods that are not yet ready, or that do not have valid metrics, are treated conservatively by the autoscaler – especially for scale-down decisions. To benefit from this behavior, define meaningful readiness checks (and consider startup probes for slow-starting services).

To use HPAs, your cluster administrator must configure cluster metrics properly:

Parameter	Description	API
CPU utilization	Number of CPU cores used. It can be used to calculate a percentage of the pod's requested CPU.	`autoscaling/v1` `autoscaling/v2`
Memory utilization	Amount of memory used. It can be used to calculate a percentage of the pod's requested memory.	`autoscaling/v2`

Table 10.6: System metrics for HPA

An HPA uses metrics and targets to manage scaling. Metrics provide the data needed to decide when to scale, while targets define the desired state the HPA aims to achieve. The HPA monitors these metrics and adjusts the number of pods to meet the target. Let's take a look at an example (available in the Git repository at `chapters/10/snippets/hpa-example.yaml`):

```
apiVersion: autoscaling/v1
kind: HorizontalPodAutoscaler
metadata:
  name: my-hpa-01
  namespace: my-namespace-01
spec:
  maxReplicas: 7
  minReplicas: 3
  scaleTargetRef:
    apiVersion: apps/v1
    kind: Deployment
    name: my-deployment-01
  targetCPUUtilizationPercentage: 75
  behavior:
    scaleDown:
      stabilizationWindowSeconds: 300
```

When you review the structure of the HPA definition, please note the following fields (all of them are important):

- `.spec.scaleTargetRef`: Defines a target that will be scaled.
- `.spec.minReplicas`: Defines a minimum number of replicas for the Deployment.
- `.spec.maxReplicas`: Defines a maximum number of replicas for the Deployment.
- `.spec.targetCPUUtilizationPercentage`: Defines when to scale the target.
- `.spec.behavior`: May have `scaleDown` and `scaleUp` behavior definitions; this is one of the most essential configuration parameters that allows you to fine-tune the scaling behavior. The best practice would be to define both `scaleDown` and `scaleUp`.

HPA is a Kubernetes API resource that automatically adjusts the number of pod replicas based on CPU and memory usage. It works in a control loop with a default sync period of 15 seconds.

During each sync, the controller manager checks the CPU and memory usage of each pod targeted by the HPA, using metrics from the resource metrics API. If a utilization target is set, the controller calculates the average usage across all pods and adjusts the number of replicas accordingly.

The HPA fetches metrics from the metrics server (`metrics.k8s.io`), and the number of replicas can change dynamically based on these metrics. HPA won't work on the Kubernetes cluster with no metrics server. Another prerequisite to make HPA work would be making sure all target pods have a resource request defined.

The `autoscaling/v2` API lets you add scaling policies to an HPA via `.spec.behavior`. These policies determine how quickly the HPA scales by setting a specific number or percentage of pods to adjust within a set time period. You can also use a stabilization window to manage scaling when metrics fluctuate.

The policy controls how quickly the HPA is allowed to scale. It limits scaling changes to a specific number of Pods per time window (for example, using `periodSeconds`) and defines how far back the HPA should consider past recommendations via stabilization windows. For a complete description of the available parameters, refer to the official documentation [10].

> A lot of users get confused by the fact that when observed usage crosses the defined threshold, HPA doesn't trigger scaling out or in. This is by design: HPA has a default tolerance of 0.1 or 10%, meaning that for scaling to take place, the usage must be outside of the (threshold-10%; threshold+10%) range.
>
> For the code snippet above, with CPU threshold of 75%, that means that replicas will be added only when usage exceeds 83% and removed when it drops below 67%. Of course, this behavior is still subject to the stabilization window.

VPA

Before we start talking about VPA, we have to mention that the VPA Operator is optional and not installed OOTB. The OCP VPA automatically analyzes CPU and memory usage for pods and adjusts their resource limits and requests accordingly. It utilizes CRs to update all pods linked to a workload, such as a Deployment, StatefulSet, or Job, in a project.

The VPA helps you determine your pods' optimal CPU and memory usage and can automatically manage these resources throughout the pod's life cycle. VPA is an API resource and a CR. The CR specifies the actions the VPA should take with pods linked to a specific workload, such as a DaemonSet or replication controller, in a project.

The VPA deployment includes a few components:

- **Recommender:** Monitors current and past resource usage to determine the optimal CPU and memory resources for the pods in a workload.
- **Updater:** Checks whether the pods have the correct resources. If not, it kills the pods so their controllers can recreate them with updated requests.
- **Admission controller:** Sets the correct resource requests on each new or recreated pod in the workload.

The default recommender analyzes CPU and memory usage to optimize resource limits and requests. It suggests reducing resources for over-provisioned pods and increasing resources for under-provisioned ones.

The VPA automatically deletes and recreates misaligned pods one at a time, ensuring no downtime. It uses a mutating admission webhook to update pods with optimized resources before they are admitted to a node. If you prefer not to delete pods automatically, you can manually update resource limits and requests based on VPA recommendations.

It is important to note that, in most enterprise environments, the VPA is run in recommendation ("Off") mode. In this mode, it provides right-sizing suggestions that platform administrators and developers can use to plan requests and limits.

By contrast, enabling the `Initial` or `Auto` update mode can be disruptive at scale; VPA may evict pods to apply new resources and can amplify scheduling pressure in large, highly utilized (overcommitted) clusters. For that reason, many teams begin with recommendation-only mode and adopt update modes selectively – per workload, with clear SLOs and defined disruption windows.

To start using it safely, please ensure you are disabling `updatePolicy`; it will allow you to review offerings and then manually apply the change. To use VPA in recommendation-only mode, set the `.spec.updatePolicy.updateMode` parameter to `"Off"`. An example is available in the GitHub repo, in `chapters/10/snippets/vpa-off-example.yaml`, for your convenience:

```
apiVersion: autoscaling.k8s.io/v1
kind: VerticalPodAutoscaler
metadata:
  name: example-vpa
  namespace: your-namespace
spec:
  targetRef:
    apiVersion: "apps/v1"
    kind: Deployment
    name: example-deployment
  updatePolicy:
    updateMode: "Off"
```

VPA is a powerful feature and deserves its own dedicated chapter. For details on the operator, CRs, and configuration parameters, refer to the official documentation [11].

Officially, Red Hat does not recommend running HPA and VPA together, because they have conflicting goals: HPA is designed to scale workloads out when average usage exceeds a certain threshold, maintaining a gap between usage and requests, while VPA aims to close that gap to minimize idle resources. This can result in a "tug-of-war" scenario where you end up with more and more replicas with smaller and smaller requests.

However, there is a way to make them work together. Just define `.spec.minReplicas` and `.spec.maxReplicas` in your HPA, and `.spec.resourcePolicy.containerPolicies[].minAllowed` in your VPA. This sets boundaries on how far both HPA and VPA can go.

Node selectors and affinity rules

In OpenShift, managing where your workloads run within a cluster is crucial for performance, reliability, and cost efficiency. This section explores how to control pod placement using node selection, affinity, and anti-affinity rules. These rules are usually applied to a Pod's parent objects, such as `Deployment`, `StatefulSet`, `ReplicaSet`, and `DaemonSet` objects.

Node selectors

Node selectors allow you to define constraints that determine which nodes a pod can be scheduled on. This is typically done using node labels and node selectors. These labels can represent various attributes, such as hardware characteristics, geographic location, or any other user-defined categorization. In the following example, the pod will only be scheduled on nodes labeled with `disktype=ssd`:

```
apiVersion: v1
kind: Pod
metadata:
  name: example-pod
spec:
  nodeSelector:
    disktype: ssd
```

Beyond simple `nodeSelector` rules, Kubernetes (and therefore OpenShift) lets you express *intent* about where pods should run. Affinity and anti-affinity rules act as scheduling policies: they guide the scheduler to place pods on particular nodes (node affinity) or near/far from other pods (pod affinity/anti-affinity). Used well, they improve availability, performance locality, and fault isolation – without hard-pinning workloads to specific hosts or chasing brittle hostnames.

Node affinity

Node affinity targets nodes by label and supports rich, set-based operators (`In`, `NotIn`, `Exists`, `DoesNotExist`, `Gt`, and `Lt`). It comes in two flavors:

- `RequiredDuringSchedulingIgnoredDuringExecution`: A hard constraint. If no node matches, the pod remains pending.
- `PreferredDuringSchedulingIgnoredDuringExecution`: A soft preference. The scheduler tries to honor it, but can place the pod elsewhere if necessary.

Please see `chapters/10/snippets/node-affinity-example.yaml` for a manifest that describes a pod that requires `disktype=ssd`.

Pod affinity and anti-affinity

Pod affinity and **pod anti-affinity** express Pod placement *relative to other Pods* that match a label selector. You can use affinity to co-locate tightly coupled components, or use anti-affinity to deliberately separate replicas to spread risk and reduce the blast radius. The `topologyKey` defines the placement domain – for example, use `kubernetes.io/hostname` for same-node behavior, or `topology.kubernetes.io/zone` to group or spread across zones. These rules also support both required (hard) and preferred (soft) modes.

By default, selectors apply within the *same namespace*; you can widen this with `namespaces` or `namespaceSelector`.

- Co-location example (with `app=frontend`): `chapters/10/snippets/pod-affinity-example.yaml`
- Separation example (away from `app=frontend`): `chapters/10/snippets/pod-antiaffinity-example.yaml`

So, the question would be when and why to use them. In production, these controls are critical:

- **High availability**: The main case, when you spread replicas across nodes or zones to avoid correlated failure.
- **Performance locality**: Land pods on nodes with the right hardware (e.g., SSD or GPU) or closer to the data path.
- **Co-location:** Place chatty, tightly coupled services together to reduce latency.

Overall, keep label taxonomies stable and meaningful; avoid over-constraining with many hard requirements that starve scheduling. Start with **preferred** rules and introduce **required** ones only where necessary. Validate behavior under failure (node drains or upgrades) and combine anti-affinity rules with PDBs so scheduling constraints don't prevent safe rollouts.

We've mentioned PDBs several times because they're essential when planning rollouts and platform maintenance on Kubernetes/OpenShift. PDBs limit **voluntary** disruptions (drains, upgrades, and restarts), so replicas remain available. In the next section, we'll explain why PDBs exist and when to use them, and show a minimal example.

PDB

A PDB limits how many Pods from a replicated workload can be taken down by voluntary actions (drains, upgrades, or rolling restarts) at the same time. It preserves availability while still letting cluster operators perform maintenance. You specify the budget with either `.spec.minAvailable` or `.spec.maxUnavailable`, using an integer or percentage; the Eviction API enforces the rule during voluntary disruptions. Take the following example:

```
apiVersion: policy/v1
kind: PodDisruptionBudget
metadata:
  name: api-pdb
  namespace: payments
spec:
  maxUnavailable: 1   # or use: minAvailable: "50%"
  selector:
    matchLabels:
      app: api       # must match your Deployment/StatefulSet labels
```

This is how the defined PDB works in practice:

- `kubectl/oc drain` and other evictions respect the PDB; if the budget would be violated, eviction is blocked.
- You can check enforcement with `kubectl/oc get pdb`: the `ALLOWED DISRUPTIONS` column shows how many Pods can be evicted right now.
- PDBs protect only against voluntary disruptions; they don't prevent unplanned outages (node crashes or kernel panics).

The common practice is to start with a small `maxUnavailable` value (often `1`) for StatefulSets or `50%` for stateless services, then tune based on SLOs and rollout speed.

Okay, it is time to wrap up.

Summary

In this chapter, we looked at how OpenShift manages application delivery from end to end. We started by looking at templates for reusable application definitions, then moved through builds, contrasting classic `BuildConfigs` with the newer Builds Operator (Shipwright-based). We showed how both integrate with the OpenShift Pipelines Operator to enable CI/CD.

Then, we compared `DeploymentConfigs` with Kubernetes Deployments and explained why Red Hat's default posture favors Deployments. From there, we reviewed rollout strategies – from rolling updates to blue-green, canary, and shadow releases – and closed with a look at scaling and placement: HPA (and, where appropriate, VPA), node selectors, affinity/anti-affinity rules, and a brief look at PDBs to ensure availability during maintenance. Taken together, these building blocks equip you to design rollouts that balance stability with agility and to operate applications at scale on OpenShift.

In the next chapter, we'll examine other common ways to deliver workloads to your clusters – specifically Helm and Kustomize, the de facto templating and configuration management standards for Kubernetes that work seamlessly on OpenShift.

References

To learn more about the topics that were covered in this chapter, take a look at the following resources:

- [1] *OpenShift documentation | Using templates*: `https://docs.redhat.com/en/documentation/openshift_container_platform/4.16/html-single/images/index#about-templates`
- [2] *OpenShift documentation | Understanding image builds*: `https://docs.openshift.com/container-platform/4.16/cicd/builds/understanding-image-builds.html`
- [3] *OpenShift documentation | Understanding build configurations*: `https://docs.openshift.com/container-platform/4.16/cicd/builds/understanding-buildconfigs.html`
- [4] *Shipwright GitHub repository*: `https://github.com/shipwright-io`
- [5] *OpenShift documentation | Builds 1.0 overview*: `https://docs.redhat.com/en/documentation/builds_for_red_hat_openshift/1.5/html/about_builds/overview-of-builds`
- [6] *Tekton documentation | Pipelines*: `https://tekton.dev/docs/getting-started/pipelines/`

- [7] *OpenShift Pipelines Operator documentation*: `https://docs.redhat.com/en/documentation/red_hat_openshift_pipelines/1.19/html/about_openshift_pipelines/about-pipelines`
- [8] *OpenShift 4.1 documentation*: `https://docs.openshift.com/container-platform/4.1/welcome/index.html`
- [9] *Keda official website*: `https://keda.sh`
- [10] *OpenShift documentation | Automatically scaling pods with the horizontal pod autoscaler*: `https://docs.redhat.com/en/documentation/openshift_container_platform/4.16/html/nodes/working-with-pods#nodes-pods-autoscaling`
- [11] *OpenShift documentation | Automatically adjust pod resource levels with the vertical pod autoscaler*: `https://docs.redhat.com/en/documentation/openshift_container_platform/4.16/html/nodes/working-with-pods#nodes-pods-vpa`
- [12] *OpenShift documentation | Deployments*: `https://docs.redhat.com/en/documentation/openshift_container_platform/4.16/html/building_applications/deployments`
- [13] *DeploymentConfig API is being deprecated in Red Hat OpenShift Container Platform 4.14*: `https://access.redhat.com/articles/7041372`
- [14] *Kubernetes 1.2 release notes*: `https://kubernetes.io/blog/2016/03/kubernetes-1-2-even-more-performance-upgrades-plus-easier-application-deployment-and-management/`

Quiz

Let's test your understanding of OpenShift 4 deployment strategies with this quick quiz:

1. What is the main difference between Deployments and `DeploymentConfigs` in OpenShift?
    a. `DeploymentConfigs` are a Kubernetes feature, while Deployments are specific to OpenShift
    b. Deployments use declarative updates, while `DeploymentConfigs` allow more control through triggers
    c. `DeploymentConfigs` cannot handle rollbacks, while Deployments can
    d. `DeploymentConfigs` use blue-green deployment by default
2. What is the `Recreate` deployment strategy primarily used for?
    a. To scale applications based on load
    b. To deploy new versions of applications with zero downtime
    c. To stop the current version before starting the new one
    d. To deploy multiple versions of an application at the same time
3. Which of the following best describes a blue-green deployment?
    a. Deploying both the old and new versions of the application to split traffic evenly
    b. Switching traffic between old and new versions seamlessly using two separate environments
    c. Slowly rolling out the new version alongside the old one to test compatibility
    d. Deploying the new version in the background without affecting the old one

4. What is the primary function of an HPA in OpenShift?
   a. Scale pods vertically by adjusting CPU or memory limits
   b. Scale the number of pods based on resource usage, such as CPU or memory
   c. Automatically increase the number of nodes in the cluster
   d. Deploy additional pods based on network traffic
5. What is the primary purpose of using the OpenShift Pipelines Operator?
   a. To build container images without a Dockerfile
   b. To manage application scaling through Kubernetes operators
   c. To define and automate CI/CD processes
   d. To handle manual application updates in production environments

Answers

1. **b.** Deployments in OpenShift follow Kubernetes' declarative model, whereas `DeploymentConfigs` provide additional control through custom triggers and hooks, allowing for more flexibility in how applications are deployed and updated.
2. **c.** The `Recreate` strategy stops the current version of an application before starting the new one, ensuring that no two versions run simultaneously. This strategy is ideal when running both versions at once could cause issues.
3. **b.** Blue-green deployment involves running two separate environments (blue for the old version and green for the new version) and switching traffic between them, allowing for seamless transitions between versions.
4. **b.** An HPA in OpenShift automatically adjusts the number of running pods based on resource metrics such as CPU or memory usage, helping applications scale dynamically under load.
5. **c.** The OpenShift Pipelines Operator is based on Tekton and enables the automation of CI/CD processes, helping streamline application delivery and updates.

Join us on Discord

For discussions around the book and to connect with your peers, join us on Discord at `http://packt.link/discordcloud` or scan the QR code below:

11

Deploying Applications with Helm and Kustomize

Now that you are familiar with the basics of OpenShift APIs and what makes up an application, as well as development considerations for OpenShift, it is time to build on that knowledge. In this chapter, you will learn about Helm, a package manager for Kubernetes and OpenShift, and how to write Helm charts for your applications that adhere to best practices and conventions. As part of that, we will also cover the process of installing, upgrading, and uninstalling Helm charts. You will also be exposed to Kustomize – a Kubernetes-native configuration management tool that allows you to define a baseline configuration for the objects that represent your application, as well as overlays that describe environment-specific differences. We will go through an exercise where we will prepare a base configuration and a number of environment-specific overlays. Finally, you will learn how to apply Kustomize configurations ("kustomizations," as they are called) using the OpenShift CLI and how to structure them in Git for versioning and collaboration.

While Helm and Kustomize are not critical to running applications in production, they simplify initial deployment and upgrades of applications, making them useful for large-scale operations.

We will cover the following topics in this chapter:

- What is Helm?
- Structure of a Helm chart
- Installing Helm charts on OpenShift
- Writing Helm charts
- Kustomize

Technical requirements

For this chapter, you will need the following:

- Bash shell
- OpenShift 4.16 cluster
- Firefox (recommended) or any other browser
- GitHub account

You can access this book's GitHub repository at `https://github.com/PacktPublishing/Learn-OpenShift-Second-Edition`.

What is Helm?

Helm [1] is the de facto package manager for Kubernetes and Kubernetes-based distributions, such as OpenShift. It is used to deploy the resources that an application is composed of as a single unit. On top of that, it provides a templating mechanism so that one chart can be adapted to different situations depending on the parameters used to instantiate it.

Kubernetes and OpenShift don't support the concept of applications natively, in that API resources that make up an application, such as Deployments, ConfigMaps, Secrets, and PersistentVolumeClaims, are treated as separate entities rather than a single unit where all the resources share a common life cycle. There are two ways to address this limitation, each with its own advantages and drawbacks, as well as use cases – Helm charts and operators:

	Helm charts	Operators
Implements new API(s)	No	Yes
Encapsulate application-specific operational logic	No	Yes
Automated deployments	Yes	Yes
Automated life cycle management	No	Yes
Automated upgrades	No	Yes
Complexity	Low	High
Intended use	Relatively simple stateless applications that need to be deployed across multiple environments with the same configuration	Complex stateful applications that involve specific operational and maintenance tasks

	Helm charts	Operators
Scope	Ensure that an application is deployed in the same fashion across multiple environments	Ensure that an application runs as required
Offer a mechanism of packaging and distribution	Yes	Yes

Table 11.1: Comparison of Helm charts and operators

Let's take a closer look at each of the preceding points:

- **Implement new API(s)**: Helm is used to apply API resources of an application; it doesn't bring any APIs of its own. While Helm charts don't require any **CustomResourceDefinitions (CRDs)** to represent applications they deploy or store their own state, they can be used to install CRDs or entire operators – these are treated as regular API resources. In fact, using Helm and operators together is a common approach in GitOps where Helm charts are used to install operators across multiple clusters via a GitOps server, such as Argo CD. Operators, on the other hand, extend the Kubernetes API server by installing new APIs that encode all application-specific tasks. For example, if you package a PostgreSQL database as a Helm chart, it can be installed as a StatefulSet to manage individual Pods, plus a ConfigMap that contains its configuration, both being Kubernetes core APIs. With an operator, you can create a CRD called, for example, DBInstance, that provides fields for configuring various parameters of PostgreSQL, including periodic volume snapshots or an upgrade strategy – something that is not easily doable with a Helm chart (*easily* being the operative word). While periodic snapshotting can be achieved by creating a CronJob that would quiesce a database, mount a volume, and take a snapshot, this is just one example. An example of such an operator is CloudNativePG [2]. Applications vary in complexity, and a lot cannot be easily accomplished and maintained using built-in APIs.
- **Encapsulate application-specific operational logic**: Helm deploys, upgrades, and uninstalls your application as a number of API objects; however, it has no knowledge about the specifics of an application, such as whether it is a stateful application, for example, a database or queue manager, or a stateless REST API. Helm assigns custom labels and annotations to the resources it manages, to keep track of different releases of the same chart and tell the chart's resources apart from other objects. However, this is where its involvement ends. An operator, on the other hand, is able to recognize that a particular application is, for instance, a PostgreSQL RDBMS that must be quiesced before taking a backup. Operators are generally best suited for applications that require a high degree of automation. This chapter focuses on Helm charts and their releases.
- **Automated deployments**: Both Helm and operators are responsible for deploying applications in an automated fashion. While Helm accepts configuration either through a file or the Helm CLI, an operator is instantiated by creating one or more **CustomResources (CRs)** that leverage one or more of the APIs (aka CRDs) provided by the operator.

- **Automated life cycle management:** Helm is useful when it comes to deploying, configuring, upgrading, and uninstalling applications on demand. However, it lacks any application-specific controls and support for continuous life cycle management. For example, how do you create a shard-based deployment of MongoDB or add a slave replica to your MariaDB Pod? How do you add a new user to a CRM? Normally, you would have to interact with an application directly by opening a shell inside its Pod or relying on its API to accomplish this. Operators, however, address all these questions by exposing corresponding controls through CRDs, which extend the OpenShift API. That is why operators are often referred to as Kubernetes-native applications. When you deploy an application as a Helm chart, from a Kubernetes or OpenShift perspective, its components are just separate API resources, so if you add a new environment variable to a ConfigMap, for example, you will have to manually redeploy the application's Pods for them to pick up the change. With an operator, however, you can configure your application to automatically redeploy its Pods when a configuration change is introduced via a ConfigMap or CR – a dedicated controller that comes with an operator, watches for any changes, and can react to them.
- **Automated upgrades:** While Helm gives you the ability to upgrade your application by changing its configuration or updating the image it runs, it does not go any further than that. First, all upgrades have to be initiated manually via the CLI. Second, Helm does not monitor the upstream repository for your application's chart to determine whether an upgrade is available. Operators, on the other hand, can be configured to either inform you of available upgrades so that you can apply them manually or apply them automatically.
- **Complexity:** Helm charts use templating to render resource manifests for applications. While templates support functions that are based on the Go templating language, they require neither programming experience nor deep knowledge of the application being wrapped in a chart. Developing operators is usually more involved because it often requires at least basic programming skills and a deep knowledge of the application. In that regard, operators can be considered a design pattern for Kubernetes-native applications.
- **Intended use:** Technically, Helm charts can be used to package and install any application; however, they don't work well for complex stateful applications that require persisting their state between changes and upgrades. Operators are better suited for that task due to their native ability to track (or "watch") changes to the application's resources and react accordingly by properly migrating data or performing other tasks.
- **Scope:** The main function of Helm, as a package manager, is to ensure that an application with all its constituent API objects is deployed in exactly the same configuration across a fleet of clusters, maybe even multiple times within the same cluster. By providing a templating language, it decouples elements that must be consistent across installations from any variations. However, it doesn't have a controller that actively monitors the state of an application, so any configuration change has to be done manually. Operators, on the other hand, do involve controllers that run in a loop in their own Pods and constantly check whether the current state of a cluster has deviated from the desired state defined in any of their CRs.

- **Offer a mechanism of packaging and distribution:** Both Helm and operators have their communities and public channels of distribution, such as Artifact Hub [3] for Helm charts and OperatorHub [4] for operators. It is not uncommon for enterprises to maintain in-house repositories where internal charts and operators are shared between departments.

Operators are discussed in more detail in *Chapter 16, Understanding Operators and the Operator Framework.*

Now that we know what Helm is used for, it is time to take a closer look at the internals of Helm charts and explore their structure.

Structure of a Helm chart

Helm uses a well-defined directory structure for all chart-related assets. A basic Helm chart consists of the following directories and files:

File or directory	Description
`Chart.yaml`	Information about a chart, including its version and the version of an application inside the chart. See [5] for a complete reference of its fields.
`LICENSE`	Licensing terms.
`README.md`	Human-readable information about the chart, including usage examples.
`values.yaml`	Parameters passed inside templates.
`templates/`	A directory with all the resources that make up the application delivered by a chart.
`templates/NOTES.txt`	Message displayed on installation, successful test run, status check, and upgrade of a chart. It can be used to tell users how to access the application that the chart installs.
`templates/test/`	Resources for testing an application. By default, this is a Pod that uses `wget` to test connectivity.
`crds/`	CRDs that extend the Kubernetes/OpenShift API.
`charts/`	Any charts that this chart depends on.

Table 11.2: Structure of a Helm chart

While some of these folders and files, such as `Chart.yaml` and `templates`, are mandatory, others, for example, `templates/NOTES.txt` and `templates/test`, are optional. Refer to [6] for a full list of mandatory and optional elements of a Helm chart.

There are two types of Helm charts:

- **Application charts**: Install applications. Such charts typically include one or more manifests for workload controllers, such as Deployment. We will be building an example of such a chart in this book as an exercise.
- **Library charts**: Provide dependencies and manifests for application charts. They don't include any workload controllers, as they are not meant to deploy any applications, but to be used by application charts.

Now let's see how charts are installed, upgraded, and uninstalled.

Installing Helm charts on OpenShift

Before we can begin working with Helm charts, we need to install the Helm CLI. There are multiple channels from which it can be obtained. The easiest way is to use your Linux distribution's package manager. However, that may not provide the most recent version. Building from the source code, on the other hand, gives you the bleeding-edge version with all the newest features (as well as bugs), but it is more involved. A good compromise between currentness and convenience is to download a binary release for your OS and CPU architecture, as shown next (the steps are copied from [7]):

```
$ curl -fsSL -o get_helm.sh https://raw.githubusercontent.com/helm/helm/main/
scripts/get-helm-3
$ chmod 700 get_helm.sh
$ ./get_helm.sh
```

Use the following command to verify the version:

```
$ helm version
```

Your version will likely vary, but it should resemble the following:

```
version.BuildInfo{Version:"v3.18.4",
GitCommit:"d80839cf37d860c8aa9a0503fe463278f26cd5e2", GitTreeState:"clean",
GoVersion:"go1.24.4"}
```

You can find the latest and older releases of Helm on Helm's GitHub page [8].

As an exercise, in the following section, we will install a (relatively) simple chart with the WordPress blog engine.

Installing Helm charts from a public repository

Before you start with any exercises in this book, export the kubeconfig for your cluster into your shell. If you followed the installation procedure from *Chapter 3, Getting Started with OpenShift*, the following command does it:

```
$ export KUBECONFIG=~/learning-ocp4/auth/kubeconfig
```

Helm can use the same kubeconfig as the `oc` and `kubectl` binaries, which will be useful later on.

Here are the steps:

1. Let's create a dedicated project:

```
$ oc new-project chapter-11-helm
```

2. The Helm CLI provides a command for searching chart repositories for keywords. For example, to find charts that have the word `wordpress` in their path, use the following command:

```
$ helm search hub wordpress --max-col-width 75
```

   The chart we need has the URL `https://artifacthub.io/packages/helm/bitnami/wordpress`. That URL, however, is not the URL of the repository itself but a link to the home page of the chart on Artifact Hub. In order to obtain the actual repository URL, you have to go to the chart's Artifact Hub page and click on **INSTALL**, which will show you how to add the chart's repository with Helm and install it:

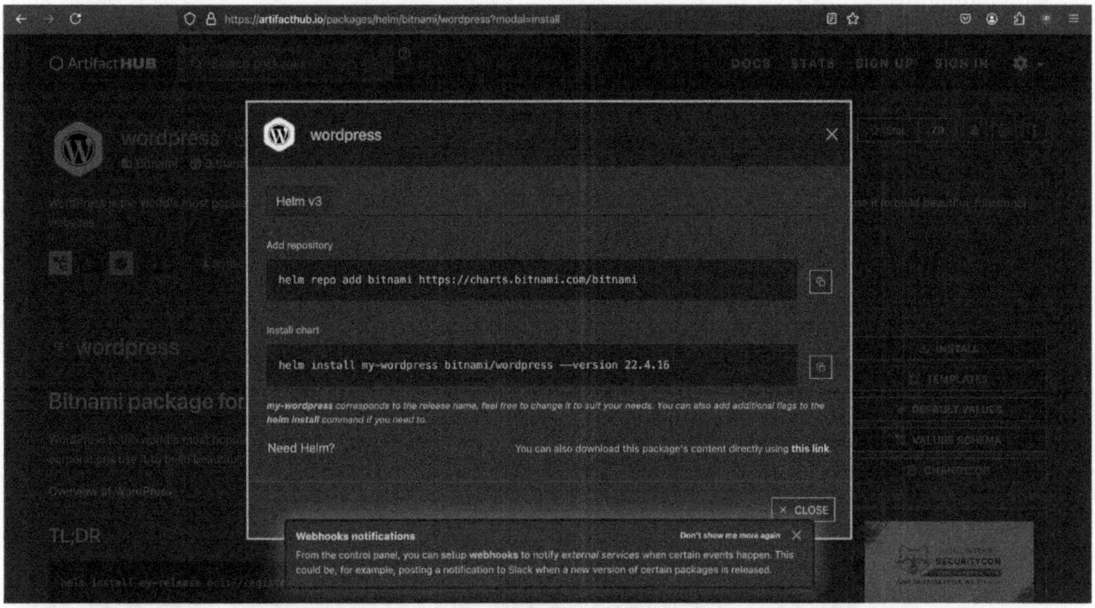

Figure 11.1: WordPress Helm chart installation instructions on Artifact Hub

3. Next, add the chart's repository as follows, giving it an arbitrary alias, for example, `bitnami`:

```
$ helm repo add bitnami https://charts.bitnami.com/bitnami
```

4. Now we can install the chart we want from this repository, referencing it by the alias we used previously:

```
$ helm install chapter-11-wp bitnami/wordpress
```

In the preceding command, `chapter-11-wp` indicates a release, a running instance of a chart's application. You can install the same chart on the same cluster multiple times under different release names. The following output indicates a successful installation:

```
NAME: chapter-11-wp
LAST DEPLOYED: Mon Jun 17 01:44:23 2024
NAMESPACE: chapter-11-helm
STATUS: deployed
REVISION: 1
TEST SUITE: None
NOTES:
CHART NAME: wordpress
CHART VERSION: 22.4.10
APP VERSION: 6.5.4
```

Figure 11.2: WordPress chart installed successfully

You can obtain the same information at any time later by using the `helm status RELEASE` command:

```
$ helm status chapter-11-wp
```

5. As you can see by running `oc get po`, the WordPress application is made up of two Pods – WordPress itself and MariaDB as its database:

```
$ oc get po
NAME                                      READY   STATUS    RESTARTS   AGE
chapter-11-wp-mariadb-0                   1/1     Running   0          84s
chapter-11-wp-wordpress-5c9c95988c-f751d  1/1     Running   0          84s
```

Figure 11.3: WordPress Pods created by the WordPress chart

> Due to Bitnami deprecating support for their non-hardened WordPress images and migrating them to a different repository (`https://hub.docker.com/r/bitnamilegacy`), the preceding Pods may fail with an image pull issue. To fix this, use the following command to update the repository for MariaDB and WordPress images:
>
> ```
> $ helm upgrade chapter-11-wp bitnami/wordpress --set
> image.repository=bitnamilegacy/wordpress,mariadb.image.
> repository=bitnamilegacy/mariadb
> ```

6. As it is, WordPress doesn't expose an endpoint that can be used to access its UI. We can change that by overriding the respective variables in the chart, which can be done via the `helm upgrade` subcommand:

```
$ helm upgrade chapter-11-wp bitnami/wordpress --set ingress.
enabled=true,ingress.hostname=wp.apps.<CLUSTER_NAME>.<DOMAIN>
```

Replace the <CLUSTER_NAME> and <DOMAIN> placeholders with the values from your environment to have Helm create a route (refer to the `install-config.yaml` file from *Chapter 3, Getting Started with OpenShift*). You can also use `oc whoami --show-console` to obtain the rest of the route.

Here, we have overridden two variables from the chart's `values.yaml` file:

Variable	Description
`ingress.enabled`	Whether to enable an ingress controller or not.
`ingress.hostname`	A hostname to express an Ingress object as. On OpenShift, an ingress controller creates a Route object with a matching hostname.

Table 11.3: WordPress chart's overridden parameters

If an upgrade is successful, you should see output similar to the following:

```
Release "chapter-11-wp" has been upgraded. Happy Helming!
NAME: chapter-11-wp
LAST DEPLOYED: Mon Jun 17 01:46:29 2024
NAMESPACE: chapter-11-helm
STATUS: deployed
REVISION: 2
TEST SUITE: None
NOTES:
CHART NAME: wordpress
CHART VERSION: 22.4.10
APP VERSION: 6.5.4
```

Figure 11.4: WordPress chart release is upgraded with new parameters

Notice that the revision was incremented to 2. Each time you upgrade or roll back a release, the revision is incremented; it can never be decreased.

7. Use the following command to list all the releases for the current namespace:

```
$ helm ls
```

It gives us a condensed version of the previous output:

```
NAME            NAMESPACE        REVISION  UPDATED                                   STATUS    CHART              APP VERSION
chapter-11-wp   chapter-11-helm  2         2024-06-17 01:46:29.109583958 -0400 EDT  deployed  wordpress-22.4.10  6.5.4
```

Figure 11.5: Updated release with an increased revision

8. Let's give our application a quick test:

```
$ curl -I wp.apps.<CLUSTER_NAME>.<DOMAIN>
```

You should get the following `HTTP/1.1 200 OK` response from Apache, which indicates that the application on the other end is up and running:

```
HTTP/1.1 200 OK
date: Mon, 17 Jun 2024 05:47:33 GMT
server: Apache
link: <http://wp.apps.ocp4.example.com/wp-json/>; rel="https://api.w.org/"
content-type: text/html; charset=UTF-8
set-cookie: 16beeab1b62e23e38c3a26534a4c3cf4=78e15e23e4e8fa24bd8e81936c6e93e1; path=/; HttpOnly
```

Figure 11.6: WordPress is serving requests

This is made possible by an API object called `Ingress` that serves as an entry point for all or part of the inbound traffic for your application.

9. Display the Ingress object with `oc get ingress`. You should see a single item in the result:

```
NAME                       CLASS    HOSTS
chapter-11-wp-wordpress    <none>   wp.apps.ocp4.example.com
```

Figure 11.7: WordPress route

If you want to see what parameters the chart we used as an example allows us to customize, run the following command:

```
$ helm show values bitnami/wordpress
```

The output of the preceding command is rather long, so we haven't provided it here for brevity. It is an exact copy of the `values.yaml` file.

Other subcommands include listing CRDs, displaying a chart's `README` file, or displaying a chart's definition from `Chart.yaml`:

```
$ helm show crds bitnami/wordpress
$ helm show readme bitnami/wordpress
$ helm show chart bitnami/wordpress
```

Our WordPress chart doesn't install any controllers or CRDs, so the first command is not expected to produce any output.

Helm chart rollbacks

Let's now imagine that you performed an upgrade by introducing a number of new values to a chart's variables, and the application is not performing as it is intended, or maybe it was a part of testing. In any case, instead of performing another upgrade using values from a previous release, you can just roll back to a corresponding revision:

1. First, you need to find out which revision you want to roll back to. For that, use the following command to view the revision history for a specific release of your chart:

```
$ helm history chapter-11-wp
```

The output should be self-explanatory, with the `superseded` status denoting all but the most recent revisions of a release:

```
REVISION  UPDATED                   STATUS      CHART              APP VERSION  DESCRIPTION
1         Mon Jun 17 01:44:23 2024  superseded  wordpress-22.4.10  6.5.4        Install complete
2         Mon Jun 17 01:46:29 2024  deployed    wordpress-22.4.10  6.5.4        Upgrade complete
```

Figure 11.8: WordPress chart revision history

By default, the maximum number of revisions is 256, but it can be changed via the `--max` option.

2. To see user-supplied values that a particular revision uses, execute the following command:

```
$ helm get values chapter-11-wp --revision <NUM>
```

   Here, `<NUM>` is the revision number, as displayed by the `helm history` command.

3. Now that we have identified a revision that we want to go back to, use the `helm rollback` command to change the current revision to `1`:

```
$ helm rollback chapter-11-wp 1
```

   The output that indicates success is very concise:

```
Rollback was a success! Happy Helming!
[[ausov@bastion wordpress]$
```

Figure 11.9: Successful rollback

4. As proof that the release was rolled back to its earlier configuration, let's see whether the Ingress object is present:

```
$ oc get ingress
```

   Since we first deployed the chart with no ingress support, it should not be surprising that we don't find it after rolling back to that initial revision:

```
[ausov@bastion wordpress]$ oc get ingress
No resources found in chapter-11-helm namespace.
```

Figure 11.10: Route is gone after rollback

5. Let's see what effect the rollback had on the current revision number:

```
$ helm ls
```

```
NAME            NAMESPACE          REVISION   UPDATED                                   STATUS
chapter-11-wp   chapter-11-helm    3          2024-06-17 02:28:32.964067209 -0400 EDT deployed
```

Figure 11.11: Release rollback confirmation

6. The effect on the revision history is as follows:

```
$ helm history chapter-11-wp
```

```
REVISION   UPDATED                    STATUS       CHART               APP VERSION   DESCRIPTION
1          Mon Jun 17 01:44:23 2024   superseded   wordpress-22.4.10   6.5.4         Install complete
2          Mon Jun 17 01:46:29 2024   superseded   wordpress-22.4.10   6.5.4         Upgrade complete
3          Mon Jun 17 02:28:32 2024   deployed     wordpress-22.4.10   6.5.4         Rollback to 1
```

Figure 11.12: Release revision history after a rollback

   Notice that even though we rolled back to revision 1, the current revision is now 3 with its description referencing the revision we "downgraded" to. This is similar to how deployment rollouts work in Kubernetes – release numbers can only go up, not down.

Dissecting a Helm chart release

One question that some of you may ask is: how does Helm keep track of all releases and their revisions? Where does it store its state? The answer is quite simple: secrets. Another mechanism that was considered by Helm developers involved the use of CRDs. However, due to the fact that some Helm users may not have permission to install them, it was decided to use the Secrets API for state persistence, as it requires the same namespace-scoped permissions as for installing charts.

Let's look at how to do it:

1. First, let's find the secret we need by listing all secrets in the current namespace:

```
$ oc get secret
```

2. The secret that stores the state of revision 1 of a release named RELEASE is named sh.helm.release.v1.<RELEASE>.v1. Let's extract its contents in the current directory:

```
$ oc extract --to . secret/sh.helm.release.v1.chapter-11-wp.v1
```

   Notice the dot (.) after --to in the preceding command. It references the current directory to which to extract the secret's content.

3. The secret contains only one key, release, which contains a gzipped descriptor of our release encoded in Base64. Let's decode it and store the output in a file named release.gz:

```
$ base64 -d release > release.gz
```

> On macOS, use base64 -di release -o release.gz or base64 -di release > release.gz. This is because macOS uses the FreeBSD version of the Base64 utility, which requires specifying an input file with the -i parameter.

4. Next, unpack it using gunzip and pipe it to any JSON parser (we used the json.tool Python module as an example, but any parser will do, for example, jq):

```
$ gunzip -c release.gz | python -m json.tool | less
```

   You will see a large JSON document that contains all information (such as Base64-encoded templates and values with defaults filled in) and metadata about the release. Because of the sheer size of the output, we're piping it to less for easier examination. Every upgrade creates a new secret to store a new release revision.

5. To conclude this exercise, use the helm uninstall command, or simply helm un:

```
$ helm un chapter-11-wp
```

Feel free to learn more by reading the blog article at [10].

Now that we know how to work with Helm charts written by a third party, the next logical step is to move on to writing our own charts. In the next section, we will develop a simple yet completely functional Helm chart that you will be able to install and share with other members of your team. Despite its simplicity, it will contain all the necessary components and be representative of how more complex charts are organized.

Writing Helm charts

Now that we have some idea of what Helm charts are and how they are structured, it is time to write a simple chart of our own. If you would rather skip all the explanation, use the following commands to copy the chart from this book's GitHub repository into your local folder:

```
$ mkdir ~/git
$ cd ~/git
$ git clone https://github.com/PacktPublishing/Learn-OpenShift-Second-Edition.
git
$ cd -
$ cp -r ~/git/Learn-OpenShift-Second-Edition/chapters/11/snippets/helm/
learning-ocp4-nginx .
$ cd learning-ocp4-nginx/
```

Next, jump to *step 12* in the *Adding templates* section, and only edit the `values.yaml` file as instructed. But if you want to put it together piece by piece, then follow along with these next steps.

Bootstrapping and exploring basic template functions

Helm provides a special command for creating a skeleton of a new chart so that you don't have to start from scratch. Let's use it to get started:

1. Let's create a basic folder structure for our new chart called `learning-ocp4-nginx`:

```
$ helm create learning-ocp4-nginx
```

2. Use the `tree` command to get a complete view of the hierarchical folder tree that was created. You may recognize file and directory names from the beginning of this chapter:

```
$ cd learning-ocp4-nginx/
$ tree
```

You should see the following hierarchy:

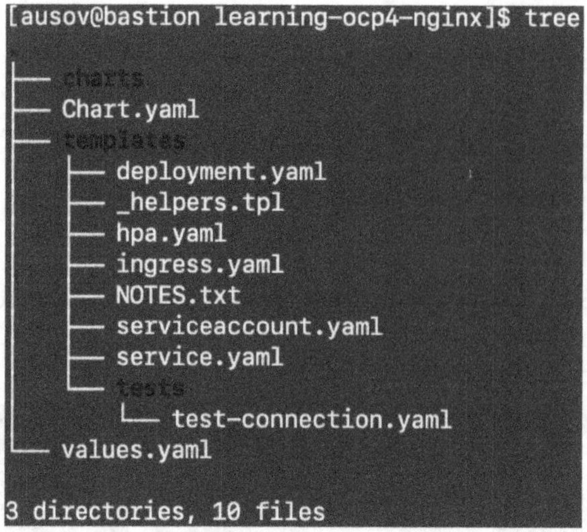

Figure 11.13: Helm chart skeleton

3. Let's start adapting it for our needs by removing the files we are not going to use or will recreate:

```
$ rm templates/*.yaml templates/NOTES.txt values.yaml
```

4. As an exercise, we will create a simple chart that will install Nginx on our demo cluster, customize its index page, and expose it to external clients. Create a metadata file named `Chart.yaml` with the contents from `chapters/11/snippets/helm/learning-ocp4-nginx/Chart.yaml` of the book's GitHub repository. The `appVersion` field in the file indicates the version of the app inside a chart, in our case, the Nginx server. For this file and any other from the rest of this chapter, you can just copy (`cp`) them over. Here's an example of cloning the repo into a local directory (unless you already have it elsewhere from previous chapters) and using its files:

```
$ mkdir ~/git
$ cd ~/git
$ git clone https://github.com/PacktPublishing/Learn-OpenShift-Second-Edition.git
$ cd -
$ cp ~/git/Learn-OpenShift-Second-Edition/chapters/11/snippets/helm/learning-ocp4-nginx/Chart.yaml .
```

5. Now let's discuss some of the basic functions offered by Helm's templating language. We will use a simple template as an example. The proper way to customize the index page of our web server is to store its contents in a ConfigMap and mount it as a volume inside the server's Pod. Create a file called `templates/cm.yml` with the contents from `chapters/11/snippets/helm/learning-ocp4-nginx/templates/cm.yml` of the book's GitHub repository, like this:

```
$ cp ~/git/Learn-OpenShift-Second-Edition/chapters/11/snippets/helm/learning-ocp4-nginx/templates/cm.yml templates/
```

Let's take a closer look at the manifest referenced previously. It contains the following elements:

Element	Description
`include`	Render a template from another file. The `learning-ocp4-nginx.fullname` function is declared in a file, `templates/_helpers.tpl`, which we will return to later in this section.
`indent`	Indent a line.
`nindent`	Same as `indent`, but with a leading newline.
`.Files.Glob`	A glob pattern that extracts the contents of files matching a certain pattern.
`AsConfig`	A helper method that injects the contents of a file as a `filename: contents` structure inside a ConfigMap. A counterpart to it, `AsSecret`, additionally encodes it in Base64.
`|`	Similar to UNIX and Linux pipelines, Helm pipelines serve as an easy way of chaining multiple functions together, sending the result of one to the input of another.

Table 11.4: Breakdown of controls from an example chart

Helm relies on the Go template language [15] and the Sprig templating engine [16]; refer to the references at the end of the chapter for more in-depth details.

Now comes the main part, where we create the rest of the templates and other files for our new chart.

Adding templates

We already created a ConfigMap template in the previous section. Now we need to add other templates and a few other files that our application will need:

1. For our application to be resilient, it needs to be managed by a workload controller. Due to its stateless nature, a Deployment object is the best choice. Prepare a file, `templates/deployment.yml`, with the contents from `chapters/11/snippets/helm/learning-ocp4-nginx/templates/deployment.yml` of the book's GitHub repository:

   ```
   $ cp ~/git/Learn-OpenShift-Second-Edition/chapters/11/snippets/helm/learning-ocp4-nginx/templates/deployment.yml templates/
   ```

   Notice the use of the `nindent` function for proper indentation on different levels of the Deployment's YAML manifest. You can also see how this manifest references parameters from the `values.yaml` file using the `.Values` object for fields that can be customized.

2. As you may recall from earlier in this book, the Nginx image we use as an example runs as root and, as such, requires the `anyuid` **security context constraint** (**SCC**). We used the `oc adm policy add-scc-to-user anyuid -z default` command to grant the default service account permission to use it. However, it can also be done by creating a role with use permission on that SCC. Let's take a file, `chapters/11/snippets/helm/learning-ocp4-nginx/templates/role.yml`, from this book's GitHub manifest and store it in a `templates/role.yml` file:

```
$ cp ~/git/Learn-OpenShift-Second-Edition/chapters/11/snippets/helm/
learning-ocp4-nginx/templates/role.yml templates/
```

3. Creating a role by itself doesn't make it useful – next, we have to create a RoleBinding that would bind that role to the dedicated service account whose manifest is provided later in this chapter. The manifest file is going to be called `templates/rolebinding.yml`; take the contents from `chapters/11/snippets/helm/learning-ocp4-nginx/templates/rolebinding.yml` of this book's GitHub repository:

```
$ cp ~/git/Learn-OpenShift-Second-Edition/chapters/11/snippets/helm/
learning-ocp4-nginx/templates/rolebinding.yml templates/
```

The `learning-ocp4-nginx.serviceAccountName` and `learning-ocp4-nginx.roleBindingName` templates referenced in the preceding manifest are defined in a special file further down.

4. It is recommended to create a dedicated service account for your application, or even multiple service accounts for different application components, so this is exactly what we are going to do, by copying the object's definition from `chapters/11/snippets/helm/learning-ocp4-nginx/templates/sa.yml` to `templates/sa.yml`:

```
$ cp ~/git/Learn-OpenShift-Second-Edition/chapters/11/snippets/helm/
learning-ocp4-nginx/templates/sa.yml templates/
```

> Using a dedicated service account instead of the default allows us to assign RBAC permissions more granularly, without potentially granting unnecessary access to the Kubernetes or OpenShift API to other Pods.

5. Next, we will need to create a service from the `chapters/11/snippets/helm/learning-ocp4-nginx/templates/svc.yml` manifest, which will be required for the next step. Store it in `templates/svc.yml`. Notice that we used the same helper template for the selector as for the deployment's selector earlier:

```
$ cp ~/git/Learn-OpenShift-Second-Edition/chapters/11/snippets/helm/
learning-ocp4-nginx/templates/svc.yml templates/
```

6. To expose our application to external users, we will need a route, whose manifest we will take from the `chapters/11/snippets/helm/learning-ocp4-nginx/templates/route.yml` file of this book's GitHub repository and store in a `templates/route.yml` file:

```
$ cp ~/git/Learn-OpenShift-Second-Edition/chapters/11/snippets/helm/
learning-ocp4-nginx/templates/route.yml templates/
```

7. The following resource is optional; however, it is recommended to include objects that can be used to verify whether your application was deployed correctly. Since Helm counts success when an application's resources have been created without API errors, it is unable to catch functional errors, when the application does not behave as intended, even though all of its Pods are running, for example. This is where it is useful to have a separate set of resources that are not a part of the application and don't get created during installation, but serve only the purpose of testing your application's proper functioning. For example, you may want to create a Pod that runs a simple `curl` or `wget` command to check connectivity to your application or parse its response for a specific body and/or header. The default test Pod uses `wget`, and the only thing we need to change is the argument passed to that command. Edit the file named `templates/tests/test-connection.yaml` to match the `chapters/11/snippets/helm/learning-ocp4-nginx/templates/tests/test-connection.yaml` file, provided in this book's GitHub repository, or just copy it over:

```
$ cp ~/git/Learn-OpenShift-Second-Edition/chapters/11/snippets/helm/
learning-ocp4-nginx/templates/tests/test-connection.yaml templates/tests/
```

8. Another file we are going to edit or copy over is `NOTES.txt`. We will customize the message that is going to be displayed on successful installation and upgrade to include the application's route, as you can see in the `chapters/11/snippets/helm/learning-ocp4-nginx/templates/NOTES.txt` file. This may not seem like much, but it demonstrates that you can include any information for the target users of your chart:

```
$ cp ~/git/Learn-OpenShift-Second-Edition/chapters/11/snippets/helm/
learning-ocp4-nginx/templates/NOTES.txt templates/
```

9. Previously, we listed the manifest for a RoleBinding object whose name contained a template construct. All templates referenced by the `include` function, including `learning-ocp4-nginx.serviceAccountName` and `learning-ocp4-nginx.roleBindingName`, are defined in the `_helpers.tpl` file, available at `chapters/11/snippets/helm/learning-ocp4-nginx/templates/_helpers.tpl`. Copy it into your `templates` directory, overwriting an existing one:

```
$ cp ~/git/Learn-OpenShift-Second-Edition/chapters/11/snippets/helm/
learning-ocp4-nginx/templates/_helpers.tpl templates/
```

10. Now that we have created all template files for our chart, we need to prepare the index file for our web application and the file that contains default values for all of our chart's parameters. Create a directory named `files`:

```
[ausov@bastion learning-ocp4-nginx]$ mkdir files
```

11. In it, create a file, files/index.html, with arbitrary content:

```
<h1>It works!</h1>
```

Or you can just take it from the repository:

```
$ cp ~/git/Learn-OpenShift-Second-Edition/chapters/11/snippets/helm/
learning-ocp4-nginx/files/index.html files/
```

12. Finally, let's recreate a file, values.yaml, with default parameter values for our chart. Copy the contents from chapters/11/snippets/helm/learning-ocp4-nginx/values.yaml. As before, replace the <CLUSTER_NAME> and <DOMAIN> placeholders with what makes sense for your environment:

```
$ cp ~/git/Learn-OpenShift-Second-Edition/chapters/11/snippets/helm/
learning-ocp4-nginx/values.yaml .
$ vi values.yaml
```

Our basic chart is now ready. Now it's time to test it in action.

Validation, installation, testing, and cleanup

One simple test that you can do to check that your chart doesn't contain any errors is to run the following command:

```
$ helm template . --debug | less
```

It will attempt to render all templates into manifest files, substituting references to values and templates, and display them. We have not provided the output here due to the size limit of this chapter.

Another useful command that checks your template for any errors and whether it follows best practices is helm lint (notice the dot indicating the current directory at the end of the following command):

```
[ausov@bastion learning-ocp4-nginx]$ helm lint .
```

As the following output indicates, there are no errors in our chart:

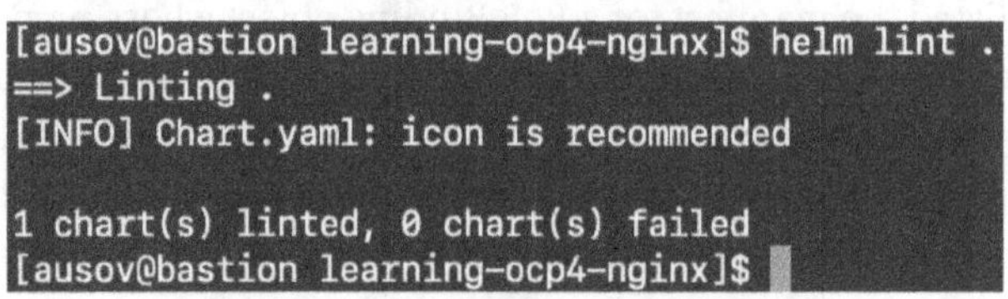

```
[ausov@bastion learning-ocp4-nginx]$ helm lint .
==> Linting .
[INFO] Chart.yaml: icon is recommended

1 chart(s) linted, 0 chart(s) failed
[ausov@bastion learning-ocp4-nginx]$
```

Figure 11.14: Chart linting successful

Now that our chart is ready, we can package and upload it to a repository for distribution, and/or install it right away. In the command that follows, chapter-11 is the release name and dot (.) is a reference to the current directory where the chart is located:

```
[ausov@bastion learning-ocp4-nginx]$ helm install chapter-11 .
```

As indicated by the following output, the chart was installed successfully, and the informational message from the `NOTES.txt` file is also displayed:

```
NAME: chapter-11
LAST DEPLOYED: Mon Jun 24 12:19:42 2024
NAMESPACE: chapter-11-helm
STATUS: deployed
REVISION: 1
NOTES:
Your application is accessible at nginx-demo.apps.ocp4.example.com
```

Figure 11.15: Demo chart installed successfully

Let's verify that the application has indeed started by executing `oc get po`:

```
NAME                                              READY   STATUS    RESTARTS   AGE
chapter-11-learning-ocp4-nginx-6864ffbd49-ddptt   1/1     Running   0          3s
```

Figure 11.16: Nginx Pod created by the demo chart

Call the URL with `index.html`:

```
$ curl nginx-demo.apps.<CLUSTER_NAME>.<DOMAIN>/index.html
```

As expected, the application responds with the content we packaged with our chart:

```
[ausov@bastion learning-op4-nginx]$ curl nginx-demo.apps.ocp4.example.com/index.html
<h1>It works!</h1>
```

Figure 11.17: Nginx deployed by the demo chart is serving requests

As mentioned earlier, `helm install` doesn't create resources defined in the `tests` folder. To run the tests, use the `helm test RELEASE_NAME` command:

```
$ helm test chapter-11
```

If you see output similar to the following, that means the test has passed:

```
NAME: chapter-11
LAST DEPLOYED: Mon Jun 24 12:19:42 2024
NAMESPACE: chapter-11-helm
STATUS: deployed
REVISION: 1
TEST SUITE:     chapter-11-learning-ocp4-nginx-test-connection
Last Started:   Mon Jun 24 16:03:02 2024
Last Completed: Mon Jun 24 16:03:04 2024
Phase:          Succeeded
NOTES:
Your application is accessible at nginx-demo.apps.ocp4.example.com
```

Figure 11.18: Demo chart passed a basic reachability test

Now, if you run oc get po again, you will see the new test Pod:

```
NAME                                              READY   STATUS      RESTARTS   AGE
chapter-11-learning-ocp4-nginx-6864ffbd49-ddptt   1/1     Running     0          3h43m
chapter-11-learning-ocp4-nginx-test-connection    0/1     Completed   0          13s
```

Figure 11.19: Test Pod left behind

Since that Pod's command doesn't start any long-running processes and just executes a one-off check, it will exit and change its status to `Completed`.

In order to package your chart for distribution, use this command:

```
$ helm package .
```

Don't forget the dot (`.`) at the end of the preceding command. It tells Helm to look for a chart's files in the current directory.

Now, if you list the contents of the current directory with `ls -ltr`, you will see a newly created archive with your chart:

```
[ausov@bastion learning-ocp4-nginx]$ ls -ltr
total 12
drwxr-xr-x. 2 ausov ausov    6 Jun 24 07:28 charts
-rw-r--r--. 1 ausov ausov  139 Jun 24 08:19 Chart.yaml
drwxr-xr-x. 2 ausov ausov   24 Jun 24 10:30 files
-rw-r--r--. 1 ausov ausov  447 Jun 24 11:56 values.yaml
drwxr-xr-x. 3 ausov ausov  177 Jun 24 12:19 templates
-rw-r--r--. 1 ausov ausov 2448 Jun 24 16:29 learning-ocp4-nginx-0.1.0.tgz
[ausov@bastion learning-ocp4-nginx]$
```

Figure 11.20: Demo chart archive ready for distribution

The `-l` option presents files as a list, `-t` sorts them by modification time, and `-r` reverses the output. This command is useful for easily identifying the most recently created or modified files, which end up at the very bottom of the list.

As the last step in our chart's life cycle, let's uninstall it and change back to the directory where we started:

```
$ helm un chapter-11
$ cd ..
```

This section marks the end of our brief discussion of Helm. While the chart we developed is very basic, the same approach always applies: first, identify the controls that you want to present to the users of your chart via parameters, and then replace the actual values in the manifest files with references to values from `values.yaml`.

Next in this chapter, we will cover Kustomize - another useful tool that provides a way to define a base configuration and environment-specific details. The section will be focused on hands-on work and code snippets, which we will upload to a brand-new Git repository at the end of this chapter, so paying attention to make sure files are put in the proper locations is critical.

Kustomize

When all you have is a single cluster, managing resources for your application is pretty trivial - you may store them in a Git repository and apply them via GitOps, making sure they always match the intended state stored in the repository. When the number of different environments and use cases grows, however, juggling different sets of manifests with environment-specific differences between them gets tiresome and error-prone. One solution to this problem is Kustomize - a CNCF graduated project that is implemented as both a `kubectl/oc` extension and a standalone binary, designed to separate common resources shared by all environments, or base, from differences (or overlays) tailored to different environments or use cases.

Applying kustomizations with the OpenShift CLI

In this exercise, we will create a Kustomize folder structure to support the following hierarchy:

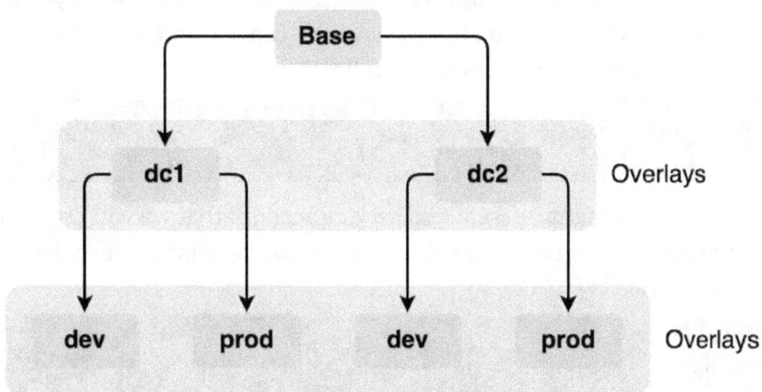

Figure 11.21: Sample Kustomize hierarchy

Here are the steps:

1. As before, let's create a separate project for this part of the chapter:

```
$ oc new-project chapter-11-kustomize
```

2. The next steps depend on whether you prefer a faster or slower route. If you'd rather skip all the details and end up with the working directory structure, just copy it from the repository, as shown next:

```
$ cp -r ~/git/Learn-OpenShift-Second-Edition/chapters/11/snippets/
kustomize/kustomize-nginx .
```

Then, jump straight to *step 14* in the *Setting up environment overlays* section, where you need to edit the `base/ingress.yml` file.

But if you're curious and are comfortable with building it step by step, start by creating a directory for all the files we're going to use during this exercise and change to it:

```
[ausov@bastion learning-ocp4]$ mkdir kustomize-nginx
[ausov@bastion learning-ocp4]$ cd kustomize-nginx
```

3. Inside that directory, create a new folder, `base`, which will contain the resources that kustomizations (stored in a different folder) will be applied to:

```
[ausov@bastion kustomize-nginx]$ mkdir base
```

Now let's populate that directory with manifests.

Preparing the base manifests

Now we're ready to create manifest files for the base of our layout:

1. Let's start with the Deployment, which will live in a file, `base/deployment.yml`, taken from the `chapters/11/snippets/kustomize/kustomize-nginx/base/deployment.yml` file of this book's repository. Assuming you already have the repository cloned from the *Writing Helm charts* section, the command would be the following:

```
$ cp ~/git/Learn-OpenShift-Second-Edition/chapters/11/snippets/kustomize/
kustomize-nginx/base/deployment.yml base/
```

2. The preceding Deployment references a service account that we will create in a separate file, `base/sa.yml` (use the `chapters/11/snippets/kustomize/kustomize-nginx/base/sa.yml` file from the repository):

```
$ cp ~/git/Learn-OpenShift-Second-Edition/chapters/11/snippets/kustomize/
kustomize-nginx/base/sa.yml base/
```

3. One part of exposing an application to external clients is to set up a service that serves as a consistent and single IP address for all communication. Prepare a file, `base/svc.yml`, using `chapters/11/snippets/kustomize/kustomize-nginx/base/svc.yml`, as a reference, or just copy it over:

```
$ cp ~/git/Learn-OpenShift-Second-Edition/chapters/11/snippets/kustomize/
kustomize-nginx/base/svc.yml base/
```

4. Another component is `Route`. In order for it to be managed by an ingress controller, so that it is always restored when deleted, we will create an Ingress object, which, in turn, will create a route upon instantiation. Take the file's contents from `chapters/11/snippets/kustomize/kustomize-nginx/base/ingress.yml` and store its definition in `base/ingress.yml`:

```
$ cp ~/git/Learn-OpenShift-Second-Edition/chapters/11/snippets/kustomize/
kustomize-nginx/base/ingress.yml base/
```

5. As in the previous exercise with Helm, we need to create a role that permits the use of the `anyuid` SCC. Create a file, `base/role.yml`, and copy the contents of `chapters/11/snippets/kustomize/kustomize-nginx/base/role.yml` to it:

```
$ cp ~/git/Learn-OpenShift-Second-Edition/chapters/11/snippets/kustomize/
kustomize-nginx/base/role.yml base/
```

6. We use the preceding role by creating a RoleBinding object, stored in a file, `chapters/11/snippets/kustomize/kustomize-nginx/base/rolebinding.yml`, that grants the permissions specified in it to the service account defined earlier. Copy its contents to `base/rolebinding.yml`:

```
$ cp ~/git/Learn-OpenShift-Second-Edition/chapters/11/snippets/kustomize/
kustomize-nginx/base/rolebinding.yml base/
```

7. Now use the following command to create two subdirectories – `base/files` (for files that are not OpenShift API manifests) and `base/patches` (for patches that customize the objects we created earlier):

```
[ausov@bastion kustomize-nginx]$ mkdir base/{fil,patch}es
```

8. There will be only one file in the `base/files` directory – `index.html` – which will be provided to our application via a ConfigMap object, which we will deal with in one of the subsequent steps. Add the following contents to it:

```
<h1>It works!</h1>
```

Or just copy it from the repository directory:

```
$ cp ~/git/Learn-OpenShift-Second-Edition/chapters/11/snippets/kustomize/
kustomize-nginx/base/files/index.html base/files/
```

9. Copy the `chapters/11/snippets/kustomize/kustomize-nginx/base/patches/deployment-scc-patch.yml` file to the `base/patches` folder:

```
$ cp ~/git/Learn-OpenShift-Second-Edition/chapters/11/snippets/kustomize/
kustomize-nginx/base/patches/deployment-scc-patch.yml base/patches/
```

It will add a special annotation to our Deployment that binds its Pods to the `anyuid` SCC. Notice the `~1` notation we used to encode `/` in the annotation's name. This is necessary in order for the patch operation to recognize it as part of the annotation, not a path separator.

> You have to create a role with the `use` verb permitted and RoleBinding objects for the service account used by the Deployment, because the preceding annotation by itself is not enough.

10. Now let's put everything we've created so far together. Take the `chapters/11/snippets/kustomize/kustomize-nginx/base/kustomization.yaml` file from this book's GitHub repository and copy it under the `base` directory:

```
$ cp ~/git/Learn-OpenShift-Second-Edition/chapters/11/snippets/kustomize/
kustomize-nginx/base/kustomization.yaml base/
```

Let's go over its contents:

- The `resources` section lists all resources that may be patched when this file is referenced by any overlays as their base. When you run `oc apply -k <DIRECTORY_WITH_KUSTOMIZE_FILE>`, it will apply all files from that list.
- The `configMapGenerator` construct is used to generate ConfigMaps from literal values, files, or environment variables. In our case, it generates a ConfigMap object from the contents of the `index.html` file using its name as the key.
- `labels` (supersedes `commonLabels`) is a list of labels and the modifiers that control their propagation through Pod templates and selectors. For example, the structure of the file tells Kustomize to include two labels – `role: frontend` and `app: nginx` – to every resource declared in the `kustomization.yaml` file. For workload controllers, of which Deployment is an example, `includeTemplates` also instructs Kustomize to include them in Pod templates, and `includeSelectors` controls whether to add them as selectors to workload resources and services as well.
- The `namespace` field sets the namespace for all resources listed in the `resources` section.
- The `patches` section describes where to apply specific patches, which can be defined either inline or in a separate file (as in our example). In the preceding snippet, we tell Kustomize to patch our deployment by adding an annotation that binds it to the `anyuid` SCC.
- Finally, `images` lists rules for overriding image names and tags by referencing them by the current names in workload resources or Pods. For example, the rule from the file just adds the `alpine` tag to the `nginx` image in our Deployment. As you will see in the next example, we could have used a different replacement name for a different scenario.

Now that we've prepared the base, let's move on to setting up overlays.

Setting up data center overlays

Overlays are how you override or extend resources defined in the base. Each overlay is a directory that contains manifests and/or patches to be applied on top of what is defined in the base. While base resources are generic and meant to provide a foundation for your project, overlays are more specific and tailored to their environments or other logical partitions. Follow these steps to create overlays for our imaginary data centers, `dc1` and `dc2`:

1. First, run the following command:

```
[ausov@bastion kustomize-nginx]$ mkdir -p overlays/dc{1,2}/base overlays/
dc2/base/patches
```

This will create a directory named `overlays`, which will hold subdirectories corresponding to different environments and data centers, just like they might in real life, with the `dc1` and `dc2` subdirectories for each of the data centers. Each of them will have a directory named `base` that will contain its own `kustomization.yaml` file referencing foundational (or base) resources for each of these data centers. On top of that, the second data center will also include a `patches` subdirectory inside `base` that will contain patches that adjust the resources from `base` according to some requirements that might exist for `dc2`.

2. Let's start filling up the structure we just created. First, we need `kustomization.yaml` for the `dc1` overlay's base, which we will take from `chapters/11/snippets/kustomize/kustomize-nginx/overlays/dc1/base/kustomization.yaml` and copy into an `overlays/dc1/base/kustomization.yaml` file:

```
$ cp ~/git/Learn-OpenShift-Second-Edition/chapters/11/snippets/kustomize/
kustomize-nginx/overlays/dc1/base/kustomization.yaml overlays/dc1/base/
```

3. Next, prepare its counterpart for `dc2`. Copy the `chapters/11/snippets/kustomize/kustomize-nginx/overlays/dc2/base/kustomization.yaml` file to `overlays/dc2/base/kustomization.yaml`:

```
$ cp ~/git/Learn-OpenShift-Second-Edition/chapters/11/snippets/kustomize/
kustomize-nginx/overlays/dc2/base/kustomization.yaml overlays/dc2/base/
```

4. The last element of the preceding base references a patch for the Deployment defined all the way at the top of our directory structure. The patch should be defined in a file, `overlays/dc2/base/patches/deployment-volume-patch.yml`, taken from the `chapters/11/snippets/kustomize/kustomize-nginx/overlays/dc2/base/patches/deployment-volume-patch.yml` file in the GitHub repository:

```
$ cp ~/git/Learn-OpenShift-Second-Edition/chapters/11/snippets/kustomize/
kustomize-nginx/overlays/dc2/base/patches/deployment-volume-patch.yml
overlays/dc2/base/patches/
```

All that the patch does is replace the path of the mount point with the Apache server's specific value, because Apache and Nginx read their web content from different locations. This is an example of how we may apply environment-specific settings to our manifests.

We now have two overlays for two of our data centers. As you may recall from *Figure 11.21*, there is a second layer to our setup – environments. We will tackle this in the next section.

Setting up environment overlays

Now let's prepare second-tier overlays for each of our overlays:

1. Essentially, we have two data centers, and each of them is split into two environments – `dev` and `prod`:

```
$ mkdir -p overlays/dc{1,2}/overlays/{dev,prod}/{fil,patch}es
```

The preceding command creates subdirectories for said overlays and two subdirectories in each of them – `files` and `patches`.

2. As before, each overlay should have its own `kustomization.yaml` file that references a base defined at some higher layer of the hierarchy. Copy the kustomization file for the dev environment of `dc1` from `chapters/11/snippets/kustomize/kustomize-nginx/overlays/dc1/overlays/dev/kustomization.yaml` to `overlays/dc1/overlays/dev/kustomization.yaml`:

```
$ cp ~/git/Learn-OpenShift-Second-Edition/chapters/11/snippets/kustomize/
kustomize-nginx/overlays/dc1/overlays/dev/kustomization.yaml overlays/
dc1/overlays/dev/
```

Notice that this kustomization file references the `overlays/dc1/base` directory as its base.

3. The next step is to prepare web content for the Nginx server that will be used to serve content from `dc1`'s dev environment – its location will be `overlays/dc1/overlays/dev/files/index.html`. Its contents are as follows:

```
<h1>DC1 DEV works!</h1>
```

Or you can simply copy it over from the repository:

```
$ cp ~/git/Learn-OpenShift-Second-Edition/chapters/11/snippets/kustomize/
kustomize-nginx/overlays/dc1/overlays/dev/files/index.html overlays/dc1/
overlays/dev/files/
```

4. The `kustomization.yaml` file we created for this overlay references a patch file, `deployment-requests-limits-patch.yml`, in the `patches` directory. Copy the `chapters/11/snippets/kustomize/kustomize-nginx/overlays/dc1/overlays/dev/patches/deployment-requests-limits-patch.yml` file to `overlays/dc1/overlays/dev/patches/deployment-requests-limits-patch.yml`:

```
$ cp ~/git/Learn-OpenShift-Second-Edition/chapters/11/snippets/kustomize/
kustomize-nginx/overlays/dc1/overlays/dev/patches/deployment-requests-
limits-patch.yml overlays/dc1/overlays/dev/patches/
```

As part of this exercise, we assume that our application requires a different amount of CPU and memory for dev and prod environments, which is explained by different amounts of traffic that they receive.

5. Now let's do the same for the prod environment and prepare another `kustomization.yaml` file under `overlays/dc1/overlays/prod`. The file's contents are available at `chapters/11/snippets/kustomize/kustomize-nginx/overlays/dc1/overlays/prod/kustomization.yaml`:

```
$ cp ~/git/Learn-OpenShift-Second-Edition/chapters/11/snippets/kustomize/
kustomize-nginx/overlays/dc1/overlays/prod/kustomization.yaml overlays/
dc1/overlays/prod/
```

6. The web content for this environment, stored in `overlays/dc1/overlays/prod/files/index.html`, will be different from the dev one:

```
<h1>DC1 PROD works!</h1>
```

   You can copy it from the repository, as before:

```
$ cp ~/git/Learn-OpenShift-Second-Edition/chapters/11/snippets/kustomize/kustomize-nginx/overlays/dc1/overlays/prod/files/index.html overlays/dc1/overlays/prod/files/
```

7. As with dev, we are going to patch our application's Deployment but give it more CPU and memory to account for a larger amount of traffic in prod. Copy the `chapters/11/snippets/kustomize/kustomize-nginx/overlays/dc1/overlays/prod/patches/deployment-requests-limits-patch.yml` file to `overlays/dc1/overlays/prod/patches/deployment-requests-limits-patch.yml`:

```
$ cp ~/git/Learn-OpenShift-Second-Edition/chapters/11/snippets/kustomize/kustomize-nginx/overlays/dc1/overlays/prod/patches/deployment-requests-limits-patch.yml overlays/dc1/overlays/prod/patches/
```

8. Now that we are finished with the `dc1` data center, let's move on to `dc2`. As with `dc1`, it will need its own `kustomization.yaml` file under `overlays/dc2/overlays/dev`, copied from `chapters/11/snippets/kustomize/kustomize-nginx/overlays/dc2/overlays/dev/kustomization.yaml`:

```
$ cp ~/git/Learn-OpenShift-Second-Edition/chapters/11/snippets/kustomize/kustomize-nginx/overlays/dc2/overlays/dev/kustomization.yaml overlays/dc2/overlays/dev/
```

9. The `dc2` overlay's kustomization file references the top-most `base` directory as its base, but similarly to `dc1`, it defines its own Deployment patch and `configMapGenerator`, as well as web content, which is defined next and stored in a `overlays/dc2/overlays/dev/files/index.html` file:

```
<h1>DC2 DEV works!</h1>
```

   The file can also be copied over using this command:

```
$ cp ~/git/Learn-OpenShift-Second-Edition/chapters/11/snippets/kustomize/kustomize-nginx/overlays/dc2/overlays/dev/files/index.html overlays/dc2/overlays/dev/files/
```

10. Next, copy the Deployment patch from `chapters/11/snippets/kustomize/kustomize-nginx/overlays/dc2/overlays/dev/patches/deployment-requests-limits-patch.yml` to `overlays/dc2/overlays/dev/patches/deployment-requests-limits-patch.yml`, which will be applied to the `dc2` dev kustomization:

```
$ cp ~/git/Learn-OpenShift-Second-Edition/chapters/11/snippets/kustomize/
kustomize-nginx/overlays/dc2/overlays/dev/patches/deployment-requests-
limits-patch.yml overlays/dc2/overlays/dev/patches/
```

11. The prod environment's kustomization file for `dc2` is provided in the `chapters/11/snippets/kustomize/kustomize-nginx/overlays/dc2/overlays/prod/kustomization.yaml` file and to be stored in `overlays/dc2/overlays/prod/kustomization.yaml`:

```
$ cp ~/git/Learn-OpenShift-Second-Edition/chapters/11/snippets/kustomize/
kustomize-nginx/overlays/dc2/overlays/prod/kustomization.yaml overlays/
dc2/overlays/prod/
```

12. As with other data centers and environments within those data centers, `dc2 prod` will serve its own web content. Store it in a `overlays/dc2/overlays/prod/files/index.html` file with the following contents:

```
<h1>DC2 PROD works!</h1>
```

Or copy it over like this:

```
$ cp ~/git/Learn-OpenShift-Second-Edition/chapters/11/snippets/kustomize/
kustomize-nginx/overlays/dc2/overlays/prod/files/index.html overlays/dc2/
overlays/prod/files/
```

13. Next, take the manifest located at `chapters/11/snippets/kustomize/kustomize-nginx/overlays/dc2/overlays/prod/patches/deployment-requests-limits-patch.yml` and copy it to a file, `overlays/dc2/overlays/prod/patches/deployment-requests-limits-patch.yml`, that defines a resource patch for our Deployment:

```
$ cp ~/git/Learn-OpenShift-Second-Edition/chapters/11/snippets/kustomize/
kustomize-nginx/overlays/dc2/overlays/prod/patches/deployment-requests-
limits-patch.yml overlays/dc2/overlays/prod/patches/
```

14. Finally, update the `base/ingress.yml` file with the correct ingress endpoint for your cluster.

Having set everything up, we can now see how Kustomize makes our lives easier.

Validation, testing, and cleanup

Now run the `tree` command and observe the directory hierarchy you have created. You should've ended up with the following structure:

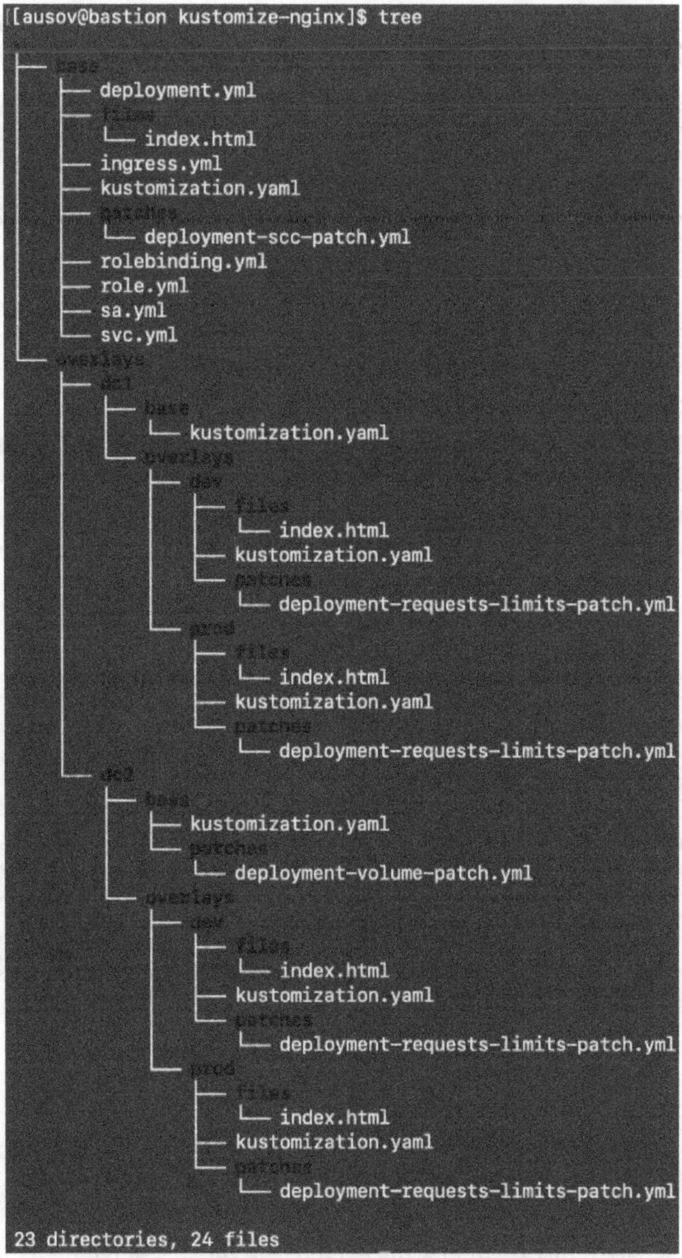

Figure 11.22: Example Kustomize directory structure

Now it's time to test our work. Use the following command to create resources for `dc1` data center's dev environment:

```
$ oc apply -k overlays/dc1/overlays/dev
```

When pointed to a directory with the `kustomization.yaml` file, the `apply -k` command combines the base and overlay, producing manifests that it then applies to a cluster:

```
serviceaccount/chapter-11-webserver created
role.rbac.authorization.k8s.io/chapter-11-use-anyuid-scc created
rolebinding.rbac.authorization.k8s.io/chapter-11-webserver-to-anyuid-scc created
configmap/chapter-11-webserver-index-page-6h8hf8g554 created
service/chapter-11-webserver created
deployment.apps/chapter-11-webserver created
ingress.networking.k8s.io/chapter-11-webserver created
```

Figure 11.23: Dev overlay for dc1 applied

Instead of querying the objects created previously by their types, such as `oc get deploy,po,sa,role,rolebinding,svc,ingress,cm`, there is an easier way of viewing them all at once. Just modify the `apply` command you ran earlier, replacing `apply` with `get`:

```
$ oc get -k overlays/dc1/overlays/dev
```

The preceding command will show you *only* objects that are declared explicitly and/or generated by Kustomize, which is especially handy if a namespace contains a lot of other unrelated resources.

As evidenced by the following screenshot, everything was applied successfully, and the application was able to start:

```
NAME                                    SECRETS   AGE
serviceaccount/chapter-11-webserver     0         6m36s

NAME                                                      CREATED AT
role.rbac.authorization.k8s.io/chapter-11-use-anyuid-scc   2024-06-26T20:22:29Z

NAME                                                                        ROLE                                AGE
rolebinding.rbac.authorization.k8s.io/chapter-11-webserver-to-anyuid-scc   Role/chapter-11-use-anyuid-scc      6m36s

NAME                                                   DATA   AGE
configmap/chapter-11-webserver-index-page-6h8hf8g554   1      6m36s

NAME                           TYPE        CLUSTER-IP     EXTERNAL-IP   PORT(S)   AGE
service/chapter-11-webserver   ClusterIP   172.30.88.45   <none>        80/TCP    6m36s

NAME                                   READY   UP-TO-DATE   AVAILABLE   AGE
deployment.apps/chapter-11-webserver   1/1     1            1           6m36s

NAME                                           CLASS    HOSTS                               ADDRESS
ingress.networking.k8s.io/chapter-11-webserver   <none>   website-demo.apps.ocp4.example.com   router-default.apps.ocp4.example.com
```

Figure 11.24: Kustomized resources

As a final check, send an HTTP `GET` request to the application's web server using `curl`:

```
$ curl website-demo.apps.<CLUSTER_NAME>.<DOMAIN>
$ curl -Is website-demo.apps.<CLUSTER_NAME>.<DOMAIN> | grep server
```

As you may remember, we didn't kustomize the default web server's implementation, which is Nginx, so we can see it in the reply:

```
[ausov@bastion kustomize-nginx]$ curl website-demo.apps.ocp4.example.com
<h1>DC1 DEV works!</h1>
[ausov@bastion kustomize-nginx]$ curl -Is website-demo.apps.ocp4.example.com | grep server
server: nginx/1.25.5
```

Figure 11.25: Application for dev in dc1 is responding

When we want to delete everything that we have set up, all it takes is using the `delete` subcommand, referencing the same `overlays` directory:

```
$ oc delete -k overlays/dc1/overlays/dev
```

Now let's repeat this exercise, but this time for a different data center and environment, `dc2` and `prod`, respectively:

```
$ oc apply -k overlays/dc2/overlays/prod
```

Go ahead and invoke the route of our application and check the value of the `server` header:

```
$ curl website-demo.apps.<CLUSTER_NAME>.<DOMAIN>
$ curl -Is website-demo.apps.<CLUSTER_NAME>.<DOMAIN> | grep server
```

Unlike `dc1 dev`, here we see that we have an Apache web server running instead of Nginx:

```
[ausov@bastion kustomize-nginx]$ curl website-demo.apps.ocp4.example.com
<h1>DC2 PROD works!</h1>
[ausov@bastion kustomize-nginx]$ curl -Is website-demo.apps.ocp4.example.com | grep server
server: Apache/2.4.59 (Unix)
```

Figure 11.26: Application for prod in dc2 is responding

As a reminder, this is accomplished by the following files:

- `overlays/dc2/base/kustomization.yaml`: Overrides the Deployment's image
- `overlays/dc2/base/patches/deployment-volume-patch.yml`: Changes the web content's mount point inside the Deployment's Pod(s)

As before, let's delete all the resources that were created to get back to a clean slate:

```
$ oc delete -k overlays/dc2/overlays/prod
```

So far, we have used Kustomize through the oc client. However, Kustomize is a separate tool and implements a binary of its own that you can download, install, and use locally:

```
$ cd
$ curl -s https://raw.githubusercontent.com/kubernetes-sigs/kustomize/master/hack/install_kustomize.sh | bash
$ sudo mv kustomize /usr/local/bin/
$ cd -
$ kustomize version
```

As a usage example, the following command takes the path to a base or overlay as an argument and renders all manifests from the base with kustomizations applied:

```
$ kustomize build overlays/dc2/overlays/prod/ | less
```

This approach may be useful for testing if all manifests are rendered correctly.

The next section deals with setting up a framework for a successful collaboration around Kustomize.

Basic kustomization workflow

Collaboration is an important part of development, be it complex applications or Kubernetes object manifests. It is challenging to support a code base in an organization with presence in multiple environments that span public/private clouds and virtualization platforms. Separation of concerns is a logical way to approach this problem.

Organizing kustomizations in Git

In this model, there may be one or more engineers working on the base part of the hierarchy and several engineers who are focused on kustomizations for individual environments and/or cloud/virtualization providers. One technical implementation of this approach is **Git submodules** [17], which this section will focus on. To demonstrate this, we will use GitHub as it is a popular choice for version tracking and collaboration. However, the steps are similar for other platforms, such as GitLab:

1. First, create two new repositories – one for your base resources and another for overlays. Click on your profile picture and then **Your profile** | **Repositories** | **New** and fill out the **Repository name** field. You may change the repository to public or leave it as private:

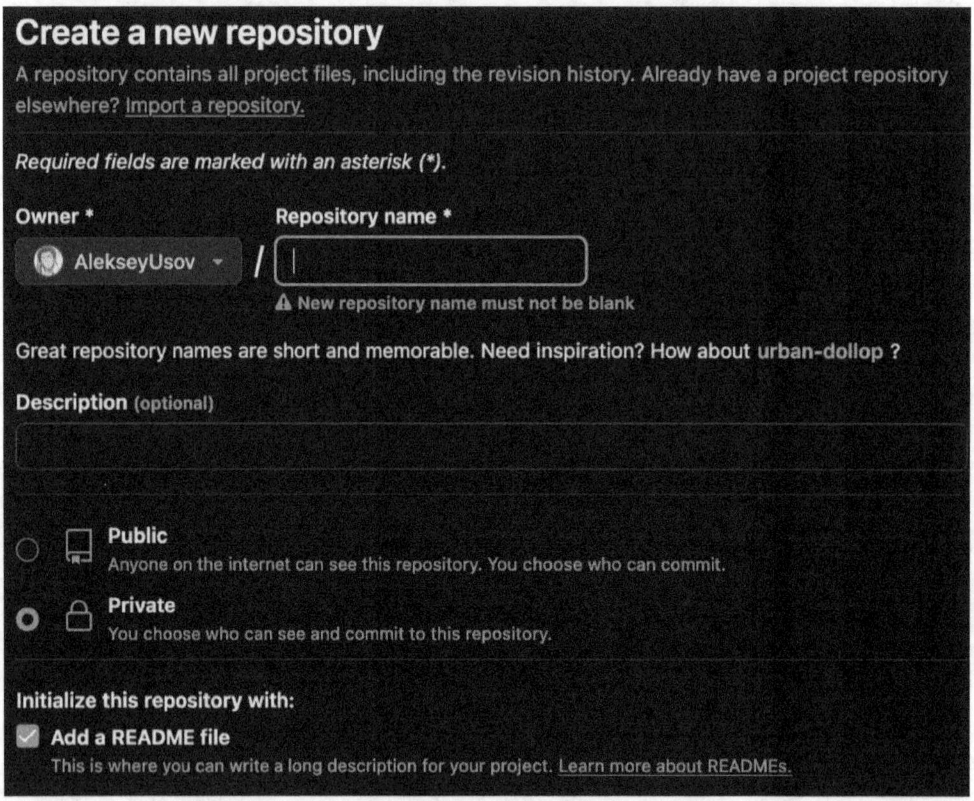

Figure 11.27: Creating a new repository in GitHub

In this section of the chapter, we use the names `learning-ocp4-kustomize-base` and `learning-ocp4-kustomize-overlays` for the base and overlays, respectively.

2. The next step is to add a public SSH key to your account so that you can interact with your repositories using the SSH protocol. Again, start with your profile picture, then navigate to **Settings** | **[Access] SSH and GPG keys** | **New SSH key** and paste your public key in the **Key** field, giving it a descriptive title:

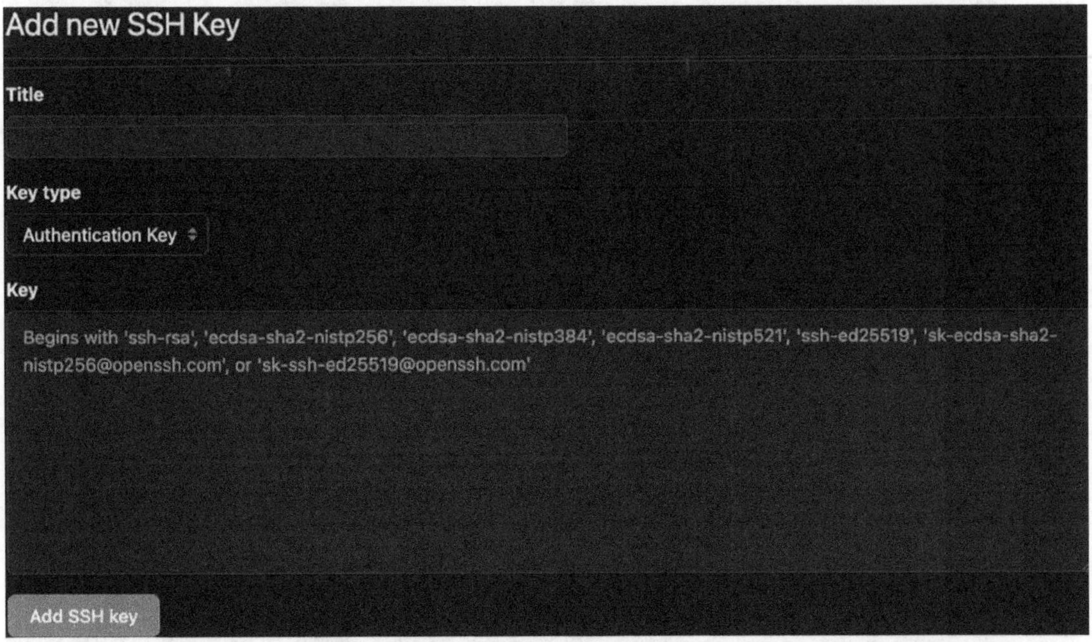

Figure 11.28: Adding an SSH key to a GitHub account

3. Now that we're done configuring GitHub, let's set everything up on our local machine. It is recommended to create a dedicated directory for all your Git projects (if you haven't already created one). Let's do so and change to it:

```
[ausov@bastion kustomize-nginx]$ mkdir ~/git
[ausov@bastion kustomize-nginx]$ cd ~/git/
```

4. You will also need to install the `git` client, if it isn't present already (use a command specific to your Linux distribution's package manager, for example, `apt-get install` for Debian-based systems or `yum`/`dnf install` for Fedora derivatives):

```
[ausov@bastion git]$ sudo yum -yq install git
```

5. Now we can clone the repositories, each at this point containing only a single file, `README.md`, added automatically when you created them:

```
[ausov@bastion git]$ git clone git@github.com:AlekseyUsov/learning-ocp4-kustomize-base.git
[ausov@bastion git]$ git clone git@github.com:AlekseyUsov/learning-ocp4-kustomize-overlays.git
```

6. Recursively (`-r`) copy the contents of the top-most `overlays` directory to the corresponding repository and change to it:

```
[ausov@bastion git]$ cp -r ~/learning-ocp4/kustomize-nginx/overlays/*
learning-ocp4-kustomize-overlays/
[ausov@bastion git]$ cd learning-ocp4-kustomize-overlays
```

7. Stage (add) the changes, commit them, and push them:

```
[ausov@bastion learning-ocp4-kustomize-overlays]$ git add .
[ausov@bastion learning-ocp4-kustomize-overlays]$ git commit -m 'Added
overlays'
[ausov@bastion learning-ocp4-kustomize-overlays]$ git push
```

> Notice the dot (`.`) at the end of the `git add .` command. It means "recursively stage all files and directories in the current directory."

8. Now let's upload the base. Change to the `base` repository and copy the contents of the top-most `base` directory inside it:

```
[ausov@bastion learning-ocp4-kustomize-overlays]$ cd ../learning-ocp4-
kustomize-base
[ausov@bastion learning-ocp4-kustomize-base]$ cp -r ~/learning-ocp4/
kustomize-nginx/base .
```

9. Now, in order to add the `overlays` repository as a submodule to the `base` repository, run the following command:

```
[ausov@bastion learning-ocp4-kustomize-base]$ git submodule add git@
github.com:AlekseyUsov/learning-ocp4-kustomize-overlays.git overlays
```

10. Use the `tree` command to check that the resulting hierarchy matches the structure depicted in *Figure 11.21*.

11. Before we submit the changes to GitHub, let's inspect how Git tracks this submodule. Take a look inside the hidden file named `.gitmodules` and use the `git diff` command to examine how Git sees our submodule:

```
[ausov@bastion learning-ocp4-kustomize-base]$ cat .gitmodules
[ausov@bastion learning-ocp4-kustomize-base]$ git diff --cached overlays/
[ausov@bastion learning-ocp4-kustomize-base]$ git diff --cached
--submodule
```

This is what the output of these commands looks like in our lab:

```
[ausov@bastion learning-ocp4-kustomize-base]$ cat .gitmodules
[submodule "overlays"]
        path = overlays
        url = git@github.com:AlekseyUsov/learning-ocp4-kustomize-overlays.git
[ausov@bastion learning-ocp4-kustomize-base]$
[ausov@bastion learning-ocp4-kustomize-base]$ git diff --cached overlays/
diff --git a/overlays b/overlays
new file mode 160000
index 0000000..fbc0c33
--- /dev/null
+++ b/overlays
@@ -0,0 +1 @@
+Subproject commit fbc0c333c7f2b6c09bb0833b7136c9492fe11a17
[ausov@bastion learning-ocp4-kustomize-base]$ git diff --cached --submodule
diff --git a/.gitmodules b/.gitmodules
new file mode 100644
index 0000000..09cf35d
--- /dev/null
+++ b/.gitmodules
@@ -0,0 +1,3 @@
+[submodule "overlays"]
+       path = overlays
+       url = git@github.com:AlekseyUsov/learning-ocp4-kustomize-overlays.git
Submodule overlays 0000000...fbc0c33 (new submodule)
[ausov@bastion learning-ocp4-kustomize-base]$
```

Figure 11.29: Git submodule as seen by Git

Based on the preceding output, we can see the following:

- The URL (`url`) from where the submodule's code will be cloned when we recursively clone the `base` repository.
- The path where the submodule's code will be cloned locally.
- A reference to the submodule's `commit` ID. The `overlay` repository was recognized by Git as a subproject, which means that it will not be staged when we run `git add .`.

12. Now let's stage (add), commit, and push the updates to the `base` repository:

```
[ausov@bastion learning-ocp4-kustomize-base]$ git add .
[ausov@bastion learning-ocp4-kustomize-base]$ git commit -am 'Added base resources and overlays submodule'
[ausov@bastion learning-ocp4-kustomize-base]$ git push
```

13. Let's see what it looks like on GitHub. Go to the base repository's page:

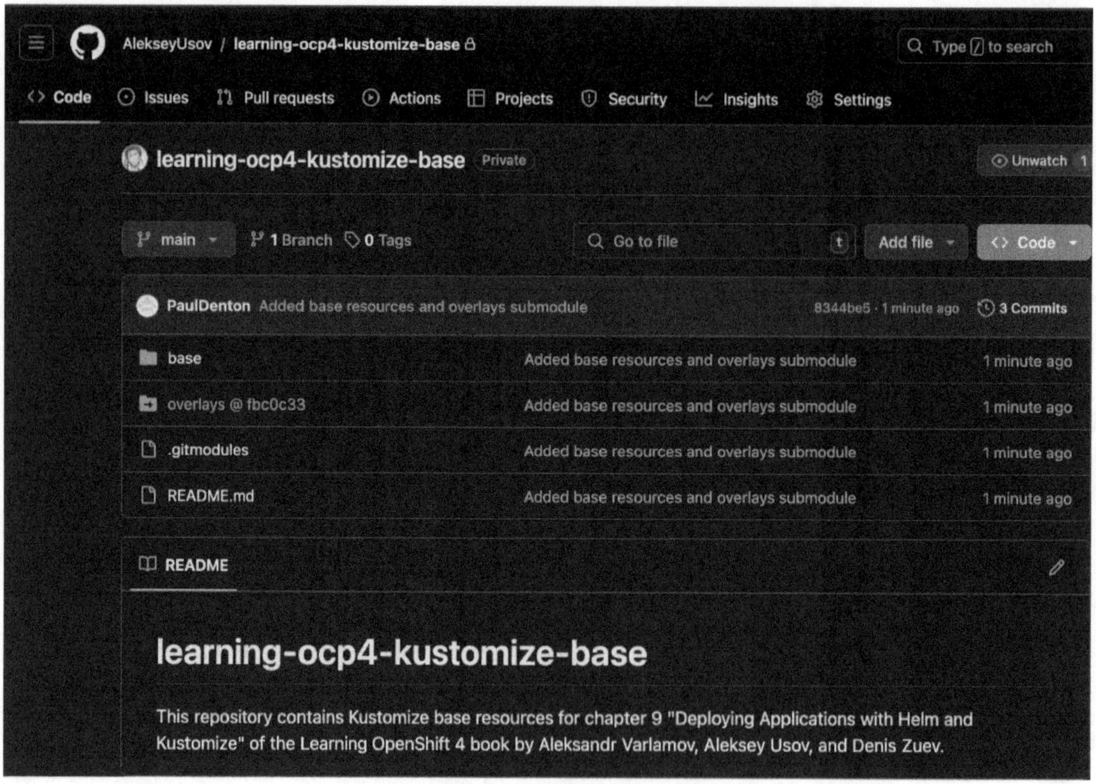

Figure 11.30: Git submodule on GitHub

Notice that instead of a regular subfolder that would contain overlays, had we not split the base and overlays into two different projects, we have a reference to the commit ID of the `overlays` project.

Workflow demo

Now let's imagine that we are collaborating with another developer. While we manage the base resources, they work on environment-specific details. Since we only have one local machine, we will simulate this scenario with two separate directories:

1. First, we are going to clone the `base` repository as though we are going to use its manifests to spin up an application in one of our environments. Change back to the `git` directory and clone the `base` repository into a directory under the same name. This is necessary because otherwise, Git would throw an error that the `learning-ocp4-kustomize-base` directory already exists, so we would have to use a different name. Again, this is only due to the nature of our exercise, where we use the same machine and shared directory for all our projects:

```
[ausov@bastion learning-ocp4-kustomize-base]$ cd ..
[ausov@bastion git]$ git clone git@github.com:AlekseyUsov/learning-ocp4-kustomize-base.git base
```

2. Change inside the new directory and view the project's structure:

```
[ausov@bastion git]$ cd base/
[ausov@bastion base]$ tree
```

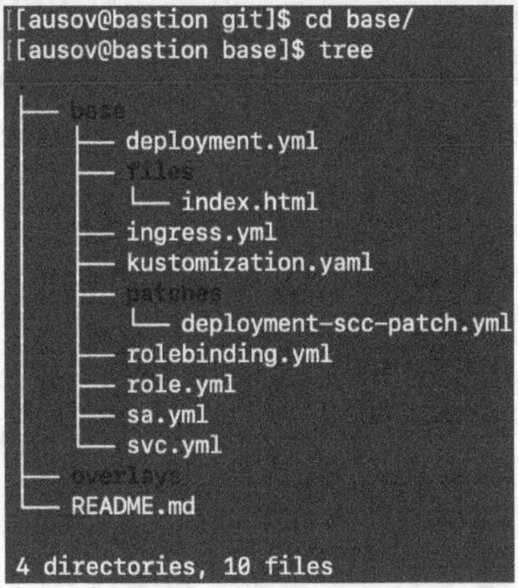

Figure 11.31: Base structure

Strange: there are no overlays, just an empty directory. This is because we didn't clone the project recursively, which we could have done with the `--recurse-submodules` option. We can still do that later; all it takes is the following command:

```
[ausov@bastion base]$ git submodule update --init
```

3. In our imaginary scenario, one of the developers noticed that the application keeps getting killed by an OOM killer due to the low memory limit or being throttled on CPU. Placing ourselves in their shoes, let's change into the `overlays` repository, located one directory layer above. In the real world, this would be that developer's machine:

```
[ausov@bastion base]$ cd ../learning-ocp4-kustomize-overlays/
```

4. Change the CPU and memory limits in the `dc1/overlays/prod/patches/deployment-requests-limits-patch.yml` patch file to `1200m` and `1.5Gi`, respectively. Commit and push the changes:

```
[ausov@bastion learning-ocp4-kustomize-overlays]$ git commit -am
'Increased CPU and RAM limits for DC1 prod'
[ausov@bastion learning-ocp4-kustomize-overlays]$ git push
```

> Since we are not adding any new files, we can combine staging and committing into one operation by adding an `-a` (add) argument to the `git commit` command.

5. Switching back to the original developer who works on base resources, navigate to the submodule's directory inside the `base` repository, switch to the `main` branch, pull the updates, and verify them:

```
[ausov@bastion learning-ocp4-kustomize-overlays]$ cd ../base/overlays
[ausov@bastion overlays]$ git branch main
[ausov@bastion overlays]$ git pull
[ausov@bastion overlays]$ git log -1 -p
```

As you can see, our changes have successfully been consolidated into our base project by means of a submodule:

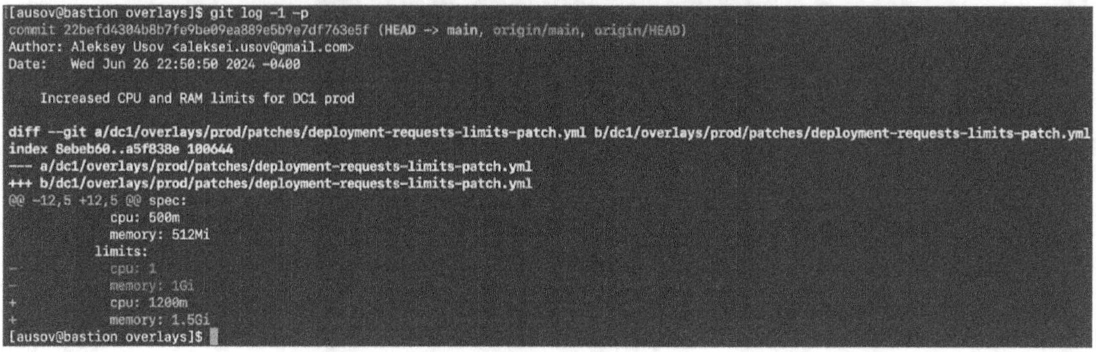

```
[ausov@bastion overlays]$ git log -1 -p
commit 22befd4304b8b7fe9be09ea889e5b9e7df763e5f (HEAD -> main, origin/main, origin/HEAD)
Author: Aleksey Usov <aleksei.usov@gmail.com>
Date:   Wed Jun 26 22:50:50 2024 -0400

    Increased CPU and RAM limits for DC1 prod

diff --git a/dc1/overlays/prod/patches/deployment-requests-limits-patch.yml b/dc1/overlays/prod/patches/deployment-requests-limits-patch.yml
index 8ebeb60..a5f838e 100644
--- a/dc1/overlays/prod/patches/deployment-requests-limits-patch.yml
+++ b/dc1/overlays/prod/patches/deployment-requests-limits-patch.yml
@@ -12,5 +12,5 @@ spec:
             cpu: 500m
             memory: 512Mi
           limits:
-            cpu: 1
-            memory: 1Gi
+            cpu: 1200m
+            memory: 1.5Gi
[ausov@bastion overlays]$
```

Figure 11.32: Git change log

This is how two or more developers can easily share responsibilities and collaborate on kustomizations to applications. Although convenient, using submodules is not the only way of implementing that – you can also use the same repository.

This concludes the topic of Kustomize and this chapter. Remember that each tool has its own limitations, and Kustomize is no exception. While it may be convenient for small-to-medium-scale projects, it doesn't scale very well and may become hard to maintain as your scope grows. Another caveat to keep in mind is that, unlike Helm, Kustomize doesn't support templating, and it is more like a simple configuration management tool.

Summary

In this chapter, we have explored two important tools for deploying applications to OpenShift and Kubernetes – Helm and Kustomize. Helm is a full-blown package manager for Kubernetes that mimics the features found in its OS-level counterparts, such as `apt`, `yum`, or Zipper: dependency resolution, metadata, installation/uninstallation, upgrades, repository management/search, and integrity validation via signatures. Its powerful templating engine enables you to apply the same chart to different scenarios, potentially installing multiple instances of it on the same cluster.

Kustomize, on the other hand, is there to help you when you have a common set of manifests for your environments, but when each of these environments (or overlays) has subtle differences. It doesn't have a templating mechanism, so applying it at scale may be complicated (the number of files to track grows very quickly with the number of different sites, environments, and so on).

Both Helm and Kustomize lend themselves well to collaboration when different members of the same team can work on charts and library charts or on base and overlays for Kustomize. Such collaboration is typically facilitated by a version control system such as Git and CI/CD pipelines with an approval workflow.

In the next chapter, we will discuss how logging works in OpenShift and what extra components are typically used in OpenShift to collect, store, visualize, and ship logs to a different location.

References

To learn more about the topics that were covered in this chapter, take a look at the following resources:

- [1] *Helm project's home page*: `https://helm.sh/`
- [2] *CloudNativePG*: `https://cloudnative-pg.io/`
- [3] *Artifact Hub*: `https://artifacthub.io/`
- [4] *OperatorHub*: `https://operatorhub.io/`
- [5] *The Chart.yaml File*: `https://helm.sh/docs/topics/charts/#the-chartyaml-file`
- [6] *The Chart File Structure*: `https://helm.sh/docs/topics/charts/#the-chart-file-structure`
- [7] *Installing Helm*: `https://helm.sh/docs/intro/install/`
- [8] *Helm CLI releases*: `https://github.com/helm/helm/releases/latest`
- [9] *how to add helm hub repo with helm 3.x*: `https://github.com/helm/hub/issues/208`
- [10] *Helm Under The Hood: Storage Using Secrets*: `https://codeengineered.com/blog/2020/helm-secret-storage/`
- [11] *Role-based access to security context constraints*: `https://docs.redhat.com/en/documentation/openshift_container_platform/4.16/html/authentication_and_authorization/managing-pod-security-policies#role-based-access-to-ssc_configuring-internal-oauth`
- [12] *Composing and Customizing Resources*: `https://kubernetes.io/docs/tasks/manage-kubernetes-objects/kustomization/#composing-and-customizing-resources`
- [13] *Kubectl and Kustomize CLI reference*: `https://kubectl.docs.kubernetes.io/references/`
- [14] *Kubectl and Kustomize guides*: `https://kubectl.docs.kubernetes.io/guides/`
- [15] *Go template documentation*: `https://pkg.go.dev/text/template?utm_source=godoc`
- [16] *Sprig Function Documentation*: `https://masterminds.github.io/sprig/`
- [17] *Git Tools - Submodules*: `https://git-scm.com/book/en/v2/Git-Tools-Submodules`

Quiz

Test your understanding of Helm and Kustomize with this quick quiz. Remember, some questions may have more than one correct answer!

1. Which file contains metadata of a Helm chart?
    a. `metadata.xml`
    b. `Chart.yml`
    c. `Chart.yaml`
    d. `chart.yaml`
2. Which Git command(s) clone all submodules of a repository?
    a. `git clone -r <REPOSITORY_URL>`
    b. `git clone --recurse-submodules <REPOSITORY_URL>`
    c. `git pull --recursive <REPOSITORY_URL>`
    d. `git submodule update --init`
3. Which parameter(s) of the `labels` directive in `kustomization.yaml` control the propagation of labels to selectors?
    a. `updateSelectors`
    b. `selectors`
    c. `includeSelectors`
    d. None of the above
4. Which command(s) create resources in OpenShift from kustomizations?
    a. `oc create -k <KUSTOMIZATION_DIR>`
    b. `oc apply -k <KUSTOMIZATION_DIR>`
    c. `kustomize render <KUSTOMIZATION_DIR>`
    d. `kustomize build <KUSTOMIZATION_DIR> | oc apply -f -`

Answers

1. **c.** The correct filename is `Chart.yaml` and it is case-sensitive.
2. **b** and **d.** The question doesn't specify whether the repository is already cloned, so both b and d are correct.
3. **c.** The only correct answer is `includeSelectors`; the others are non-existent.
4. **b** and **d.** We used the `oc apply -k` command several times during the course of this chapter, and although we haven't used the `kustomize build KUSTOMIZATION_DIR | oc apply -f -` command, it will work too as the `build` subcommand produces rendered manifests with kustomizations applied that can be passed to either `oc apply` or `oc create`.

Part 3

Logging, Monitoring, Observability, and Advanced OpenShift Services

This part's goal is to teach you how to monitor your applications, as well as to centrally manage and search different types of logs to assist with troubleshooting. It continues with a discussion about service meshes and how they help pinpoint bottlenecks and cascading errors in a microservice architecture. Finally, you will learn about other services provided by OpenShift that can enhance the developer experience. This chapter is critical, as observability is one of the most important considerations of any enterprise. Also, certain business cases can greatly benefit from services not included in a basic installation of OpenShift.

This part of the book includes the following chapters:

12

Logging in OpenShift

Applications running on OpenShift and its various subsystems produce a large amount of log data, which has to be collected, stored, indexed, and analyzed. Log management is necessary not just for developers and infrastructure engineers, but for compliance as well. This can be done locally, using a storage backend managed by its own operator, or by forwarding logs to a remote system, such as Loki, Elasticsearch, Amazon CloudWatch, Apache Kafka, Splunk **HTTP Event Collector** (**HEC**), or syslog. In this chapter, you will learn about the architecture of logging in OpenShift, its components, such as Loki and Vector, as well as how to configure OpenShift to send logs to a centralized location for further analysis and retention. Its importance is emphasized by the fact that the need for centralized log storage and analysis grows with the number of applications and is a regulatory requirement in all major jurisdictions.

We'll cover the following main topics:

- Understanding logging
- Configuring logging

Technical requirements

In this chapter, you will need the following:

- Internet access
- Bash shell (other shells work as well)
- OpenShift 4.16 (preferably a multinode cluster, similar to the one we built in *Chapter 3*, *Getting Started with OpenShift*)
- Firefox (recommended) or any other web browser
- An active Red Hat subscription to view Red Hat KB articles

Access to this book's GitHub repository can be found at `https://github.com/PacktPublishing/Learn-OpenShift-Second-Edition`.

Understanding logging

Logs are the data produced by well-designed software at runtime. They can tell us a lot about an application's operation, its health, how much stress it's under, and sometimes even leak sensitive data when improperly configured. All of that makes logs indispensable for troubleshooting, forensics, and auditing. In OpenShift, log data is produced not just by applications running on a cluster, but by OpenShift's internal components as well. This brings us to the topic of organizing logs that originate from many sources in a distributed environment.

Challenges of managing logs in a distributed environment

In today's complex IT landscape, applications and infrastructure are increasingly distributed across multiple servers, virtual machines, and containers. This distributed nature brings with it a host of challenges when it comes to managing logs.

One of the most significant issues is log sprawl. With numerous components generating logs, the volume of log data can quickly become overwhelming. Managing logs across different servers, each with its own log format and retention policies, can be a daunting task. This complexity often leads to data fragmentation, making it difficult to correlate events across different systems.

In a distributed environment, a single user action or system event can trigger multiple log entries across various components. To understand the complete picture and troubleshoot issues effectively, it's crucial to correlate these logs. However, this can be a time-consuming and error-prone process without the right tools and infrastructure.

The lack of centralized log management often results in inefficient troubleshooting and performance analysis. When logs are scattered across multiple systems, identifying the root cause of an issue can be a needle-in-a-haystack scenario. Moreover, without a unified view of log data, it's challenging to monitor application performance, detect anomalies, and optimize resource utilization.

The benefits of centralized logging

To address the challenges outlined, centralized logging emerges as a crucial solution. By aggregating logs from various sources into a single repository, organizations can gain a comprehensive view of their IT environment. Centralized logging offers the following benefits:

- **Improved troubleshooting and problem-solving:** Centralized logging provides a unified platform to search, filter, and analyze logs from different components. This enables IT teams to quickly identify the root cause of issues by correlating log entries across systems. With advanced search capabilities, they can easily pinpoint specific events, errors, or performance bottlenecks.
- **Enhanced security and compliance:** Log data is invaluable for security investigations. Centralized logging helps organizations comply with regulatory requirements by ensuring proper log retention and access control. By analyzing log data, security teams can detect suspicious activities, identify potential threats, and respond promptly to incidents.
- **Better application performance monitoring:** Centralized logging empowers organizations to gain insights into application performance. By analyzing log data, IT teams can monitor response times, error rates, and resource utilization. This information is essential for identifying

performance bottlenecks, optimizing resource allocation, and ensuring optimal application performance.

Real-world use cases

To illustrate the tangible benefits of centralized logging, let's explore some real-world scenarios:

- **E-commerce company:** A large e-commerce company was struggling with frequent application crashes and slow performance. By implementing centralized logging, they were able to quickly identify the root cause of issues, such as database overload or network congestion. This led to significant improvements in website uptime and customer satisfaction.
- **Financial institution:** To comply with strict regulatory requirements, a financial institution needed to maintain detailed logs of all transactions and system activities. Centralized logging helped them meet compliance standards by providing a centralized repository for log data, ensuring proper retention, and enabling efficient audits.
- **Cloud-native application development team:** A development team building cloud-native applications faced challenges with debugging and troubleshooting in a dynamic containerized environment. Centralized logging provided a unified view of logs from different containers, allowing them to quickly identify and resolve issues, accelerating the development cycle.

By understanding the challenges of managing logs in a distributed environment and recognizing the compelling benefits of centralized logging, organizations can make informed decisions about their log management strategy. In the next section, we will explore how the **Cluster Logging Operator** (**CLO**) and other operators can help implement centralized logging in OpenShift 4.

Configuring logging

Setting up a centralized logging solution on OpenShift requires several steps, which include installing necessary operators and creating certain **Custom Resources** (**CRs**). In this section, we will walk you through this process step by step, and by the end of it, we will have a fully functional log management engine running on our cluster.

When deciding on the location (local versus remote), backend, and storage size, the following factors must be considered:

- Who is going to be the **owner** of the data? Is it application developers or security people who have their own log store?
- **Regulatory requirements** – for instance, is it allowed to send logs to a public cloud provider?
- **Data retention** – how much data do we want to keep? While application developers may only need a day's worth of data, especially for non-production environments, regulators usually have very strict requirements as to how far back in time they must be able to search the logs for auditing purposes.
- **Log verbosity** – the granularity of our logs. Higher verbosity means a larger volume of data, which has a big impact on the storage backends' size.
- **Types of logs to collect:** OpenShift clusters generate logs of the following types:

- **Application**: Produced by application containers running in non-default namespaces.
- **Infrastructure**: Produced by workloads running in `openshift-*`, `kube-*`, and `default` namespaces.
- **Audit**: Produced by each node's audit subsystem (`auditd`), as well as `openshift-apiserver` and `kube-apiserver` services.

On a high level, the process of configuring logging on OpenShift consists of three steps:

1. Installing a log store operator, unless you plan on sending all logs to a remote system. We will use the Loki operator, which is the recommended log store provider in OpenShift.
2. Installing the CLO for collecting logs.
3. Installing the **Cluster Observability Operator** (COO) for enhanced monitoring and visualization.

Elasticsearch and its operator, long used as a log storage backend, were deprecated in OpenShift 4.8/Logging 5.4.3, and now the recommended backend is provided by the **Loki** Operator, which we will install and configure as the log store backend in this section. Before OpenShift 4.8, the default logging stack included Elasticsearch as a log store and search engine, Fluentd for collecting logs from nodes, and Kibana for visualizing them. Kibana comes as a separate service with its own dashboards. Loki, on the other hand, integrates itself into the OpenShift console via a plugin, so logs can now be accessed from the same UI. Developed by Grafana Labs, it was designed to resemble Prometheus.

Now that we have a high-level plan, let's start by installing the Loki operator to store logs collected from our cluster's components and applications.

Installing the Loki operator

Follow these steps to deploy the Loki Operator on OpenShift:

1. First, go to **OperatorHub** and type `loki` in the search bar. We will use the official operator supported by Red Hat:

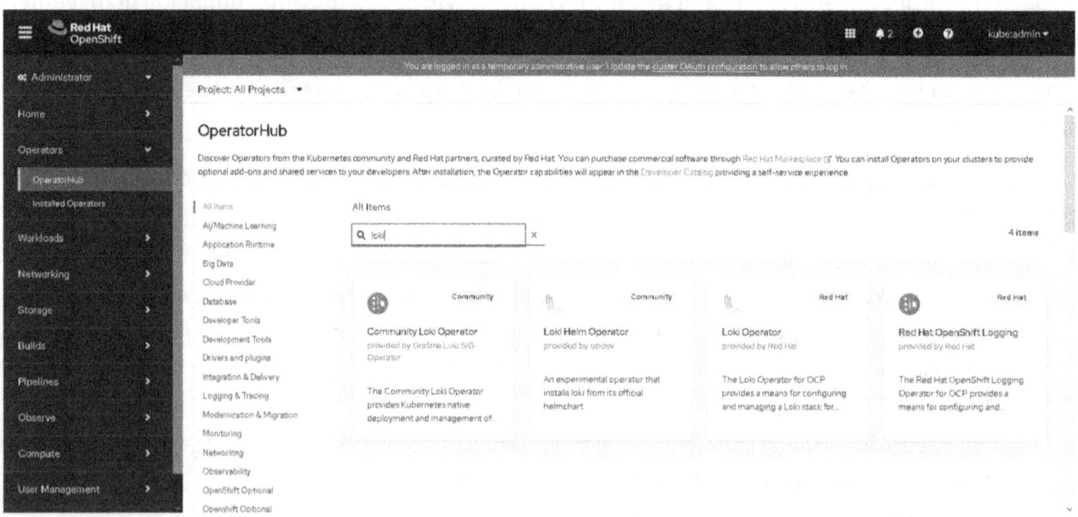

Figure 12.1: Finding Loki Operator in OperatorHub

2. After clicking on the operator's tile and then **Install**, you will have the opportunity to select the update channel, version, installation mode, and other settings. We recommend enabling cluster monitoring on the operator's target namespace and changing **Update approval** to **Manual** to have more control over updates:

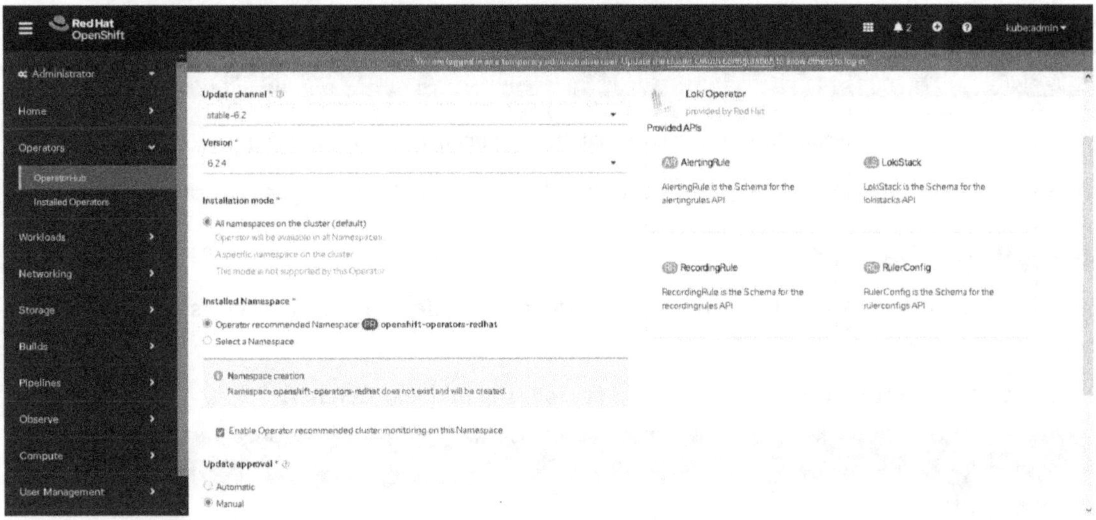

Figure 12.2: Loki Operator's target namespace, cluster monitoring, and update approval

3. Click **Install** again and wait for an install plan to get generated. Use the following command to view the operator's `OperatorGroup`, `Subscription`, and `InstallPlan` resources:

```
$ oc get og,sub,ip -n openshift-operators-redhat
```

You should see output similar to the following screenshot:

```
NAME                                                                  AGE
operatorgroup.operators.coreos.com/openshift-operators-redhat-jgqk9   30s

NAME                                                 PACKAGE         SOURCE              CHANNEL
subscription.operators.coreos.com/loki-operator      loki-operator   redhat-operators    stable-6.2

NAME                                              CSV                      APPROVAL   APPROVED
installplan.operators.coreos.com/install-zngkh    loki-operator.v6.2.4     Manual     false
```

Figure 12.3: Install plan is generated and requires manual approval

4. Use the following command to approve the install plan:

```
$ oc patch ip/install-zngkh -p '{"spec": {"approved": true}}' --type
merge -n openshift-operators-redhat
```

5. Now list pods in the operator's namespace:

```
$ oc get po -n openshift-operators-redhat
```

About a minute after approving the plan, the operator should install, and you will see a single pod running:

```
NAME                                            READY   STATUS    RESTARTS   AGE
loki-operator-controller-manager-75f9cf44df-hcdln   2/2     Running   0          51s
```

Figure 12.4: Loki Operator controller manager is up and running

Now that we have installed the log store operator, let's move on to the logging operator.

Installing the CLO

The next step is to install the CLO, which will perform log collection. The process is similar to installing the Loki Operator:

1. Go to **OperatorHub** and type `openshift logging` in the search bar:

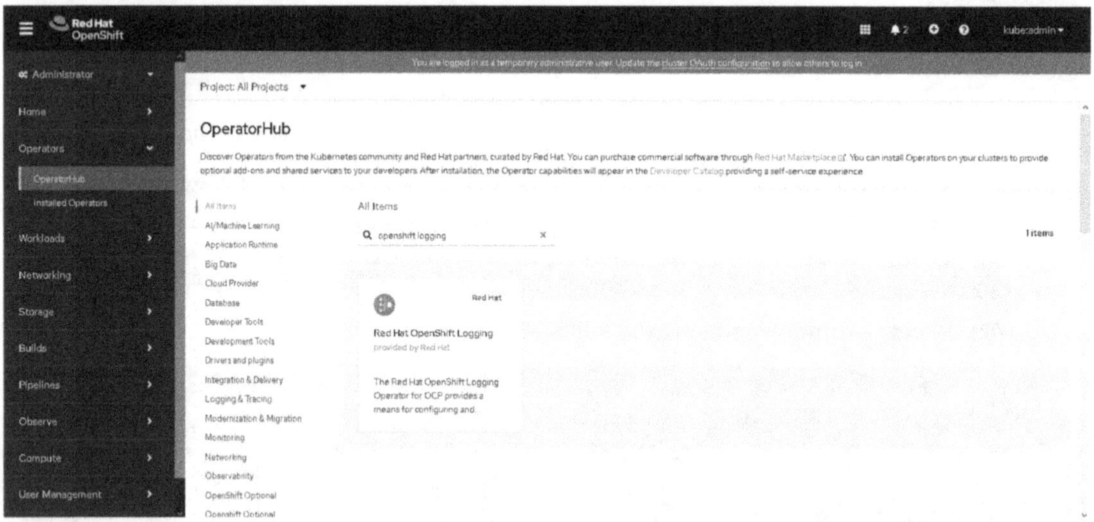

Figure 12.5: Finding OpenShift Logging Operator in OperatorHub

2. Click on the **Red Hat OpenShift Logging** tile and then click **Install.** Then enable cluster monitoring on the operator's namespace and change **Update approval** to **Manual:**

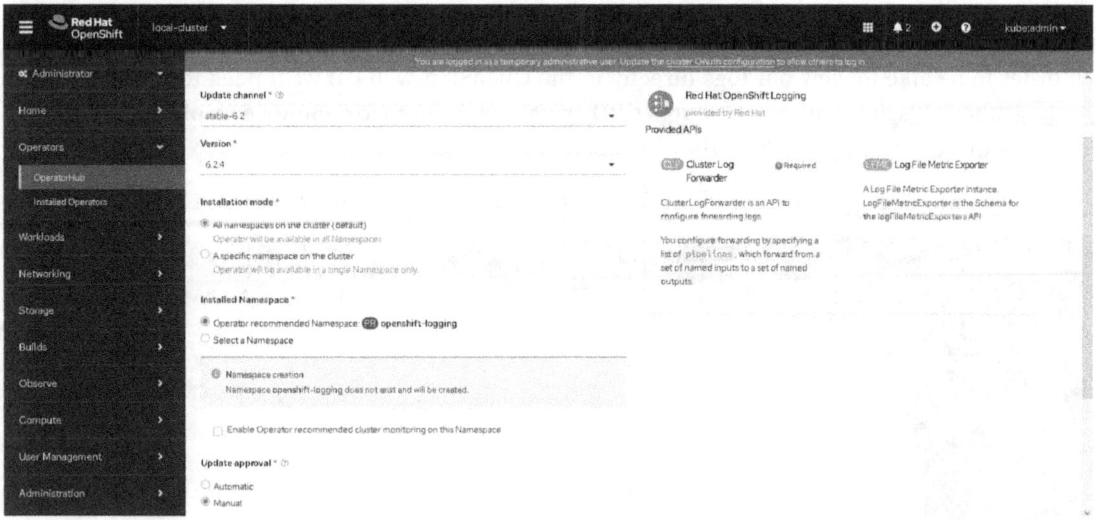

Figure 12.6: Logging Operator's target namespace, cluster monitoring, and update approval

3. Click **Install** again and wait for the **Operator Lifecycle Manager** (**OLM**) to generate an install plan (this may take a few minutes). As usual, we will be approving it from the command line, so switch to the terminal and use the following command to find its name:

```
$ oc get ip -n openshift-logging
```

Approve it (remember to use the install plan from the output of the preceding command):

```
$ oc patch ip/install-9744q -p '{"spec": {"approved": true}}' --type
merge -n openshift-logging
```

In about a minute, list pods in the `openshift-logging` namespace:

```
$ oc get po -n openshift-logging
```

As with the Loki Operator, you should see only one pod running:

```
NAME                                     READY   STATUS    RESTARTS   AGE
cluster-logging-operator-6bf57f755-vmf75   1/1     Running   0          11s
```

Figure 12.7: CLO pod is up and running

At this point, you should have both operators ready, so now we can leverage them to create the logging stack, starting from the Loki Operator.

Installing the COO

In order to be able to view our logs directly in the OpenShift web UI, we'll need to install the COO. Among other APIs, it installs the UIPlugin CRD, which can be used to deploy a console plugin that will visualize the logs stored in Loki in the web console.

1. As with other operators, find the COO in **OperatorHub** by typing `observability`:

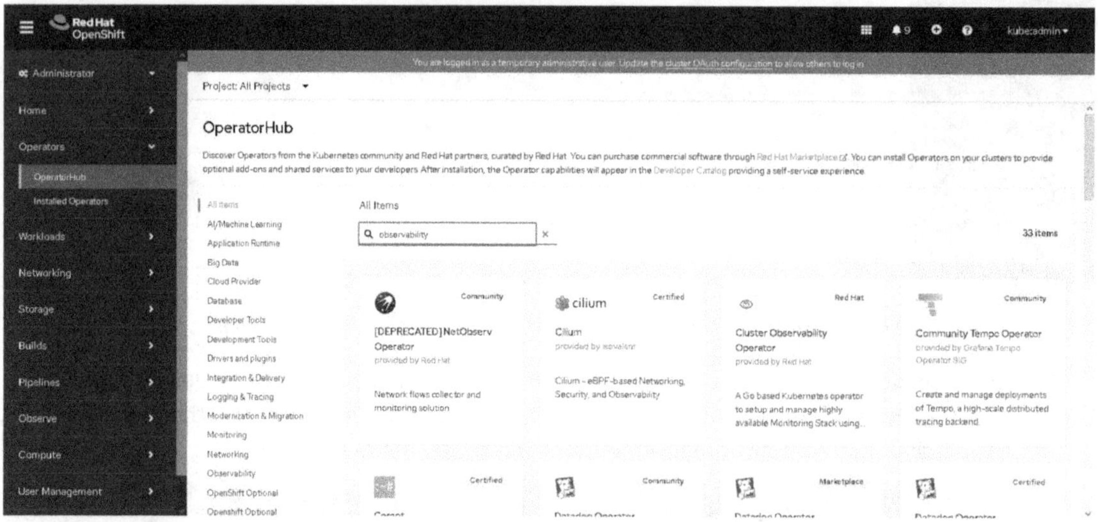

Figure 12.8: Finding Cluster Observability Operator in OperatorHub

2. Click on the operator's tile to see its channel, version, and general information. Click **Install**, and on the next page, leave all settings at their defaults, except for enabling cluster monitoring on the operator's namespace:

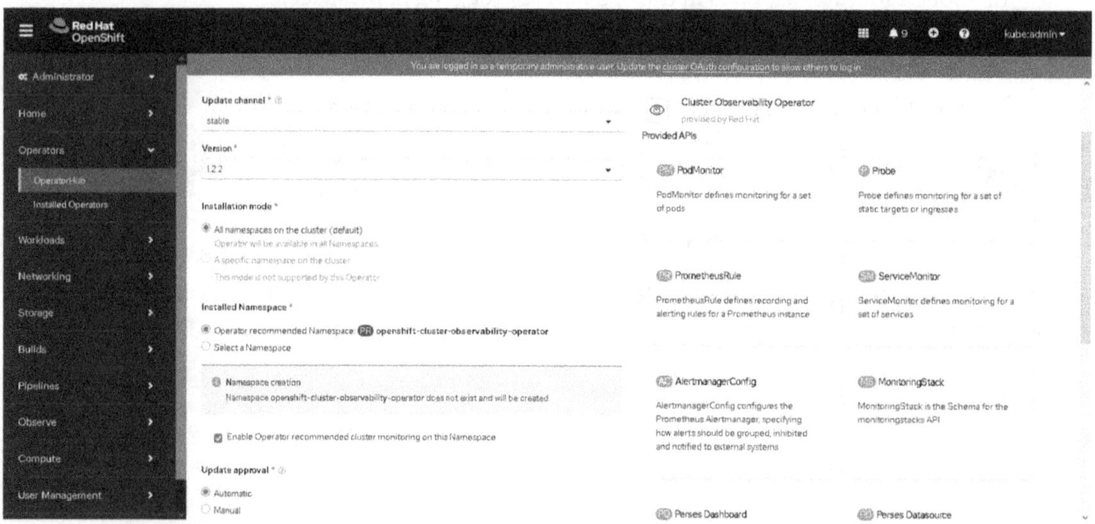

Figure 12.9: COO's target namespace, cluster monitoring, and update approval

3. Click **Install** again and wait for the operator to install. Since we didn't set the approval strategy to manual this time, the install plan will be approved by OLM automatically. Check pods of the operator with this command:

```
$ oc get po -n openshift-cluster-observability-operator
```

In a minute or so, you'll see the operator's pods up and running:

```
[ausov@bastion kustomize-nginx]$ oc get po -n openshift-cluster-observability-operator
NAME                                                      READY   STATUS    RESTARTS   AGE
obo-prometheus-operator-57596c5f4f-p8j8j                  1/1     Running   0          26s
obo-prometheus-operator-admission-webhook-6f5b995c48-gpsq5   1/1     Running   0          25s
obo-prometheus-operator-admission-webhook-6f5b995c48-pjjm4   1/1     Running   0          25s
observability-operator-6dc655c757-pbmjp                   1/1     Running   0          25s
perses-operator-756cb4b7bd-vpxb6                          1/1     Running   0          25s
```

Figure 12.10: COO pods are up and running

Now that we have all three operators in place, we can configure them, starting with creating a LokiStack CR.

Creating a LokiStack instance

Loki log store is an alternative to Elasticsearch. It uses an object store, such as AWS S3, Google Cloud Store, Azure, Minio, OpenStack Swift, or ODF to store data. Since we already installed ODF back in *Chapter 8, Working with Persistent Storage*, and used it to provide the internal registry with persistent storage, it is only logical to use it for logging too. As opposed to Elasticsearch, Loki uses deferred (at rest) indexing for complex fields, which results in better performance during ingestion. The high-level process of configuring Loki involves creating an object store bucket and creating a LokiStack CR. Let's walk through these steps together:

1. First, since we will be leveraging ODF as the object store provider, we need to create an **Object Bucket Claim** (**OBC**). Use a manifest from `chapters/12/snippets/obc-loki-bucket.yml` of this book's GitHub repository:

```
$ oc create -f chapters/12/snippets/obc-loki-bucket.yml
```

This will result in ODF creating a corresponding **Object Bucket** (**OB**) resource and binding it to our OBC. On top of that, it will create a Secret and ConfigMap for storing access credentials and endpoint information, respectively. You can use the following command to see all these objects for yourself:

```
$ oc get obc,ob,secret,cm -n openshift-logging
```

2. Use the following commands to extract object store details and store them in the current shell session's environment variables for later use. The names of the variables are self-explanatory:

```
$ BUCKET_PORT=$(oc get -o jsonpath='{.data.BUCKET_PORT}' cm/loki-bucket
-n openshift-logging)
$ BUCKET_HOST=$(oc get -o jsonpath='{.data.BUCKET_HOST}' cm/loki-bucket
-n openshift-logging)
```

```
$ BUCKET_NAME=$(oc get -o jsonpath='{.data.BUCKET_NAME}' cm/loki-bucket
-n openshift-logging)
$ ACCESS_KEY_ID=$(oc get -o jsonpath='{.data.AWS_ACCESS_KEY_ID}' secret/
loki-bucket -n openshift-logging | base64 -d)
$ SECRET_ACCESS_KEY=$(oc get -o jsonpath='{.data.AWS_SECRET_ACCESS_KEY}'
secret/loki-bucket -n openshift-logging | base64 -d)
```

If the `base64` utility is not available on your system, you can also use `oc extract`, for example:

```
$ SECRET_ACCESS_KEY=$(oc extract --keys AWS_SECRET_ACCESS_
KEY --to - secret/loki-bucket -n openshift-logging)
```

This command extracts data from ConfigMaps and Secrets and automatically decodes them, without relying on `base64`.

3. Now create a secret that will be used by Loki to locate and access the object store:

```
$ oc create secret generic logging-loki-s3 --from-literal=access_key_
id="${ACCESS_KEY_ID}" --from-literal=access_key_secret="${SECRET_
ACCESS_KEY}" --from-literal=bucketnames="${BUCKET_NAME}" --from-
literal=endpoint="https://${BUCKET_HOST}:${BUCKET_PORT}" -n
openshift-logging
```

4. Let's take a look at the `chapters/12/snippets/lokistack-logging-loki.yml` file from this book's repository, which defines a LokiStack instance. Two things of note in this manifest are the following:

   - `.spec.tls.caName` and `.spec.tls.caKey` are to prevent the `x509: certificate signed by unknown authority` error on the ingester's side when connecting to the object store.
   - Every component defines a node selector and a corresponding toleration to schedule it on infra nodes.

   A more complete explanation of the LokiStack schema is offered at [4], along with other information.

5. Create the Loki stack:

```
$ oc create -f chapters/12/snippets/lokistack-logging-loki.yml
```

6. Rolling everything out should take up to 5 minutes, with the ingester usually taking the longest. Use the following command to verify the deployment:

```
$ oc get po -o wide -n openshift-logging
```

   You should see eight pods (aside from the logging operator's pod) running, one per component (the only exception being the gateway):

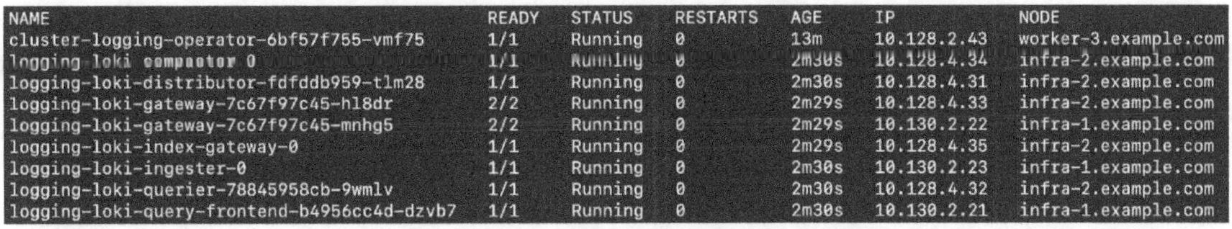

Figure 12.11: LokiStack is up and running

Notice that all pods created by our LokiStack instance are running on infra nodes, as specified by its manifest's node selector and tolerations.

The Loki ingester pod (`logging-loki-ingester-0`) is the last to become ready and usually takes less than 2 minutes to start.

If you're using a storage backend other than ODF, refer to [3] for additional instructions.

Now that we have the log store configured, we can complete the section on logging by creating a `ClusterLogForwarder` instance that will deploy log collectors for forwarding data to Loki.

Creating a ClusterLogForwarder instance

The primary responsibility of a `ClusterLogForwarder` object is to specify parameters for log collection and rules for forwarding logs either to a local backend store (such as Loki) or to a remote system. Without the latter, the local store is used. As of Logging 6.2, which is the most recent release of Logging at the time of writing this chapter, log collectors are based on the **Vector** upstream project. Compared to deprecated Fluentd, Vector is a newer and more performant implementation written in Rust with a focus on lower memory footprint, higher **Logs per Second** (**LPS**) count, and better scalability, albeit at the cost of somewhat higher CPU usage. Unlike Fluentd, it indexes only labels associated with logs, not logs themselves, resulting in better performance and storage effectiveness. There is a good comparative analysis [1] of the two, plus Fluent Bit, that we recommend reading.

Follow these steps as we walk you through the process of setting up log collection and forwarding:

1. Start by creating a **Service Account** (**SA**) that will be used by collectors. Depending on what types of logs you want to collect, you'll need to create cluster role bindings between this SA and specific cluster roles installed by the CLO. These cluster roles are as follows:

    - `collect-infrastructure-logs`: Contains permissions to perform the `collect` verb on the `logs` resource named `infrastructure` from `logging.openshift.io` and `observability.openshift.io` API groups.
    - `collect-application-logs`: Contains permissions to perform the `collect` verb on the `logs` resource named `application` from `logging.openshift.io` and `observability.openshift.io` API groups.
    - `collect-audit-logs`: Contains permissions to perform the `collect` verb on the `logs` resource named `audit` from `logging.openshift.io` and `observability.openshift.io` API groups.

> Back in *Chapter 5, Navigating Authentication and Authorization,* we mentioned that there is no complete list of all verbs supported by OpenShift API Server and that these verbs are meaningless without the API server knowing how to interpret them. That means you can even define a cluster role or a role with an arbitrary verb, and the server will accept it. The `collect` verb is one such example of a custom verb that is not interpreted (mapped to an HTTP method) out of the box by the API server.

Since in this exercise we will be collecting all types of logs, we will need to create an SA and bind it to all three cluster roles, plus one cluster role that allows writing logs (`logging-collector:write-logs`). The following command will create such an account and bindings from manifests stored in this book's GitHub repository:

```
$ oc create -f chapters/12/snippets/sa.yml -f chapters/12/snippets/
clusterrolebindings.yml
```

2. Open the `chapters/12/snippets/clf-instance.yml` file from this book's repository and examine the CLF instance manifest contained therein. We would like you to take note of the following parameters:

   - Unlike LokiStack's components, notice how we didn't override the node selector for collectors because they are meant to run on every node, collecting data. That said, we still needed to add `.spec.collector.tolerations`, because we need collectors to run on infra nodes too, just not exclusively.
   - The `.spec.serviceAccount` field references the service account we created earlier, bound to cluster roles for log collection.
   - The `.spec.outputs` field is a list of destinations or downstream channels for collected logs. In our example, we use a LokiStack instance as an output; however, OpenShift Logging 6.2 supports many more, including Amazon CloudWatch, Azure Monitor, Kafka, Splunk, and Syslog. If your logging backend is not natively supported (yet), you can always use `http`.
   - The `.spec.pipelines` field is a list of pipelines that wire inputs and outputs together. We don't have any user-defined inputs in our CLF instance, because we only need to collect logs from built-in sources.
   - To prevent the annoying `x509: certificate signed by unknown authority` error in the Loki ingester, we also need to point collectors to the right CA certificate that was used to issue the ODF object endpoint's (`s3.openshift-storage.svc:443`) service certificate. This CA is stored in the ConfigMap called `openshift-service-ca.crt` in the `openshift-config` namespace.

As proof, we invite you to check it for yourself:

1. First, start a simple pod from the `netshoot/nicolaka` image, which contains a lot of useful tools for network troubleshooting and diagnostics, including `openssl`:

```
$ oc run -it netshoot --image nicolaka/netshoot -- bash
```

2. Once inside, run this command to check the ODF object endpoint's certificate:

```
$ openssl s_client -connect s3.openshift-storage.svc:443 | grep
issuer
```

You will see the issuer's **Canonical Name** (**CN**), which looks like this:

```
openshift-service-serving-signer@1754206383
```

3. Next, exit the pod and extract the CA certificate from the ConfigMap, decode it, and extract the issuer:

```
$ oc extract --keys service-ca.crt --to - cm/openshift-service-ca.
crt -n openshift-config | openssl x509 -noout -issuer
```

You're expected to see the same issuer as when you ran `openssl` inside the `netshoot` pod, which should explain why we needed to reference this ConfigMap and its key in our CLF manifest. The problem is explained in more detail in [2].

4. Let's clean up after our experiment:

```
$ oc delete po/netshoot
```

3. Now that we've examined the CLF's structure, let's create the instance:

```
$ oc create -f chapters/12/snippets/clf-instance.yml
```

4. Give it 3 minutes or so and check what pods have been created:

```
$ oc get po -o wide -n openshift-logging
```

You should see nine collector pods deployed – one for each node:

```
cluster-logging-operator-6bf57f755-vmf75    1/1   Running   0    17h   10.128.2.43    worker-3.example.com
instance-7fxrp                              1/1   Running   0    16h   10.129.2.171   worker-1.example.com
instance-b9gck                              1/1   Running   0    16h   10.131.0.28    worker-2.example.com
instance-cs7gm                              1/1   Running   0    16h   10.128.2.45    worker-3.example.com
instance-gppp7                              1/1   Running   0    16h   10.128.4.37    infra-2.example.com
instance-jnx29                              1/1   Running   0    16h   10.129.1.13    master-2.example.com
instance-lbbzg                              1/1   Running   0    16h   10.130.2.25    infra-1.example.com
instance-q686q                              1/1   Running   0    16h   10.130.1.74    master-3.example.com
instance-tjrz7                              1/1   Running   0    16h   10.128.1.230   master-1.example.com
instance-vsc8c                              1/1   Running   0    16h   10.131.2.26    infra-3.example.com
logging-loki-compactor-0                    1/1   Running   0    17h   10.128.4.34    infra-2.example.com
logging-loki-distributor-fdfddb959-tlm28    1/1   Running   0    17h   10.128.4.31    infra-2.example.com
logging-loki-gateway-7c67f97c45-hl8dr       2/2   Running   0    17h   10.128.4.33    infra-2.example.com
logging-loki-gateway-7c67f97c45-mnhg5       2/2   Running   0    17h   10.130.2.22    infra-1.example.com
logging-loki-index-gateway-0                1/1   Running   0    17h   10.128.4.35    infra-2.example.com
logging-loki-ingester-0                     1/1   Running   0    17h   10.130.2.23    infra-1.example.com
logging-loki-querier-78845958cb-9wmlv       1/1   Running   0    17h   10.128.4.32    infra-2.example.com
logging-loki-query-frontend-b4956cc4d-dzvb7 1/1   Running   0    17h   10.130.2.21    infra-1.example.com
```

Figure 12.12: Log collectors are up and running

Whenever you see pods distributed like this across all or a subset of nodes, think DaemonSets. Check for any DaemonSets with the following command:

```
$ oc get ds -n openshift-logging
```

Indeed, all collector pods are managed by DaemonSets, which is a standard pattern for running CSI/CNI/special hardware drivers, log collectors, or monitoring agents:

```
NAME       DESIRED   CURRENT   READY   UP-TO-DATE   AVAILABLE   NODE SELECTOR
instance   9         9         9       9            9           kubernetes.io/os=linux
```

Figure 12.13: Collector pods are managed by a DaemonSet

Notice that the default node selector targets only RHEL/CoreOS nodes. By default, OpenShift Logging does not support Windows nodes.

Lastly, we need to create an instance of the `UIPlugin` CRD that will provide visibility into the log data by seamlessly integrating with the OpenShift web UI.

Creating a UIPlugin instance

The final piece of the puzzle is a `UIPlugin` instance that will deploy a web console plugin and configure OpenShift to use it, so that we can view logs collected by CLF and stored in an object store provided by ODF in the OpenShift web UI.

Adding a plugin is as easy as running the following command, which uses a `UIPlugin` manifest from our book's GitHub repository:

```
$ oc create -f chapters/12/snippets/uiplugin.yml
```

If you check pods in the `openshift-cluster-observability-operator` namespace now, you will notice that a new pod, `logging-xxxxxxxxxx-xxxxx`, was created (at the top of the list):

```
NAME                                                    READY   STATUS    RESTARTS   AGE
logging-6dc676bd59-8nlgg                                1/1     Running   0          16s
obo-prometheus-operator-57596c5f4f-p8j8j                1/1     Running   0          2m43s
obo-prometheus-operator-admission-webhook-6f5b995c48-gpsq5   1/1     Running   0          2m42s
obo-prometheus-operator-admission-webhook-6f5b995c48-pjjm4   1/1     Running   0          2m42s
observability-operator-6dc655c757-pbmjp                 1/1     Running   0          2m42s
perses-operator-756cb4b7bd-vpxb6                        1/1     Running   0          2m42s
```

Figure 12.14: UIPlugin pod is up and running

Now open the OpenShift console, and you'll see a **Web console update is available** popup in the top-right corner. Click on **Refresh web console** and navigate to the new **Observe** > **Logs** menu. By default, application logs will be displayed:

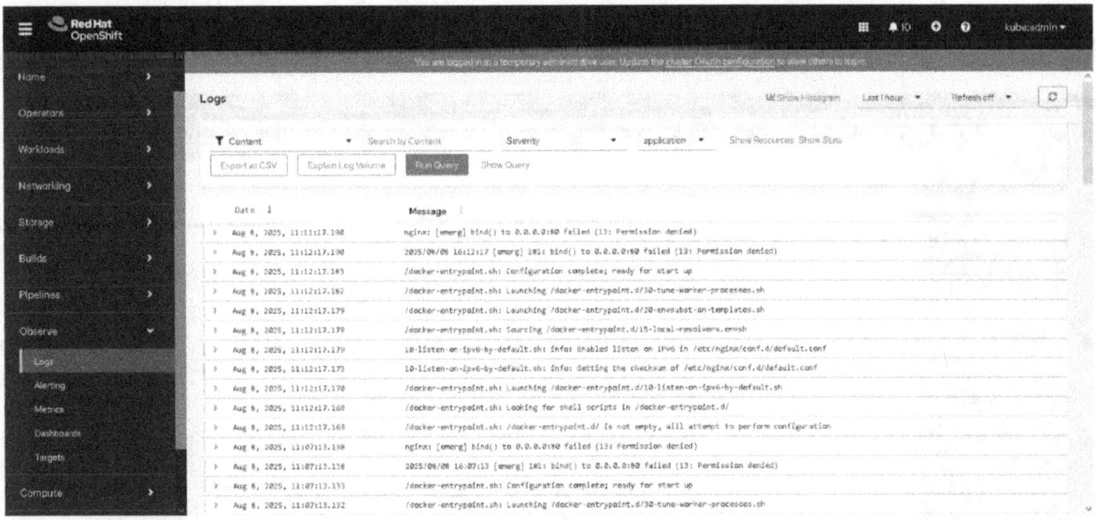

Figure 12.15: Application logs can be accessed through the OpenShift web UI

Since this is a demo cluster, we barely have any applications running; however, you can still see entries from pods we deployed in previous chapters, mostly produced by the Nginx web server. While not particularly impressive, this demo is still representative of how accessing logs works with OpenShift Logging.

You can expand any entry from the results to view its metadata and the message itself:

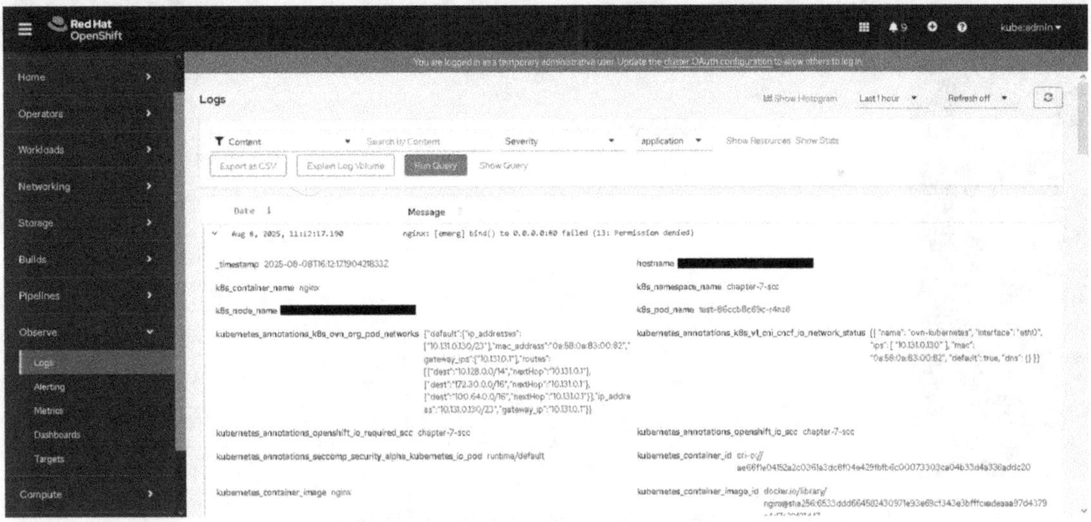

Figure 12.16: Logs and their metadata are available for examination

Some of the fields are not shown on the screenshot due to space limitations, and zooming out would make it even less readable than it already is.

Infrastructure logs are accessed and examined from the same panel – just select **infrastructure** from the drop-down menu at the top:

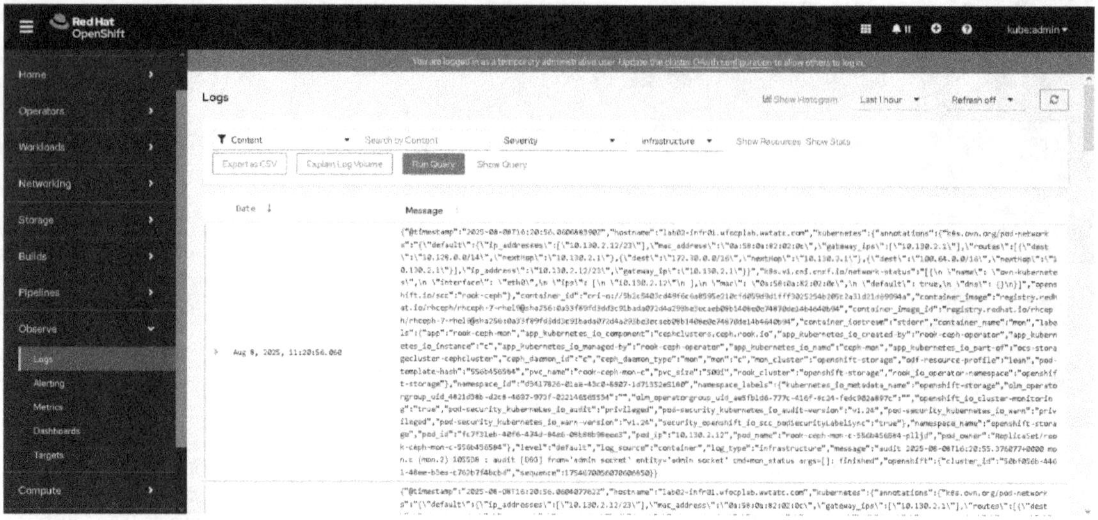

Figure 12.17: Infrastructure logs from OpenShift internal components

Since we configured our `ClusterLogForwarder` resource to collect audit logs as well, you can view them on the same panel:

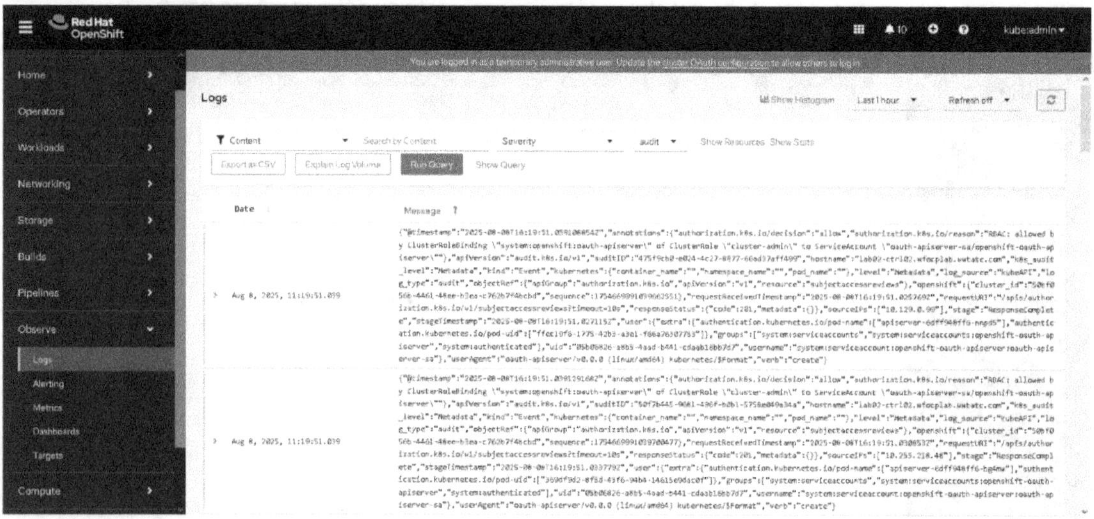

Figure 12.18: Audit logs recorder by OpenShift API Server

With the console plugin, you can filter logs by content, namespaces, pods, or individual containers. The query editor is also available for complex search queries.

So far, we have configured cluster logging with an internal log store. The setup in our lab is basic, but sufficient for small environments. For production use, however, you have to do proper size planning and possibly log filtering. The latter is done in the same `ClusterLogForwarder` resource that configures log forwarding to internal, such as Loki, or external destinations, such as Google Cloud Logging or Amazon CloudWatch. With the ClusterLogForwarder API, you can send all or different types of logs to different destinations, maintaining a smaller set of data locally. For example, you can forward all log types to a remote system, at the same time saving application logs produced in specific namespaces or even by specific pods to a local store [5]. Due to the limitations of our lab, we didn't cover this part of logging; however, we encourage you to explore this on your own using the official documentation.

Warning!

With default settings, a large volume of logs produced by your applications may cause performance issues and even disruptions in your cluster. Make sure to perform capacity planning and tune the logging stack's internal buffers to avoid potential issues and pay attention to metrics. Use [6] as a guide on performance and reliability tuning,

Summary

In this chapter, we discussed why centralized logging is important in enterprises and how large volumes of logs are shipped to dedicated systems such as Splunk, for long-term storage, indexing, and search. Commercial log management solutions, such as Splunk, for example, usually come with their own search engines that can be queried using special query languages. In the case of Splunk, this language is called **Search Processing Language** (**SPL**) and is used for searching, manipulating, and filtering data.

In OpenShift, logging involves three operators: the Loki operator, which manages the object store for log retention, the **Cluster Logging Operator** (**CLO**), which adds an API called ClusterLogForwarding from the `observability.openshift.io` group to OpenShift, and the **Cluster Observability Operator** (**COO**), which brings a number of APIs for enhanced monitoring with it, including UIPlugin, which taps into LokiStack and presents the data to the OpenShift web console.

Logging is but one part of observability – an umbrella concept that includes monitoring and tracing as well. In the next chapter, we will focus on another component of observability – monitoring.

References

To learn more about the topics that were covered in this chapter, take a look at the following resources:

- [1] *Who is the winner – Comparing Vector, Fluent Bit, Fluentd performance*: `https://medium.com/ibm-cloud/log-collectors-performance-benchmarking-8c5218a08fea`
- [2] *How to configure Loki Object Storage CA certificate in RHOCP 4*: `https://access.redhat.com/solutions/7006107`
- [3] *How to configure object storage for Loki*: `https://access.redhat.com/articles/7006275`
- [4] *Installing log storage*: `https://docs.redhat.com/en/documentation/openshift_container_platform/4.16/html/logging/log-storage#installing-log-storage`
- [5] *Configuring log forwarding*: `https://docs.redhat.com/en/documentation/openshift_container_platform/4.16/html/logging/log-collection-and-forwarding#configuring-log-forwarding`

- [6] *Performance and reliability tuning*: `https://docs.redhat.com/en/documentation/openshift_container_platform/4.16/html/logging/performance-and-reliability-tuning`

Quiz

Test your understanding of logging in OpenShift with this quick quiz. Remember, some questions may have more than one correct answer!

1. What are the primary benefits of centralized logging? Select all that apply:
    a. Easier root cause analysis in distributed systems
    b. Storing logs at origin (locally) is no longer needed
    c. Improved audit and compliance
    d. Performance profiling
2. What is the primary function of the **Cluster Logging Operator** (CLO) in OpenShift 4?
    a. Manages container orchestration
    b. Automates the deployment and management of the logging stack
    c. Provides network security
    d. Monitors resource utilization
3. What is the correct sequence of steps when creating a LokiStack instance?
    a. Create an **Object Bucket** (OB) > Create a LokiStack object referencing the OB
    b. Create an **Object Bucket Claim** (OBC) > Extract object store details from a Secret and ConfigMap associated with the OBC > Create a secret with object store details > Create a LokiStack object referencing the secret
    c. Create access credentials using the log store's API > Store access credentials in a secret > Create a LokiStack object referencing the secret
    d. Create access credentials using the log store's API > Store access credentials in a secret > Create a LokiStack object with access credentials embedded in its definition
4. Which object storage provider is NOT supported by the Loki Operator?
    a. Amazon S3
    b. Alibaba **Object Storage Service** (OSS)
    c. Red Hat OpenShift Data Foundation
    d. Minio
5. Which log collector implementation is best suited for large volumes of data?
    a. Fluentd
    b. Statsd
    c. Vector
    d. Collectd

Answers

1. **a**, **c**, and **d**. Refer to the *The benefits of centralized logging* section for more details. Although remote log stores offer significantly more capacity, that doesn't negate the need to store a subset of data locally for faster and easier access.
2. **b**. The sole function of the CLO is to automate the lifecycle of the logging stack.
3. **b**. Refer to the *Configuring logging > Creating a LokiStack instance* section for more details.
4. **b**. Although supported by Loki itself, Alibaba OSS is not yet supported by its operator. All others are available as object store backends.
5. **c**. Vector was developed with low memory usage and storage efficiency in mind, thanks to its lightweight indexes, if compared to Fluentd. Statsd and collectd, on the other hand, are used to collect system and application metrics, respectively.

Join us on Discord

For discussions around the book and to connect with your peers, join us on Discord at `http://packt.link/discordcloud` or scan the QR code below:

13

Monitoring in OpenShift

In the previous chapter, we configured centralized logging to capture textual event data. Monitoring complements that by capturing time-series numeric data, providing the quantitative insight needed for capacity planning and SLO compliance.

In this chapter, you will learn what Prometheus is and how to configure the Prometheus-based monitoring solution, available on OpenShift by default. It also offers a few examples of important cluster-level metrics, as well as explains how to enable monitoring for user-defined projects. Finally, it shows you how to create expressions in **Prometheus Query Language** (**PromQL**) for complex queries and use dashboards to identify and interpret business-critical indicators. All these skills are important for providing stakeholders, developers, and SREs with the necessary tools to observe business-critical application metrics and the underlying infrastructure.

We'll cover the following main topics:

- Cluster monitoring stack
- Querying metrics with PromQL
- Using Alertmanager for notifications
- Monitoring business applications
- Creating custom dashboards with Grafana
- Production considerations

Let's get started!

Technical requirements

In this chapter, you will need the following:

- Bash shell
- OpenShift 4.16 (preferably a multinode cluster, similar to the one we built in *Chapter 3*, *Getting Started with OpenShift*)

- Firefox (recommended) or any other web browser
- An active Red Hat subscription to view Red Hat KB articles

You can access this book's GitHub repository at `https://github.com/PacktPublishing/Learn-OpenShift-Second-Edition`.

Cluster monitoring stack

Like logging and tracing, monitoring is another part of observability; an umbrella term for tools and technologies used to gain insight into the inner workings of a system, such as logs, metrics, traces, and other indicators that assist in detecting issues before they start to have an impact on business. Unlike logging, monitoring is not concerned with arbitrary textual diagnostic information produced by applications. Instead, it collects and processes various metrics emitted by those applications. Metrics are numerical indicators that reflect certain aspects of an application's execution, such as the number of processed requests, resource consumption, and so on. Metrics are crucial for business because they enable it to calculate **performance key indicators (PKIs)** and commit to a certain **service-level agreement (SLA)**, which is basically a contract between a platform provider and consumers. For example, such a contract may stipulate that 95% of requests to the API should complete within 5 seconds or the platform should have an availability of no less than 99.99%. Observability in general is also critical for debugging, troubleshooting, and profiling applications. OpenShift 4 comes with a built-in monitoring solution based on Prometheus [1], an open source monitoring and alerting system. Originally developed by Matt T. Proud and Julius Volz at SoundCloud in 2012 [2] and adopted by CNCF in 2016 (right after Kubernetes), Prometheus was designed to address the limitations around monitoring solutions of the time, specifically StatsD and Graphite. The most distinctive features of Prometheus are as follows:

- Multidimensional data model with labels attached to every metric, inspired by OpenTSDB. [3]
- Powerful query language able to slice data across different dimensions.
- Works by pulling metrics over HTTP from a `/metrics` (default) endpoint on targets every minute (default), with push supported through an intermediary gateway.
- Standalone and has no external dependencies.
- Scales to tens of millions of active data series.
- Supports both auto-discovery of targets and static configuration.

Due to its scalability and operational simplicity, Prometheus became a de facto standard for cloud-native monitoring, where it supports service discovery through many cloud providers and tools, including Kubernetes, Azure, Amazon EC2, Zookeeper, HashiCorp Consul, PuppetDB, Docker, Linode, DigitalOcean, and many others. Most components of Prometheus are written in Go, with some using Python, Ruby, and Java. Prometheus is at the core of OpenShift monitoring solution [4], and it comes preconfigured with a large number of cluster-level metrics that provide operational insight into the health of OpenShift, with support for the monitoring of user-defined projects, where it can collect application-specific metrics, enabled by any of the supported libraries. These libraries are available for a wide range of languages, including Python, Java, and Ruby, to name a few. Unofficial third-party language bindings also exist for Node.js, .NET, and even Bash. Sending metrics from the NGINX server and the Tarantool database is supported too through a Lua client. Performance-wise, it has a negligible impact on all but the most latency-sensitive applications. Prometheus stores metrics as time-series data, where each data point (aka measurement) is stored with its timestamp and an arbitrary number of labels (aka dimensions).

> Prometheus is not an event logging system. If you need to extract metrics from logs or events, the Loki log store backend has a feature called metric queries to accomplish that, as described in [5]. We discussed Loki in more detail in *Chapter 12, Logging in OpenShift*.

The architecture of the OpenShift monitoring stack for cluster monitoring is depicted in the following figure:

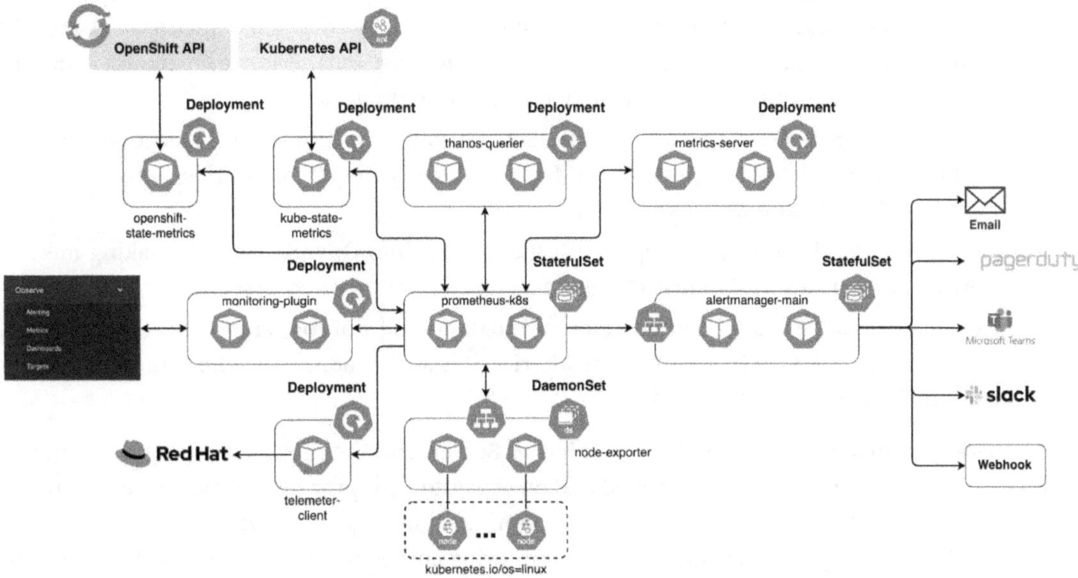

Figure 13.1: OpenShift core monitoring components

There are additional components, such as Thanos Ruler (involved in the monitoring of user-defined projects). We will discuss them later in this chapter.

OpenShift cluster monitoring components perform the following functions:

- **Prometheus: A time-series database** (**TSDB**) and rule evaluation engine that is at the core of the OpenShift monitoring solution. Multiple Prometheus instances are supported, scraping metrics from targets independently, with deduplication performed by **Alertmanager**. Requires persistent storage for short-term data retention. For long-term retention, Prometheus can be configured to send data to an external system [6].

- **Alertmanager**: Receives alerts from Prometheus (and Thanos Ruler, if monitoring of user-defined projects is enabled) and sends notifications to external systems, such as email or Slack. Supports HA mode with multiple Alertmanager instances forming a cluster and synchronizing notifications and alert silences between each other using the **Memberlist** HashiCorp library. If synchronization fails due to loss of connectivity, however, some alerts may be duplicated. Requires persistent storage for long-term retention of data.
- **Kube State Metrics**: Creates metrics for Kubernetes API objects.
- **OpenShift State Metrics**: Supplements Kube State Metrics with data for OpenShift-specific APIs. This is an OpenShift-specific component, and its versioning policy is aligned with that of OpenShift.
- **Thanos Querier**: Aggregates and deduplicates cluster metrics and metrics received via Thanos Ruler from user-defined projects.
- **Metrics Server**: Aggregates CPU and memory usage and exposes them in `Node` and `Pod` objects under the `metrics.k8s.io/v1beta1` API for consumption by other tools, such as HPA and VPA (covered in more detail in *Chapter 10, Deployment to OpenShift*). Prior to OpenShift 4.16, this function was performed by a component called **Prometheus Adapter.**
- **Node Exporter**: Implemented as a DaemonSet that collects machine-level metrics from OpenShift nodes. That data includes CPU/RAM usage, various filesystem metrics, network-related metrics, OS information, and so on.
- **Monitoring Plugin**: Integrates OpenShift monitoring into OpenShift UI by making metrics, alerts, alerting rules, and metrics targets available under the *Observe* section.
- **Telemeter Client**: Sends a limited amount of data to Red Hat for remote health monitoring of your cluster [7]. Like OpenShift State Metrics, it is an OpenShift-specific component and is versioned identically to OpenShift.

Prometheus, Alertmanager, Thanos Querier, Metrics Server, and the monitoring plugin run in two pods each, with members of each pair scheduled on separate nodes for resiliency. This is controlled by the `podAntiAffinity` setting, which you can examine with `oc get -o yaml` on the corresponding StatefulSet or Deployment. In addition, all monitoring components run in the `system-cluster-critical` priority class and, in case of a resource contention, can be preempted only by node critical services, such as OpenShift and Kubernetes API servers, controller manager, scheduler, CoreDNS, and CSI drivers. You can list all pods that have this priority and their namespaces using the following command, but we also need to export the `kubeconfig` file of the cluster we have built in *Chapter 3, Getting Started with OpenShift*, into the current shell first:

```
$ export KUBECONFIG=~/learning-ocp4/auth/kubeconfig
$ oc get po -o jsonpath='{range .items[*]}{@.metadata.namespace}{"\n"}
{@.metadata.name}{"\n"}{@.spec.priority}{"\n"}{end}' -A | grep -B 2 2000000000
```

The priority specified in the `system-cluster-critical` priority class may be different in your lab. To make sure you get the correct output from the preceding command, check the priority first with the `oc get -o jsonpath='{.value}{"\n"}' pc/system-cluster-critical` command.

Prometheus supports two types of rules:

- **Recording:** Define computationally expensive or frequently used expressions for which a new time series is generated. Especially useful for dashboards that invoke the same expression on a periodic basis.
- **Alerting:** Define conditions for which alerts are triggered.

In OpenShift, Prometheus, Alertmanager, and other components of the monitoring stack are managed by the **Cluster Monitoring Operator** (**CMO**). The CMO is deployed by the **Cluster Version Operator** (**CVO**), a higher-level cluster operator that manages the lifecycle of OpenShift core operators. You can review its current state with `oc get -o yaml co/monitoring`. We will discuss the CVO in more detail in *Chapter 16, Understanding Operators and the Operator Framework*. Use the following command to list all CRDs managed by the CMO:

```
$ oc get co/monitoring -o jsonpath='{.status.relatedObjects[*].resource}{"\n"}'
| sed 's/ /\n/g' | grep -v namespace
```

You should see the following CRDs:

CRD	Description
`AlertmanagerConfig`	Describes the desired configuration of an `Alertmanager` instance. Specifies alert receivers, alert inhibition rules, routes for connecting alerts and receivers, and time windows for when alerts should be active or silenced, as well as alert grouping rules.
`Alertmanager`	Mostly specifies parameters that directly map to the `alertmanager-main` StatefulSet's fields, in addition to the `AlertManagerConfig` discovery settings and other Alertmanager peers (if any) to form a cluster. In a default configuration, there is only one instance of Alertmanager named `main`.
`Probe`	Identifies monitoring targets using static (hostnames or IP addresses) or dynamic (Ingress) service discovery.
`Prometheus`	Defines a Prometheus StatefulSet with settings for metrics scraping, sharding, service monitors selectors, and TSDB, among others.
`PrometheusRule`	Defines Prometheus recording and alerting rules.
`ServiceMonitor`	Configures Prometheus to scrape metrics from a configurable endpoint exposed by an application through its `Service` object.
`PodMonitor`	Configures Prometheus to scrape metrics from a configurable endpoint exposed by an application directly on its pod.
`ThanosRuler`	Defines a Thanos Ruler deployment for the monitoring of user-defined projects, including Thanos Querier endpoints and retention settings.

Table 13.1: OpenShift monitoring APIs

See the same list with `oc api-resources --api-group monitoring.coreos.com`.

Out of the box, Prometheus on OpenShift monitors the following cluster services, aside from its own components:

- CoreDNS
- Integrated image registry
- etcd
- HAProxy Ingress
- Kubernetes API
- Kubernetes controller manager
- Kubernetes scheduler
- OpenShift API
- Machine API
- OpenShift controller manager
- OVN Kubernetes
- **Operator Lifecycle Manager** (**OLM**), which we will cover in *Chapter 16*, *Understanding Operators and the Operator Framework*

You can list PrometheusRule instances for all components across all namespaces via `oc get promrule -A`. Additional services deployed on OpenShift, such as **OpenShift Data Foundation** (**ODF**), may ship with their own Prometheus rules, thus being responsible for their own monitoring.

Unlike other components of observability, such as logging, distributed tracing, network observability, power monitoring, and Red Hat's build of OpenTelemetry, the monitoring stack follows the same release cycle as OpenShift core operators and is updated together with OpenShift.

Moving monitoring components to dedicated nodes

When first deployed during cluster installation, monitoring components (except for operator pods) run only on worker nodes, with the exception of DaemonSet-managed Node Exporter pods, which run on all nodes thanks to a "blanket" `{"operator":"Exists"}` toleration that covers all possible node taints. You can see this for yourself with this command:

```
$ oc get po -o wide -n openshift-monitoring
```

You're expected to see something like this at this early stage:

```
NAME                                                   READY   STATUS    RESTARTS   AGE     IP              NODE
alertmanager-main-0                                    6/6     Running   0          6d4h    10.131.0.13     worker-2.example.com
alertmanager-main-1                                    6/6     Running   0          6d4h    10.129.2.27     worker-1.example.com
cluster-monitoring-operator-6d6fdc795f-nv66f           1/1     Running   0          6d5h    10.128.0.25     master-1.example.com
kube-state-metrics-769bbb9c6c-5sc6h                    3/3     Running   0          6d4h    10.129.2.20     worker-1.example.com
metrics-server-69f9cd4f7b-458jr                        1/1     Running   0          5d6h    10.129.2.41     worker-1.example.com
metrics-server-69f9cd4f7b-5kzrm                        1/1     Running   0          5d6h    10.128.2.13     worker-3.example.com
monitoring-plugin-5b9f6df695-w8d62                     1/1     Running   0          6d4h    10.131.0.12     worker-2.example.com
monitoring-plugin-5b9f6df695-zpctb                     1/1     Running   0          6d4h    10.129.2.26     worker-1.example.com
node-exporter-62wjw                                    2/2     Running   0          6d4h    10.253.218.53   infra-3.example.com
node-exporter-8bnl5                                    2/2     Running   0          6d5h    10.253.218.50   master-3.example.com
node-exporter-cgzcf                                    2/2     Running   0          6d5h    10.253.218.49   master-2.example.com
node-exporter-gypk5                                    2/2     Running   0          6d4h    10.253.218.52   infra-2.example.com
node-exporter-lsnqk                                    2/2     Running   0          6d5h    10.253.218.54   worker-1.example.com
node-exporter-m7g74                                    2/2     Running   0          6d5h    10.253.218.48   master-1.example.com
node-exporter-nnhjs                                    2/2     Running   0          6d4h    10.253.218.51   infra-1.example.com
node-exporter-wwzsp                                    2/2     Running   2          6d5h    10.253.218.56   worker-3.example.com
node-exporter-x89j7                                    2/2     Running   2          6d5h    10.253.218.55   worker-2.example.com
openshift-state-metrics-7ccfd9b44-6r7tt                3/3     Running   0          6d4h    10.129.2.21     worker-1.example.com
prometheus-k8s-0                                       6/6     Running   0          6d4h    10.129.2.28     worker-1.example.com
prometheus-k8s-1                                       6/6     Running   0          6d4h    10.131.0.7      worker-2.example.com
prometheus-operator-6f4b4dd654-kz4sf                   2/2     Running   0          6d5h    10.130.0.64     master-3.example.com
prometheus-operator-admission-webhook-7f766b8555-tqkmj 1/1     Running   0          6d4h    10.129.2.22     worker-1.example.com
prometheus-operator-admission-webhook-7f766b8555-xjsc2 1/1     Running   0          6d4h    10.131.0.11     worker-2.example.com
telemeter-client-74f596d5bb-59vgw                      3/3     Running   0          5d21h   10.129.2.30     worker-1.example.com
thanos-querier-54cbd654b4-dp4zj                        6/6     Running   0          6d4h    10.129.2.23     worker-1.example.com
thanos-querier-54cbd654b4-qnxl4                        6/6     Running   0          6d4h    10.131.0.8      worker-2.example.com
```

Figure 13.2: Initial placement of the cluster monitoring stack

Use the following command to list the Node Exporter tolerations:

```
$ oc get -o jsonpath='{.spec.template.spec.tolerations}{"\n"}' ds/node-exporter
-n openshift-monitoring
```

This is the output you should expect to see:

```
[{"operator":"Exists"}]
```

As for the other components, ideally, they should be moved to dedicated infrastructure nodes in order to separate their management from business applications and optimize subscription usage. Red Hat maintains a list [8] of internal OpenShift services that can be scheduled on dedicated nodes without disqualifying them from subscription exemption. Configuration overrides of the OpenShift monitoring stack are stored in a ConfigMap called `cluster-monitoring-config` in the `openshift-monitoring` namespace. It contains a single key, `config.yaml`, whose value is a dictionary with each element providing placement and storage (if supported) settings for a specific component. We will use it in this chapter to reschedule all monitoring components to infrastructure nodes and optionally provide them with persistent storage.

Use the file located at `chapters/13/snippets/cm-cluster-monitoring-config-ephemeral.yml` in this book's GitHub repository to permanently reschedule all components of the monitoring stack on dedicated infrastructure nodes.

> If you already configured ODF persistent storage, as per *Chapter 8, Working with Persistent Storage*, use the `chapters/13/snippets/cm-cluster-monitoring-config-persistent.yml` file instead. For other storage backends, modify the manifest to use a proper `StorageClass`.

Now, apply the file and watch the scheduler do its magic:

```
$ oc create -f chapters/13/snippets/cm-cluster-monitoring-config-ephemeral.yml
$ watch -n1 oc get po -o wide -n openshift-monitoring
```

In a few minutes, you will see that all components (except the CMO controller pod) were moved successfully:

```
NAME                                                   READY   STATUS    RESTARTS   AGE     IP              NODE
alertmanager-main-0                                    6/6     Running   0          67s     10.128.4.55     infra-2.example.com
alertmanager-main-1                                    6/6     Running   0          67s     10.130.2.37     infra-1.example.com
cluster-monitoring-operator-6d6fdc795f-nv66f           1/1     Running   0          6d6h    10.128.0.25     master-1.example.com
kube-state-metrics-6dfdd7869c-hnr2s                    3/3     Running   0          32m     10.130.2.32     infra-1.example.com
metrics-server-865c48cd78-n48pd                        1/1     Running   0          32m     10.130.2.34     infra-1.example.com
metrics-server-865c48cd78-njqlb                        1/1     Running   0          32m     10.128.4.50     infra-2.example.com
monitoring-plugin-7f6989fc85-b2v2x                     1/1     Running   0          32m     10.130.2.35     infra-1.example.com
monitoring-plugin-7f6989fc85-qfckl                     1/1     Running   0          32m     10.128.4.52     infra-2.example.com
node-exporter-62wjw                                    2/2     Running   0          6d4h    10.253.218.53   infra-3.example.com
node-exporter-8bnl5                                    2/2     Running   0          6d5h    10.253.218.50   master-3.example.com
node-exporter-cgzcf                                    2/2     Running   0          6d5h    10.253.218.49   master-2.example.com
node-exporter-ggpk5                                    2/2     Running   0          6d4h    10.253.218.52   infra-2.example.com
node-exporter-lsnqk                                    2/2     Running   0          6d5h    10.253.218.54   worker-1.example.com
node-exporter-m7g74                                    2/2     Running   0          6d5h    10.253.218.48   master-1.example.com
node-exporter-nnhjs                                    2/2     Running   0          6d4h    10.253.218.51   infra-1.example.com
node-exporter-wwzsp                                    2/2     Running   2          6d5h    10.253.218.56   worker-3.example.com
node-exporter-x89j7                                    2/2     Running   2          6d5h    10.253.218.55   worker-2.example.com
openshift-state-metrics-dc77c6d6b-vk8dr                3/3     Running   0          32m     10.128.4.48     infra-2.example.com
prometheus-k8s-0                                       6/6     Running   0          73s     10.128.4.54     infra-2.example.com
prometheus-k8s-1                                       6/6     Running   0          73s     10.130.2.36     infra-1.example.com
prometheus-operator-86c658f6f9-jdk52                   2/2     Running   0          4m32s   10.128.4.53     infra-2.example.com
prometheus-operator-admission-webhook-55bb6cbd65-5knjq 1/1     Running   0          32m     10.128.4.46     infra-2.example.com
prometheus-operator-admission-webhook-55bb6cbd65-wdw7r 1/1     Running   0          32m     10.130.2.31     infra-1.example.com
telemeter-client-7d95c6bfd7-zcksq                      3/3     Running   0          32m     10.128.4.51     infra-2.example.com
thanos-querier-67ccdb6774-j55wz                        6/6     Running   0          32m     10.128.4.49     infra-2.example.com
thanos-querier-67ccdb6774-vlckd                        6/6     Running   0          32m     10.130.2.33     infra-1.example.com
```

Figure 13.3: Cluster monitoring components moved to infra nodes

If you used the `chapters/13/snippets/cm-cluster-monitoring-config-persistent.yml` manifest, you can also see PVs created for Prometheus and Alertmanager with this command:

```
$ oc get pvc -n openshift-monitoring
```

Since both Prometheus and Alertmanager are controlled by StatefulSets, each replica has its own storage, making it four in total:

```
NAME                                      STATUS   VOLUME                                     CAPACITY   ACCESS MODES   STORAGECLASS
alertmanager-main-db-alertmanager-main-0  Bound    pvc-3f54389c-2ea9-490b-aa58-99b6012b433c   20Gi       RWO            ocs-storagecluster-ceph-rbd
alertmanager-main-db-alertmanager-main-1  Bound    pvc-21240f4f-2cbd-4e37-83a1-14ad6fd2608b   20Gi       RWO            ocs-storagecluster-ceph-rbd
prometheus-k8s-db-prometheus-k8s-0        Bound    pvc-cbdeb0f9-e042-4b52-aba3-007a1755a6f9   40Gi       RWO            ocs-storagecluster-ceph-rbd
prometheus-k8s-db-prometheus-k8s-1        Bound    pvc-5207b43d-59ab-4722-8bbc-5066fc97fa1f   40Gi       RWO            ocs-storagecluster-ceph-rbd
```

Figure 13.4: Persistent storage provisioned for Prometheus and Alertmanager

If you are content with the default settings of the monitoring stack, you don't have to create the `cluster-monitoring-config` ConfigMap. Should you notice that your configuration doesn't have an effect, examine the ConfigMap for any typos (`storageClassName`, etc.) or indentation errors. If the configuration is invalid, the CMO will report the `Degraded=True` condition in its status. After you make the necessary changes, it may take the CMO up to 5 minutes to notice and apply them. Full configuration reference for cluster monitoring components is available at [9].

Built-in cluster monitoring entities

The OpenShift monitoring solution comes preconfigured with various metrics, targets, dashboards, and alerting rules that give you insight into the operation of the cluster and its components. All features of monitoring in OpenShift are exposed through the **Observe** menu in both the **Administrator** and **Developer** perspectives of the UI. Let's walk through what is available in that part of the UI.

Metrics

If you click on **Observe | Metrics**, you will see a graph editor where you can enter a PromQL expression for one or more of your metrics and results of the expression for all data points in the metric's time series will be presented as a graph above the editor. You can also enter additional queries by clicking **Add query** and superimposing them on the same chart.

Prometheus supports metrics of the following types:

- **Counter:** A cumulative incremented value that can only go up or be reset to `0`. It is a good candidate for metrics that represent a total amount of something, for example, the total number of HTTP requests.
- **Gauge:** A metric type that represents the current state of a system and can go up and down, such as a temperature or pressure. Good examples would be the number of Unix processes or the current RAM/CPU usage.
- **Histogram:** Samples observed values and counts them in buckets of configurable sizes, with each bucket representing a range of values. A classic use case for it is network latency: a histogram can count the number of requests that take less than 0.1 seconds to complete, less than 0.2, including the previous range, and so on. We will see an example of such a metric later in this chapter.
- **Summary:** Similarly to histograms, counts the received samples in buckets; however, it has lower resolution, and data from multiple instances of the same process cannot be aggregated in Prometheus, because summaries are calculated on the applications' side. They are useful when bucket boundaries cannot be determined in advance. More on differences between histograms and summaries at [10].

Let's see what node and pod metrics are provided by the metrics server. First, run `oc get nodemetrics`. In the output, you will see CPU and RAM usage for every node:

```
NAME                    CPU           MEMORY        WINDOW
master-1.example.com    1619960405n   12218204Ki    20.104s
master-2.example.com    1421471781n   10683772Ki    10.011s
master-3.example.com    2239493143n   10891336Ki    10.064s
infra-1.example.com     416852774n    9667464Ki     10.039s
infra-2.example.com     427786502n    10330060Ki    20.019s
infra-3.example.com     316646565n    5733496Ki     20.015s
worker-1.example.com    147300957n    4206056Ki     20.046s
worker-2.example.com    141465034n    4138892Ki     10.01s
worker-3.example.com    148681298n    3764248Ki     20.025s
```

Figure 13.5: Node metrics

We can also check for pod metrics in the openshift-monitoring namespace via `oc get podmetrics -n openshift-monitoring` (output truncated for brevity):

```
NAME                                           CPU        MEMORY     WINDOW
alertmanager-main-0                            3178548n   107964Ki   10.872s
alertmanager-main-1                            2551684n   110516Ki   15.667s
cluster-monitoring-operator-6d6fdc795f-nv66f   907710n    94028Ki    18.702s
kube-state-metrics-6dfdd7869c-hnr2s            3656165n   104648Ki   10.933s
metrics-server-865c48cd78-n48pd                2259237n   53424Ki    25.71s
metrics-server-865c48cd78-njqlb                2229215n   50792Ki    13.664s
monitoring-plugin-7f6989fc85-b2v2x             0          2364Ki     13.509s
monitoring-plugin-7f6989fc85-qfckl             13073n     2364Ki     13.998s
node-exporter-62wjw                            3605451n   38928Ki    14.272s
node-exporter-8bnl5                            4041627n   53368Ki    13.095s
```

Figure 13.6: Pod metrics

The preceding commands query the Metrics API directly and present the data in a raw format, suitable for consumption by other systems.

Other useful commands include `oc adm top no` (displays node CPU and RAM usage stats):

```
NAME                    CPU(cores)   CPU%   MEMORY(bytes)   MEMORY%
master-1.example.com    662m         18%    11975Mi         80%
master-2.example.com    594m         16%    10136Mi         68%
master-3.example.com    472m         13%    10581Mi         71%
infra-1.example.com     491m         6%     9498Mi          30%
infra-2.example.com     541m         7%     10169Mi         32%
infra-3.example.com     268m         3%     5595Mi          18%
worker-1.example.com    204m         2%     4107Mi          13%
worker-2.example.com    132m         1%     4056Mi          13%
worker-3.example.com    168m         2%     3687Mi          11%
```

Figure 13.7: Node metrics (alternate)

And `oc adm top po -n openshift-kube-apiserver` (displays pod CPU and RAM usage stats in the `openshift-kube-apiserver` namespace):

```
NAME                                         CPU(cores)   MEMORY(bytes)
kube-apiserver-guard-master-1.example.com    0m           0Mi
kube-apiserver-guard-master-2.example.com    0m           0Mi
kube-apiserver-guard-master-3.example.com    0m           0Mi
kube-apiserver-master-1.example.com          249m         4797Mi
kube-apiserver-master-2.example.com          117m         5027Mi
kube-apiserver-master-3.example.com          76m          3715Mi
```

Figure 13.8: Pod metrics (alternate)

Both present essentially the same information as `oc get nodemetrics` and `oc get podmetrics`, as all of them obtain it from the same source (Prometheus Adapter); however, `oc adm top` presents it in a more user-friendly and less precise format, which makes it very useful in troubleshooting capacity issues, but does not offer the maximum level of precision. Learn more about metrics exposed by `oc adm top` at [11].

Metrics are used to build dashboards, which is where we are moving next.

Dashboards

The **Observe | Dashboards** section gives you access to built-in dashboards that provide insight into the core components of your cluster. You can view CPU/RAM usage, network bandwidth, and storage IOPS in the context of workloads, pods, individual containers, or relative to node capacity, among many others. For example, the **Kubernetes | Compute Resources | Workload** dashboard allows you to see per-pod resource consumption for specific workloads filtered by namespaces:

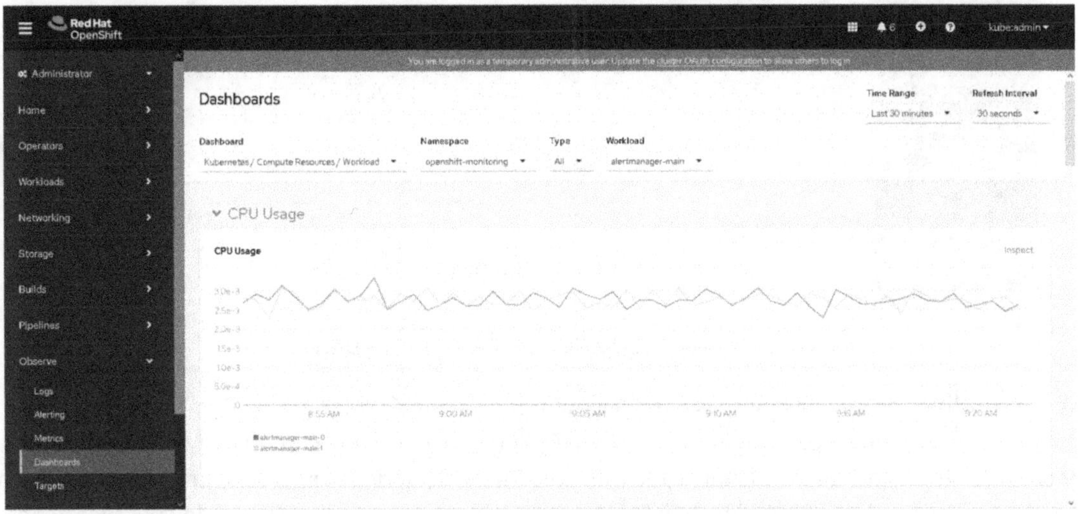

Figure 13.9: OpenShift monitoring, workload metrics

By clicking **Inspect** in the top-right corner of the chart, you will be redirected to the **Metrics** section, where you can view the PromQL expression that is used to plot the chart:

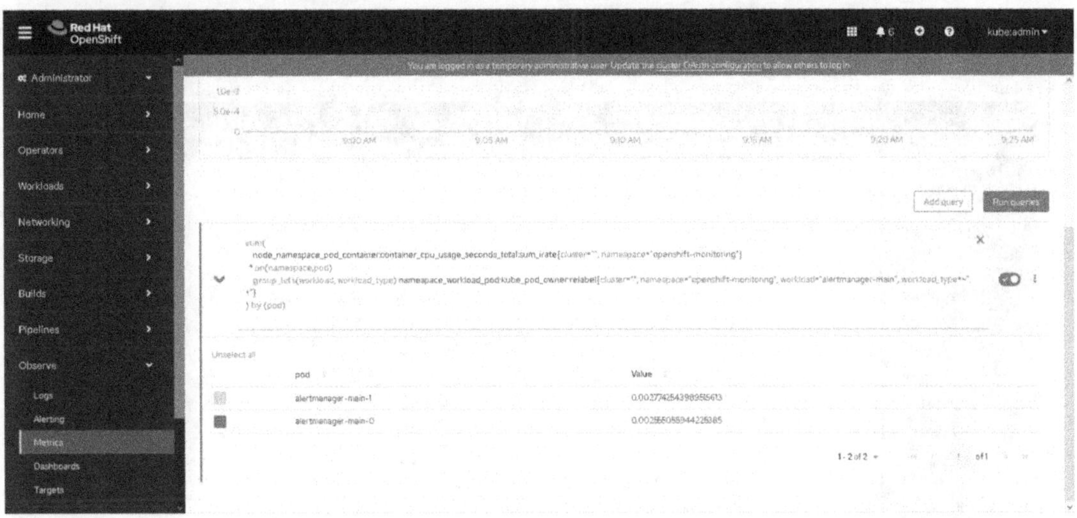

Figure 13.10: OpenShift monitoring, query editor

If you are interested in a more detailed picture of resource consumption down to an individual container, use the **Kubernetes | Compute Resources | Pod** dashboard:

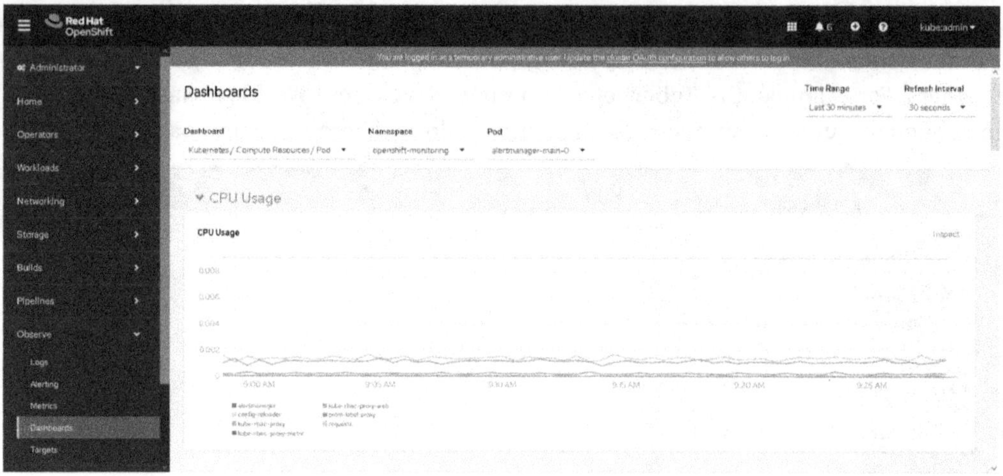

Figure 13.11: OpenShift monitoring, CPU usage dashboard

As useful as they are, all dashboards in the OpenShift monitoring stack are read-only and don't allow for any customizations. One way to bypass this limitation is to use the community-powered Grafana operator to deploy a Grafana instance and then add Thanos Querier as its data source. This approach was first mentioned in a 2020 blog article [12] and is also laid out in the KB article [13]. Please note that this solution is not supported by Red Hat under the terms of its SLA. We will, however, configure it closer to the end of this chapter because of its educational value.

Metrics targets

The CMO creates targets for endpoints of all internal components so that Prometheus can scrape their metrics. You can view all targets and their associated monitors at **Observe | Targets**:

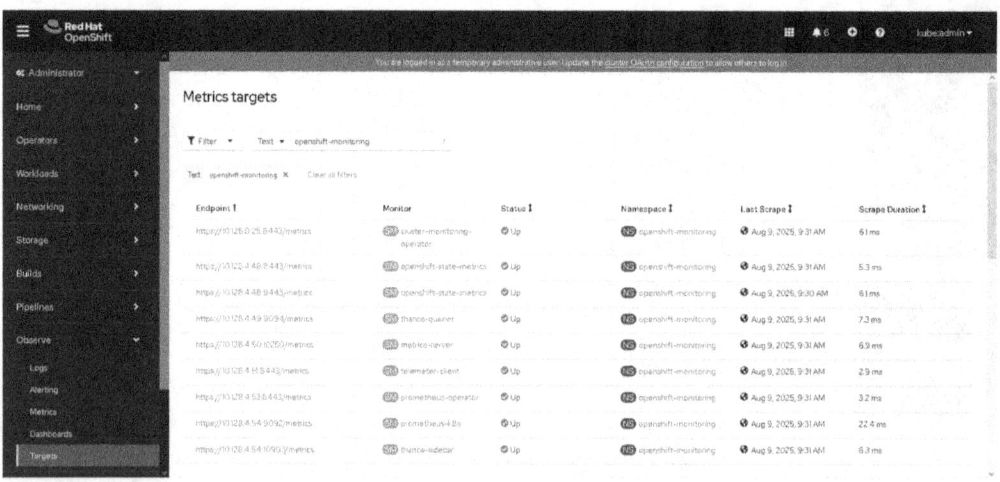

Figure 13.12: OpenShift monitoring, metrics targets exposed by service monitors

Each target endpoint corresponds to a single `ServiceMonitor` that can be identified by clicking on the endpoint. You can also list monitors with `oc get smon -n openshift-monitoring`, assuming you want to see service monitors in the `openshift-monitoring` namespace.

Alerting

All built-in and user-defined alerting rules are available in the **Observe** | **Alerting** section. From there, you can filter rules by their source (**Platform** for core platform and **User** for user-defined rules), severity, name, arbitrary labels, or state:

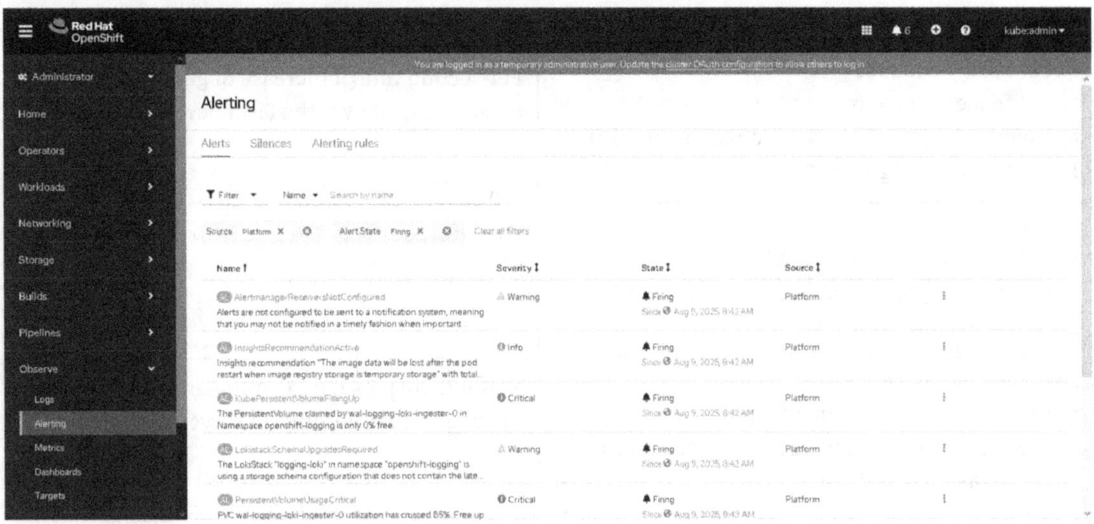

Figure 13.13: OpenShift monitoring, alerts

By clicking on an individual alert, you can access its graph, labels, remediation instructions, and a link to the rule that triggered it. Every alerting rule corresponds to a `PrometheusRule` resource and includes a PromQL expression that defines the condition for firing an alert, for how long the condition should be met before Prometheus dispatches an alert, and a description that uses templating to embed various labels into the alert's message to provide specifics about what triggered the alert. You can also silence individual alerts for a specific period of time or practically indefinitely.

Querying metrics with PromQL

As you saw in the previous section, the **Observe** | **Metrics** part of the web UI contains a query editor where you can input PromQL expressions to be evaluated by Prometheus and immediately view the result of that expression's evaluation on a chart. In this section, we will cover the basics of PromQL, such as the selection of time series for a metric, functions, and operators.

Let's take a look at some of the examples of using PromQL:

Query	Description
`etcd_requests_total{namespace="openshift-apiserver",type="routes.route.openshift.io",operation="get"}`	Returns time series for the `etcd_requests_total` metric with specific namespace, type, and operation labels. In practical terms, it shows the total number of `get` requests to `etcd` for `route` objects from different API server pods in the `openshift-api-server` namespace.
`rate(etcd_requests_total{namespace="openshift-apiserver",type="routes.route.openshift.io",operation="get"}[1h])`	Per-second rate of increase of `get` requests to `etcd` averaged over the last hour.
`sum(etcd_requests_total{namespace="openshift-apiserver",type="routes.route.openshift.io",operation="get"})`	Total number of `get` requests to `etcd` from all API server pods.
`increase(etcd_requests_total{namespace="openshift-apiserver",type="routes.route.openshift.io",operation="get"}[1h])`	Absolute increase in the number of `get` requests to `etcd` from different API server pods.
`etcd_requests_total{namespace="openshift-apiserver",type!="routes.route.openshift.io",operation=~"create|update|delete"}`	Total number of `create`, `update`, and `delete` requests to `etcd` from API servers for non-`route` objects.
`etcd_requests_total{namespace="openshift-apiserver",type="routes.route.openshift.io",operation=~"get|list"} >= 2000`	Show only time series for `read` operations on routes with sample values greater than or equal to `2000`.
`sum by (operation,apiserver) (etcd_requests_total)`	Total number of requests to `etcd` per API verb and API server type (Kubernetes, OpenShift, or OAuth).
`sum without (container,endpoint,instance,job,namespace,pod,prometheus,service,type) (etcd_requests_total)`	Same as above.
`histogram_quantile(0.9, sum by(le,operation) (rate(etcd_request_duration_seconds_bucket[5m])))`	90th percentile `etcd` request latency over the last 5 minutes for every operation (`get`, `list`, `listWithCount`, `create`, `update`, and `delete`).

Query	Description
`max_over_time(etcd_requests_total{namespace="openshift-apiserver",operation="get"}[30m])`	The maximum number of `get` operations on all resources over the last 30 minutes.
`min_over_time(etcd_requests_total{namespace="openshift-apiserver",operation="get"}[30m])`	The minimum number of `get` operations on all resources over the last 30 minutes.
`avg_over_time(etcd_requests_total{namespace="openshift-apiserver",operation="get"}[30m])`	Average number of `get` operations on all resources over the last 30 minutes.

Table 13.2: PromQL sample queries

The following table lists the functions used in our examples:

Function	Description
`rate()`	It calculates the change frequency of a metric value over a configurable time window. It can be used only with counters.

`min_over_time()`
`max_over_time()`
`avg_over_time()`
	It calculates the minimum, maximum, and average value, respectively, of a metric over a configurable period of time.

`histogram_quantile()`	Based on a distribution of values within a histogram, it calculates the value within the histogram that corresponds to a specific quantile. Useful, for example, for identifying potential outliers, such as requests that take longer than usual or slow requests experienced by a small number of clients.
`sum()`	It calculates a sum over all time series for all labels.
`increase()`	This is the absolute increase of a time series.

Table 13.3: Example PromQL functions

Due to the limitations of this book, we are not covering PromQL syntax, functions, and operators in their entirety, which are explained in great detail in [14]. A cheat sheet of PromQL usage examples that encompass a wide variety of different use cases is available at [15]. Refer to [16] for a complete list of PromQL functions with usage examples.

Using Alertmanager for notifications

Just being able to see alerts in the OpenShift web console is not enough; we need a mechanism for delivering them to concerned teams with arbitrary combinations of severity levels, namespaces, applications, and cluster core components. Alertmanager works by receiving alerts from Prometheus and Thanos Ruler and dispatching them to external receivers. It also takes care of silencing alerts, managing alert dependencies, and notification rate limiting. Alertmanager supports email, PagerDuty, Microsoft Teams, Slack, WeChat, and many other types of receivers. For an unsupported API, you can always use a webhook receiver that sends a `POST` request with the alert contents sent in the body. For a full list of supported endpoints, consult [17]. By default, Prometheus evaluates rules every minute, which adds a delay to firing rules.

Alertmanager natively supports more than 10 external systems for notification, with email being one of the oldest and most widely used. Configuring it is very simple and has been covered by countless blog articles and documentation pages, so in this book, we decided to do something more interesting and use one of the less popular receivers: Telegram. This instant messenger is a relatively new addition to the list, having been introduced at the end of 2022. Follow these steps to configure Alertmanager to send notifications to a Telegram channel:

1. First, extract the current Alertmanager configuration of the main instance:

   ```
   $ oc extract --to . secret/alertmanager-main -n openshift-monitoring
   ```

2. The next step is to edit it to configure receivers and alert routing for those receivers. For that, we will need a chatbot and a channel. Go to `https://telegram.me/BotFather` and request a bot (when a dialog window opens, type `/newbot` to start a conversation and then provide a name and username for your bot). You will get a bot token in response; save it somewhere for now.
3. Next, create a channel by clicking on the pencil or burger icon at the top left, and then on **New Channel**.
4. Open a chat with your bot and click on your bot's picture at the top of the chat, click **Add to Group or Channel**, and select the channel you created in the previous step (make sure that **Admin Rights** and **Manage Messages** are enabled, if present).
5. Depending on the Telegram version and flavor that you use, you may need to open your channel's settings instead (three vertical dots in the top-right corner), then click **Manage Channel | Administrators | Add Administrator**, type the name of your bot, click on the name of your bot, and click **Save | Close | Save**.
6. Now, send a message or two into the channel and run the following command:

   ```
   $ curl -s https://api.telegram.org/bot<YOUR_BOT_TOKEN>/getUpdates |
   python3 -m json.tool
   ```

   Take note of the `chat_id` value (starts with -), as you will need it later.

7. Now, edit the `alertmanager.yaml` file created in *step 1* by adding the following code snippet to the list of receivers (replace the placeholders in uppercase with your `bot_token` and `chat_id` values, respectively):

```
- "name": "telegram-bot"
  telegram_configs:
  - api_url: https://api.telegram.org
    bot_token: YOUR_BOT_TOKEN
    chat_id: YOUR_CHAT_ID
    parse_mode: ''
```

8. Also, add this to the list of routes at the very bottom:

```
  - "matchers":
    - "severity = warning"
    "receiver": "telegram-bot"
```

   To avoid typos, you can just copy the `chapters/13/snippets/alertmanager.yaml` file, which is located in this book's GitHub repository.

9. To apply the configuration, load it back into the `alertmanger-main` secret:

```
$ oc set data secret/alertmanager-main --from-file alertmanager.yaml -n
openshift-monitoring
```

10. The configuration will be loaded live, and Alertmanager's pods will not restart. If you have any warning alerts firing in your cluster, in a few moments, you should receive notifications for them:

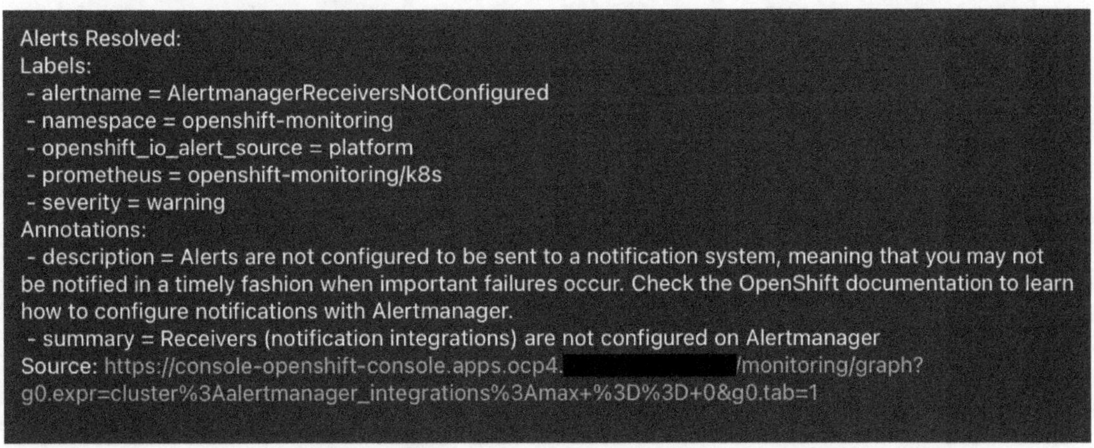

Figure 13.14: Alert notification received in Telegram

Unless you configured a custom receiver beforehand, you should have at least one warning firing: `AlertmanagerReceiversNotConfigured`. If you set everything up correctly, you will be notified of its resolution now that you have configured the receiver.

You can configure other receivers in a similar fashion; for example, follow [18] to set up a classic email receiver. By configuring multiple receivers and binding them to alerts of specific severities and with specific labels, you can also send different types of alerts to appropriate response teams.

Monitoring business applications

By default, Prometheus in OpenShift monitors only the cluster's core services. Enabling monitoring for an arbitrary business application running in a user-defined project requires two steps (in any order):

- In order for Prometheus to scrape metrics from your application, the application must expose them first. Configure your application to send desired metrics by using a Prometheus library for your application's language. This process is commonly referred to as **code instrumentation**.
- Create a `PodMonitor` or `ServiceMonitor` for your application's pods or services, respectively. This will tell the Prometheus instance deployed in the `openshift-user-workload-monitoring` namespace to start querying (or "scraping") your application's endpoint(s) for metric data.

The monitoring of user-defined projects is backed by the following components deployed in the `openshift-user-workload-monitoring` namespace:

- **Prometheus**: A separate instance of the monitoring system and TSDB configured for the monitoring of user-defined projects.
- **Thanos Ruler**: A rule and alerting evaluation engine, deployed as a separate process for user-defined projects. Sends metrics to **Thanos Querier** for aggregation and deduplication.
- **Alertmanager**: A separate instance of the Alertmanager processing system, which can be optionally deployed in the `openshift-user-workload-monitoring` namespace. Receives alerts from Prometheus and Thanos Ruler. If absent, the `main` Alertmanager instance from the `openshift-monitoring` namespaces will be used.

The configuration of the monitoring substack for user-defined projects is controlled by the `user-workload-monitoring-config` ConfigMap in the `openshift-user-workload-monitoring` namespace. Unlike its counterpart in the `openshift-monitoring` namespace, this ConfigMap is created automatically when the monitoring of user-defined projects is enabled.

Enabling and customizing monitoring for user-defined projects

The monitoring stack in every OpenShift cluster is configured for monitoring core components, which is usually sufficient for administrators and SREs. The monitoring of business applications is supported, too, but must be enabled first [20]. Here is a graphical representation of the part of the monitoring stack responsible for monitoring user-defined workloads:

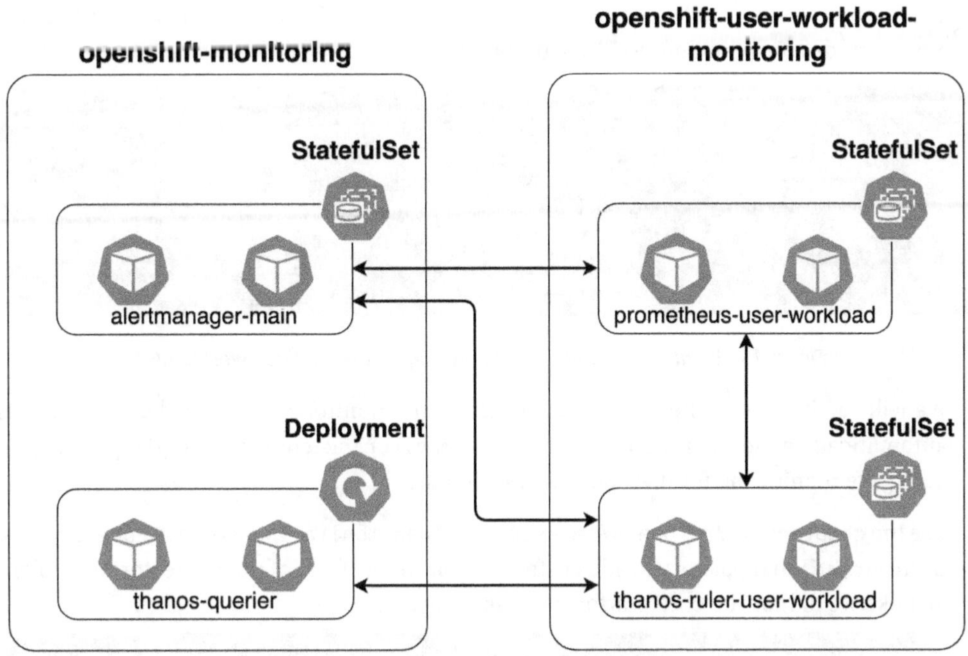

Figure 13.15: Monitoring components for user-defined projects

The preceding figure assumes that the `main` Alertmanager instance is used to route alerts for applications in user-defined projects.

To enable monitoring for user-defined projects, follow these steps:

1. First, add `enableUserWorkload: true` under `data/config.yaml` in the `cluster-monitoring-config` ConfigMap. You can use an updated `chapters/13/snippets/cm-cluster-monitoring-config-ephemeral-user-workload-enabled.yml` file from this book's GitHub repository:

```
$ oc apply -f chapters/13/snippets/cm-cluster-monitoring-config-ephemeral-user-workload-enabled.yml
```

> If you configured ODF persistent storage as per *Chapter 8*, *Working with Persistent Storage*, use the `chapters/13/snippets/cm-cluster-monitoring-config-persistent-user-workload-enabled.yml` file instead. For other storage backends, modify the manifest to use proper storage classes.

2. Run the following command in 1–2 minutes to see the status of Prometheus, Thanos Ruler, their pods, and PVCs:

```
$ oc get prom,ruler,po,pvc -o wide -n openshift-user-workload-monitoring
```

You should see that both components are available. Notice that their pods are running on worker nodes for now, and no PVCs are present:

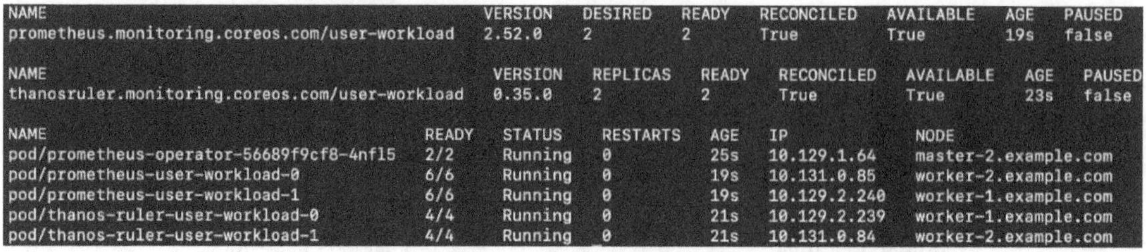

Figure 13.16: Initial placement of monitoring for user-defined workloads

We will rectify this in the next step. Enabling the monitoring of user-defined projects also automatically generated the `user-workload-monitoring-config` ConfigMap that is used to configure monitoring for user-defined workloads.

3. Use the `chapters/13/snippets/cm-user-workload-monitoring-config-ephemeral.yml` file from our GitHub repository to add customizations in the form of node selectors and tolerations, just like we did for the core platform monitoring stack:

```
$ oc apply -f chapters/13/snippets/cm-user-workload-monitoring-config-ephemeral.yml
```

> If you previously configured ODF persistent storage, as per *Chapter 8, Working with Persistent Storage*, use the `chapters/13/snippets/cm-user-workload-monitoring-config-persistent.yml` file instead. For other storage backends, modify the manifest to use proper storage classes.

4. Wait 1–2 minutes again and run the following command to check the monitoring components:

```
$ oc get prom,ruler,po,pvc -o wide -n openshift-user-workload-monitoring
```

Both Prometheus and Thanos Ruler should be available and running on infrastructure nodes now with PVCs configured:

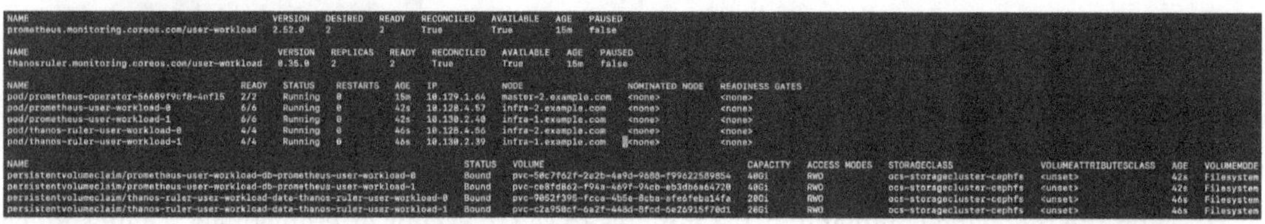

Figure 13.17: Updated placement and provisioned persistent storage for monitoring for user-defined workloads

Now that we have the monitoring of user-defined projects enabled, we can deploy a sample application and create a `ServiceMonitor` to configure Prometheus to scrape its metrics:

1. First, use the `prometheus-demo-ns.yml`, `prometheus-demo-deploy.yml`, and `prometheus-demo-svc.yml` files from the `chapters/13/snippets` directory of this book's GitHub repository to create a sample application:

```
$ oc create -f chapters/13/snippets/prometheus-demo-ns.yml -f chapters/13/snippets/prometheus-demo-deploy.yml -f chapters/13/snippets/prometheus-demo-svc.yml
```

2. Use the `oc get po,svc,ep -n prometheus-demo-app` command to verify the deployment:

```
NAME                                      READY   STATUS    RESTARTS   AGE
pod/prometheus-demo-app-6f747fb847-lz2wq  1/1     Running   0          12s

NAME                          TYPE        CLUSTER-IP      EXTERNAL-IP   PORT(S)    AGE
service/prometheus-demo-app   ClusterIP   172.30.175.84   <none>        8080/TCP   12s

NAME                            ENDPOINTS           AGE
endpoints/prometheus-demo-app   10.129.2.243:8080   12s
```

Figure 13.18: Demo application components

3. The application has already been instrumented with an appropriate library to expose metrics at the `/metrics` canonical path. Now, we need to create a `ServiceMonitor`. A `chapters/13/snippets/prometheus-demo-smon.yml` file has already been prepared for you:

```
$ oc create -f chapters/13/snippets/prometheus-demo-smon.yml
```

By creating a `ServiceMonitor`, we instructed the monitoring stack to scrape metrics from the `/metrics` canonical path. We didn't have to instrument our application with a Prometheus library, because it was already built into our sample application.

Let's now verify that our application is sending metrics when requested:

1. First, open an interactive shell session inside one of the Prometheus pods in the `openshift-user-workload-monitoring` namespace and send an HTTP `GET` request to the `/metrics` endpoint of the application:

```
$ oc exec -it prometheus-user-workload-0 -n openshift-user-workload-monitoring -- bash
$ curl prometheus-demo-app.prometheus-demo-app.svc:8080/metrics
```

You should see the following metrics, although the actual values may be different:

```
# HELP http_request_duration_seconds Duration of all HTTP requests
# TYPE http_request_duration_seconds histogram
http_request_duration_seconds_bucket{code="200",handler="found",method="get",le="0.005"} 0
http_request_duration_seconds_bucket{code="200",handler="found",method="get",le="0.01"} 0
http_request_duration_seconds_bucket{code="200",handler="found",method="get",le="0.025"} 0
http_request_duration_seconds_bucket{code="200",handler="found",method="get",le="0.05"} 0
http_request_duration_seconds_bucket{code="200",handler="found",method="get",le="0.1"} 0
http_request_duration_seconds_bucket{code="200",handler="found",method="get",le="0.25"} 0
http_request_duration_seconds_bucket{code="200",handler="found",method="get",le="0.5"} 0
http_request_duration_seconds_bucket{code="200",handler="found",method="get",le="1"} 0
http_request_duration_seconds_bucket{code="200",handler="found",method="get",le="2.5"} 0
http_request_duration_seconds_bucket{code="200",handler="found",method="get",le="5"} 0
http_request_duration_seconds_bucket{code="200",handler="found",method="get",le="10"} 0
http_request_duration_seconds_bucket{code="200",handler="found",method="get",le="+Inf"} 0
http_request_duration_seconds_sum{code="200",handler="found",method="get"} 0
http_request_duration_seconds_count{code="200",handler="found",method="get"} 0
# HELP http_requests_total Count of all HTTP requests
# TYPE http_requests_total counter
http_requests_total{code="200",method="get"} 0
http_requests_total{code="404",method="get"} 0
# HELP version Version information about this binary
# TYPE version gauge
version{version="v0.4.2"} 1
```

Figure 13.19: Metrics exposed by the demo application

Notice that the `http_request_duration_seconds` metric is a histogram (as indicated by its `TYPE` value on the next line); every bucket corresponds to a range of response latencies of the application. Since we have just deployed the application and it has barely processed any requests yet, all buckets have the same value. Again, this is made possible by using a Prometheus library to instrument the application's code so that it exposes metrics over HTTP. Had it used an endpoint other than `/metrics`, we would have to adjust it in the `ServiceMonitor` to match.

2. Before we move on, send some requests to the app's webroot by running the following command a few times to generate some activity that can be seen in a dashboard on the next step:

```
$ curl prometheus-demo-app.prometheus-demo-app.svc:8080
```

3. Exit the pod's shell by pressing *Ctrl* + *D* or running `exit`.
4. If you now navigate to **Observe** | **Targets** again and start typing the name of our demo namespace, you will see the metrics target listed with a status of **Up**:

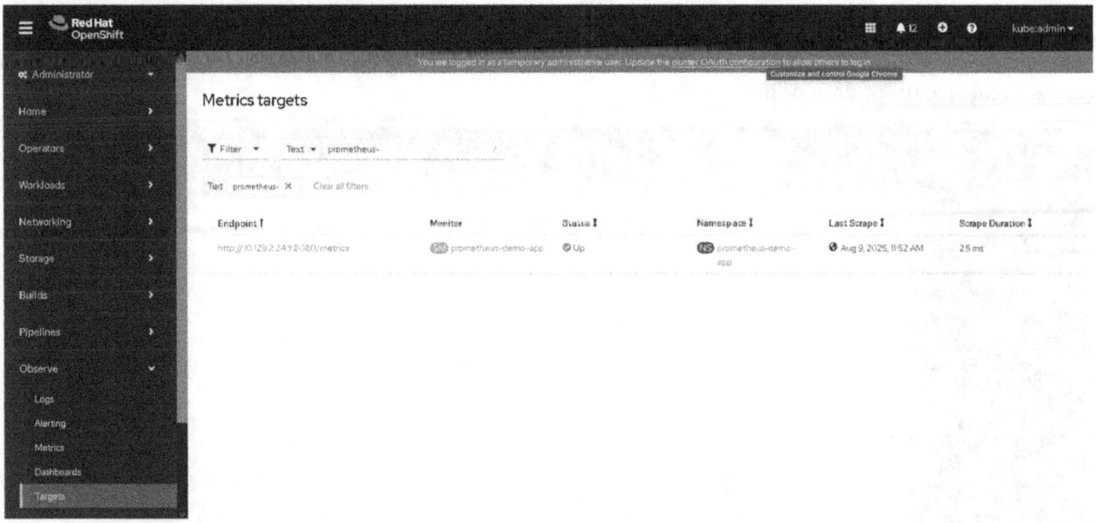

Figure 13.20: Metrics target for the demo application in the OpenShift web UI

By clicking on it, you can view its endpoints, of which there is just one – the IP address of the application's pod paired with its only port, `8080`:

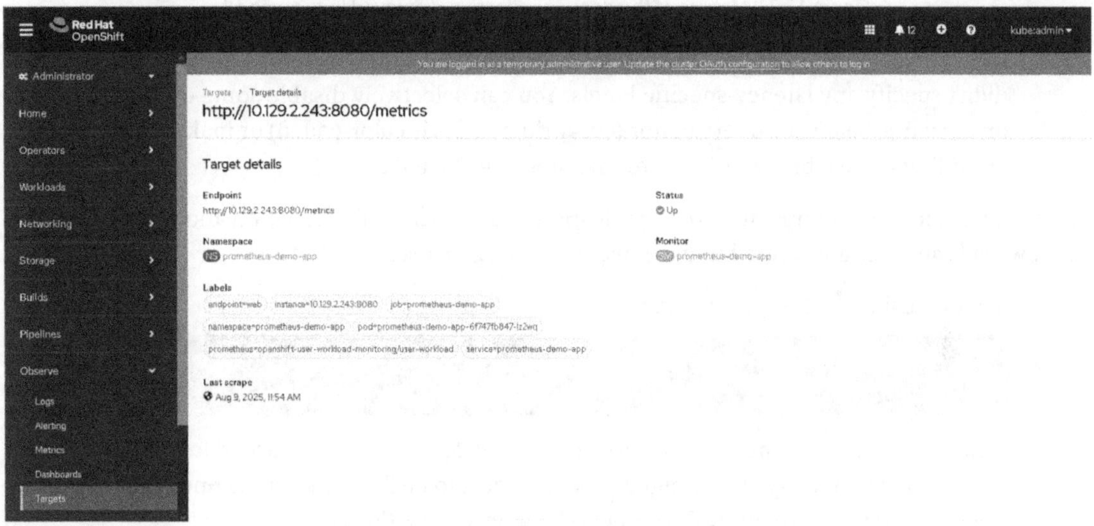

Figure 13.21: Web UI view of the metrics endpoint exposed by the applications

5. Now that the metrics are being collected, we can query them via the web console. Go to **Observe | Metrics** and type the following in the query field below the plot:

```
http_request_duration_seconds_bucket{namespace="prometheus-demo-app"}
```

6. Set the refresh interval to 30 seconds to match the metrics scraping interval from the `ServiceMonitor`. Click **Run queries**, and you should see a simple chart that shows the historical stream of data points:

Figure 13.22: Metrics of the demo application displayed in the web UI

The expression in the preceding screenshot returns all time series for the metric, because we didn't specify any latency-specific labels. You can selectively disable some of the time series on the panel below the query editor (every time series is color-coded) or make it more specific by adding more labels within `{}`, for example, `le="0.05"`.

As an experiment, let's interact with our application and see what effect it has on another metric. This time, we will not exec anywhere but use **port forwarding** instead:

1. Set it up using the following command:

```
$ oc port-forward deploy/prometheus-demo-app 8080:8080 -n prometheus-
demo-app
```

Now, every time we send a request to local port `8080`, it will be forwarded to the same port in the pod. For simplicity, we configure the local port to be the same as the one that the application is listening on, but they don't necessarily have to be the same.

2. Next, in another terminal session, start an infinite loop of sending HTTP `GET` requests to our application with a 1-second interval and leave it running for 10–20 seconds to generate some requests:

```
$ while true; do curl localhost:8080; sleep 1; done
```

3. Terminate both the loop and port-forwarding with *Ctrl* + *C* and open the query editor. Enter the following and click **Run queries**:

```
http_requests_total{namespace="prometheus-demo-app"}
```

You should see a chart that shows an increase in the request count for the `200` status code:

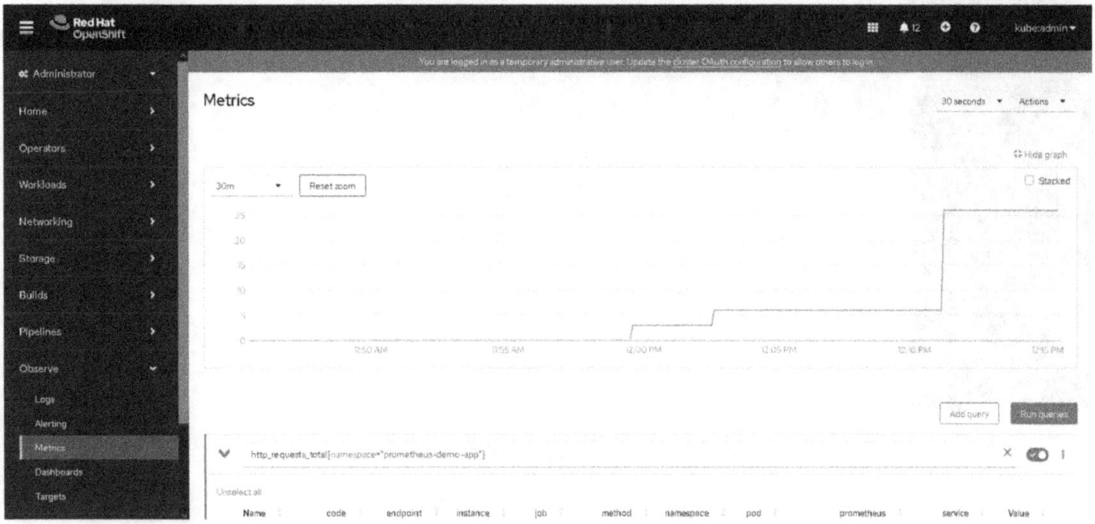

Figure 13.23: Updated metrics of the demo application reflected in the web UI

In a real-world scenario with lots of graphs for different status codes overlaying on top of each other, you would want to make the chart show only successful requests by adding the `code="200"` label to the expression.

4. So let's create a custom rule for that metric. The manifest is stored in the `chapters/13/snippets/prometheus-demo-promrule.yml` file of this book's GitHub repository for your convenience. The rule defined in the manifest is triggered when the total number of HTTP `GET` requests to any endpoint other than `/metrics` with a status code of `200` exceeds 10. Create the rule:

```
$ oc create -f chapters/13/snippets/prometheus-demo-promrule.yml
```

> Rules for user-defined projects can only use metrics from the same namespace or from core platform components. Metrics from other projects require separate local rules.

5. Next, navigate to **Observe | Alerting**, remove the **Source: Platform** filter, and start typing `TooManyHTTPRequests` until the alert shows up (you can also use the **Source: User** filter):

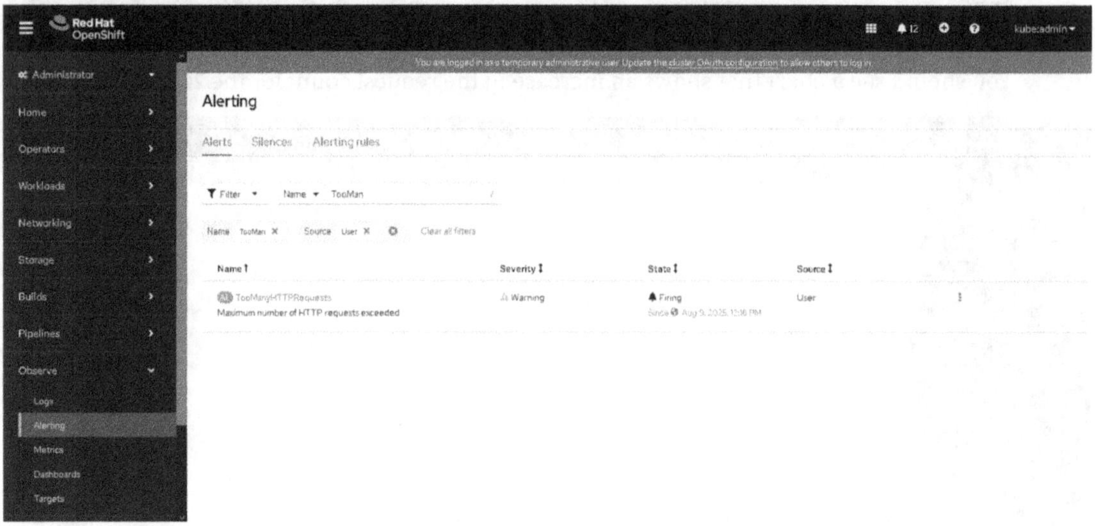

Figure 13.24: Demo application alert firing

If you check the alert within a minute of creating it, it may be in a **Pending** state, which means it is waiting for the period specified in `.spec.groups[].rules[].for` before it fires.

6. Click on it, and you will see the plot showing data points selected by the rule's PromQL expression:

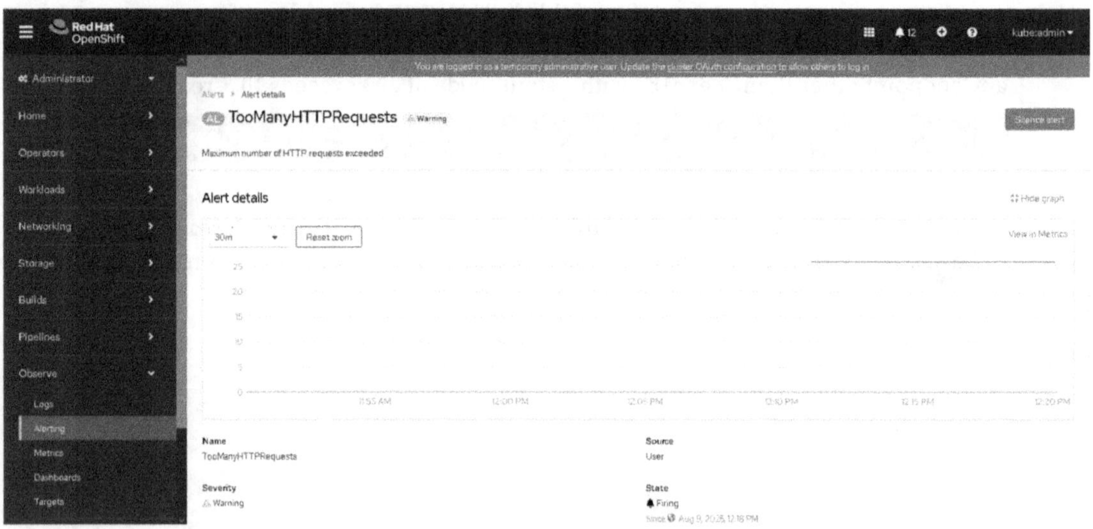

Figure 13.25: TooManyHTTPRequests plot

By now, you should have received an alert in the channel that you configured previously for alerts of a warning severity. If you followed our exercises so far, that would be a Telegram channel:

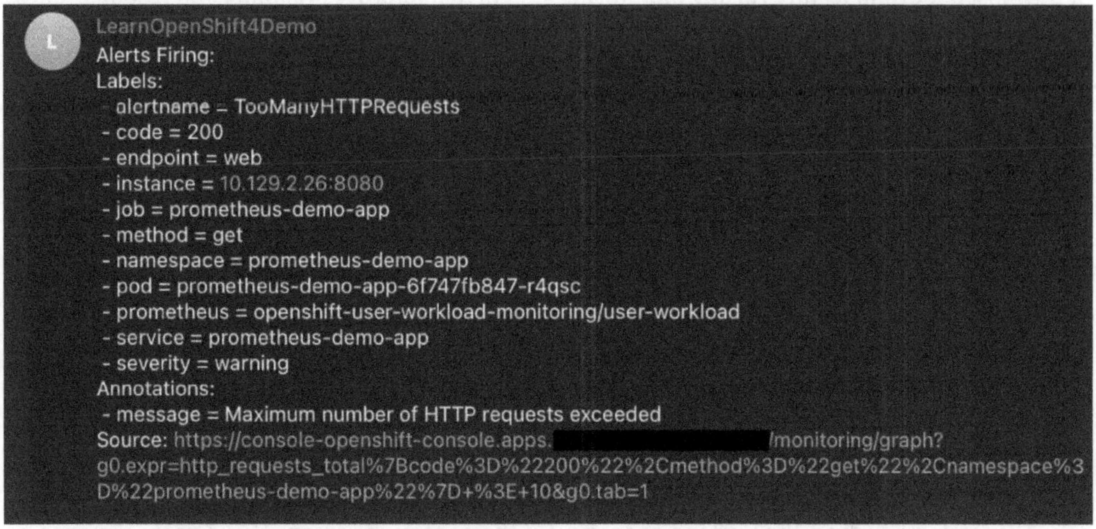

Figure 13.26: An alert about the demo application received in Telegram

You can use any combination of these labels to configure alert routing rules. To prevent an alert from firing, for example, while you are working on a resolution, you can silence it in the Alerting UI at **Observe** | **Alerting**, clicking on the alert, and specifying for how long you want to silence it.

As a wrap-up on the subject of alerting, here are some of the best practices that we recommend following when writing your own alerting rules:

- Concentrate on symptoms, not causes. Implementing rules for every possible underlying cause results in many alerts that are difficult to maintain and likely will not be comprehensive enough anyway. An alert should only notify you about apparent symptoms of a problem, which should be investigated further.
- Include severity levels in your alerts in order to route them to the proper response teams.
- Carefully implement alert routing to avoid sending irrelevant alerts to recipients. As experience shows, too many alerts cause people to lose focus, which impacts response time.
- Try to keep the number of rules to a minimum, only focusing on scenarios that are important to the business.
- Always provide a clear message for your alerts. It should mention the likely cause of a problem and possible remedies. Use core platform alerts as a guide; they all include links to remediation runbooks and use templating to include component-specific labels in the message to provide more information.

There is also a good read on alerting in general by Rob Ewaschuk [19], a former Google SRE.

Creating custom dashboards with Grafana

The ability to create custom dashboards tailored to technical teams, analysts, and stakeholders is one of the most important features of any monitoring system that improves visibility and responsiveness. Earlier in this chapter, we mentioned that the OpenShift UI does not provide controls for customizing existing or adding new dashboards and suggested that the community-supported Grafana can be used to pull metrics from Thanos Querier and build custom dashboards. The author of this chapter had several customers asking about this, so we decided to include it in this book. Now, let's walk through the process of setting it up together.

First, we need to install the Grafana operator:

1. Go to **Operators | OperatorHub**, type `grafana` in the search box, and click on **Grafana Operator** provided by Grafana Labs. Since this operator is not supported by Red Hat, you will have to accept the disclaimer to proceed. Click **Install**, then **Install** again to accept default parameters (the operator will be installed in the `openshift-operators` namespace). When installation begins, click on **View installed Operators in Namespace openshift-operators** and wait until its status changes to **Succeeded.**
2. Now that the operator is ready, we can create an instance of Grafana. In the list of installed operators, click on the Grafana operator. On the operator's screen, click **Create instance** on the Grafana tile (you may need to scroll all the way down to see it). Switch to YAML view, then change the name to `grafana-demo`, as well as dashboards and folders labels to match, and specify a route that you will use to access Grafana. Take note of the default user and password (**root/start**) and click **Create** to create the instance. You can find a complete Grafana instance manifest at `chapters/13/snippets/grafana-demo.yml` in this book's GitHub repository. Feel free to use it as a reference when editing the object in the UI, or just go ahead and create an object from it via `oc create`.
3. Next, we need to grant the Grafana instance's service account the permission to access metrics on the cluster level:

```
$ oc adm policy add-cluster-role-to-user cluster-monitoring-view -z
grafana-demo-sa -n openshift-operators
```

4. The next step is to create a token that Grafana will use to authenticate itself to Thanos Querier:

```
$ oc create token grafana-demo-sa --duration 8760h -n openshift-operators
```

5. Another required component is a data source, which encapsulates the endpoint address and authentication details for where to fetch metrics from – in our case, Thanos Querier. On the Grafana operator's screen, select **Grafana Datasource** at the top (scroll to the right if you can't see it), then select **Create Grafana Datasource**. In the YAML editor, add the token from the previous step, and update the endpoint URL and labels according to the `chapters/13/snippets/grafanadatasource-sample.yml` manifest in this book's GitHub repository.

6. In the OpenShift console (in the **Administrator** perspective), navigate to **Networking | Routes**, make sure that the `openshift-operators` namespace is selected, and click on the hostname of your route. Log in with the default username and password (`root/start`), then go to **Connections | Data sources** and confirm that the data source you added is present. Admin credentials can also be obtained using the following command:

```
$ oc extract --to - secret/grafana-demo-admin-credentials -n openshift-
operators
```

7. If the datasource is not showing up, check the `GrafanaDatasource` object you created:

```
$ oc get -o yaml grafanadatasource/grafanadatasource-sample -n openshift-
operators
```

   If no typos or mistakes were made, you should see something like this:

```
status:
  conditions:
  - lastTransitionTime: "2025-08-10T07:18:03Z"
    message: Datasource was successfully applied to 1 instances
    observedGeneration: 1
    reason: ApplySuccessful
    status: "True"
    type: DatasourceSynchronized
  hash: ff0021fe01d38f17d4253da0b5c1ac226b54fa60622734eff8b41ca519843007
  lastResync: "2025-08-10T07:23:03Z"
  uid: 6b455a42-be97-474b-8517-4d47ccd6d55a
```

Figure 13.27: GrafanaDataSource was successfully applied and synchronized

8. Go back to the Grafana UI and try refreshing the page – the datasource should show up. You may need to wait for up to 5 minutes (`.spec.resyncPeriod`) before it shows up.

Now, let's create our first dashboard:

1. Click on **Dashboards | Create Dashboard | Add visualization** and select our only datasource (named `prometheus` by default).
2. On the **Query** tab (below the panel that says **No data**), select the `http_requests_total` metric, select **namespace** in **Label filters**, and set the value to `prometheus-demo-app`.
3. Click **Run queries**, and a graph for the metric will be displayed above. At the top right, you can also choose a visualization for the metric, for example, **Time series** (default) or **Histogram**. Change the time range to encompass our last experiment with sending HTTP requests to our application, then click **Save dashboard**.
4. On the right-hand side, give this panel a title (for example, `Demo App Total HTTP Requests`), then click **Save dashboard**. Give a title to your dashboard, for example, `Demo App Dashboard`, then click **Save | Back to dashboards**. You should see something similar to the following:

Figure 13.28: A panel and a dashboard for the demo application in Grafana

We have just successfully configured our first dashboard with a single chart.

As a conclusion to our exercise, let's simulate traffic to our application again and see how it is reflected on the dashboard:

1. First, change the refresh rate to **5s** in the top-right corner so that you can see changes as soon as possible. Next, use the following already familiar command to set up local port forwarding:

```
$ oc port-forward deploy/prometheus-demo-app 8080:8080 -n prometheus-
demo-app
```

2. Open a separate terminal and send 60 HTTP `GET` requests to the `/` endpoint of our demo application with a 1-second interval:

```
$ for i in $(seq 1 60); do curl localhost:8080; sleep 1; done
```

You should start seeing the change in the graph with a 5–10-second delay (you might want to change the span to the last 5 minutes and set the refresh interval to **30s** or lower to make the changes stand out):

Figure 13.29: Demo application's activity is reflected on the Grafana dashboard

You can now terminate the `oc port-forward` command from the first step by pressing *Ctrl* + *C*.

We have just created a simple dashboard for our demo application that updates in near-real time and tracks the total number of HTTP `GET` requests and responses with different status codes. By adding additional labels to the dashboard's query, you can make more specific dashboards, for example, for displaying only HTTP `404` responses. While simplistic, it is representative of how you would create dashboards for your business applications.

Production considerations

Proper capacity planning, sizing, and availability configuration are important to prepare the monitoring stack for production use. Incorrect planning may result in missing data points, with duplicate alerts at best and disruptions to other workloads running on the same nodes at worst. The following is a list of the items that you may want to consider for a production deployment:

- Moving monitoring components to dedicated nodes using node selectors [21] and tolerations [22]. This will free up resources for business applications, separate management concerns, and save on subscription costs.
- Deploying a separate `Alertmanager` instance for user-defined workloads. This will reduce the load on the `main` instance in the `openshift-monitoring` namespace and is beneficial for a large number of user-defined projects.
- Configuring retention size and period for Prometheus [23]. By default, Prometheus purges data blocks every 15 days for core cluster components and every 24 hours for user-defined workloads. If you specify retention size too, data will be purged based on both policies, whichever is met first.
- Configuring the retention period for Thanos Ruler. By default, it retains metrics data for 24 hours. The complete procedure is outlined at [24].

- Configuring persistent filesystem storage for Prometheus, Alertmanager, and Thanos Ruler that is large enough for the configured retention period and size (Prometheus), as well as for the number of rules evaluated and the number of samples generated by them (Thanos Ruler). This will make sure that collected metrics, as well as alerts and alert silences, survive pod restarts and prevent duplicate notifications. Keep in mind that monitoring components can only use filesystem storage (`.spec.volumeMode: Filesystem` in a PVC ensures that it will be formatted) and require a POSIX-compliant filesystem if pre-formatted storage is provided. Use [25] as a reference.
- Configuring requests and limits for monitoring components. This will ensure that they are always scheduled on the nodes that have the requested amount of CPU and RAM, at the same time making sure that they cannot use up all available node capacity. Examples are available at [26].
- Sending core and/or user-defined metrics data to an external system for long-term storage using the remote write feature. Supported receivers include Kafka, Amazon Timestream, Elasticsearch, Splunk, and New Relic, among others. The full list of supported endpoints is available at [27]. Depending on the capacity of a remote system in question, you may also want to adjust queue settings on the Prometheus side using the `config.yaml/prometheusK8s/queueConfig` section to avoid throttling, as explained at [28] and [29].
- Scaling up monitoring components to increase performance and availability.
- Configuring the uncompressed body size limit for scraped cluster metrics. This is to prevent the main Prometheus instance from consuming an excessive amount of memory if one of its targets sends too much data in one data point. It is controlled by a parameter called `enforceBodySizeLimit` of `prometheusK8s` in the `cluster-monitoring-config` ConfigMap. By default, there is no limit. Refer to [30] to learn more.
- Adding cluster ID labels to core and/or user-defined metrics. It is common for businesses to have multiple OpenShift clusters for different environments, classes of applications, and **lines of business** (**LOBs**), so sorting out and correlating metrics sent to a central remote system from different clusters may become untenable. Adding a unique cluster-specific label to metrics sent by Prometheus on each cluster lets you query metrics based on the cluster they came from. Details are provided at [31].

Not all these recommendations must necessarily be followed for every production deployment. Consider which ones make sense for your environment and can be maintained with relatively low operational overhead. A more complete list of configuration options with details can be found at [32].

Summary

Now that this chapter is over, it's time to look back at what we've learned. We started with a brief explanation of the role that monitoring plays in observability, and we then briefly discussed the history behind Prometheus, a de facto standard for metric collection and processing. Next, we listed all the components of the core monitoring stack in OpenShift and then configured it with persistent storage and moved it to dedicated infra nodes. As part of the same discussion, we looked into PromQL and examined monitoring-related sections in the OpenShift web console.

As a separate exercise, we configured our first alert receiver in Alertmanager. We picked Telegram as it is less covered in public sources, and observed how notifications are displayed in our channel.

Next, we moved on to monitoring user-defined applications with service monitors and Prometheus rules. The exercise was based on a simple demo app that we deployed to illustrate those concepts.

Finally, we installed Grafana community operator and created Grafana with a `GrafanaDatasource` to tap into the monitoring data stored in Thanos and visualize it. We also built a simple dashboard that tracks the total number of HTTP requests to our demo application, showing how Grafana can be used to build panels and dashboards for different teams within your organization. The scale, of course, is different; however, the concept remains the same.

In the next chapter, we will discuss yet another part of observability – distributed tracing. It is usually used alongside service mesh, which is what we're going to start our discussion with.

References

To learn more about the topics that were covered in this chapter, take a look at the following resources:

- [1] *Prometheus upstream project*: `https://prometheus.io/`
- [2] *Prometheus: Monitoring at SoundCloud*: `https://developers.soundcloud.com/blog/prometheus-monitoring-at-soundcloud`
- [3] *OpenTSDB – The Scalable Time Series Database*: `https://opentsdb.net/`
- [4] *About OpenShift Container Platform monitoring*: `https://docs.redhat.com/en/documentation/monitoring_stack_for_red_hat_openshift/4.16/html/about_monitoring/about-ocp-monitoring`
- [5] *Metric queries*: `https://grafana.com/docs/loki/latest/query/metric_queries/`
- [6] *Configure remote write storage*: `https://docs.redhat.com/en/documentation/monitoring_stack_for_red_hat_openshift/4.16/html/configuring_core_platform_monitoring/configuring-metrics#configuring-remote-write-storage_configuring-metrics`
- [7] *About remote health monitoring*: `https://docs.redhat.com/en/documentation/openshift_container_platform/4.16/html/support/remote-health-monitoring-with-connected-clusters#about-remote-health-monitoring`
- [8] *Subscription requirements for OpenShift*: `https://www.redhat.com/en/resources/self-managed-openshift-subscription-guide#section-4`
- [9] *ClusterMonitoringConfiguration*: `https://docs.redhat.com/en/documentation/monitoring_stack_for_red_hat_openshift/4.16/html/config_map_reference_for_the_cluster_monitoring_operator/config-map-reference-for-the-cluster-monitoring-operator#clustermonitoringconfiguration`
- [10] *Histograms and summaries*: `https://prometheus.io/docs/practices/histograms/`
- [11] *Using oc adm top to Monitor Memory Usage*: `https://www.redhat.com/en/blog/using-oc-adm-top-to-monitor-memory-usage`
- [12] *Custom Grafana dashboards for Red Hat OpenShift Container Platform 4*: `https://www.redhat.com/en/blog/custom-grafana-dashboards-red-hat-openshift-container-platform-4`

- [13] *Custom Grafana Dashboard for custom metrics*: https://access.redhat.com/solutions/5335491
- [14] *Querying basics*: https://prometheus.io/docs/prometheus/latest/querying/basics/
- [15] *PromQL Cheat Sheet*: https://promlabs.com/promql-cheat-sheet/
- [16] *Query functions*: https://prometheus.io/docs/prometheus/latest/querying/functions/
- [17] *Alertmanager configuration | General receiver-related settings*: https://prometheus.io/docs/alerting/latest/configuration/#receiver
- [18] *Email receiver configuration*: https://prometheus.io/docs/alerting/latest/configuration/#email_config
- [19] *My Philosophy on Alerting* by R. Ewaschuk: https://docs.google.com/document/d/199PqyG3UsyXlwieHaqbGiWVa8eMWi8zzAn0YfcApr8Q/edit
- [20] *Configuring user workload monitoring*: https://docs.redhat.com/en/documentation/monitoring_stack_for_red_hat_openshift/4.16/html/configuring_user_workload_monitoring/index
- [21] *Using node selectors to move monitoring components*: https://docs.redhat.com/en/documentation/monitoring_stack_for_red_hat_openshift/4.16/html/monitoring_key_concepts/key-concepts#using-node-selectors-to-move-monitoring-components_key-concepts
- [22] *Assigning tolerations to monitoring components*: https://docs.redhat.com/en/documentation/monitoring_stack_for_red_hat_openshift/4.16/html-single/configuring_core_platform_monitoring/index#assigning-tolerations-to-monitoring-components_configuring-performance-and-scalability
- [23] *Modifying the retention time and size for Prometheus metrics data*: https://docs.redhat.com/en/documentation/monitoring_stack_for_red_hat_openshift/4.16/html/configuring_core_platform_monitoring/storing-and-recording-data#modifying-retention-time-and-size-for-prometheus-metrics-data_storing-and-recording-data
- [24] *Modifying the retention time for Thanos Ruler metrics data*: https://docs.redhat.com/en/documentation/monitoring_stack_for_red_hat_openshift/4.16/html/configuring_user_workload_monitoring/storing-and-recording-data-uwm#modifying-the-retention-time-for-thanos-ruler-metrics-data_storing-and-recording-data-uwm
- [25] *Configuring persistent storage*: https://docs.redhat.com/en/documentation/monitoring_stack_for_red_hat_openshift/4.16/html/configuring_core_platform_monitoring/storing-and-recording-data#configuring-persistent-storage_storing-and-recording-data
- [26] *Managing CPU and memory resources for monitoring components*: https://docs.redhat.com/en/documentation/monitoring_stack_for_red_hat_openshift/4.16/html/configuring_core_platform_monitoring/configuring-performance-and-scalability#managing-cpu-and-memory-resources-for-monitoring-components_configuring-performance-and-scalability
- [27] *Remote Endpoints and Storage*: https://prometheus.io/docs/operating/integrations/#remote-endpoints-and-storage
- [28] *Example remote write queue configuration*: https://docs.redhat.com/en/documentation/

monitoring_stack_for_red_hat_openshift/4.16/html/configuring_core_platform_monitoring/configuring-metrics#example-remote-write-queue-configuration_configuring-metrics

- [29] *Remote write tuning*: https://prometheus.io/docs/practices/remote_write/#remote-write-tuning
- [30] *Setting the body size limit for metrics scraping*: https://docs.redhat.com/en/documentation/monitoring_stack_for_red_hat_openshift/4.16/html/configuring_core_platform_monitoring/configuring-performance-and-scalability#setting-the-body-size-limit-for-metrics-scraping_configuring-performance-and-scalability
- [31] *Creating cluster ID labels for metrics*: https://docs.redhat.com/en/documentation/monitoring_stack_for_red_hat_openshift/4.16/html/configuring_core_platform_monitoring/configuring-metrics#creating-cluster-id-labels-for-metrics_configuring-metrics
- [32] *Configuring core platform monitoring*: https://docs.redhat.com/en/documentation/monitoring_stack_for_red_hat_openshift/4.16/html/configuring_core_platform_monitoring/index
- [33] *Prometheus WhatsApp API integration*: https://github.com/infobip/prometheus-whatsapp-tutorial

Quiz

Test your understanding of application monitoring with this quick quiz:

1. What is the default endpoint used by Prometheus to pull metrics from targets?
    a. `/`
    b. `/metrics`
    c. `/api`
    d. `/prometheus`
2. What is the name of the ConfigMap that stores the configuration of the OpenShift core monitoring stack?
    a. `openshift-monitoring-config`
    b. `cluster-monitoring-config`
    c. `user-workload-monitoring-config`
    d. `prometheus-config`
3. What is the name of the ConfigMap that stores the configuration for monitoring user-defined workloads?
    a. `user-workload-monitoring-config`
    b. `openshift-user-workload-monitoring`
    c. `user-workload-config`
    d. `cluster-monitoring-config`

4. Which object needs to be created for a direct scraping of metrics from an application?
    a. `ServiceMonitor`
    b. `PodMonitor`
    c. `Probe`
    d. None of the above
5. Which receiver is NOT natively supported by Prometheus?
    a. Email
    b. Amazon **Simple Notification Service** (SNS)
    c. WhatsApp
    d. Discord

Answers

1. **b.** Although the `/metrics` endpoint is used by default, it can be changed.
2. **b.** To configure the OpenShift cluster monitoring stack, you need to update the `cluster-monitoring-config` ConfigMap.
3. **a.** Configuration of the monitoring of user-defined projects is done through the `user-workload-monitoring-config` ConfigMap.
4. **b.** Although both `ServiceMonitor` and `PodMonitor` objects can be used to configure Prometheus for metrics scraping, the latter is used specifically for direct access to metrics and does not involve a `Service` object, targeting pods directly using their labels.
5. **c.** Although WhatsApp is not (yet) natively supported as a receiver, you can use a generic `webhook_config` to send your alerts to WhatsApp; there is a project on GitHub [33] that does exactly that (untested), if you're willing to go an extra mile.

14

Understanding Service Mesh and Distributed Tracing

In this chapter, we'll introduce service mesh and distributed tracing and show how they map to OpenShift. A service mesh adds a dedicated layer for service-to-service communication – making it easier to apply consistent policies for security and traffic management – while distributed tracing helps you follow a single request across multiple services so you can pinpoint where latency and errors originate.

We'll focus on Red Hat OpenShift Service Mesh and how it fits into real enterprise operations: installing and understanding the operator-driven architecture, onboarding workloads safely, and using the platform tooling to troubleshoot production-style issues. As more organizations adopt microservices, these capabilities become less of a "nice to have" and more of a baseline for operating reliably at scale.

This chapter covers the following topics:

- Handling microservice architecture challenges
- Exploring the Service Mesh Operator
- Exploring Istio and Maistra
- Setting up Kiali
- Tracing with Jaeger and Tempo
- Exploring the Envoy proxy

Let's get started!

Technical requirements

In this chapter, you will need the following:

- Internet access
- Bash shell (other shells work as well)
- A multi-node OpenShift cluster – for example, OpenShift on vSphere, built in *Chapter 3, Getting Started with OpenShift* (recommended)

- OpenShift Data Foundation, installed and configured according to *Chapter 8*, *Working with Persistent Storage*, or any other S3-compatible object store
- Firefox (recommended) or any other web browser
- An active Red Hat subscription to view Red Hat **Knowledgebase** (**KB**) articles

You can access this book's GitHub repository at `https://github.com/PacktPublishing/Learn-OpenShift-Second-Edition`.

Handling microservice architecture challenges

As you've noticed throughout the book, switching from monolithic to microservice architectures has revolutionized software development, offering scalability, flexibility, and faster deployment cycles. OpenShift is an excellent platform for running microservices, but this shift also introduces challenges that teams must address to leverage their potential fully. Let's briefly discuss the key challenges microservices bring:

- **Management complexity**: Managing numerous microservices, each with different languages and tools, adds deployment and monitoring challenges, requiring robust orchestration.
- **Network reliability**: Microservices rely on network communication, which introduces latency and potential failures that can disrupt the system.
- **Observability**: Monitoring microservices is difficult due to their distributed nature, necessitating advanced tools for logs, metrics, and traces.
- **Service discovery**: Scaling services demands efficient discovery mechanisms to avoid hard-coding endpoints.
- **Security**: More services increase the attack surface, requiring encryption and consistent security management.
- **Testing and debugging**: Microservices complicate testing and debugging due to complex, difficult-to-predict interactions.
- **Deployment and versioning**: Independent deployments challenge version compatibility across services, risking system disruptions.
- **Data management**: Distributed data complicates consistency and synchronization, requiring careful management.

Service meshes bring components that reduce management complexity and improve visibility and security for microservices communication. Red Hat's implementation of Istio brings all the necessary functionality in the best possible, enterprise-ready ways. The sections that follow will describe the key components of Red Hat OpenShift Service Mesh.

Service meshes and tracing solutions

A service mesh abstracts service-to-service networking and provides consistent controls for security, connectivity, and observability. In OpenShift, Red Hat delivers these capabilities through the **OpenShift Service Mesh Operator**, which packages and integrates established open source projects including **Istio** and **Envoy**.

By introducing an additional layer in the request path, a service mesh provides a great deal of flexibility – especially for traffic management and policy enforcement – but it can also make troubleshooting harder if you don't have the right visibility. This is where tools such as Jaeger and Kiali become essential:

- **Jaeger** offers distributed tracing capabilities, enabling detailed tracking of service requests and identifying performance bottlenecks and latency issues.
- **Kiali** provides powerful visualization tools to monitor the service mesh, view traffic flows, and understand service dependencies, enhancing overall observability.

Navigating microservice architectures is challenging, but with the right platform capabilities, it becomes manageable. A service mesh (Istio/Envoy) combined with strong observability (Jaeger/Kiali) gives you the foundation to secure service-to-service traffic, shape and control requests, and debug problems across multiple hops. In the rest of this chapter, we'll explore how these components fit together in OpenShift – starting with the OpenShift Service Mesh Operator and the architecture it installs and manages.

Exploring the Service Mesh Operator

Red Hat OpenShift Service Mesh provides a consistent way to manage service-to-service communication in microservice architectures. It adds a transparent layer on top of existing applications – typically without requiring code changes – by intercepting network traffic between services and applying policy in a uniform, platform-managed way.

Microservices break enterprise applications into modular services, which improves independent deployment and scaling. The trade-off is operational complexity: as the number of services grows, it becomes harder to secure service-to-service traffic, control request behavior (timeouts, retries, routing), and troubleshoot failures and latency across multiple hops. A service mesh addresses this by inserting proxies into the request path so traffic can be secured, routed, observed, and controlled consistently.

Built on the open source Istio project (with Envoy as the data-plane proxy), OpenShift Service Mesh provides the following core capabilities:

- **Traffic management:** Controls routing and reliability behavior (for example, traffic shifting, retries, and timeouts).
- **Service identity and security:** Establishes strong service identity and secures service-to-service communication (commonly with mTLS).
- **Policy enforcement:** Defines and distributes policies (for example, mTLS mode and authorization rules) that the sidecar proxies enforce consistently across services and namespaces.
- **Telemetry and observability:** Produces standardized metrics, logging, and traces to help you understand dependencies and detect issues quickly.

Under the hood, the mesh typically deploys an Envoy sidecar proxy alongside application pods to intercept inbound and outbound traffic. The control plane distributes configuration to these proxies, which then enforce routing, security, and telemetry behavior in the data plane.

Let's take a closer look at the components that make up OpenShift Service Mesh.

OpenShift Service Mesh architecture

Let's look at the component diagram of Service Mesh; it shows the data flow at a high level, as well as the main components we will discuss in this chapter.

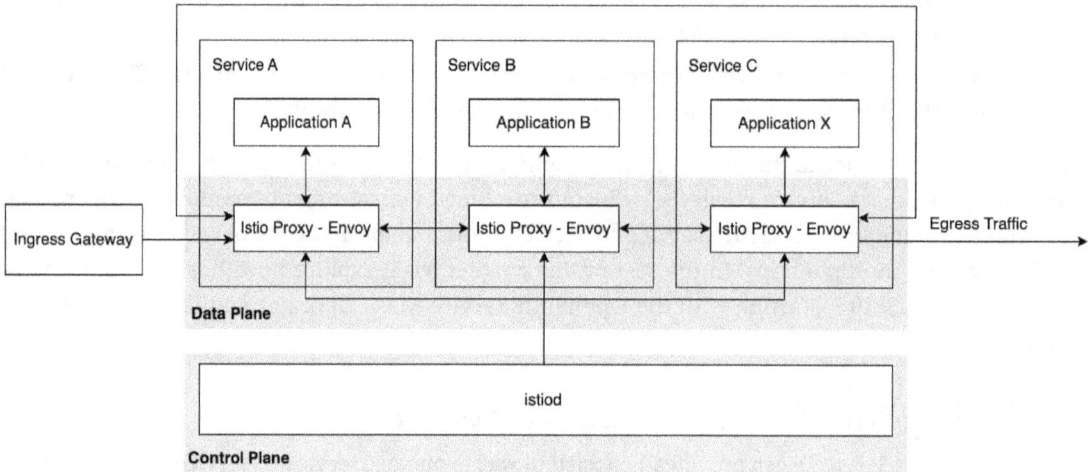

Figure 14.1: Overview of the Service Mesh architecture

The two main components of the Service Mesh architecture are the **data plane** and the **control plane**. The data plane uses Envoy proxies to manage traffic between services, while the control plane configures these proxies for tasks such as policy enforcement, routing, and service discovery. We will start with the data plane and move on to the control plane, and discuss them in detail.

Data plane

The data plane is made up of intelligent proxies that run alongside application containers in pods, intercepting and controlling all inbound (ingress) and outbound (egress) network communication between microservices in the service mesh. These include the following:

- **Envoy proxies:** The core of the data plane, these Envoy containers manage all service traffic, ensuring secure and efficient communication. They also collect service traffic metrics.
- **Sidecar proxies:** Deployed alongside applications in the same pod, these proxies handle inbound and outbound communication for each specific workload.
- **Mesh gateways:** Specialized load-balancing proxies for managing external HTTP/TCP connections. These come in two types:
    - **Ingress gateway:** Manages traffic entering the mesh, enabling monitoring and routing.
    - **Egress gateway:** Handles traffic leaving the mesh, applying rules to outgoing traffic.

In summary, the data plane uses Envoy proxies to control and manage all service communication, providing traffic control, security, and metrics collection.

Control plane

The control plane manages and configures proxies in the data plane. It also handles policy enforcement, service discovery, and the configuration of routing rules.

Istiod is the core of Istio's control plane, consolidating components such as Citadel, Galley, and Pilot into one. It translates routing rules into Envoy configurations, manages service discovery, configurations, and certificates, and injects sidecar proxies into workloads. Istiod can function as a **certificate authority** (CA) for secure mTLS or integrate with an external CA. Its key sub-components are as follows:

- **Pilot**: Configures proxies at runtime
- **Citadel**: Manages issuance and rotation of certificates
- **Galley**: Validates and manages Istio configurations

In summary, Istiod powers the control plane, orchestrating the configuration and management of data plane proxies to ensure secure, efficient, and reliable communication between microservices.

Operator bundled solutions

Red Hat OpenShift Service Mesh bundles the following Istio add-ons as part of the product:

- **Kiali**: A management console for OpenShift Service Mesh, offering dashboards, observability, configuration, and validation tools. It visualizes the mesh's structure, health, and traffic, integrating with Grafana for metrics and Jaeger for tracing.
- **Prometheus**: A monitoring solution that stores telemetry data from the service mesh, supplying metrics, health status, and topology to Kiali.
- **Jaeger**: A distributed tracing platform that tracks requests across services to help monitor and troubleshoot microservices.
- **Elasticsearch**: Used by Jaeger for persistent storage of trace data.
- **Grafana**: Provides advanced queries, metrics analysis, and dashboards for service mesh data, optionally used with Kiali.

Some of these components are covered in the book, and some of them, such as Kiali, Tempo, and Jaeger, will be covered in this chapter alongside Istio/Maistra. For context, Maistra is an opinionated distribution of Istio designed to work with OpenShift. It combines Kiali, Jaeger, and Prometheus into a platform managed according to the OperatorHub lifecycle.

> **Warning!**
>
> Starting with Red Hat OpenShift Service Mesh 2.5, Jaeger and the OpenShift Elasticsearch Operator are deprecated and will be removed in future releases. Red Hat will provide bug fixes and support, but no new enhancements. The new alternative is the Red Hat OpenShift distributed tracing platform, Tempo.

OpenShift Service Mesh Operator versions

Red Hat OpenShift Service Mesh is a rapidly evolving component, with frequent updates to both the operator and the underlying Istio/Envoy stack. Within the OpenShift 4 ecosystem, there are currently two supported Service Mesh streams: 2.x and 3.x. Service Mesh 2.x (for example, 2.5 and 2.6) remains fully supported and widely deployed in production environments; it is based on the Maistra distribution and tracks Istio up to version 1.18, together with Kiali and Envoy.

Service Mesh 3.x is the newer major stream. It is built directly from the upstream Istio project (starting with Istio 1.24 in Service Mesh 3.0 and newer in later releases), uses a new operator derived from the community Sail operator, and introduces modern capabilities such as tighter Kubernetes Gateway API integration and, in recent versions, support for Istio's ambient (sidecar-less) mode.

At the time of writing, Service Mesh 2.x is still common in existing OpenShift 4 deployments, and Red Hat provides a documented migration path from 2.x to 3.x.

In this book, we will focus primarily on Service Mesh 2.x: it is the mesh version that most of you are likely to encounter today and provides a solid foundation for understanding day-to-day operations. Where relevant, we will call out the key differences and new capabilities introduced in Service Mesh 3.x so that you can plan and execute a future migration with confidence.

Service Mesh Operator components and their versions

At the time of writing, the latest version of the Operator is 2.5.2, which has the following core components:

- Istio 1.18.5
- Envoy proxy 1.26.8
- Kiali 1.73.8

The Red Hat OpenShift Service Mesh Operator supports multiple service mesh control plane versions. However, the Operator version does not determine the version of your deployed service mesh.

The version you use is determined by the `ServiceMeshControlPlane` version, which is specified in the `spec.version` field. This field controls the architecture and configuration settings for installing and deploying the service mesh. We will soon explore the deployment process to see how it is implemented.

> **Warning!**
>
> There are several key differences and unique features between Red Hat Service Mesh and OSS Istio, with most of them designed to ensure better alignment between Service Mesh and OpenShift. For a detailed comparison, please refer to the official documentation [1].

Installing and configuring the Service Mesh Operator

Let's start by discussing the deployment process, focusing first on the different deployment models available.

Understanding the various deployment models

Red Hat Service Mesh supports three deployment models:

- Multitenant deployment
- Cluster-wide deployment
- Federated deployment

In the following sections, we will briefly discuss them and define when to choose a specific one. Please note that the most common deployment model is the multitenant deployment model, and we will focus on it in more detail later, but before we do, let's briefly describe each available model.

Multitenant deployment model

As described previously, the multitenant deployment model is the default for Red Hat OpenShift Service Mesh, using a multitenant Operator to manage the Service Mesh control plane. It offers flexibility and isolation with namespace-specific configurations.

These are the model specifics:

- Multiple independent teams (tenants) share one cluster
- Each tenant has its own control plane (own Istio/SMCP) in a separate namespace
- Often implemented using **ServiceMeshControlPlane** (**SMCP**) per namespace or per team
- Administrative control split:
    - **Cluster admin**: Oversees all SMCPs (control planes)
    - **Tenant admin**: Manages their own Service Mesh, Kiali, and Jaeger

Choose this model for the following use cases:

- You need strong isolation between teams/apps, which is usually true for most **OpenShift Container Platform** (**OCP**) clusters
- Teams have different lifecycle needs, mTLS requirements, or configurations (e.g., rate limits)
- It is ideal for platform teams supporting multiple app teams or business units in the same cluster

These are some trade-offs:

- Higher resource overhead (each tenant has its own control plane)
- Operational complexity increases with more tenants
- Suitable for shared clusters with soft multi-tenancy

Cluster-wide mesh deployment model

Also known as the single-tenant model, it has a Service Mesh control plane that monitors resources across the entire cluster.

These are the model specifics:

- A single Service Mesh control plane manages all namespaces in a cluster
- All services/namespaces are enrolled in one service mesh instance

Choose this model for the following use cases:

- You have a single team or tightly coupled services
- You prefer simpler operations and centralized management
- It is good for smaller organizations or single-team ownership

These are some trade-offs:

- Less flexibility, as all services share the same policies, telemetry, and trust boundaries
- One mistake or some broken configuration can affect all services across the cluster
- Not great for team autonomy and/or security boundaries

By default, namespaces are labeled `istio-injection=enabled`, which can be modified in the `spec.labelSelectors` field of the `ServiceMeshMemberRoll` resource. Starting with OpenShift Service Mesh 2.5, you can migrate from a multitenant to a cluster-wide mesh, as explained at [2].

Federated deployment model

The federated model is the most advanced; it enables sharing services and workloads between meshes in different administrative domains.

These are the model specifics:

- Multiple clusters each have their own service mesh, connected through mesh federation
- Each mesh will be configured separately
- Certificate generation, metrics, and tracing stay local to each mesh
- It uses multi-mesh gateways and trust domains for cross-cluster communication
- The model assumes minimal trust and no remote Kubernetes API access

Choose this model for the following use cases:

- You have multi-cluster or hybrid cloud environments
- You need high availability or disaster recovery across regions
- You need regulatory compliance, latency-sensitive apps, or global services

These are some trade-offs:

- Most complex to operate and secure
- Requires careful trust configuration, certificate management, and inter-mesh policies
- Needs Red Hat Service Mesh Federation (introduced in later versions such as OSSM 2.x+)

So, as discussed before, let's focus on the most common multitenant deployment model and move on to install and configure it.

Deploying a multitenant service mesh in OpenShift

Multitenant deployment suits enterprise environments where OpenShift cluster resources are divided among multiple applications. This division ensures that each application is isolated, enhancing security and management.

We would need to deploy a few Operators to ensure we have the full `ServiceMesh` stack available:

- OpenShift Service Mesh Operator
- Kiali Operator
- Tempo Operator
- Red Hat OpenShift distributed tracing platform (Jaeger)

> **Warning!**
>
> Starting with Red Hat OpenShift Service Mesh 2.5, the Jaeger tracing platform is deprecated and will be removed in a future release. Red Hat will provide bug fixes and support during the current release lifecycle, but no enhancements. As an alternative, you can use the Tempo tracing platform.

Red Hat OpenShift Service Mesh Operator

As with many other solutions, the Service Mesh Operator and its components are installed via an operator controlled by the Operator Lifecycle Manager and available via Red Hat OpenShift OperatorHub. As of August 2025, two releases of **Red Hat Service Mesh (RHSM)** are available: 2 and 3. RHSM 2 is an older, stable product, based entirely on Maistra. RHSM 3, on the other hand, tracks upstream Istio instead and exposes controls through different **custom resource definitions (CRDs)**. In this book, we chose to focus on RHSM 2 as a more stable, familiar, and proven solution that is still in wide use by many large organizations – banks in particular.

In the *Technical requirements* section, we recommended that you perform this and the following exercises on the multi-node OpenShift cluster that we built in *Chapter 3, Getting Started with OpenShift*, and configured in *Chapter 8, Working with Persistent Storage*. This is because OpenShift Service Mesh requires a significant amount of resources that may not be available on your system. If, however, you choose OpenShift Local as your platform, make sure that you give its VM extra CPU, memory, and disk storage before you proceed:

```
$ crc stop
$ crc config set memory 24000
$ crc config set cpus 8
$ crc config set disk-size 45
$ crc start
```

Even with these changes, you may still observe instability of the VM while running Service Mesh, which is why we recommend a multi-node cluster.

Let's quickly deploy the Operator and move on to the control plane deployment:

1. Log in to the OpenShift UI as an administrator or `kubeadmin`.
2. Go to **Operators** | **OperatorHub** and search for `Service Mesh 2`.
3. Switch an active namespace to `openshift-operators`.
4. Then, click on **Red Hat OpenShift Service Mesh 2:**

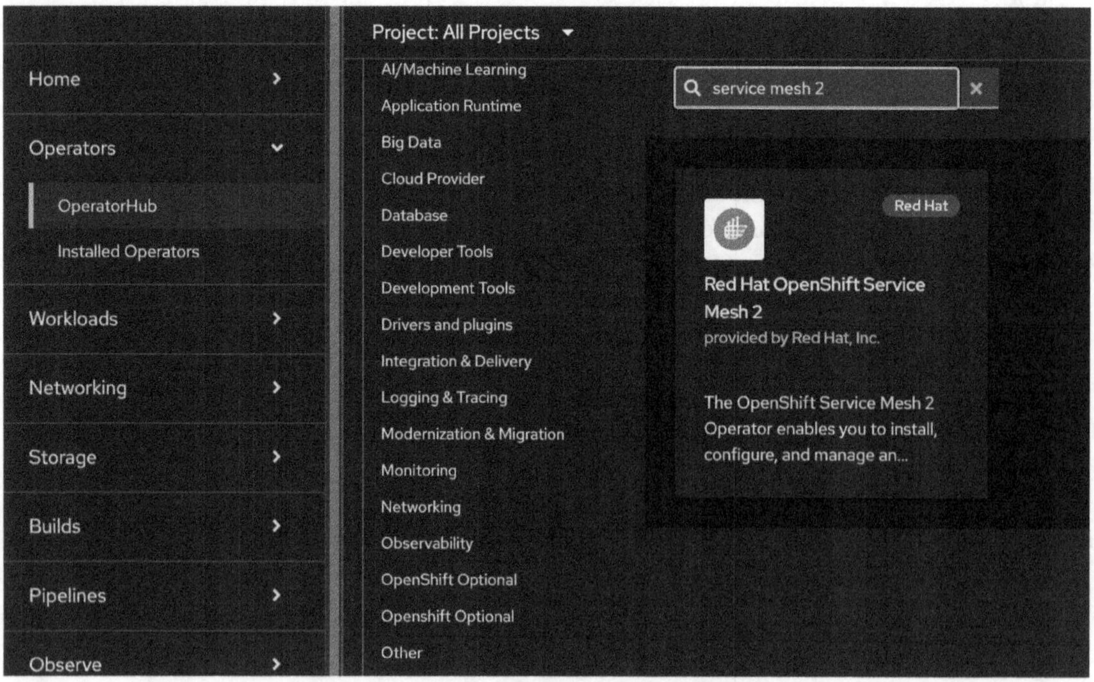

Figure 14.2: Searching on OperatorHub

5. It will open an installation page for you. Click the blue **Install** button; the UI will show you all the parameters available for the Operator. Review the available parameters, paying particular attention to the following:
   - **Installation Mode: All namespaces on the cluster (default)**
   - **Installed Namespace:** `openshift-operators`
   - **Update Approval: Automatic**

> You can use **Manual** approval. The deployment process won't change much, but you will gain more control over Operator installation and your cluster status.

6. On the right side of the screen, you will see a list of APIs that the Operator provides: **Istio Service Mesh Control Plane, Istio Service Mesh Member**, and **Istio Service Mesh Member Roll.** Carefully review the available APIs and configurations and click **Install.** For further steps, we will finally switch from the web UI to the OC CLI.
7. Wait until the Operator is installed. You can also click on **Installed Operators** on the left.

> We have observed on a few occasions that if you navigate to **Operators | Installed Operators** shortly after creating the subscription, you may notice that the Operator has a status of `Unknown`, and if you click on the Operator's name, you will see the following message:
>
> ```
> This operator cannot be updated. The health of CatalogSource
> "redhat-operators" is unknown. It may have been disabled or
> removed from the cluster.
> ```
>
> This error is typically transitive. Check whether `CatalogSource` is online, and if it is, just wait for a few minutes (it can take up to 10). The subscription's status should update to `BundleUnpacking`, and then an `InstallPlan` should be generated.

Most Operators can be installed via the OC CLI, or in a declarative way via some GitOps solutions, such as ArgoCD or Red Hat GitOps Operator. Let's try to execute a deployment of other required Operators in this chapter via the OC CLI. The first Operator would be Kiali. As we mentioned before, Kiali is a management console for OpenShift Service Mesh.

Kiali Operator provided by Red Hat

Let's deploy the Kiali Operator provided by Red Hat, which will control the Kiali configuration and workloads. Let's use the OC CLI to do the deployment:

1. Log in to your cluster via the OC CLI as `kubeadmin` (or any cluster admin-level user):

```
$ oc login <PUBLIC_API_ENDPOINT> -u <USERNAME OR TOKEN>
```

2. Create a Kiali Operator subscription from the `chapters/14/snippets/kiali-operator.yaml` file of this book's repository (it will be created in the `openshift-operators` namespace, as most of the subscriptions reside there):

```
$ oc create -f chapters/14/snippets/kiali-operator.yaml
```

3. Now, you can check its installation status by running the following command:

```
$ oc get sub -n openshift-operators kiali-ossm -o yaml | grep
CatalogSourcesUnhealthy -B 1
```

   You should see `status: "False"`, which means there are no unhealthy catalog sources, and installation can proceed. If, however, the `CatalogSource` error mentioned earlier didn't manifest itself, the output will be empty.

4. So, the Operator is installed. You can always check the status of operators via the UI, but it is quite handy to be able to check it via the OC CLI. For example, you can use the following command to monitor the progress of installation:

```
$ watch -n1 oc get po -n openshift-operators
```

   You should see one additional running pod for the Kiali Operator, besides Istio.

Now that Kiali is installed, let's move on to installing the Tempo Operator as a distributed tracing solution.

Tempo Operator

A Tempo Operator controls Tempo's lifecycle. In the following sections, we will discuss Tempo, a new distributed tracing solution. For now, let's focus on the Operator's installation and discuss the configuration of Tempo in a dedicated section later.

We will install the Operator using the same declarative method of deployment as we did for the Kiali Operator, by creating a `.yaml` definition file and applying it via the OC CLI:

1. Log in to your cluster via the OC CLI as `kubeadmin` (or a cluster admin-level user), unless authenticated already:

```
$ oc login –u <OR by using token>
```

2. Create a project/namespace for the Tempo Operator:

```
$ oc create ns openshift-tempo-operator
```

3. Create an Operator group and subscription for the Tempo Operator from manifests in this book's repository:

```
$ oc create -f chapters/14/snippets/tempo-operator-group.yaml
$ oc create -f chapters/14/snippets/tempo-operator-subs.yaml
```

4. You can check the status of the Tempo Operator group, subscription, and Operator in the same way as you did for the Kiali Operator, or via the web UI; just log in to the UI, go to **Operators | Installed Operators**, and ensure that you are in the openshift-tempo-operator namespace. For a CLI-based approach, use this command:

```
$ watch -n1 oc get po -n openshift-tempo-operator
```

There will be one controller pod running.

Red Hat OpenShift distributed tracing platform

Currently, there are two tracing solutions you can use: Jaeger- and Tempo-based. The Jaeger-based one will be completely replaced by a Tempo-based one soon. We will deploy both for learning purposes.

We will start by using Jaeger and then see how we can migrate the Service Mesh control plane to Tempo. It is something you will likely do in enterprise environments, so it may be pretty useful:

1. Log in to your cluster via the OC CLI as kubeadmin (or a cluster admin-level user), unless authenticated already:

```
$ oc login -u <OR by using token>
```

2. Create a new namespace called openshift-distributed-tracing:

```
$ oc create ns openshift-distributed-tracing
```

3. Create an Operator group and subscription for the Jaeger operator from manifests in this book's repository:

```
$ oc create -f chapters/14/snippets/jaeger-tracing-operatorgroup.yaml
$ oc create -f chapters/14/snippets/jaeger-tracing-operator-subs.yaml
```

Use the following command to monitor installation progress:

```
$ watch -n1 oc get po -n openshift-distributed-tracing
```

In the end, there will be a single controller pod running.

4. You can check the status of the Operator either via the OC CLI or the UI. We hope you are already comfortable with this operation, but if you feel you need a recap, please look at how we did it for the Kiali and Tempo Operators.

When all the Operators are available, we can create an Istio Service Mesh control plane. In the next section, we will create a control plane, review some critical parameters, and ensure successful deployment.

Exploring Istio and Maistra

Let's first talk about Maistra again. Maistra is an open source version of Istio made for OpenShift environments. It includes several improvements that make it work especially well with OCP.

Here are some key benefits of Maistra:

- **Integrated management:** Maistra works seamlessly with OpenShift's management tools, making it easy to manage both the service mesh and the overall OpenShift environment.
- **Enhanced security:** Maistra uses OpenShift's strong security features, such as built-in authentication and authorization, to ensure that your service mesh is secure.
- **Simplified installation and upgrades:** The Maistra Operator makes it easier to install, configure, and upgrade the service mesh components.
- **CRDs:** Maistra uses OpenShift-specific CRDs to offer more flexible and detailed configuration options for the service mesh.
- **Improved monitoring and logging:** Maistra integrates with OpenShift's monitoring and logging tools, providing detailed insights into service mesh components and workloads.

These features make Maistra a more efficient and cohesive solution for organizations using OpenShift.

Maistra API objects

Before we proceed to create a Service Mesh control plane, let's stop for a second and talk about the core API objects that Maistra operates with and the roles these objects play. Let's list the main API objects and their roles:

- `ServiceMeshControlPlane`: Defines the configuration for the entire Service Mesh control plane, specifying how components should be deployed and configured.
- `ServiceMeshMemberRoll`: Lists the namespaces that are part of the service mesh, allowing for selective mesh membership.
- `VirtualService`: Configures routing rules for a service, allowing you to control how requests are routed within the mesh.
- `DestinationRule`: Specifies policies that apply to traffic intended for a service after routing has occurred, such as load balancing and connection pool settings
- `Gateway`: Defines entry points into the mesh, typically used to manage external traffic coming into the service mesh.
- `PeerAuthentication`: Configures authentication policies for workloads, specifying mutual TLS settings and other authentication requirements.
- `AuthorizationPolicy`: Specifies access control policies for workloads, defining who can access what resources and under what conditions.
- `Sidecar`: Provides fine-grained control over the sidecar proxies, allowing customization of the sidecar configuration for specific namespaces or workloads.

By understanding these key API objects and their roles, you can effectively manage and configure your Maistra service mesh, ensuring that it operates smoothly and meets your specific requirements.

Deploying the control plane

In this section, we will go through a few simple steps to deploy the control plane and make all the Operators we deployed work. Before we proceed, let's define some prerequisites:

- The control plane requires a separate namespace called `istio-system`
- The control plane version must be v2.5 or above to have the latest features
- The multitenant control plane mode is required to have some isolation
- The following add-ons are needed: Monitoring, Tracing, and Observation

> **Warning!**
>
> In an enterprise environment, please consider deploying `ServiceMesh` components on infrastructure nodes, as explained in [3].

Great, we are now ready and can proceed with the control plane deployment:

1. Log in to your cluster via the OC CLI as `kubeadmin` (or a cluster admin-level user), unless authenticated already:

```
$ oc login -u <OR by using token>
```

2. Create a project/namespace for the Tempo Operator:

```
$ oc create ns istio-system
```

3. Create a `ServiceMeshControlPlane` instance from a manifest in this book's repository:

```
$ oc create -f chapters/14/snippets/istio-control-plane.yaml
```

4. That's it! Let's wait for some time (around 5–10 minutes), get some tea, and then check the status of the control plane (`oc get smcp -n istio-system` works too):

```
$ oc get ServiceMeshControlPlane -n istio-system
NAME    READY   STATUS            PROFILES      VERSION   AGE
basic   9/9     ComponentsReady   ["default"]   2.5.12    75s
```

> Feel free to run `oc describe smcp -n istio-system` to get the detailed status of the control plane and its settings in a human-readable format.

If all the control plane resources are ready (`STATUS: ComponentsReady`), we are good to go, and Service Mesh is fully functional and ready. It may take about two minutes for all of the components of the control plane to become ready.

Let's now move forward and talk about all the components we have: a management and observability console (Kiali), tracing (Jaeger and Tempo), and the monitoring stack.

Setting up Kiali

In this section, we will drill down into the Kiali UI and see what information it provides.

As we discussed before, Kiali is a key observability tool for Istio, offering a clear view of service mesh infrastructure. It visualizes mesh topology, microservice interactions, and application health, providing insights into traffic, metrics, and issues.

With integration to tools such as Jaeger and Prometheus, Kiali improves visibility and control for efficient microservice management in Kubernetes.

Kiali web console

Let's use the Kiali console to validate your Service Mesh installation. This is something you will often do in your environment when working with RHSM:

1. Log in to your cluster via the OC CLI as `kubeadmin` (or a cluster admin-level user), unless authenticated already:

```
$ oc login -u <OR by using token>
```

2. Get the route that the Kiali web console uses with the following command:

```
$ oc -n istio-system get route kiali -o jsonpath='https://{.spec.host}
{"\n"}'
```

3. Copy the URL and open it in your browser; you can use your OCP cluster-level login for logging in:

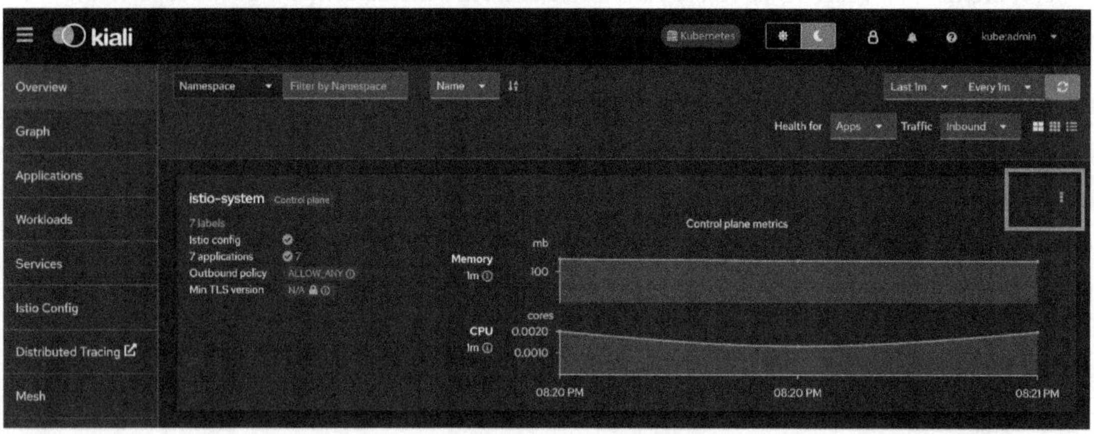

Figure 14.3: Kiali UI overview

4. If you click on the three dots in the upper-right corner of the **istio-system** widget, it will show you a few links you may use very often: **Graph**, **Applications**, **Workloads**, **Services**, and **Istio Config**. These links are also available on the left menu, but there are a few more links to the Grafana dashboards; please check them and keep in mind that they are always nearby, so keep them handy. For example, if you click on **Istio Control Plane Dashboard**, the request will open

another tab on your browser, which leads to an **out-of-the-box** (**OOTB**) Grafana dashboard with all the necessary data, after you accept the certificate exception and authorize the `grafana` service account to access the information about your user:

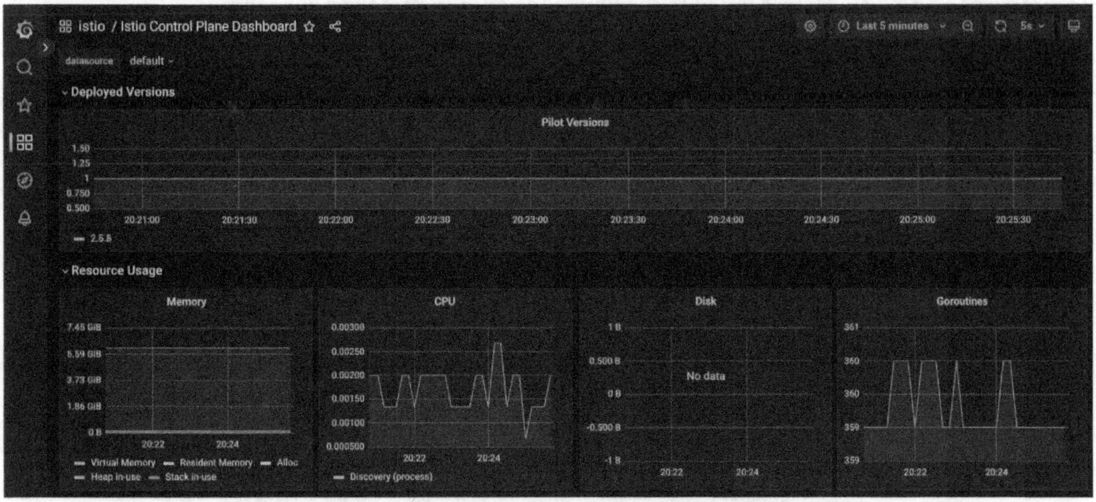

Figure 14.4: Grafana Istio Control Plane Dashboard

So, now you have the monitoring information about your control plane and know where to find links to Grafana to get even more details than Kiali itself provides. On the left, there is also a menu item called **Distributed Tracing**, which points to Jaeger's web UI (as with Grafana, you will have to accept the certificate exception and authorize access to your user).

> If the **Distributed Tracing** menu item is not displayed, try hard-refreshing the page with *Ctrl* + *R*. This is likely because you opened the Kiali console too quickly.

But we have no applications that use Service Mesh, and thus, no information. Let's deploy an application and see how it all works.

Service Mesh members: Bookinfo

Now that you have a Service Mesh control plane and all the components available, you can add some applications to the mesh. To do so, Service Mesh provides you with a few options:

- Specifying the project name in a `ServiceMeshMemberRoll` resource
- Configuring label selectors in a `ServiceMeshMemberRoll` resource
- Creating a `ServiceMeshMember` resource in a project

The first option is the most common approach for Istio in OpenShift environments, so we'll focus on that, but you are welcome to check out the other options outlined at [4].

Historically, the main demo application for Istio is a *BookInfo* application; the same application is available for Maistra, which includes all the necessary tuning for OpenShift. We will use this application to demonstrate the Service Mesh. We will perform the following steps using the OpenShift CLI. To simplify the next steps, let's log in to the cluster as administrator or `kubeadmin`:

1. Create a new project called `bookinfo`:

```
$ oc new-project bookinfo
```

2. Create a `ServiceMeshMemberRoll` (`smmr`) resource from a manifest we prepared for you in this book's GitHub repository:

```
$ oc create -f chapters/14/snippets/smmr-example.yaml
```

3. Next, let's check the `ServiceMeshMemberRoll` status:

```
$ oc get smmr -n istio-system -o wide
```

   You should see a `Configured` status:

```
NAME      READY   STATUS       AGE   MEMBERS
default   1/1     Configured   10s   ["bookinfo"]
```

Figure 14.5: ServiceMeshMemberRoll status

4. Deploy the `bookinfo` application:

```
$ oc apply -n bookinfo -f https://raw.githubusercontent.com/Maistra/
istio/maistra-2.5/samples/bookinfo/platform/kube/bookinfo.yaml
```

5. Create the ingress gateway and `VirtualService` objects:

```
$ oc -n bookinfo apply -f https://raw.githubusercontent.com/Maistra/
istio/maistra-2.5/samples/bookinfo/networking/bookinfo-gateway.yaml
```

6. Create default destination rules:

```
$ oc apply -n bookinfo -f https://raw.githubusercontent.com/Maistra/
istio/maistra-2.5/samples/bookinfo/networking/destination-rule-all.yaml
```

7. Check the status of the application itself (ensure that all pods are started and running):

```
$ oc get pods -n bookinfo -o custom-columns="NAME:.metadata.name,STATUS:.
status.phase"
```

8. Get the Istio gateway address and then get the URL of the product page:

```
$ oc -n istio-system get route istio-ingressgateway -o jsonpath='{.spec.
host}{"\n"}'
```

9. Now, using the output from the previous command, create a URL, like this:

```
http://istio-ingressgateway-istio-system.apps.cluster.example.com/
productpage
```

10. Then, open it in your browser:

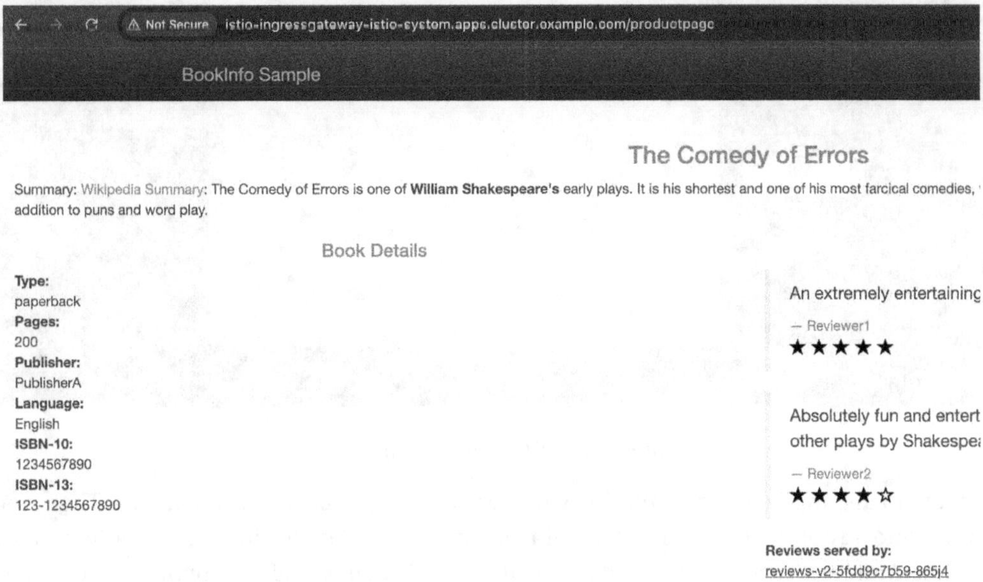

Figure 14.6: BookInfo UI

11. In the upper-right corner, click **Sign in** and log in with the following credentials:

    - **Username:** `admin`
    - **Password:** `admin`

    Ensure that you click a few links on the UI of the application to generate some communication between the application's components. Simply refreshing the page also does the trick.

Congratulations! Your application is now up and running, utilizing Service Mesh for internal communication and Service Mesh Ingress Gateway as part of the external communication path.

Once you initiate the first request and Service Mesh handles the communication, you will have access to a comprehensive communication graph, monitoring information, and other application details.

Please don't hesitate to go through the menus and then get back to your Kiali web UI to check what has changed. Select **Graph** on the left and set **Namespace** to `bookinfo`. You should see a graph of requests and a lot of information about your queries:

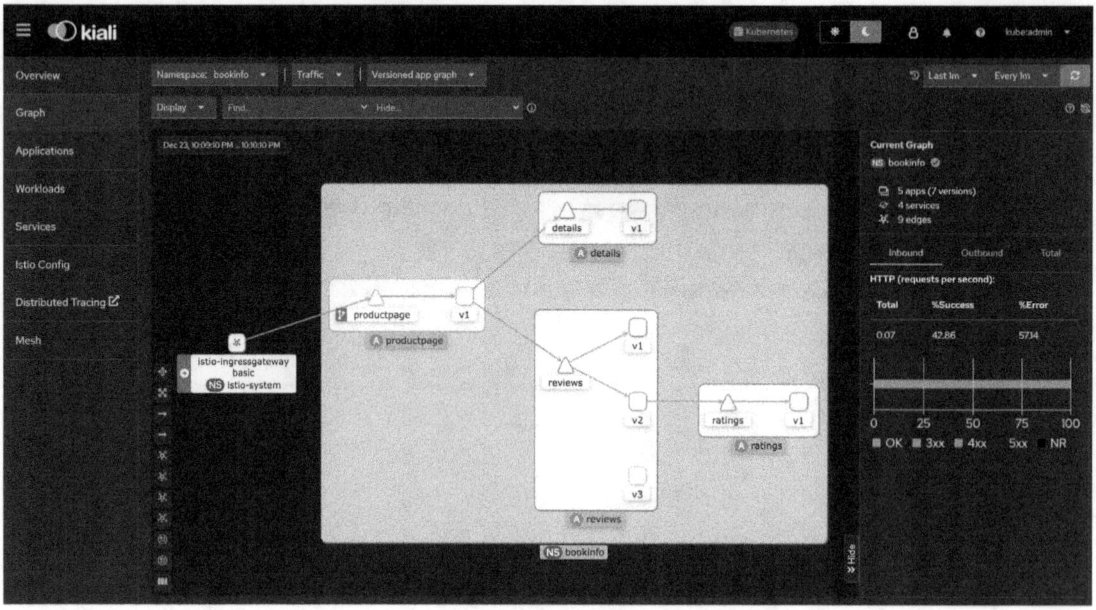

Figure 14.7: Kiali UI – BookInfo application

If you move to the **Applications** menu, you will see a list of the `bookinfo` components. Then, you can drill down into any of the components and find some specific data for it, such as traffic details, protocols, access attempt success ratio, and reach details for **Inbound** and **Outbound** metrics. There are many menu items; let's talk about them so you can navigate them more efficiently.

Kiali web console items

If you are already familiar with Kiali, you can skip this section, but if this is something new for you, please go ahead and review what menu items we have:

Menu Item	Description
Overview	Visualization of key performance data, including inbound communication for Service Mesh members, high-level control plane metrics (CPU and RAM), and service health monitoring with options for detailed analysis.
Graph	**Namespace Graph** shows communication within a namespace, highlighting service interactions. You can switch between the following: • **Service Graph:** Focuses on service-to-service communication • **Workload Graph:** Displays interactions between workloads • **App Graph:** Visualizes application-level communication paths
Applications	Lists all applications in the service mesh, showing health status, traffic, and associated workloads and services.

Menu Item	Description
Workloads	Shows all workloads in the mesh with metrics, health status, and details on associated pods, services, and applications.
Services	Lists all services in the mesh with traffic, health status, and associated workloads, enabling performance monitoring and interaction tracking.
Istio Config	Displays all Istio config objects (e.g., `VirtualService`, `DestinationRule`, and `Gateway`) and allows for creating new Service Mesh objects via the UI. **Config Validation** identifies issues in Istio configuration to ensure a healthy service mesh.
Distributed Tracing	Integrates with Jaeger for detailed distributed tracing, allowing you to track requests through the mesh and identify performance bottlenecks and errors.

Table 14.1: Kiali web console items

You are a hero! If you are reading these lines, then you deployed an RHSM Operator, Kiali, Jaeger, Tempo, and Grafana, and made them all work together by creating a control plane. You also deployed your first application, which uses Istio, and checked its status via Kiali.

Now, it's time to shift focus from the application and explore migrating tracing from Jaeger to Tempo, a newer tracing solution that will soon replace Jaeger. We'll compare both solutions and guide you through the migration process.

Tracing with Jaeger and Tempo

Why is tracing important for Istio and microservices? Tracing the flow of requests across microservices is crucial for diagnosing performance issues and ensuring reliability. Solutions such as Jaeger and Tempo provide the visibility needed to monitor these interactions.

In this section, we'll talk about Jaeger and Tempo and then simulate updating your environment and replacing Jaeger with Tempo.

Jaeger

Jaeger is a widely used tool for tracing and monitoring, helping developers track and analyze request paths through complex systems. It provides valuable insights into latency, service dependencies, and performance bottlenecks.

Our initial control plane deployment uses Jaeger, and as we just described, Kiali's UI points to the Jaeger UI when you click on the **Distributed Tracing** menu item. Let's navigate there and see what kind of data Jaeger provides:

1. Get your Kiali UI address again, in case you closed it:

```
$ oc -n istio-system get route kiali -o jsonpath='https://{.spec.host}
{"\n"}'
```

2. Find the **Distributed Tracing** menu item and click on it:

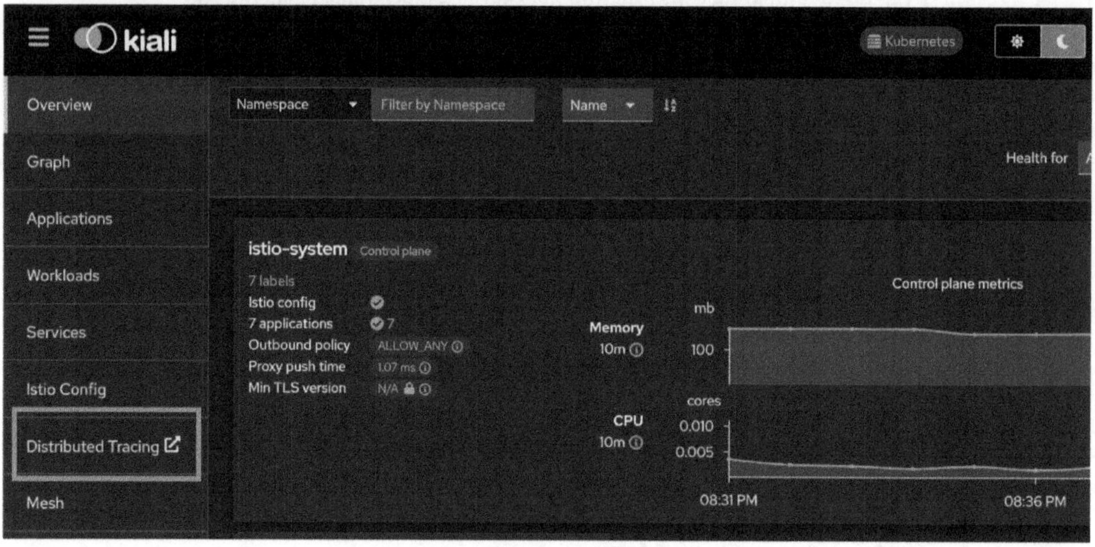

Figure 14.8: Kiali UI – Distributed Tracing link

3. The browser will forward you to the `jaeger-istio-system` route. Click the **Log in with OpenShift** button. Accept the certificate exceptions and click **Allow selected permissions** on the **Authorize Access** page to allow the Jaeger UI proxy's service account access to your account's information (`user:info`) and permissions (`user:check-access`). Then, you will be redirected to Jaeger's UI.
4. The default tab of the Jaeger UI is **Search**, which makes sense, since Jaeger exists to supply you with traces and allow you to search through them. On the menu to the left, set **Service** to **productpage.bookinfo**, set **Lookback** to **Last 2 Days**, and click **Find Traces**.
5. Jaeger will show you a list of traces, which will correlate with the last attempts to access our demo application's UI. You can generate more; just try to access your `bookinfo` application and execute a few actions there, such as logging in with admin credentials.

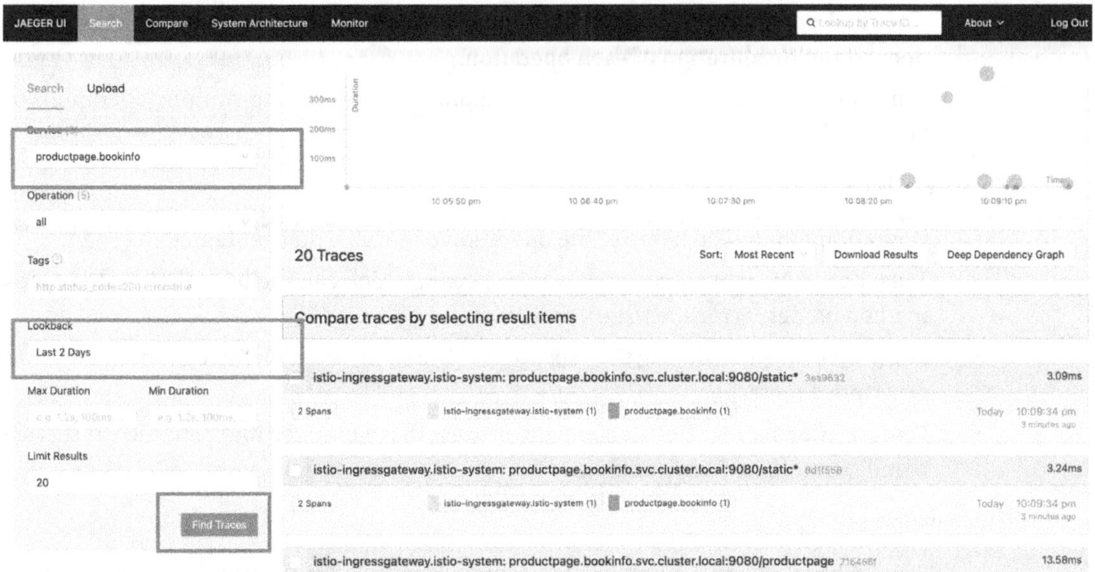

Figure 14.9: Jaeger UI overview

Click on one of the available traces. Jaeger will drill down into the trace and show you the following:

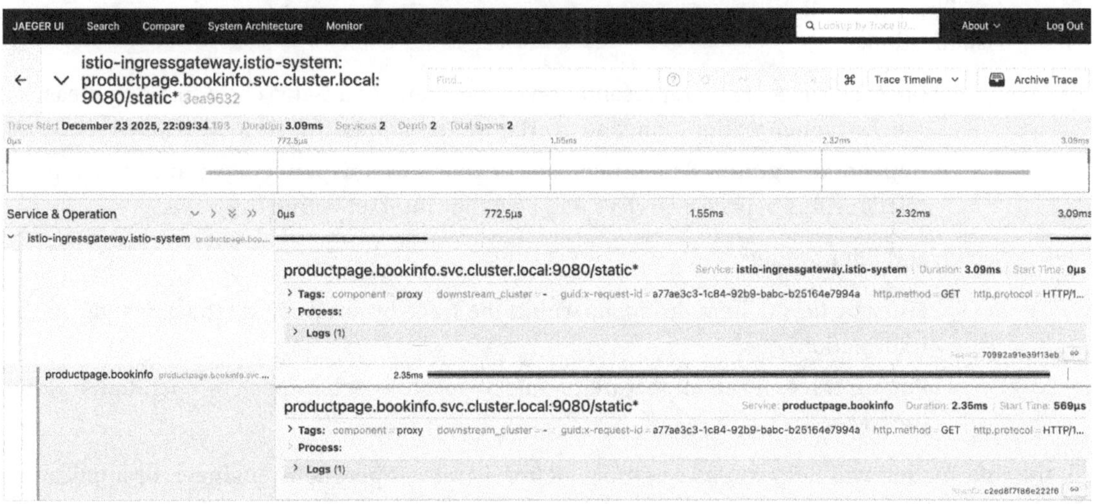

Figure 14.10: Jaeger UI trace info

So, when you click on one of the traces in Jaeger, you will be presented with detailed information about the trace. Here are the key elements and information that Jaeger will show:

- **Trace timeline:**
    - **Spans:** Each span represents a unit of work in the trace. The timeline will show all spans in a hierarchical order, indicating the sequence and nested nature of operations.

    - **Start and end times:** The precise start and end times for each span, allowing you to understand the duration of each operation.
    - **Durations:** The duration of each span, helping to identify long-running operations or bottlenecks.
- **Span details:**
    - **Operation name:** The name of the operation or service that generated the span.
    - **Tags:** Key-value pairs associated with the span, which can include HTTP status codes, method names, error messages, and more.
    - **Logs:** Events logged during the execution of the span, often including timestamps and descriptive messages.
    - **Process information:** Details about the process that generated the span, such as service name, version, and environment.
- **Trace overview:**
    - **Service breakdown:** A summary of all services involved in the trace, showing the number of spans per service and their total duration.
    - **Critical path:** Highlights the critical path of the trace, indicating the sequence of operations that determine the overall latency.
- **Visualization:**
    - **Gantt chart:** A visual representation of the spans as a Gantt chart, making it easy to see the sequence, duration, and overlap of operations.
    - **Dependency graph:** Sometimes, Jaeger provides a dependency graph showing the relationships between services and how they interact within the trace.
- **Search and filter options:**
    - **Filter by tags:** Filters the spans within the trace by specific tags to narrow down the information.
    - **Find in trace:** A search feature to quickly locate specific spans or operations within the trace.

All the information will help you as a platform administrator, operations engineer, or application developer to diagnose performance issues, identify bottlenecks, and understand the flow of requests through their microservices architecture.

For more information on using Jaeger, you can refer to the documentation on distributed tracing in OpenShift [5].

Alright, Tempo is here again; let's talk about it and then execute the migration.

Tempo

Tempo is emerging as a robust alternative to Jaeger, designed to handle high volumes of tracing data with efficiency and scalability. As we transition from Jaeger to Tempo, we aim to leverage Tempo's advanced capabilities to enhance our observability stack.

As of November 3, 2025, Jaeger is no longer supported on OpenShift, so please consider using Tempo instead, as the deprecation notice from Red Hat is already out there, and Tempo is stable and available.

For learning purposes, we made our control plane use Jaeger, but now it's time to see whether we can reconfigure it to work with Tempo instead.

Migration to Tempo

Let's do the control plane reconfiguration via the OC CLI to make the object's backup quicker and simpler and avoid any unnecessary UI diving.

> **Warning!**
>
> Before you proceed, please ensure that you have **OpenShift Data Foundation (ODF)** deployed and available; Tempo in the `TempoStack` configuration requires an S3-compatible backend to store the tracing data. You can potentially use any other S3-compatible storage provider, such as MinIO; however, deploying such a solution is outside the scope of this book.

If the preceding warning is okay and the S3 prerequisite is addressed, go ahead and execute these steps:

1. Log in to the OCP cluster via the OC CLI as `kubeadmin` or another administrator-level user, unless logged in already.
2. Switch the current project to `istio-system`:

```
$ oc project istio-system
```

3. Now, make a copy of your current `ServiceMeshControlPlane` object:

```
$ oc -n istio-system get ServiceMeshControlPlane basic -o yaml > smcp-bkp.yaml
$ cp smcp-bkp.yaml smcp-tempo.yaml
```

4. You will notice the definition of `ServiceMeshControlPlane` is large, but we need to make just a few changes there. In the `spec` section of `smcp-tempo.yaml`, let's add `meshConfig` and change `tracing.type` to `None`. Also, we recommend cleaning up runtime data, such as `creationTimestamp`, `finalizers`, `generation`, `resourceVersion`, `uid`, `ownerReferences`, and `status` (we have an example of why this is a good practice later in this chapter). For your convenience, we prepared an updated definition in `chapters/14/snippets/smcp-tempo.yaml`.

5. We also need to create a `ServiceMeshMemberRoll` object for Tempo; let's make a backup of the current config:

```
$ oc get ServiceMeshMemberRoll default -o yaml > smmr-bkp.yaml
```

6. Now, you can either copy it (`cp smmr-bkp.yaml smmr.yaml`) and edit it, or just get an updated definition that we prepared for you: `chapters/14/snippets/smmr.yaml`.
7. Let's apply new `ServiceMeshControlPlane` and `ServiceMeshMemberRoll` objects:

```
$ oc replace -f smcp-tempo.yaml
$ oc replace -f smmr.yaml
```

8. Now, we need to reconfigure Kiali to make it work with Tempo instead of Jaeger. Make a backup:

```
$ oc get Kiali kiali -o yaml > kiali-tempo.yaml
```

9. Open `kiali-tempo.yaml` with your favorite editor and change `.spec.external_services.tracing` as follows:

```
apiVersion: kiali.io/v1alpha1
kind: Kiali
...output omitted...
spec:
  external_services:
    tracing:
      query_timeout: 30
      enabled: true
      in_cluster_url: 'http://tempo-simplest-query-frontend.tracing-
system.svc.cluster.local:16686'
      ...output omitted...
      url: 'tempo-simplest-query-frontend-tracing-system.apps.<your-
cluster-name>.<domain>'
      use_grpc: false
```

Or, just use the file we prepared for you: `chapters/14/snippets/kiali-tempo.yaml`. Don't forget to update the route in `.spec.external_services.grafana.url` to match your cluster's domain.

10. Apply the new Kiali configuration:

```
$ oc replace -f kiali-tempo.yaml
```

11. Create a new project called `tracing-system` and switch to it (the OC CLI will do it automatically):

```
$ oc new-project tracing-system
```

12. If you have ODF installed, create an S3 `ObjectBucketClaim` object (provided in `chapters/14/snippets/tempo-s3.yaml`) using a Noobaa `StorageClass`:

```
$ oc create -f chapters/14/snippets/tempo-s3.yaml
```

13. Similarly to how we did it when allocating object storage for LokiStack in *Chapter 12*, *Logging in OpenShift*, run the following commands to extract object store details and store them in the current shell's environment variables:

```
$ BUCKET_HOST=$(oc get -o jsonpath='{.data.BUCKET_HOST}' cm/tempo-s3 -n tracing-system)
$ BUCKET_NAME=$(oc get -o jsonpath='{.data.BUCKET_NAME}' cm/tempo-s3 -n tracing-system)
$ ACCESS_KEY_ID=$(oc get -o jsonpath='{.data.AWS_ACCESS_KEY_ID}' secret/tempo-s3 -n tracing-system | base64 -d)
$ SECRET_ACCESS_KEY=$(oc get -o jsonpath='{.data.AWS_SECRET_ACCESS_KEY}' secret/tempo-s3 -n tracing-system | base64 -d)
```

> If you're using something besides ODF for object storage, you will need to create a bucket on that provider and obtain the values for the `BUCKET_HOST`, `ACCESS_KEY_ID`, and `SECRET_ACCESS_KEY` variables from that provider. Set the preceding variables accordingly. Depending on the provider, you will likely have to change the protocol schema to `https` in the command that follows.
>
> Due to limitations of this book, we're not covering all S3-compatible backends.

14. Create a secret that Tempo will use to look up the location and access credentials of the object store:

```
$ oc create secret generic tempo-s3-secret --from-literal=access_key_id="${ACCESS_KEY_ID}" --from-literal=access_key_secret="${SECRET_ACCESS_KEY}" --from-literal=bucket="${BUCKET_NAME}" --from-literal=endpoint="http://${BUCKET_HOST}" -n tracing-system
```

For your reference, the secret's template is also provided in `chapters/14/snippets/tempo-secret.yaml`.

15. Create a `TempoStack` instance definition that references the secret we just created. Use the `chapters/14/snippets/tempo-stack.yaml` file from this book's repository:

```
$ oc create -f chapters/14/snippets/tempo-stack.yaml
```

16. The last step is to create a Telemetry object for Service Mesh. We have prepared a `chapters/14/snippets/mesh-telemetry.yaml` file that you can use:

```
$ oc create -f chapters/14/snippets/mesh-telemetry.yaml
```

17. That's it! Let's check the status of `ServiceMeshControlPlane` and `TempoStack`:

```
$ oc get ServiceMeshControlPlane -n istio-system
NAME    READY   STATUS            PROFILES      VERSION   AGE
basic   8/8     ComponentsReady   ["default"]   2.5.12    88m
$ oc get TempoStack -o wide
NAME       AGE   TEMPO VERSION   MANAGEMENT
simplest   33s   2.7.2           Managed
```

The deployment is ready, and the Service Mesh now uses Tempo as the distributed tracing solution. You can find more details on available configurations and approaches in the official documentation [6].

Now, let's talk about the data plane, specifically Envoy. What is it, and how does it work? Proceed to the next section to find the answer.

Exploring the Envoy proxy

While working with the `bookinfo` example, you may have noticed some additional containers in every pod. These are Envoy proxies. Run the following command to verify that Envoy is present within each pod in the `bookinfo` namespace:

```
$ oc get pods -n bookinfo -o jsonpath="{range .items[*]}{.metadata.name}{'\t'}
{range .spec.containers[*]}{.name}{','}{end}{'\n'}{end}"
```

You should see something similar to this:

```
details-v1-c4655f497-5lv75         details,istio-proxy,
productpage-v1-8cf579d89-79mtl     productpage,istio-proxy,
ratings-v1-5688565545-p25h7        ratings,istio-proxy,
reviews-v1-6fd4d9bb79-9rd95        reviews,istio-proxy,
reviews-v2-5fdd9c7b59-kgnb2        reviews,istio-proxy,
reviews-v3-6dfcb45d95-zpcll        reviews,istio-proxy,
```

> If the preceding command produces an error such as `error parsing jsonpath "{range, unclosed action` after copying and pasting, delete and retype single and double quotes.

So, what is the Istio proxy? The Istio proxy is, in fact, Envoy. Envoy is a high-performance open source edge and service proxy designed for cloud-native applications. It serves as the data plane component in service meshes such as Istio and Maistra, managing all network traffic between microservices.

Here is the list of Envoy functions:

- **Proxying and load balancing:** Envoy proxies incoming and outgoing traffic for microservices and balances load across service instances to ensure high availability and reliability.
- **Service discovery:** Envoy dynamically discovers services and endpoints, allowing it to route traffic efficiently without hardcoding IP addresses.

- **Traffic management**: It manages traffic flow with advanced rules for retries, circuit breaking, and rate limiting, maintaining resilience and stability.
- **Observability**: Envoy provides extensive observability features, including metrics, distributed tracing, and logging, helping to monitor service performance and diagnose issues.
- **Security**: It enhances security with **mutual TLS (mTLS)** for encrypted communication, and policies for authentication and authorization.
- **Protocol support**: It supports various protocols, such as HTTP/1.1, HTTP/2, gRPC, and TCP, making it versatile for different application scenarios.
- **Configuration management**: Configurable via APIs, Envoy adapts dynamically to changing environments, with zero-downtime configuration updates.

In the `bookinfo` application, Envoy sidecars are injected into each pod, ensuring that all traffic flows through Envoy, which enforces policies and gathers telemetry data. This sidecar model, combined with a control plane such as Istio or Maistra, allows for the centralized management of traffic rules, security policies, and observability settings.

Envoy's role in handling these critical aspects ensures reliable, secure, and observable interactions between services, significantly contributing to the robustness of the service mesh.

Envoy is a compelling solution that can do a lot just as a standalone component; please refer to the official Envoy documentation [7] for more details.

Before we move on to the next section, let's take a moment to explore one of the powerful features Service Mesh offers: the ability to simulate various network conditions without making real changes to the network itself. This capability is highly valuable for testing applications under different scenarios.

Application testing with Istio

When an application is deployed, we may use the built-in functionality of Service Mesh to introduce some delays and inject errors; you may need to use this functionality for testing purposes. It is all available out of the box and can simply be configured by using default Maistra API objects or CRDs that we already briefly described.

Introducing delays

You can introduce delays into your service mesh traffic using a `VirtualService` configuration. This is useful for testing how your application behaves under network latency conditions. Let's quickly tune the existing `VirtualService` we made during the `bookinfo` deployment:

1. Switch to the `bookinfo` project:

```
$ oc project bookinfo
```

2. Dump the `bookinfo` virtual service:

```
$ oc get VirtualService bookinfo -o yaml > bookinfo-vs.yam
```

3. Make a backup of the `bookinfo` virtual service:

```
$ cp bookinfo-vs.yaml bookinfo-vs-bkp.yaml
```

4. Edit the `bookinfo-vs.yaml` file as follows (or use the `chapters/14/snippets/bookinfo-vs-delay.yaml` manifest from this book's GitHub repository):

```
apiVersion: networking.istio.io/v1beta1
kind: VirtualService
metadata:
  annotations:
...output omitted...
  name: bookinfo
  namespace: bookinfo
spec:
  gateways:
  - bookinfo-gateway
  hosts:
  - '*'
  http:
  - match:
    - uri:
        exact: /productpage
    - uri:
        prefix: /static
    - uri:
        exact: /login
    - uri:
        exact: /logout
    - uri:
        prefix: /api/v1/products
    fault:
      delay:
        percentage:
          value: 80
        fixedDelay: 5s
    route:
    - destination:
        host: productpage
        port:
          number: 9080
```

The preceding configuration will introduce a delay of 5 seconds for 80% of requests.

5. Replace the object:

```
$ oc replace -f bookinfo-vs.yaml
```

That's it! We have a delay definition; let's proceed further and add some errors.

Injecting errors

To introduce some errors, we will use the same steps (*steps 1–3*) in the previous exercise as for the delays, but in this case, instead of adding `fault.delay`, we will add `fault.abort`, and generate an HTTP error with code `500` with 50% probability:

1. Open `bookinfo-vs.yaml` and change it as follows (or use the `chapters/14/snippets/bookinfo-vs-error.yaml` manifest from this book's GitHub repository):

```
apiVersion: networking.istio.io/v1beta1
kind: VirtualService
metadata:
  annotations:
...output omitted...
  name: bookinfo
  namespace: bookinfo
spec:
  gateways:
  - bookinfo-gateway
  hosts:
  - '*'
  http:
  - match:
    - uri:
        exact: /productpage
    - uri:
        prefix: /static
    - uri:
        exact: /login
    - uri:
        exact: /logout
    - uri:
        prefix: /api/v1/products
    fault:
      delay:
        percentage:
          value: 80
        fixedDelay: 5s
```

```
      abort:
        percentage:
          value: 50
        httpStatus: 500
    route:
    - destination:
        host: productpage
        port:
          number: 9080
```

2. Then, just replace the object again:

```
$ oc replace -f bookinfo-vs.yaml
```

You might get this error with manifests that you exported and updated manually:

```
Error from server (Conflict): error when replacing "/
home/<USERNAME>/bookinfo-vs-bkp.yaml": Operation cannot be
fulfilled on virtualservices.networking.istio.io "bookinfo": the
object has been modified; please apply your changes to the latest
version and try again
```

If you do, remove `resourceVersion` from the object's metadata and rerun the preceding command. It is generally recommended to clean up any runtime parameters from manifests, as they bloat them at best, and interfere with `apply`/`replace` at worst, as we've just seen. If you're curious, there is a Red Hat KB article [9] describing the problem. Consider this when adopting GitOps, which relies purely on a declarative approach and runs `apply`/`replace` under the hood.

Sometimes, you may also encounter this error when modifying YAML manifests in the OpenShift UI. The cause is the same; while you were editing the object, its version was updated by OpenShift (the `status` field), and when you try to apply your updates with an outdated version, you get this error. The solution is to click **Reload** to update the version and then click **Save** again.

That's it! Congratulations! Now, when you try to access the application's endpoint, you'll likely experience a delay and may see the message `fault filter abort`, which means the configuration works as expected. The rollback for these changes is also straightforward; just replace `VirtualService` with the backed-up copy: `oc replace -f bookinfo-vs-bkp.yaml`.

This marks the end of our introduction to OpenShift Service Mesh and distributed tracing. Keep in mind that running Service Mesh and tracing in production is a lot different than in a lab, so proper capacity planning and ongoing tuning are necessary. One recommendation is to specify resource requests and limits in `ServiceMeshControlPlane` for such components of Service Mesh as Pilot and Envoy. For more, feel free to consult [8].

Summary

Congratulations! You've made it to the end of the chapter! Here, we covered all the key concepts of Service Mesh: why it's needed, its core components, how to deploy them, and the powerful features it offers. We also walked through deploying a real application utilizing Service Mesh, solidifying your understanding of its practical use.

Let's quickly run through the quiz and move on to other important services that you may need to know about for the successful management of Red Hat OpenShift.

References

To learn more about the topics that were covered in this chapter, take a look at the following resources:

- [1] *Service mesh and Istio differences*: `https://docs.redhat.com/en/documentation/openshift_container_platform/4.16/html/service_mesh/service-mesh-2-x#ossm-vs-community`
- [2] *About migrating to a cluster-wide mesh:* `https://docs.redhat.com/en/documentation/openshift_container_platform/4.16/html/service_mesh/service-mesh-2-x#ossm-about-about-migrating-to-cluster-wide_ossm-deployment-models`
- [3] *About control plane components and infrastructure nodes*: `https://docs.redhat.com/en/documentation/openshift_container_platform/4.16/html/service_mesh/service-mesh-2-x#ossm-about-control-plane-components-and-infrastructure-nodes_ossm-create-smcp`
- [4] *Adding services to a service mesh*: `https://docs.redhat.com/en/documentation/openshift_container_platform/4.16/html/service_mesh/service-mesh-2-x#ossm-create-mesh`
- [5] *Red Hat OpenShift Distributed Tracing Platform architecture*: `https://docs.redhat.com/en/documentation/openshift_container_platform/4.16/observability/distributed_tracing/distr-tracing-tempo-architecture#distr-tracing-tempo-architecture_distr-tracing-tempo-architecture`
- [6] *Distributed tracing documentation*: `https://docs.redhat.com/en/documentation/openshift_container_platform/4.16/html/distributed_tracing/distr-tracing-tempo-installing`
- [7] *Envoy documentation*: `https://www.envoyproxy.io/docs/envoy/v1.31.0/`
- [8] *Performance and scalability*: `https://docs.redhat.com/en/documentation/openshift_container_platform/4.16/html/service_mesh/service-mesh-2-x#ossm-performance-scalability`
- [9] *How to resolve "the object has been modified; please apply your changes to the latest version and try again" error when running oc apply command in RHOCP 4*: `https://access.redhat.com/solutions/6428441`

Quiz

Let's test your understanding of Red Hat Service Mesh with this quick quiz:

1. What is Maistra in the context of Red Hat Service Mesh?
    a. A cloud storage solution
    b. An open source distribution of Istio tailored for OpenShift
    c. A container orchestration tool
    d. A security framework for microservices
2. What distributed tracing backends are currently available for Red Hat Service Mesh?
    a. Envoy and Maistra
    b. Jaeger and Kafka
    c. Tempo and Jaeger
    d. Istio and Zipkin
3. What is the primary role of Envoy in Red Hat Service Mesh?
    a. Managing persistent storage
    b. Handling network traffic between microservices
    c. Deploying container images
    d. Managing access control policies
4. Which feature is NOT provided by Red Hat OpenShift Service Mesh?
    a. Service discovery
    b. Load balancing
    c. Application deployment
    d. End-to-end authentication
5. How can you expose a service outside of Red Hat OpenShift Service Mesh?
    a. By using a `Gateway` resource
    b. By using a `PodDisruptionBudget` resource
    c. By using a `PersistentVolume` resource
    d. By using a `ConfigMap` resource

Answers

1. **b**. Maistra is an open source distribution of Istio specifically tailored for use with Red Hat OpenShift. It integrates the features of Istio with the OpenShift platform, providing service mesh functionality in a way optimized for OpenShift environments.
2. **c**. Red Hat Service Mesh supports both Jaeger and Tempo as distributed tracing backends. Jaeger is the traditional solution, while Tempo is a newer alternative that integrates well with modern observability stacks.
3. **b**. Envoy is a proxy that handles all network traffic between microservices in Red Hat Service Mesh, providing traffic management, load balancing, and security features.
4. **c**. Red Hat OpenShift Service Mesh provides features such as service discovery, load balancing, and end-to-end authentication. However, application deployment is handled by OpenShift itself, not by Service Mesh.
5. **a**. A `Gateway` resource in Red Hat Service Mesh is used to expose services externally, enabling inbound and outbound traffic control for the mesh. Other options, such as `PodDisruptionBudget`, `PersistentVolume`, and `ConfigMap`, are unrelated to external service exposure.

Join us on Discord

For discussions around the book and to connect with your peers, join us on Discord at `http://packt.link/discordcloud` or scan the QR code below:

15

Exploring Additional Services in OpenShift

This chapter discusses several additional offerings that are not essential to running OpenShift, but are still useful enough to warrant their own chapter. These services include serverless, Windows containers, an integrated registry, and GitOps. They serve different purposes, and the goal of this chapter is to make you aware of their capabilities and situations where they can be of use. You will learn what serverless computing is and how to create serverless functions in OpenShift, how to run Windows-native workloads in OpenShift in Windows containers, how to provide the integrated image registry with persistent storage, and finally, how to use ArgoCD to deploy applications consistently locally and across multiple clusters.

We'll cover the following main topics:

- Serverless
- Windows containers
- Integrated registry
- GitOps

Let's begin!

> OpenShift is at the core of a diverse ecosystem of additional components that can be deployed on it to supplement its capabilities, so we can't realistically cover them all in a single book, let alone one chapter.

Technical requirements

In this chapter, you will need the following:

- Bash shell
- OpenShift 4.16:
    - **Serverless section**: OpenShift Local/OpenShift on VMware vSphere from *Chapter 3, Getting Started with OpenShift*
    - **Windows Containers, integrated registry, and GitOps sections**: OpenShift on VMware vSphere from *Chapter 3, Getting Started with OpenShift*
- Firefox (recommended) or any other web browser
- An active Red Hat subscription to view Red Hat KB articles

You can access this book's GitHub repository at `https://github.com/PacktPublishing/Learn-OpenShift-Second-Edition`.

Serverless

OpenShift provides extensive flexibility, which also introduces significant complexity in managing deployments. As an alternative approach, large companies such as Google introduced serverless for Kubernetes, known as **Knative**, in July 2018. This model offers a different perspective on how applications can be deployed and organized, focusing on simplifying deployment and scaling by abstracting the underlying infrastructure.

For OpenShift, Knative became available as part of the **Red Hat OpenShift Serverless** offering, which was introduced with the release of OpenShift 4.2 in October 2019. This integration allowed OpenShift users to leverage Knative's capabilities within the OpenShift ecosystem, providing a robust platform for building and managing serverless applications.

In the following table, you can see which Red Hat OpenShift editions include Serverless:

Edition	Inclusion
OpenShift Kubernetes Engine	No
OpenShift Container Platform	Yes
OpenShift Platform Plus	Yes

Table 15.1: OpenShift Serverless availability matrix

The Red Hat OpenShift Serverless Operator offers a suite of APIs that facilitate running containers, microservices, and functions in a serverless manner. Serverless Operator provides the following features:

- **Easy to get started:** Provides simple developer experience for deploying and running cloud-native applications on Kubernetes with powerful abstractions.

- **Immutable revisions:** Deploy new features using canary, A/B, or blue-green testing with gradual traffic rollout.
- **Flexible language and runtime support:** Use any programming language or runtime, including Java, Python, Go, JavaScript, Quarkus, Spring Boot, or Node.js.
- **Automatic scaling:** No need to configure replica numbers or idling behavior. Applications automatically scale to zero when idle and up to meet demand, with built-in reliability and fault tolerance.
- **Event-driven applications:** Allows you to build loosely coupled, event-triggered, distributed applications that connect to various built-in or third-party event sources, powered by operators.
- **Hybrid cloud ready:** Provides portable serverless functionality that runs anywhere **OpenShift Container Platform** (**OCP**) runs, allowing you to leverage data locality and SaaS as needed.

Now that we know the basics, it's time to deploy the Serverless Operator and create a sample application.

Deploying Knative Serving

The Serverless Operator is not coming out of the box, but can be easily deployed from the Red Hat Ecosystem Catalog via OperatorHub; let's deploy it and create a simple serverless application:

1. Go to **OperatorHub** and search for `knative`, then click on the **Red Hat OpenShift Serverless** pictogram:

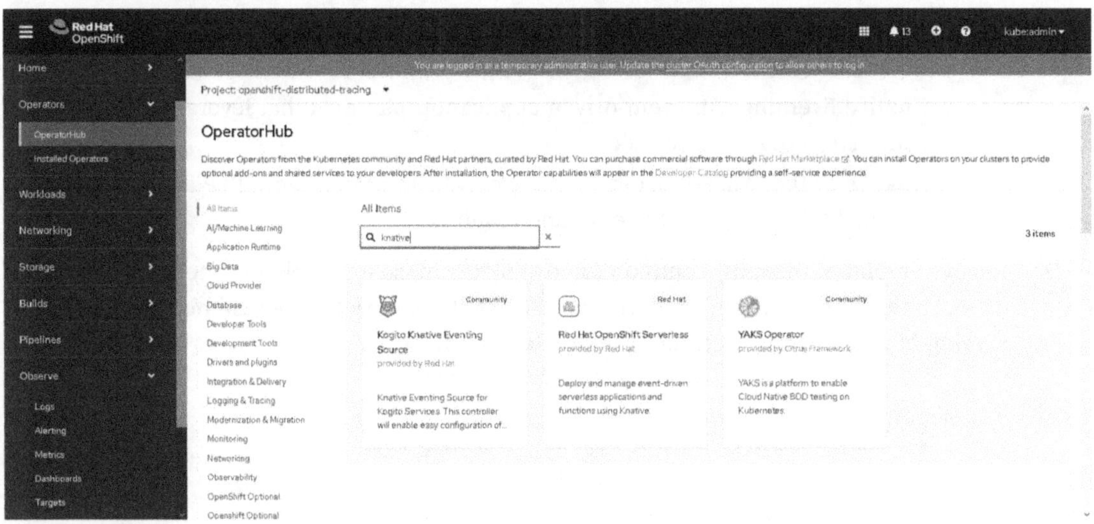

Figure 15.1: Finding OpenShift Serverless Operator in OperatorHub

2. Click the **Install** button, then **Install** again, and installation will start; wait till the Operator's status changes to **ready for use**, then click on **View Operator**:

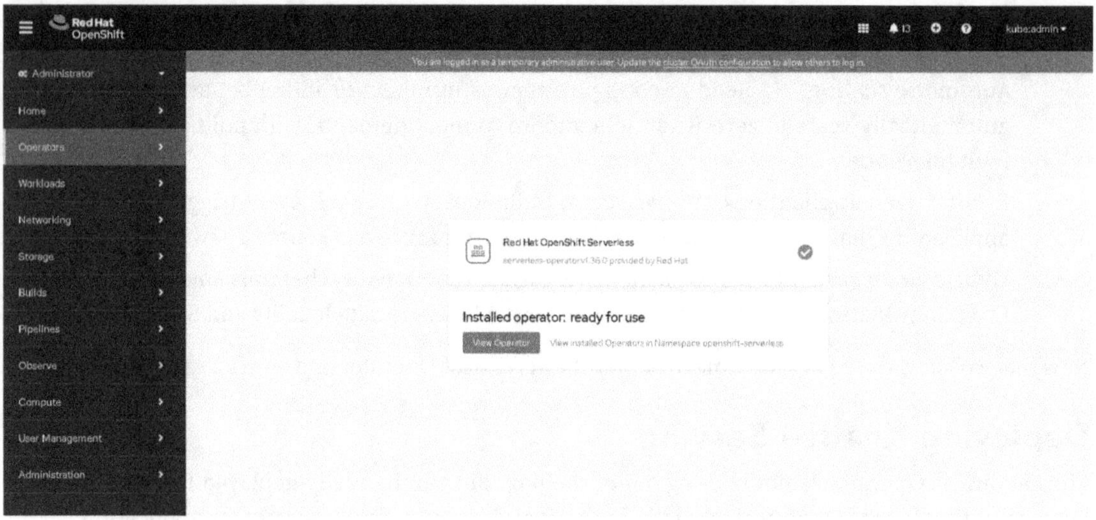

Figure 15.2: Installing OpenShift Serverless Operator from OperatorHub

On the Operator's page, you will see three provided APIs:

- **Knative Serving**: A platform for streamlined application deployment, traffic-based auto-scaling from zero to *N*, and traffic-split rollouts.
- **Knative Eventing**: An event-driven application platform that leverages **CloudEvents** with a simple HTTP interface.
- **Knative Kafka**: An extension to Knative Eventing, merging HTTP accessibility with Apache Kafka's proven efficiency and reliability.

3. Knative Serving is the most common Knative platform, so let's pick this one and create it. To do so, change the project to `knative-serving` and then click **Create instance** on the **Knative Serving** pictogram, and then click the **Create** button:

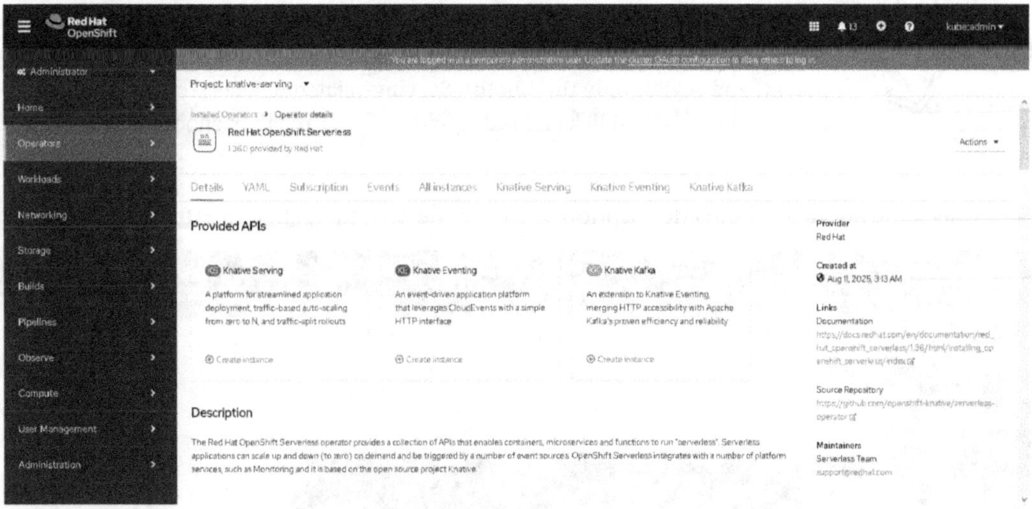

Figure 15.3: APIs provided by OpenShift Serverless

> The Knative `Service` object can only be created in the `knative-serving` namespace.

Now that you have Knative Serving deployed, you can create an application by using the Knative CLI or via the web UI, in the **Developer** or **Administrator** perspective.

Creating a sample application

For now, let's do it from the UI, so please follow these steps:

1. Go to the **Serverless** > **Serving** menu on the left, and click **Create** > **Service**:

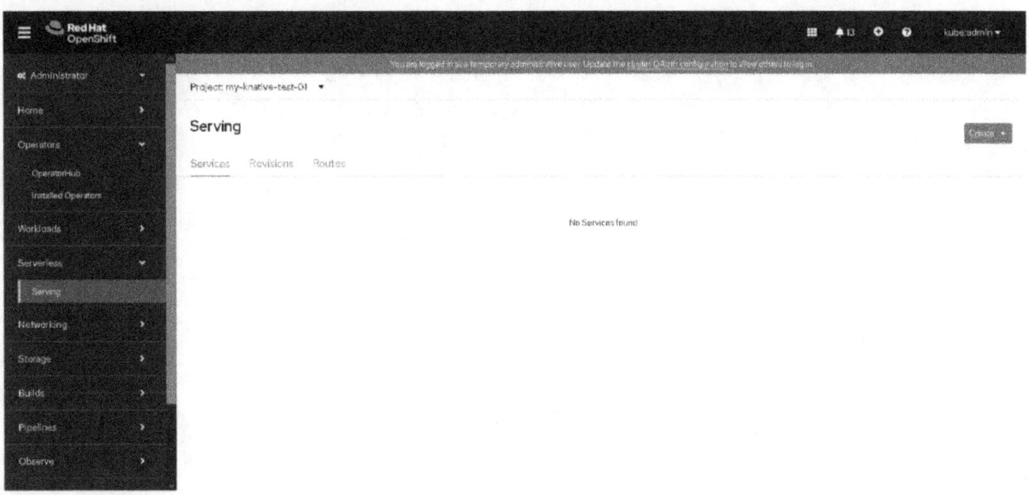

Figure 15.4: Creating a Knative Serving resource

> Make sure you are using a new project to make the deployment steps more transparent, and review only the Knative Serving-related objects. You can create it directly in the web UI – click on the drop-down menu and then choose **Create Project.**

2. Check the **Service Schema** description and other details, then click **Create:**

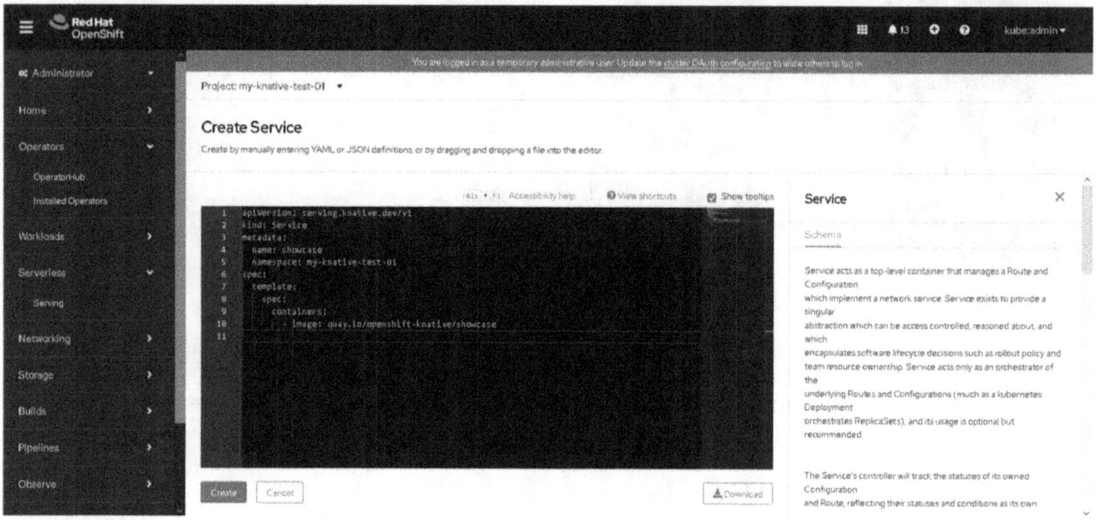

Figure 15.5: YAML representation of a Knative Service object

An **Admission Webhook** warning may pop up for a few seconds, but it can be safely ignored. As you may remember from *Chapter 7*, *Application Security and Isolation*, this is caused by the **Pod Security Admission** (**PSA**) webhook that detected the `restricted` **Pod Security Standard** (**PSS**) in `warn` mode on our namespace. This is yet another example of how PSA and PSS can protect your cluster from potentially insecure workloads.

3. The Knative `Service` deployment will take a couple of seconds, then you can reach your application via a route available on the service's page to the right, under **URL:**

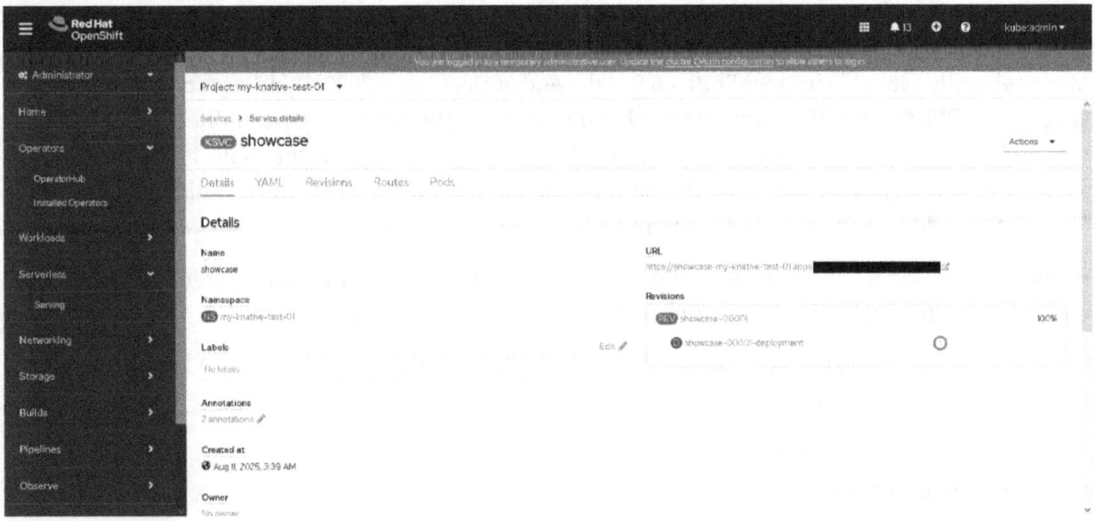

Figure 15.6: Knative Service details

When you click on the URL, the sample application's page will open:

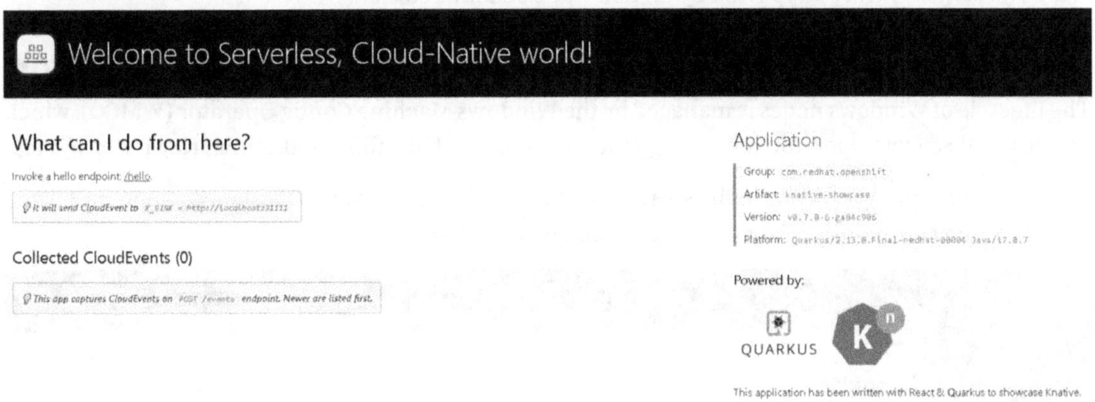

Figure 15.7: Sample Knative Service application

Please use the official documentation at [1] to drill down into the Serverless Operator's configuration options.

You can follow the official guide at [2] to install the kn CLI if you want to deploy Knative via CLI.

This was but a brief introduction to the world of serverless in OpenShift. It does not cover everything that the Serverless Operator has to offer, so we recommend checking with the documentation to explore it further.

The next topic we're going to cover is how to run containerized Windows applications on OpenShift.

Windows containers

Made generally available in OpenShift 4.6.8 at the end of December 2020, Windows containers brought support for Windows-native containerized applications to the realm of OpenShift. Another product that aims to bridge the gap between Linux and Windows workloads in OpenShift is OpenShift Virtualization (generally available since OpenShift 4.5); however, it is geared toward different use cases. More information on their differences can be found in [3].

In this section, we will configure a demo Windows node, connect it to our cluster, and schedule a simple application on it. The whole process boils down to the following steps:

- Installing and setting up the Windows Machine Config Operator
- Creating Windows VM template
- Creating Windows MachineSet
- Running workloads

The topics that follow will guide you through all these steps, and at the end of this section, you will have a working Windows application running on your cluster and capable of serving requests.

Windows containers are supported by all Red Hat OpenShift editions.

Installing and setting up the Windows Machine Config Operator

The lifecycle of Windows nodes is managed by the **Windows Machine Config Operator** (**WMCO**), which can be installed from OperatorHub. Let's go over the process of installing and configuring it step by step:

1. Start by typing `windows` in the search bar. You should see two WMCO instances – one supported by the community, and another provided by Red Hat:

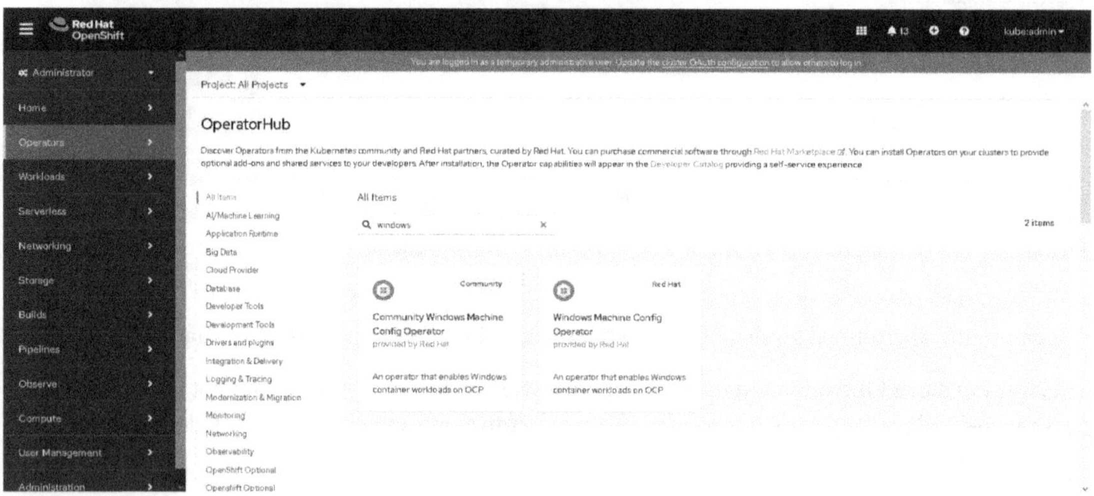

Figure 15.8: Finding Windows Machine Config Operator in OperatorHub

If you have a Red Hat subscription and would like to have official support, click on the tile tagged **Red Hat**; otherwise, you can use the community-supported version. There is no technical difference between the two.

2. On the operator's page, you will see the usage instructions that explain in detail how to enable Windows workloads. You can also select the channel and operator version:

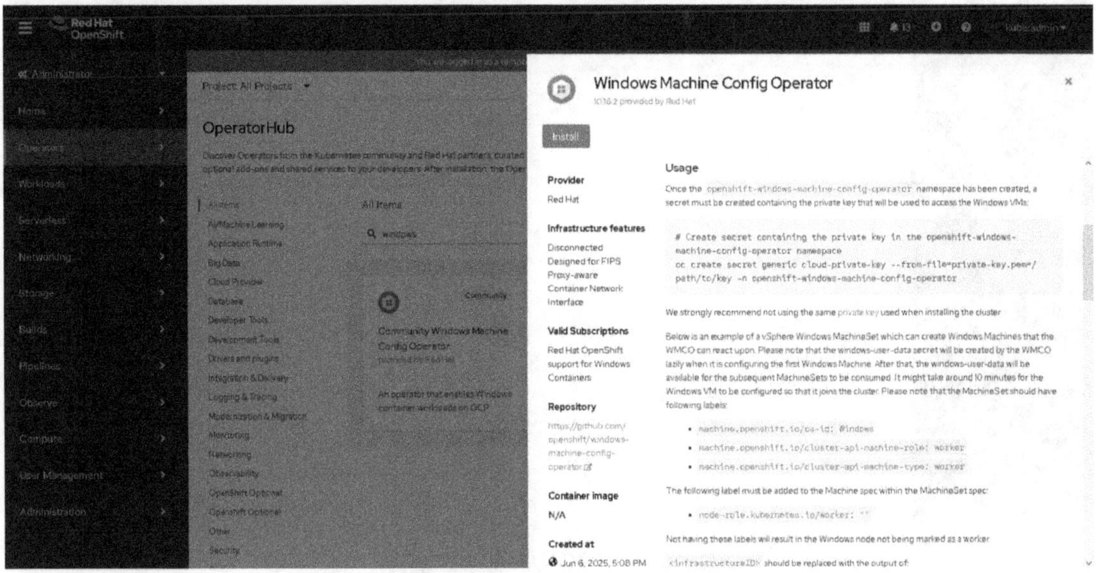

Figure 15.9: Windows Machine Config Operator details and configuration instructions

At the time of writing this chapter, the latest WMCO version available through the stable channel is 10.16.2. Leave them at their defaults and click **Install**.

> You can also access these instructions, as well as the list of available channels and versions, by directly examining the `packagemanifest` resource from the `openshift-marketplace` namespace:
>
> ```
> $ oc get packagemanifest/windows-machine-config-operator -o
> yaml -n openshift-marketplace
> ```

3. On the next screen, you will notice that the operator doesn't install any APIs, only a controller. We recommend installing the operator in the default namespace, `openshift-windows-machine-config-operator`. Also, enable cluster monitoring on the namespace and set **Update approval** to **Manual**:

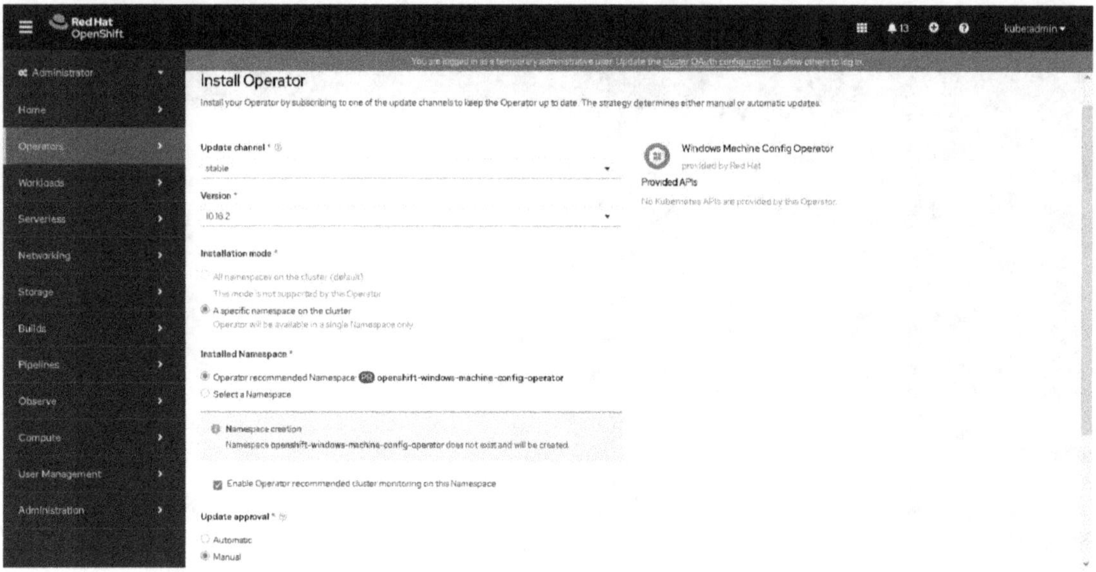

Figure 15.10: WMCO installation page

> Enabling cluster monitoring on a namespace adds the `openshift.io/cluster-monitoring: "true"` label to it behind the scenes. We also recommend selecting the **Manual** approval strategy because it allows for better control over upgrades, which is important in a production environment where upgrades can sometimes cause disruptions.

4. Click **Install** again.

   Installation will begin, and in about a minute, you will be prompted to approve the installation plan:

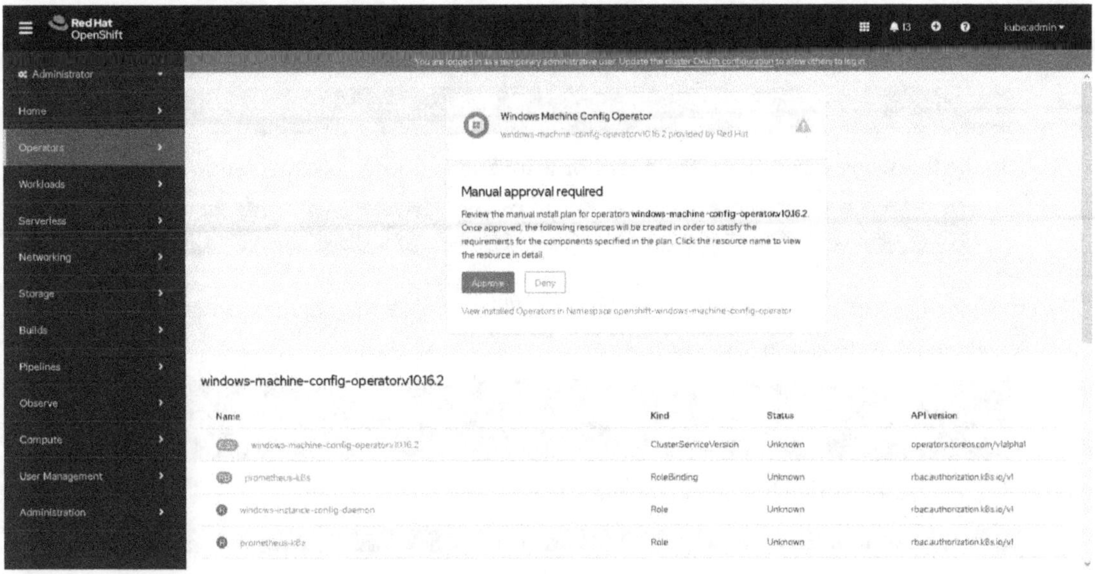

Figure 15.11: WMCO installation requires manual approval

5. Click **Approve** and wait for the operator to finish installing. The following message will be displayed indicating progress:

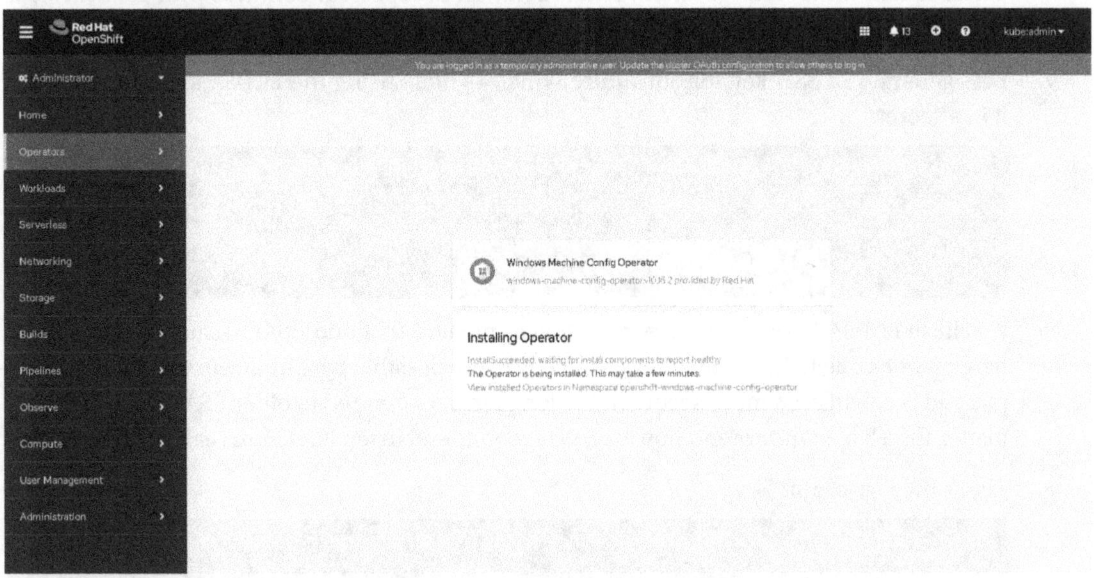

Figure 15.12: WMCO installation in progress

6. When the UI reports success, you can go to your terminal and check whether the operator pod is running using the following command:

```
$ oc get po -n openshift-windows-machine-config-operator
```

In the following screenshot, the operator is up and running, as expected:

```
NAME                                                READY   STATUS
windows-machine-config-operator-67f95b9b5d-dr6pk    1/1     Running
```

Figure 15.13: WMCO pod is running

Let's check its logs nonetheless:

```
$ oc logs -l name=windows-machine-config-operator -n openshift-windows-
machine-config-operator
```

You may notice the following error message:

```
unable to create signer from private key secret: Secret \"cloud-private-key\" not found"
```

Figure 15.14: WMCO cannot find the expected secret with the private SSH key

As stated on the operator's details in OperatorHub, it expects to find a secret named `cloud-private-key` containing a private SSH key for connection to Windows machines in order to perform their initial configuration, so this behavior is expected. Continue with the next steps to finalize WMCO configuration.

7. Let's generate an SSH key for our future Windows node using the ECDSA algorithm and put it in a secret:

```
$ ssh-keygen -t ecdsa -N '' -f ~/.ssh/id_ecdsa_win
$ oc create secret generic cloud-private-key --from-file=private-key.
pem=/home/ausov/.ssh/id_ecdsa_win -n openshift-windows-machine-config-
operator
```

We chose ECDSA here (other common choices include DSA and RSA) because it offers more performance due to its smaller keys, which is made possible by **elliptic curve** (EC) cryptography and is considered more secure in the long term, compared to older RSA. It doesn't really matter for a lab environment; however, we recommend using ECDSA in real-world scenarios.

8. Check the logs again:

```
$ oc logs -l name=windows-machine-config-operator -n openshift-windows-
machine-config-operator
```

Now that the secret is there, you should see the following message indicating the creation of another secret, `windows-user-data`:


```
{"level":"info","ts":"2025-08-11T12:40:08Z","logger":"controller.secret","msg":"s
ecret not found, creating the secret","secret":{"name":"cloud-private-key","names
pace":"openshift-windows-machine-config-operator"},"name":"windows-user-data"}
```


Figure 15.15: Another secret is generated

9. Use the following command to display the secret `windows-user-data` that was created in the `openshift-machine-api` namespace:

```
$ oc get secret windows-user-data -n openshift-machine-api
```

As you can see, the secret is present:

```
NAME                TYPE     DATA   AGE
windows-user-data   Opaque   1      2m53s
```

Figure 15.16: The windows-user-data secret generated by WMCO

We will examine its contents later in this section.

In a real-world scenario, you would probably use GitOps, Ansible, or some other automation to pre-create the `openshift-windows-machine-config-operator` namespace and the secret in advance to avoid that error. However, we felt that doing it post-factum would provide a better learning experience.

Now that we have WMCO installed and configured, we can work on creating a base VM template that WMCO will use to provision nodes.

Creating a Windows VM template

As of 10.16.2, WMCO supports two methods of adding Windows nodes:

- **Windows MachineSet objects:** Creating a `MachineSet` object that uses a base generic image to spin up new nodes, enabling scalability in a cloud. Cluster autoscaling is supported for Windows nodes via the `ClusterAutoscaler` and `MachineAutoscaler` APIs.
- **Bring-Your-Own-Host (BYOH)**: Add an existing Windows host to your OpenShift cluster. This method involves configuring key-based SSH access on the Windows side and a ConfigMap named `windows-instances` on the side of OpenShift, which is explained in more detail in [4]. Supported since OpenShift 4.8.

We chose the first method for our demonstration, as it lends itself to a more scalable solution that, from our experience, is used by businesses more often than BYOH. Since this approach relies on a base image, we will have to prepare it first. Different infrastructure platforms use different methods; for VMware vSphere, that means preparing a VM template. Follow these steps to obtain an evaluation copy of Windows Server 2022 and create a VM template from it:

1. Download Windows Server 2022 Datacenter Evaluation ISO from `https://info.microsoft.com/ww-landing-windows-server-2022.html` [5]. You will be asked to provide some information about yourself, such as your first/last name, company name, and phone number. Then pick the 64-bit edition ISO. You can also try using a direct link: `https://go.microsoft.com/fwlink/p/?LinkID=2195280&clcid=0x409&culture=en-us&country=US` [6].

2. For the steps that follow, you will need a datastore where the Windows ISO can be stored. Create a folder for your Windows image, if it doesn't already exist, and use the **UPLOAD FILES** option to upload the ISO you obtained before (at the moment of writing this, the file was named `SERVER_EVAL_x64FRE_en-us.iso`):

Figure 15.17: Creating a Windows Server ISO folder on a VMware vSphere datastore

The ISO is 4.75 GB in size, so the process may take a while, depending on your internet connection. In one of our labs, it took about 1 hour, while in the other, it was just a couple of minutes.

3. Next, we will start a new VM from ISO. Select the VM folder where you want your VM template to live (we suggest choosing **Templates** or similar) > **Actions** > **New Virtual Machine.** Configure it as follows:

   - **Select a creation type: Create a new virtual machine**
   - **Select a name and folder**: Provide a name and confirm your selection of a VM folder
   - **Select a compute resource**: Select an ESXi cluster and resource pool
   - **Select storage**: Choose a datastore and keep VM Storage Policy at Datastore Default
   - **Select compatibility**: No changes (usually set to **ESXi 7.0 U2 and later**)
   - **Select a guest OS**: Microsoft Windows Server 2022 (64-bit)
   - **Customize hardware/virtual hardware:**
     - **CPU:** 8 (same as for other workers)
     - **Memory**: 32 GB (same as for other workers)
     - **New Hard Disk**: 100 GB (same as for other workers)
     - **New Network:** Same one as for other OpenShift nodes
     - **New CD/DVD Drive: Datastore ISO File** > select the ISO you uploaded, check **Connect At Power On**
     - **Customize hardware / VM Options: Boot Options** > **Firmware: BIOS**
   - Ready to complete: **FINISH**

4. Now power up the VM and open its console. You may catch the *Loading files...* message, followed by the Windows logo, and a progress circle. In a minute or two, you should be presented with the Windows installation screen below:

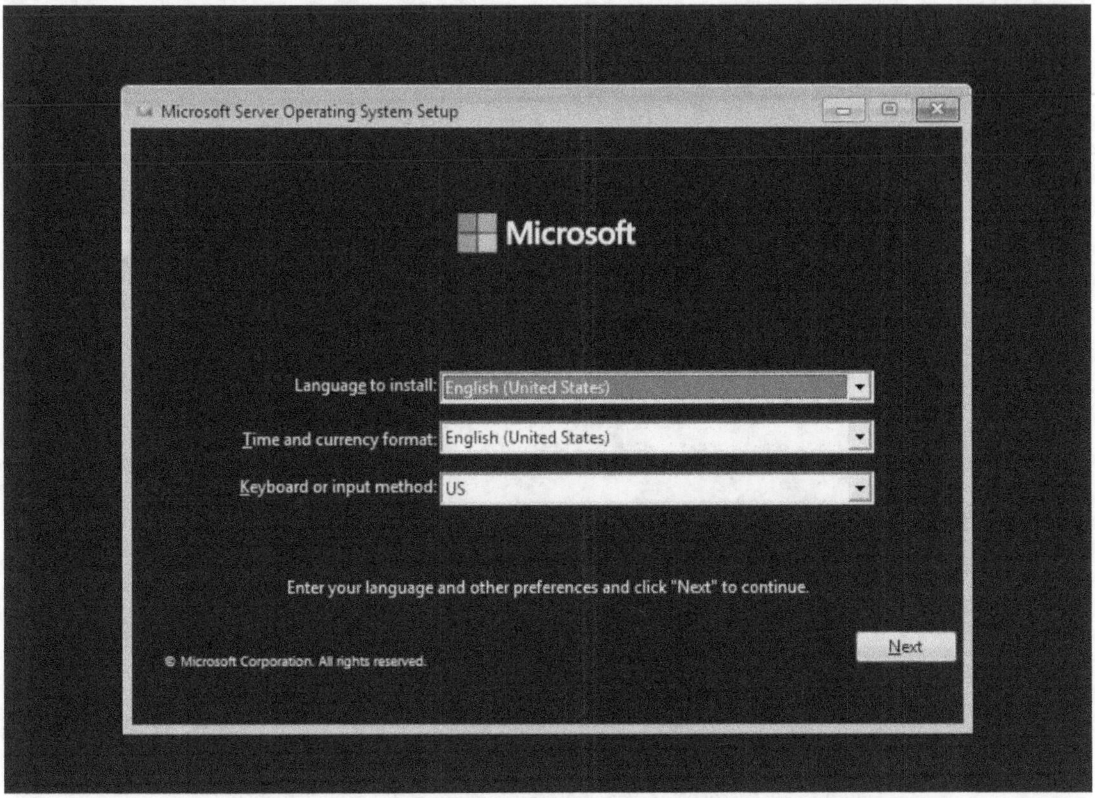

Figure 15.18: Microsoft Server Operating System Setup – region

5. We are going to keep it as simple as possible, so click **Next** > **Install now** (or use the *Alt* + *I* or *Option* + *I* shortcut):

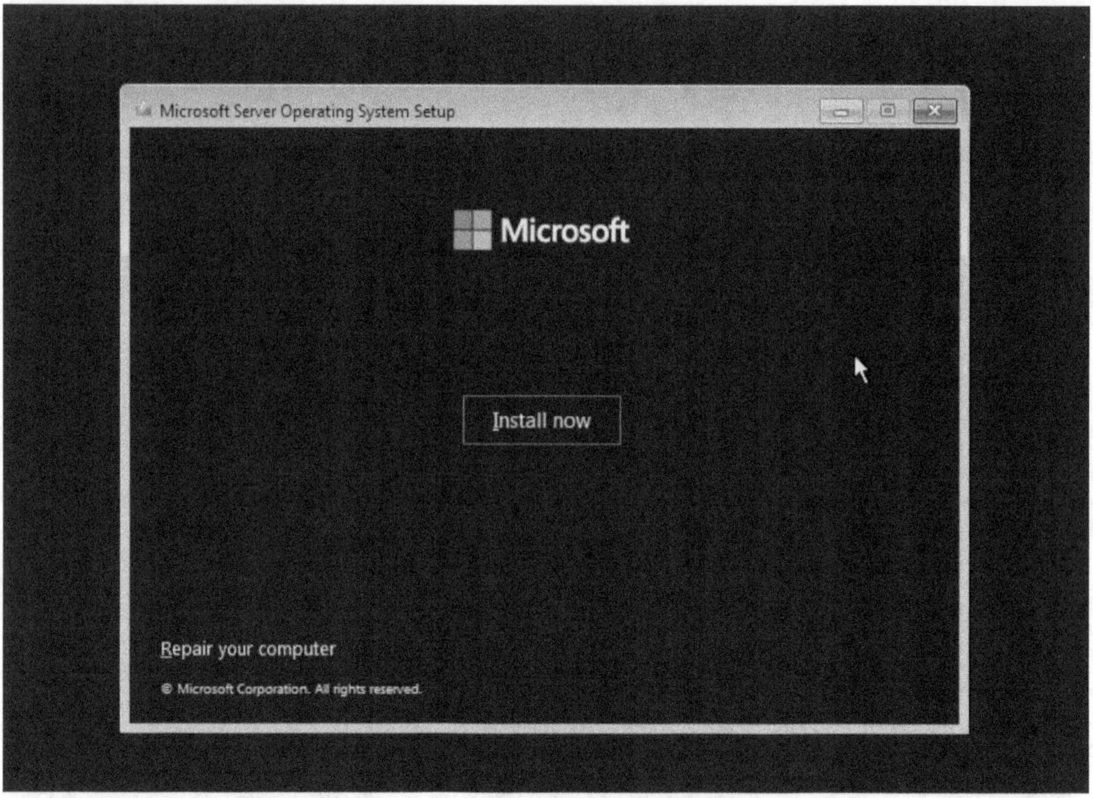

Figure 15.19: Microsoft Server Operating System Setup – ready to install

You will see the **Setup Starting** message.

6. Since this machine will be used only as a container runtime environment and not a full-blown desktop workstation, we will select the **Windows Server 2022 Datacenter Evaluation** option. That will install a Windows Core environment without a GUI, which reduces the footprint of the VM and speeds up the installation. Click **Next** (*Alt* + *N* or *Option* + *N* shortcut):

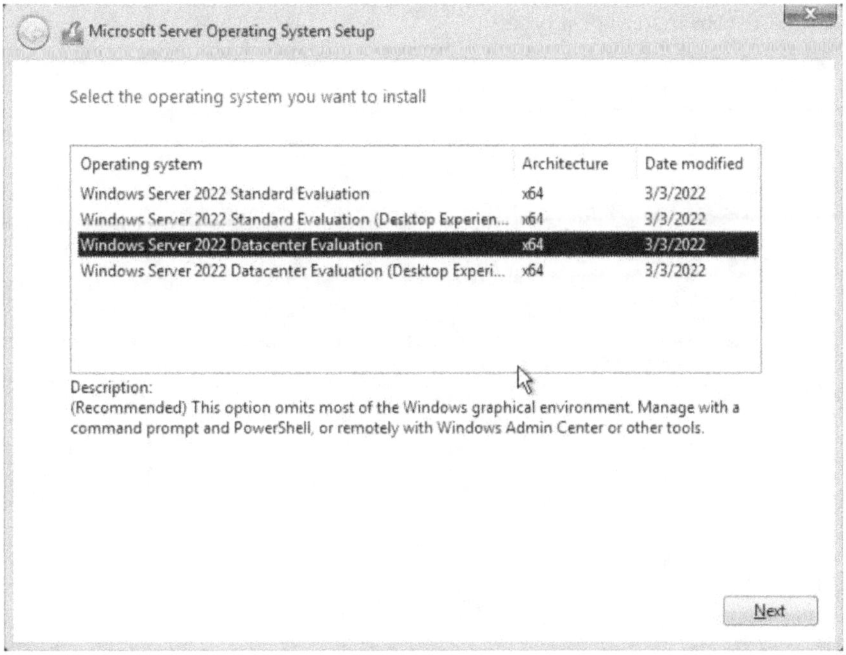

Figure 15.20: Microsoft Server Operating System Setup – Windows Server edition

7. Accept the license agreement (we suggest reading it first) and click **Next** (*Alt* + *N* or *Option* + *N* shortcut):

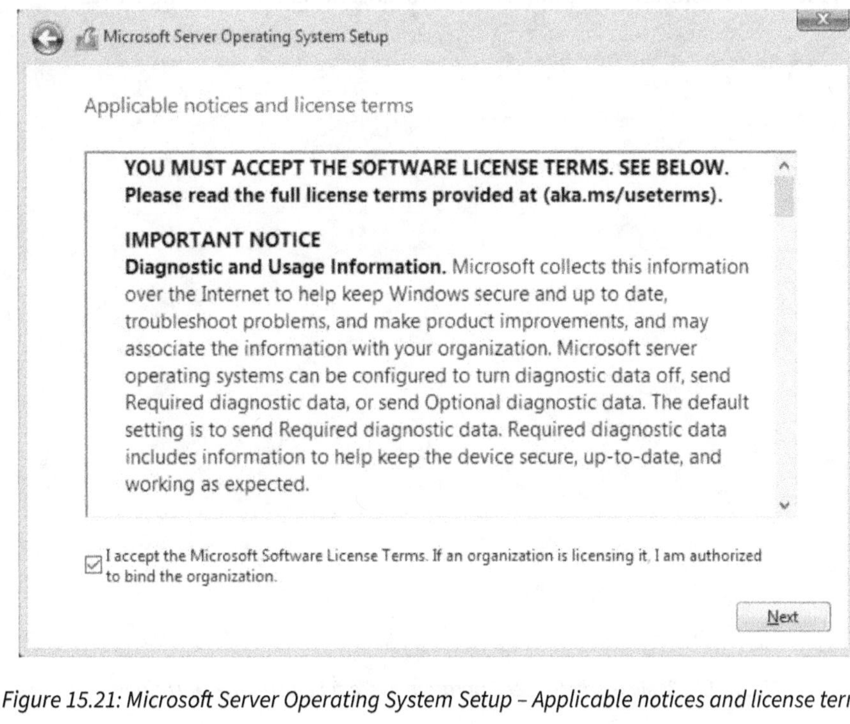

Figure 15.21: Microsoft Server Operating System Setup – Applicable notices and license terms

8. Select the **Custom** installation type:

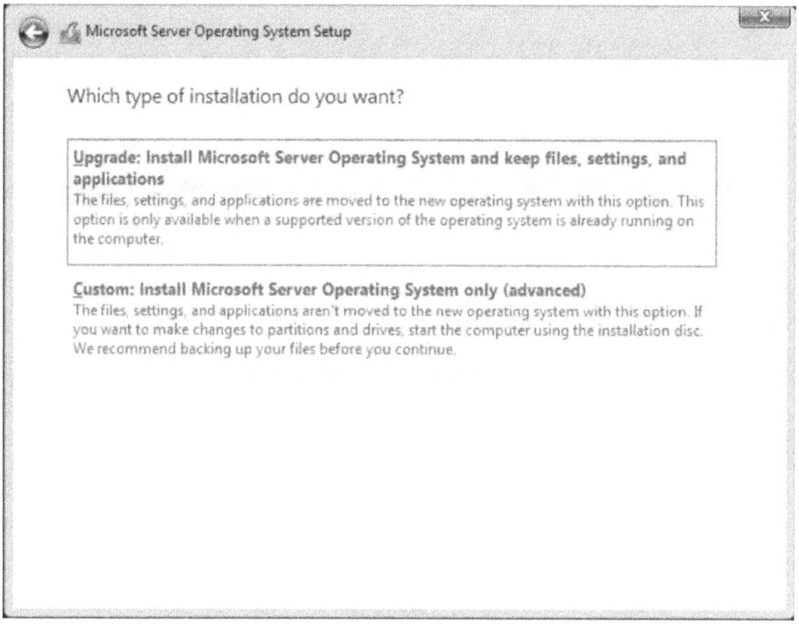

Figure 15.22: Microsoft Server Operating System Setup – Installation type

This is where you have an opportunity to apply a custom partitioning scheme to the storage of your VM. We recommend keeping it as it is to save time, and clicking **Next**:

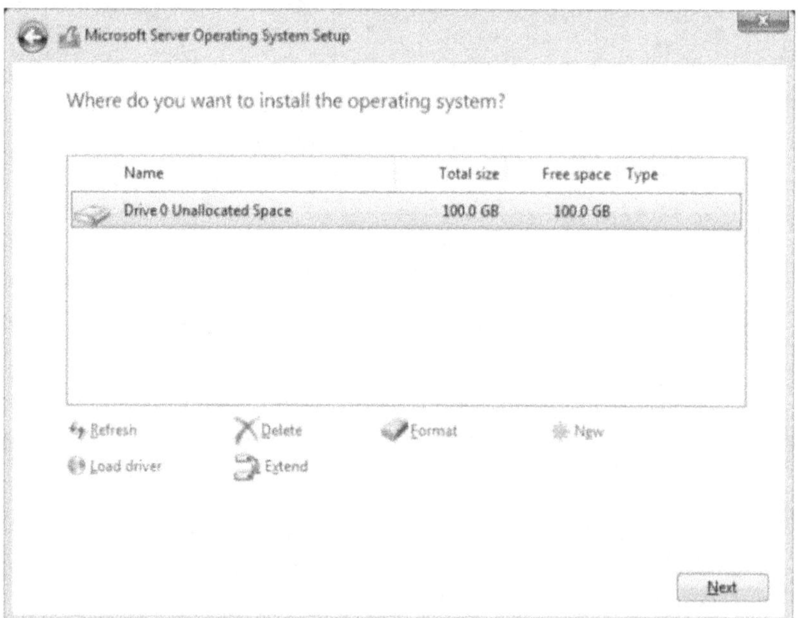

Figure 15.23: Microsoft Server Operating System Setup – disk partitioning

Now, the installation will commence. The entire process shouldn't take more than 5–10 minutes (it took about 4 minutes in our lab):

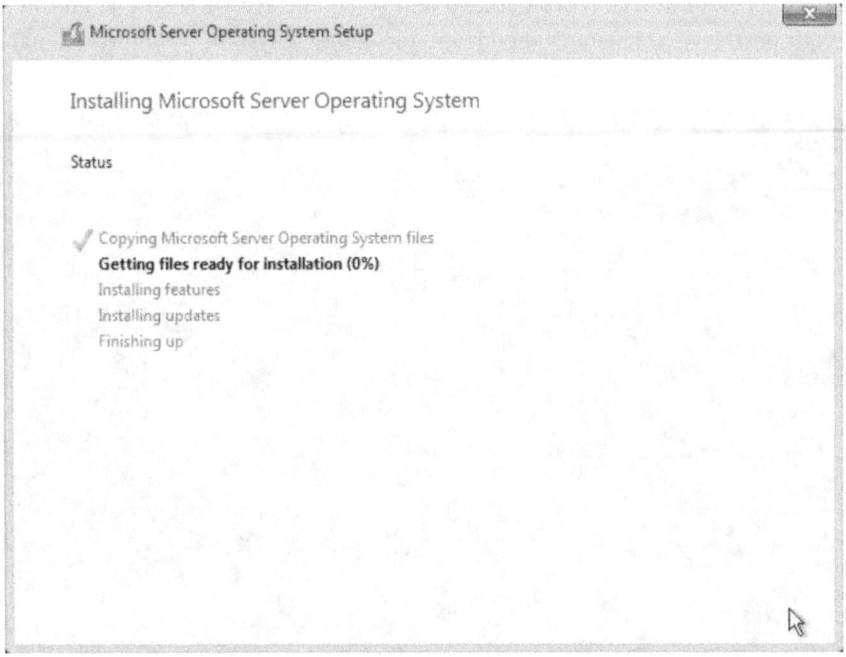

Figure 15.24: Microsoft Server Operating System Setup – Installing

9. After the installation is finished and the VM restarts, you will be asked to change your `Administrator` password on first login:

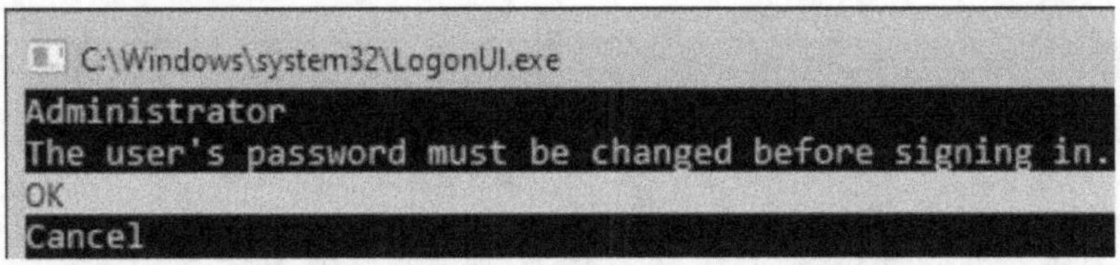

Figure 15.25: Setting up the Administrator password on first login

Hit **OK** and type your new password twice. Pressing *Enter* doesn't result in a newline, so use the down arrow key to switch to the next field. If you don't see * appearing as you type your password, click on the `cmd.exe` window and try again. Hit **OK** again when the prompt says that your password has been changed, and the `SConfig` system configuration panel will start:

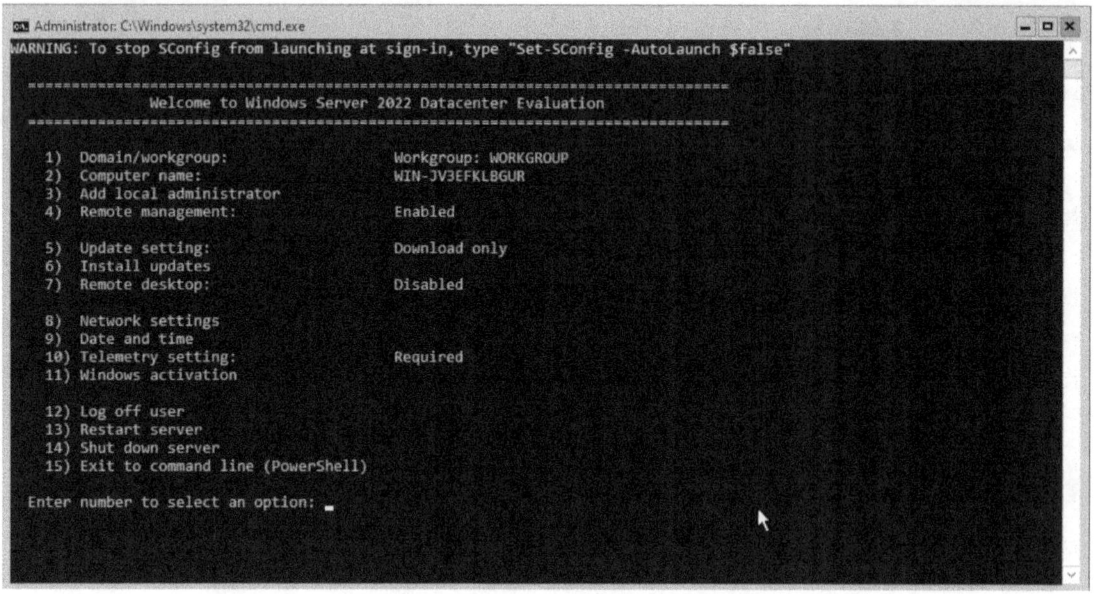

Figure 15.26: SConfig startup menu

10. Select **2** and enter a new computer name. Select **Y** at the restart prompt to apply the change:

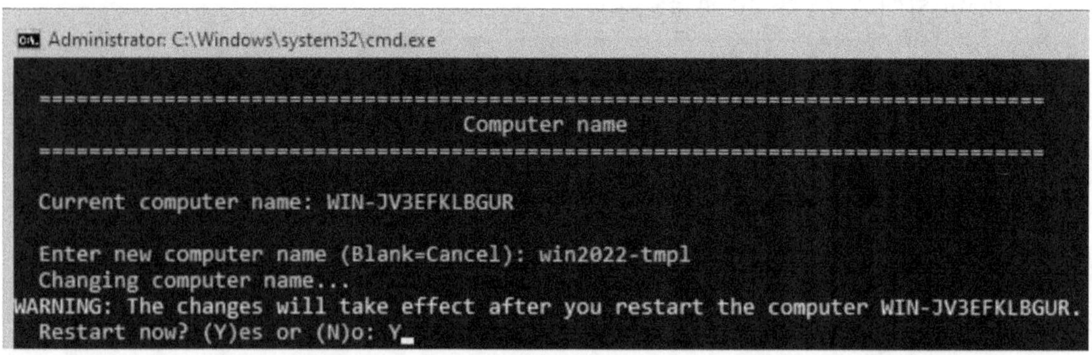

Figure 15.27: Changing the computer name in SConfig

11. When the VM comes back, type in your `Administrator` password and select **15** to start the PowerShell command interpreter:

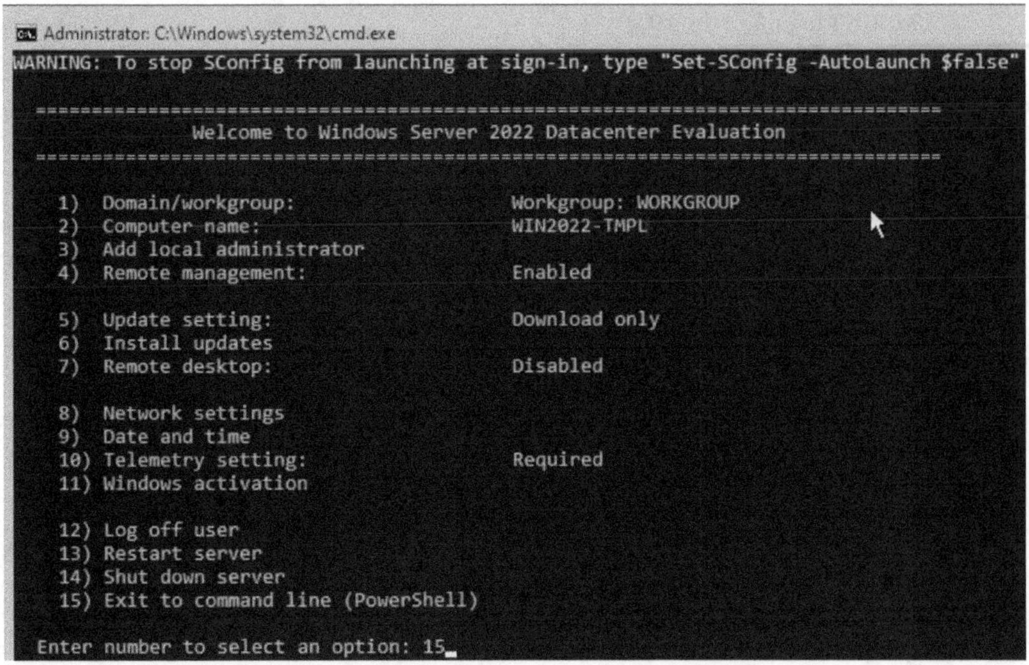

Figure 15.28: Launching PowerShell from SConfig

Use the **Send Ctrl+Alt+Delete** button in the upper-right corner of the console if prompted to unlock the terminal.

12. The next step is to install VMware guest tools for Windows. For Windows Server 2022 LTSC, only 11.0.6 or newer versions are supported. Right-click on the VM > **Guest OS** > **Install VMware Tools...**:

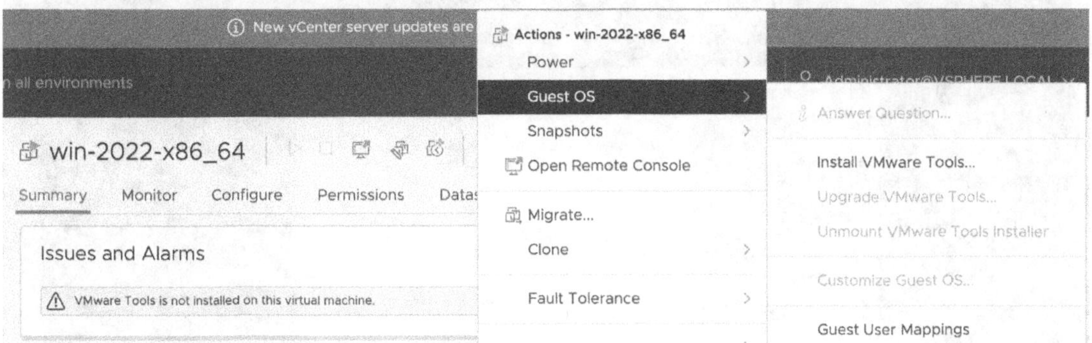

Figure 15.29: Mounting the VMware Tools ISO – 1

Click **MOUNT** to mount the ISO:

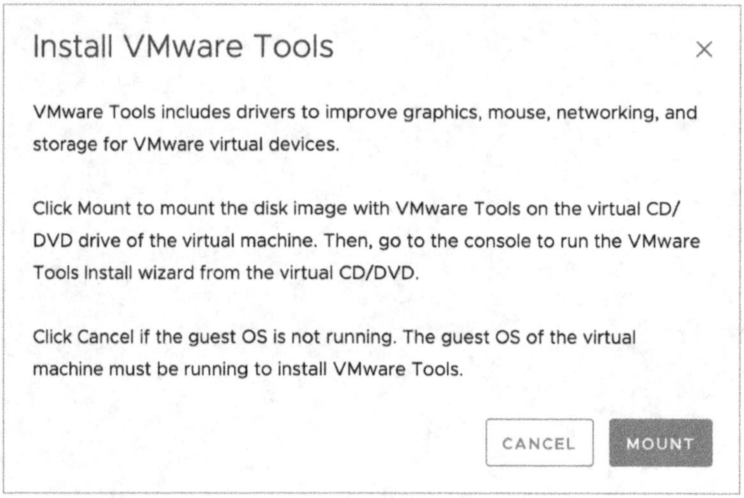

Figure 15.30: Mounting the VMware Tools ISO – 2

13. In the terminal, type `D:\setup.exe`. The prompt will return almost immediately, making it look like the command silently failed or started something in the background, but the wizard is actually obstructed by the terminal; move the latter aside and bring the wizard to the front. Click **Next > Next (Typical) > Install > Finish:**

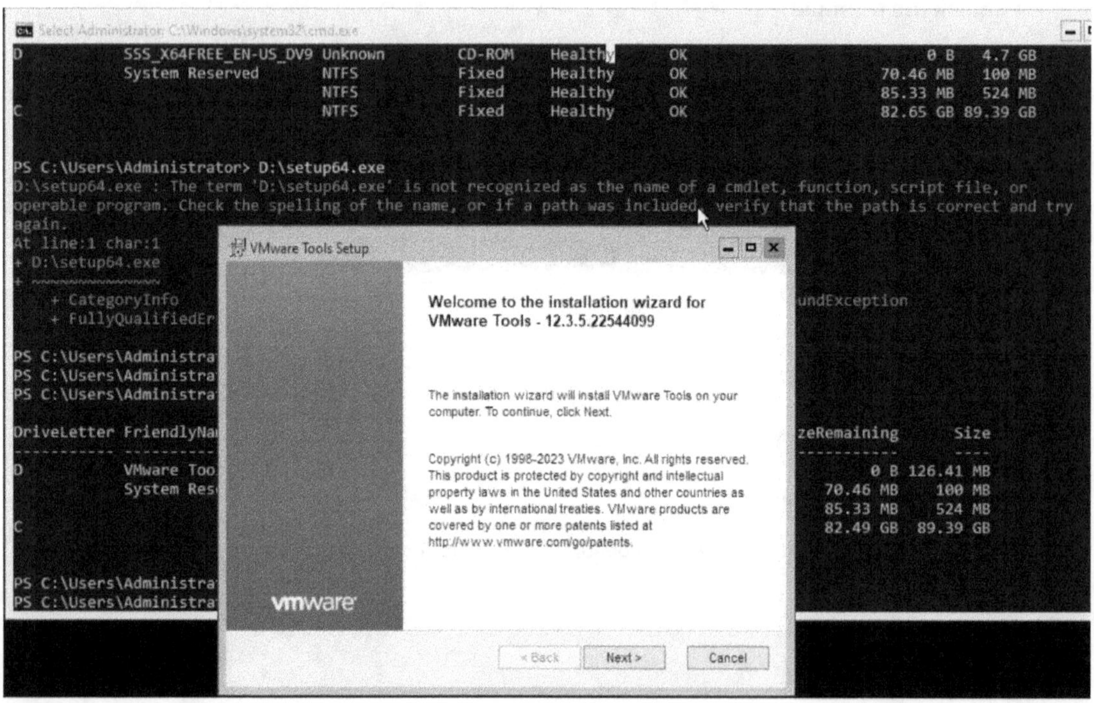

Figure 15.31: Starting the VMware Tools setup wizard

When prompted to restart the VM after installation, answer **Yes**.

14. When the VM is back online, log in and select **15** again in `SConfig`. Use the following command to check the status of the `VMTools` Windows service:

```
PS C:\Users\Administrator> Get-Service -Name VMTools
```

The service should be up and running:

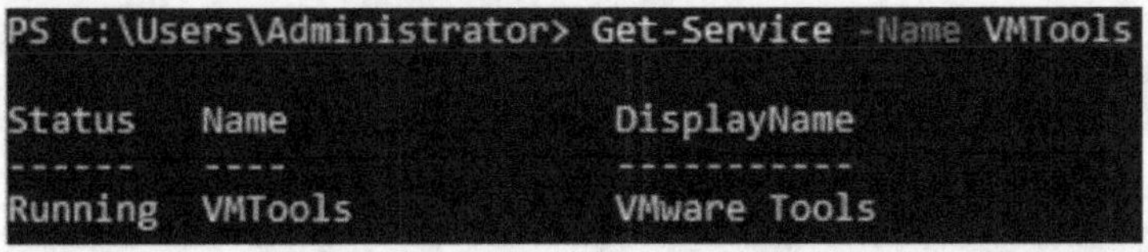

Figure 15.32: Checking the status of the VMTools Windows service

15. Next, use Notepad to open a new `tools.conf` file in the `C:\ProgramData\VMware\VMware Tools` directory:

```
PS C:\Users\Administrator> notepad.exe 'C:\ProgramData\VMware\VMware
Tools\tools.conf'
```

Answer **Yes** to the question about creating a new file and add the line `exclude-nics=` to the file, as shown here:

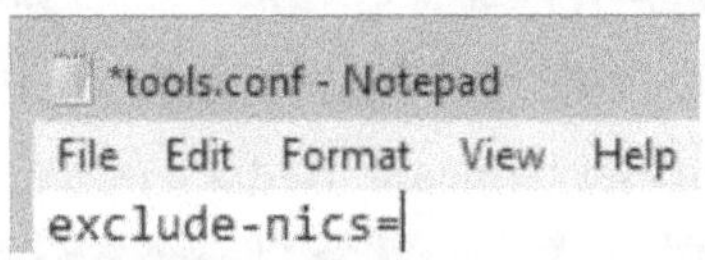

Figure 15.33: Explicitly setting the list of excluded NICs to an empty string in the VMTools configuration file

This will make sure that `VMTools` doesn't ignore a new vNIC that will be created for the hybrid overlay network `10.224.0.0/14`, which we configured specifically for the WMCO when installing OpenShift in *Chapter 3, Getting Started with OpenShift*.

Save and close the file.

16. Use the following cmdlet to check the availability of the OpenSSH client and server programs:

```
PS C:\Users\Administrator> Get-WindowsCapability -Online | Where-Object
Name -like 'OpenSSH*'
```

You should see that, unlike `OpenSSH.Client`, `OpenSSH.Server` is not currently installed:

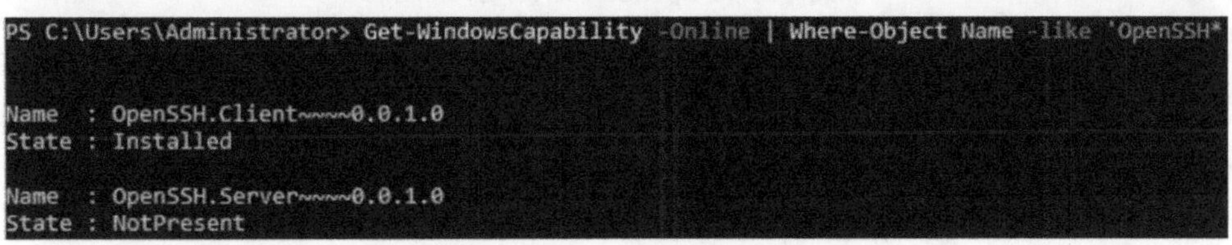

Figure 15.34: Checking for available OpenSSH Windows capabilities

17. Run the following cmdlet to install the `OpenSSH.Server` capability, if not present:

```
PS C:\Users\Administrator> Add-WindowsCapability -Online -Name OpenSSH.
Server
```

When it is complete, you should see the following output (you may need to hit *Enter* if it hangs):

Figure 15.35: OpenSSH server is installed

18. Now, enable the service to start on boot and start it (no output is expected for either operation):

```
PS C:\Users\Administrator> Set-Service -Name sshd -StartupType
'Automatic'
PS C:\Users\Administrator> Start-Service sshd
```

Check whether the OpenSSH server has started:

```
PS C:\Users\Administrator> Get-Service -Name sshd
```

This is what you're expected to see:

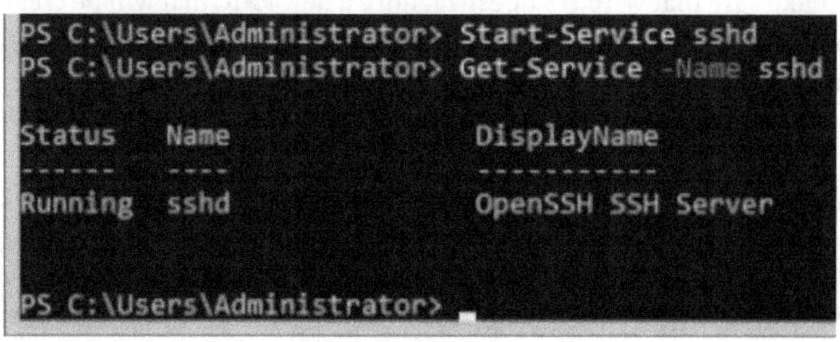

Figure 15.36: OpenSSH server is running

19. A new firewall rule should have been automatically configured to allow SSH through the local firewall. Check it with the following cmdlet:

    ```
    PS C:\Users\Administrator> Get-NetFirewallRule -name 'OpenSSH-Server-In-TCP'
    ```

    Here is what you should see if it does exist:

```
PS C:\Users\Administrator> Get-NetFirewallRule -name 'OpenSSH-Server-In-TCP'


Name                          : OpenSSH-Server-In-TCP
DisplayName                   : OpenSSH SSH Server (sshd)
Description                   : Inbound rule for OpenSSH SSH Server (sshd)
DisplayGroup                  : OpenSSH Server
Group                         : OpenSSH Server
Enabled                       : True
Profile                       : Any
Platform                      : {}
Direction                     : Inbound
Action                        : Allow
EdgeTraversalPolicy           : Block
LooseSourceMapping            : False
LocalOnlyMapping              : False
Owner                         :
PrimaryStatus                 : OK
Status                        : The rule was parsed successfully from the store. (65536)
EnforcementStatus             : NotApplicable
PolicyStoreSource             : PersistentStore
PolicyStoreSourceType         : Local
RemoteDynamicKeywordAddresses : {}
```

Figure 15.37: Checking whether inbound SSH connections are allowed through the local firewall

20. The next step is to add a firewall rule for inbound connections to the kubelet at port `10250/TCP`:

    ```
    PS C:\Users\Administrator> New-NetFirewallRule -DisplayName
    'ContainerLogsPort' -LocalPort 10250 -Enabled True -Direction Inbound
    -Protocol TCP -Action Allow -EdgeTraversalPolicy Allow
    ```

    The following output indicates success:

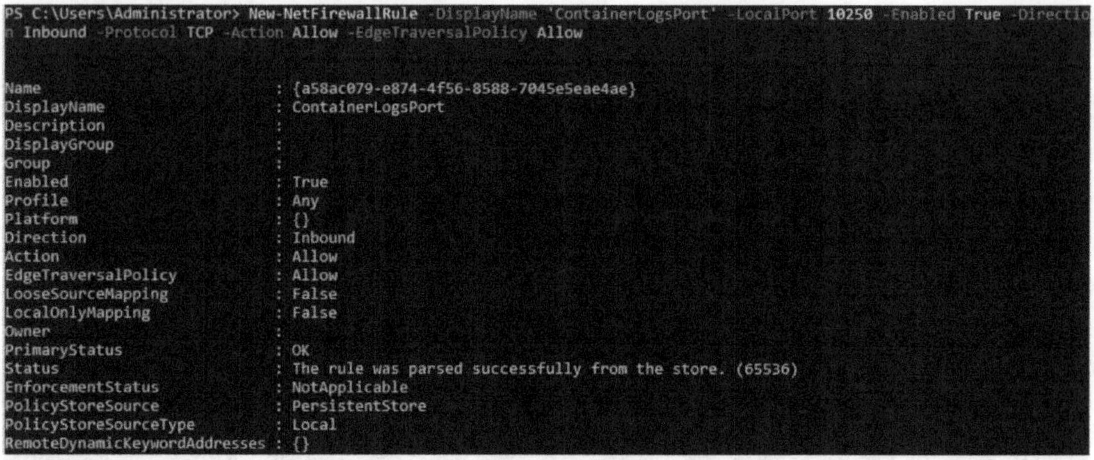

Figure 15.38: Adding a kubelet firewall rule

21. Now, we need to configure key-based authentication over SSH to our VM so that new machines that will be cloned from it can be configured over SSH via the private key that we stored in the `cloud-private-key` secret earlier. Copy the public part of the key to the VM over SSH. Now that we have configured SSH on the VM, we can connect to it securely by providing the `Administrator` password:

```
$ scp ~/.ssh/id_ecdsa_win.pub administrator@VM_IP:
```

You can find out the IP address of your VM by typing `ipconfig`:

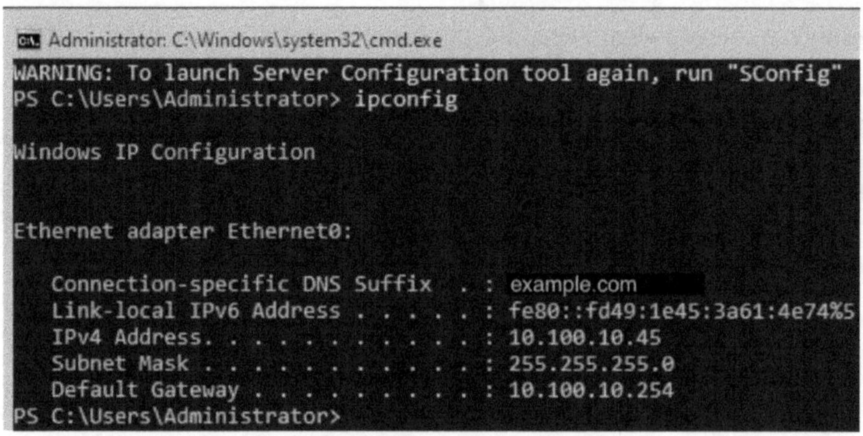

Figure 15.39: Obtaining the Windows VM's IP address

Here's what it looks like from our bastion host, where we generated the key:

```
The authenticity of host '10.100.10.45 (10.100.10.45)' can't be established.
ED25519 key fingerprint is SHA256:ahPrk9PQIcxQKgyXyxCtc01Q+ItFZh821AI1cyEa80M.
This key is not known by any other names
Are you sure you want to continue connecting (yes/no/[fingerprint])? yes
Warning: Permanently added '10.100.10.45' (ED25519) to the list of known hosts.
administrator@10.100.10.45's password:
id_ecdsa_win.pub                                    100%  195   395.2KB/s   00:00
```

Figure 15.40: Copying the public SSH key to our Windows instance

22. Confirm the location of your public key with the `Get-ChildItem` cmdlet (the equivalent of `ls -l` in Linux/Unix):

```
PS C:\Users\Administrator> Get-ChildItem


    Directory: C:\Users\Administrator


Mode                 LastWriteTime         Length Name
----                 -------------         ------ ----
d-r---         8/11/2025   7:51 AM                3D Objects
d-r---         8/11/2025   7:51 AM                Contacts
d-r---         8/11/2025   7:51 AM                Desktop
d-r---         8/11/2025   7:51 AM                Documents
d-r---         8/11/2025   7:51 AM                Downloads
d-r---         8/11/2025   7:51 AM                Favorites
d-r---         8/11/2025   7:51 AM                Links
d-r---         8/11/2025   7:51 AM                Music
d-r---         8/11/2025   7:51 AM                Pictures
d-r---         8/11/2025   7:51 AM                Saved Games
d-r---         8/11/2025   7:51 AM                Searches
d-r---         8/11/2025   7:51 AM                Videos
-a----         8/11/2025   8:51 AM            195 id_ecdsa_win.pub
```

Figure 15.41: Listing files in the current directory in PowerShell

23. Use the following PowerShell commands to add the key to the file of authorized `Administrator` keys and adjust its permissions:

```
PS C:\Users\Administrator> $authorizedKey = Get-Content -Path .\id_ecdsa_
win.pub
PS C:\Users\Administrator> Add-Content -Force -Path C:\ProgramData\ssh\
administrators_authorized_keys -Value $authorizedKey;icacls.exe C:\
ProgramData\ssh\administrators_authorized_keys /inheritance:r /grant
Administrators:F /grant SYSTEM:F
```

The expected output should show the successful processing of the file:

```
PS C:\Users\Administrator> $authorizedKey = Get-Content -Path .\id_ecdsa_win.pub
PS C:\Users\Administrator> Add-Content -Force -Path C:\ProgramData\ssh\administrators_authorized_keys -Value $authorized
Key;icacls.exe C:\ProgramData\ssh\administrators_authorized_keys /inheritance:r /grant Administrators:F /grant SYSTEM:F
processed file: C:\ProgramData\ssh\administrators_authorized_keys
Successfully processed 1 files; Failed processing 0 files
PS C:\Users\Administrator>
```

Figure 15.42: Adding a public key to the list of authorized Administrator keys

24. Now try and SSH into your Windows VM:

```
$ ssh -i ~/.ssh/id_ecdsa_win administrator@VM_IP
$ administrator@OCP4-B66ZC-WINW C:\Users\Administrator>powershell
```

It should let you in without a password:

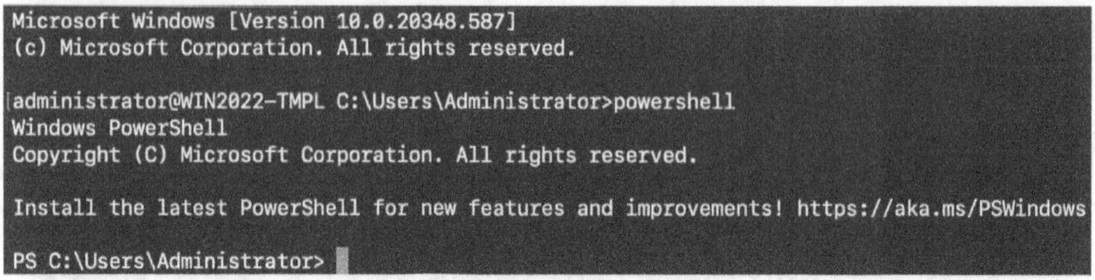

Figure 15.43: Successfully signed it to a Windows VM via SSH

25. It is a good practice to install the latest updates, for which we will need a package provider. Use the following cmdlet to install the NuGet provider, which interacts with repositories hosted at `https://www.nuget.org/`:

```
PS C:\Users\Administrator> Get-PackageProvider -Name nuget -Force
```

It should produce the following output:

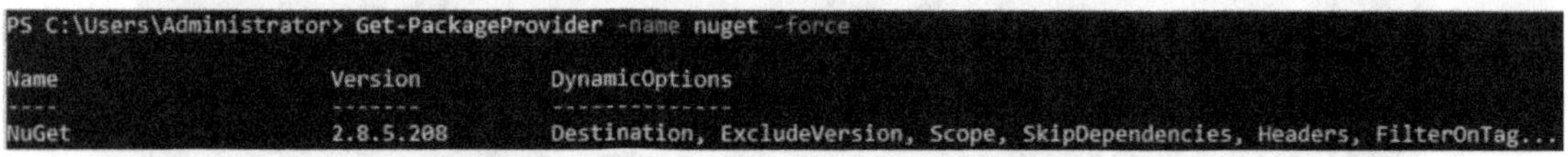

Figure 15.44: Installing the NuGet package provider

26. Now, install the `PSWindowsUpdate` module (no output is expected):

```
PS C:\Users\Administrator> Install-Module PSWindowsUpdate -confirm:$false
-Force
```

27. The next step is to download and install Windows updates:

```
PS C:\Users\Administrator> Get-WindowsUpdate -Install -acceptall
-IgnoreReboot
```

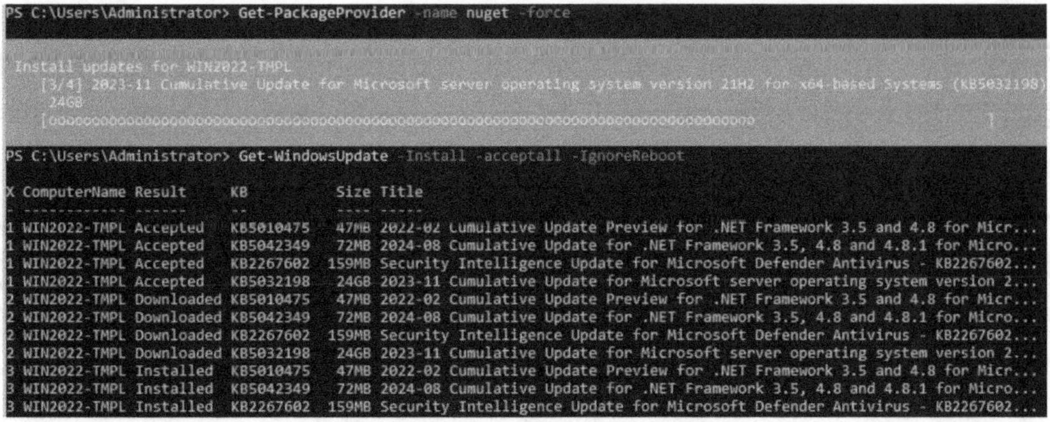

Figure 15.45: Installing Windows updates

> If you decide to continue from when you logged in over SSH and got to this point, you're likely to see this error when trying to install updates: `Get-WindowsUpdate : Access is denied. (Exception from HRESULT: 0x80070005 (E_ACCESSDENIED))`. This is expected, as you can't run Windows updates from a remote session, so you'll have to switch back to the VM's console in vSphere. A more in-depth explanation is provided at [7].

28. When it's done, examine the list of installed updates (we only had four) and restart the machine, as suggested by the message at the bottom of the output (**Reboot is required, but do it manually**):

```
PS C:\Users\Administrator> Restart-Computer -Force
```

Before restarting, Windows will display the following message:

Figure 15.46: Windows cleaning up before restart

29. When the machine restarts, log back in and rerun the command that installs updates to make sure all updates have been applied. You may need to repeat the update-and-restart cycle several times until there are no updates left to install, but usually, one more time when it installs Windows Defender updates is enough.
30. Windows containers on VMware vSphere support only Windows Server 2022 LTSC, build `10.0.20348.681` (`KB5012637`) and newer, so one extra check we can do is confirm that our server meets these requirements:

```
PS C:\Users\Administrator> (Get-ItemProperty -Path C:\Windows\System32\
hal.dll).VersionInfo.FileVersion
```

This is the version we have in our lab after installing all updates:

```
PS C:\Users\Administrator> (Get-ItemProperty -Path C:\Windows\System32\hal.dll).VersionInfo.FileVersion
10.0.20348.2031 (WinBuild.160101.0800)
PS C:\Users\Administrator>
```

Figure 15.47: Checking the Windows build number

To finalize preparing our Windows golden image, we need to generalize it by removing all machine-specific details, such as IP configuration and log files. This is done using the tool called **Sysprep**, which consumes an XML file with settings, cleans up all transient configuration, and powers the VM down. Follow these steps to prepare a Windows image using Sysprep:

1. We have prepared a `sysprep` configuration file in `chapters/15/snippets/unattend.xml` in this book's GitHub repository. Change the `Administrator` password inside the file (near the bottom) and copy it to the VM:

   ```
   $ scp -i ~/.ssh/id_ecdsa_win chapters/15/snippets/unattend.xml
   administrator@VM_IP:
   ```

2. Next, run Sysprep as shown here to create a generic VM template:

   ```
   PS C:\Users\Administrator> C:\Windows\System32\Sysprep\sysprep.exe /
   generalize /oobe /shutdown /unattend:.\unattend.xml
   ```

   Sysprep will start displaying its progress:

   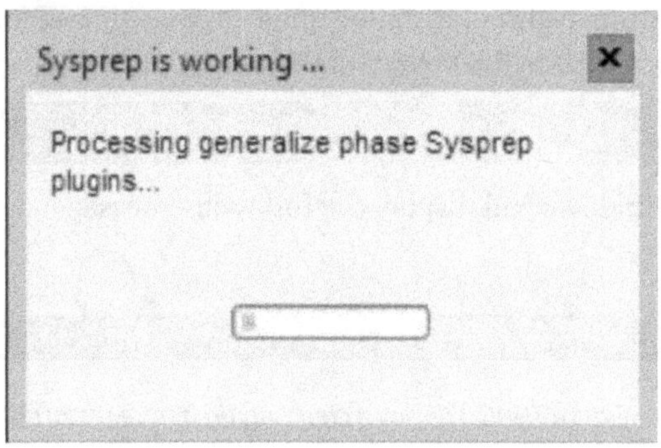

   Figure 15.48: Running Sysprep

   When it's done, Sysprep will power off the VM.

3. Now, clone the golden image to a VM template in vSphere (**Actions** > **Clone** > **Clone to Template...**):

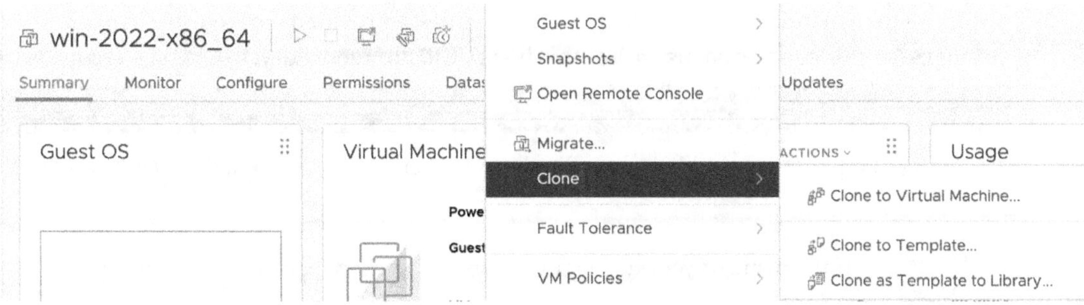

Figure 15.49: Cloning the template to a VM template

4. Configure the clone as follows:
   - **Select a name and folder**: Specify a name for your template, for example, `win-2022-x86_64-tmpl`, and select the folder to store it in (we used `Templates`).
   - **Select a compute resource**: Select an ESXi cluster and a resource pool.
   - **Select storage**: Choose a datastore (same as for the source VM).
   - **Ready to complete: FINISH**. That will kick off the template creation process, which will be completed shortly.

Now that we have a Windows base image for all our machines, it is time to move on to creating a Windows MachineSet that will be minting out nodes from that template.

Creating Windows MachineSet

As we discussed in *Chapter 6, Exploring Scalability with OpenShift*, a MachineSet is a controller that provisions machines from the same VM image in a cloud provider, akin to how a ReplicaSet spawns multiple pods from the same pod template. By generalizing machine configuration in the form of a VM template and automating node provisioning via MCO/WMCO, OpenShift makes it much cheaper in terms of time and effort to create and decommission nodes. Much like pod replicas, machines become expendable in case of any issues; replacing a faulty node is often faster than fixing it, although that doesn't negate the necessity of a post-mortem analysis.

MachineSets that manage standard CoreOS and RHEL machines have been around since the inception of OpenShift 4 back in June 2019, and with the introduction of Windows containers, they can now be used to provision Windows nodes too. With Windows, they serve the same purpose of maintaining a stable set of nodes running the same OS, although they manage Windows configuration differently.

Now, let's create a new MachineSet that will be using the template we prepared in the previous section to provision new Windows nodes:

1. First, we need to obtain our cluster's infrastructure ID:

```
$ oc get -o jsonpath='{.status.infrastructureName}{"\n"}' infrastructure/
cluster
```

2. Next, create a Windows MachineSet from a manifest provided for you in `chapters/15/snippets/machineset-windows.yml` of this book's GitHub repository:

```
$ oc create -f chapters/15/snippets/machineset-windows.yml
```

Make sure to replace placeholders accordingly and specify the VM template we created earlier.

> If the name of your network contains any / characters, they must be encoded as `%2f`.

3. Now, list the MachineSets and their machines:

```
$ oc get machine,machineset -n openshift-machine-api
```

If everything was done correctly, a new machine should start provisioning almost immediately:

```
NAME                                                    PHASE          TYPE   REGION   ZONE   AGE
machine.machine.openshift.io/ocp4-zlkjz-winworker-vn882   Provisioning                          28s

NAME                                                DESIRED   CURRENT   READY   AVAILABLE   AGE
machineset.machine.openshift.io/ocp4-zlkjz-winworker   1         1                             28s
```

Figure 15.50: Windows machine provisioning in progress

You can quickly locate the VM in vSphere and open its console if you're curious. Log in as Administrator and run `ipconfig` to check whether the VM was able to obtain an IP address through DHCP:

```
Administrator: C:\Windows\system32\cmd.exe
WARNING: To launch Server Configuration tool again, run "SConfig"
PS C:\Users\Administrator> ipconfig

Windows IP Configuration


Ethernet adapter Ethernet0:

   Connection-specific DNS Suffix  . : example.com
   Link-local IPv6 Address . . . . . : fe80::fd49:1e45:3a61:4e74%5
   IPv4 Address. . . . . . . . . . . : 10.100.10.45
   Subnet Mask . . . . . . . . . . . : 255.255.255.0
   Default Gateway . . . . . . . . . : 10.100.10.254
PS C:\Users\Administrator>
```

Figure 15.51: Checking the Windows node's auto-assigned IP configuration before it joins a cluster

You can use the following command to watch as the node joins your cluster and becomes ready:

```
$ watch -n1 oc get no,machine,machineset -n openshift-machine-api
```

The following screenshot was taken shortly after a new node reported to the control plane:

```
NAME                           STATUS                       ROLES                   AGE   VERSION
master-1.example.com           Ready                        control-plane,master    8d    v1.29.6+aba1e8d
master-2.example.com           Ready                        control-plane,master    8d    v1.29.6+aba1e8d
master-3.example.com           Ready                        control-plane,master    8d    v1.29.6+aba1e8d
infra-1.example.com            Ready                        infra                   8d    v1.29.6+aba1e8d
infra-2.example.com            Ready                        infra                   8d    v1.29.6+aba1e8d
infra-3.example.com            Ready                        infra                   8d    v1.29.6+aba1e8d
worker-1.example.com           Ready                        worker                  8d    v1.29.6+aba1e8d
worker-2.example.com           Ready                        worker                  8d    v1.29.6+aba1e8d
worker-3.example.com           Ready                        worker                  8d    v1.29.6+aba1e8d
ocp4-zlkjz-winworker-vn882     NotReady,SchedulingDisabled  worker                  30s   v1.29.14+7cf4c05

NAME                                                   PHASE          TYPE   REGION   ZONE   AGE
machine.machine.openshift.io/ocp4-zlkjz-winworker-vn882   Provisioning                             28s

NAME                                                 DESIRED   CURRENT   READY   AVAILABLE   AGE
machineset.machine.openshift.io/ocp4-zlkjz-winworker   1         1                              28s
```

Figure 15.52: Windows node joining cluster

If you examine the logs of the WMCO, you will see the progress of provisioning and the node's IP address:

```
$ oc logs -l name=windows-machine-config-operator -n openshift-windows-
machine-config-operator
```

The output should be similar to what is shown here:

```
{"level":"info","ts":"2025-08-11T17:10:15Z","logger":"wc 10.100.10.45","msg":"configuring"}
{"level":"info","ts":"2025-08-11T17:11:11Z","logger":"wc 10.100.10.45","msg":"rebooting instance"}
{"level":"info","ts":"2025-08-11T17:11:31Z","logger":"wc 10.100.10.45","msg":"transferring files"}
{"level":"info","ts":"2025-08-11T17:12:25Z","logger":"controllers.certificatesigningrequests","msg":"CSR contents
are invalid for approval by WMCO","CSR":"csr-m72lp"}
{"level":"info","ts":"2025-08-11T17:12:26Z","logger":"controllers.certificatesigningrequests","msg":"CSR contents
are invalid for approval by WMCO","CSR":"csr-7scm5"}
{"level":"info","ts":"2025-08-11T17:12:40Z","logger":"wc 10.100.10.45","msg":"configured","service":"windows-insta
nce-config-daemon","args":"controller --windows-service --log-dir C:\\var\\log\\wicd --kubeconfig C:\\k\\wicd-kube
config --namespace openshift-windows-machine-config-operator --ca-bundle C:\\k\\ca-bundle.crt"}
{"level":"info","ts":"2025-08-11T17:12:46Z","logger":"wc 10.100.10.45","msg":"rebooting instance"}
{"level":"info","ts":"2025-08-11T17:13:36Z","logger":"controllers.certificatesigningrequests","msg":"CSR contents
are invalid for approval by WMCO","CSR":"csr-4d6kf"}
{"level":"info","ts":"2025-08-11T17:14:25Z","logger":"nc 10.100.10.45","msg":"instance has been configured as a wo
rker node","version":"10.16.2-a9b66e7"}
{"level":"info","ts":"2025-08-11T17:14:25Z","logger":"metrics","msg":"Prometheus configured","endpoints":"windows-
exporter","port":9182,"name":"metrics"}
```

Figure 15.53: Monitoring the Windows node's initialization from WMCO logs

By running `oc get csr`, you can also check the CSRs that were created and approved as the node joined the cluster:

```
NAME          AGE     SIGNERNAME                                          REQUESTOR
                              REQUESTEDDURATION   CONDITION
csr-4d6kf     2m35s   kubernetes.io/kube-apiserver-client               system:node:ocp4-zlkjz-winworker-vn882
                             24h                  Approved,Issued
csr-7scm5     3m45s   kubernetes.io/kubelet-serving                     system:node:ocp4-zlkjz-winworker-vn882
                             <none>               Approved,Issued
csr-m72lp     3m46s   kubernetes.io/kube-apiserver-client-kubelet   system:serviceaccount:openshift-machine-c
onfig-operator:node-bootstrapper   <none>          Approved,Issued
```

Figure 15.54: Checking CSRs generated by the Windows node's kubelet

In about three minutes, the node becomes ready to run workloads:

```
NAME                                  STATUS   ROLES                  AGE   VERSION
node/master-1.example.com             Ready    control-plane,master   8d    v1.29.6+aba1e8d
node/master-2.example.com             Ready    control-plane,master   8d    v1.29.6+aba1e8d
node/master-3.example.com             Ready    control-plane,master   8d    v1.29.6+aba1e8d
node/infra-1.example.com              Ready    infra                  8d    v1.29.6+aba1e8d
node/infra-2.example.com              Ready    infra                  8d    v1.29.6+aba1e8d
node/infra-3.example.com              Ready    infra                  8d    v1.29.6+aba1e8d
node/worker-1.example.com             Ready    worker                 8d    v1.29.6+aba1e8d
node/worker-2.example.com             Ready    worker                 8d    v1.29.6+aba1e8d
node/worker-3.example.com             Ready    worker                 8d    v1.29.6+aba1e8d
node/ocp4-zlkjz-winworker-vn882       Ready    worker                 93s   v1.29.14+7cf4c05

NAME                                                    PHASE     TYPE   REGION   ZONE   AGE
machine.machine.openshift.io/ocp4-zlkjz-winworker-vn882   Running                          6m16s

NAME                                                  DESIRED   CURRENT   READY   AVAILABLE   AGE
machineset.machine.openshift.io/ocp4-zlkjz-winworker  1         1         1       1           6m16s
```

Figure 15.55: Windows node is ready

4. When we were installing WMCO, we noticed that when we created the `cloud-private-key` secret, the operator created another secret named `windows-user-data` in the `openshift-machine-api` namespace. Let's now examine it using the following command:

```
$ oc extract --to - secret/windows-user-data -n openshift-machine-api
```

You should see a rather large block of code stored inside:

```
# userData
<powershell>function Get-RandomPassword {
            Add-Type -AssemblyName 'System.Web'
            return [System.Web.Security.Membership]::GeneratePassword(16, 2)
        }

        # Check if the capi user exists, this will be the case on Azure, and will be used instead of Administrator
        if((Get-LocalUser | Where-Object {$_.Name -eq "capi"}) -eq $null) {
            # The capi user doesn't exist, ensure the Administrator account is enabled if it exists
            # If neither users exist, an error will be written to the console, but the script will still continue
            $UserAccount = Get-LocalUser -Name "Administrator"
            if( ($UserAccount -ne $null) -and (!$UserAccount.Enabled) ) {
                $password = ConvertTo-SecureString Get-RandomPassword -asplaintext -force
                $UserAccount | Set-LocalUser -Password $password
                $UserAccount | Enable-LocalUser
            }
        }

        Add-WindowsCapability -Online -Name OpenSSH.Server~~~~0.0.1.0
        $firewallRuleName = "ContainerLogsPort"
        $containerLogsPort = "10250"
        New-NetFirewallRule -DisplayName $firewallRuleName -Direction Inbound -Action Allow -Protocol TCP -LocalPort $containerLogsPort -EdgeTraversalPolicy Allow
        New-NetFirewallRule -DisplayName "WindowsExporter" -Direction Inbound -Action Allow -Protocol TCP -LocalPort "9182" -EdgeTraversalPolicy Allow
        Set-Service -Name sshd -StartupType 'Automatic'
        Start-Service sshd
        (Get-Content -path C:\ProgramData\ssh\sshd_config) | ForEach-Object {
        $_.replace('#PubkeyAuthentication yes','PubkeyAuthentication yes').replace('#PasswordAuthentication yes','PasswordAuthentication no')
        } | Set-Content -path C:\ProgramData\ssh\sshd_config
        $authorizedKeyFilePath = "$env:ProgramData\ssh\administrators_authorized_keys"
        New-Item -Force $authorizedKeyFilePath
        echo "ecdsa-sha2-nistp256 AAAAE2VjZHNhLXNoYTItbmlzdHAyNTYAAAAIbmlzdHAyNTYAAABBBHPGso/QpUAX6kiZn0D+ktyTO+wPRH2GfI99cvnmKa0jKG0nqjXadLZiwvFuaJskjlX8j6UF0iNysI4jyo/CI3s=
"| Out-File $authorizedKeyFilePath -Encoding ascii
        $acl = Get-Acl C:\ProgramData\ssh\administrators_authorized_keys
        $acl.SetAccessRuleProtection($true, $false)
        $administratorsRule = New-Object system.security.accesscontrol.filesystemaccessrule("Administrators","FullControl","Allow")
        $systemRule = New-Object system.security.accesscontrol.filesystemaccessrule("SYSTEM","FullControl","Allow")
        $acl.SetAccessRule($administratorsRule)
        $acl.SetAccessRule($systemRule)
        $acl | Set-Acl
        Restart-Service sshd</powershell>
<persist>true</persist>
```

Figure 15.56: Windows node's initialization script

If you look closely, you will notice that these are basically the same commands that we executed earlier while preparing our Windows golden image. Much like `worker-user-data`, which is used to perform the initial configuration of CoreOS machines, `windows-user-data` is used to preconfigure Windows machines. The difference between them is that CoreOS machines apply their configurations using Ignition; however, Ignition is not supported by Windows, which is why it relies on executing a PowerShell script over SSH.

5. If you SSH into your new Windows worker one more time and run `ipconfig` again, you should see a new vNIC show up, with an IP address allocated from the hybrid overlay network `10.224.0.0/14`, which we configured way back when installing our cluster:

```
PS C:\Users\Administrator> ipconfig

Windows IP Configuration


Ethernet adapter vEthernet (Ethernet0):

   Connection-specific DNS Suffix  . : example.com
   Link-local IPv6 Address . . . . . : fe80::af6:39ad:9f82:f1e5%8
   IPv4 Address. . . . . . . . . . . : 10.100.10.45
   Subnet Mask . . . . . . . . . . . : 255.255.255.0
   Default Gateway . . . . . . . . . : 10.100.10.254

Ethernet adapter vEthernet (VIPEndpoint):

   Connection-specific DNS Suffix  . : example.com
   Link-local IPv6 Address . . . . . : fe80::a7af:a6c1:9929:2019%24
   IPv4 Address. . . . . . . . . . . : 10.224.0.162
   Subnet Mask . . . . . . . . . . . : 255.255.255.0
   Default Gateway . . . . . . . . . :
PS C:\Users\Administrator>
```

Figure 15.57: Checking the Windows node's auto-assigned IP configuration after it joins a cluster

6. Let's run the following cmdlet to confirm that Kubernetes agents, overlay network service, and container runtime are up and running:

```
PS C:\Users\Administrator> Get-Process | ?{ $_.ProcessName -match
"kube|overlay|containerd" }
```

As you can see, Windows nodes use `containerd` as their container runtime:

```
PS C:\Users\administrator> Get-Process | ?{ $_.ProcessName -match "kube|overlay|containerd" }

Handles  NPM(K)    PM(K)      WS(K)     CPU(s)     Id  SI ProcessName
-------  ------    -----      -----     ------     --  -- -----------
    172      15    31416      37556      19.25   4288   0 containerd
    232      18    41856      50864      31.77   4852   0 hybrid-overlay-node
    452      32    55544      81240     390.39   3008   0 kubelet
     90       8    12312       6020       0.08   2488   0 kube-log-runner
     87       8    12472       6132       0.03   3056   0 kube-log-runner
    265      20    37708      49696      31.44   2180   0 kube-proxy


PS C:\Users\administrator>
```

Figure 15.58: Checking container runtime and Kubernetes services on a Windows node

We have just created a Windows MachineSet, which provides a simple mechanism for adding more Windows nodes with no manual configuration whatsoever. The next step is to start using the node we have to run pods, which is what the next section is dedicated to.

Running Windows workloads

Up until this point, we have been preparing the necessary infrastructure for our sample Windows application. Now that we have everything ready, we can deploy our first Windows workload on our cluster. In the steps that follow, we will prepare YAML manifests for a standard set of API objects that make up an application:

1. First, you will need to make sure that your application is placed on the Windows node we created. Being a completely different execution runtime from CoreOS, Windows nodes have a special taint that prevents other workloads from accidentally getting scheduled onto them. Technically, we could specify a corresponding toleration and a node selector in our application's controller, such as `Deployment`, but a better way is to use a resource called `RuntimeClass`, which represents tolerations and node selectors for a workload of a particular type – in our case, Windows. Inspect the YAML manifest we have prepared for you in `chapters/15/snippets/runtimeclass-win.yml` of this book's GitHub repository. To understand why we specified those labels in the `nodeSelector`, run the following command to obtain a YAML representation of your Windows node:

    ```
    $ oc get -o yaml no/WIN_NODE_NAME
    ```

    Notice the labels present in the node's manifest:

    ```
    labels:
      beta.kubernetes.io/arch: amd64
      beta.kubernetes.io/instance-type: vsphere-vm.cpu-8.mem-32gb.os-unknown
      beta.kubernetes.io/os: windows
      kubernetes.io/arch: amd64
      kubernetes.io/hostname: ocp4-zlkjz-winworker-vn882
      kubernetes.io/os: windows
      node-role.kubernetes.io/worker: ""
      node.kubernetes.io/instance-type: vsphere-vm.cpu-8.mem-32gb.os-unknown
      node.kubernetes.io/windows-build: 10.0.20348
      node.openshift.io/os_id: Windows
    name: ocp4-zlkjz-winworker-vn882
    ```

    Figure 15.59: Windows node's default labels

    Specifically, the `node.kubernetes.io/windows-build` label corresponds to a specific Windows edition – in this case, Windows Server 2022 (build number `10.0.20348`). For example, Windows Server 2019 nodes supported by earlier versions of the WMCO would have the build number `10.0.17763`.

    When a workload uses a particular `RuntimeClass`, its node selectors and tolerations are merged with what is specified in the `RuntimeClass`, with any conflicts preventing scheduling, so a pod would remain in the `Pending` state.

    `RuntimeClass` is a cluster-scoped resource, so it's best to be created before any namespace-scoped objects that follow.

2. Next, we need to create a very simple manifest for the namespace. You may examine its YAML definition in `chapters/15/snippets/ns.yml` of this book's GitHub repository.
3. Since our application is a simple stateless service with each replica being completely identical to the others, we will use the `Deployment` API. The manifest is available at `chapters/15/snippets/deployment.yml`. Let's go over some of its elements.

   The pod template contained in this deployment starts a simple web server that listens on the standard HTTP port and responds with a short message indicating its OS. Three fields of the manifest, however, are of particular interest to us:

   - `.spec.template.spec.containers[].image`: This uses the Windows Server 2022 Core base image from the **Long-Term Servicing Channel** (**LTSC**). It is important that the base image build for your Windows application exactly matches the build of the node's OS.
   - `.spec.template.spec.os.name`: This is used to set the Windows-specific security context on your application's container. Currently, only Windows and Linux are supported.
   - `.spec.template.spec.runtimeClassName`: This is the name of the `RuntimeClass` we created earlier. This is where your deployment will take tolerations and node selectors from, so you don't have to specify them here.
4. Since pod IP addresses are ephemeral (they change when a pod is recreated) and you may have more than one replica, you need a `Service` object that will act as a single point of access for potentially multiple instances of your application and provide a stable IP whose lifecycle is independent of that of your application's pods. Open the `chapters/15/snippets/svc.yml` file and examine it.
5. In order for your application to be reachable for clients from outside OpenShift, you will need a route that references the preceding `Service` object as well. Its manifest is stored in `chapters/15/snippets/route.yml` of this book's repository. Make sure to replace the `CLUSTER_NAME` and `DOMAIN` placeholders accordingly.
6. Finally, pass all manifests you created to the `oc create` command, as shown here (the order matters):

```
$ oc create -f chapters/15/snippets/runtimeclass-win.yml -f chapters/15/snippets/ns.yml -f chapters/15/snippets/deployment.yml -f chapters/15/snippets/svc.yml -f chapters/15/snippets/route.yml
```

   The warning about the security context generated by PSA (discussed in *Chapter 7, Application Security and Isolation*) can be safely ignored.

   We could've just used the `oc expose` command on our deployment to create a service and then use it again on the service to create a route, which would save us some space (and maybe a tree); however, there is a reason why we used a declarative approach for this exercise. There will be more on this in the *GitOps* section of this chapter.

7. Now, let's see whether our application was scheduled on the correct node and was able to start. Use the already familiar command shown here:

```
$ oc get po -o wide -n windows-demo
```

If you didn't make any mistakes, your pod should've successfully started on the Windows node:

```
NAME                             READY   STATUS    RESTARTS   AGE   IP           NODE
win-webserver-589d574f-jbv5m     1/1     Running   0          26s   10.224.0.3   ocp4-zlkjz-winworker-vn882
```

Figure 15.60: Workload running on a Windows node

Again, note the pod's IP address; it was allocated from `10.224.0.0/14`, the hybrid overlay network we created back in *Chapter 3, Getting Started with OpenShift*.

8. Run another command to issue a `GET /` request to the application:

```
$ curl win-test.apps.ocp4.example.com
```

The web server running inside the container should reply with a simple text message that we configured earlier:

```
<html><body><H1>Running on Windows Server 2022 Datacenter Edition</H1></
body></html>
```

9. To wrap this up, let's clean up and delete our application:

```
$ oc delete -f chapters/15/snippets/runtimeclass-win.yml -f chapters/15/
snippets/ns.yml
```

We are not deleting other resources explicitly, as they will be cleaned up as part of the namespace's deletion process, which may take about a minute.

At this point, we can conclude that everything is working as intended and complete this exercise. However, there is one loose end we haven't tied up yet. You may recall that when we prepared the manifest for a `RuntimeClass` and examined its structure, there was one field we didn't discuss: `.handler`. Its value is set to `runhcs-wcow-process`, but where exactly did it come from? To answer this question, let's SSH into our Windows node and switch to PowerShell:

```
$ ssh -i ~/.ssh/id_ecdsa_win administrator@VM_IP
$ administrator@OCP4-B66ZC-WINW C:\Users\Administrator>powershell
```

As mentioned earlier, Windows nodes use `containerd` as a container runtime. On Linux, its main configuration file is located at `/etc/containerd/config.toml`. On Windows, its location is not well documented, so we have to scour the `C:\` drive to find it. Use the following cmdlet to start a recursive search of `C:\` for all files whose names end with `.toml`:

```
PS C:\Users\Administrator> Get-ChildItem -Path C:\ -Include *.toml -File
-Recurse -ErrorAction SilentlyContinue
```

The following screenshot shows the search result, as well as one unsuccessful attempt to find the file:

```
Microsoft Windows [Version 10.0.20348.2113]
(c) Microsoft Corporation. All rights reserved.

administrator@OCP4-B66ZC-WINW C:\Users\Administrator>powershell
Windows PowerShell
Copyright (C) Microsoft Corporation. All rights reserved.

Install the latest PowerShell for new features and improvements! https://aka.ms/PSWindows

PS C:\Users\Administrator> Get-ChildItem -Path C:\ -Include config.toml -File -Recurse -ErrorAction SilentlyContinue
PS C:\Users\Administrator> Get-ChildItem -Path C:\ -Include *.toml -File -Recurse -ErrorAction SilentlyContinue


    Directory: C:\k\containerd


Mode                 LastWriteTime         Length Name
----                 -------------         ------ ----
-a----          9/5/2024   1:57 AM           6027 containerd_conf.toml
```

Figure 15.61: Locating the containerd configuration file on a Windows node

Now that we know the location of the file, let's examine it for any clues using the `Get-Content` cmdlet:

```
PS C:\Users\Administrator> Get-Content C:\k\containerd\containerd_conf.toml
```

Specifically, we're interested in the part shown here:

```
[plugins."io.containerd.grpc.v1.cri".containerd.runtimes.runhcs-wcow-process]
  base_runtime_spec = ""
  container_annotations = []
  pod_annotations = []
  privileged_without_host_devices = false
  privileged_without_host_devices_all_devices_allowed = false
  runtime_engine = ""
  runtime_path = ""
  runtime_root = ""
  runtime_type = "io.containerd.runhcs.v1"
```

Figure 15.62: The containerd default runtime handler

As you may notice, `runhcs-wcow-process` is the name of a runtime defined in the `containerd` configuration file. In a customized configuration, you can define your own runtime and reference it in your `RuntimeClass`.

This is the default configuration, and the name of the default `containerd` runtime is not directly documented anywhere, so we recommend taking note of it.

We have just deployed our first, albeit simple, Windows application on our OpenShift cluster. Now, you can deploy more applications, scale the Windows MachineSet manually, and even set up cluster autoscaling for your Windows nodes, which is discussed in more detail in *Chapter 6, Exploring Scalability with OpenShift*. We will now be wrapping up the discussion of Windows containers with a brief review of their limitations.

Limitations

Although generally available since December 2020, Windows containers are still not as mature as traditional Linux containers. WMCO and the way in which networking, access controls, and runtime security are handled by Windows impose certain limitations, most of which are presented in the following table:

Product	Support
Red Hat OpenShift Builds	No
Red Hat OpenShift Service Mesh	No
Red Hat OpenShift Pipelines	No
Red Hat OpenShift Serverless	No
Red Hat OpenShift Local	No
Calico	Not supported for OpenShift 4.6 and newer due to the Windows Machine Config Bootstrapper binary (`wmcb.exe`), which Calico relied on, having been replaced with WMCO
Windows Server 2019 LTSC	Partial: version 1809 is supported, but only on the following platforms: • **Amazon Web Services** (**AWS**) • Microsoft Azure • Bare metal or provider agnostic (with `platform: none` in the `install-config.yaml`)
Windows Server 2022 LTSC	Partial: build `10.0.20348.681` or later
DeploymentConfigs	No
Dual NICs	No
Huge pages	No
`clusterNetwork` CIDR addresses of class E (from `240.0.0.0`)	No
Privileged containers	No
Custom `hybridOverlayVXLANPort`	Only for Windows Server 2022 LTSC
Red Hat Insights cost management	No

Product	Support
Monitoring of user-defined projects	No
Horizontal Pod Autoscaling (HPA)	No
Vertical Pod Autoscaling (VPA)	No
MachineConfigs and MachineConfigPools	No
Hyper-V isolation mode	No, only process mode is supported [8]

Table 15.2: Windows containers support matrix

Despite these limitations, the work on Windows containers continues, and support for more features/products is likely to be added in future releases. More on the limitations of Windows containers in Kubernetes can be found at [9].

Another extra component that we are going to tackle in this chapter is the integrated registry, which we already briefly covered earlier in this book. In this chapter, we will approach it once again, this time, from the persistence and availability perspective.

Integrated registry

If you have followed the book, you may remember that we switched the integrated registry to the `Managed` state and configured it with `emptyDir` storage due to its simplicity back in *Chapter 9, Developing for OpenShift*. It is, however, unsuitable for production due to its ephemeral nature, which is what we're going to rectify in this section.

Although this registry is included in OpenShift by default to support build infrastructure, we included its discussion here as well so that we could properly configure it when we have a storage backend and infra nodes configured. Back in *Chapter 8, Working with Persistent Storage*, we installed an enterprise-grade storage backend for our cluster. We will now use it to configure the Image Registry Operator that manages OpenShift's integrated image registry:

1. First, we need to create a **PersistentVolumeClaim** (**PVC**) that requests storage from the `ocs-storagecluster-cephfs` storage class that is backed by CephFS, network file storage, and apply it. Use the `chapters/15/snippets/pvc-image-registry.yml` file from this book's repository:

```
$ oc apply -f chapters/15/snippets/pvc-image-registry.yml
```

2. It is always a good idea to check that the resource was created successfully:

```
$ oc get pvc -n openshift-image-registry
```

The PVC should be in the Bound state:

```
[ausov@bastion learning-ocp4]$ oc get pvc -n openshift-image-registry
NAME             STATUS   VOLUME                                     CAPACITY   ACCESS MODES   STORAGECLASS
image-registry   Bound    pvc-74b9893c-04d3-4eba-907a-e79010678d1f   30Gi       RWX            ocs-storagecluster-cephfs
```

Figure 15.63: A PVC for the image registry was created

The PVC we just created was immediately bound to a PV that ODF created for us. This behavior is governed by the `volumeBindingMode` field (in this case, `Immediate`) from the `StorageClass` definition. As the name suggests, in the `WaitForFirstConsumer` mode, a PV is allocated only when a pod that references the corresponding PVC is created.

3. Check whether any registry pods are running by executing the following command:

```
$ oc get po -l docker-registry=default -n openshift-image-registry
```

If you configured it back in *Chapter 9*, then you should see a single pod. If not, there will be none.

4. Next, inspect the `chapters/15/snippets/config-imageregistry-cluster.yml` manifest from this book's repository. When you install OpenShift 4 using the UPI method, the registry is configured with `.spec.managementState: Removed`. Should you decide later that you don't need it, you can always switch it back to `Removed`.
5. As part of this configuration, we will also be moving registry pods to the dedicated infra nodes we created way back in *Chapter 4, Post-Install Configuration*. In addition, note that we're setting `emptyDir: none`, effectively removing it if it was enabled before.

Apply the manifest as `patch`:

```
$ oc patch --patch-file chapters/15/snippets/config-imageregistry-
cluster.yml --type merge config.imageregistry/cluster
```

The following message indicates success:

```
config.imageregistry.operator.openshift.io/cluster patched
```

6. Check the `openshift-image-registry` namespace again after a minute or two:

```
$ oc get po -l docker-registry=default -n openshift-image-registry
```

Registry pods should redeploy:

```
NAME                              READY   STATUS    RESTARTS   AGE   IP            NODE
image-registry-66f45cd84-5nbgh    1/1     Running   0          66s   10.131.2.31   infra-3.example.com
image-registry-66f45cd84-7qkbt    1/1     Running   0          66s   10.130.2.42   infra-1.example.com
image-registry-66f45cd84-jr9fm    1/1     Running   0          66s   10.128.4.59   infra-2.example.com
```

Figure 15.64: Image registry is up and running with the new storage volume provided by ODF

7. Notice that the OpenShift scheduler also placed them on different infra nodes, as specified in `.spec.affinity.podAntiAffinity`. We haven't addressed the same problem with ingress pods, because HA is configured by default in the form of `topologySpreadConstraints`:

   ```
   $ oc get -o yaml deploy/router-default -n openshift-ingress
   ```

   Look for this section of the manifest:

```
tolerations:
- effect: NoExecute
  key: node-role.kubernetes.io/infra
topologySpreadConstraints:
- labelSelector:
    matchExpressions:
    - key: ingresscontroller.operator.openshift.io/hash
      operator: In
      values:
      - 5cddc7ff4b
  maxSkew: 1
  topologyKey: topology.kubernetes.io/zone
  whenUnsatisfiable: ScheduleAnyway
```

Figure 15.65: High availability configuration for the router

This was the last time we will touch the integrated registry. Now, let's move on to another extra service that you can rely on.

GitOps

GitOps is a pattern of operations that relies on the declarative state of applications or infrastructure stored in a Git repository, which is treated as the single source of truth for configuration. CI/CD pipelines then run tests of those declarative manifests and apply them. In the world of Kubernetes and OpenShift, this involves a controller that periodically polls a remote Git repository for changes and makes sure that the actual state of a cluster matches what is defined in Git. This approach has the following benefits:

- Familiar CI/CD tools, such as Jenkins, can be used to apply software development practices to infrastructure management.
- It provides consistency across all environments and cloud/on-premise platforms.
- It improves visibility, with all changes tracked in Git and easily auditable.
- It allows you to safeguard against manual changes that reconcile any differences (aka **configuration drift**) between the actual and desired states.

Two dominant GitOps solutions are ArgoCD and FluxCD. They are very similar and serve the same purpose of enforcing the desired state of your applications and infrastructure. In this section, we will be briefly covering the OpenShift GitOps offering from Red Hat, based on the upstream ArgoCD project. This is meant only as a short introduction, though, because the topic of GitOps is so vast that it deserves its own book, so we invite you to familiarize yourself closely with ArgoCD using the official documentation at [10].

Installing OpenShift GitOps Operator

OpenShift GitOps includes several controllers, among which are application and application set controllers, and a number of APIs, such as `ArgoCD`, `Application`, `ApplicationSet`, and `AppProject`, all belonging to the `argoproj.io` API group. In OpenShift 4, they are distributed in the form of an operator available through OperatorHub. The following table shows the support of GitOps across different Red Hat OpenShift editions:

Edition	Inclusion
OpenShift Kubernetes Engine	No
OpenShift Container Platform	Yes
OpenShift Platform Plus	Yes

Table 15.3: OpenShift GitOps availability matrix

Let's get to practice and install GitOps on our cluster:

1. First, navigate to OperatorHub and type `OpenShift GitOps` in the search bar. You should see the only available operator matching the search:

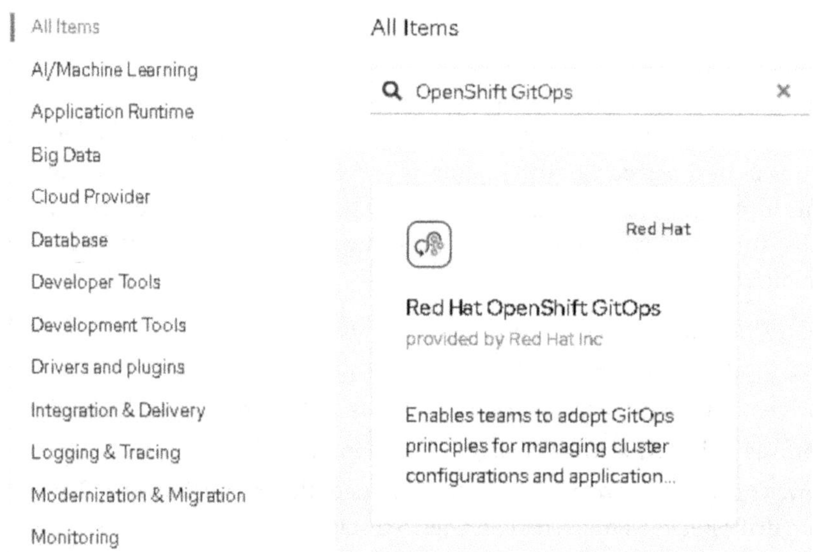

Figure 15.66: Finding the OpenShift GitOps Operator in OperatorHub

2. Click on the operator's tile, accept all default options, and click **Install**. You can change **Update approval** to **Manual**, in which case you will have to approve the generated installation plan:

Figure 15.67: GitOps Operator installation in progress

3. Click **Approve** if you selected the **Manual** update approval:

Figure 15.68: The GitOps Operator's installation requires manual approval

4. Wait until the Operator reports successful installation and refresh the web console when prompted to do so.

Now, let's do a few simple checks to confirm that the operator is installed and ready:

1. Check the `operator` pod in the `openshift-gitops-operator` namespace:

```
$ oc get po -n openshift-gitops-operator
```

You should see the controller manager pod running with two containers, as shown here:

```
NAME                                                          READY   STATUS
openshift-gitops-operator-controller-manager-56db547655-vx241   2/2     Running
```

Figure 15.69: GitOps operator's controller manager pod is up and running

2. Check the default `argocd` instance, `Application/ApplicationSet` controllers, and other internal components:

```
$ oc get po,argocd -n openshift-gitops
```

You should see the following pods, among which are a GitOps server for serving user requests and Redis for maintaining internal state and tracking jobs:

```
NAME                                                        READY   STATUS    RESTARTS   AGE
pod/cluster-dcb955578-jrhgn                                 1/1     Running   0          49s
pod/gitops-plugin-56cb6b8c79-2w427                          1/1     Running   0          49s
pod/openshift-gitops-application-controller-0               1/1     Running   0          46s
pod/openshift-gitops-applicationset-controller-69d988d55-gspp4   1/1     Running   0          46s
pod/openshift-gitops-dex-server-764c9dd9dd-drtv9            1/1     Running   0          46s
pod/openshift-gitops-redis-6c9f9f8867-4vxbz                 1/1     Running   0          47s
pod/openshift-gitops-repo-server-68f75db696-hqprk           1/1     Running   0          47s
pod/openshift-gitops-server-b44647855-h85qn                 1/1     Running   0          46s

NAME                                      AGE
argocd.argoproj.io/openshift-gitops       49s
```

Figure 15.70: The ArgoCD instance's pods, up and running

3. Check routes with the following command:

```
$ oc get route -n openshift-gitops
```

You should see a single route:

```
NAME                      HOST/PORT
openshift-gitops-server   openshift-gitops-server-openshift-gitops.apps.ocp4.example.com
```

Figure 15.71: GitOps default routes

4. The default `ServiceAccount` used by the ArgoCD application controller has permissions to create and modify a number of cluster resources. However, as part of our exercise, we will have to create a resource that is not a part of this list. The proper way would be to create a custom `ClusterRole` and bind it to the service account or create a non-default `AppProject` instance that includes a whitelist of resources it is allowed to manage; however, these are more advanced concepts. Since the goal of this section is to get you started with GitOps quickly, we can grant it `cluster-admin` access for now so that the controller can manage all resources:

```
$ oc adm policy add-cluster-role-to-user cluster-admin -z openshift-gitops-argocd-application-controller -n openshift-gitops
```

Keep in mind, however, that this is insecure and is considered a bad practice.

5. There are two ways to authenticate in the GitOps web UI: using OpenShift OAuth credentials or the admin account. The latter requires a password that is stored as a secret in the `openshift-gitops` namespace, where the default `argocd` instance is installed. Obtain the password as shown here:

```
$ oc extract --to - secret/openshift-gitops-cluster -n openshift-gitops
```

6. Now, open your preferred web browser and go to the route identified earlier; in a default installation, it should look similar to `https://openshift-gitops-server-openshift-gitops.apps.ocp4.example.com`. Accept the untrusted self-signed certificate (unless you replaced it in *Chapter 4, Post-Install Configuration*) and log in with the `admin` user and the extracted password.

   Another way to authenticate is via the OpenShift OAuth server. Click on the **LOG IN VIA OPENSHIFT** button and then on **User:info - Allow selected permissions.**

   Now, if you check **Settings** > **Clusters**, you will see the only cluster managed by this instance of GitOps – the local one, `https://kubernetes.default.svc`, identified by the Kubernetes API service's internal DNS name:

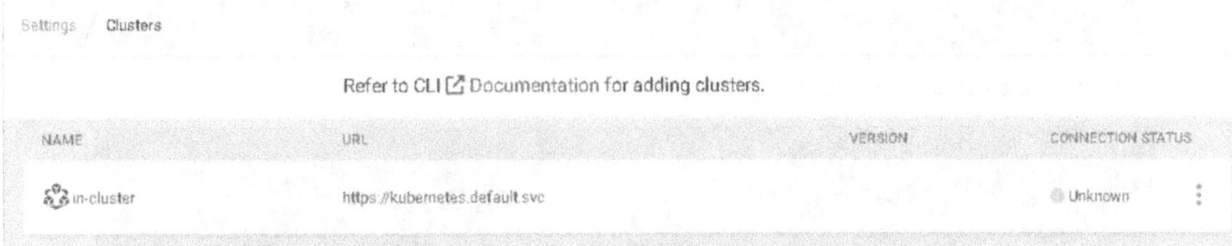

Figure 15.72: Local cluster is configured by default in ArgoCD Settings > Clusters

Now that we have set up GitOps on our cluster, we can create our first application and observe how ArgoCD keeps its configuration consistent with manifests stored in a remote repository.

Creating a simple application

One of the APIs provided by OpenShift GitOps is `Application`, a collection of objects that make up an application and are meant to be managed as a single entity. The term "application" does not necessarily mean application in a traditional sense of the word, which is a running process performing a specific business function (or functions) and capable of serving requests from clients. It can be something as simple as a single manifest to be applied to a cluster resource – for example, to enable `etcd` encryption or configure the integrated image registry. In this exercise, we will use GitOps to create the Windows-based application that we deployed earlier in the *Windows containers* section. This is why we chose a purely declarative approach of deploying it from YAML manifests – so that they can be stored in Git and used by ArgoCD here. Follow these steps to end up with a working ArgoCD application:

1. First, we will need to create a repository in GitHub for our manifests. We have already tackled this in *Chapter 11, Deploying Applications with Helm and Kustomize,* so you should be familiar with the process. Go to `https://github.com/`, click the **New** green button on the left, and on the **Create a new repository** page, provide a **Repository name** value (we named ours `windows-containers-demo`). You can optionally make it private or keep it public (default) and choose to add a README file. Click **Create repository,** and we are done here.
2. Next, on your new repository's page, click **Code**, select **SSH**, and click **Copy URL to clipboard** – we will need it later. Unless you have already done so, refer to *Chapter 11, Deploying Applications with Helm and Kustomize > Kustomize > Organizing Kustomizations in Git* on how to add an SSH key to your account to avoid access issues.

3. Now, let's clone the empty repository to our local system, change to it (cd), copy our application's assets over (cp), stage (add) the changes, commit them, and finally, push:

```
$ git clone git@github.com:AlekseyUsov/windows-containers-demo.git ~/git/windows-containers-demo
$ cd ~/git/windows-containers-demo
$ cp -t ~/git/windows-containers-demo ~/git/Learn-OpenShift-Second-Edition/chapters/15/snippets/{svc,deployment,runtimeclass-win,route,ns}.yml
$ git add .
$ git commit -m 'Added Windows demo assets'
$ git push
```

Here is the expected output of the last command:

```
Enumerating objects: 8, done.
Counting objects: 100% (8/8), done.
Delta compression using up to 2 threads
Compressing objects: 100% (7/7), done.
Writing objects: 100% (7/7), 1.65 KiB | 1.65 MiB/s, done.
Total 7 (delta 0), reused 0 (delta 0), pack-reused 0 (from 0)
To github.com:AlekseyUsov/windows-containers-demo.git
   cdd8297..51a8577  main -> main
```

Figure 15.73: Pushing application assets to Git

4. Now, go to GitHub again and refresh the repository's page. You should see the changes you just uploaded:

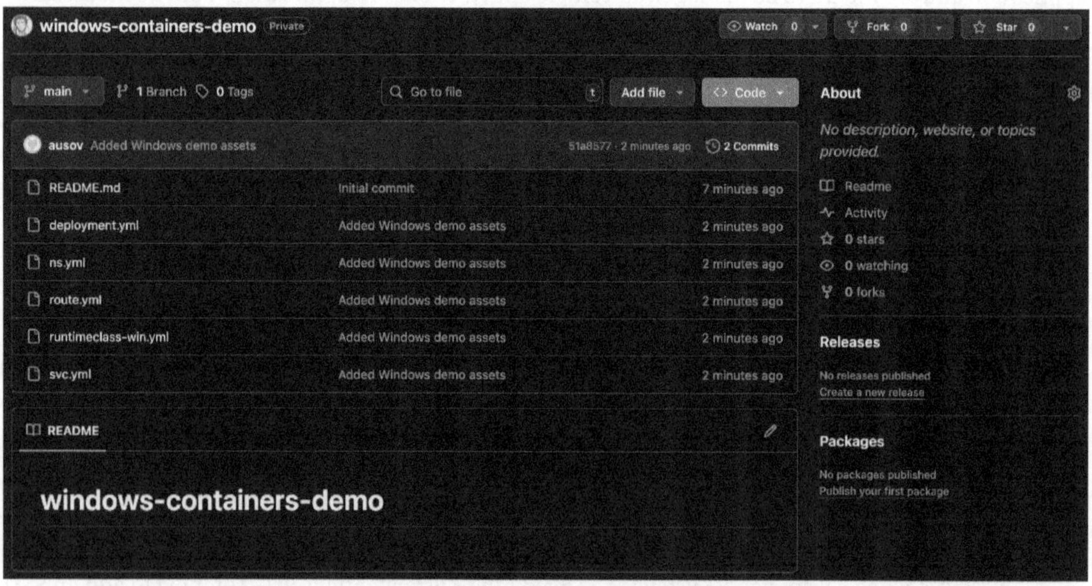

Figure 15.74: GitHub repository with application assets uploaded

5. If your repository is private, you need to tell ArgoCD how to authenticate it first. Go back to the ArgoCD UI and click **Settings** > **Repositories** > **+ CONNECT REPO**. Fill in the fields of the form as follows:

    - **Choose your authentication method: VIA SSH**
    - **CONNECT REPO USING SSH / Name:** `windows-containers-demo` (optional)
    - **CONNECT REPO USING SSH / Project:** `default`
    - **CONNECT REPO USING SSH / Repository URL:** SSH URL of the GitHub repository you created earlier
    - **CONNECT REPO USING SSH / SSH private key data:** Copy the contents of your private key file (e.g., `~/.ssh/id_rsa`) and paste it here; it must correspond to the same public key that you added to your GitHub account earlier

    For a public repository, you can just skip to *step 8*.

6. Click **CONNECT**. Your repo should now appear in the list and have a **CONNECTION STATUS** value of **Successful**:

Figure 15.75: A repo is added and connected in ArgoCD

7. Now, switch back to the ArgoCD UI and click **Applications** on the left (or you can just click on three vertical dots next to your repo and select **Create application**):

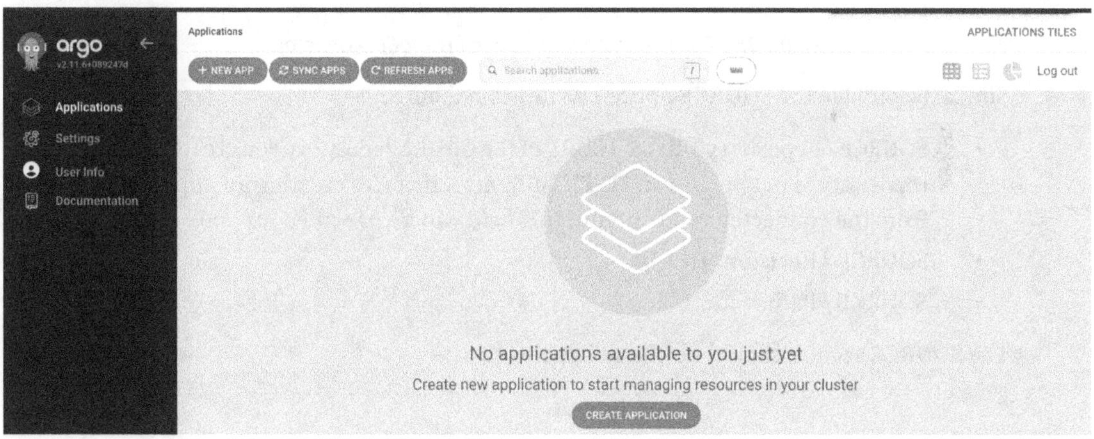

Figure 15.76: Applications dashboard in ArgoCD

8. Click on the **CREATE APPLICATION** button and fill out the **GENERAL** options according to the following instructions:

    - **GENERAL / Application Name:** `windows-containers-demo`
    - **GENERAL / Project Name:** `default`

- **GENERAL / SYNC POLICY: Automatic**
- **GENERAL / SELF HEAL:** Checked

Here is the corresponding screenshot of the **GENERAL** section:

Figure 15.77: Creating an application in ArgoCD – General

9. Similarly, provide the **SOURCE** options as described here:

   - **SOURCE / Repository URL:** SSH URL of the GitHub repository you created earlier. If your repository is public, use an HTTP URL. Also, if you're creating an application directly from the connected repo's menu, this field will be pre-filled for you.
   - **SOURCE / Revision: HEAD.**
   - **SOURCE / Path:** `.` (dot).

   The **SOURCE** section should now look like this:

Figure 15.78: Creating an application in ArgoCD – Source

10. Also, provide the **DESTINATION** details where you want ArgoCD to create your application. A destination is defined as a combination of an OpenShift cluster and namespace (for namespace-scoped resources). Use the following:
    - **DESTINATION / Cluster URL:** `https://kubernetes.default.svc`
    - **DESTINATION / Namespace**: Since we have a separate manifest that defines a target namespace for our application, we will leave it empty:

Figure 15.79: Creating an application in ArgoCD – Destination

11. Finally, click **CREATE** at the top, and you should see your application in the dashboard:

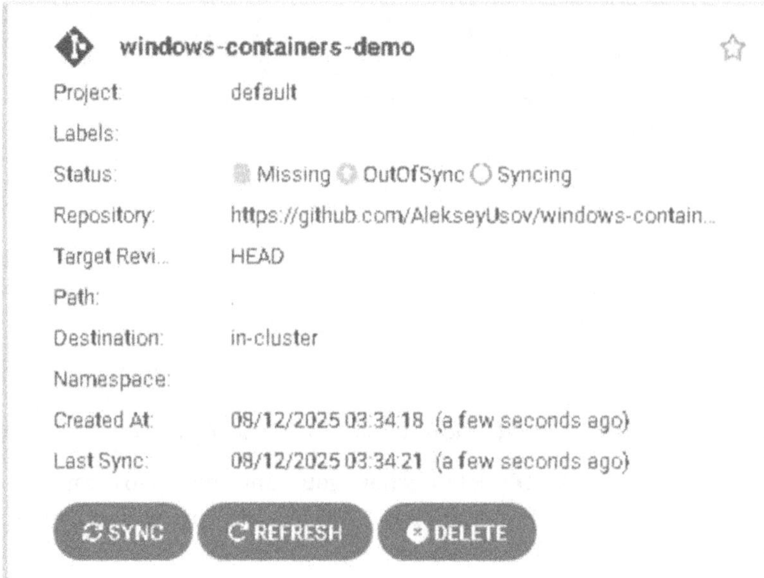

Figure 15.80: Application sync in progress

Wait until ArgoCD creates all the resources and the application reports as **Healthy** and **Synced:**

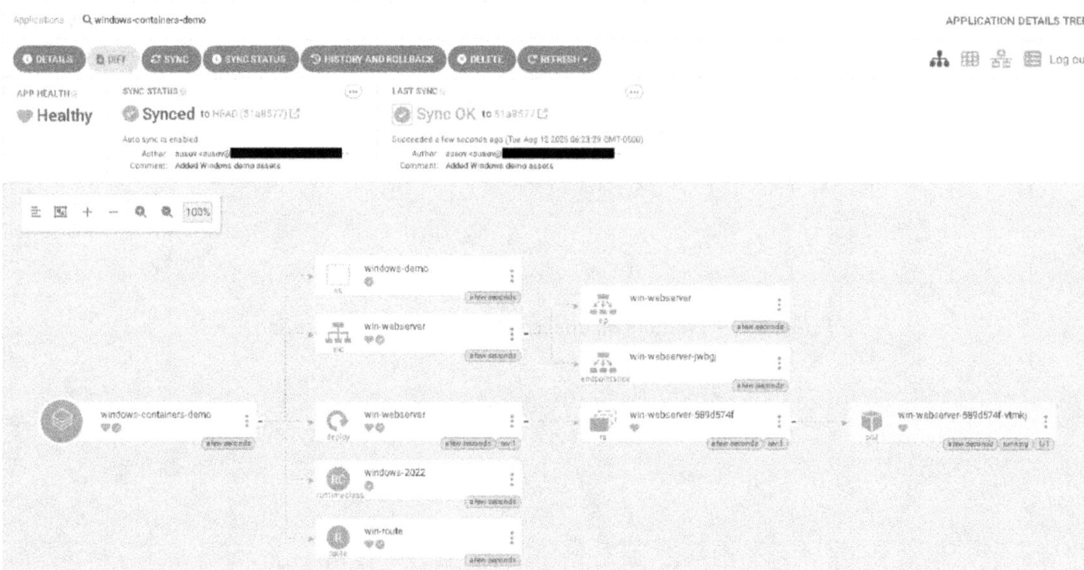

Figure 15.81: Application is synced and healthy

Every application in ArgoCD has two indicators: sync status and health. Sync status reports any discrepancies between the desired state of your application as defined in Git and the actual state as applied to the cluster, with any reconciliation errors. Health, on the other hand, reflects the state of the application itself, which generally means that all resources have been successfully created, and all pods (if any) are running. For example, if your application defines a Deployment and ArgoCD was able to successfully create it, the sync status will be **Sync OK**; however, if a pod created by that Deployment is unable to start for any reason (no suitable node was found, image pull error, missing Secret/ConfigMap, etc.), ArgoCD will mark it as **Unhealthy**. In short, sync status is concerned with admission of a resource, and health is with its runtime.

12. Let's confirm that ArgoCD created our application from the CLI as well:

```
$ oc get po -o wide -n windows-demo
```

As in the section on Windows containers, you should see a single replica running on your Windows nodes, as specified via node selector and tolerations in the `RuntimeClass`:

```
NAME                            STATUS    IP           NODE
win-webserver-589d574f-vtmkj    Running   10.224.0.15  ocp4-zlkjz-winworker-vn882
```

Figure 15.82: Application is successfully deployed by ArgoCD

Due to the page width limits, we used the following command to produce the more succinct output shown previously:

```
$ oc get po -o custom-columns=NAME:.metadata.name,STATUS:.status.
phase,IP:.status.podIP,NODE:.spec.nodeName -n windows-demo
```

You, however, can just use the first option.

13. Just seeing our application being created is not particularly interesting, as there are many ways to do that without involving any extra controllers. ArgoCD also makes sure that the state of our application matches that stored in Git by reverting any out-of-band changes, including those introduced manually. Let's test this by trying to scale our application to two replicas and immediately listing them:

```
$ oc scale deploy/win-webserver --replicas 2 -n windows-demo
$ oc get po -o wide -n windows-demo
```

As you can see, the newly created replica was immediately terminated, because ArgoCD detected the change to the Deployment's replica count and reverted it:

```
NAME                            READY   STATUS
win-webserver-589d574f-tfzdr    0/1     Terminating
win-webserver-589d574f-vtmkj    1/1     Running
```

Figure 15.83: ArgoCD reconciles changes to the number of replicas

If you're quick, you may be able to catch it in the **Terminating** status.

14. Now, let's try and delete the Deployment altogether and immediately check for pods:

    ```
    $ oc delete deploy/win-webserver -n windows-demo
    $ oc get po -o wide -n windows-demo
    ```

    The result is the same – ArgoCD reconciled the difference by recreating the Deployment (you can tell by the `AGE` column that it was just recreated):

    ```
    NAME                          READY   STATUS    RESTARTS   AGE
    win-webserver-589d574f-ks6q5  1/1     Running   0          4s
    ```

    Figure 15.84: ArgoCD restores the deleted Deployment

    The same application can be created across multiple clusters, ensuring consistency at scale. With ArgoCD, you can also deploy Helm charts, providing different values depending on your target environment.

15. As we established earlier, GitOps is characterized by relying on a Git repository as the central source of truth, so every change must go through Git in order to be applied. Let's introduce a minor yet representative update to our application. Change replicas from **1** to **3** and edit the service's response in the `deployment.yml` file to `Running 3 replicas on Windows Server 2022 Datacenter Edition`. Run `git diff` to review your changes. Your output should be similar to the following:

```
diff --git a/deployment.yml b/deployment.yml
index 197aa20..080a13e 100644
--- a/deployment.yml
+++ b/deployment.yml
@@ -9,7 +9,7 @@ spec:
   selector:
     matchLabels:
       app: win-webserver
-  replicas: 1
+  replicas: 3
   template:
     metadata:
       labels:
@@ -23,7 +23,7 @@ spec:
         command:
         - powershell.exe
         - -command
-        - $listener = New-Object System.Net.HttpListener; $listener.Prefixes.Add('http://*:80/'); $listene
r.Start();Write-Host('Listening at http://*:80/'); while ($listener.IsListening) { $context = $listener.Get
Context(); $response = $context.Response; $content='<html><body><H1>Running on Windows Server 2022 Datacent
er Edition</H1></body></html>'; $buffer = [System.Text.Encoding]::UTF8.GetBytes($content); $response.Conten
tLength64 = $buffer.Length; $response.OutputStream.Write($buffer, 0, $buffer.Length); $response.Close(); };
+        - $listener = New-Object System.Net.HttpListener; $listener.Prefixes.Add('http://*:80/'); $listene
r.Start();Write-Host('Listening at http://*:80/'); while ($listener.IsListening) { $context = $listener.Get
Context(); $response = $context.Response; $content='<html><body><H1>Running 3 replicas on Windows Server 20
22 Datacenter Edition</H1></body></html>'; $buffer = [System.Text.Encoding]::UTF8.GetBytes($content); $resp
onse.ContentLength64 = $buffer.Length; $response.OutputStream.Write($buffer, 0, $buffer.Length); $response.
Close(); };
         securityContext:
           windowsOptions:
             runAsUserName: "ContainerAdministrator"
```

Figure 15.85: Making legitimate changes to application resources in Git

16. Stage (`-a`) and commit your changes, then push:

```
$ git commit -am 'Increased the number of replicas and changed response'
$ git push
```

17. Now, execute the following command and wait:

```
$ watch -n1 oc get po -o wide -n windows-demo
```

In no more than 3 minutes (default sync period), GitOps will update its local copy of the repo from GitHub and reconcile the differences between the declared and actual states:

```
NAME                                READY   STATUS    RESTARTS   AGE
win-webserver-79b8556767-2cksw      1/1     Running   0          57s
win-webserver-79b8556767-4snlh      1/1     Running   0          60s
win-webserver-79b8556767-zc4vs      1/1     Running   0          63s
```

Figure 15.86: ArgoCD updates the running instances of an application to match its manifests in Git

Remember that updates to the number of replicas in a deployment trigger a new rollout and creation of a new `ReplicaSet`, so the pod created by the previous `ReplicaSet` will be gone.

18. Let's check the response from the application:

```
$ curl win-test.apps.ocp4.example.com
```

Changes to the web content should have been applied as well:

```
[ausov@bastion windows-containers-demo]$ curl win-test.apps.ocp4.example.com
<html><body><H1>Running 3 replicas on Windows Server 2022 Datacenter Edition</H1></body></html>
```

Figure 15.87: Application returns updated response

To make reconciliation take place more frequently, you can set the `timeout.reconciliation` parameter in the `argocd-cm` ConfigMap to a lower value, such as `1m`. More in [11].

We have just updated the configuration of our GitOps-managed application solely by pushing changes to Git, without any manual changes to its live instance on OpenShift. The GitOps application controller handled them for us.

We encourage you to explore other options that can be used with your ArgoCD application. After you're done experimenting, feel free to delete the ArgoCD application by clicking on **DELETE** at the top and confirming foreground deletion. Although this will delete the application from OpenShift as well, there is a configuration option to prevent that.

Summary

Congratulations! You've made it through one of the biggest chapters of this book. Let's do a quick recap of what we've learned.

We saw how serverless applications can be deployed on OpenShift using Knative. To that end, we installed the OpenShift Serverless operator that is based on the open source Knative project. We created a `KnativeServing` resource and then a Service from the `serving.knative.dev` API group (not to be confused with a Service from the core API group), which deployed a serverless application on our cluster.

Next, we installed the Windows Machine Config Operator to create and manage Windows nodes so that we can run Windows-based workloads, such as .NET, on our cluster. That was followed by creating a base Windows Server 2022 VM template in VMware vSphere and a Windows `MachineSet`. As part of the same exercise, we also deployed a demo application on a new Windows node.

The integrated registry is included by default; however, it can be configured with persistent storage and moved to dedicated nodes, like other infrastructure services that we covered earlier in this book.

Finally, we explored the benefits of GitOps and how the OpenShift GitOps operator, based on the ArgoCD upstream project, can be used to enforce the configuration of your applications or the entire cluster by checking with manifests stored in a version control system and remediating any configuration drift. We used the demo application from the discussion of Windows containers as an example.

In the next chapter, we will turn our attention to another important topic: operators and the Operator Framework. We will explore operators in more detail, discuss the problems they were designed to address, and even build our own operator.

References

To learn more about the topics that were covered in this chapter, take a look at the following resources:

- [1] *Red Hat OpenShift Serverless 1.36*: `https://docs.redhat.com/en/documentation/red_hat_openshift_serverless/1.36`
- [2] *Installing the Knative CLI*: `https://docs.redhat.com/en/documentation/red_hat_openshift_serverless/1.36/html/installing_openshift_serverless/installing-kn`
- [3] *Strategies for Moving .NET Workloads to OpenShift Container Platform*: `https://www.redhat.com/en/blog/strategies-for-moving-.net-workloads-to-openshift-container-platform`
- [4] *Configuring a BYOH Windows instance*: `https://docs.redhat.com/en/documentation/openshift_container_platform/4.16/html/windows_container_support_for_openshift/byoh-windows-instance#configuring-byoh-windows-instance`
- [5] *Evaluate Windows Server 2022*: `https://info.microsoft.com/ww-landing-windows-server-2022.html`
- [6] *Download Windows Server 2022 64-bit edition*: `https://go.microsoft.com/fwlink/p/?LinkID=2195280&clcid=0x409&culture=en-us&country=US`
- [7] *Access Denied installing updates remotely with Powershell*: `https://superuser.com/questions/1728641/access-denied-installing-updates-remotely-with-powershell`

- [8] *Isolation modes of Windows containers*: `https://learn.microsoft.com/en-us/virtualization/windowscontainers/manage-containers/hyperv-container`
- [9] *Compatibility and limitations of Windows containers*: `https://kubernetes.io/docs/concepts/windows/intro/#limitations`
- [10] *ArgoCD documentation*: `https://argo-cd.readthedocs.io/en/stable/`
- [11] *Configure applications sync frequency on GitOps / ArgoCD on RHOCP4*: `https://access.redhat.com/solutions/7012592`
- [12] *Argo CD sync failed due to GitOps service account user forbidden error in RHOCP 4*: `https://access.redhat.com/solutions/7007638`
- [13] *OpenShift GitOps sync is failing in user namespace*: `https://access.redhat.com/solutions/6012601`
- [14] *Enabling Windows container workloads*: `https://docs.redhat.com/en/documentation/openshift_container_platform/4.16/html/windows_container_support_for_openshift/enabling-windows-container-workloads`
- [15] *Creating a Windows machine set on vSphere*: `https://docs.redhat.com/en/documentation/openshift_container_platform/4.16/html/windows_container_support_for_openshift/creating-windows-machine-sets#creating-windows-machineset-vsphere`
- [16] *Running Windows Containers in Openshift 4.8*: `https://myopenshiftblog.com/running-windows-containers-in-openshift-4-8/`
- [17] *Quick start guide to the smallest OpenShift cluster for Windows workload*: `https://www.opensourcerers.org/2023/08/21/quick-start-to-smallest-openshift-cluster-for-windows-workload/`
- [18] *Creating a Windows Template for use with OpenShift Windows Machine Config Operator*: `https://xphyr.net/post/creating_windows_template/`
- [19] *How to Install VMware Tools on Windows Server Core VM*: `https://www.prajwaldesai.com/install-vmware-tools-on-windows-server-core/`
- [20] *Scheduling Windows container workloads*: `https://docs.redhat.com/en/documentation/openshift_container_platform/4.16/html/windows_container_support_for_openshift/scheduling-windows-workloads`
- [21] *OpenShift 4.7: Windows Container Support for Red Hat OpenShift on vSphere*: `https://www.redhat.com/en/blog/windows-container-support-for-red-hat-openshift-on-vsphere`
- [22] *Use Windows PowerShell to search for files*: `https://devblogs.microsoft.com/scripting/use-windows-powershell-to-search-for-files/`
- [23] *Windows Machine Config Operator on GitHub*: `https://github.com/openshift/windows-machine-config-operator/tree/v10.16.0`
- [24] *Announcing Windows Container Support for Red Hat OpenShift*: `https://www.redhat.com/en/blog/announcing-general-availability-for-windows-container-workloads-in-openshift-4.6`
- [25] *WMCO on GitHub*: `https://github.com/openshift/windows-machine-config-operator?tab=readme-ov-file`
- [26] *How to add toleration for the "non-OCS" taints to the OpenShift Data Foundation pods?*: `https://access.redhat.com/articles/6408481`

Quiz

Test your understanding of additional OpenShift services with this quick quiz. Remember, some questions may have more than one correct answer!

1. Which OpenShift Serverless API is responsible for autoscaling functions, including down to zero, and splitting traffic to different revisions?
    a. Knative Eventing
    b. Knative Kafka
    c. Knative Serving
    d. None of the above
2. Which Windows editions are supported by Windows Machine Config Operator?
    a. Windows 10
    b. Windows Server 2016
    c. Windows Server 2019
    d. Windows Server 2022
3. What is the name of the secret that contains the initialization script for Windows nodes?
    a. `worker-user-data`
    b. `windows-user-data`
    c. `windows-init`
    d. `win-provision`
4. What is the resource type and name of the object that is used to configure the OpenShift internal image registry?
    a. `operator.imageregistry/cluster`
    b. `config.imageregistry.operator.openshift.io/cluster`
    c. `config.imageregistry.openshift.io/cluster`
    d. `config.imageregistry/cluster`
5. Which OpenShift GitOps API object describes a set of related resources to be managed as a single unit?
    a. `ArgoApp`
    b. `Application`
    c. `ApplicationSet`
    d. `AppProject`

Answers

1. **c.** We created a Knative Serving object at the beginning of this chapter.
2. **c** and **d.** Only Windows Server 2019 and 2022 are officially supported; mainstream support for Windows Server 2016 ended on January 11, 2022.
3. **b.** The `windows-user-data` secret is stored in the `openshift-machine-api` namespace.
4. **b** and **d.** They are actually the same resource, with **b** being its fully-qualified name.
5. **b.** The correct answer is `Application`. `ApplicationSet` is a higher-level entity that describes a single application deployed across a fleet of clusters, `AppProject` is a project in ArgoCD (not to be confused with OpenShift Project), and `ArgoApp` does not exist.

Answers

Part 4

Extending, Maintaining, and Upgrading OpenShift

This is the last part of the book, where you will learn how to develop custom APIs and add them to OpenShift to manage applications natively. When you complete this section, you will have a full understanding of operators and be able to develop a simple operator of your own, and perform maintenance, upgrades, and troubleshoot issues with a cluster.

This part of the book includes the following chapters:

16

Understanding Operators and the Operator Framework

Throughout this book, we have used a number of operators to deploy various applications – **OpenShift Data Foundation (ODF)**, Serverless, **Windows Machine Config Operator (WMCO)**, and others. We also briefly mentioned operators as a way of packaging, automating, and distributing applications. Now it is time to discuss them in more detail. In this chapter, we will establish the definition of an operator, problems that operators were designed to address, and a few examples. Next, we will move on to discuss how operators are distributed and two ways of installing them on OpenShift – from the web console and the CLI. Cluster operators will be discussed as well, with slightly more focus on some of the most important ones. We will wrap this chapter up with an introduction to operator development, specifically the Operator Framework, and some of the things that have to be taken into account when planning the development of a new operator.

While this chapter covers everything you need to know to install and manage operators on OpenShift and introduces you to the resources you will need, should you decide to write an operator of your own, exploring all caveats of operator development is outside the scope of this chapter due to the limitations of the book. We will, however, show you how to create a simple operator that responds to events and manages the lifecycle of the nginx web server.

We'll cover the following main topics:

- What is an operator?
- Operator Framework
- Developing a simple operator
- Cluster Version Operator

Let's get started!

Technical requirements

In this chapter, you will need the following:

- Bash shell
- The `make` utility (installation instructions provided)
- Docker 17.03+ or Podman (installation instructions provided)
- A third-party Image registry with read/write access (quay.io, for example)
- OpenShift 4.16
- Firefox (recommended) or any other web browser
- An active Red Hat subscription to view Red Hat KB articles

This book's GitHub repository can be found at `https://github.com/PacktPublishing/Learn-OpenShift-Second-Edition`.

What is an operator?

We briefly discussed operators in *Chapter 11, Deploying Applications with Helm and Kustomize*, in the context of how they compare to Helm charts. Compared to Helm charts, operators are not just distribution packages; they also automate the entire lifecycle of an application, including installation, management, configuration changes, upgrades, and uninstallation.

First introduced in a 2016 CoreOS blog post [1], operators were proposed as a mechanism of encapsulating operational knowledge in software. Each operator is made up of one or more **custom resource definitions** (**CRDs**) that extend the OpenShift API and one or more controllers that run in their own pods and watch the **custom resources** (**CRs**) created from those CRDs. Like regular business applications, controllers run as containerized processes; however, they interact with OpenShift or Kubernetes API to watch for their resources and react accordingly, which is why they are often referred to as Kubernetes-native applications. An operator controller constantly monitors the actual state of the cluster and compares it to the desired state described in its CRs, which is called an **operator pattern**.

Operators work by translating the high-level configuration details of their applications, defined in CRs, into low-level actions coded in their controllers. For example, a stateful application such as a database, message broker, or monitoring system must be scaled and upgraded according to very specific procedures. Before the advent of operators, all these tasks were either performed manually or automated on top of OpenShift at best. That automation would often take the form of shell scripts or Ansible playbooks. By codifying these actions in the form of a Kubernetes-native application distributed as a container image and presenting high-level controls in the form of one or more CRD, we no longer have to treat our application as a set of Kubernetes core objects, such as a Deployment, ConfigMap, and Service. Instead, we can manage it using a dedicated CR that can also be subject to RBAC rules for granular access control. Another advantage of this approach is that operators are written by those who know their applications best – developers or SRE engineers. You can find more on the philosophy behind operators at [2] - [7].

Now that we have established the definition of an operator, we can discuss how they are distributed and installed.

Operator Framework

The Operator Framework is a toolkit that combines developer-focused tools, Kubernetes APIs, and other abstractions to build, test, package, and run custom controllers as operators. It is made up of three components:

- **Operator Software Development Kit (SDK)**: For building, testing, and packaging operators.
- **Operator Lifecycle Manager (OLM)**: For deploying and managing operators in Kubernetes.
- **OperatorHub**: For sharing operators with the community or your team.

Let's discuss each of them in more detail.

Operator SDK

The Operator SDK [8] is a set of runtime libraries, helpers, and API abstractions that allow you to build, test, run, and package your operators. It facilitates the connection between Kubernetes APIs and the business logic of a packaged application. With the Operator SDK, you can implement the controller logic for your operator using the following built-in plugins:

- **Go**: Gives you the most flexibility, as you can write custom controller logic directly in Go.
- **Ansible**: Executes an Ansible role every time a CR is created, updated, or deleted.
- **Helm**: Relies on a Helm chart to provide internal logic for the operator's controller. It exposes the chart's parameters from `values.yaml` as CRD fields. We will use this method for building a simple operator as a demonstration.

All these options have their pros and cons. For example, with Go, you can code an operator that reacts almost instantly to any configuration change and offers a wide range of capabilities, but it requires Go programming skills. Ansible and Helm, on the other hand, are easier to get started with, but such operators are slower to react to events and are limited in their capabilities.

Let's discuss capabilities provided by operators in a bit more detail. In terms of how much control you have over an operator-managed application and how much manual involvement it requires, the Operator Framework recognizes five capability levels:

Level	Description	Examples
I (Basic Install)	The operator reads the configuration from the `spec` section of one or more of its CRs, creates all necessary resources, such as Deployments, ConfigMaps, and others, waits for the application to become ready, and reports updates in the `status` section of the CR(s).	Deploying a web server, blogging platform, or stateless API. Creating a persistent volume, deploying a database, and initializing its schema. Changing the public hostname of a stateless web-based application.

Level	Description	Examples
II (Seamless Upgrades)	An application can be upgraded by changing its version in a CR or by upgrading the operator itself. The necessity to perform an upgrade or its availability can be reported through the `status` section of that CR. The operator also ensures the integrity of data during upgrades, as well as preventing data loss and disruptions.	Gracefully shutting down a PostgreSQL database, upgrading its engine, and migrating the database schema, if necessary.
III (Full Lifecycle)	An operator can create and restore backups of an application, implement failovers and failbacks, and perform complex application-aware configuration and intelligent scaling.	Backing up a relational database by flushing its log and quiescing writes beforehand. Adding extra shards to a MongoDB database. Adding extra members to a RabbitMQ cluster.
IV (Deep Insights)	The operator exposes metrics about its own health and application-specific metrics. It is also capable of sending alerts and emitting application-specific events.	A PostgreSQL operator tracking persistent volume usage and sending alerts when running out of space. A database or message broker operator exposing performance and usage metrics – for example, the number of **transactions per second** (**TPS**) or number of messages in a queue. A RabbitMQ operator emitting events on the addition of a new cluster member.
V (Auto Pilot)	The operator is capable of autoscaling its managed application in response to changing load based on its metrics (number of queries/transactions per second, persistent volume usage, etc.), auto-healing the application to a certain degree, taking actions to prevent potential issues, and maintaining the performance profile of the application.	Increasing the number of shards for a MongoDB instance to improve performance for a large number of documents. Adding a slave read-only replica to a relational database. Rebuilding an index of a relational database when query execution time increases.

Table 16.1: Operator capability levels

Visually, these levels can be represented as a pyramid where Level I represents foundational capabilities that every Kubernetes-native application must support to be qualified as an operator, and each subsequent level brings additional features:

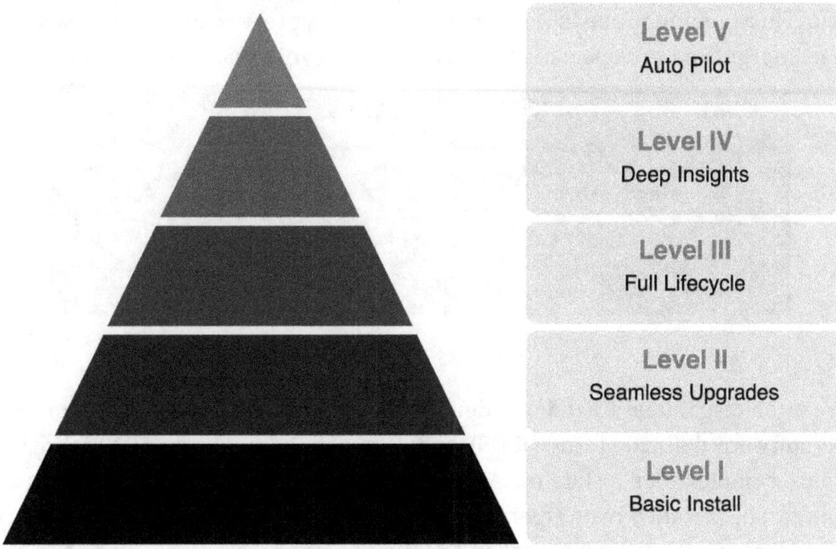

Figure 16.1: Operator capability levels

Here are some good practices for developing and running operators:

- Do not run their controllers as root, unless they require privileged access.
- Use a dedicated service account for each controller instead of `default`.
- Use a separate CR for any user-provided configuration.
- Operators should not register their CRDs themselves – this is the OLM's job.
- Use OpenAPI Specification for your operator's CRDs or validating admission webhooks for validating CRs and rejecting invalid changes.
- A given CRD should be owned only by a single operator.
- If your application consists of multiple components that perform their own business tasks, they should be managed by their own operators.
- Each CRD provided by your operator should be owned by its own controller that may run as a separate reconciliation loop inside the same container as other controllers.
- Do not hardcode any namespaces or resource names into your operators.
- Use semantic versioning (`major.minor.patch`) to indicate potentially backwards incompatible and breaking changes.
- If your operator requires CRDs provided by another operator, it should not install the dependent operator itself but rely on the OLM instead. If another operator is specified as a dependency, the OLM handles the dependency resolution.
- Use operator SDKs, such as the Operator SDK [8], Kubebuilder [9], or shell-operator [10].

Read more on operator development practices at [11] and [12].

Operator Lifecycle Manager

All non-default operators installed by users and administrators are managed by the **Operator Lifecycle Manager (OLM)**. For this reason, they are sometimes called OLM-based operators. The controller part of the OLM runs in a pod in the `openshift-operator-lifecycle-manager` namespace, which can be viewed with the `oc get po -n openshift-operator-lifecycle-manager` command:

```
NAME                                        READY   STATUS
catalog-operator-6b86ff957f-nq752           1/1     Running
collect-profiles-29250120-vntbs             0/1     Completed
collect-profiles-29250135-t4qz5             0/1     Completed
collect-profiles-29250150-grdjl             0/1     Completed
olm-operator-78f995c8cf-5tbsc               1/1     Running
package-server-manager-86df486665-2tdx4     2/2     Running
packageserver-77469469b5-ml52j              1/1     Running
packageserver-77469469b5-rhz48              1/1     Running
```

Figure 16.2: OLM pods

Operators are often distributed by **independent software vendors (ISVs)** and automate specific software, such as **software-defined storage (SDS)**, **software-defined network (SDN)** fabrics, or anything else that is more complex than a stateless API layer or web application. Earlier in this book, we saw how operators can be installed from OperatorHub – a publicly available operator registry. Generally, the process involves selecting the channel and version of an operator, specifying the namespace (if supported by the operator), selecting the update strategy (manual or automatic), and enabling cluster monitoring on the operator's namespace – all performed in the OpenShift web console. If a manual update strategy is chosen, you also need to approve an InstallPlan – again, from the same console. The process is relatively straightforward, and we have followed it a few times; however, installation through the web console often offers a limited number of configuration options and is impractical to automate. The CLI approach, however, automates very well and provides more flexibility for complex operators without introducing significant complexity. The OLM relies on the following APIs:

API	Short Name	Description
`CatalogSource`	`catsrc`	A repository of metadata, such as ClusterServiceVersions (CSVs), CRDs, and operator packages, that contains references to external operator manifests. Used by the OLM to discover and install operators and resolve dependencies.
`ClusterServiceVersion`	`csv`	Contains an operator's metadata, its CRs, core APIs, and RBAC objects required for the operator to function. Each release of an operator is represented by its own CSV.
`InstallPlan`	`ip`	Includes a list of CRs and other objects that will be installed with a particular CSV. Depending on the setting for `.spec.installPlanApproval` in an operator's Subscription, it may be approved automatically or require manual approval.

API	Short Name	Description
`OLMConfig`	-	Controls the OLM features described in Table 16.3.
`OperatorGroup`	`og`	Configures RBAC resources so that operators installed in the same namespace can watch resources in other namespaces.
`OperatorCondition`	`condition`	Allows an add-on operator to communicate its status and events back to the OLM, indicating successful installation, upgrade readiness, and others. The OLM, in turn, can override the state reported by the operator – for example, its upgrade readiness.
`Subscription`	`sub`	An object that represents an intention to install a specific version of an operator from a specific channel. A channel is a stream of updates that is used to deliver updates to an operator. Different channels usually vary by their support level, maturity (e.g., rc-1.0), and stability (e.g., stable-4.16).

Table 16.2: OLM APIs

The following table describes features that can be controlled by the OLMConfig CRD:

Option	Description
`.spec.features.disableCopiedCSVs`	Toggles copied (or "stub") CSVs. When an operator is installed, a CSV copy is created in all namespaces targeted by its OperatorGroup. On large clusters with hundreds or even thousands of namespaces and operators, this may lead to increased memory and etcd usage, which is why a toggle was introduced. Two downsides of turning it off are the loss of discovery, because operators can then only be discovered in the namespaces they are installed in, and a degraded UX experience, because the OLM uses copied CSVs to render operator-related pages in the web console. More on it in [13].
`.spec.features.packageServerSyncInterval`	Controls the interval used by `packageserver` pods in the `openshift-operator-lifecycle-manager` namespace to check the status of catalog sources. It allows you to maintain the balance between responsiveness to catalog updates and CPU usage.

Table 16.3: OLMConfig options

OperatorGroup's function is to allow operators sharing the same namespace access their CRs in their target namespaces or across an entire cluster, as specified in the OperatorGroup. As such, the list of target namespaces must be supported by the operator's `installModes` specified in its PackageManifest; otherwise, the operator's CSV will transition into a failed state. A CSV copy is created by the OLM in each namespace watched by an operator. Operators may support one or more `installModes` from the following list:

- `OwnNamespace`: An operator only watches resources in its resident namespace.
- `SingleNamespace`: An operator watches resources in a namespace where it is not installed.
- `MultiNamespace`: An operator watches resources in multiple namespaces.
- `AllNamespaces` (default): An operator has visibility into all namespaces.

There can only be one OperatorGroup in a namespace where new CSVs are created (copied CSVs don't count); otherwise, the OLM will emit a `TooManyOperatorGroups` event with the message `csv created in namespace with multiple operatorgroups, can't pick one automatically.`

Now, check for existing CatalogSources by executing the following command:

```
$ oc get catsrc -n openshift-marketplace
```

You should see four sources available:

```
[ausov@bastion ocp4-lab2]$ oc get catsrc -n openshift-marketplace
NAME                  DISPLAY               TYPE   PUBLISHER   AGE
certified-operators   Certified Operators   grpc   Red Hat     9d
community-operators   Community Operators   grpc   Red Hat     9d
redhat-marketplace    Red Hat Marketplace   grpc   Red Hat     9d
redhat-operators      Red Hat Operators     grpc   Red Hat     9d
```

Figure 16.3: Default CatalogSources

Let's examine the `redhat-operators` entry:

```
$ oc get -o jsonpath='{.spec.image}{"\n"}' catsrc/redhat-operators -n
openshift-marketplace
```

The image you see in the output contains a snapshot of a catalog index used by the OLM to locate operators and their versions:

```
registry.redhat.io/redhat/redhat-operator-index:v4.16
```

Figure 16.4: Full address of the Red Hat catalog index image

The image in this example is tagged as `v4.16`, which corresponds to the version of our cluster. When a cluster is updated, the **Cluster Version Operator** (**CVO**) bumps the tag to the target version, so that only compatible operators and their versions can be installed.

Installing an operator from the CLI

Like any other API object, OLM resources can be created directly from YAML or JSON. Installing an operator from the CLI on OpenShift involves the following steps:

1. Inspecting a `PackageManifest` object that corresponds to the operator you want to install in order to determine which channels, versions, and install modes are supported by the operator.
2. Creating an `OperatorGroup` object that specifies target namespace(s) for the operator or all namespaces (if supported).
3. Creating a `Subscription` resource by filling out the fields for channel, version, source catalog, and install plan approval strategy.
4. Approving the generated install plan, if a manual approval strategy was specified.

You can learn more about the OLM by following the links at [14] and [15].

Let's use the APIs listed previously to locate, install, configure, and uninstall an arbitrary operator. For this exercise, we will use the 3scale operator as an example, but any other will work too.

1. First, let's see what channels, versions, and installation modes the 3scale operator supports by running the following command (you can also use `jq .` for parsing the output):

```
$ oc get packagemanifest/3scale-operator -o jsonpath='{.status.
channels[0].currentCSVDesc.installModes}' -n openshift-marketplace |
python -m json.tool
```

As the output shows, the operator supports most installation modes, except `MultiNamespace`:

```
[
    {
        "supported": true,
        "type": "OwnNamespace"
    },
    {
        "supported": true,
        "type": "SingleNamespace"
    },
    {
        "supported": false,
        "type": "MultiNamespace"
    },
    {
        "supported": true,
        "type": "AllNamespaces"
    }
]
```

Figure 16.5: Installation modes supported by the 3scale operator

2. Next, you will create an OperatorGroup so that the OLM generates all required RBAC entities for the operator. To that end, we will use the `chapters/16/snippets/og-3scale.yml` file provided in this book's GitHub repository. We will configure the operator to watch the same namespace it is installed in, which corresponds to the `OwnNamespace` installation mode.

> In case of a large number of target namespaces or when they are not known in advance, you can specify them using an equality-based (`.spec.selector.matchLabels`) and/or set-based (`.spec.selector.matchExpressions`) selector instead of listing them explicitly. This will only work for operators that support the `MultiNamespace` installation mode.
>
> This approach lends itself to scenarios where you want to enable a new user or team using specific namespaces to create operator CRs without targeting all namespaces. All you need to do is create a namespace and label it by doing `oc label ns/<NAMESPACE> <KEY>=<VALUE>` so that it matches the OperatorGroup's selector. In about a minute, the OLM will create a new copy of the operator's CSV in that namespace.
>
> If both `targetNamespaces` and `selector` are used, however, the former (explicit listing) will take priority.

As was mentioned earlier in this chapter, when you configure an OperatorGroup to target more than one namespace, it copies the CSV from the OperatorGroup's resident namespace to all target namespaces. It also strips the `olm.targetNamespaces` annotation from every copy, so as not to leak the names of target namespaces to every user.

3. The task of an OperatorGroup is to create necessary RBAC rules for the operator, allowing it to watch its resources in target namespaces. Let's create a new namespace for the 3scale operator and the OperatorGroup, of which the operator will be the only member:

```
$ oc adm new-project openshift-3scale-operator
$ oc create -f chapters/16/snippets/og-3scale.yml
```

4. Now list ClusterRoles that the OLM has generated:

```
$ oc get clusterrole | grep 3scale
```

When an OperatorGroup is created, the OLM generates three ClusterRoles:

```
olm.og.3scale-operator.admin-8JWzHtlD2sKlPEBBzurahyC14BfdG4d1SbViZI
olm.og.3scale-operator.edit-8KZzBoEZUDkPCBqrWCYim95Y2ZUf4em6uxirt2
olm.og.3scale-operator.view-1iGdzqPeDRH5L1FsNgonSvG2uwuWMu1IPGTCDH
```

Figure 16.6: ClusterRoles generated by the OLM for the 3scale operator

For now, these roles do not contain any rules. We will revisit them after we have installed the 3scale operator.

5. An operator is installed by subscribing to one of its channels and optionally specifying the desired CSV, as well as other parameters. Let's extract them so that we can create a proper `Subscription` object. First, use the following command to list the channels and versions provided within each channel:

```
$ oc get packagemanifests 3scale-operator -o jsonpath='{.status.
channels[*]}' -n openshift-marketplace | jq [.name,.currentCSV]
```

Here is an output from our lab environment:

```
[
  "threescale-2.14",
  "3scale-operator.v0.11.13"
]
[
  "threescale-2.15",
  "3scale-operator.v0.12.3"
]
[
  "threescale-mas",
  "3scale-operator.v0.12.1-mas"
]
```

Figure 16.7: Channels and CSVs provided by the 3scale operator

For this exercise, let's pick the `3scale-operator.v0.12.3` CSV from the `threescale-2.15` channel.

6. Next, we will need the name of the catalog source that provides this operator:

```
$ oc get packagemanifests 3scale-operator -o jsonpath='{.status.
catalogSource}{"\n"}' -n openshift-marketplace
```

The name of the catalog source is `redhat-operators`. Now we can put together our subscription. For simplicity, a complete manifest is provided at `chapters/16/snippets/sub-3scale.yml` of this book's repository. Just in case there is a newer CSV by the time you're reading this, we recommend checking it first.

For the sake of learning, we set `.spec.installPlanApproval` to `Manual` in order to demonstrate how to approve an InstallPlan manually yet again, but this time we will review it from the CLI before giving it a green light.

7. Use the following command to create a subscription:

```
$ oc create -f chapters/16/snippets/sub-3scale.yml
```

8. Run the following command to check for a new InstallPlan:

```
$ oc get ip -n openshift-3scale-operator
```

Usually, a few seconds later, an InstallPlan is generated (there may still be a transient issue with the CatalogSource, mentioned in previous chapters):

```
NAME            CSV                          APPROVAL   APPROVED
install-6xmlc   3scale-operator.v0.12.0      Manual     false
```

Figure 16.8: InstallPlan pending approval

Before we approve it, let's extract all the names and types of resources that come with this plan by using the following command:

```
$ oc get -o jsonpath='{.status.plan[*].resource}' ip/install-xxxxx -n
openshift-3scale-operator | jq -r [.kind,.name]
```

The output was cut to save space:

```
[
  "ClusterServiceVersion",
  "3scale-operator.v0.12.3"
]
[
  "CustomResourceDefinition",
  "activedocs.capabilities.3scale.net"
]
[
  "CustomResourceDefinition",
  "developerusers.capabilities.3scale.net"
]
[
  "Service",
  "threescale-operator-controller-manager-metrics-service"
]
[
  "CustomResourceDefinition",
  "apimanagerrestores.apps.3scale.net"
]
```

Figure 16.9: The contents of the 3scale InstallPlan (abbreviated)

9. To complete the installation, we need to approve the InstallPlan:

```
$ oc patch --type merge -p '{"spec": {"approved": true}}' ip/install-
xxxxx -n openshift-3scale-operator
```

10. Once the plan is approved, a new CSV is generated, and an operator pod is created. As the operator controller in the pod initializes, the CSV will go through the following phases: **Pending** > **InstallReady** > **Installing** > **Succeeded**. Use the following command to wait for a controller manager pod to start:

```
$ watch -n1 oc get po -n openshift-3scale-operator
```

At this point, the controller pod should be up and running:

```
NAME                                                   READY   STATUS
threescale-operator-controller-manager-v2-7f4d5cf4cd-9w6hz   1/1     Running
```

Figure 16.10: 3scale operator controller manager pod running

We can also use the `oc get crd | grep 3scale` command to list the installed CRDs:

```
activedocs.capabilities.3scale.net
apimanagerbackups.apps.3scale.net
apimanagerrestores.apps.3scale.net
apimanagers.apps.3scale.net
applicationauths.capabilities.3scale.net
applications.capabilities.3scale.net
backends.capabilities.3scale.net
custompolicydefinitions.capabilities.3scale.net
developeraccounts.capabilities.3scale.net
developerusers.capabilities.3scale.net
openapis.capabilities.3scale.net
products.capabilities.3scale.net
proxyconfigpromotes.capabilities.3scale.net
tenants.capabilities.3scale.net
```

Figure 16.11: APIs added to OpenShift by the 3scale operator

Now, let's examine the RBAC objects that were created by the OLM for the 3scale operator. First, use the `oc get clusterrole | grep 3scale` command again to list all ClusterRoles that have *3scale* in their names:

```
developerusers.capabilities.3scale.net-v1beta1-admin
developerusers.capabilities.3scale.net-v1beta1-crdview
developerusers.capabilities.3scale.net-v1beta1-edit
developerusers.capabilities.3scale.net-v1beta1-view
olm.og.3scale-operator.admin-8JWzHtlD2sKlPEBBzurahyC14BfdG4d1SbViZI
olm.og.3scale-operator.edit-8KZzBoEZUDkPCBqrWCYim95Y2ZUf4em6uxirt2
olm.og.3scale-operator.view-1iGdzqPeDRH5L1FsNgonSvG2uwuWMu1IPGTCDH
openapis.capabilities.3scale.net-v1beta1-admin
openapis.capabilities.3scale.net-v1beta1-crdview
openapis.capabilities.3scale.net-v1beta1-edit
openapis.capabilities.3scale.net-v1beta1-view
```

Figure 16.12: ClusterRoles generated by the OLM

The output is too big to provide here in its entirety, so we have shown only a part of it. However, even with the limited output, you may notice a pattern here. The roles named olm.og.<OPERATORGROUP_NAME>.admin-<HASH> were the only ClusterRoles generated right after we had created the OperatorGroup. When we first checked them, they were empty. You can also see new roles that follow the naming scheme <CRD>.<API_GROUP>-<API_VERSION>-admin|crdview|edit|view. These cluster roles were created by the OLM after the operator's CSV was registered as a member of the OperatorGroup, and there are 4 roles per CRD.

Now let's take a look inside one of the ClusterRoles that were created first:

```
$ oc get -o yaml clusterrole/olm.og.3scale-operator.edit-<HASH>
```

There are two things of interest there. First, it is an aggregation rule that looks up all cluster roles that match the selector and adds their rules into the rules section, overwriting any preexisting rules. For brevity, we've shown only the first selector:

```
aggregationRule:
  clusterRoleSelectors:
  - matchLabels:
      olm.opgroup.permissions/aggregate-to-e613b59dfc80a528-edit: "true"
```

Figure 16.13: Example of an aggregation rule

Another is the rules section, which was populated from a matching cluster role by a controller running as part of the OpenShift control plane. Again, this is not the entire rules section, but a small part of it:

```
rules:
- apiGroups:
  - capabilities.3scale.net
  resources:
  - developerusers
  verbs:
  - create
  - update
  - patch
  - delete
```

Figure 16.14: ClusterRole rules for a specific CRD

We can easily find the source of these rules if we just look up that cluster role using the selector we saw earlier and examine its manifest:

```
$ oc get clusterrole -l olm.opgroup.permissions/aggregate-to-<CRD_HASH>-edit="true"
$ oc get -o yaml clusterrole/developerusers.capabilities.3scale.net-v1beta1-edit
```

There is only one role matching the aggregation rule, which makes it pretty simple to understand the relationship between all those cluster roles. For the `OwnNamespace` installation mode, the following aggregated ClusterRoles are created:

ClusterRole	Aggregation Rule Selectors
olm.og.<OPERATORGROUP_NAME>.admin-<HASH>	olm.opgroup.permissions/aggregate-to-<CRD_HASH>-admin: "true"
olm.og.<OPERATORGROUP_NAME>.edit-<HASH>	olm.opgroup.permissions/aggregate-to-<CRD_HASH>-edit: "true"
olm.og.<OPERATORGROUP_NAME>.view-<HASH>	olm.opgroup.permissions/aggregate-to-<CRD_HASH>-view: "true"

Table 16.4: Aggregated ClusterRoles generated by the OLM

For every CRD installed by an operator, the OLM generates the following ClusterRoles, which are "plugged into" the three aggregated cluster roles, as well as the built-in OpenShift cluster roles:

<table>
<tr><th>ClusterRole</th><th>Verbs</th><th>Aggregation Labels</th></tr>
<tr><td><CRD>.<API_GROUP>-<API_VERSION>-admin</td><td>- '*'</td><td>olm.opgroup.permissions/aggregate-to-<CRD_HASH>-admin: "true"

rbac.authorization.k8s.io/aggregate-to-admin: "true"</td></tr>
<tr><td><CRD>.<API_GROUP>-<API_VERSION>-crdview</td><td>- get</td><td rowspan="2">olm.opgroup.permissions/aggregate-to-<CRD_HASH>-view: "true"

rbac.authorization.k8s.io/aggregate-to-view: "true"</td></tr>
<tr><td><CRD>.<API_GROUP>-<API_VERSION>-view</td><td>- get
- list
- watch</td></tr>
<tr><td><CRD>.<API_GROUP>-<API_VERSION>-edit</td><td>- create
- update
- patch
- delete</td><td>olm.opgroup.permissions/aggregate-to-<CRD_HASH>-edit: "true"

rbac.authorization.k8s.io/aggregate-to-edit: "true"</td></tr>
</table>

Table 16.5: CRD-specific roles generated by the OLM

The following figure illustrates the logical relationship between all these objects, using `edit` cluster roles of the operator as an example:

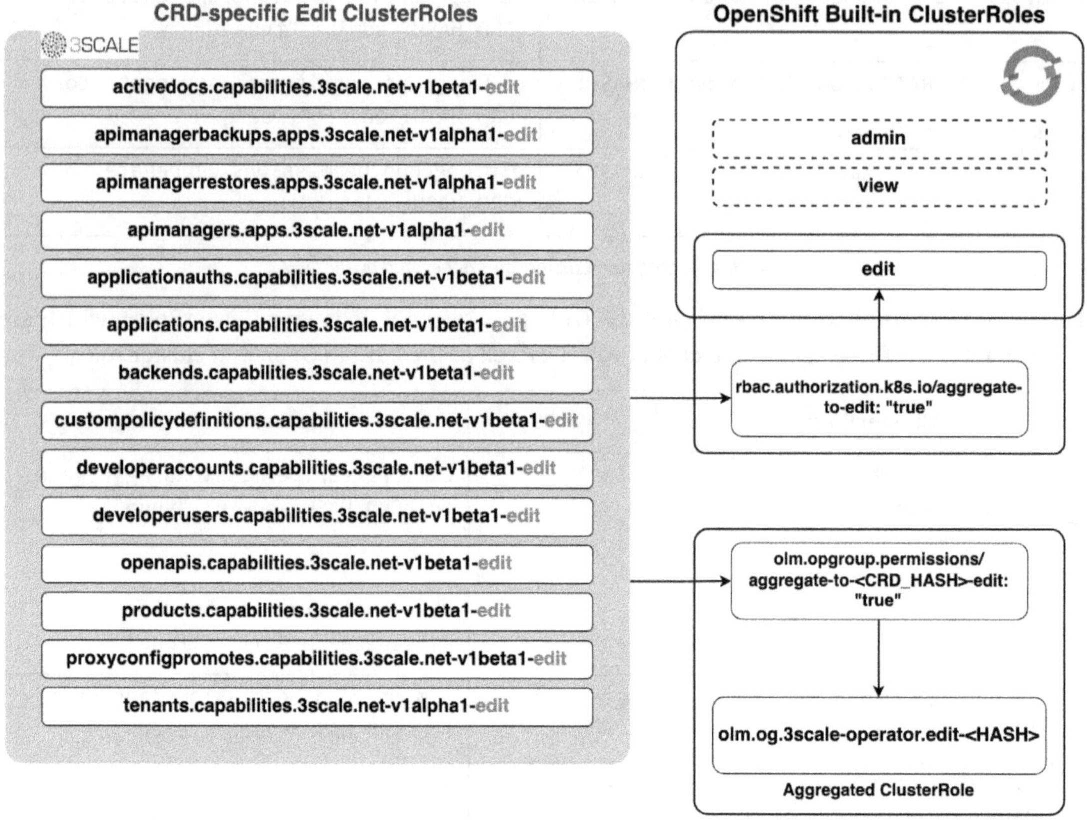

Figure 16.15: Logical relationships between aggregated and CRD-specific ClusterRoles

There are additional roles and role bindings generated for installation modes other than `AllNamespaces`. Consult the relevant documentation section at [16] for more details.

Scheduling operator pods on specific nodes

Just like regular pods, operator pods can be configured to run only on specific nodes using node selectors and tolerate node taints with tolerations. This is configured in a given operator's `Subscription` resource:

```
spec:
<OMITTED>
  config:
    affinity:
      nodeAffinity:
```

```
        preferredDuringSchedulingIgnoredDuringExecution:
        - weight: 100
          preference:
            matchExpressions:
            - key: node-role.kubernetes.io/infra
              operator: Exists
      tolerations:
      - key: node-role.kubernetes.io/infra
        effect: NoExecute
```

We used this feature of OLM back in *Chapter 8*, *Working with Persistent Storage*, to move the ODF controller manager's pod to an infrastructure node as a demo.

After you make the change to the manifest file and run `oc apply -f <FILE>`, the configuration will be applied immediately, which can be verified by checking the name of the node that was assigned to an operator's controller pod:

```
$ oc get po threescale-operator-controller-manager-v2-xxxxxxxxxx-xxxxx -o
jsonpath='{.spec.nodeName}{"\n"}' -n openshift-3scale-operator
```

You may expect an output similar to this (your node may be different):

```
$ oc get po \
> threescale-operator-controller-manager-v2-6b86c6d6bb-lkfc6 \
> -o jsonpath='{.spec.nodeName}{"\n"}' \
> -n openshift-3scale-operator
infra-1.ocp4.example.com
```

Figure 16.16: Finding out the resident node of the operator's controller pod

The Subscription API also supports `podAffinity` and `podAntiAffinity` rules. Use the `oc explain sub.spec.config.affinity` command for more details.

You can also remove preexisting node or pod affinity rules or the entire config section by explicitly setting them to an empty object, for example: `config: {}`.

We have just learned how to install any operator from the CLI, discussed various entities involved in operator installation, saw how the OLM manages RBAC for its managed operators, and how to schedule operator pods on reserved nodes using node affinity and tolerations. Now that we are done with the command line, it is time to launch a web browser and familiarize ourselves with OperatorHub.

OperatorHub

OperatorHub [17] is a public registry that maintains the global index and packages for all operators provided by the community and ISVs. It is available directly from Red Hat OpenShift in the form of a web interface, from which operators can be installed in a point-and-click fashion. Following is a screenshot of OperatorHub's landing page, with some of the operators presented:

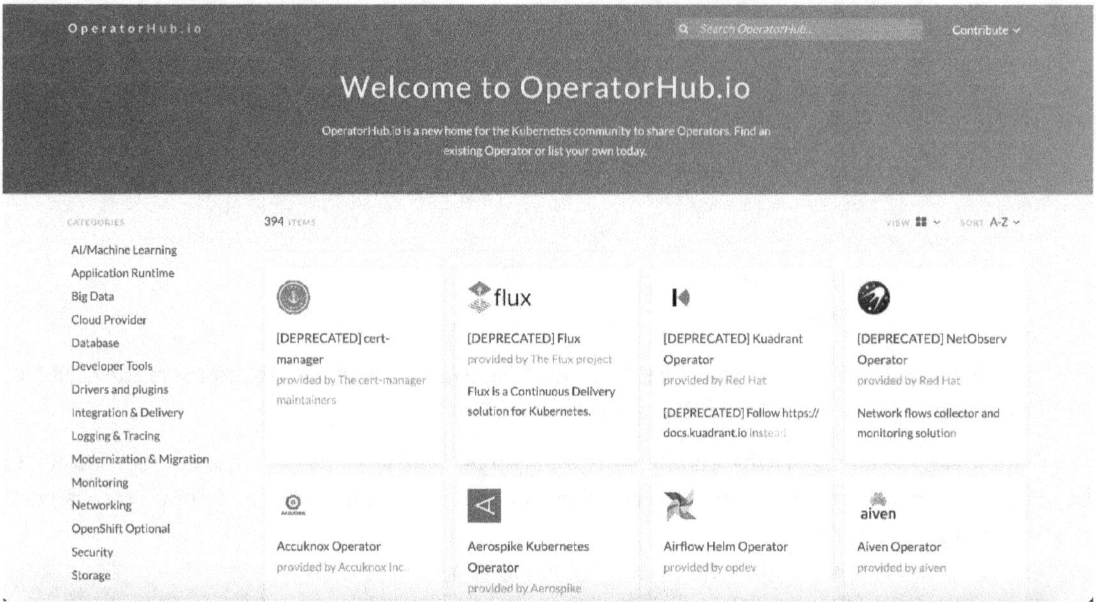

Figure 16.17: OperatorHub landing page

If you click on any operator's tile, you will be shown its installation instructions on OLM-enabled Kubernetes clusters:

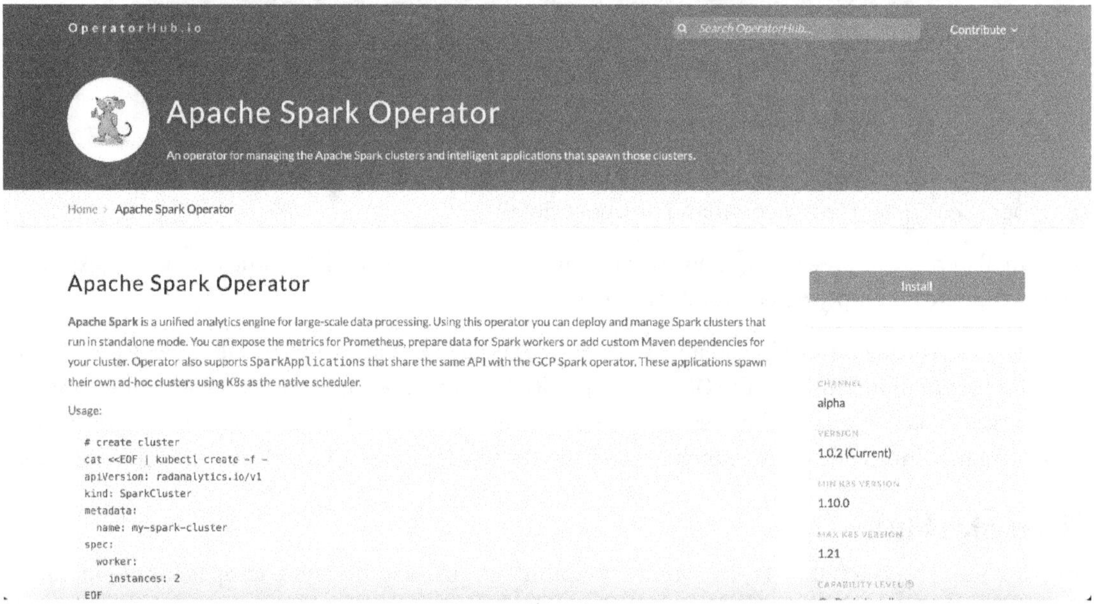

Figure 16.18: Operator details in OperatorHub

In the OpenShift web UI, all operators available through OperatorHub are divided into the following categories, reflected on an operator's tile:

Category	Description
Red Hat Operators	Operators packaged and provided by Red Hat.
Certified Operators	Operators provided and supported by ISVs and packaged for distribution through a partnership with Red Hat.
Red Hat Marketplace (superseded by Red Hat Ecosystem Catalog as of April 1, 2025)	Operators that can be purchased through Red Hat Ecosystem Catalog [18] – for example, OpenShift Data Foundation.
Community Operators	Community-maintained operators. Since they don't come from Red Hat, these operators are not entitled to any support from Red Hat.

Table 16.6: Operator categories in OperatorHub

In the Red Hat Ecosystem Catalog, you can also examine individual operators for their capability level, compatibility with OpenShift, documentation, and support terms:

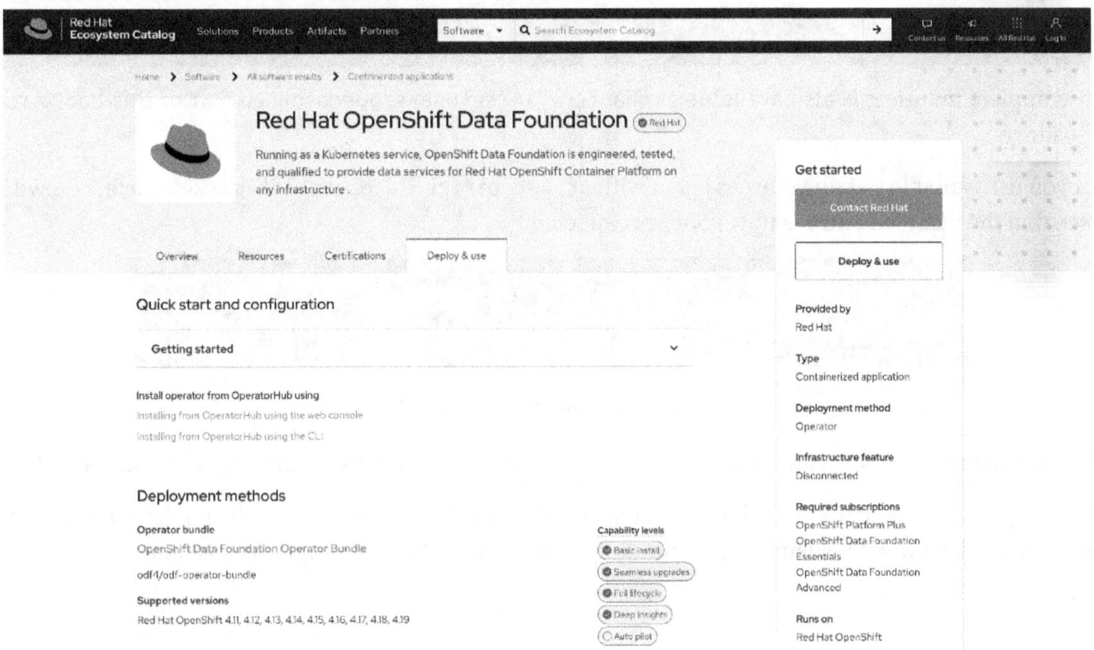

Figure 16.19: Red Hat Ecosystem Catalog

To find only products delivered as operators, first scroll down to **Software products based on your needs**, then click on **Browse all software** and select **Operator** in **Deployment Method**.

On a lower level, OperatorHub is managed by the Marketplace Operator running in the `openshift-marketplace` namespace:

```
$ oc get po -n openshift-marketplace | grep marketplace-operator
```

The Marketplace Operator's configuration is exposed through the OperatorHub CR named `cluster`, which can be examined using the `oc get -o yaml operatorhub/cluster` command.

In the preceding configuration, you can choose to disable all default CatalogSources (`.spec.disableAllDefaultSources: true`) or individually. In that case, you would probably want to configure your own sources if you are operating in an air-gapped environment. In order to selectively disable some of the sources, use the following snippet:

```
apiVersion: config.openshift.io/v1
kind: OperatorHub
metadata:
  name: cluster
spec:
  sources:
  - name: community-operators
    disabled: true
```

Store it in a file named `operatorhub.yml` and apply the following:

```
$ oc apply -f operatorhub.yml
```

A complete manifest is also available at `chapters/16/snippets/operatorhub.yml` of this book's repository.

If you list available CatalogSources again with `oc get catsrc -n openshift-marketplace`, you will see that the disabled entry is now gone, as expected:

```
NAME                  DISPLAY               TYPE   PUBLISHER
certified-operators   Certified Operators   grpc   Red Hat
redhat-marketplace    Red Hat Marketplace   grpc   Red Hat
redhat-operators      Red Hat Operators     grpc   Red Hat
```

Figure 16.20: Community CatalogSource disabled

In a similar manner, you can disable other sources and enable your own, after they have been created.

You may want to roll back your changes using `oc edit` or edit the file and reapply it before moving on, even though we won't be using any community operators for the remainder of this book.

> To remove a section's contents completely, set its value to `{}` – for example, `spec: {}`.

Developing a simple operator

As you may remember, we wrote a basic Helm chart for the nginx web server back in *Chapter 11, Deploying Applications with Helm and Kustomize*. While useful in deploying all resources required by the application, such as a Deployment to manage the server's pods, ConfigMap to provide web content, and Route to provide external connectivity, it does not manage the lifecycle of nginx. Every time we need to make a change, we need to install a new release of the chart by overriding its values exposed through the `values.yaml` file because Helm treats our application as a collection of manifests rendered from templates. By packaging it as an operator, we can control it via a special CR, editing it just like we would any other OpenShift API object.

The Operator SDK comes with a CLI implemented as a single binary that can generate all of the boilerplate code for a specific plugin – Helm, Ansible, or Go. Execute the following commands to download the Operator SDK binary for your machine's CPU architecture and OS and add it to your `$PATH`:

```
$ export ARCH=$(case $(uname -m) in x86_64) echo -n amd64 ;; aarch64) echo -n
arm64 ;; *) echo -n $(uname -m) ;; esac)
$ export OS=$(uname | awk '{print tolower($0)}')
$ export OPERATOR_SDK_DL_URL=https://github.com/operator-framework/operator-
sdk/releases/download/v1.41.1
$ curl -LO ${OPERATOR_SDK_DL_URL}/operator-sdk_${OS}_${ARCH}
$ chmod +x operator-sdk_${OS}_${ARCH}
$ sudo mv operator-sdk_${OS}_${ARCH} /usr/local/bin/operator-sdk
```

> At the time of writing this chapter, `v1.41.1` was the most recent release of the Operator SDK; however, you may want to check its GitHub page for any updates when you're reading this.

If you followed the steps correctly, this command will print the Operator SDK's version information:

```
$ operator-sdk version
```

The Operator SDK requires Docker or Podman to build, push, and run operator images, and `make` to execute build targets specified in a `Makefile` that it generates in your local project. Install them both with the following command:

```
$ sudo yum -yq install docker make
```

If the installation is successful, it will not produce any output (`-q` or `--guiet`).

In systems that are kept up to date, the Docker CLI is emulated via Podman, so you can use both `docker` and `podman` commands. If your image registry requires authentication, you will need to authenticate before continuing:

```
$ podman login docker.io
```

You will see a `Login Succeeded!` message if authentication was successful. Due to its simplicity, we use a private Docker Hub repository for this exercise; however, Quay and others will work as well.

Since our registry requires authentication, we need to configure a pull secret so that OpenShift is able to download images and run them. This can be done either per project or globally. Follow these steps to add our registry's credentials to the cluster-wide dictionary of pull secrets [19]:

1. First, extract the current contents of the global pull secret named `pull-secret` from the `openshift-config` namespace and store it in `global-pull-secret.json`:

```
$ oc get secret/pull-secret --template='{{index .data ".dockerconfigjson"
| base64decode}}' -n openshift-config > global-pull-secret.json
```

2. Next, use the following oc subcommand to log into an external registry and add credentials to the JSON file we created in the previous step:

```
$ oc registry login --registry=docker.io  --auth-
basic='<USERNAME>:<PASSWORD>' --to global-pull-secret.json
```

3. Finally, load the updated JSON data into the secret:

```
$ oc set data secret/pull-secret --from-file=.dockerconfigjson=global-
pull-secret.json -n openshift-config
```

It will take about 3 mins for the MCO to update the global pull secret in `/var/lib/kubelet/config.json` on all nodes. Updates to the global pull secret do not trigger node drain or reboot. You can monitor the progress with this already familiar command:

```
$ watch -n1 oc get mcp
```

Now we can use the Operator SDK to build an operator. Follow these steps:

1. Start by creating a new directory for our project and changing into it:

```
$ mkdir ocp4-nginx-operator && cd ocp4-nginx-operator
```

2. Next, run the following command to generate a skeleton directory structure with files required for building a new operator. Notice that we point it to the Helm chart we wrote earlier in this book:

```
$ operator-sdk init --plugins helm --domain packt.com --group web
--version v1alpha1 --kind Nginx --helm-chart ../learning-ocp4-nginx
```

The preceding command initializes a project for a Helm-based operator that watches the `Nginx.web.packt.com/v1alpha1` CustomResource, as well as Kustomize manifests for deploying the operator in OpenShift and RBAC rules in `config/rbac/role.yaml`:

```
INFO[0000] Writing kustomize manifests for you to edit...
INFO[0000] Creating the API:
$ operator-sdk create api --group web --version v1alpha1 --kind Nginx --helm-chart ../learning-ocp4-nginx
INFO[0000] Writing kustomize manifests for you to edit...
Created helm-charts/learning-ocp4-nginx
Generating RBAC rules
WARN[0000] The RBAC rules generated in config/rbac/role.yaml are based on the chart's default manifest. Some r
ules may be missing for resources that are only enabled with custom values, and some existing rules may be ove
rly broad. Double check the rules generated in config/rbac/role.yaml to ensure they meet the operator's permis
sion requirements.
```

Figure 16.21: Bootstrapping a project with operator-sdk init

3. Let's take a closer look at the structure of a new project with `ls -ltr`:

```
-rw-r--r--.  1 ausov ausov   194 Aug 12 13:40 Dockerfile
-rw-r--r--.  1 ausov ausov 10132 Aug 12 13:40 Makefile
drwx------. 11 ausov ausov   148 Aug 12 13:40 config
drwxr-xr-x.  3 ausov ausov    33 Aug 12 13:40 helm-charts
-rw-r--r--.  1 ausov ausov   191 Aug 12 13:40 watches.yaml
-rw-------.  1 ausov ausov   546 Aug 12 13:40 PROJECT
```

Figure 16.22: Files generated as part of the skeleton project

The file named `watches.yaml` defines mappings of CRs to their Helm charts:

```
# Use the 'create api' subcommand to add watches to this
file.
- group: web.packt.com
  version: v1alpha1
  kind: Nginx
  chart: helm-charts/learning-ocp4-nginx
#+kubebuilder:scaffold:watch
```

Figure 16.23: The contents of watches.yaml

A complete reference for all available options can be found at [20]. You are also welcome to examine the contents of the `config` directory, which contains operator-related manifests and kustomizations for applying them – having read *Chapter 11, Deploying Applications with Helm and Kustomize*, you should possess the necessary knowledge.

Another file worth looking into is `PROJECT`, which is a project descriptor used by `operator-sdk` to correctly identify a project's type – Helm, Ansible, or Go:

```
# Code generated by tool. DO NOT EDIT.
# This file is used to track the info used to scaffold your project
# and allow the plugins properly work.
# More info: https://book.kubebuilder.io/reference/project-config.html
domain: packt.com
layout:
- helm.sdk.operatorframework.io/v1
plugins:
  manifests.sdk.operatorframework.io/v2: {}
  scorecard.sdk.operatorframework.io/v2: {}
projectName: ocp4-nginx-operator
resources:
- api:
    crdVersion: v1
    namespaced: true
  domain: packt.com
  group: web
  kind: Nginx
  version: v1alpha1
```

Figure 16.24: The contents of PROJECT

The next file, `Dockerfile`, specifies build instructions for our operator's controller image:

```
# Build the manager binary
FROM quay.io/operator-framework/helm-operator:v1.41.1

ENV HOME=/opt/helm
COPY watches.yaml ${HOME}/watches.yaml
COPY helm-charts  ${HOME}/helm-charts
WORKDIR ${HOME}
```

Figure 16.25: The contents of Dockerfile

As specified in the preceding file, both the `watches.yaml` file and the `helm-charts` directory are copied to `/opt/helm`, where an operator expects to find them. As for the `helm-charts` directory, it contains a copy of our Helm chart. We could have specified a `tar.gz` archive instead of a directory when we ran `operator-sdk init` – in that case, it would have been extracted automatically.

Lastly, `Makefile` defines build targets for our project that we will invoke during this exercise – we encourage you to examine it to understand the configuration of different targets, as it is too long to provide here. Make note of two environment variables referenced in the file – `IMG` and `BUNDLE_IMG`. We will be overriding them when invoking some of the build targets later.

4. Next, edit the `config/rbac/role.yaml` file and add `- "routes/custom-host"` at the end, right after the line `"routes"`. This is required so that our operator, running under its own ServiceAccount, can update the hostname in our application's `Route` object, as explained at [21].

5. Now all that's left for us to do is build our operator's image from the `Dockerfile` and push it to our registry. To that end, we will override the `IMG` and `BUNDLE_IMG` environment variables referenced by the `Makefile` and execute both `docker-build` and `docker-push` targets:

   ```
   $ export IMG=docker.io/alekseyusov/ocp4-nginx-operator:v0.0.1
   $ make docker-build docker-push
   ```

   The preceding command will trigger `docker build -t ${IMG}` and `docker push ${IMG}` commands.

Technically, our operator is ready and can be run on our local machine with just a single command:

```
$ make install run
```

That will start a controller process in the foreground from the image we built in the previous step, which is a good way to check if your operator is able to start at all:

```
/usr/local/bin/kustomize build config/crd | kubectl apply -f -
customresourcedefinition.apiextensions.k8s.io/nginxes.web.packt.com created
/home/ausov/ocp4-lab2/ocp4-nginx-operator/bin/helm-operator run
{"level":"info","ts":"2025-08-12T14:53:45-04:00","logger":"cmd","msg":"Version","Go Version":"go1.24.
3","GOOS":"linux","GOARCH":"amd64","helm-operator":"v1.41.1","commit":"69ee6d4077ff769a8513571343a96f
3cb8ca35ef"}
{"level":"info","ts":"2025-08-12T14:53:45-04:00","logger":"cmd","msg":"Watching all namespaces"}
{"level":"info","ts":"2025-08-12T14:53:45-04:00","logger":"helm.controller","msg":"Watching resource"
,"apiVersion":"web.packt.com/v1alpha1","kind":"Nginx","reconcilePeriod":"1m0s"}
{"level":"info","ts":"2025-08-12T14:53:45-04:00","logger":"controller-runtime.metrics","msg":"Startin
g metrics server"}
{"level":"info","ts":"2025-08-12T14:53:45-04:00","logger":"controller-runtime.metrics","msg":"Serving
 metrics server","bindAddress":":8080","secure":false}
{"level":"info","ts":"2025-08-12T14:53:45-04:00","msg":"starting server","name":"health probe","addr"
:"[::]:8081"}
{"level":"info","ts":"2025-08-12T14:53:45-04:00","msg":"Starting EventSource","controller":"nginx-con
troller","source":"kind source: *unstructured.Unstructured"}
{"level":"info","ts":"2025-08-12T14:53:45-04:00","msg":"Starting Controller","controller":"nginx-cont
roller"}
{"level":"info","ts":"2025-08-12T14:53:45-04:00","msg":"Starting workers","controller":"nginx-control
ler","worker count":2}
```

Figure 16.26: Starting an operator's controller locally

Press *Ctrl* + *C* to terminate the reconciliation loop.

Since we are running on OpenShift 4, it is only natural to let the OLM do the heavy lifting of installing our operator and registering its CRD. For that, OLM will need a bundle image containing our operator's metadata and all the objects it requires, such as Deployment, ConfigMap, Route, and others. Let's override the location of a bundle image defined by the `BUNDLE_IMG` environment variable, then build and push a bundle image for our operator:

```
$ export BUNDLE_IMG=docker.io/alekseyusov/ocp4-nginx-operator-bundle:v0.0.1
$ make bundle bundle-build bundle-push
```

The bundle target will prompt you for basic information about your operator that will be used to categorize it in a registry, such as OperatorHub, and provide its users with some useful information, such as the vendor's URL and email addresses of its maintainers.

```
/usr/local/bin/operator-sdk generate kustomize manifests -q

Display name for the operator (required):
> Learn OpenShift 4 Demo Nginx Operator

Description for the operator (required):
> A simple Helm-based operator that deploys Nginx on OpenShift 4

Provider's name for the operator (required):
> Packt

Any relevant URL for the provider name (optional):
>

Comma-separated list of keywords for your operator (required):
> helm,openshift,nginx,operator

Comma-separated list of maintainers and their emails (e.g. 'name1:email1, name2:email2') (required):
> Aleksey Usov:ausov@example.com
```

Figure 16.27: Providing operator's information for OperatorHub

The same target will also generate a number of local resources required by the controller manager process that will be created from this image, including bundle/manifests, which contains CSV and RBAC objects, and config/crd/bases/<GROUP>.<DOMAIN>_<KIND>es.yaml, which contains an OpenAPI specification for our operator's CRD.

The command will also generate two other files: bundle.Dockerfile and bundle/metadata/annotations.yaml. Let's examine them in more detail. You can see from bundle.Dockerfile that all manifests and metadata are copied inside the bundle image:

```
FROM scratch

# Core bundle labels.
LABEL operators.operatorframework.io.bundle.mediatype.v1=registry+v1
LABEL operators.operatorframework.io.bundle.manifests.v1=manifests/
LABEL operators.operatorframework.io.bundle.metadata.v1=metadata/
LABEL operators.operatorframework.io.bundle.package.v1=ocp4-nginx-operator
LABEL operators.operatorframework.io.bundle.channels.v1=alpha
LABEL operators.operatorframework.io.metrics.builder=operator-sdk-v1.41.1
LABEL operators.operatorframework.io.metrics.mediatype.v1=metrics+v1
LABEL operators.operatorframework.io.metrics.project_layout=helm.sdk.operatorframework.io/v1

# Labels for testing.
LABEL operators.operatorframework.io.test.mediatype.v1=scorecard+v1
LABEL operators.operatorframework.io.test.config.v1=tests/scorecard/

# Copy files to locations specified by labels.
COPY bundle/manifests /manifests/
COPY bundle/metadata /metadata/
COPY bundle/tests/scorecard /tests/scorecard/
```

Figure 16.28: The contents of bundle.Dockerfile

The `bundle/metadata/annotations.yaml` file defines the same annotations as are specified on the image itself with the `LABEL` instructions:

```
annotations:
  # Core bundle annotations.
  operators.operatorframework.io.bundle.mediatype.v1: registry+v1
  operators.operatorframework.io.bundle.manifests.v1: manifests/
  operators.operatorframework.io.bundle.metadata.v1: metadata/
  operators.operatorframework.io.bundle.package.v1: ocp4-nginx-operator
  operators.operatorframework.io.bundle.channels.v1: alpha
  operators.operatorframework.io.metrics.builder: operator-sdk-v1.41.1
  operators.operatorframework.io.metrics.mediatype.v1: metrics+v1
  operators.operatorframework.io.metrics.project_layout: helm.sdk.operatorframework.io/v1

  # Annotations for testing.
  operators.operatorframework.io.test.mediatype.v1: scorecard+v1
  operators.operatorframework.io.test.config.v1: tests/scorecard/
```

Figure 16.29: The annotations set on the operator's image

Now that we have both operator and operator bundle images in a registry, we can switch to our OpenShift cluster:

1. First, let's create a project for our operator:

   ```
   $ oc new-project nginx-operator-demo
   ```

2. Next, run the following command to create a file-based catalog that uses our bundle image as an index image and install the nginx operator using the OLM:

   ```
   $ operator-sdk run bundle docker.io/alekseyusov/ocp4-nginx-operator-
   bundle:v0.0.1
   ```

   In a separate terminal session, use the following command to monitor operator pods as they come up:

   ```
   $ watch -n1 oc get po -n nginx-operator-demo
   ```

   You are expected to see two running pods, one of which is the operator controller manager that runs the operator image referenced by `${IMG}` in the `Makefile`:

```
NAME                                                              READY   STATUS      RESTARTS   AGE
c8550df88f6882bebdb55b3c1bcfcbcdaa1c1297d47fa3290ae7da7bc7p2vxj   0/1     Completed   0          96s
docker-io-alekseyusov-ocp4-nginx-operator-bundle-v0-0-1           1/1     Running     0          107s
ocp4-nginx-operator-controller-manager-786ff4b77-d9sr5            1/1     Running     0          33s
```

Figure 16.30: CatalogSource and controller pods of the new operator

3. Now check for installed CSVs with `oc get csv`. As you can see, one of the installed CSVs represents a specific version of our operator (in the middle):

```
[ausov@bastion ocp4-nginx-operator]$ oc get csv
NAME                                       DISPLAY                                        VERSION    REPLACES                                   PHASE
cluster-logging.v6.2.4                     Red Hat OpenShift Logging                      6.2.4      cluster-logging.v6.2.3                     Succeeded
cluster-observability-operator.v1.2.2      Cluster Observability Operator                 1.2.2      cluster-observability-operator.v1.2.1      Succeeded
grafana-operator.v5.18.0                   Grafana Operator                               5.18.0     grafana-operator.v5.15.1                   Succeeded
jaeger-operator.v1.65.0-3                  Red Hat OpenShift distributed tracing platform 1.65.0-3   jaeger-operator.v1.65.0-2                  Succeeded
kiali-operator.v2.11.1                     Kiali Operator                                 2.11.1     kiali-operator.v1.89.1                     Succeeded
loki-operator.v6.2.4                       Loki Operator                                  6.2.4      loki-operator.v6.2.3                       Succeeded
ocp4-nginx-operator.v0.0.1                 Learn OpenShift 4 Demo Nginx Operator          0.0.1                                                 Succeeded
openshift-builds-operator.v1.5.0           Builds for Red Hat OpenShift Operator          1.5.0      openshift-builds-operator.v1.4.1           Succeeded
openshift-gitops-operator.v1.17.0          Red Hat OpenShift GitOps                       1.17.0     openshift-gitops-operator.v1.16.2          Succeeded
openshift-pipelines-operator-rh.v1.19.2    Red Hat OpenShift Pipelines                    1.19.2     openshift-pipelines-operator-rh.v1.19.1    Succeeded
serverless-operator.v1.36.0                Red Hat OpenShift Serverless                   1.36.0     serverless-operator.v1.35.0                Succeeded
servicemeshoperator.v2.6.9                 Red Hat OpenShift Service Mesh 2               2.6.9-0    servicemeshoperator.v2.6.8                 Succeeded
tempo-operator.v0.16.0-2                   Tempo Operator                                 0.16.0-2   tempo-operator.v0.13.0-1                   Succeeded
```

Figure 16.31: CSV installed by the new operator

Other CSVs were created for operators that were installed in the `AllNamespaces` mode in previous chapters.

For each operator, there are also corresponding OperatorGroup, Subscription, and InstallPlan objects that can be viewed with `oc get og,sub,ip`:

```
NAME                                                AGE
operatorgroup.operators.coreos.com/operator-sdk-og  3m16s

NAME                                                               PACKAGE               SOURCE                        CHANNEL
subscription.operators.coreos.com/ocp4-nginx-operator-v0-0-1-sub   ocp4-nginx-operator   ocp4-nginx-operator-catalog   operator-sdk-run-bundle

NAME                                          CSV                          APPROVAL   APPROVED
installplan.operators.coreos.com/install-k97zg   ocp4-nginx-operator.v0.0.1   Manual     true
```

Figure 16.32: OperatorGroup, Subscription, and InstallPlan generated by `operator-sdk`

Let's inspect the `Subscription` resource more closely:

```
$ oc get -o yaml sub/ocp4-nginx-operator-v0-0-1-sub
```

From the following output, we can tell that our operator was installed from the `ocp4-nginx-operator-catalog` CatalogSource located in the `nginx-operator-demo` namespace and the operator's version, among other details:

```
spec:
  channel: operator-sdk-run-bundle
  installPlanApproval: Manual
  name: ocp4-nginx-operator
  source: ocp4-nginx-operator-catalog
  sourceNamespace: nginx-operator-demo
  startingCSV: ocp4-nginx-operator.v0.0.1
```

Figure 16.33: The contents of the new operator's subscription

The CatalogSource for our operator was created by the `operator-sdk bundle` command and can be viewed with the `oc get catsrc` command:

```
NAME                          DISPLAY                 TYPE   PUBLISHER
ocp4-nginx-operator-catalog   ocp4-nginx-operator     grpc   operator-sdk
```

Figure 16.34: CatalogSource generated by operator-sdk

Run the following command to see the internal IP address of the catalog:

```
$ oc get -o jsonpath='{.spec.address}{"\n"}' catsrc/ocp4-nginx-operator-catalog
```

It will print a pair, `<IP>:50051` – for example, `10.131.1.33:50051`.

Now list all pods in the current project and their IPs:

```
$ oc get po -o jsonpath='{range .items[*]}{.metadata.name} - {.status.podIP} -
{.spec.containers[0].ports[0].containerPort}{"\n"}{end}'
```

In the output, you will see a pod that runs the registry:

```
c8550df88f6882bebdb55b3c1bcfcbcdaa1c1297d47fa3290ae7da7bc7p2vxj - 10.131.1.34 -
docker-io-alekseyusov-ocp4-nginx-operator-bundle-v0-0-1 - 10.131.1.33 - 50051
ocp4-nginx-operator-controller-manager-786ff4b77-d9sr5 - 10.131.1.35 -
```

Figure 16.35: IP addresses and ports of created pods

Now that we have the operator up and running, we can create a CR that represents the desired state of our application. If you look inside the `config/samples/web_v1alpha1_nginx.yaml` file, you will see that it contains a copy of the contents from the `values.yaml` file from the Helm chart that we built our operator from. Update the domain in `.spec.route.host` to match your cluster, then create the CR, and watch for an nginx pod to come up:

```
$ oc create -f config/samples/web_v1alpha1_nginx.yaml
$ watch -n1 oc get po -n nginx-operator-demo
```

The pod should be able to start normally:

```
NAME                                                              READY   STATUS
c8550df88f6882bebdb55b3c1bcfcbcdaa1c1297d47fa3290ae7da7bc7p2vxj   0/1     Completed
docker-io-alekseyusov-ocp4-nginx-operator-bundle-v0-0-1           1/1     Running
nginx-sample-learning-ocp4-nginx-77f45d8cc5-skz5x                 1/1     Running
ocp4-nginx-operator-controller-manager-786ff4b77-d9sr5            1/1     Running
```

Figure 16.36: Nginx pod created in response to creating a Nginx CR

If you see the controller manager pod getting killed with an `OOMKilled` status, try increasing its memory limit from the default `128Mi` to `256Mi` in the operator's CSV and delete the pod so that it's re-created:

```
$ oc edit csv/ocp4-nginx-operator.v0.0.1
$ oc delete po -l app.kubernetes.io/name=ocp4-nginx-operator
```

We have to edit the CSV because any changes to the deployment will be reset by the OLM to match the CSV. After a new pod is created, give it a couple of minutes to settle down and then check its memory usage with the `oc adm top po` command that we introduced you to in *Chapter 13, Monitoring in OpenShift*. In our lab, it stabilized around 180-200Mi. Since this usage is fairly consistent, we could've increased the request to match the limit or set the limit to, say, 512Mi and requests to 256Mi so that the pod always has that amount of memory reserved for it.

This also works as an example of sizing requests and limits for business applications to avoid overprovisioning. Ideally, you want your requests to be slightly above normal usage (95p or 99p) and limits to allow for occasional spikes. Setting proper requests and limits is more of an art than a science because it involves striking a balance between the stability of applications and the cost of extra hardware required when you set requests too high. It is not a one-time adjustment, but a recurring process.

As you may recall, the Helm chart that we used as a foundation for this operator creates a default route so that our server can be accessed immediately without any extra configuration. Check for it with `oc get route`:

```
NAME                                 HOST/PORT
nginx-sample-learning-ocp4-nginx     nginx-demo.apps.ocp4.example.com
```

Figure 16.37: Route created by our Nginx operator on processing the Nginx CR

As expected, the route was created, so let's use it to send a simple `GET` request to validate the application:

```
$ curl nginx-demo.apps.ocp4.example.com
```

The response body should contain the text stored in a ConfigMap deployed as part of our application:

```
<h1>It works!</h1>
```

We can also view the CR we created earlier with `oc get nginx`:

```
nginx-sample   42s
```

Now, let's change the target state of our application and see how our operator reacts to it. Change the desired number of replicas for nginx to 2 and immediately observe the change by running the following commands:

```
$ oc patch --type merge -p '{"spec": {"replicaCount": "2"}}' nginx/nginx-sample
$ watch -n1 oc get po
```

In a few seconds, a new pod is created, matching the observed state of the application to the desired state specified in the CR:

```
NAME                                                              READY   STATUS
c8550df88f6882bebdb55b3c1bcfcbcdaa1c1297d47fa3290ae7da7bc7p2vxj   0/1     Completed
docker-io-alekseyusov-ocp4-nginx-operator-bundle-v0-0-1           1/1     Running
nginx-sample-learning-ocp4-nginx-77f45d8cc5-f71f8                 1/1     Running
nginx-sample-learning-ocp4-nginx-77f45d8cc5-skz5x                 1/1     Running
ocp4-nginx-operator-controller-manager-6f78cd9b99-fqsqr           1/1     Running
```

Figure 16.38: The demo operator reacting to the change in CR

Let's try something else. Change the hostname in the nginx CR for exposing our application:

```
$ oc patch --type merge -p '{"spec": {"route": {"host": "nginx-test.apps.ocp4.
example.com"}}}' nginx/nginx-sample
$ watch -n1 oc get route
```

Just as quickly, the default route has changed to reflect the configuration in CR:

```
NAME                                HOST/PORT
nginx-sample-learning-ocp4-nginx    nginx-test.apps.ocp4.example.com
```

Figure 16.39: Route updated by the nginx operator

Let's test it again with `curl nginx-test.apps.ocp4.example.com`. Just like before, the request should succeed.

To clean up, run the following commands – they will delete the CR, which will also delete all components of our application, remove the operator with all its related resources, including its CatalogSource, and finally delete the namespace:

```
$ oc delete -f config/samples/web_v1alpha1_nginx.yaml
$ make undeploy
$ oc delete project nginx-operator-demo
```

We have just built a ready-to-use Helm-based operator. Although limited and not representative of all the benefits offered by operators, it should serve as a good foundation for you to start developing operators of your own and then transitioning to something more complex. We encourage you to explore other methods of developing operators, such as Ansible [22] and especially Go [23]. In case Python is more up your alley, we recommend looking into Kopf [24]. And if you are interested in transforming your own charts to operators, see [25] and [26] for detailed instructions.

Now that we are done with the OLM and OLM-managed operators, let's take a look at another class of operators in OpenShift.

Cluster Version Operator

OpenShift 4 implements its cluster-critical functions in the form of various **ClusterOperators** (**COs**) that, just like add-on operators, expose their configuration settings through their own CRs. For example, the Image Registry Operator manages the lifecycle of the OpenShift integrated registry, reading its desired configuration from the `config.imageregistry.operator.openshift.io` CR named `cluster`. It supports parameters for persistent storage, management state, pod placement, and rollout strategy.

Just like the OLM manages the lifecycle of add-on operators, the CVO does the same for cluster operators. Specifically, it performs the following functions:

- Periodically checks the remote **OpenShift Update Service** (OSUS) for available upgrade paths, storing supported target versions in the `.status.availableUpdates` of the ClusterVersion object.
- If the current cluster version does not match the version requested in `.spec.desiredUpdate`, the CVO initiates a cluster upgrade by downloading the target release image that contains resource manifests for all COs. It then reconciles all COs to their target versions as specified in the manifests. COs, on their end, are responsible for upgrading their CRs.

Like other operators, the CVO runs in its own pod in the `openshift-cluster-version` namespace and can be seen by running the `oc get po -n openshift-cluster-version` command:

```
[ausov@bastion learning-ocp4]$ oc get po -n openshift-cluster-version
NAME                                      READY   STATUS    RESTARTS       AGE
cluster-version-operator-66bd7b5b7b-b716m 1/1     Running   1 (60d ago)    60d
[ausov@bastion learning-ocp4]$
```

Figure 16.40: CVO controller pod

If we run `oc get clusterversion`, we will see the current state of the CVO, stored in a ClusterVersion object named `version`:

```
NAME      VERSION   AVAILABLE   PROGRESSING   SINCE   STATUS
version   4.16.8    True        False         76d     Cluster version is 4.16.8
```

Figure 16.41: Current state of the ClusterVersion object

You can examine its structure with the following command:

```
$ oc get -o yaml clusterversion/version
```

Although it is possible to start an upgrade by patching the ClusterVersion resource with a desired image, architecture, and version, it is recommended to use the `oc adm upgrade` command or Web UI. If you must use a declarative approach (for example, as part of a GitOps workflow), however, be aware of the caveats outlined in the output of `oc explain clusterversion.spec.desiredUpdate`.

By default, CVO manages the lifecycle and updates of all COs. You can, however, override that behavior for a specific resource in the `.spec.overrides` section of the ClusterVersion object. Keep in mind that doing so puts your cluster in an unsupported state and disables upgrades for that component. While useful for troubleshooting and testing configuration changes that otherwise would be reset by the operator, it should be used with care. Use `oc explain clusterversion.spec.overrides` to learn more.

More detailed information on the CVO is available at [27]. The upgrade process is discussed in more detail in *Chapter 17, Upgrading OpenShift*.

Troubleshooting cluster operators

Every ClusterOperator reports five useful parameters in the output of `oc get co`:

- `VERSION`: Reflects the current version of an operator and is updated during upgrades. By monitoring cluster operators as they increase their versions, you can tell how close an upgrade process is to completion.
- `AVAILABLE`: Whether the resources managed by an operator are healthy.
- `PROGRESSING`: Whether an operator is working to reconcile its desired and actual states.
- `DEGRADED`: Whether an operator is able to make progress and recover from an error. If `True`, a manual intervention is required.
- `MESSAGE`: A message that gives a clue as to the cause of a problem.

Your success in troubleshooting cluster operator issues will depend on your ability to identify resources owned by a particular operator and verify their state. When one or more COs report `True` in the `DEGRADED` column, usually the following procedure applies:

1. First, do `oc describe co/<CLUSTER_OPERATOR>` on the failing operator and look for the `Related Objects` field – it lists all resources managed and watched by the operator, including namespaces. For example, let's examine the definition of the Ingress operator with `oc describe co/ingress`:

```
Related Objects:
  Group:
  Name:        openshift-ingress-operator
  Resource:    namespaces
  Group:       operator.openshift.io
  Name:
  Namespace:   openshift-ingress-operator
  Resource:    ingresscontrollers
  Group:       ingress.operator.openshift.io
  Name:
  Namespace:   openshift-ingress-operator
  Resource:    dnsrecords
  Group:
  Name:        openshift-ingress
  Resource:    namespaces
  Group:
  Name:        openshift-ingress-canary
  Resource:    namespaces
```

Figure 16.42: Resource watched by the Ingress CO

As you can tell from the output, the operator manages resources in three namespaces – `openshift-ingress-operator`, `openshift-ingress`, and `openshift-ingress-canary`. We will not be diving deep into what resources are located in each of them and will instead focus on a single namespace as an example – `openshift-ingress-operator`.

2. You can also see all conditions of the operator, their states, and when the most recent transitions to or from that state occurred. For example, let's take a look at the following condition:

```
Conditions:
  Last Transition Time:  2025-08-03T09:43:32Z
  Message:               The "default" ingress controller reports Available=True.
  Reason:                IngressAvailable
  Status:                True
  Type:                  Available
```

Figure 16.43: The Ingress CO reports Available

The `.status.conditions` field lists all conditions supported by an object of a particular type. ClusterOperators have their own possible conditions; other objects, such as pods, have theirs. Each condition has the following fields (as seen in the output of `oc get -o yaml`):

- `Type`: Type of a condition that describes a specific aspect of an object. In the case of COs, common examples include `Available`, `Degraded`, `Upgradable`, and `Progressing`.
- `Reason`: A short machine-readable string that tells why the condition changed status.
- `Message`: A more detailed message for administrators or operations that describes the problem.
- `LastTransitionTime`: The last time a condition changed status.
- `Status`: `True`, `False`, or `Unknown`; indicates whether a condition is currently being met.

3. Let's check for the IngressController object with the following command:

```
$ oc get ingresscontroller -n openshift-ingress-operator
```

There is only one resource of that type, named `default`:

```
default   76d
```

4. Inspect the YAML definition of the IngressController/default object:

```
$ oc get -o yaml ingresscontroller/default -n openshift-ingress-operator
```

Note the fields `.status.availableReplicas` and `.status.selector`:

```
availableReplicas: 3
selector: ingresscontroller.operator.openshift.io/deployment-ingresscontroller=default
```

This tells us that the object manages three pods identified by the preceding selector. This is a lead worth pursuing.

5. Search for pods labeled `ingresscontroller.operator.openshift.io/deployment-ingresscontroller=default` across all namespaces:

```
$ oc get po -l ingresscontroller.operator.openshift.io/deployment-ingresscontroller=default -A
```

The search should yield three (your number may vary) replicas:

```
NAMESPACE           NAME                              READY   STATUS
openshift-ingress   router-default-6f64c57455-mxdxn   1/1     Running
openshift-ingress   router-default-6f64c57455-qfphz   1/1     Running
openshift-ingress   router-default-6f64c57455-vphlv   1/1     Running
```

Figure 16.44: Ingress pods are up and running

As you can see, they are all running in our lab, but if there were any issues, such as scheduling problems, you would see them here. In that case, we would proceed to look into events with `oc get ev` or pod logs (`oc logs`), if pods are able to start, but keep crashing (`CrashLoopBackOff`).

Keep in mind that all cluster operators are different, and they manage different resources; however, the course of action outlined should help you in identifying the cause of any common issue with cluster operators. For a complete list of cluster operators and their functions, refer to [28].

Summary

This concludes the chapter on operators and the OLM. We started by discussing the problem of managing the lifecycle of applications and the limitations of Helm and the built-in APIs of OpenShift. All of that called for a more automated solution in the form of an operator that bundles the logic of managing an application with the application itself and exposes controls through one or more CRDs.

We also discussed how the **Operator Lifecycle Manager** (**OLM**) manages user-installed operators, APIs it provides, and configuration controls that it provides.

Next, we looked at how operators are built and explored the use of the Operator SDK to create a simple operator that deploys and manages nginx from the Helm chart we wrote earlier in this book. This gave us an opportunity to revisit the concepts of Helm and Kustomize and build on the knowledge we've obtained.

Finally, we learned what **cluster operators** (**COs**) are, how the **Cluster Version Operator** (**CVO**) manages their lifecycle and upgrades. We also briefly discussed common CO troubleshooting methods and how cluster upgrades work. The next chapter naturally continues this discussion in more detail with a few diagrams that show how the CVO determines viable upgrade paths and all possible transitions between conditions of a CO.

References

To learn more about the topics that were covered in this chapter, take a look at the following resources:

- [1] *Introducing Operators: Putting Operational Knowledge into Software*: `https://www.redhat.com/en/blog/introducing-operators-putting-operational-knowledge-into-software`
- [2] *What is an operator*: `https://operatorframework.io/what/`
- [3] *What is a Kubernetes operator?*: `https://www.redhat.com/en/topics/containers/what-is-a-kubernetes-operator`
- [4] *Operators over easy: an introduction to Kubernetes Operators*: `https://www.redhat.com/en/blog/operators-over-easy-introduction-kubernetes-operators`

- [5] *O'Reilly: Kubernetes Operators: Automating the Container Orchestration Platform*: `https://www.redhat.com/rhdc/managed-files/cl-oreilly-kubernetes-operators-ebook-f21452-202001-en_2.pdf`
- [6] *Operator pattern*: `https://kubernetes.io/docs/concepts/extend-kubernetes/operator/`
- [7] *Operators overview*: `https://docs.redhat.com/en/documentation/openshift_container_platform/4.16/html/operators/operators-overview`
- [8] *Operator SDK*: `https://sdk.operatorframework.io/`
- [9] *Kubebuilder*: `https://book.kubebuilder.io/`
- [10] *Shell-operator*: `https://github.com/flant/shell-operator`
- [11] *Best practices for building Kubernetes Operators and stateful apps*: `https://cloud.google.com/blog/products/containers-kubernetes/best-practices-for-building-kubernetes-operators-and-stateful-apps`
- [12] *Operator Best Practices*: `https://sdk.operatorframework.io/docs/best-practices/best-practices/`
- [13] *Operator Framework enhancements: Toggle Copied CSVs*: `https://github.com/operator-framework/enhancements/blob/master/enhancements/olm-toggle-copied-csvs.md`
- [14] *Operator Lifecycle Manager*: `https://olm.operatorframework.io/`
- [15] *Operator Lifecycle Manager concepts and resources*: `https://docs.redhat.com/en/documentation/openshift_container_platform/4.16/html/operators/understanding-operators#olm-understanding-olm`
- [16] *Role-based access control*: `https://docs.redhat.com/en/documentation/openshift_container_platform/4.16/html/operators/understanding-operators#olm-operatorgroups-rbac_olm-understanding-operatorgroups`
- [17] *OperatorHub*: `https://operatorhub.io/`
- [18] *Red Hat Ecosystem Catalog*: `https://catalog.redhat.com/en`
- [19] *Updating the global cluster pull-secret*: `https://docs.redhat.com/en/documentation/openshift_container_platform/4.16/html/images/managing-images#images-update-global-pull-secret_using-image-pull-secrets`
- [20] *Define Watches in Helm-based operators*: `https://sdk.operatorframework.io/docs/building-operators/helm/reference/watches/`
- [21] *User without cluster-admin role cannot modify the Route's hostname*: `https://access.redhat.com/solutions/6620061`
- [22] *Ansible Operator Tutorial*: `https://sdk.operatorframework.io/docs/building-operators/ansible/quickstart/`
- [23] *Go Operator Tutorial*: `https://sdk.operatorframework.io/docs/building-operators/golang/tutorial/`
- [24] *Kopf: Kubernetes Operators Framework*: `https://kopf.readthedocs.io/en/stable/`
- [25] *Operator SDK tutorial for Helm-based Operators*: `https://docs.redhat.com/en/documentation/openshift_container_platform/4.16/html/operators/developing-operators#osdk-helm-tutorial`

- [26] *Helm Operator Tutorial*: `https://sdk.operatorframework.io/docs/building-operators/helm/tutorial/`
- [27] *Cluster Version Operator*: `https://github.com/openshift/cluster-version-operator?tab=readme-ov-file`
- [28] *Cluster Operators reference*: `https://docs.redhat.com/en/documentation/openshift_container_platform/4.16/html/operators/operator-reference`

Quiz

Test your understanding of operators and the Operator Framework with this quick quiz.

1. Which resource does the OLM use to configure RBAC rules for an operator?
    a. `Subscription`
    b. `InstallPlan`
    c. `OperatorGroup`
    d. `OLMConfig`
2. What will happen if you create more than one OperatorGroup in the same namespace?
    a. It won't be created at all
    b. All CSVs created in that namespace will transition into the `Failed` phase and a `TooManyOperatorGroups` event will be emitted
    c. All CSVs created in that namespace will transition into the `Failed` phase and an `UnsupportedOperatorGroup` event will be emitted
    d. Nothing
3. Which command is used to initialize a project and create boilerplate code for a new operator?
    a. `operator-sdk init`
    b. `operator-sdk bootstrap`
    c. `operator-sdk create api`
    d. `operator-sdk create`
4. If we specify both `targetNamespaces` and `selector` in the same OperatorGroup, how will the OLM interpret this?
    a. Effectively, they will be merged
    b. An error will be thrown, because these two fields are mutually exclusive
    c. `selector` will take priority
    d. `targetNamespaces` will take priority
5. Which field of a cluster operator lists all objects managed by that operator?
    a. Managed Objects
    b. Related Objects
    c. Managed Resources
    d. Related Resources

6. What is the capability level of the sample operator that we built in this chapter?
    a. Level I
    b. Level II
    c. Level III
    d. Level IV
    e. Level V

Answers

1. **c.** The purpose of an OperatorGroup is to set up RBAC rules in target namespaces for its member operators, each represented by a CSV.
2. **b.** There can only be one OperatorGroup in a namespace; otherwise, all CSVs in that namespace will assume a failure condition with reason *TooManyOperatorGroups*.
3. **a.** The `operator-sdk init` command bootstraps a new project by creating a minimal directory structure and necessary files.
4. **d.** When both `.spec.targetNamespaces` and `.spec.selector` are specified in the same OperatorGroup, the latter is ignored.
5. **b.** The Related Objects field, as presented in the output of the `oc describe` command, can be used to track down all resources watched by a particular ClusterOperator.
6. **b.** An easy way to determine this is to ask if the operator supports taking backups of our application. Since that operator was created from a Helm chart that doesn't offer that capability by design, then it must be either Level I or II, because any subsequent level requires capabilities from all previous levels. The operator can install a nginx instance, which is a very basic feature provided by Level I. We also previously established that we can easily change the hostname of our managed application by editing the operator's Nginx CR, and the operator will update a `Route` object accordingly. That corresponds to **b**, Level II.

Join us on Discord

For discussions around the book and to connect with your peers, join us on Discord at `http://packt.link/discordcloud` or scan the QR code below:

17

Upgrading OpenShift

In this chapter, we'll dive into the specifics of OpenShift upgrades and the critical role of planning. We'll explore which OpenShift versions are best suited for large enterprise environments, and which versions align more with the needs of fast-growing organizations and start-ups. We'll also cover the key questions of when and how to upgrade, emphasizing the importance of thorough planning. This is particularly crucial for enterprise platforms such as OpenShift, which leads the market in managing containerized applications.

By the end of this chapter, you will know the following:

- The release cadence and life cycle of OpenShift
- Safe upgrade paths and how to plan them effectively
- How to execute an upgrade with hands-on steps

You might wonder why we are focusing so much on upgrades. OpenShift is a complex and ever-evolving platform, and as its steward, you're responsible for overseeing its overall health, managing its features, and ensuring it's running optimally. Ultimately, you will be the one deciding when it's time for an upgrade, and this chapter will equip you to make that call with confidence.

In this chapter, we'll cover the following topics:

- Exploring the release cadence of OpenShift
- Understanding upgrade paths
- Cluster upgrade
- Considerations regarding downgrades

Let's get started!

Technical requirements

For the exercises in this chapter, you will need the following:

- Internet access
- Bash shell (other shells work as well)
- OpenShift Cluster (CRC/OpenShift local won't work)
- Firefox (recommended) or any other web browser
- An active Red Hat subscription to view Red Hat KB articles, the OpenShift Update Graph, and access the update server's API endpoint

Exploring the release cadence of OpenShift

Red Hat OpenShift is an enterprise-grade containerization platform that typically hosts numerous business-critical applications and customer-facing services. Throughout this book, we have extensively covered standardization, planning, and architecture. Now, it's time to discuss how to keep your platform up to date and leverage the standards provided by Red Hat.

Red Hat provides a product life cycle for **OpenShift Container Platform** (**OCP**) to help customers and partners effectively plan, deploy, and support their infrastructure. This life cycle is published for transparency, though exceptions may occur.

OpenShift v4 follows a phased life cycle, supporting at least four minor versions at any time. Each minor version has a fixed support period from its release, with varying levels of support and maintenance. Red Hat aims to release updates every four months, giving customers ample time to plan.

Life cycle phases

Let's describe the main life cycle phases, with a precise look at **Extended Update Support** (**EUS**). EUS is typically available for all even-numbered minor releases, which is crucial for enterprise deployments. Large companies often have slower internal upgrade cycles and complex governance, leading to slower upgrades. Therefore, using odd-numbered releases can cause your environment to run out of support time and create unnecessary back and forth with vendor support.

Let's quickly cover the life cycle phases. There are two main logical parameters for these phases – the duration of the life cycle phase, which is self-explanatory, and coverage, which describes the updates and the versions you can expect in this stage:

- **Full Support phase:**
    - **Duration:** Starts at the GA of the minor version and ends 6 months or 90 days after the next minor release GA, whichever is later.
    - **Coverage:** Includes critical security updates, urgent bug fixes, and other periodic updates. Customers must upgrade to the latest supported patch version for these updates.

- **Maintenance Support phase:**
    - For OpenShift 4.12 and newer:
        - **Duration:** Begins after Full Support and lasts 18 months post-GA.
        - **Coverage:** Provides critical security updates and selected high-priority bug fixes. Other updates are at Red Hat's discretion.
    - For OpenShift 4.7 to 4.11:
        - **Duration:** Starts after Full Support and lasts 12 months. Adjusted if Full Support exceeds 6 months, totaling 18 months combined.
        - **Coverage:** Similar to newer versions with discretionary additional updates.
    - After Maintenance Support, software and documentation remain available, but technical support is limited to upgrade assistance
- **EUS phase:**
    - For OpenShift 4.8 and later (all even-numbered minor releases):
        - **Duration:** Adds six months after Maintenance Support.
        - **Coverage:** Includes critical security updates and urgent bug fixes. EUS allows staying on the same minor release for up to 24 months.
        - **Specifics:** EUS is included with specific Red Hat OpenShift subscriptions and as an add-on for others. It is available across multiple architectures from OpenShift 4.14.
- **EUS Term 2 phase:**
    - For OpenShift 4.14 and later:
        - **Duration:** Adds 12 months of support after EUS.
        - **Coverage:** Extends minor release life cycle to 36 months with critical updates and urgent fixes.
- **Extended Life phase:**
    - For OpenShift 4.8 only:
        - **Coverage:** Provides access to existing content and limited technical support without new updates.
        - **Specifics:** This additional support is available as an optional add-on.

Please take a look at the Red Hat documentation page [1] and save it in your bookmarks; it will be your trusted companion when you plan deployments and upgrades.

Understanding upgrade paths

As you can see, there are multiple different life cycle phases and many details in the way Red Hat releases the OCP; the upgrades from version to version are also slightly specific and usually require some additional work and consideration.

Let's talk about upgrade paths and some key concepts regarding upgrades in general.

Versioning and channels

First, let's discuss versioning. There are the following:

- **Minor and major releases:** OCP upgrades are categorized into major (e.g., 3.x to 4.x) and minor (e.g., 4.6 to 4.7) releases.
    - Major releases usually coincide with fundamental architectural changes – for example, OpenShift 2's proprietary broker-and-gear architecture with cartridges, the move to Docker and Kubernetes in OpenShift 3, and the operator-driven, declarative control plane introduced in OpenShift 4.
    - Minor versions lead the user through changes in the sub-components of the OCP platform.
- **Patch versions:** Patch versions (e.g., 4.6.1 to 4.6.2) typically involve bug fixes and minor improvements. These upgrades are usually straightforward and less disruptive.

OpenShift also uses a few more concepts that are important when you configure a cluster and define its upgrade strategy:

- **EUS:** As discussed earlier, EUS is available for even-numbered minor releases (e.g., 4.8 and 4.10). EUS allows a longer support period, making it easier for enterprises to manage upgrades over a more extended period.
- **Upgrade channels:** The OCP uses upgrade channels to manage how updates are delivered. Channels are categorized as stable, fast, or candidate, indicating the stability and testing level of the updates.

Let's stop for a second and talk about the upgrade channels in more detail. This concept is very similar to upgrades in the Linux world – you can stay with older and more stable versions, move to the modern versions, or even switch to the candidate channel and use the latest versions with all the new features and, of course, bugs.

Let's discuss upgrade channels in more detail:

- **Stable:** The stable channel receives updates with a delay and a gradual rollout. Red Hat evaluates new releases using feedback and telemetry, support cases, and customer clusters that send telemetry and Insights data. This delay, which can range from several hours to about a day for patch and CVE fixes, allows additional validation. If issues are detected, upgrades to that version may be blocked in both the fast and stable channels, and a new version may be promoted as the preferred upgrade target.

- **Fast:** The fast channel is updated with new patch versions as soon as Red Hat declares them generally available. Use this channel if you want to receive updates as early as possible, for example, in pre-production environments that send telemetry to Red Hat. The fast channel includes all patch updates but does not typically recommend upgrades to the next minor release when it becomes available.
- **Candidate:** This channel supplies you with the release candidate versions of the components. In most cases, you won't use it, but if you are running some labs or developing some software for OpenShift, it may be the way to go.

You could use the stable channel for production and the fast channel for pre-production environments that send telemetry and data insights to Red Hat. This allows Red Hat to observe the impact of updates on configurations similar to yours. Future releases may adjust the pace at which updates move from the fast channel to the stable channel based on this feedback.

Customers can switch between fast and stable channels at any time. Channels only offer safe upgrade suggestions and will never suggest a dangerous upgrade. If you switch to the candidate channel after installing a GA version, you might see a warning saying that the current version is not recognized. You can safely switch back to a GA channel. You can learn more about stable and other channels in [2]. Even though the article was originally written for OpenShift 4.2, it is still relevant.

Upgrade path and tools

So, what is an upgrade path? An upgrade path defines the sequence of steps in the upgrade process, specifying which versions should be upgraded to subsequent versions and detailing the necessary actions at each stage. OpenShift provides an upgrade recommendation service that identifies your current version and guides you through the appropriate path within your chosen channel to reach the next release.

> Depending on how critical your environment is and the level of support you have with Red Hat, you may consider opening a proactive case with support before executing an upgrade.

Red Hat supplies the customer with multiple tools that help to define the upgrade path. The most important ones to know are the OpenShift Update Graph [3] and the update server's API endpoint [4]. The OpenShift web UI also provides some high-level information.

Warning!

There is no direct upgrade procedure for major releases. You cannot upgrade from OCP 3 to OCP 4 with a single click or a simple sequence of actions due to significant architectural and component changes. Instead, you must *migrate* your cluster, which involves deploying a new OCP 4 cluster and moving all applications to it. This process may sometimes require a significant redesign of the applications.

These tools are crucial because sometimes you cannot upgrade directly from one version to another. In some cases, you might need to upgrade to a newer version if a direct upgrade path is unavailable.

Perfect! We've just covered upgrade paths and are ready to move on to the update process itself. But before we dive in, let's take a brief detour to discuss the Cincinnati graph. While it's not mandatory to understand it, having a basic grasp of it will give you a more complete view of how OpenShift upgrades work.

Cincinnati graph data

Now that we understand what an upgrade path is, how does it actually work? At the core is Cincinnati – an update protocol designed to manage and automate updates for software projects. It defines a method for representing transitions between different releases, allowing clients (such as OpenShift clusters) to automatically upgrade from one version to another in a controlled and reliable way.

Cincinnati graph data is structured information that defines the relationships and transitions between different software versions. This data is organized in a graph format with the following:

- **Nodes:** Each node represents a specific software version
- **Edges:** The edges between nodes indicate valid upgrade paths

The OpenShift Update Service uses Cincinnati graph data to determine and recommend appropriate upgrade paths for clusters. This ensures updates are applied smoothly and safely by only allowing upgrades that are compatible and tested.

The generic graph for a specific minor version may look a bit complicated:

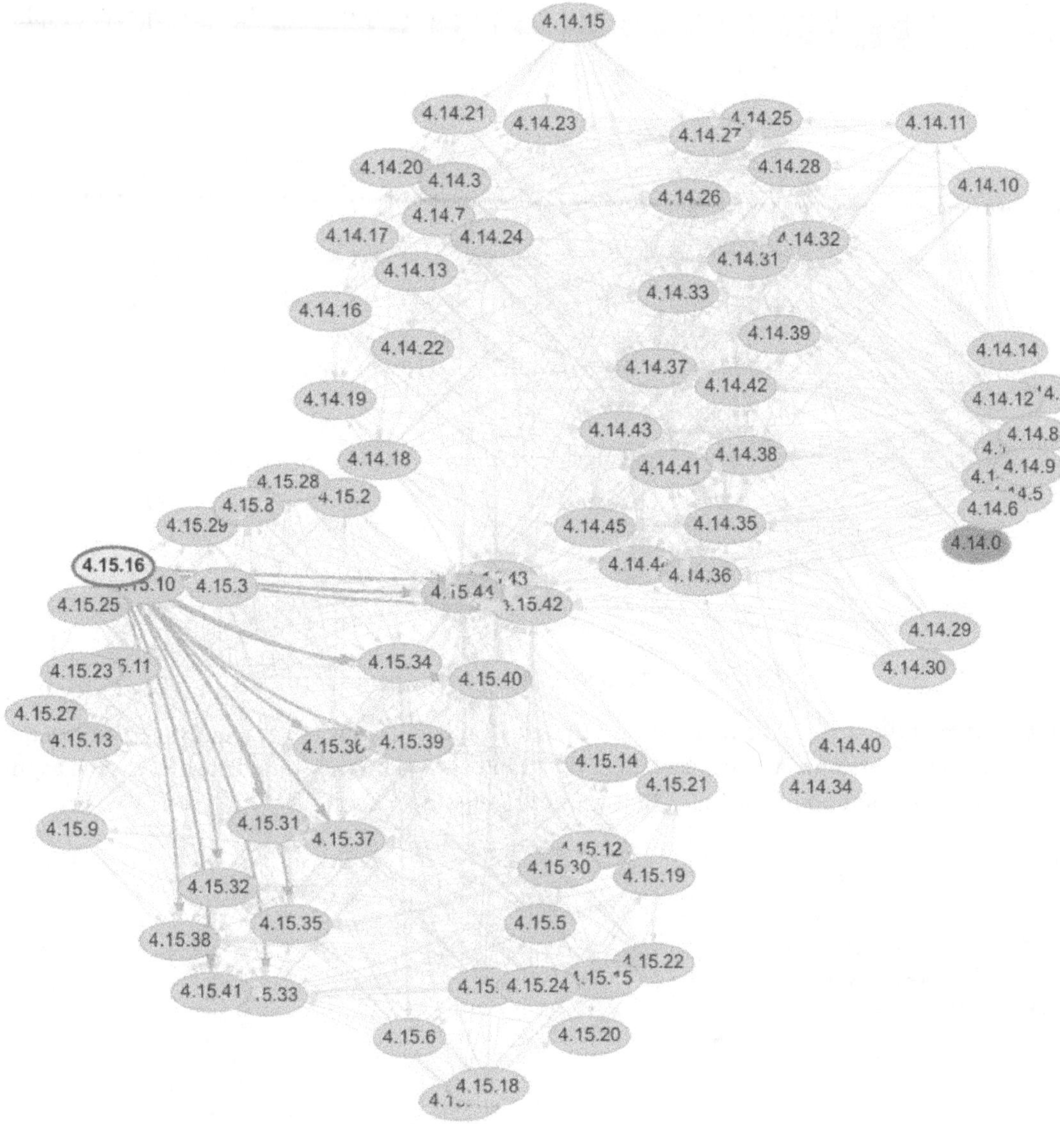

Figure 17.1: An example of a Cincinnati graph

So, it is better to stick with the path representation and recommendations Red Hat may provide and use the graph to drill down into details and see from what versions of Red Hat OpenShift you can jump to the target version.

Let's look at the upgrade path and recommendations generated by the Red Hat OCP Update Graph:

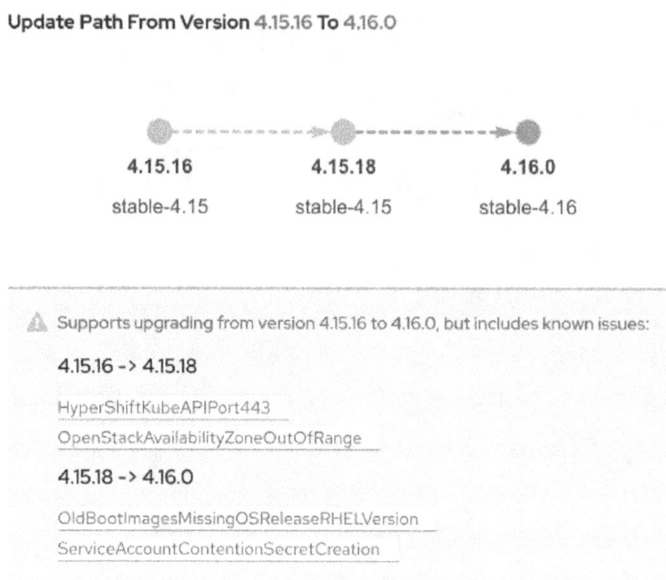

Figure 17.2: OpenShift UI – update path

At the bottom of the screen, the Red Hat OCP Update Graph will show the graph, where you can navigate through the versions. Another benefit of the graph view is links to version artifacts such as the **OpenShift CLI** (oc) and the `openshift-install` utility, as shown here:

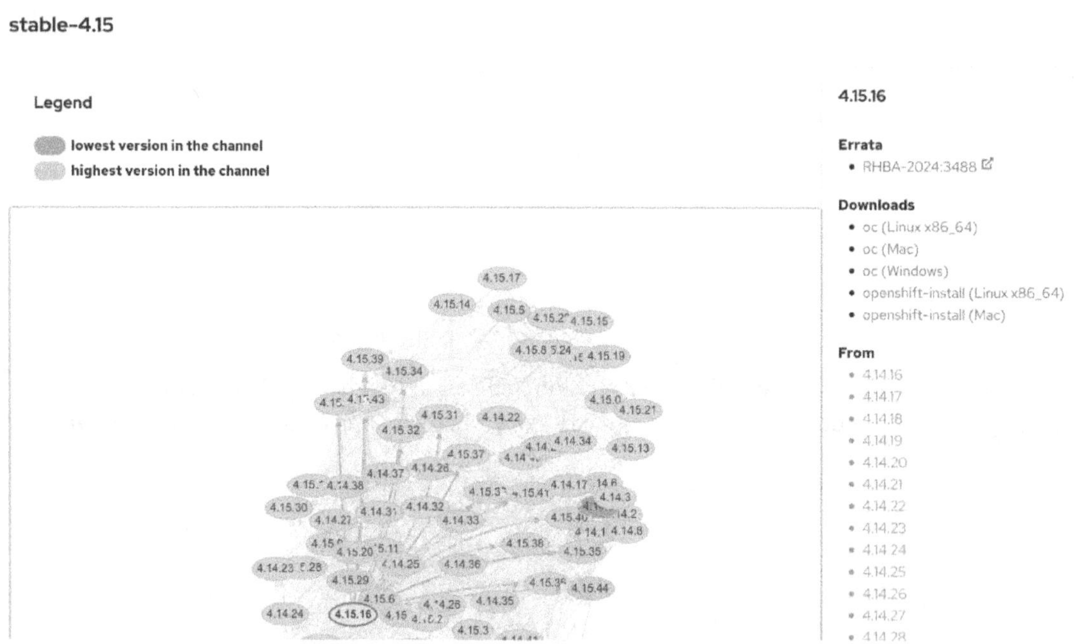

Figure 17.3: OpenShift UI – Cincinnati graph

Let's move forward. We'll take a look at how the path is represented in the OpenShift web UI and plan and execute the upgrade for our lab cluster. You can try to do the same thing using the lab environment on the VMware platform or any other platform; please note that the upgrade won't work for **CodeReady Containers** (CRC), which is now called OpenShift Local. When you have looked at the Cincinnati graph, let's move forward, see how it is used inside the OpenShift UI, and discuss and execute the upgrade process.

Cluster upgrade

With OCP 4, updating a cluster is straightforward and can be done through a single operation using either the web console or oc. Administrators can access new update options in the web console by navigating to **Administration | Cluster Settings** or using the `oc adm upgrade` command.

Red Hat's public **OpenShift Update Service** (**OSUS**) [5] provides a graph of update options based on official OpenShift release images. By default, clusters are configured to connect to OSUS and receive information about available updates. OSUS uses the Cincinnati graph mentioned earlier to validate and show the upgrade paths.

An update begins when a cluster administrator or an automatic update controller edits the **custom resource** (CR) of the **cluster version operator** (CVO) to specify a new version. The CVO then retrieves the target release image from the registry and applies the changes to the cluster.

The target release image includes manifest files for all cluster components in a specific OCP version. During an update, the CVO applies these manifests in stages called **runlevels**. Most manifests support a cluster operator, which may perform tasks to align with its new version. The CVO monitors the status of each resource and the states reported by all cluster operators, proceeding with the update only when all manifests and operators in the current runlevel are stable. Once the control plane is updated, the **machine config operator** (MCO) updates the operating system and the configuration of each node in the cluster.

Let's move on and talk about OSUS and the critical role it plays in upgrade procedures.

OpenShift Update Service

OSUS helps to manage updates for the OCP, including **Red Hat Enterprise Linux CoreOS** (**RHCOS**). OSUS uses a **Directed Acyclic Graph** (**DAG**) to represent the update paths. In this graph, vertices represent update payloads for cluster components and edges indicate safe update transitions between versions.

CVO in your cluster communicates with OSUS to determine valid updates and paths based on the current cluster version and the update graph. When an update is requested, the CVO fetches the corresponding release image from `quay.io`, a registry where the release artifacts are hosted as container images.

To ensure compatibility, each released artifact undergoes a verification process. This release verification pipeline checks compatibility with supported cloud platforms, system architectures, and other component packages. The pipeline's status page for releases designed for AMD64 architecture is available at [6]. Once a release passes these checks, OSUS makes it available and notifies the administrator that it is ready for deployment.

During continuous update mode in OpenShift, two controllers are active:

- **Payload controller**: This controller continuously updates and applies payload manifests to the cluster. It monitors the status of the operators, indicating whether they are available, upgrading, or failing.
- **Update service controller**: This controller checks with OSUS to see whether new updates are available.

During an update, the MCO applies new configurations to the cluster machines. Here's a breakdown of the process:

1. **Cordoning nodes**: The MCO cordons off nodes, marking them unavailable for scheduling. The number of nodes cordoned at a time is specified in each `MachineConfigPool` with the `maxUnavailable` field, which defaults to `1`.
2. **Updating nodes**: Nodes are updated alphabetically by zone, based on the `topology.kubernetes.io/zone` label. Within each zone, the oldest nodes are updated first. If zones are not used (e.g., in bare-metal deployments), nodes are updated by age, starting with the oldest.
3. **Applying configuration and rebooting**: The MCO applies the new configuration to the selected nodes and reboots them. This process repeats the number of nodes specified by the `maxUnavailable` field until all nodes are updated.

> If you use **Red Hat Enterprise Linux (RHEL)** machines as workers, the MCO does not update the kubelet. You must first update the OpenShift API on these machines before updating the kubelet.

Now that you are aware of OSUS, it is time to talk about the CVO.

Cluster Version Operator

The CVO monitors cluster operators and components, collecting status information about the cluster version and its operators. This status includes condition types that inform administrators about the health and state of the OCP cluster. To understand whether the cluster is healthy, upgrading, or stuck, administrators should look at the conditions exposed by the Cluster Version Operator on the ClusterVersion object – let's take a look at these conditions:

- CVO's condition types:
  - `Available`: Indicates that an operator is functional. If `False`, a part of the operand is not working and needs administrator attention.
  - `Progressing`: Indicates that an operator is rolling out new code or making changes. It does not display `True` when reconciling a known state but does when responding to state changes.
  - `Degraded`: Indicates persistent issues where an operator's current state doesn't match its required state. This condition requires administrator intervention and does not occur during normal updates.

- Additional condition types include the following:
    - `Failing`: Indicates the cluster cannot reach its desired state and is unhealthy, requiring administrator intervention.
    - `Invalid`: Indicates an error in the cluster version preventing the server from taking action. The CVO only reconciles the current state while this condition is set.
    - `RetrievedUpdates`: Indicates whether updates have been retrieved from the update server. It is `Unknown` before retrieval, `False` if updates failed or couldn't be retrieved, and `True` if the updates are recent and accurate.
    - `ReleaseAccepted`: Indicates that the requested release payload was successfully loaded and verified without failure.
    - `ImplicitlyEnabledCapabilities`: Indicates there are enabled capabilities that were not requested by the user. The CVO does not support disabling capabilities if previously managed resources are involved.

You will be working with the CVO whenever you plan, perform, or troubleshoot cluster upgrades. To make those processes easier, the following diagram illustrates how CVO conditions usually change over time and the typical reasons behind those changes.

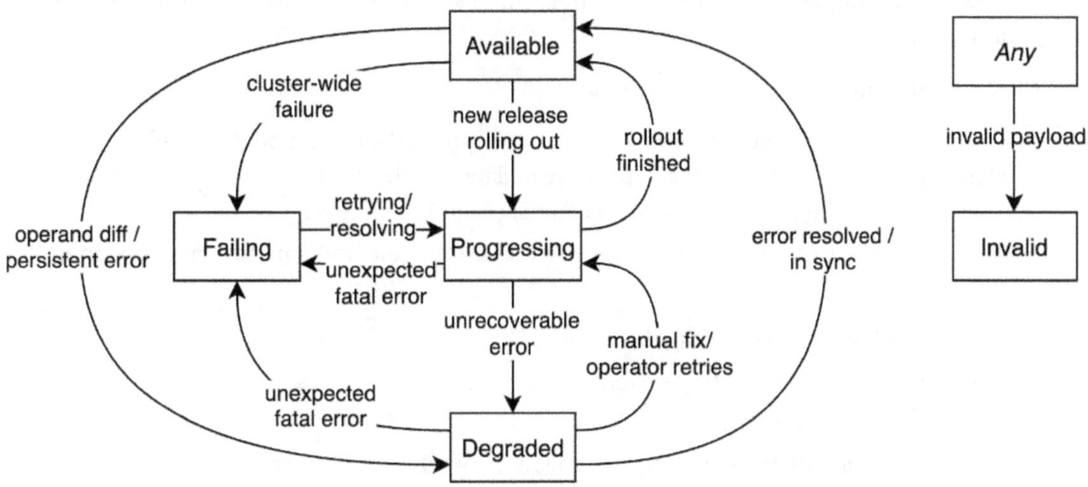

Figure 17.4: CVO conditions graph

Great! You now have a good understanding of all the components involved in the upgrade process, which is an excellent start. Now, let's dive into how to estimate the upgrade time – a crucial factor in planning and setting realistic expectations with other teams and management. So, how can we approach this estimation? Let's explore what guidance Red Hat provides to support this step.

Cluster upgrade duration

The time it takes to update OCP varies based on deployment topology. This guide explains the factors that affect update duration and helps you estimate how long updates will take in your environment.

Several factors can impact how long it takes to update your OpenShift cluster:

- **Node reboots:**
    - The value of `MaxUnavailable` in `MachineConfigPool`.
    - The minimum number or percentages of replicas set in the **pod disruption budgets (PDBs)** of protected applications.
    - Whether the nodes are physical or virtual. Bare-metal nodes typically take longer to reboot and initialize, sometimes 5-7 minutes or even longer.

> **Warning!**
>
> The default setting for `maxUnavailable` is `1` for all the machine config pools in OCP. It is recommended that you do not change this value and update one control plane node at a time. *Do not change this value to 3 for the control plane pool.*

- **Number of nodes:** The total number of nodes in the cluster impacts the update time.
- **Node health:** The overall health of the cluster nodes also influences update duration.
- **The number of pods** in a cluster. The more there are in a cluster, the longer it takes to drain a single node.

In OCP, the cluster update happens in two phases:

- **CVO update deployment:** The CVO retrieves and applies the target update release image to the cluster. All components running as pods are updated during this phase, while host components are updated by the MCO. This process can take 60 to 120 minutes.
- **MCO node updates:** The MCO updates each control plane and compute node by doing the following:
    - Cordoning and draining the nodes
    - Updating the operating system
    - Rebooting the nodes
    - Uncordoning the nodes and rescheduling workloads on them

Red Hat provides clear reference diagrams [7] that illustrate the upgrade sequence across cluster components and the typical duration of each step. It also documents a practical formula you can use to estimate how long an upgrade is likely to take in your environment:

Cluster update time = CVO target update payload deployment time + (# node update iterations x MCO node update time)

For example, cluster update time = 60 + (3 x 5) = 75 minutes.

Cluster upgrade

Before we start an upgrade, we need to define what version of OpenShift we are currently running and see (more easily via the web UI) what channel is in use and what upgrade path is available.

Every upgrade procedure in an Enterprise environment should start with a few initial steps:

1. Read the release notes [8] for the target release and plan your time accordingly.
2. Create a proactive support case if your subscription level allows.
3. Read the upgrade documentation [9] and check for any API deprecations.
4. Migrate deprecated APIs, as explained in [10].
5. Assess conditional update risks; see [11] for details.
6. Back up `etcd`, as explained in [12].
7. Select versions recommended by OSUS.
8. Resolve any critical alerts on the cluster.
9. Verify that the cluster is in an upgradable state:
    a. All nodes are `Ready`.
    b. Cluster operators and MachineConfigPools are `Healthy`.
    c. You can execute `oc get no,co,mcp,clusterversion` to check the health.
10. Make sure there are enough spare nodes available.
11. Ensure the cluster's PDBs are appropriately configured.

In step 11, it's worth noting that incorrectly configured PDBs may block cluster upgrades, making MCO unable to drain a node. This happens when deleting a pod to drain the node would violate the `minAvailable` or `maxUnavailable` settings of the PDB. If you notice that draining a particular node takes too long, you can try draining it manually and see whether there are any warnings related to PDBs.

In our case, the cluster is running 4.15.16, and we will upgrade to the latest 4.16.z release that the update graph marks as an available/recommended target for our cluster.

> If you initially deployed OCP 4.16.x, then *Stage C* is optional.

Let's proceed further and upgrade the cluster.

Stage A – Preparing for an upgrade

Let's follow the steps from the previous section and check a couple of things via the oc CLI (you will use an administrator-level user for all the upgrade steps):

1. Back up `etcd`:

    1. Start a debug session as root for a control plane node:

        ```
        $ oc debug --as-root node/<node_name>
        ```

    2. Change your root directory to `/host` in the debug shell:

        ```
        sh-4.4# chroot /host
        ```

    3. Run the `cluster-backup.sh` script in the debug shell:

        ```
        /usr/local/bin/cluster-backup.sh /home/core/assets/backup
        ```

        At this point, it is a good idea to copy the backup to a secure location, either with `scp` (if SSH is enabled) or with `oc cp`.

    4. Exit the debug session by typing `exit` or pressing *Ctrl* + *D* twice, first to exit `chroot` and second to exit the session itself.

2. Check that all nodes are healthy and in the `Ready` status with `oc get nodes`:

```
$ oc get nodes
NAME                          STATUS   ROLES                  AGE   VERSION
master-1.cluster.example.com   Ready    control-plane,master   40d   v1.28.10+a2c84a5
master-2.cluster.example.com   Ready    control-plane,master   40d   v1.28.10+a2c84a5
master-3.cluster.example.com   Ready    control-plane,master   40d   v1.28.10+a2c84a5
worker-1.cluster.example.com   Ready    worker                 40d   v1.28.10+a2c84a5
worker-2.cluster.example.com   Ready    worker                 40d   v1.28.10+a2c84a5
worker-3.cluster.example.run   Ready    worker                 40d   v1.28.10+a2c84a5
```

Figure 17.5: Node readiness check

3. Check that all the cluster operators are healthy with `oc get co`:

```
$ oc get co | head
NAME                        VERSION   AVAILABLE   PROGRESSING   DEGRADED   SINCE   MESSAGE
authentication              4.16.29   True        False         False      11h
baremetal                   4.16.29   True        False         False      15d
cloud-controller-manager    4.16.29   True        False         False      15d
cloud-credential            4.16.29   True        False         False      15d
cluster-autoscaler          4.16.29   True        False         False      15d
config-operator             4.16.29   True        False         False      15d
console                     4.16.29   True        False         False      15d
control-plane-machine-set   4.16.29   True        False         False      15d
csi-snapshot-controller     4.16.29   True        False         False      15d
```

Figure 17.6: Operator readiness check

When you run the `oc get co` command, you expect to see the list of cluster operators and their status. If every entry in the `DEGRADED` column is `False` and every entry in the `AVAILABLE` column is `True`, the cluster is healthy and ready for an upgrade. The `VERSION` column will display the version of OpenShift you are currently running.

If you see something unexpected, such as nodes not being ready or operators failing, please do not upgrade your cluster. Instead, reach out to Red Hat for support.

> **Warning!**
>
> Upgrading from OpenShift Data Foundation version 4.15 to 4.16 is blocked due to a known issue. Only fresh deployments of OpenShift Data Foundation 4.16 are currently supported. This limitation will be removed in the upcoming OpenShift Data Foundation 4.16.z release. See [13].

Stage B – Defining an upgrade path

Let's continue by defining the upgrade path for our cluster:

1. Log in to the OpenShift web UI using `kubeadmin` or another administrator-level account.
2. Navigate to **Administration | Cluster Settings** on the left side of the screen.
3. Now, let's check the current version and channel on the **Details** page:

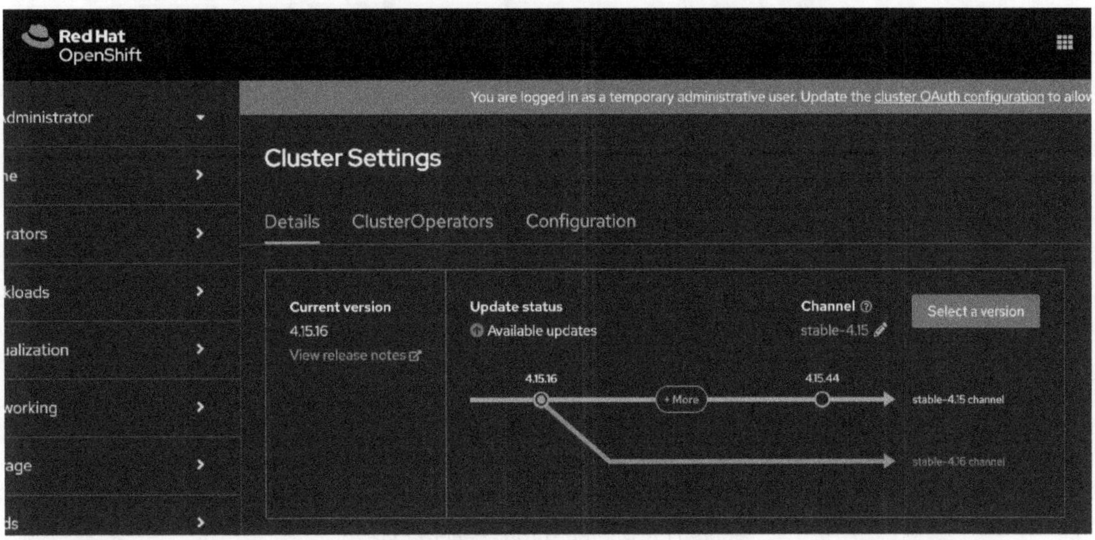

Figure 17.7: Cluster upgrade state

4. Go to the Red Hat OCP Update Graph [3] and make the following selections:
    - **Current Channel: stable-4.15**
    - **Architecture: x86_64**
    - **Current OpenShift Version: 4.15.16**
    - **Target OpenShift Version: 4.16.32**

> Please note that the version will probably be different when you read this book; please act accordingly.

This is shown here:

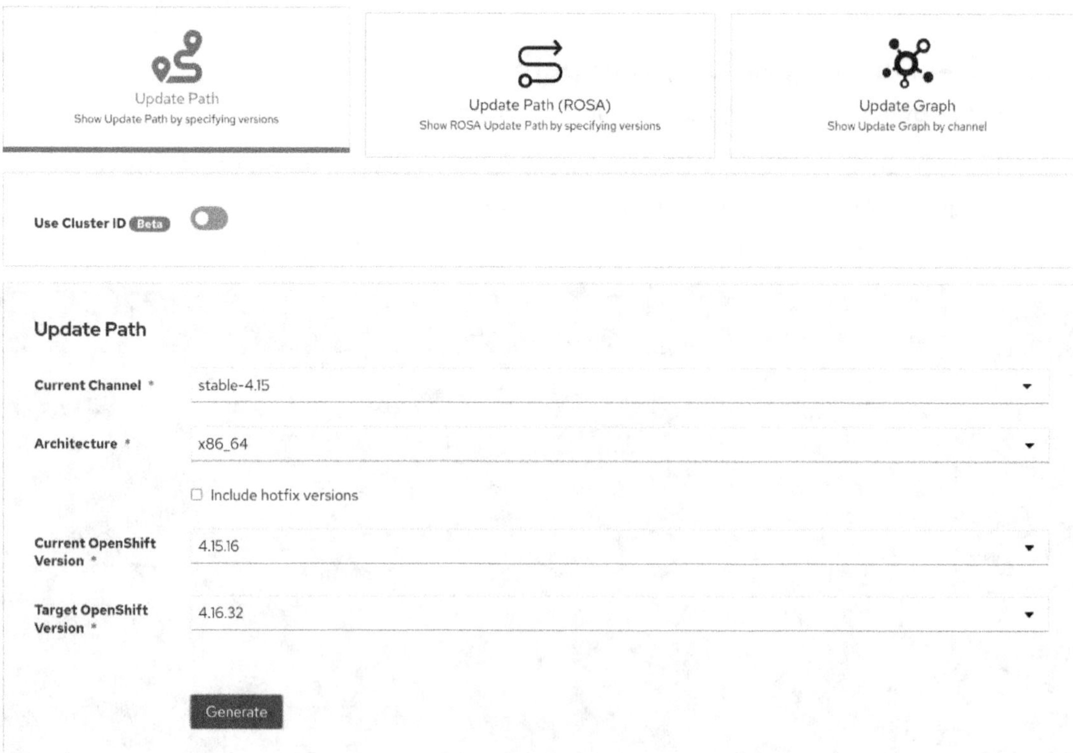

Figure 17.8: Upgrade graph generation – A

5. Then click **Generate** and review recommendations (switch to the **Web** tab for simplicity):

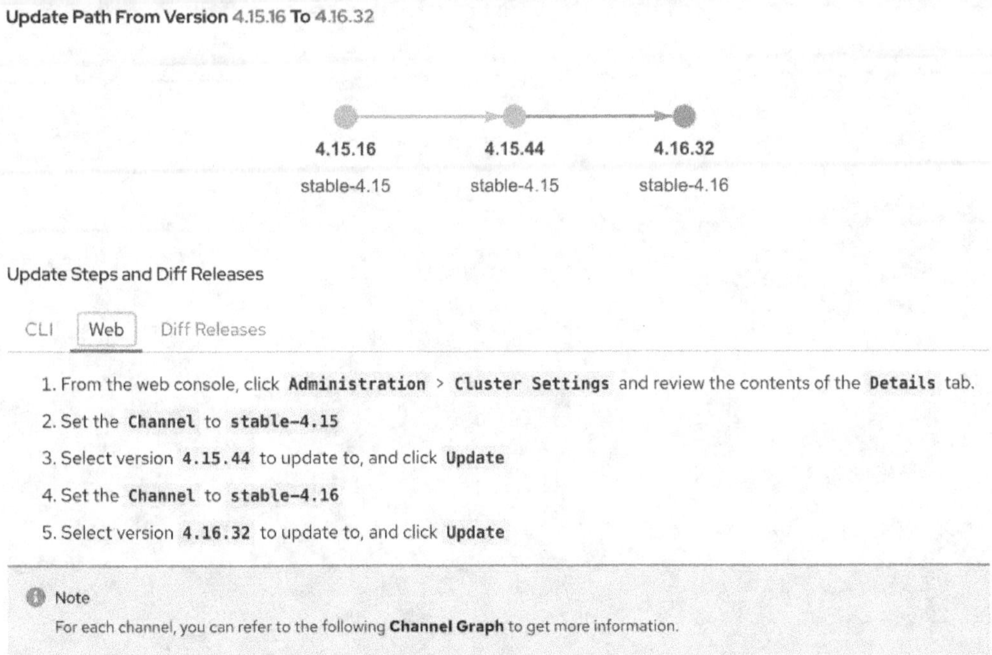

Figure 17.9: Upgrade Graph Generation – B

Perfect! Let's proceed with the recommended steps: upgrade to a patch version and then upgrade the minor version. Please note that the application allows you to move straight to 4.16.32.

Stage C – Upgrading to the recommended patch version

This is how we upgrade to the recommended patch version:

1. Log in to the OpenShift web UI using `kubeadmin` or another administrator-level account.
2. Go to **Administration** | **Cluster Settings** and review the **Details** tab; the channel should already be `stable-4.15`, so we do nothing with it.
3. Click on the **Select a version** button and then pick the recommended one: `4.15.44`.
4. Then, click **Upgrade** and you will see the following screen:

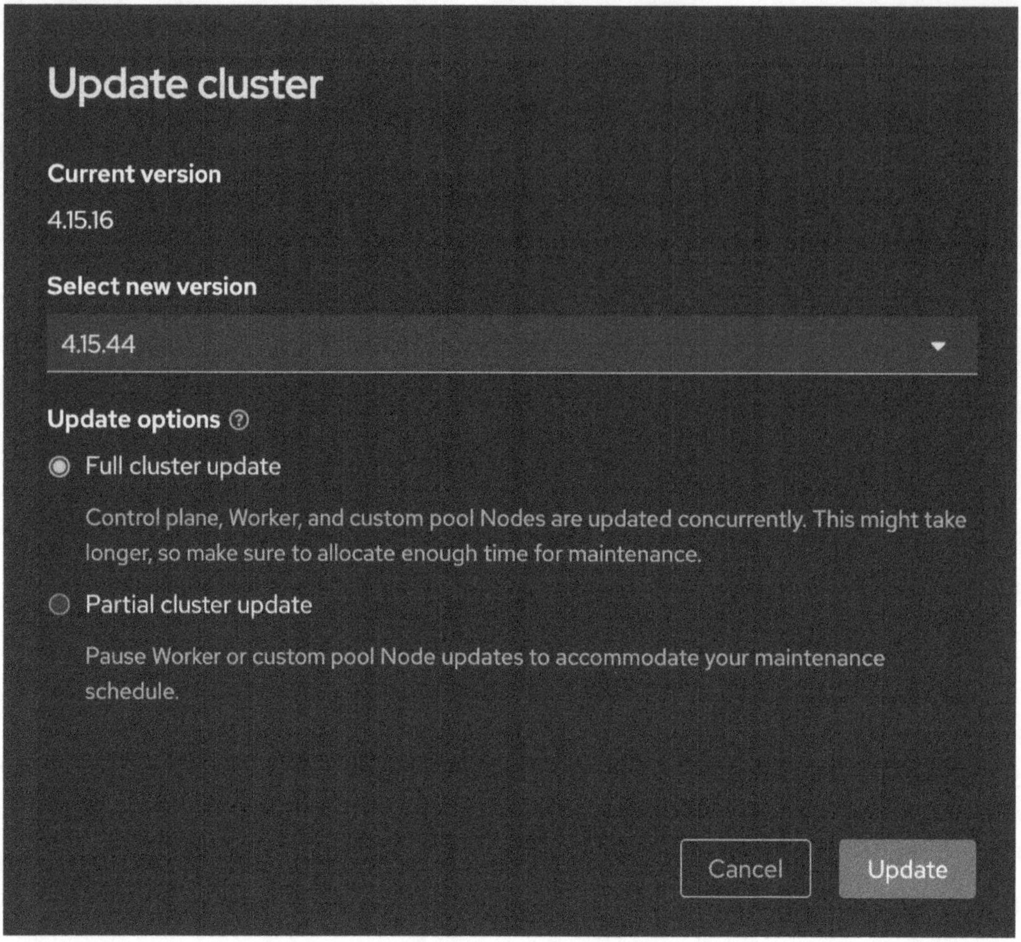

Figure 17.10: Version selection

Wait for a couple of minutes, and the UI will show you a banner that notifies you that the upgrade procedure has started:

Figure 17.11: Cluster upgrade notification

As soon as the upgrade starts, the **Administration | Cluster Settings | Details** page will show the upgrade status. Now you can leave the operators to do the upgrade, checking the status from time to time and, in the meantime, making a coffee or writing some scripts. The upgrade for six nodes – three control planes and three workers – may take up to 60 minutes but usually takes about 30-40 minutes. As the UI suggests, and as we discussed before, the upgrade will handle the cluster operators first, then control plane nodes, then worker nodes.

Please look at the following screenshot, which describes the upgrade status. In this case, 2 out of 33 cluster operators have already been upgraded:

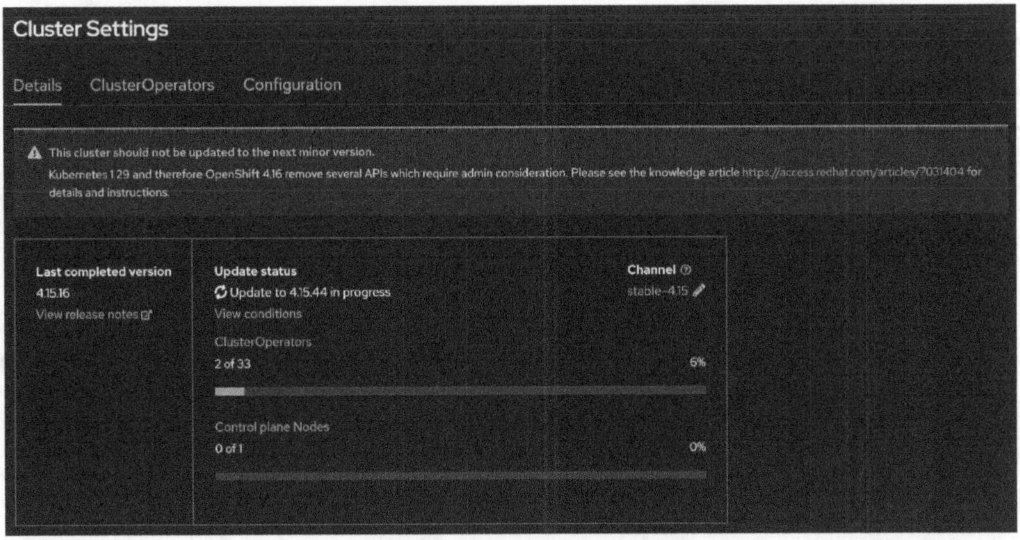

Figure 17.12: Upgrade process status

Please be patient and do not reboot your cluster nodes. Eventually, stage C will end with the following result:

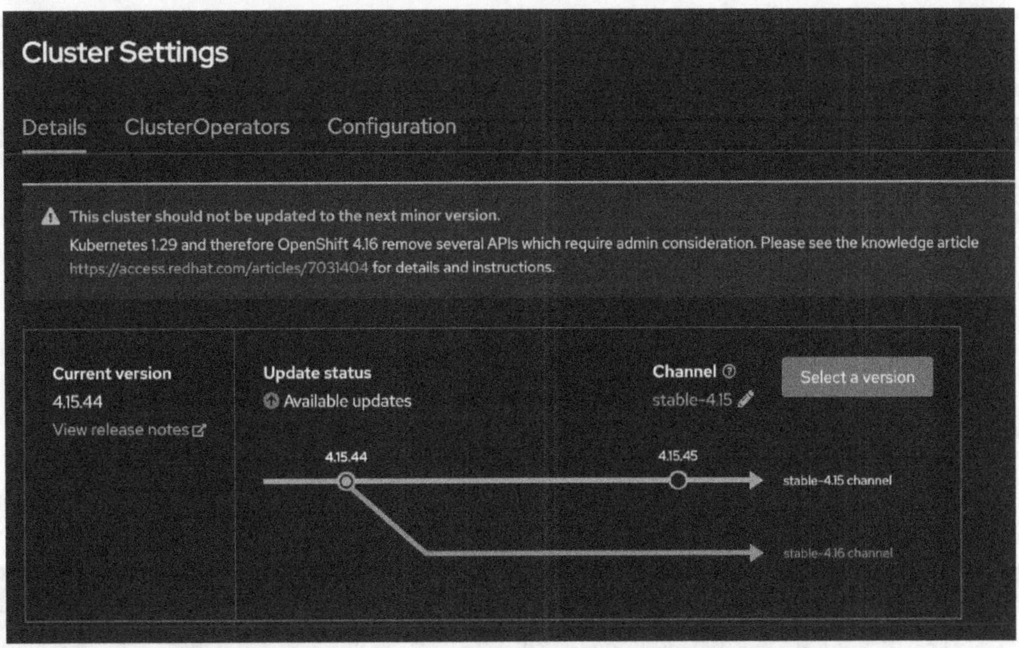

Figure 17.13: Upgrade finalization

As you may have noticed, the graph has a fork, and we need to switch a channel and move to version 4.16 as we planned. Let's proceed to stage D, checking whether the cluster can be upgraded.

Stage D – Upgrading to the recommended minor version

If you are upgrading to 4.16, you may need to review the article at [14].

The article says that two API are removed in Kubernetes 1.29, which is a base version for OCP 4.16; the document says: "*Kubernetes 1.29 removed the following deprecated APIs. If your cluster, or any idle workloads or tools use any of these APIs, you must migrate them to the appropriate new version before upgrading to OpenShift Container Platform 4.16.*"

For example, here is the table for the deprecated APIs:

Resource	API	Notable changes
`Flowschemas`	`flowcontrol.apiserver.k8s.io/v1beta2`	No
`prioritylevelconfigurations`	`flowcontrol.apiserver.k8s.io/v1beta2`	Yes

Table 17.1: Deprecated APIs

So, what changes? `flowSchemas` and `priorityLevelConfigurations` are part of the Kubernetes **API Priority and Fairness** (**APF**) feature, which helps manage the flow of requests to the Kubernetes API server, ensuring fair usage and the prioritization of requests. Please review the definition of the change on the Kubernetes documentation page [15]. Let's run the following command and see whether the `flowcontrol.apiserver.k8s.io/v1beta2` API is being used:

```
$ oc get apirequestcounts flowschemas.v1beta2.flowcontrol.apiserver.k8s.io
```

If the requests show nothing, we are good to go and there is nothing to migrate currently.

Alternatively, you can also run just a simple command such as this and see what versions of the API are being used:

```
$ oc get apirequestcounts | grep flowcontrol
flowschemas.v1beta3.flowcontrol.apiserver.k8s.io
prioritylevelconfigurations.v1beta3.flowcontrol.apiserver.k8s.io
```

Figure 17.14: Flow control v1beta2 check

So, we see no `flowcontrol.apiserver.k8s.io/v1beta2`. Let's acknowledge that we have completed the evaluation and move forward:

```
$ oc -n openshift-config patch cm admin-acks --patch \
'{"data":{"ack-4.15-kube-1.29-api-removals-in-4.16":"true"}}' --type=merge
```

Now, if you navigate back to the OpenShift web UI and go to **Administration** | **Cluster Settings**, you will notice there are no warnings anymore, and it seems we are ready to move forward. But, before we do this, please ensure that you run through all the important checks again:

- You have an `etcd` backup
- Cluster operators are in good shape
- Nodes are in good shape
- There are no major events or errors

Now, let's proceed with the following steps:

1. Change the channel version: Click **Channel**, select **stable-4.16**, and click **Save**.

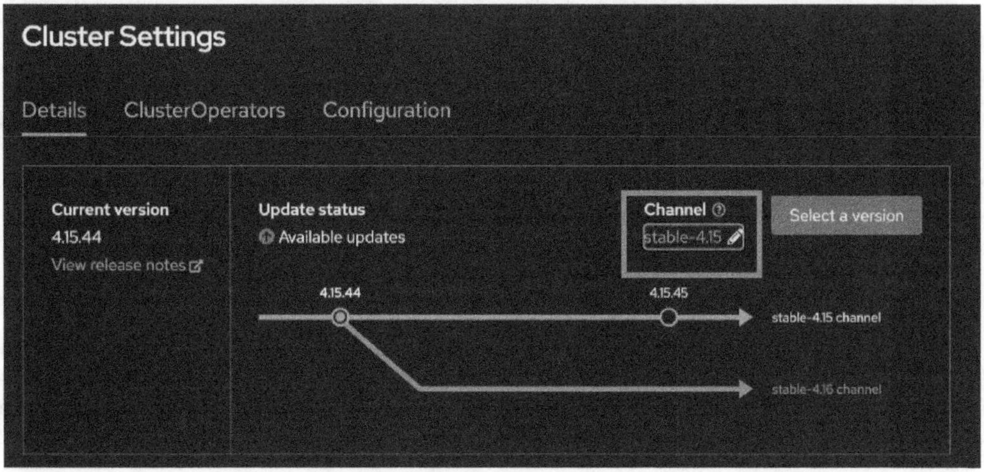

Figure 17.15: Channel version

2. Now the data on the web UI has changed, and it seems our cluster is upgradable:

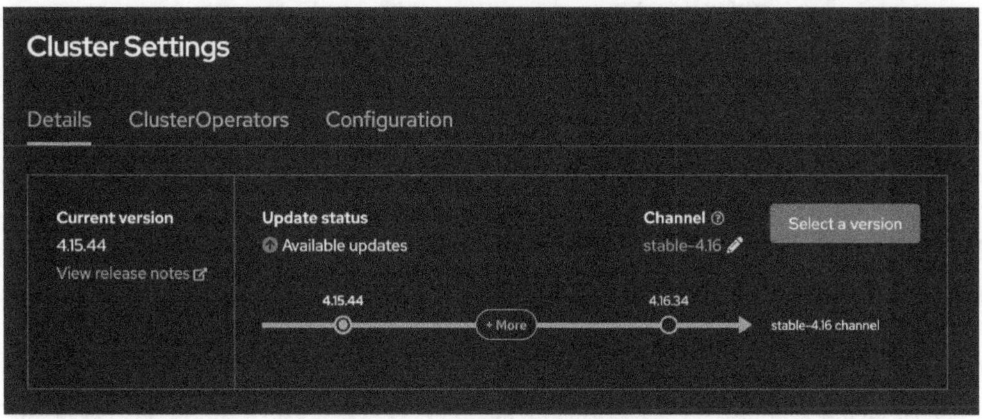

Figure 17.16: An updated upgrade path

3. Click **Select a version** | **Select new version**, select **4.16.32**, and click the **Update** button.

This is it; now we need to wait again for the cluster to be updated. The upgrade procedure will take some time. As soon as the upgrade is finished, you can review the status of the cluster on the same, familiar page: **Administration | Cluster Settings**.

Optional stage – Troubleshooting

We expect your upgrade will go smoothly and won't generate any problems, but in real life, you may face issues such as a stalled upgrade procedure or an unavailable API or UI. This is why a proactive support case may be a great idea. What would you do if the upgrade failed? You have to collect information and share it with Red Hat Support. It is important to know what information to get:

1. Gather the `must-gather` output:

   ```
   $ oc adm must-gather
   ```

2. Gather the `ClusterVersion` history:

   ```
   $ oc describe clusterversions/version
   ```

There are other ways to gather more information or even fix the upgrade; it all depends on how deeply you know the OCP and Kubernetes. We will cover some essential approaches and tools in the next chapter of this book.

Considerations regarding downgrades

It is essential to include this section in the book, but there is very little to say. Downgrades are not officially supported by OpenShift 4. Please do not plan them in production, but you are welcome to experiment in the lab at your own risk. Please check the KB article [16] for more details.

Summary

Now, you are familiar with OpenShift upgrade procedures and some potential hiccups. We still encourage you to keep in touch with the Red Hat team while working on cluster upgrades in your enterprise environment – proactive support cases help to improve your and your users' experience.

We recommend you have a go at the chapter quiz and proceed to the next chapter, where we will talk about how exactly to open support cases and work with Red Hat Support, supplying the Red Hat experts with the most relevant and useful data.

References

To learn more about the topics that were covered in this chapter, take a look at the following resources:

- [1] *Red Hat OpenShift Container Platform Life Cycle Policy*: `https://access.redhat.com/support/policy/updates/openshift/`
- [2] *OpenShift 4.2 Upgrades phased roll out*: `https://access.redhat.com/articles/4495171`
- [3] *Red Hat OpenShift Container Platform Update Graph*: `https://access.redhat.com/labs/ocpupgradegraph/update_path/`

- [4] Update server's API endpoint: https://api.openshift.com/api/upgrades_info/v1/graph
- [5] *OpenShift Update Service: Update Manager for Your Cluster*: https://www.redhat.com/en/blog/openshift-update-service-update-manager-for-your-cluster
- [6] OpenShift 4 release status: https://amd64.ocp.releases.ci.openshift.org
- [7] *Understanding OpenShift Container Platform update duration*: https://docs.redhat.com/en/documentation/openshift_container_platform/4.16/html/updating_clusters/understanding-openshift-updates-1#understanding-openshift-update-duration
- [8] RHOCP 4.16 release notes: https://docs.redhat.com/en/documentation/openshift_container_platform/4.16/html-single/release_notes/index
- [9] *Preparing to update to OpenShift Container Platform 4.16*: https://docs.redhat.com/en/documentation/openshift_container_platform/4.16/html/updating_clusters/preparing-to-update-a-cluster#updating-cluster-prepare
- [10] Deprecated API migration guide: https://kubernetes.io/docs/reference/using-api/deprecation-guide/#v1-29
- [11] *Assessing the risk of conditional updates*: https://docs.redhat.com/en/documentation/openshift_container_platform/4.16/html/updating_clusters/preparing-to-update-a-cluster#update-preparing-conditional_updating-cluster-prepare
- [12] *Backing up etcd*: https://docs.redhat.com/en/documentation/openshift_container_platform/4.16/html/backup_and_restore/control-plane-backup-and-restore
- [13] *Updating OpenShift Data Foundation*: https://docs.redhat.com/en/documentation/red_hat_openshift_data_foundation/4.16/html-single/updating_openshift_data_foundation/index
- [14] *Preparing to upgrade to OpenShift Container Platform 4.16*: https://access.redhat.com/articles/7031404
- [15] *Flow control resources*: https://kubernetes.io/docs/reference/using-api/deprecation-guide/#flowcontrol-resources-v129
- [16] *Is it possible to downgrade a version in OpenShift Container Platform 4?*: https://access.redhat.com/solutions/4777861
- [17] *The Ultimate Guide to OpenShift Update for Cluster Administrators*: https://www.redhat.com/en/blog/the-ultimate-guide-to-openshift-update-for-cluster-administrators

Quiz

Let's test your knowledge with a few simple questions about the topics covered in this chapter:

1. What is the primary purpose of the **cluster version operator** (CVO) during an OpenShift update?
    a. Deploying new applications
    b. Managing the cluster's upgrade process and collecting status conditions from operators
    c. Handling persistent storage configuration
    d. Monitoring network traffic

2. Which command should you use to check whether your OpenShift cluster is upgradable?
    a. `oc get secrets`
    b. `oc describe clusterversion/version`
    c. `oc adm upgrade`
    d. `oc get pods`
3. What role does the **machine config operator** (**MCO**) play during an OpenShift update?
    a. It manages the deployment of new applications
    b. It handles updating the machine configuration and rebooting nodes
    c. It monitors the network traffic
    d. It collects logs from all nodes
4. Which step is *not* recommended before performing an upgrade on an OpenShift cluster?
    a. Ensuring the cluster is in an upgradable state
    b. Backing up `etcd`
    c. Addressing all critical alerts
    d. Changing `maxUnavailable` to `3` for the control plane pool
5. Which of the following is a crucial factor that affects the duration of an OpenShift cluster update?
    a. The number of cluster administrators
    b. The `maxUnavailable` value in the machine config pool
    c. The number of ReplicaSets
    d. The number of services

Answers

1. **b**. The **cluster version operator** (**CVO**) is responsible for managing OpenShift cluster updates, coordinating the update process across cluster components, and collecting feedback from operators about their status. It is not responsible for deploying apps, handling storage, or monitoring traffic.
2. **b**. The `oc describe clusterversion/version` command shows the current OpenShift version and upgrade availability. It shows you the current state, desired version, available updates, and upgrade history. Other options, such as `oc get nodes` and `oc get pods`, do not show the upgrade status.
3. **b**. The MCO applies configuration changes to nodes (e.g., kernel arguments, CRI-O settings, and certificates) and orchestrates node reboots when necessary. It ensures that the nodes meet the desired state during an upgrade.
4. **d**. Changing `maxUnavailable` to `3` for control plane nodes is dangerous – you risk taking down the quorum for `etcd` (which usually requires at least 2 out of 3 masters to remain available). Control plane upgrades are done conservatively, usually one at a time. The other steps (ensuring upgradeable state, backing up `etcd`, and addressing alerts) are strongly recommended.

5. **b.** The `maxUnavailable` parameter of a `MachineConfigPool` value controls how many nodes can be updated (rebooted) at once. A low value (e.g., `1`) means updates proceed slowly (one at a time); increasing it speeds up updates but can impact availability. It's a direct factor in upgrade pacing.

18

Troubleshooting and Maintenance

OpenShift 4 is a sophisticated platform composed of numerous subsystems, each playing a critical role across the control plane, infrastructure, and worker nodes. When configured according to Red Hat's guidelines and best practices, OpenShift generally provides a stable and reliable environment. However, even with a well-configured setup, the complexity of the platform, microservices, and applications means that issues can occasionally arise, necessitating careful troubleshooting and maintenance.

In this chapter, we offer practical guidance on how to address common challenges within OpenShift 4. We'll delve into a range of tools and techniques designed to help you maintain the smooth operation of your clusters. Whether it's diagnosing issues, applying necessary fixes, or customizing configurations, the insights here will equip you with the knowledge to ensure that your OpenShift environment remains robust and resilient.

For the current chapter, we assume you have a `cluster-admin` role and can connect to your nodes and see all the workload on the cluster. Some tools and approaches may also work for unprivileged users within their namespaces, but with a user who has a `cluster-admin` role, for example, `kubeadmin`, you will definitely see and be able to do more.

In this chapter, we'll cover the following topics:

- Using the debug shell
- Accessing CoreOS via SSH
- Introducing persistent changes to CoreOS
- Using `must-gather`
- The sos report command
- Debugging pods

Let's get started!

Technical requirements

In this chapter, you will need the following:

- Bash or another shell.
- OpenShift 4.16 cluster. Please consider using a dedicated (multi-node or single-node) cluster for the section on RHOCS layering. If you plan to skip it, feel free to use OpenShift Local (CRC).
- Firefox (recommended) or any other browser.
- An active Red Hat subscription, to view Red Hat KB articles.

You can access this book's GitHub repository at `https://github.com/PacktPublishing/Learn-OpenShift-Second-Edition`.

Using the debug shell

Like any complex system, OpenShift sometimes needs debugging. When issues occur, the person managing the cluster may need to run commands on failing pods or nodes. We also need to consider that SSH should not be used for node access whenever possible, for the reasons that we mentioned back in *Chapter 3, Getting Started with OpenShift, Installation Methods > Prerequisites > SSH*. So, how can you access a node for service actions or debugging without using SSH? The solution is the **debug shell** – a universal tool for debugging nodes and pods.

It lets you interact with containers directly, giving you access to logs, running processes, and the filesystem. You can use it to troubleshoot problems such as environment configuration errors and missing files, or to check the state of a running container. In this section, we'll cover how to start a debug session, navigate within the shell, and use common commands for effective troubleshooting.

Before we dive into the debug shell and all the debugging approaches, let's summarize the reasons why the debug shell is preferred and encouraged by Red Hat:

- `oc debug` goes through the API server and is fully audited and gated by RBAC.
- Users won't "hand-tweak" nodes. The MCO manages RHCOS; SSH edits can cause unexpected configuration drift.
- Debug pods/containers are temporary, so you leave no long-lived changes or credentials behind.
- It avoids managing SSH keys and opening inbound ports to nodes. Nevertheless, most enterprises consider SSH as the last resort and "break glass" access.

We will discuss SSH further in the chapter; for now, let's focus on the recommended and safer debug approach.

Debugging nodes

Before you jump into the debug shell, you would probably need to review your cluster's nodes' status and maybe see some basic information about them; let's quickly recap what commands may be useful:

- To get a list of nodes, run the following:

```
$ oc get nodes
```

- Get nodes' CPU and RAM utilization by running the following:

```
$ oc adm top nodes
```

- To see the full node spec, run this:

```
$ oc get node/<NODENAME> -o yaml
```

- For a human-readable summary with the related events, use this:

```
$ oc describe node/<NODENAME>
```

Please note, the same pattern will work for other resources, for example: oc get pod/<POD> -n <NAMESPACE> -o yaml and oc describe pod/<POD> -n <NAMESPACE>.

So why would you use describe over get? It summarizes key fields (conditions, capacity/allocations, taints, etc.) and appends the object's relevant events at the bottom, which is often the fastest way to spot scheduling, image-pull, or probe issues.

Let's try these commands. For starters, get a list of nodes via oc get nodes. When you get a list of nodes, pick one of the masters (or any available nodes you have) and try to get the resource consumption status for it, like this:

```
$ oc adm top node master-3.cluster.example.com
```

In the output, you will see some essential information about CPU and memory usage on the node; it may be a good starting point for the debug, together with oc adm top node.

Let's pretend the node is our debug target and we think something may be wrong with it – for example, some networking issues are happening, but we don't know whether this is a closed port or maybe DNS doesn't work well.

So, let's start the debug shell and jump into the host:

1. Run the debug command against your target node, oc debug node/master-3.cluster.example.com, and wait for the prompt like this:

```
Temporary namespace openshift-debug-bzrrh is created for debugging node...
Starting pod/apiclusterexamplecom-debug-v9476 ...
To use host binaries, run `chroot /host`

Pod IP: 192.168.55.190
If you don't see a command prompt, try pressing enter.

sh-5.1#
```

Figure 18.1: Starting debug container on a node

What happened? oc created a temporary namespace and a debug pod, with extensive privileges, which allows you to use it as a bridge into the host OS we are going to debug.

If you open a parallel terminal session and execute the following command, you will see what exactly differentiates the debug pod from other regular pods:

```
$ oc get pod -n openshift-debug-<id> <debug-pod-name> -o yaml
```

Look at the output of the preceding commands and note some of the specifics of the debug pod:

- `.spec.containers[].securityContext` has `privileged: true` and `runAsUser: 0`
- `.spec.containers[].volumeMounts` has an entry named `host`, which points to the host's `/host` directory
- The pod also has a special `priorityClassName` to ensure that it won't be preempted by a regular application pod
- `hostIPC`, `hostNetworks`, and `hostPID` are also enabled so that the pod has direct access to the node

So, the debug pod is super privileged, which allows us to access the host filesystem and all processes on the node.

2. Let's go back to the initial console and check the command the debug pod offered us to run: `` To use host binaries, run `chroot /host` ``. If you run the command, you will change the root of the active shell to the host's root directory.

Congratulations! You're now on the host and can execute low-level commands such as `crictl ps` and others, which will help you manage the node, its operating system, and the containers running on it. You can also use familiar `systemctl` commands to check the low-level services' statuses, for example, `systemctl is-active kubelet` or `systemctl status kubelet`.

> There are a few more commands and approaches you may want to try. You can use `journalctl` on a node to collect bootstrap logs: `journalctl -b -f -u bootkube.service`; you can also use `oc adm node-logs` to gather audit, API server, and other logs, as well.

Debugging pods

You can use the `oc debug` command for pods that are failing. This command allows you to start a debug pod with root access, based on the deployment or configuration of the problematic pod. Normally, pods run with non-root privileges, but running a troubleshooting pod with temporary root access can be helpful for investigating issues.

Let's create a deployment and use `oc debug` to troubleshoot it. We'll use two terminal sessions: one for the debug session and another to review the debug pod and its structure, just like we did with the node debug. Follow these steps:

1. Let's create a namespace and some deployment inside by running `oc new-project debug-test` and `kubectl create deployment hello-node --image=registry.k8s.io/e2e-test-images/agnhost:2.43 -- /agnhost serve-hostname`:

```
$ oc new-project debug-test
Now using project "debug-test" on server "https://api.cluster.example.com:6443".

You can add applications to this project with the 'new-app' command. For example, try:

    oc new-app rails-postgresql-example

to build a new example application in Ruby. Or use kubectl to deploy a simple Kubernetes application:

    kubectl create deployment hello-node --image=registry.k8s.io/e2e-test-images/agnhost:2.43 -- /agnhost serve-hostname

$ kubectl create deployment hello-node --image=registry.k8s.io/e2e-test-images/agnhost:2.43 -- /agnhost serve-hostname
deployment.apps/hello-node created
```

Figure 18.2: Project and deployment creation

2. Wait until all the objects are ready, and check their status by using the `oc get all` command. When the `hello-node` deployment is ready, you can run `oc get deployment.apps/hello-node -o yaml` and review the configuration; please note the `command` section:

```
        - command:
          - /agnhost
          - serve-hostname
```

3. So, the container starts with the `/agnhost serve-hostname` command. Apparently, it also uses the image we just specified: `registry.k8s.io/e2e-test-images/agnhost:2.43.` Let's remember that.
4. Run `oc debug` against the deployment, such as `oc debug deployment.apps/hello-node`:

```
$ oc debug deployment.apps/hello-node
Warning: would violate PodSecurity "restricted:latest": allowPrivilegeEscal
n=false), unrestricted capabilities (container "agnhost" must set securityC
must set securityContext.runAsNonRoot=true), seccompProfile (pod or contain
calhost")
Starting pod/hello-node-debug-h6k56, command was: /agnhost serve-hostname
Pod IP: 10.129.0.55
If you don't see a command prompt, try pressing enter.
/ #
```

Figure 18.3: Debugging a deployment via the oc debug command

Okay, so the debug console is available, but let's take a look at the namespaces and see what new objects there are.

5. If you run the `oc get pods` command in a separate terminal, you will see a new debug pod that you just started:

```
$ oc project debug-test && oc get pods
Already on project "debug-test" on server "https://api.cluster.example.com:6443".
NAME                         READY   STATUS    RESTARTS   AGE
hello-node-8dd54cb99-5kj7m   1/1     Running   0          106s
hello-node-debug-km6hq       1/1     Running   0          54s
```

Figure 18.4: Changing the project and listing pods

6. Let's take a look at the configuration of the debug pod by running oc get pod/<pod-name> -o yaml and reviewing the command it uses. It still uses the same image, registry.k8s.io/e2e-test-images/agnhost:2.43. But what has changed?

   Right, there is no more command to be executed on start; the pod is using /bin/sh as the command, which allows you to jump into the container and run some manual tests and application debug. So, in the debug shell, you can run the desired application manually and see the logs it produces:

   Figure 18.5: Manual application execution

   Then, you can press *Ctrl* + *C* and exit from the debug pod; OpenShift will clean it up after you. Please remember, you can always run a debug pod with broader privileges if needed. In such a case, you may need to do it via an additional flag:

```
$ oc debug deployment/hello-node --as-root -n debug-test
```

> **Warning!**
>
> In real-life scenarios, you might lose access to your SSH session on the bastion host or encounter issues with your oc CLI session. When this happens, a debug pod may become stuck. It's good practice to regularly check your cluster for stale debug pods, especially in large environments.

When a debug pod refuses to start but you still need access to the node, fall back to your trusty standby: SSH. Treat it as your "break-glass" option: a direct, low-level way to reach the host when OpenShift tooling isn't cooperating. In the next section, we will talk about how to access OpenShift nodes via SSH.

Accessing CoreOS via SSH

As we mentioned, there are times when a debug pod just isn't enough. In such situations, you may need to fall back on the non-recommended, yet still available option: SSH.

So, let's look at why SSH and what cases will lead you to using it:

- The API server or kubelet is unreachable, so oc debug hangs.
- Some networking or storage issues prevent the debug pod from scheduling.
- There are out-of-band tasks, such as firmware/BIOS, disks/bootloader issues, and so on.

Before we jump into the how-to, let's recap why Red Hat (and, most likely, your security team) prefers oc-based tooling over direct SSH:

- Nodes are meant to be immutable and operator-managed: The **Machine Config Operator** (**MCO**) owns the host image; ad hoc changes risk being overwritten or blocking upgrades.
- Manual edits create configuration drift: Untracked changes can push a node or its entire MachineConfigPool (**MCP**) into a Degraded state. In case you need a quick reminder of what MCPs are, we discussed them in more detail in *Chapter 4, Post-Install Configuration*.
- SSH access is audited and visibly flagged: When you log in, the node is annotated and tainted, so everyone knows it was accessed bypassing the API.
- Security and compliance are stronger with oc tooling: oc debug is subject to cluster RBAC and auditing, whereas SSH circumvents those controls.

In short, we aim to do the following:

- Manage nodes through operators rather than by hand.
- Leverage built-in RBAC, auditing, and logging for transparency and security.
- Keep port 22 open only for true break-glass scenarios, and then only from a tightly controlled bastion or jump host.

With that in mind, let's look at the safest way to open an SSH session when it really is the only way forward.

> **Warning!**
>
> To SSH into your cluster nodes, you must ensure that you've kept the SSH keys used during the installation process. If you lose these keys, regaining access to the nodes will be difficult. Please ensure you save your installation logs and SSH keys.

Let's try to connect to CoreOS via SSH:

1. Obtain a list of nodes and get the IP of the target one (let's use master3 for this example):

```
$ oc get node master3 -o wide.
```

   Please note, we are using -o wide in this example, to have IP addresses printed, but you can always run oc get node <NODENAME> -o yaml to obtain all the details from there.

2. Get the target node IP address and navigate to the folder where you have the openshift-install binary and all the deployment artifacts (if you followed the instructions, it will likely be ~/learning-ocp4) or point the SSH client to the proper SSH key, for example, ssh -i ~/.ssh/id_rsa core@10.100.10.43:

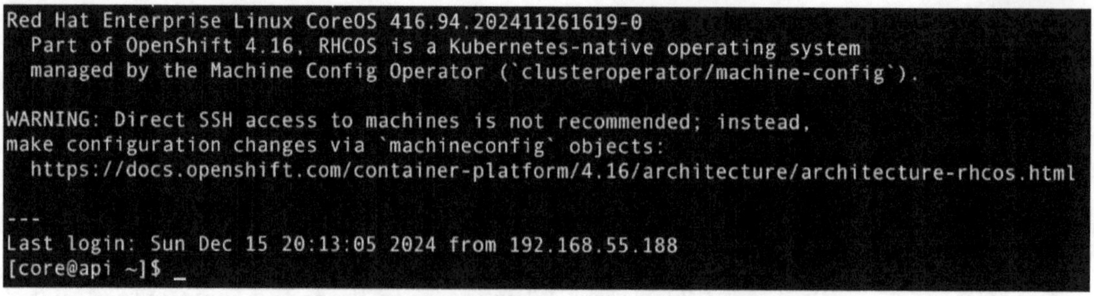

Figure 18.6: SSH session and the warning from Red Hat

Note that the version of CoreOS reported in the **message of the day** (**MOTD**) indicates the minor release of OpenShift (`416` -> `4.16`) that it was built for, the RHEL version it is based on (`94` -> `9.4`), as well as the timestamp of the build in the format YYYYMMDDHHMM, and the build/hotfix number. You can find the mapping between OCP releases and CoreOS versions at [1].

As you may have noticed, there's a path to the private key we're using. However, since it's in the default folder with the default name, you don't need to specify it. You can simply run `ssh core@<NODE_IP_ADDRESS>`.

3. Another important thing is that we are using the built-in user `core` here, so to drill down into the node status, services, and running containers, you may need to switch to `root`. You can do so via `sudo su -`, as you would do on a regular Linux system, to follow the best practices.

   Now, let's get back to the MOTD and the warning we see when we log in (it is probably still on your screen, but you can always check it with `cat /etc/motd`). So, what does the MOTD say? It notifies you of the following:

   - The node is managed by the MCO
   - You shouldn't apply any changes manually

Let's move forward and take a look at the options on how you can apply the persistent changes with the MCO.

Introducing persistent changes to CoreOS

As you noticed in the output of the MOTD, the Red Hat team is warning you against making any changes to CoreOS directly on the host OS level, but why? The reason is that CoreOS is designed to be an immutable, lightweight operating system. It's tightly integrated with OpenShift, and any manual changes can lead to inconsistencies, unsupported configurations, and potential issues during updates or patches.

Red Hat's recommended approach is to manage the system through the OpenShift platform itself, using its tools and APIs, which ensures that any modifications are consistent, supported, and do not compromise the stability or security of your cluster.

In the MOTD, you have the name of the operator that should be used – the MCO. So, what is the MCO?

OpenShift 4 is an operator-focused platform, and the MCO extends that to the operating system itself, managing updates and configuration changes to essentially everything between the kernel and kubelet.

The MCO is an open source solution; you can get additional information and check out the source code at [2].

The MCO in OpenShift manages and updates cluster node configurations using three key components:

- `machine-config-controller`: This component coordinates machine upgrades from the control plane, monitoring all nodes and managing their configuration updates to ensure smooth and consistent changes.
- `machine-config-daemon`: This component is running on each node; this daemonset applies configuration changes as defined by `MachineConfig`. When a new `MachineConfig` is detected, the node drains its pods, applies the update, and reboots (when a reboot is required to apply the change). These updates, delivered through Ignition files and containers, are crucial for keeping OpenShift and Red Hat CoreOS in sync.
- `machine-config-server`: This daemonset running on control plane nodes provides Ignition configuration files to control plane and worker nodes as they join the cluster, ensuring that they are correctly configured from the start.

Together, these components automate and standardize configuration changes and updates across the OpenShift cluster, following Red Hat's best practices for both the platform and RHCOS.

So, what CRDs does the MCO provide you with to control CoreOS on nodes and OCP in general? Here they are:

CRD	Description
`MachineConfig`	This CRD represents the desired configuration for a set of nodes. It includes specifications such as OS updates, kernel parameters, systemd units, and other configurations that should be applied to the nodes.
`MachineConfigPool`	This CRD groups together nodes that share the same configuration. It ensures that all nodes in the pool receive the same `MachineConfig`. It's useful for applying configurations to specific types of nodes, such as workers or masters.
`ContainerRuntimeConfig`	This CRD is used to manage and configure the container runtime on the nodes. It allows administrators to adjust settings related to the container runtime, such as log size limits, storage, and more.

CRD	Description
`KubeletConfig`	This CRD is used to manage and customize the configuration of the kubelet, which is the component on each node responsible for interacting with the container runtime and communicating a node's status back to the control plane. You can use it to adjust settings such as CPU management, memory reservations, and other node-level parameters.

Table 18.1: CRDs

`MachineConfig` and `MachineConfigPool` would be your main resources to work with; they are already familiar to you since they were used when you configured the infrastructure nodes back in *Chapter 4, Post-Install Configuration*.

`KubeletConfig` and `ContainerRuntimeConfig` are a bit more specific and would be required when you do some fine-tuning for your clusters, such as handling nodes in an overcommitted state or tuning some kubelet limits.

In your day-to-day job, you will likely work with three: `MachineConfig` (`mc`), `MachineConfigPool` (`mcp`), and `KubeletConfig`.

So, what kind of operations would you do via the MCO? Let's summarize:

- Creating new nodes
- Modifying existing nodes
- Configuring SELinux
- Adding kernel configuration
- Adding SSH keys
- Disabling/enabling SSH
- Some other OS-level configuration

Please review the Red Hat blog [3] and the official documentation [4] to see some handy examples.

Let's now review some default objects that will exist on your cluster right after deployment:

1. Get a list of `MachineConfigPools` by running `oc get mcp`. As usual, you can use the short name for the CRD to save typing (`mcp` instead of `MachineConfigPool`).
2. Typically, you'll have two `MachineConfigPools`: one for masters and another for workers. If your cluster also includes Infrastructure nodes, you may choose to create an additional `MachineConfigPool` for them too, as explained in *Chapter 4, Post-Install Configuration*.
3. If you run the `oc get machineconfig` (or just `oc get mc`) command, you will see a list of applied configurations, which should also be familiar to you from the infrastructure nodes experiment:

Figure 18.7: Listing MachineConfigs

Okay, perfect! Let's change something, maybe by using the `KubeletConfig` CRD:

1. First, let's check whether any of them exist by running the following command: `oc get kubeletconfig`; we are expecting to see no resources yet.
2. Now, let's create a definition and name the file `kubeletconfig.yaml`. We will configure kubelet to allow us to run 260 pods per node; the default value is 250, so we will bump it to 260.

   To keep it simple, just copy the content of the example from our Git: `chapters/18/snippets/kubeletconfig.yaml`.

   You may want to reach an even higher workload density. There are valid configurations where companies run up to 500 pods per node (for example, see [5]).

3. Create a `KubeletConfig` from the file you just made, for example, `oc create -f chapters/18/snippets/kubeletconfig.yaml`.
4. Now, if you run `oc get mcp`, you will see that the `MachineConfigPool` worker started updating; you can also run `oc get mc | grep kube` and see that you got a new configuration:

```
$ oc get mc | grep kube
01-master-kubelet                 4bb3364914c4dbcdfcc08b0914f402cdd38f014f   3.4.0   11d
01-worker-kubelet                 4bb3364914c4dbcdfcc08b0914f402cdd38f014f   3.4.0   11d
97-master-generated-kubelet       4bb3364914c4dbcdfcc08b0914f402cdd38f014f   3.4.0   11d
97-worker-generated-kubelet       4bb3364914c4dbcdfcc08b0914f402cdd38f014f   3.4.0   11d
98-master-generated-kubelet       4bb3364914c4dbcdfcc08b0914f402cdd38f014f   3.4.0   11d
98-worker-generated-kubelet       4bb3364914c4dbcdfcc08b0914f402cdd38f014f   3.4.0   11d
99-worker-generated-kubelet       4bb3364914c4dbcdfcc08b0914f402cdd38f014f   3.4.0   2m27s
```

Figure 18.8: Filtering out MachineConfigs generated for kubelet

Congratulations! This is how you can introduce changes to the running components configuration; the process is fairly straightforward.

But what if you need to install something? Let's talk about this case as well.

RHCOS layering

Imagine you need to add a specific driver for your hardware or install mandatory software as part of the operating system. However, **Red Hat CoreOS** (**RHCOS**) is *stateless*, meaning it doesn't retain changes after a reboot. How would you achieve this?

RHCOS lets you extend the base image by layering additional images on top of the stateful original image. This approach creates a custom layered image with all RHCOS features, plus the added ones needed for specific reasons.

To create a custom layered image, you use a Containerfile and apply it to nodes with a custom object. If required, you can easily remove the custom image by deleting this object.

With RHCOS image layering, you can install **Red Hat Package Manager** (**RPM**) packages into your base image, so your custom content runs alongside RHCOS. The MCO deploys and monitors these custom layered images just like it does with the standard RHCOS image, giving you more flexibility in managing your RHCOS nodes.

Once you apply a custom layered image to your cluster, you assume responsibility for those images and nodes. While Red Hat continues to maintain the base RHCOS image on standard nodes, you are responsible for maintaining and updating the custom layered images and handling any issues that arise from the customizations you've added.

There are two options to do so:

- **Out-of-cluster layering**: The primary method is called out-of-cluster layering, which is the standard way to add customizations to your clusters. With this approach, you create a Containerfile that references an OCP image and the RPMs you want to include. You then build the layered image in your environment and push it to your repository. More details on out-of-cluster layering can be found in the official documentation at [6].

  In your cluster, you create a `MachineConfig` object for the targeted node pool that points to the new image. The MCO then overrides the base RHCOS image with the new one specified by `osImageURL` in `MachineConfig`, and the node boots using this custom image.

- **On-cluster layering**: With on-cluster layering, you create a `MachineOSConfig` object that includes the Containerfile and other relevant parameters. The build process takes place entirely within your cluster, and the resulting custom layered image is automatically pushed to your repository. It is then applied to the `MachineConfig` pool specified in the `MachineOSConfig` object. This approach keeps the entire process contained within your cluster.

  You can get more detailed information about the on-cluster layering approach in the official documentation at [7].

Warning!

Currently, on-cluster image layering is a Technology Preview feature only. Technology Preview features are not supported with Red Hat production **service-level agreements (SLAs)** and might not be functionally complete. Red Hat does not recommend using them in production.

So, with the layering, you can apply **hot fixes**, install RHEL packages, and bring in some third-party packages. For example, for third-party package installation via the out-of-cluster method, the Containerfile/Dockerfile would look like this:

```
FROM quay.io/openshift-release-dev/ocp-v4.0-art-dev@sha256...
RUN rpm-ostree install https://dl.fedoraproject.org/pub/epel/epel-release-
latest-9.noarch.rpm && \
    rpm-ostree install ncdu && \
    ostree container commit
```

A Containerfile is essentially the same (or almost the same) as a Dockerfile. The change in naming was made for various reasons, but the concept remains unchanged; it serves as a definition used to build a container image. Please see [8] for details on their similarities and differences.

Take note of the `FROM` value; this points to the specific base CoreOS image. To ensure compatibility, you must obtain the correct image for your specific cluster version. You can do this by running the following command:

```
$ oc adm release info --image-for rhel-coreos
```

Let's try to build the layer with the `ncdu` tool [9] as an example and apply it by following the out-of-cluster layering. For this step, please ensure the integrated image registry is up and running using the following:

```
$ oc get pods -n openshift-image-registry -l docker-registry=default
```

We are expecting it to be up and running.

> For the following procedure to work, we recommend you try it on either the multi-node cluster that we built in *Chapter 3, Getting Started with OpenShift*, or a single-node cluster. We have observed issues with OpenShift Local (CRC) not being able to reboot in our lab and other problems, which don't seem to be connected to insufficient CPU or memory. Given that CRC is not completely reliable, we decided to give you a fair warning.

Now, we can execute the following steps to generate and apply a layer:

1. Let's create a new project by running the following:

   ```
   $ oc new-project layering-test
   ```

2. Create an image stream and get its status, as shown in the figure that follows:

   ```
   $ oc -n layering-test create is ncdu-epel && oc -n layering-test get is ncdu-epel
   ```

Figure 18.9: ImageStream status

3. Create a tag using the following:

   ```
   $ oc -n layering-test tag image-registry.openshift-image-registry.svc:5000/layering-test/ncdu-epel:latest ncdu-epel:latest
   ```

4. Get the base image to be used by running this command:

   ```
   $ oc adm release info --image-for rhel-coreos
   ```

5. Now, we can create a `BuildConfig` file. Please use the example file named `buildconfig.yaml` from Git (do not create anything from it, we must edit it first): `chapters/18/snippets/buildconfig.yaml`.

6. Make sure you update a base image in the following places of the YAML, by using the output from *step 4*:

```
spec.strategy.dockerStrategy.from.name
spec.source.dockerfile - FROM
```

7. Create the `Buildconfig` file itself with this well-known command:

```
$ oc create -f buildconfig.yaml
```

8. Run a build and follow it:

```
$ oc start-build ncdu-epel --follow
```

9. Save the part of the output of the command that shows you the image that the build prepared for you:

Figure 18.10: Image successfully pushed to our image stream in the integrated registry

10. Execute the following command to allow an MCO `ServiceAccount` to read the image:

```
$ oc policy add-role-to-user system:image-puller
system:serviceaccount:openshift-machine-config-operator:machine-os-puller
-n layering-test
```

11. Now, we can create a `MachineConfig`, for example, name the file `ncdu-epel-mc.yaml`. As usual, to simplify the process, we have a file in Git; please update `spec.osImageURL` with the image you just built following *step 8*. You can get the example from Git: `chapters/18/snippets/ncdu-epel-mc.yaml`.

    Also, if you're using OpenShift Local or a single-node OpenShift cluster, make sure to update the `machineconfiguration.openshift.io/role` label to `master`, because in OpenShift Local, the node named `crc` is managed by the master MCP, not the worker MCP.

12. Create a `MachineConfig` from the definition you just made and ensure that the worker MCO started the update process for the worker MCP, as usual, by running the following:

```
$ oc create -f ncdu-epel-mc.yaml
```

13. You can follow the status of MCP by running `oc get mcp` and just waiting until the MCP is in an `UPDATED: True` state.

Let's quickly check whether the layering was done successfully:

1. First, connect to the node – you can do it via SSH or `oc debug` (let's use `oc debug`, as it is the recommended way):

   ```
   $ oc debug node/<node-name>
   ```

   You are expecting an output like this:

   ```
   $ oc debug node/bc-24-11-63-77-3c
   Temporary namespace openshift-debug-pdrtn is created for debugging node...
   Starting pod/bc-24-11-63-77-3c-debug-4wntl ...
   To use host binaries, run `chroot /host`
   Pod IP: 192.168.88.100
   If you don't see a command prompt, try pressing enter.
   sh-5.1#
   ```

   Figure 18.11: Opening a debug shell on a node to verify changes

2. Now, you can run `chroot /host`, as suggested:

   ```
   # chroot /host
   ```

3. There is no specific output from the preceding command; it will silently change the root directory for you, and now we are ready to check whether the new package is available:

   ```
   $ rpm -q ncdu
   ```

   This will show you the version of `ncdu` you just added:

   ```
   sh-5.1# rpm -q ncdu
   ncdu-1.22-1.el9.x86_64
   ```

   Figure 18.12: A new RPM was added to the base image

4. That's it! You can run now the application and ensure that it can run:

   ```
   $ ncdu
   ```

You should see a summary of disk space usage for all directories starting from /:

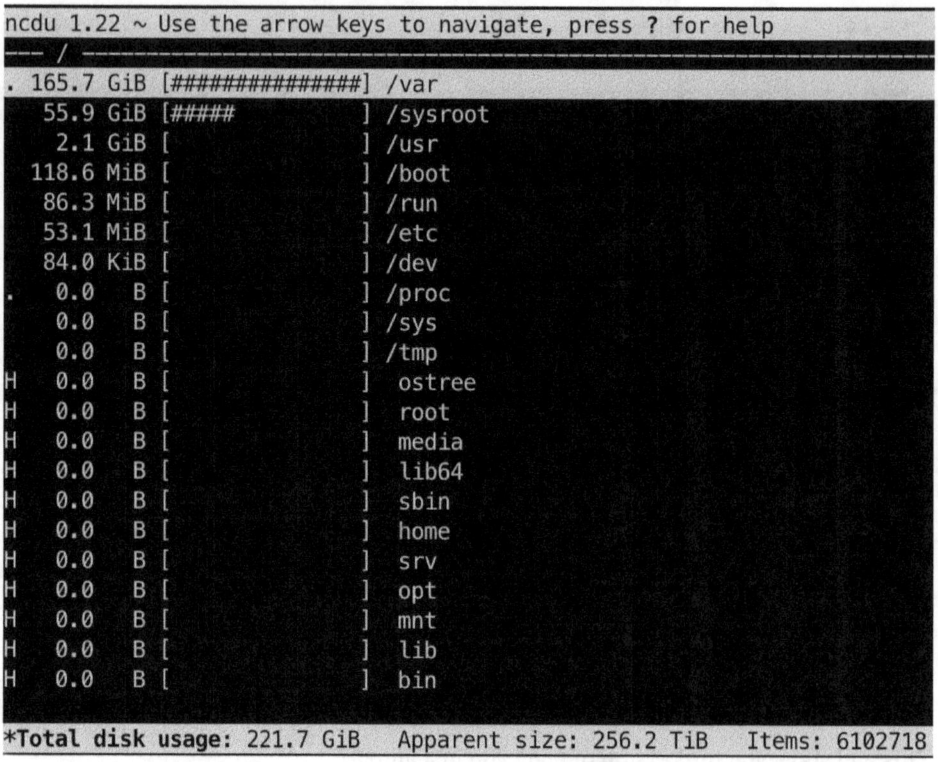

Figure 18.13: Running the added utility as a test

Congratulations, you made a permanent change to the OS package set on your nodes!

Now you know all you need to successfully debug your nodes and pods, make permanent changes, and onboard more useful tools if you need them.

But, as you know, situations can be different, and sometimes you require the vendor's support. To provide you with high-class support, Red Hat Support will ask you to provide debug information – usually, there are two reports that are required by default: the `must-gather` report and `sos report`. If you supply the case with this information, your overall experience of support communication will be much better, as you will help the team better understand what happens on the low level and avoid unnecessary back and forth. Let's talk about both.

Using must-gather

When troubleshooting issues in OpenShift, having the right information is essential. The `must-gather` tool helps by collecting important diagnostic data from your cluster. Whether you're working with support teams or analyzing issues on your own, `must-gather` gives you a clear snapshot of your environment. In this section, we'll learn how to use `must-gather` to quickly gather the data you need to diagnose and solve problems.

You can run `must-gather` using the `oc adm must-gather` command. This command needs to be executed by a user with `cluster-admin` privileges, as we've discussed; most tools and actions are handled by users with this level of access.

The `must-gather` tool collects nearly everything you might need, packing it into a folder; you can expect a lot of files, folders, and ZIP archives there. This folder can then be shared with Red Hat Support or analyzed by you. It gathers all resource definitions and logs from your services, providing a comprehensive view of your cluster.

If you run `oc adm must-gather` with no flags, it will pull a default image and collect all the information it can find; you can expect a lot of output, but please run it and check what it does and what the log says. Sometimes it may be a lot of data; it is essential to remember that you can tune it.

The `oc adm must-gather` command uses up to 30% of the container's storage. Once this limit is reached, the container stops, and you will lose the results of the gathering. You can fix this by changing the default limit like this:

```
$ oc adm must-gather --volume-percentage <storage_percentage>
```

There is another trick you must know about, which will help you save your time and storage: you can always use special `must-gather` images for specific components. The list of images is available in the official Red Hat documentation at [10].

You can also use `must-gather` as the centralized instrument to gather audit and other logs from the nodes; for this purpose, you can run a command such as the following:

```
$ oc adm must-gather -- /usr/bin/gather_audit_logs
```

This may be a crucial step when, for example, you are trying to find some steps somebody executed.

If you look under `/usr/bin` of your host by running the `oc adm must-gather -- ls /usr/bin` command, you will find many other binaries with the `gather_` prefix. For example, run `oc adm must-gather -- ls /usr/bin 2>&1 | grep gather_` as follows:

```
$ oc adm must-gather -- ls /usr/bin 2>&1 | grep gather_
[must-gather-t842k] POD 2025-08-14T19:25:33.869213176Z gather_apirequestcounts
[must-gather-t842k] POD 2025-08-14T19:25:33.869213176Z gather_aro
[must-gather-t842k] POD 2025-08-14T19:25:33.869213176Z gather_audit_logs
[must-gather-t842k] POD 2025-08-14T19:25:33.869213176Z gather_core_dumps
[must-gather-t842k] POD 2025-08-14T19:25:33.869213176Z gather_etcd
[must-gather-t842k] POD 2025-08-14T19:25:33.869213176Z gather_haproxy_config
[must-gather-t842k] POD 2025-08-14T19:25:33.869213176Z gather_ingress_node_firewall
[must-gather-t842k] POD 2025-08-14T19:25:33.869213176Z gather_insights
[must-gather-t842k] POD 2025-08-14T19:25:33.869213176Z gather_kas_startup_termination_logs
[must-gather-t842k] POD 2025-08-14T19:25:33.869213176Z gather_machineconfig_ondisk
[must-gather-t842k] POD 2025-08-14T19:25:33.869213176Z gather_metallb
[must-gather-t842k] POD 2025-08-14T19:25:33.869213176Z gather_monitoring
[must-gather-t842k] POD 2025-08-14T19:25:33.869213176Z gather_network_logs
[must-gather-t842k] POD 2025-08-14T19:25:33.869213176Z gather_network_logs_basics
[must-gather-t842k] POD 2025-08-14T19:25:33.869213176Z gather_nmstate
[must-gather-t842k] POD 2025-08-14T19:25:33.869213176Z gather_olm
[must-gather-t842k] POD 2025-08-14T19:25:33.869213176Z gather_osus
[must-gather-t842k] POD 2025-08-14T19:25:33.869213176Z gather_podnetworkconnectivitycheck
[must-gather-t842k] POD 2025-08-14T19:25:33.869213176Z gather_ppc
[must-gather-t842k] POD 2025-08-14T19:25:33.869213176Z gather_ppc_single_node
[must-gather-t842k] POD 2025-08-14T19:25:33.869213176Z gather_priority_and_fairness
[must-gather-t842k] POD 2025-08-14T19:25:33.869213176Z gather_profiling_node
[must-gather-t842k] POD 2025-08-14T19:25:33.869213176Z gather_service_logs
[must-gather-t842k] POD 2025-08-14T19:25:33.869213176Z gather_service_logs_util
[must-gather-t842k] POD 2025-08-14T19:25:33.869213176Z gather_sriov
[must-gather-t842k] POD 2025-08-14T19:25:33.869213176Z gather_vsphere
[must-gather-t842k] POD 2025-08-14T19:25:33.869213176Z gather_windows_node_logs
```

Figure 18.14: Dedicated binaries for collecting data about specific OpenShift subsystems

You are welcome to test them in your lab and review the resulting folders and files.

Okay, now you know how to get the OCP-specific logs and statuses, but what about the underlying operating system? If you are a long-time RHEL user, you probably faced this utility before in your practice, and I have good news for you – it is still with us, in the form of `sos report`. If this is something new for you, this is an extremely useful tool that helps you get information about your OS.

The sos report command

Since all nodes in your OpenShift clusters run on either RHCOS or RHEL, it's essential to collect debug data from these operating systems when troubleshooting issues. One of the key tools for this task is `sos report`, which gathers comprehensive configuration details, system information, and diagnostic data from RHEL and RHCOS systems.

This standardized data can be shared with Red Hat Support to assist in diagnosing issues. In some cases, Red Hat Support may specifically request a `sos report` archive from an OpenShift node, particularly when system logs or node-specific data not covered by `oc adm must-gather` need to be reviewed.

Using sos report is straightforward, but let's walk through the process. First, connect to the target node either via SSH or by using the oc debug command. Both approaches have been discussed, so choose the one that best fits your situation and preferences. For this example, we'll proceed with oc debug to avoid using SSH:

1. Get a list of your nodes using `oc get nodes`.
2. Pick one node and start a debug container, then run `chroot /host`.
3. In a shell, run the `toolbox` script, which will start a container with debug and diagnostics tools. By default, it uses the `registry.redhat.io/rhel9/support-tools` image.
4. Collect a report by running `sos report --all-logs`.

If you want to interactively upload your report file to the case, you can use the same command but with the `--upload` flag, as in this example:

```
# sos report --batch --upload --case-id 01234567
```

For cases when you already have a report file to upload, you can use the following:

```
# sos upload --upload-target redhat --case-id 01234567 sosreport-*.tar.xz
```

Please use the reference link at [11] to read more about the sos command.

The `--upload` option was first introduced in `sos-3.9` and is available in RHEL 7.9+.

You may have used `redhat-support-tool` to upload files to Red Hat Support cases before. This utility was officially deprecated as of RHEL 8 and is not shipped in RHEL 9+, which CoreOS is based on. See Red Hat's memo [12] and the **Red Hat Support Tool (RHST)** deprecation guide [13].

> For support cases, you may also need your cluster ID; to obtain it, you can run `oc get clusterversion -o jsonpath='{.items[].spec.clusterID}{"\n"}'`.

Perfect! Now you know how to gather everything the Red Hat Support team might request. This is awesome, but let's also discuss some common Kubernetes and OpenShift hiccups you can encounter with everything running on it – pod conditions and why they may change.

Debugging pods

Now that we have covered debug tooling and why you may prefer the debug shell over SSH, it is time to look at how workloads behave on a cluster. You may have encountered some of these statuses and conditions of pods during your journey through the book, even though we have tried to put the steps in a way so that the picture you have is as complete as possible.

Effective troubleshooting starts with a clear mental model of the pod's lifecycle. In OpenShift, pods move through a small set of phases (`Pending`, `Running`, `Succeeded`, `Failed`, and `Unknown`), while each container inside a pod transitions through states (`Waiting`, `Running`, and `Terminated`) with reasons such as `ImagePullBackOff` or `CrashLoopBackOff`.

In the next couple of pages, we will try to turn these phases and states into a decision tree – what they all mean, how to diagnose them, and how to act – whether that's fixing image pulls, unblocking PVCs, adjusting requests/limits, or resolving SCCs and probe issues.

Pod phases

The pod's lifecycle contains a few phases, which are usually self-explanatory, because Kubernetes developers and architects thought about us as practitioners and made them simple to understand. Let's take a look:

- `Pending`: The pod is accepted by the cluster, but not yet scheduled
- `Running`: At least one container is running, restarting, or starting
- `Succeeded`: All containers exited with a code of `0` and `restartPolicy` not set to `Always`
- `Failed`: A container exited with a non-zero exit code and won't restart (per its `restartPolicy`)
- `Unknown`: The node is unreachable, or the kubelet is not reporting a status

Let's present these phases in a simple diagram and discuss what can trigger the phase change. Please note: the diagram includes **Terminating**, but this is not a phase. A pod can be deleted from any phase and will show `Terminating` while the cleanup is in progress. Now, let's look at the diagram:

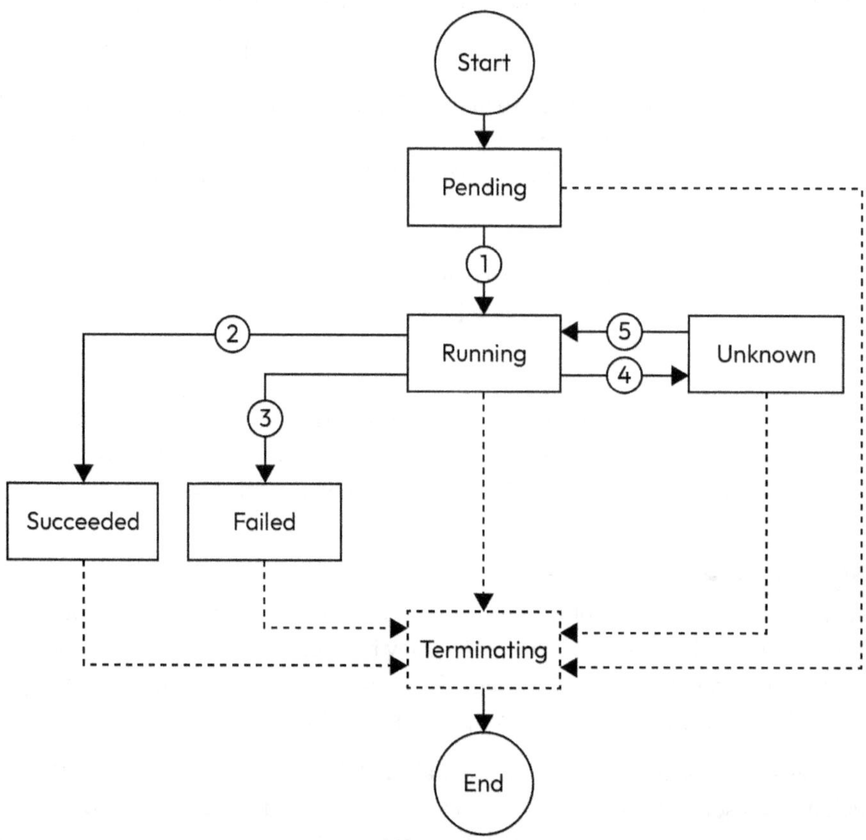

Figure 18.15: State diagram of pod phases

What do the numbers on the arrows mean? Here is the definition:

1. Pending to Running: Scheduled; containers started
2. Running to Succeeded: All containers exited with 0 and restartPolicy not set to Always
3. Running to Failed: Non-zero exit and not restarted per restartPolicy
4. Running to Unknown: Node/kubelet unreachable
5. Unknown to Running: Node/kubelet reports again

That's it! We have a few phases for pods, and it looks simple enough. But, as we briefly discussed previously, containers inside a pod will also have states (Waiting, Running, and Terminated) with reasons. Let's dig a bit deeper.

States and reasons

Containers will have states and reasons such as CrashLoopBackOff, ImagePullBackOff, ErrImagePull, CreateContainerConfigError, CreateContainerError, OOMKilled, and so on – these reasons are the best clues that will help you fix a problem. Let's take a look at them and define what they mean and how you can assess them.

First, let's enumerate the most common commands you will run for debugging:

- List pods and their phases: oc get pods -n <NAMESPACE> -o wide
- Check reasons and events: oc describe pod/<POD> -n <NAMESPACE>
- Check logs of the main container: oc logs pod/<POD> -n <NAMESPACE>
- Check logs from a previous crash: oc logs -p pod/<POD> -n <NAMESPACE> -c <CONTAINER>
- Check events: oc get events -n <NAMESPACE> --sort-by=.lastTimestamp (or oc events, which sorts events by timestamp already)

Now, with these commands in mind, let's talk about the most common states and reasons, and what you check when they happen:

Reason (state)	What it means	What to check/fix
ImagePullBackOff/ ErrImagePull (Waiting)	The image cannot be pulled	Verify the image name/tag and registry reachability; check events in oc describe pod. Ensure that a pull secret is attached to the service account: oc secrets link sa/<SERVICEACCOUNT> <PULL-SECRET> --for=pull -n <NAMESPACE>. Another common cause of this issue is that an image simply may not exist.
CreateContainerConfigError (Waiting)	Invalid pod spec (missing/renamed Secret/ConfigMap/ volume/envFrom)	Confirm that the referenced Secret/ ConfigMap/volume/key exists: oc get secret,cm -n <NAMESPACE>; fix mounts/ env references; re-apply.

Reason (state)	What it means	What to check/fix
CreateContainerError / RunContainerError (Waiting)	Runtime could not start the container	Check command/arguments/entrypoint, file paths/permissions, and image health. Read events in oc describe pod for the exact failure; correct the spec or image.
CrashLoopBackOff (Waiting after Running)	Process starts, then repeatedly exits	Usually indicates a problem with the application. Inspect the previous crash: oc logs -p pod/<POD> -c <CONTAINER> -n <NAMESPACE>. Validate config/env, credentials, and service dependencies; review probes/timeouts that may kill the app too early.
OOMKilled (Terminated)	Container exceeded its memory limit	Increase memory limit or reduce usage; check ResourceQuota/LimitRange; verify app memory behavior (e.g., JVM heap), check memory usage with oc adm top po. Redeploy with adjusted requests/limits.
Probe failed (see Events: Readiness/Liveness/Startup)	App is unhealthy or probe is misconfigured	Verify the probe's path/scheme (for httpGet probes), port, timeoutSeconds, and initialDelaySeconds. Align thresholds with the real startup time of your application and confirm that the endpoint actually returns expected codes.
Pod has unbound immediate PersistentVolumeClaims (Pending)	PVC not bound (storage not ready)	Run oc get pvc -n <NAMESPACE> to see if there are any PVCs in the Pending phase; confirm that StorageClass and provisioner are healthy; check capacity, accessModes, volumeMode, and any topology constraints.
0/x nodes are available (Pending)	Unschedulable (no suitable node)	Review taints/tolerations, nodeSelector/affinity, requested CPU/memory vs. node capacity, quotas/limits, and PDBs. Use oc describe pod (check events) and oc describe node/<NODE>.

Reason (state)	What it means	What to check/fix
`denied by SCC (see Events)`	Blocked by security context constraints	Preferred remediation is to adjust `securityContext` of a pod and/or its container(s) (e.g., `runAsNonRoot`, `fsGroup`, capabilities, etc.) to fit the restricted SCC. Bind to a less-restrictive SCC only when justified and documented.
`Network plugin/CNI setup failed (Events)`	Pod sandbox/CNI initialization failed	Check node readiness and CNI DaemonSet health; review `NetworkPolicy` that may block `init`; investigate CNI/controller logs.
`Denied by Pod Security Admission (PSA)`	Pod or container's security context is too permissive and is not allowed by a pod security standard defined in the namespace's labels	Remediate all security context violations reported by PSA (usually can be seen as a warning right after you try creating a pod or in the events) and reapply.

Table 18.2: Container states and remediations

You can keep this table handy, and it will likely help you to handle most of the pod/container issues you may encounter.

> Do not hesitate to engage Red Hat Support – whether it's planning your production or pre-production environment, or planning to execute a debug process. All the information you gather will help you make your experience with Red Hat OpenShift better.

Summary

Congratulations, you've made it! This chapter marks the end of this book and your journey through OpenShift from basics to advanced concepts. Let's briefly summarize what we have learned.

In this chapter, we addressed common questions that crop up during troubleshooting, such as where to start or what tools to use. To that end, we examined how to use `oc debug` to troubleshoot node- or pod-level issues and how to proceed if we have SSH enabled, as well as discussed concerns around the use of SSH with OpenShift. We also investigated how to introduce persistent changes to CoreOS in the form of extra RPMs and configuration. As part of that topic, we looked at such APIs as `MachineConfig`, `MachineConfigPool`, and `KubeletConfig`, and practiced with CoreOS layering.

Next, we talked about how to engage Red Hat to resolve issues – specifically, how to provide its support with all necessary diagnostic data using `oc adm must-gather` and `sos report`.

Our final stop on this journey was the discussion of pod troubleshooting and different phases, states, and reasons. Learning about them helped us understand various reasons that may impede a pod's startup or lead to it crashing, and how to resolve these problems.

While these tasks are not a part of daily operations, thanks to OpenShift's stability and enterprise-grade reliability, it's crucial to be prepared for complex scenarios that may arise in real-world deployments. Understanding these tools equips you with the ability to troubleshoot effectively when needed.

That's it! We have come a long way and covered a lot of ground. We started with a conceptual discussion of containers, their benefits, and used them as a segue to the topic of Kubernetes and OpenShift. Furthermore, we then jumped straight into installing our first multi-node OpenShift cluster on vSphere and making some day-2 configuration changes. In the chapters that followed, we practiced installing Helm charts and using Kustomize, explored authentication and authorization, scalability, and security, briefly talked about serverless, enabled Windows workloads and GitOps, discussed operators, and even built a simple operator of our own. Finally, we discussed cluster upgrades, cluster operators, and troubleshooting.

We hope you enjoyed reading this book and following the exercises we prepared as much as we enjoyed writing it. It is our strong conviction that there is always more to learn, and we learned some useful information ourselves along the way. We're certain that this book will be useful not only to complete newcomers who are just starting with OpenShift, but also to seasoned experts.

On that note, goodbye and good luck!

References

To learn more about the topics that were covered in this chapter, take a look at the following resources:

- [1] *RHEL Versions Utilized by RHEL CoreOS and OCP*: `https://access.redhat.com/articles/6907891`
- [2] *Machine Config Operator's GitHub page*: `https://github.com/openshift/machine-config-operator`
- [3] *How to Handle OpenShift Worker Nodes Resources in Overcommitted State*: `https://www.redhat.com/en/blog/how-to-handle-openshift-worker-nodes-resources-in-overcommitted-state`
- [4] *Managing nodes*: `https://docs.redhat.com/en/documentation/openshift_container_platform/4.16/html/nodes/working-with-nodes#nodes-nodes-managing`
- [5] *OpenShift Scale: Running 500 Pods Per Node*: `https://www.redhat.com/en/blog/500_pods_per_node`
- [6] *Using out-of-cluster layering to apply a custom layered image*: `https://docs.redhat.com/en/documentation/openshift_container_platform/4.16/html/machine_configuration/mco-coreos-layering#coreos-layering-configuring_mco-coreos-layering`
- [7] *Using on-cluster layering to apply a custom layered image*: `https://docs.redhat.com/en/documentation/openshift_container_platform/4.16/html/machine_configuration/mco-coreos-layering#coreos-layering-configuring-on_mco-coreos-layering`

- [8] *Containers GitHub repository, Containerfile*: https://github.com/containers/common/blob/main/docs/Containerfile.5.md
- [9] *NCurses Disk Usage*: https://dev.yorhel.nl/ncdu
- [10] *Gathering data about specific features*: https://docs.redhat.com/en/documentation/openshift_container_platform/4.16/html/support/gathering-cluster-data#gathering-data-specific-features_gathering-cluster-data
- [11] *How can I use sos to upload reports and other files?*: https://access.redhat.com/solutions/3592?#sosupload
- [12] *Red Hat Access: Red Hat Support Tool*: https://access.redhat.com/articles/445443
- [13] *Red Hat Support Tool (RHST) Deprecation Guide*: https://access.redhat.com/articles/6960871

Quiz

Let's test your understanding of OpenShift 4 debug processes and tools with this quick quiz:

1. You need a single command to collect a comprehensive, support-ready diagnostic bundle (resources, events, operator logs, and selected node details) from the entire OpenShift cluster across all namespaces. Which do you use?
    a. Use the `oc get logs` command to collect logs from the cluster
    b. Use `oc adm logs-gather` to automatically gather all logs
    c. Manually connect to each node and gather logs using `scp`
    d. Use the `oc adm must-gather` command to collect diagnostics and logs from the entire cluster
2. What is the purpose of the `sosreport` tool in OpenShift troubleshooting, and when should it be used?
    a. It is used for generating a performance report of OpenShift clusters
    b. It collects only application logs for review by Red Hat Support
    c. It is used exclusively for gathering metrics from OpenShift monitoring tools
    d. It collects system configuration, logs, and diagnostic information from RHEL or RHCOS nodes, and is used when detailed system-level data is needed
3. What steps should you take if an OpenShift node becomes `NotReady`?
    a. Remove the node from the cluster and add it back
    b. Immediately escalate to Red Hat Support without further investigation
    c. Install additional memory on the node to resolve readiness issues
    d. Check node status, review logs using `journalctl -xe`, ensure adequate resources, and consider restarting the node or its services

4. What type of information does `sosreport` collect from an OpenShift node?

    a. Only application-level logs from OpenShift pods
    b. Network traffic data between OpenShift pods
    c. System configuration details, logs, and diagnostic data from the underlying OS (RHEL or RHCOS)
    d. Kubernetes object definitions and YAML configurations

5. How can you view logs from the previous instance of a container that is `CrashLooping`?

    a. Use `oc logs -f pod/<pod> -n <NAMESPACE>`
    b. Use `oc get events -n <NAMESPACE> --sort-by=.lastTimestamp`
    c. Use `oc exec -it pod/<POD> -- tail -n 100 /var/log/app.log`
    d. Use `oc logs --previous -c <CONTAINER> pod/<pod> -n <NAMESPACE>`

Answers

1. **d.** The `oc adm must-gather` command is a comprehensive tool provided by OpenShift to collect logs and diagnostics from an entire cluster, including logs from nodes, pods, and other components. It is a recommended way to collect detailed troubleshooting data.
2. **d.** The `sosreport` tool is primarily used to collect system-level data, including logs, configurations, and diagnostics, from **Red Hat Enterprise Linux** (**RHEL**) or **Red Hat CoreOS** (**RHCOS**) nodes.
3. **d.** When a node becomes `NotReady`, the first step is to investigate the cause by checking the node's status and logs using commands such as `journalctl -xe` or inspecting specific services such as the kubelet and `crio`.
4. **c.** The `sosreport` tool is designed to collect detailed information about the system, such as configuration files, logs, and diagnostic data from the OS (RHEL or RHCOS). This makes it an invaluable resource for troubleshooting OS-level issues that may impact OpenShift nodes.
5. **d.** Using `-p` or `--previous` allows you to inspect logs from the previous instance of the container; this is a very handy and underrated feature.

19

Unlock Your Exclusive Benefits

Your copy of this book includes the following exclusive benefits:

DRM-Free PDF Version

Download DRM-free PDF and ePub copies of this book.

7-Day Packt Library Access

Get 7-day unlimited access to 8,000+ books and videos. No credit card required.

Available for first-time Packt+ trial users only.

Next-Gen Reader Access

Read this book on Packt Reader with progress sync, dark mode and note-taking.

Follow the guide below to unlock them. The process takes only a few minutes and needs to be completed once.

Unlock this book's free benefits in 3 easy steps

Step 1

Keep your purchase invoice ready for *Step 3*. If you have a physical copy, scan it using your phone and save it as a PDF, JPG, or PNG.

For more help on finding your invoice, visit `https://www.packtpub.com/en-us/unlock?step=1`.

> **Note:** If you bought this book directly from Packt, no invoice is required. After *Step 2*, you can access your exclusive content right away.

Step 2

Scan the QR code or go to `packtpub.com/unlock`.

On the page that opens (similar to *Figure 19.1* on desktop), search for this book by name and select the correct edition.

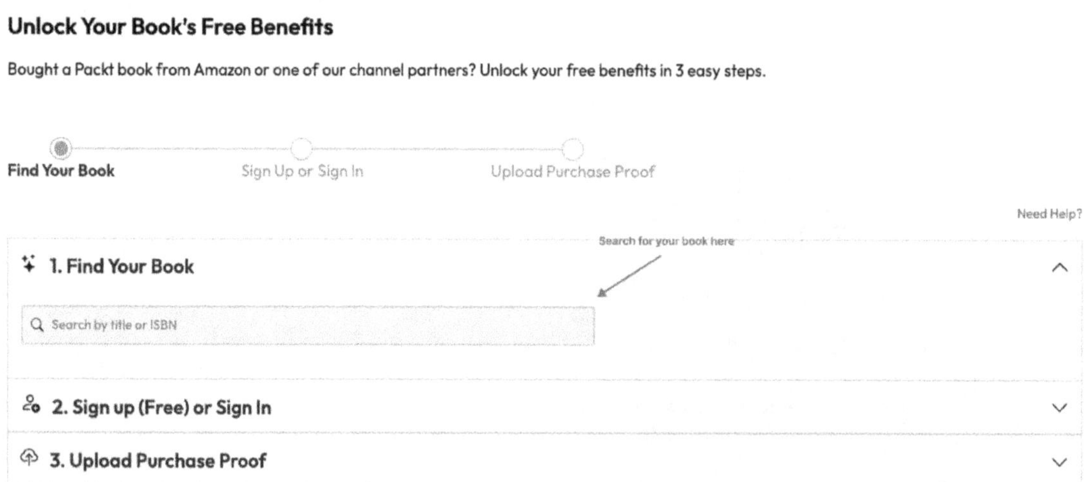

Figure 19.1: Packt unlock landing page on desktop

Step 3

After selecting your book, sign in to your Packt account or create one for free. Then upload your invoice (PDF, PNG, or JPG, up to 10 MB). Follow the on-screen instructions to finish the process.

Need Help

If you get stuck and need help, visit `https://www.packtpub.com/unlock-benefits/help` for a detailed FAQ on how to find your invoices and more. This QR code will take you to the help page.

Note: If you are still facing issues, reach out to `customercare@packt.com`.

Stay Sharp in Cloud and DevOps – Join 44,000+ Subscribers of CloudPro

CloudPro is a weekly newsletter for cloud professionals who want to stay current on the fast-evolving world of cloud computing, DevOps, and infrastructure engineering.

Every issue delivers focused, high-signal content on topics like:

- AWS, GCP & multi-cloud architecture
- Containers, Kubernetes & orchestration
- Infrastructure as Code (IaC) with Terraform, Pulumi, etc.
- Platform engineering & automation workflows
- Observability, performance tuning, and reliability best practices

Whether you're a cloud engineer, SRE, DevOps practitioner, or platform lead, CloudPro helps you stay on top of what matters, without the noise.

Scan the QR code to join for free and get weekly insights straight to your inbox:

https://packt.link/cloudpro

Other Books You May Enjoy

If you enjoyed this book, you may be interested in these other books by Packt:

Modern DevOps Practices

None Agarwal

ISBN: 978-1-80056-238-7

- Become well-versed with AWS ECS, Google Cloud Run, and Knative
- Discover how to build and manage secure Docker images efficiently
- Understand continuous integration with Jenkins on Kubernetes and GitHub actions
- Get to grips with using Spinnaker for continuous deployment/delivery
- Manage immutable infrastructure on the cloud with Packer, Terraform, and Ansible
- Explore the world of GitOps with GitHub actions, Terraform, and Flux CD

Mastering DevOps on Microsoft Power Platform

Uroš Kastelic, József Zoltán Vadkerti

ISBN: 978-1-83588-084-5

- Gain insights into ALM and DevOps on Microsoft Power Platform
- Set up Power Platform pipelines and environments by leveraging best practices
- Automate, test, monitor, and secure CI/CD pipelines using DevSecOps tools, such as VS Code and GitHub Advanced Security, on Power Platform
- Enable pro-developer extensibility using fusion development to integrate Azure and Power Platform
- Provision enterprise landing zones and build well-architected workloads
- Discover GenAI capabilities in Power Platform and support ChatOps with the copilot stack

Packt is searching for authors like you

If you're interested in becoming an author for Packt, please visit authors.packt.com and apply today. We have worked with thousands of developers and tech professionals, just like you, to help them share their insight with the global tech community. You can make a general application, apply for a specific hot topic that we are recruiting an author for, or submit your own idea.

Share your thoughts

Now you've finished *Learn OpenShift, Second Edition,* we'd love to hear your thoughts! Scan the QR code below to go straight to the Amazon review page for this book and share your feedback or leave a review on the site that you purchased it from.

https://packt.link/r/1835882412

Your review is important to us and the tech community and will help us make sure we're delivering excellent quality content.

Index

A

B

C

I

J

K

N

O

P

Q

R

S

www.ingramcontent.com/pod-product-compliance
Lightning Source LLC
LaVergne TN
LVHW060010210926
848481LV00013B/3679